Warman's

AMERICAN RECORDS

2nd Edition

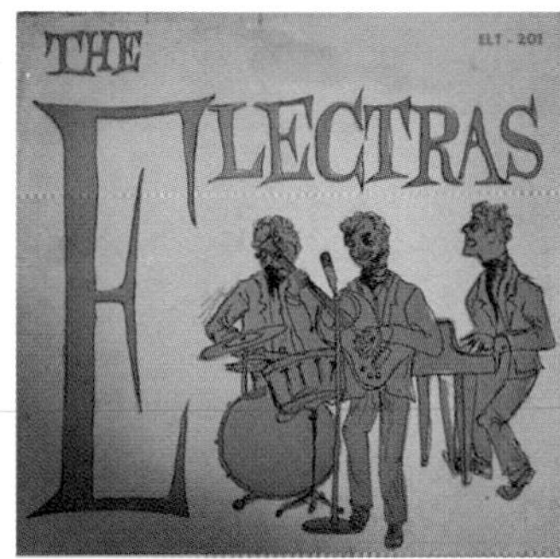

CHUCK MILLER

Edited by Tracy L. Schmidt

Identification and Price Guide

Published by

700 East State Street • Iola, WI 54990-0001
715-445-2214 • 888-457-2873
www.krause.com
Our toll-free number to place an order or obtain a free catalog is (800) 258-0929.

Library of Congress Catalog Number: 2004093900

ISBN: 0-87349-814-3

Designed by Jamie Griffin

Edited by Tracy L. Schmidt

The Electras title page image: During the 2004 Presidential election, it was revealed that the bass player for The Electras was Democratic senator and Presidential candidate John Kerry, causing near-mint record copies to sell for over $2,000. Kerry recorded this album with six of his preparatory school buddies in 1961, selling most of their 500 copies pressed to their classmates. $800, good condition.

Printed in the United States

DEDICATION/ACKNOWLEDGMENTS

Even though my name is on the spine of this book, that doesn't mean I wrote this book myself. There were dozens of people who, both personally and professionally, helped me get this book off the ground, allowed me to photograph their collections and archives, and guided me in the completion of a dream I thought might never come to fruition.

Finding rare records to add to this book was difficult, but not impossible.

Special thanks go to the various record stores and dealers who allowed me to photograph everything from Robert Johnson Vocalions to Bob Dylan cover variations. These include Last Vestige Music Store in Albany, N.Y.; Val Shively's House of Oldies in Pa.; Rockaway Records in Los Angeles, Calif.; Blue Note Records in North Miami Beach, Fla. (and the Blue Note Record Shop in Albany, N.Y.); various dealers and collectors throughout the Internet who helped provide many of the rare photos that you see in this book. Thanks to all.

This book could not be written without the guidance and support of Krause Publications and *Goldmine* magazine, with whom I have been associated for the past eight years. A hearty thanks to the staff of *Goldmine* magazine, including former editor Greg Loescher, assistant editor Cathy Bernardy, former editor Michael Metzger, and former assistant editor Irwin Soonachan. Each of these people, as well as those behind the scenes at *Goldmine*, have guided me throughout my continued association with the magazine. A big thank you also to the staff of the book division at Krause Publications, including research director Tim Neely, book editor Tracy Schmidt, and acquisitions editor Paul Kennedy.

Many of the record shows I attended while working on this project contained dealers and experts who were more than willing to help answer, explain, and demonstrate concepts and collecting tips that could be passed to you. Many thanks also go to those who sent rare images from their own personal collection, who took the time to take a snapshot or forward a photocopy (or even the original records) to me. Special thanks go to Mark Roberts of Ultimix Records; David S. Carne; John Tefteller; Eric Schwartz; Jon "Bermuda" Schwartz; Philip Schwartz and the members of the Keystone Record Collector Club; Lindsay Thomas Morgan; Jim Wright; Henry Sapoznik; Charles Essmeier, Jr.; Tom Grosh; Clark Favrille; Tom Kelly; Russell Shor; Mark Berresford; Ed Guy; Russ Harrington; DCC Compact Classics; Val Shively; Bob Szuszzewicz; Bruce Spizer, and Mark Pisani. Much appreciation also goes to my "Board of Advisors," whose valuable expertise in musical collecting genres made this book happen. Make sure you visit their page and ask them any questions that were not covered in my book. I'm sure they have all the answers.

A special thanks to Brad Paisley, who was kind enough to write the foreword to this book. Brad's shared observations are a special contribution, and I am honored that he helped out.

There have been three generations of Millers who helped to make this project a success. Both my grandmother, Betty Miller, and my aunt, Elaine Miller, have scoured the New England yard sales and flea markets and collector's shops for 30 years, and have found some significant treasures for my collection. Thanks to my mother-in-law, Doris Robinson, who used the power of inter-library loan to help me find dozens of books and research materials for this project. And a special thanks to my wife, Vicki, without whose support this book could never have been finished, and who never lost faith in me.

And a special thanks to you, the person holding this book now. I want to hear from you about *Warman's American Records*. I want your ideas, your opinions, and your stories about your collection. There may be a monetary value placed on a record because of its age, its rarity, or the rare performance by a soon-to-be superstar. But with records, there is also an emotional bond. These are songs you heard at your senior prom or when you were cruising down the highway in your '65 GTO, '73 Pinto, or in your 2001 Nissan Altima.

I'm also looking forward to hearing from you—let me know what you liked or didn't like about this book and its contents, and let me know what records and genres should be considered for future volumes of this book.

Chuck Miller
c/o O&A
54 State Street
Albany NY 12207-2501
email: boardwalk7@aol.com
http://www.chuckthewriter.com

Mary Wells' first two Motown 45s, "Bye Bye Baby" and "I Don't Want to Take a Chance" were released on this early version of the Motown label ("I Don't Want to Take a Chance" was also released with the "Map of Detroit" artwork). Notice that in addition to putting their street address on the 45, Motown also added their telephone number as well.

$50, *NM condition*

Contents

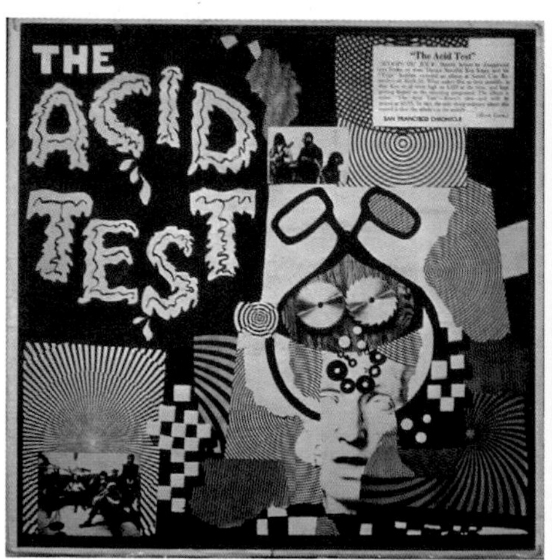

THE
ACID
TEST

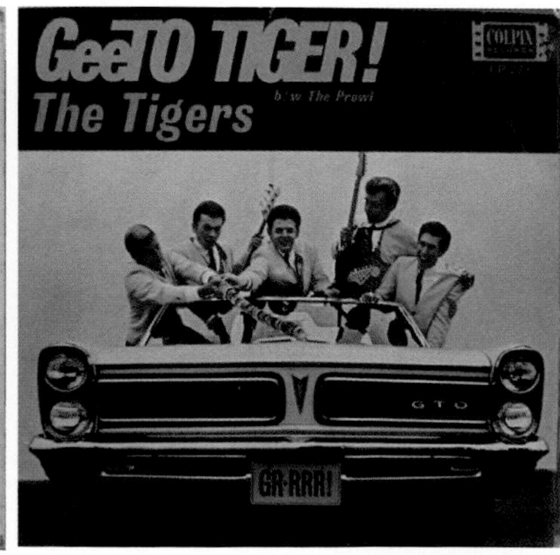

GeeTO TIGER!
The Tigers
COLPIX
GR-RRR!

SHE'S A RAINBOW
LONDON
THE ROLLING STONES

Foreword

I'm a record collector, and have been since the second grade. Back then, my collection included everything from Waylon Jennings singing the theme to "The Dukes of Hazzard," to the J. Geils Band's "Centerfold." These were the songs I grew up with, and all my classmates had them as well. All those records—both my collection of 45s, and the albums my family loved to listen to—helped influence my choice to become a musician.

Brad Paisley, country music superstar and record collector.

Photo credit: Russ Harrington, Russ Harrington Studios, Nashville, Tenn.

My first big break came when I performed Saturday nights at the Capitol Music Hall in Wheeling, West Virginia, as part of the house band backing up the country music superstars on the Saturday night Jamboree USA shows. While there were popular artists coming in from Nashville and other major cities, Wheeling always had its own country music legends who pressed their own records and sold them to adoring fans. Doc Williams' old records are very collectible—he and his wife, Chickie, have performed throughout the East Coast with their band, the Border Riders. I even bought my first pair of cowboy boots from Doc Williams' souvenir store. And Slim Lehart, the guitar-strumming "Wheeling Cat," will always be a part of my musical heritage. I still remember performing with Slim every time Biggie Beyer, the Marshall County Commissioner in West Virginia, would have a benefit fundraiser. It was neat to be around these guys, and their old albums and 45s are getting harder to find today.

I still buy records all the time. We have a couple of great record stores here in Nashville, including The Great Escape and Phonolux. On our honeymoon, my wife and I drove up and down the West Coast. In San Luis Obispo, California, we went into these record stores and bought all these classic old records—Buck Owens, Jimmy Dickens, and the rest.

I love collecting album art—if an album cover makes me laugh or catches my eye—I often pick it up. You can get great albums at a reasonable price that still sound great. How can you pass up a corny album cover like "Satan is Real" by the bluegrass/gospel duo, the Louvin Brothers, from 1960? It's a picture of them in white suits with flames all around them, and a cardboard-cutout Satan in the background.

Many of my hits are still being pressed as 45s. At first, I didn't think they still made 45s. I thought it was somebody the record company hired, who takes it on as a project and makes singles for people to have. It's great that 45s are still manufactured, and no matter what, when you can see the grooves in a record, you know that music is stored in those grooves.

If you're a new record collector, I would recommend you start with buying the old stuff that you love listening to, and then expand out. If you love jazz music, then look at the era and take a look at artists and sounds that were cool. Collect within your budget, but don't be afraid to purchase a record that might have some great previously undiscovered songs.

I hope that you enjoy *Warman's American Records*. Chuck Miller is a knowledgeable record collector and music historian, and this book is a great guide to either begin your own record collection—or to find out if those old records you listened to as a kid have some collectible value today.

—Brad Paisley

While Brad Paisley's albums are only available on compact disc, several of his hit songs, including "I'm Gonna Miss Her" and "Who Needs Pictures," are available on 45s.

***$4**, NM condition*

Doc and Chickie Williams' song and poem "Beyond the Sunset/Should You Go First and I Remain" has been covered by several country music performers, including Hank Williams Sr. and Johnny Cash.

***$40**, NM condition*

Charlie and Ira Louvin's album Satan is Real *was also issued as a series of four-song 45-RPM extended-play singles. The record company also kept the duo's striking album art on the 45 jackets.*

***$75**, VG+ condition*

Introduction

Welcome to the updated new edition of *Warman's American Records*. If you've purchased this book, or even if you're in a bookstore thumbing through this introduction, it's a good assumption that you either have a record collection, or are considering starting one.

Granted, the records that are part of your "collection" may have been in your attic for years, or your brother went to college and said you could have them. You've seen them at flea markets, yard sales, estate sales, and specialized weekend sales. Some of them have sold at auctions for thousands of dollars. Others sit forlornly in old boxes and crates, unsold for even the "50 cents" price on the crate cover. Perhaps you heard a song on the radio, and wanted a copy of that song for your own listening pleasure. Or your enjoyment of a particular singer's catalog might persuade you to purchase their recordings on name recognition alone.

Vocal harmony groups of the early 1950s, especially Federal label recordings by the Midnighters, the Dominoes, or the Royals, are very collectible. This song, "Work With Me Annie," was reportedly too salacious for airplay, yet it spawned a series of answer records, as well as a cover version by Georgia Gibbs, "Dance With Me Henry." **$50**, *VG+ condition*

For the past 100 years, this music has been stored on records. Whether these records are cylindrical or circular; whether they were pressed on shellac, vinyl, styrene, flexible plastic, celluloid, or metallic soap; whether those records contain the operatic acrobatics of Enrico Caruso or the axe-playing dexterity of Eddie Van Halen, records are part of our culture and history. Before motion pictures and radio, cylinder records have captured the earliest voices and speeches, giving us in the 21st century the opportunity to hear our 19th-century ancestors. Records have survived wars, economic depressions, oil embargoes, and the changing tastes of the general population. And against all odds, records have even survived the digital technology of compact discs—the very equipment that would have sent vinyl records into extinction.

A record is a work of art, not just in sound, but in appearance as well. Album covers have long doubled as fine art, as evidenced in 1939 when Alex Steinweiss created the first artworks for Columbia 78 RPM folios. Holding a record in your hand, you can see the grooves and inherently know that the song starts when the grooves wind tight on the disc—when the grooves space apart, there is silence until they tighten up again. What looks like a simple black circle with a pretty picture in the center, can contain melodies and lyrics as complex as an All-Star midnight jam.

Like you, I am also a record collector. Since 1975, when my grandmother bought me a box of 45s from a flea market, I've been hooked. Over the next 30 years, I've visited record stores, used record shops, flea markets, conventions, record shows, estate sales, the Internet, my grandmother's basement, almost anywhere records could be found. There's been treasure and trash in all my searches, and sometimes when I think I've seen too many copies of "Have You Never Been Mellow" or "Weekend in New England," I would find a rare record, almost forgotten by its original owners, looking for a collector to take it home.

Ronnie Spector's 1977 record "Say Goodbye to Hollywood" was an all-star affair—the song was penned by Billy Joel, and as can be seen on this hard-to-find picture sleeve, the backup musicians were none other than Bruce Springsteen's E Street Band. Picture sleeve **$12.50**, *VG+ condition*

By using this book, you will discover the wonders of colored vinyl and picture discs—how they're made and the special appeal collectors have for them. You'll learn about ring wear, edge warps, scratches, mispressings, cue burn, bootlegs, stickers, counterfeits, and reproductions. Perhaps you'll find you have an even greater appreciation for you collection.

Terminology and Grading

Just as the Eskimos and skiers have numerous terms for snow, record collectors have numerous terms and nicknames for their records: Discs. Platters. 7-inchers. 12-inchers. LPs. 45s. Golden Oldies. Stacks of Wax. Frisbees. Whatever term we use for them, not all records are the same—there are often variations in label art, lyrics, song order, condition, and playability.

The best and most accepted method of grading a record is by using the *Goldmine* grading system. This system is used by dealers and collectors alike, and offers a universal standard for collectors. There are many different factors involved in grading a record—the physical condition of the album jacket or picture sleeve; the visual condition of the record; and if possible, how the record sounds when played on a turntable with a properly calibrated stylus and balanced tonearm. For visual quality, look at the record under a strong light. Take into consideration how the label looks, if there are any scratches, scuffs, cracks, or discolorations on the record's grooved portion.

After you've examined the disc, give it a grade based on the following requirements:

MINT (M). The record is perfect. No flaws, scratches, or scuffs on the grooves. Mint jackets are clean and crisp, with no disfigurations whatsoever. There is an argument that even a record coming straight out of the factory to your hands cannot be completely "mint" like a coin or a stamp, and therefore the "mint" grade should be used rarely, if at all.

NEAR MINT (NM) or **MINT-MINUS** (M-). The record is as close to perfect as possible. No marks whatsoever on the grooves. The label is clean, unmarked, and unscuffed. There is no ring wear on the album cover or on the picture sleeve. There is no background surface noise on the disc. Some dealers will not give a record a grade higher than "near-mint," as it may be their belief that no record can ever be truly "perfect." For purposes of this book, "near-mint" will be the standard for which all other conditions will be based. This figure is approximately the highest a dealer will sell a record in such condition.

This near-mint copy of Heart's "Magic Man" looks pristine. Notice the label colors are bright and crisp; and the grooves show no wear.

***$8**, NM condition*

VERY GOOD PLUS (VG+). The record has been played, but by someone who took extremely good care of his or her record collection. There might be some slight "scuffs" or "warps" on the grooves; which on a VG+ record should not affect the sound quality when played. You may see a faint outline of ring discoloration on the album jacket or picture sleeve (ring discoloration occurs when albums are stored together on a shelf, and time causes some of the album artwork to rub off, causing a circular "ring" on the album jacket). There might be a tiny dent in the corner of the album cover, or a small split in one of the jacket's seams. If a record has one or two of these flaws, it is considered "VG+"—just missing the final cut for Near Mint. Records in VG+ condition should sell for approximately half of the same record in NM condition.

VERY GOOD (VG). Records in this condition have more pronounced defects. You'll hear a small hiss when you play the record, but you'll still be able to hear the music without difficulty. There may be scratches on the record, but they won't affect the record's playability. The album cover may have more pronounced ringwear or a bigger split in one of the seams. There might be the residue of a mailing label or sticker on the album cover or on the label. Part of the label may have scratches or may have lost some adherence to the vinyl.

A "very good" record may have one or two of these defects or aberrations, but not all of them. Records in VG condition should sell for approximately 25% of the same record in NM condition. If your record is in NM condition and you wish to sell it to a dealer, he may only pay you the VG price so that he can make a profit with the disc in a future transaction. Most music collectible books will not list values for less than VG condition, and this book is one of them.

This "good" copy of Heart's "Magic Man" shows some wear on the label, especially in the green background, as well as a slight tear along the label hole.

***$3**, Good condition*

GOOD or GOOD PLUS (G, G+). You can play a "good" or "good plus" record on your turntable and listen to the music. You might not mind that the record was formerly owned by Stacy Davis of Anaheim, California (you know that because she affixed a mailing sticker on the record label, covering up the label trademark). You will need some tape to repair the splits in two of the album jacket seams. The jacket or picture sleeve will have severe ring wear, rips, folds, gouges, or damage from water or some other stain.

There may be cracks in the record, which will cause a pop when the needle passes over it. The record might have a moderate warp, which might affect the tonearm's operation. The record may have been pressed off-center, causing the tonearm to sway back and forth like a hypnotist's pendant. Or the label itself may have been pressed off-center, so much so that the paper itself actually touches the runout grooves. The scratches on the record give a "recorded near a bonfire" quality to the song. If the disc is made of styrene, the grooves of the record may have turned white from constant play

A rule of thumb is that if you have been looking for this record for most of your life, and you find it in this condition, you should buy it only with the mindset that you will keep looking for a better copy, and eventually use the record now in your collection as a backup copy. If the record was once certified multiplatinum, that means there are millions of copies of this record somewhere, you can pass on this "well-loved" or "gently used" copy someday. Records in G or G+ condition should sell for approximately 10% of the same record in NM condition.

This is a "fair" copy of Heart's "Magic Man." Notice the label shows severe wear patterns, the colors have worn away, somebody penned a "1" on the label—and if the label looks this distressed, imagine the numerous plays that have worn down the grooves.
25¢, *Fair condition*

POOR or FAIR (P, F). These records have little collector value. The record label has magic marker or crayon all over it, or decorated with stamps and stickers and other defacings. The record is cracked to the point where pieces of the groove are missing. The edge warps look like mountain peaks, and playing the record will cause your tonearm to fly out of the grooves.

If the album jacket hasn't fallen apart, it's holding on by a couple of unsplit corners. There's graffiti on the front cover—if not the previous owner's name, some artwork defacing the singer or least favorite band member. Or a young lady has decided Mick Jagger is her favorite Rolling Stone, and the lipstick prints near his picture on the album cover are clear proof. The 45s picture sleeve is wrinkled and splitting, or its center may have been cut out. Unless this record is an extremely rare piece that would normally sell for four figures in NM condition, one should pay no more than a few pennies—if at all—for records in this condition.

It is not always the case that the record's condition is caused by the care—or lack thereof—of the purchaser or owner. Sometimes a record company's quality control division misses a mispressed or off-center 45. The glue on a 45 label may have lost its adherence due to age, and the label may have simply fallen off the record.

Other Definitions in this Book

MONO. The record was produced in monaural sound, one audio channel of music. Virtually all records made before the 1950s, and many records up until the late 1960s, were produced in mono.

This Toto 45 is a common record to begin with, but someone in the record company's "quality control" department let this mispressing, with a center hole an inch out of true, appear on store shelves. Records like these are only collectible as curiosities, and are nearly impossible to play or listen to without aspirin.
25¢, *Poor condition*

STEREO. The record was produced in stereophonic sound, offering two distinct audio channels of music. Widespread use of stereo record production began in the mid-1950s. Until the late 1960s, you could purchase your choice of records in either mono or stereo (not all monaural phonographs could play stereo records).

ELECTRONICALLY CHANNELED STEREO or **FAKE STEREO**. Sometimes used by producers to turn a mono track into a stereo track—the left channel might include all the bass notes, while the right channel might incorporate all the higher-frequency instruments and vocals.

QUADRAPHONIC. In the early 1970s, some record companies experimented with quadraphonic sound, allowing specially-designed phonographs to play sounds into four different speakers.

A **PICTURE DISC** is an album or 45 that has a photograph or artwork pressed into the vinyl. Usually a picture disc has a representation of the album's original front cover on the vinyl; other times the record contains photographs of the band members or representative artwork. Depending on the artwork, a picture disc can also exist in non-circular formats (the grooves will remain circular, but the perimeter of the record may be uniquely shaped).

A **PICTURE SLEEVE** is a special paper holder for 45s. It often contains specialized artwork and a photo of the artist or group. In near-mint condition, some picture sleeves can attain a value worth more than the records they once contained. You may also see a 45 stored in a **COMPANY SLEEVE**, which often contains an artistic representation of the record company's trademark logo. A 45 may also appear in a generic **WHITE SLEEVE**, or in a generic **CARDBOARD SLEEVE** (mostly sold by record supply companies), or in no sleeve at all.

Several record companies, including Capitol, Vee Jay, Brunswick, and Decca, pressed their labels with rainbow art, often called a "color bar" (straight line or arrow of rainbow) or a "color band" (a rainbow around the label's perimeter). Besides their visual aesthetics, color-banded labels are harder to counterfeit than solid-colored labels.
$25, *NM condition*

When the last song on a record is played, the needle will ride the **RUNOUT GROOVE** to an infinite loop bordering the label. A record's **DEAD WAX** or **TRAIL-OFF VINYL** is the black, grooveless area surrounding the label, and often contains engraved mastering numbers and the mastering agent's initials or company name. Sometimes the dead wax contains cryptic messages from the band, phrases or messages designed to entertain, confuse, titillate, or mystify.

HIS MASTER'S VOICE or **NIPPER** refers to the dog and gramophone logo of RCA Victor Records. Other labels will have artwork representing the label's headquarters—a map of Detroit

(Motown), the Sears Tower in Chicago (Mercury, mid-1970's), or a Burbank street lined with palm trees (Warner Bros, mid-1970s).

The location of logos or text record label may be referenced in terms of a clock face. "12 o'clock" means at the top of the record label; "6 o'clock" means at the bottom of the record label.

A vinyl album is usually stored in an **INNER SLEEVE**. This is usually made of paper, plastic or some other protective compound, and protects the album when it is stored in its **OUTER SLEEVE** or **COVER**. Inner sleeves can contain liner notes, song lyrics, fan club information, and/or photographs of other records in a record company's catalog.

How dare you list my favorite song as only worth a couple of dollars! Don't you know this song is one of the greatest of all time? The singer is a legend! That record should be worth millions!

One of the biggest myths and fallacies about record collecting is that an artist's most significant work will be the most desirable and collectible. Sometimes that's true, sometimes it isn't. I would never argue that the Beach Boys' greatest songs—"Good Vibrations," "I Get Around," "Wouldn't It Be Nice," and "Surfer Girl" are classics. But even a near-mint copy of "Good Vibrations" is only worth $15. Meanwhile, a song they recorded in 1971, "Cool, Cool Water" (Reprise 0998) can command a near-mint price tag of $80. It was a minor hit on the Beach Boys' custom label Brother, and it was poorly distributed. So for Beach Boys collectors, this song is hard to find. And their earliest recording of "Surfin" can command $200-$300 dollars on the Candix label, and four times as much on the "X" label, both the names of a record company the group was associated with before their major-label signing with Capitol.

Another record myth is that because of the popularity of compact discs, nobody makes vinyl records any more. Actually, more titles are available on vinyl today than were in the past ten years. Even though record production decreased in the 1990s, some artists have always released their singles and albums on vinyl, as well as on compact disc and on cassette (Pearl Jam, R.E.M., and Madonna, to name a few). Artists such as Bruce Springsteen, Eminem, Sean Paul, and the White Stripes have released their current popular albums on vinyl, mostly as two-LP sets to capably fit a CDs worth of material. Most hip-hop records are available as 12" vinyl dance mixes, allowing a budding hip-hop maven the opportunity to spin discs on his own wheels of steel.

Even Brad Paisley, who wrote the foreword to my book, has had several of his hits available as 45s. Some 45s are being pressed to serve two markets, the United States and the United Kingdom—both countries have millions of vinyl-playing jukeboxes that, without a steady stream of 45s to play and to generate an income for their owners, would eventually enter obsolescence.

And still another myth about collecting is that in order to keep a record in near-mint condition, it should never be played or even touched. If you've spent $100 on a rare non-sealed record, wouldn't you like to know what's on it, to hear its treasured buried in the grooves? Well, if you have a good turntable with a well-adjusted tonearm and proper stylus—and if you properly clean the record after each playing—and you're making a personal copy to your cassette player so that you can listen to this album in a non-eroding format, then that's fine. If you properly store your vinyl with care and attention, your records can maintain their near-mint or VG+ grade for years, even decades.

Yet another myth about record collecting is that these prices are hard and fast—no dickering, no bargaining, and that's that. Since records are considered collectibles the same way trading cards and rare coins are considered collectible, prices can fluctuate. And like trading cards, some records can increase in value depending on where—or to whom—they are sold. The average music lover wouldn't know who Timothy McNealy is to save his life; but a funk music collector could pay as much as $700 for a copy of McNealy's funk groove "Sagittarius Black."

What's the deal with those numbers and letters in the runout grooves?

The dead wax in the runout grooves of albums often contains an undecipherable series of numbers and letters, but in many cases that alphanumeric code can tell you when and where a particular album was pressed, and whether it was one of the first pressings out of the factory. Knowledge of such information can increase the value of your record, and can help you in purchasing a record that is rarer than its print run would normally indicate.

First, some explanation of what happens after an artist records an album. The tapes are edited, remixed, and recorded onto a "master tape," which is carefully timed for the length of one side of an album. Metal stampers, which will be used to press the vinyl into records, are made from the master tape.

RCA's 45s and LPs contain an alphanumeric code in the runout groove. If you look at the accompanying photo of SSgt. Barry Sadler's "Ballads of the Green Berets" album, you can see the digitally enhanced code "SPRM 6184 3S" in the dead wax at the record's lower left. ***$10**, NM condition*

Before 1955, the first two alphanumeric characters in the code corresponded with the year of the original master tape. The first letter, "A" through "E", represents the decade of the master tape's creation, while the second character would be a number representing the year within that decade. "D9", for example, means the master was made in 1949, while "E3" means 1953.

Beginning in 1955, RCA scrapped the two-character identification system. Now the master tape's year of creation would be represented by a single letter—"F" for 1955, "G" for 1956, and so on. The letters "I," "O," "Q," and "V" are skipped in this sequence, so the pattern runs like this:

(F-1955) (G-1956) (H-1957) (J-1958) (K-1959) (L-1960) (M-1961) (N-1962) (P-1963) (R-1964) (S-1965) (T-1966) (U-1967) (W-1968) (X-1969) (Y-1970) (Z-1971). So an "S" recording means Sadler recorded his album in 1965.

The fourth letter of the RCA code corresponds with the recording format, "M" or "P" for mono, "Y" or "S" for stereo. So now we know this album is a mono pressing from 1965.

The four-digit number in the middle means that this album side was created with the 6,183rd master tape produced by RCA.

The last numbers, followed by a final "S," indicate which generation metal stamper was used to create the album. An indication of "1S" means the record was pressed with the first generation of stampers made for that album. This example has "3S"—meaning the pressing plants wore out two stampers before this record was even made. Since stampers wear out at different rates, it is not uncommon to find one side of a record with a higher or lower stamper number than the other.

After examining the code, if you want to find out where the record was made, look in another area of the dead wax, usually on the opposite side of the label from the code. There you will find a machine stamped or hand-drawn letter "I," "H," or "R". RCA records stamped with an "H" were made in their Hollywood, California factory. An "I" means the records were pressed in Indianapolis. And if the dead wax letter is "R," the record was manufactured in RCA's plant in Rockaway, New York.

This coding system works for RCA releases; other record companies used different numbering methods. For some collectors, stamper numbers are the DNA code of a record. With it, they can determine a record's history, its audio content, even the home factory and date when it was pressed.

Record Collecting and the Internet

There is no doubt that the Internet has changed the way most record collectors acquire those rare and hard-to-find titles. Those same collectors, who five years ago went from show to show, now purchase rare records with a click of the mouse and a mailed money order. Sites like eBay.com, Gemm.com, and Bidville.com have helped unite collectors with rare titles, and many record stores now handle a brisk business in online sales.

If you do buy records on the Internet, either with an auction or from a sale, make sure you work with a reputable dealer. Ask about money-back guarantees if you're not satisfied with the product received. If the seller does not offer insurance, especially on 78s or cylinders, offer to pay the insurance yourself. Since buyers cannot physically see the record, only a photograph or digital image of that record, quality descriptions and communications are key.

Without viewing photographs in an Internet auction, you wouldn't know that this Ugly Ducklings 45, which would normally sell for $60-$75 dollars in near-mint condition, has been defaced with someone's magic marker initials.
***$30**, Good condition*

Also make sure that your seller will safely pack and ship the record. For example, I wanted to include a copy of the Davis Sisters' 78 "I Forgot More Than You'll Ever Know About Him," but the copy I won at an Internet auction arrived poorly packed, and broken in half.

Since a potential buyer can only see the record via photographs provided by the seller, it is important to ask questions and request photographs of a record, especially one for which you are willing to pay top dollar. An Internet seller should take as many photos as is reasonable, if you are seriously interested in purchasing a record online. You don't need 100 photos of every conceivable angle, but if you hear the words "small pen mark on cover," you want to see a photograph of the item to determine how many pairs of antenna, buck teeth, and shiners did the previous ballpoint artist give to that otherwise rare Beatles' album.

Why Isn't My Favorite Album or Artist or Genre Listed In This Price Guide?

First off, I have no bad feelings for any musical artist or group. And I would love to list every single album ever made, every 45 ever pressed, every picture sleeve ever printed. Such a book would be the size of the New York City phone directory, would cost at least $500 apiece, and would kill more trees than a California wildfire.

Warman's American Records was written for beginning and intermediate record collectors. It's for people who want to start their own record collection. It's for new collectors who want to visit a record collecting show, and make educated purchases without fear of overspending.

For more information on specific types of record collecting, and to find out more about the artists, singers, and genres, each subdivision of this book contains a bibliography, specific magazines, and Internet Web pages loaded with discographies, discussions, and downloadable data.

Most of all, this book was written to explain why certain records are collectible, while others are not. The quality of the artist's work is not necessarily equal to the record's collectible price. Sometimes a lyric is changed during a song's print run; sometimes a record was yanked off the market, leaving only a few copies in the hands of eager collectors. On the other hand, sometimes an album may stay in print for decades, with only a variation in label art or vinyl thickness as an identifying clue.

How to Read the Prices and Information in This Book

At the end of each chapter is a representative list of various artists and recordings in that genre or format. The artist's name is listed first, then the various formats in which that artist's music is available. For listings, the artist's record company and catalog are listed first, then the A-side and/or B-side of the release, any distinguishing information (promo only, colored vinyl, limited print run), and the year of release if available.

Two prices will then be listed—the higher value is the "near-mint" or "NM" value, or the amount one should expect to pay for a clean, nearly perfect copy. The second value, "very-good-plus," or "VG+," is a shade below near-mint, and might have a blemish or two. A good rule of thumb is that the more a record shows wear and use, the less a collector will pay for it.

If an artist has several releases with a single record company, that company's label name is listed first (RCA Victor, Warner Bros., Motown, Sugarhill), then the songs released by that company are listed below. When an artist or group moves to another label, the new label is listed and several titles from that artist are listed in conjunction with same.

There was a chapter on something in the first edition of this book, but it's not in this edition. What gives? Is it not collectible any more?

Those records are still collectible, even if the listings or genres were removed form this update. As much as I would have loved to keep every chapter from the first edition in this update, there were dozens of chapters that didn't get in the first time around because of the original edition's timeframe (focusing on records made post-1950).

So what's new in this book?

For one thing, this book now contains information on several previously overlooked record collecting genres. Some of these genres are "cross-collectible titles," meaning that these records are prized by other hobbyists who would not otherwise be interested in music.

These new chapters include:

Childrens' Records: The first records we ever owned; whether they contained stories or songs, were pressed on colored vinyl, or needed a special phonograph attachment, this chapter will bring a smile to your face.

Bootleg Pressings: Records that were never officially authorized by the artists or the established record companies. Some of these pressings have enormous historical significance and interest, but can unauthorized pressings be truly collectible?

Bob Dylan: First perceived as a poet of the folk generation; today, he is considered one of the greatest songwriters America has ever produced.

45s : A chapter devoted to the history of the 45 RPM format. How did this 7-inch, big-holed record become a dominant force in music for over 50 years?

Psychedelic Releases: Music mixed with a dreamscape, both imaginary and pharmaceutically assisted.

Swing: Featuring the big bands orchestras that helped win the war.

In addition, several chapters were expanded from the previous edition to include and incorporate records that were made before 1950, including rare photos of records for which only a few copies exist today. The chapter on picture discs now features striking and brilliant shots of Vogue Picture Discs, while the colored vinyl section features two of the oldest swirl-vinyl pressings, both commemorative issues from the first World War.

Other chapters from the previous edition were combined into a more cohesive section. For example, the chapters on Philles Records and Cameo-Parkway Records are now part of "Rock and Roll" a chapter devoted to collecting music from 1955 to the end of 1963, before the Beatles appeared on American shores.

How were the prices arrived at for this book?

Darts. Plain and simple. I used the same dartboard from the last time I worked on this book, since it worked so well the first time.

Actually, the prices for the records in this book were arrived at from various sources from within the Krause Publications family of books, including *The Standard Catalog of American Records* (3rd Edition), *The Goldmine Price Guide to 45 RPM Records* (3rd Edition), *The Goldmine Record Album Price Guide* (3rd Edition), *The Goldmine Promo Record and CD Price Guide*, *The Goldmine 45 RPM Picture Sleeve Price Guide*, *The Goldmine Country Western Record and CD Price Guide*, *The Goldmine Price Guide to Alternative Records*, *The Goldmine Heavy Metal Price Guide*, and *The Goldmine Jazz Album Price Guide*.

Within these books, the authors were in contact with thousands of used record shops, sifted through millions of advertisements and auction results, and listened to legions of record collectors. While these prices may constitute an educated listing of millions of titles, they should only be considered a reference guide and in no way a listing of iron-clad prices. Krause Publications does not set prices for records; it only reflects the trends shown in the marketplace for collectible and desirable vinyl. The publishers of *Warman's® American Records* do not buy and sell records. So therefore, none of the items in this book are "offers to buy" or "offers to sell" from Krause Publications, F&W Publishing, *Warman's® American Records*, or this author.

Chuck Miller
c/o O&A
54 State Street
Albany NY 12207-2501
email: boardwalk7@aol.com
http://www.chuckthewriter.com

Buying and selling promotional records on the Internet is not an easy project. Some of the language on white label promos actually states that the record is the property of the original issuing company, who can at any time request that the record be returned from the radio station. Some record companies have kept an eye on Internet auctions, and any auctions with the terms "white label promo" or "WLP" may get cancelled. Some artists also look at Internet auctions for promo copies, because the records that were originally not for sale are now trading hands for cash; cash that the artist does not receive. The debate on whether promotional records can be sold on the secondary market continues to this day.

***$100**, NM condition*

Section 1

The Art Of Presentation: Formats

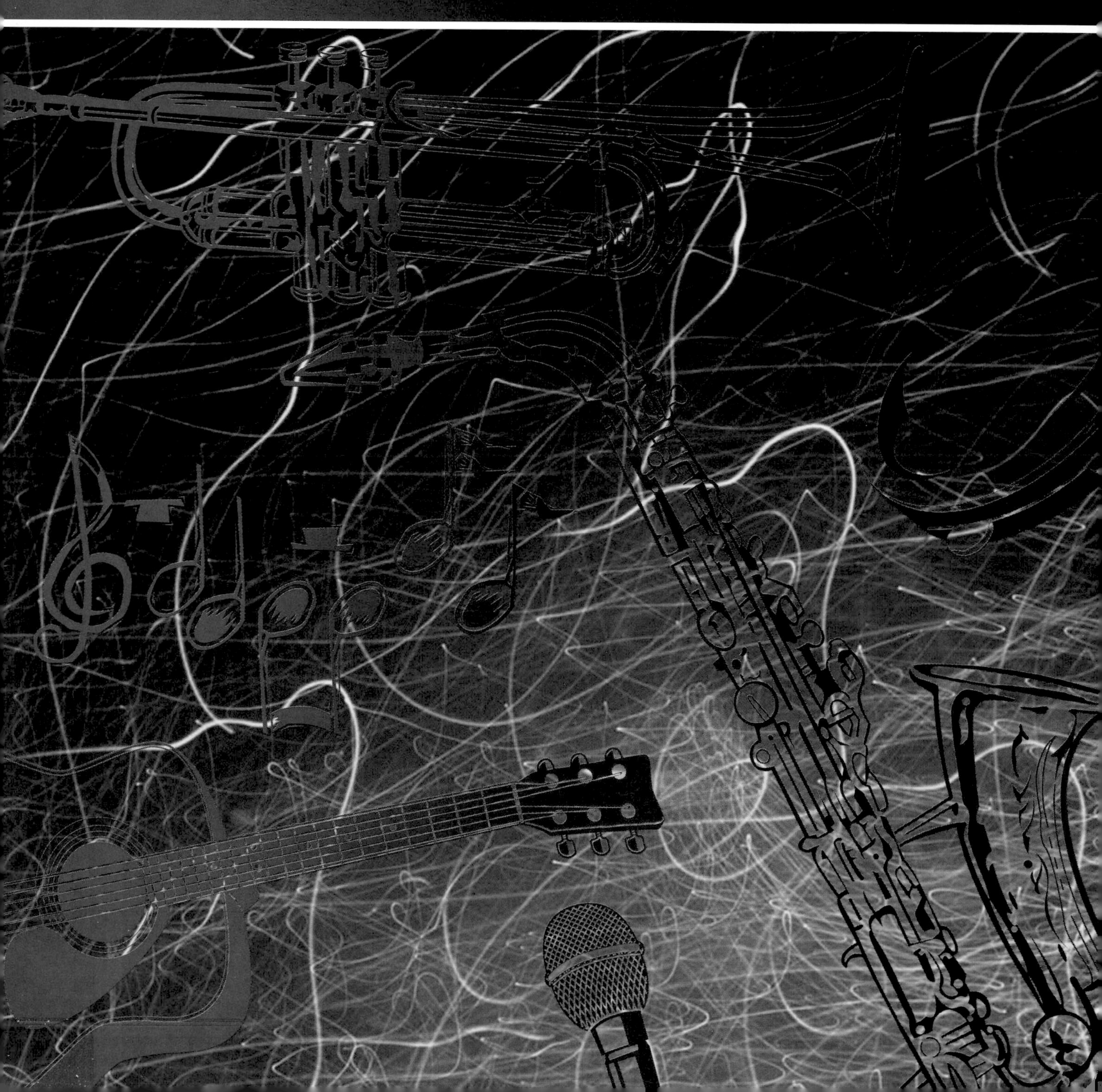

CHAPTER 1

45s

History

They are seven inches in diameter, often pressed from polyvinyl chloride or polystyrene. Bearing two concentric grooves, one on each side of the disc, they provide anywhere from 90 seconds to eight minutes of preserved sound. The grooves lead to a circular paper label, with information on the artist, the song on that side, and possibly a picture of a dog staring at a gramophone, two concentric red-yellow swirls, a stylized map of Detroit, a rooster crowing at a musical scale, or any number of artistic statements. It was born from an attempt to keep a record company's market share solvent; it developed into the predominant format for single-song musical enjoyment, and today, still holds an importance and fascination among collectors of popular music.

Up until the mid-1940s, the predominant format for popular music was the 10-inch, 78 RPM record, an unchallenged format for nearly half a century. But despite their popularity, 78s suffered from two inherent limitations: because of their high rotation speed, 78s could only hold three to four minutes of music on each side. And because most 78s were still made of fragile shellac (a resin produced by tiny red beetles in Thailand), discs could easily break and crack if dropped.

RCA Victor developed the 7-inch, 45 RPM record as an alternative to their rival Columbia's 33-1/3 RPM 12-inch record. Light, durable and easy to manufacture, 45s became the outlet for pop songs, available to music lovers at an affordable price. By the mid-1950s, 45s had proven their

Unlike most 1970s singles, Bruce Springsteen's "Born to Run" 45 was released in its original 4:25 length, mostly because Springsteen produced the record in such a way that it was difficult to edit down to a three-minute length.
***$20**, NM condition*

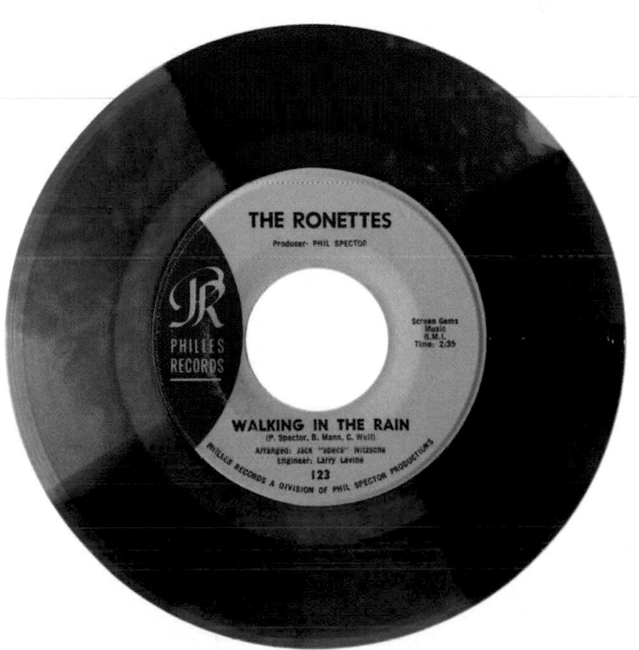

From the collection of John Tefteller.

*Several 45s and LPs were pressed by factory employees as one-of-a-kind "after hours" pressings, made from leftover colored-vinyl pellets. The record's visual beauty notwithstanding, values for these discs are highly speculative because only a few copies of any certain title exist. Speculative value in NM condition, **$250**.*

durability, eventually forcing the 78 RPM platter off the market. By 1959, American 78s had disappeared from store shelves. Other countries kept manufacturing 78s—Canada pressed some titles into 1960; while India made 78s until at least 1966, including some Beatles 78s.

RCA Victor added a large 1-1/2" diameter hole in the center of their 45s so their records would be incompatible with phonographs manufactured for 78s or the new 33-1/3s, and could only be played on RCA Victor's line of "Victrola" dropchanger phonographs. This forced phonograph manufacturers to devise a line of spindle column attachments that could hold a stack of 45s, dropping them in the proper order of song play. Of course, RCA Victor was more than willing to create a line of column spindle attachments, if it would help sell their 45 line.

To fill the hole—literally—many companies manufactured single-use adapters. Made of plastic, zinc, or steel; these implements could be snapped into a record's center hole, allowing the music to be heard on a thin-spindled phonograph. The first adapters were manufactured by the Webster Electric Company of Chicago, and were made of zinc. By the 1960s, plastic adapters by Hutchison, Duotone, and Recoton commanded the market. Metal adapters returned to prominence in the 1970s, as Pfanstiehl created a flat zinc adapter that was perfect for dance remix DJ use.

While most 45s in the 1950s and early 1960s were pressed in black vinyl, with monaural sound, there were small print runs of colored vinyl 45s, mostly in a translucent red hue. Some companies even experimented with special stereo 45s, creating an entire new label to trumpet the record's improved fidelity and realistic sound. Many artists re-recorded their classic hits for these stereo pressings, some of which contain variations in phrasing or instrument use. Between 1955 and 1984, the 45 RPM record continued its dominance as a popular music format. But by 1984, the 45s very existence was threatened by the rise in popularity of other new formats.

A red vinyl 45 is, with only a few exceptions, worth much more than its black vinyl counterpart. This pressing by Snooky Pryor can sell for as much as $2,500 in near-mint condition.

***$1,500**, VG+ condition*

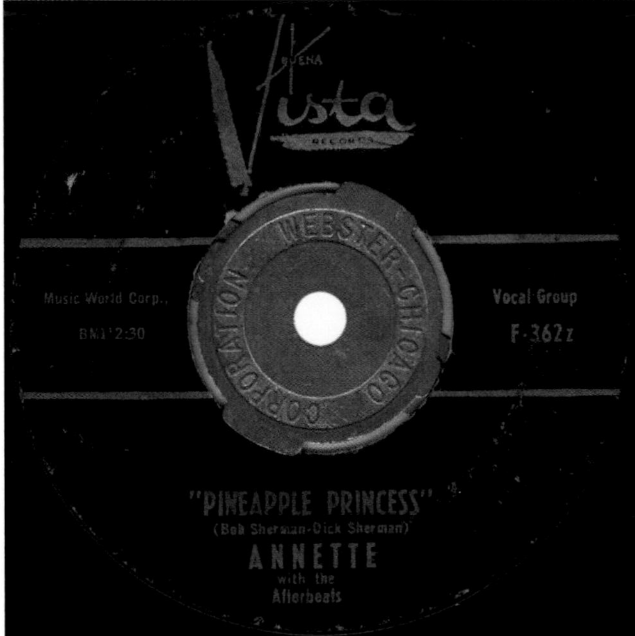

Unlike plastic adapters, which can pop out with a simple tap, metal adapters like this Webster spacer can actually lower the value of a collectible 45; if the adapter is not carefully removed from the record, it could leave notches in the hole rim.

***$5**, Fair condition*

When the Fleetwoods recorded "Come Softly To Me" for a stereo single release, one can hear a jingling sound in the distance. That sound is actually Fleetwoods' member Gary Troxel shaking car keys to help keep the tempo consistent, as the group originally recorded the song a cappella.

***$50**, NM condition*

In 1984, the compact disc made its first appearance in stores. An instant success, the CD eventually overtook sales of albums and 45s, and as consumers replaced their phonographs with CD players, record companies eventually whittled production of albums from millions per title to a few thousand pressings per title. Many companies, instead of making 45s, manufactured cheap "cassingles," a cassette in a thin cardboard sleeve. In addition to that, stores were told they could no longer send unsold 45s back to the record companies for profit or credit, meaning that the stores were stuck with the records, whether they sold or not. With all that, sales of vinyl 45s dropped to near-extinction by the early 1990s.

That's not to say, however, that 45s were completely eliminated. Country music fans could still get their favorite artists' songs on 45—in fact, for years Garth Brooks continued to have his hits pressed on 45s rather than on cassette singles. Several musical acts, including Madonna, R.E.M., and Pearl Jam, still made 45s for their fans who had turntables.

Jukeboxes also helped keep the humble 45 alive. In the opening credits of the TV series *Happy Days*, one sees a jukebox loading a 45 onto a mechanical turntable. In fact, the proliferation of jukeboxes around the world is one of the reasons why some companies continue to make 45s, long after other formats have been discontinued. Without a steady stream of new 45s, the jukeboxes would not generate income for their owners. For that reason, many pressings in the 1990s had the words "For Jukeboxes Only!" stamped on the label, as if to deter their sale or use otherwise.

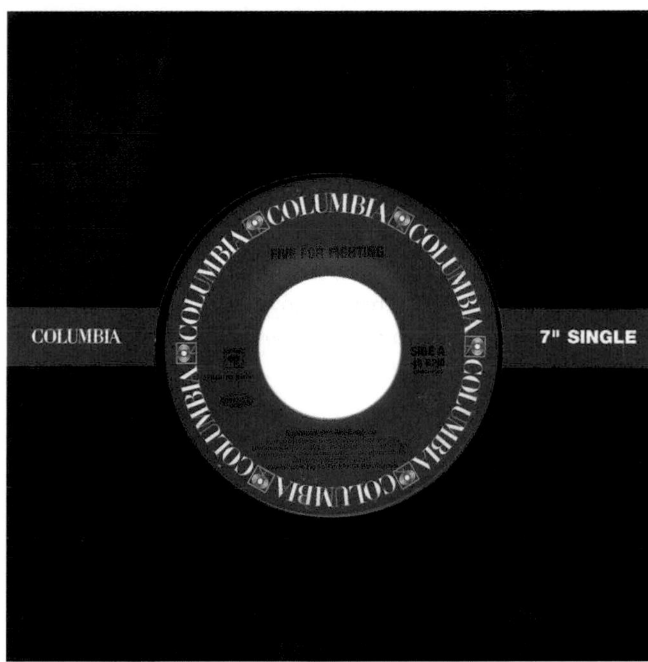

Five for Fighting's hit song "Superman (It's Not Easy)" was not only released on a 45, it was also released with Columbia's new 21st-century label design and hard-stock company sleeve.

***$8**, NM condition*

What To Look For

A good rule of thumb for collecting 45s is to examine a record for condition, rarity, and significance. Labels of 45s often suffer from ringwear and penmarks, at a rate more prevalent than LPs or 78s. Because of their thinness, 45s can also be damaged by heat warps or cracks. Pressings made from polyvinyl chloride (PVC) are much more collectible than those made from polystyrene, an injection plastic used for model kits. The sound quality on styrene pressings can decrease quickly with several plays; and styrene pressings often have spraypainted or inked labels, which wear down with even minimal use. While some American companies used cheap styrene for their pressings (including such labels as Bell, Mala, Amy, Sphere Sound, Philly Groove, and DynoVoice), Canadian 45s were all pressed on vinyl.

It can break a collector's heart to see a 45 label with pen marks, mailing stickers, duct tape, Dymo® plastic labels, medical tape, magic marker, love notes, etc., on it. Yet, even in finding these records in conditions that might be charitably graded "poor" or "are you kidding," one must consider, from an archeological standpoint, that these records may have been played over and over again by fans of a particular singer or group—and something in the song, the artist's performance, the melody, may have been extremely pleasurable to that listener.

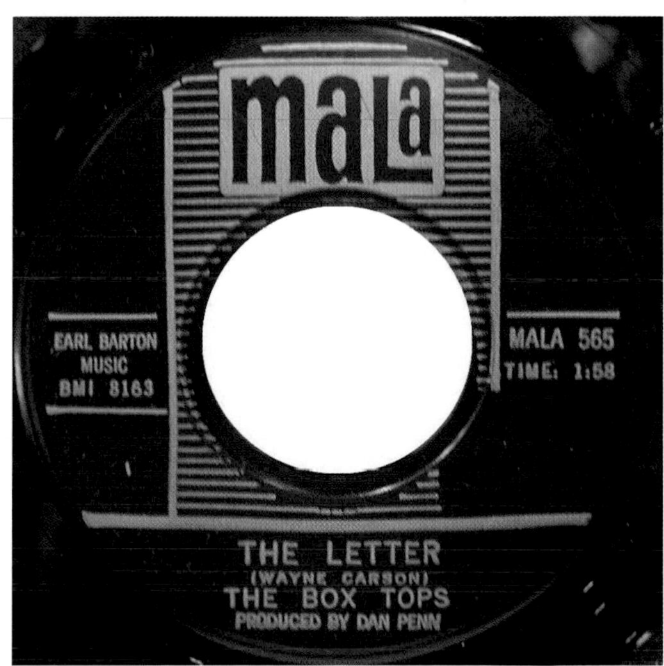

A thin styrene pressing of the Box Tops' "The Letter." Notice that the label artwork actually bleeds into the center hole. Vinyl pressings of this title do exist, depending on which independent pressing plant manufactured the 45s.

***$8**, VG+ condition*

As for "significance," one has to understand that just because a record is collectible, does not in itself mean that the performance on the record is better or worse than a lesser-priced record in an artist's catalog. The rarest recordings in an artist's catalog are usually the pressings made when they first started out, on homemade labels or regional companies, with press runs of anywhere between 200 and 1000 copies.

Books

Vourtsis, Phil, *The Fabulous Victrola "45,"* Schiffer Books, Atgeln, PA, 2002.

Neely, Tim, *Goldmine Price Guide to 45 RPM Records* (4th Edition), Krause Publications, Iola, WI, 2003.

Whitburn, Joel, *Billboard Top Pop Singles, 1955-1999*, Record Research, Menomonee Falls, WI, 2000.

Dawson, Jim and Propes, Steve, *45 RPM: The History, Heroes and Villains of a Pop Music Revolution*, Backbeat Books, San Francisco, CA, 2003.

Web Pages

Get your questions about 45s answered at the Record Collectors Guild, http://www.recordcollectorsguild.org.

Maybe the person who wrote "To My Future Husband Jan" on her Everly Brothers' "Devoted To You" eventually married Jan. We can only hope "Jan" wasn't a record collector, because copies with gouged ballpoint pen marks or felt-tip marker scribblings devalue the record to one-tenth of the price for a near-mint copy.

$2.50, *Fair condition*

One of the loudest garage bands to come out of Iowa, the band Gonn recorded this garage classic "Blackout of Greteley" in 1967. It was later reissued on the Sundazed label, allowing garage fans a chance to hear this rarity.

$400, *NM condition*

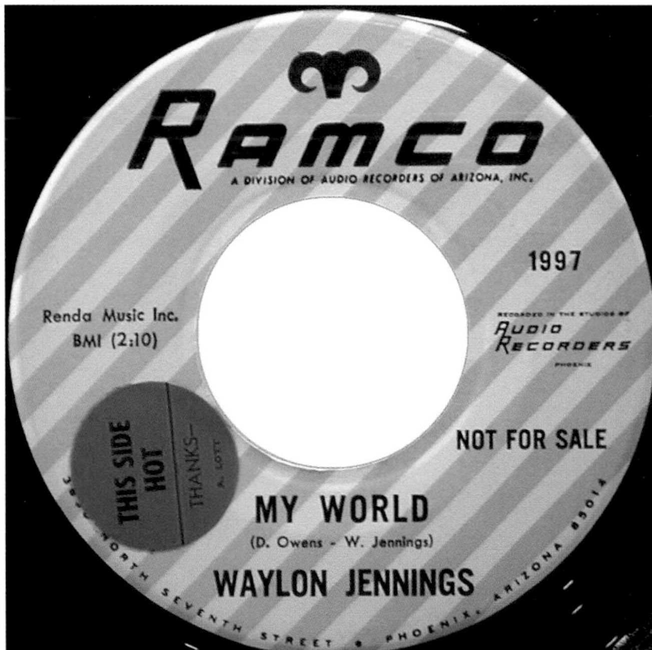

From the collection of Val Shively

This early Waylon Jennings 45, on the tiny Ramco label, is a difficult title to find today—and this pressing even contains a red sticker from an independent promoter, encouraging disc jockeys to play this previously unknown artist.

$12, *NM condition*

Further evidence that 45s are still made today, is this pressing of Kelly Clarkson's "A Moment Like This," her first major hit, from 2002.

***$4**, NM condition*

The Raspberries were one of the creators of "power pop," melodic hits with jangly guitar riffs and hooky refrains. "Go All The Way," their first hit, is one of the thickest, most heavily processed 45s made at the time.

***$6**, NM condition*

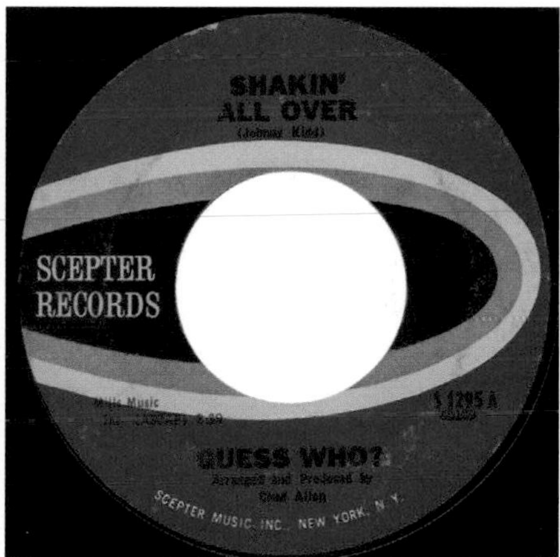

Photo Credit: Guess Who? Quality 45 from the Collection of Piers Hemmingsen.

When Chad Allan and the Expressions covered the old Johnny Kidd and the Pirates pre-British Invasion hit "Shakin' All Over," it became a major hit. Their home label Quality originally released the song with name "Guess Who?," hoping consumers might mistake the song as a Beatles record, instead of by a band from Winnipeg. Eventually Quality did list Chad Allan and the Expressions on later pressings of "Shakin' All Over," but when the song was released in America on the Scepter label, the group officially renamed themselves The Guess Who.

*(L to R) **$15**, NM condition; **$12.50**, NM condition; **$10**, VG+ condition*

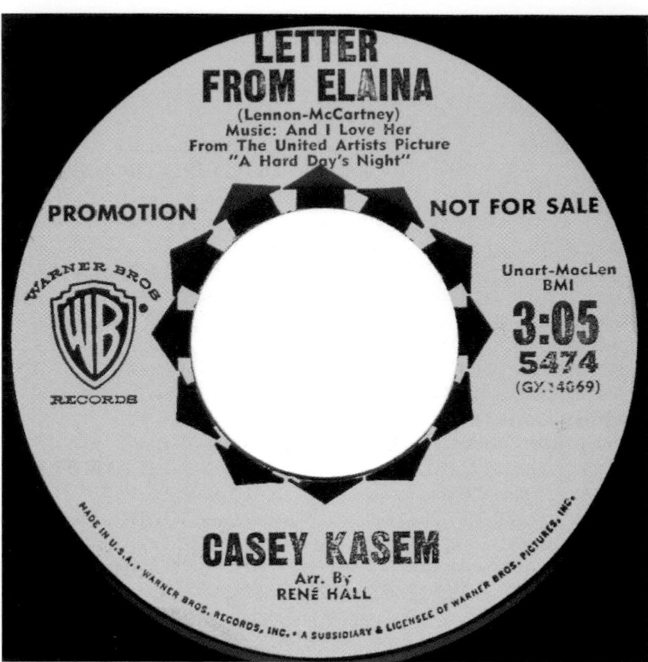

Casey Kasem, the longtime host of the radio countdown show "American Top 40," has a charted hit to his credit. With an instrumental version of "And I Love Her" as the background music, he told the story how a girl named Elaina met her favorite Beatle, George Harrison, after a Beatles concert in San Francisco.

***$8**, NM condition*

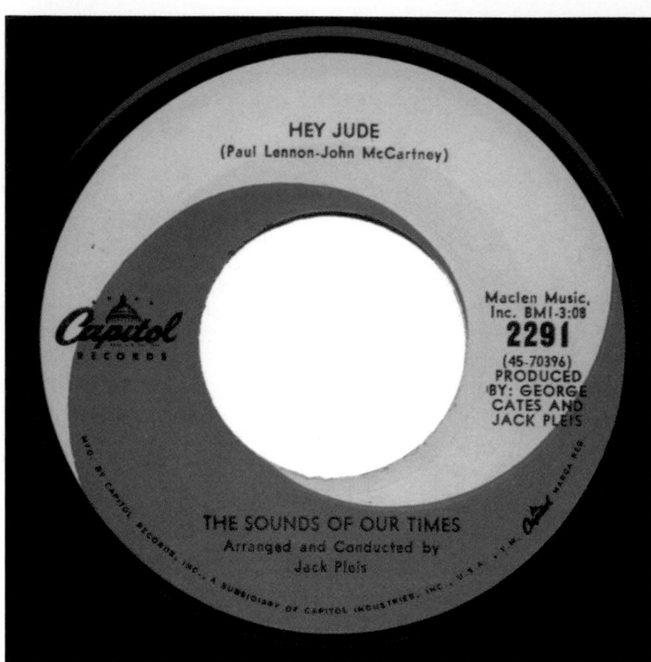

This 45 by the orchestral group Sounds of Our Times is collectible not because of its performance of "Hey Jude"—but instead, for misprinting the writers' credits as "Paul Lennon and John McCartney."

***$20**, NM condition*

ARTIST 45s — VG+ to NM

CLAY AIKEN:
RCA 54105, "This is the Night"/"Bridge Over Troubled Water," 2003 ..... **$2.00-$4.00**

THE ALLMAN BROTHERS BAND:
Capricorn 0007, "Ramblin Man"/"Pony Boy," 1973 ..... **$2.50-$5.00**

AMERICA:
Warner Bros. 7555, "A Horse With No Name"/"Everyone I Meet Is From California," 1972 ..... **$3.00-$6.00**

ED AMES:
RCA Victor 47-8483, "Try To Remember"/"Love Is Here To Stay," 1964 ..... **$4.00-$8.00**
47-9002, "My Cup Runneth Over"/"It Seems A Long, Long Time," 1966 ..... **$4.00-$8.00**

BILL ANDERSON:
Decca 31458, "Still"/"You Make It Easy," 1963 ..... **$5.00-$10.00**

ANNETTE:
Disneyland 118, "Tall Paul"/"Ma, He's Making Eyes at Me," 1959 ..... **$10.00-$20.00**
Buena Vista 336, "Jo Jo the Dog Faced Boy"/"Lonely Guitar," 1959 ..... **$10.00-$20.00**
349, "First Name Initial"/"My Heart Became of Age," 1959 ..... **$7.50-$15.00**
(with picture sleeve, add), 1959 ..... **$15.00-$30.00**
354, "O Do Mio"/"It Took Dreams," 1960 ..... **$7.50-$15.00**
(with picture sleeve, add), 1960 ..... **$15.00-$30.00**
362, "Pineapple Princess"/"Luau Cha Cha Cha," 1960 ..... **$7.50-$15.00**
(with picture sleeve, add), 1960 ..... **$15.00-$30.00**
405, "He's My Ideal"/"Mr. Piano Man," 1962 ..... **$7.50-$15.00**
(with picture sleeve, add), 1962 ..... **$15.00-$30.00**
433, "Muscle Beach Party"/"I Dream About Frankie," 1964 ..... **$7.50-$15.00**
(with picture sleeve, add), 1964 ..... **$15.00-$30.00**

THE ASSOCIATION:
Valiant 747, "Cherish"/"Don't Blame It On Me," 1966 ..... **$6.00-$12.00**
Warner Bros. 7041, "Windy"/"Sometime," 1967 ..... **$5.00-$10.00**

BACHMAN-TURNER OVERDRIVE:
Mercury 73622, "You Ain't Seen Nothin' Yet"/"Free Wheelin'," 1974 ..... **$2.00-$4.00**

THE BAY CITY ROLLERS:
Bell 45169, "Keep On Dancing"/"Alright," 1972 ..... **$5.00-$10.00**
45618, "All of Me Loves All of You"/"The Bump," 1974 ..... **$7.50-$15.00**
Arista 0149, "Saturday Night"/"Marlina," 1975 ..... **$2.00-$4.00**
(with picture sleeve, add), 1975 ..... **$3.00-$6.00**
0205, "I Only Want to Be with You"/"Write a Letter," 1976 ..... **$2.00-$4.00**
0256, "You Made Me Believe in Magic"/"Dance Dance Dance," 1977 ..... **$2.00-$4.00**

BARENAKED LADIES:
Reprise 17499, "The Old Apartment"/"Lovers in a Dangerous Time," 1997 ..... **$1.50-$3.00**
17174, "One Week"/"When You Dream," 1998 ..... **$1.50-$3.00**

THE BEAU BRUMMELS:
Autumn 8, "Laugh, Laugh"/"Still In Love With You Baby"
(if white label), 1965 ..... **$7.50-$15.00**
(if tan label, second pressing), 1965 ..... **$6.00-$12.00**

BIG BROTHER AND THE HOLDING COMPANY:
Columbia 44626, "Piece of My Heart"/"Turtle Blues," 1968 ..... **$5.00-$10.00**

BLACK OAK ARKANSAS:
Atco 6948, "Jim Dandy"/"Red Hot Lovin," 1973 ..... **$2.50-$5.00**

MICHAEL BOLTON:
RCA PB-10650, "You Make Me Feel Like Lovin' You"/"If I Had Your Lovin'" (as "Michael Bolotin"), 1976 ..... **$5.00-$10.00**
Columbia 73017, "How Am I Supposed To Live Without You"/"Forever Eyes," 1989 ..... **$1.50-$3.00**

PAT BOONE:
Mono 45s
Dot 15377, "Ain't That a Shame"/"Tennessee Saturday Night," 1955 ..... **$10.00-$20.00**
15443, "Tutti Frutti"/"I'll Be Home," 1956 ..... **$10.00-$20.00**
15472, "I Almost Lost My Mind"/"I'm in Love with You," 1956 ..... **$10.00-$20.00**

15660, "April Love"/"When the Swallows Come Back to Capistrano," 1957 ....$7.50-$15.00
15955, "Twixt Twelve and Twenty"/"Rock Boll Weevil," 1959....$7.50-$15.00
(with picture sleeve, add), 1959....................$15.00-$30.00
15982, "Fools Hall of Fame"/"The Brightest Wishing Star," 1959 ....$7.50-$15.00
(with picture sleeve, add), 1959....................$15.00-$30.00
16209, "Moody River"/"A Thousand Years," 1961....................$7.50-$15.00

Stereo 45s

Dot S-207, "Twixt Twelve and Twenty"/"Rock Boll Weevil," 1959 ....$20.00-$40.00
S-211, "Fools Hall of Fame"/"The Brightest Wishing Star," 1959 ....$20.00-$40.00
S-218, "Beyond the Sunset"/"My Faithful Heart," 1959 ....$20.00-$40.00

DAVID BOWIE:

RCA Victor APBO-0001, "Time"/"The Prettiest Star," 1973 ....$3.00-$6.00
(with rare picture sleeve, add), 1973....................$400.00-$800.00
PB-10152, "Young Americans"/"Knock on Wood," 1975.............$3.00-$6.00
PB-10441, "Golden Years"/"Can You Hear Me," 1975....................$2.00-$4.00

THE BOX TOPS:

Mala 565, "The Letter"/"Happy Times," 1967 ....$6.00-$12.00

BREAD:

Elektra 45686, "Make It With You"/"Why Do You Keep Me Waiting," 1970 ....$2.00-$4.00

THE BYRDS:

Columbia 43271, "Mr. Tambourine Man"/"I Knew I'd Want You," 1965 ....$7.50-$15.00
(with picture sleeve that promotes the Byrds' appearance on the TV show Hullabaloo, add), 1965 ....$150.00-$300.00
(if "Mr. Tambourine Man" is on both sides, red vinyl promo), 1965 ....$75.00-$150.00
43578, "Eight Miles High"/"Why," 1966 ....$6.00-$12.00
(with picture sleeve, add), 1966....................$30.00-$60.00

GLEN CAMPBELL:

Capehart 5008, "Death Valley"/"Nothin' Better Than A Pretty Woman," 1961 ....$12.50-$25.00
Capitol 5441, "Guess I'm Dumb"/"That's All Right," 1965 ....$50.00-$100.00
2302, "Wichita Lineman"/"Fate of Man," 1968....................$2.50-$5.00

THE CAPTAIN AND TENNILLE:

Butterscotch Castle 001, "The Way I Want To Touch You"/"Disney Girls" (independent first pressing), 1974 ....$40.00-$80.00
(if on Joyce 101, second pressing), 1974 ....$20.00-$40.00
(if on A&M 1624, first major label pressing), 1974....................$3.00-$6.00
(if on A&M 1725, pressed after hit "Love Will Keep Us Together," B-side is "Broddy Bounce"), 1975 ....$2.00-$4.00
(with picture sleeve for A&M 1725, add), 1975 ....$2.00-$4.00

KAREN CARPENTER:

Magic Lamp 704, "I'll Be Yours"/"Looking For Love," 1967 ....$1,000.00-$2,000.00

THE CARPENTERS:

A&M 1183, "(They Long To Be) Close To You"/"I Kept On Loving You," 1970 ....$2.50-$5.00
2735, "Yesterday Once More"/"(They Long To Be) Close To You—We've Only Just Begun," 1985....................$10.00-$20.00
(with picture sleeve, add), 1985....................$10.00-$20.00

DAVID CASSIDY:

Bell 45150, "Cherish"/"All I Want to Do Is Touch You," 1971 ....$2.50-$5.00
(with picture sleeve, add), 1971....................$3.00-$6.00
45260, "Rock Me Baby"/"Two Time Loser," 1972 ....$2.00-$4.00

THE CHAMBERS BROTHERS:

Columbia 43816, "Time Has Come Today"/"Dinah," 1966 ....$6.00-$12.00
(if on Columbia 44414, B-side is "People Get Ready"), 1968 ....$4.00-$8.00

CHILLIWACK:

Parrot 350, "I Must Have Been Blind"/"Chain Train," 1970............$4.00-$8.00
Solid Gold 712, "My Girl (Gone Gone Gone)"/"Sign Here" (Canada only), 1982 ....$4.00-$8.00
Millennium YB-11813, "My Girl (Gone Gone Gone)"/"Sign Here" (USA only), 1982 ....$2.00-$4.00

RITA COOLIDGE:

A&M 1965, "We're All Alone"/"Southern Lady," 1977....................$2.00-$4.00
(with picture sleeve, add), 1977....................$2.00-$4.00

THE COWSILLS:

MGM 13810, "The Rain, the Park and Other Things"/"River Blue," 1967 ....$5.00-$10.00
(with picture sleeve, add), 1967....................$6.00-$12.00

JOHNNY CRAWFORD:

Del-Fi 4162, "Daydreams"/"So Goes the Story," 1961....................$7.50-$15.00
(with picture sleeve, add), 1961....................$12.50-$25.00
4178, "Cindy's Birthday"/"Something Special," 1962 ....$7.50-$15.00
(with picture sleeve, add), 1962....................$12.50-$25.00
4188, "Rumors"/"No One Really Loves a Clown," 1962 ....$7.50-$15.00
(with picture sleeve, add), 1962....................$12.50-$25.00

CREEDENCE CLEARWATER REVIVAL:

Fantasy 617, "I Put A Spell On You"/"Walk on the Water," 1968 ...$4.00-$8.00
619, "Proud Mary"/"Born on the Bayou," 1969 ....$3.00-$6.00
637, "Travelin' Band"/"Who'll Stop The Rain," 1970....................$3.00-$6.00
(with picture sleeve, add), 1970....................$6.00-$12.00

JAMES DARREN:

Colpix 102, "There's No Such Thing"/"Mighty Pretty Territory," 1959 ....$7.50-$15.00
(with picture sleeve, add), 1959....................$15.00-$30.00
609, "Goodbye Cruel World"/"Valerie," 1961 ....$7.50-$15.00
(with picture sleeve, add), 1961....................$12.50-$25.00
622, "Her Royal Majesty"/"If I Could Only Tell You," 1962 ....$6.00-$12.00

THE DEFRANCO FAMILY FEATURING TONY DEFRANCO:

20th Century 2030, "Heartbeat—It's a Lovebeat"/"Sweet, Sweet Loretta," 1973 ....$2.00-$4.00
(with picture sleeve, add), 1973....................$3.00-$6.00
2088, "Save the Last Dance for Me"/"Because We Both Are Young," 1974 ....$2.00-$4.00
(with picture sleeve, add), 1974....................$3.00-$6.00

JOHN DENVER:

RCA Victor 74-0445, "Take Me Home, Country Roads"/"Poems, Prayers and Promises," 1971 ....$4.00-$8.00
74-0829, "Rocky Mountain High"/"Spring," 1972 ....$2.50-$5.00
(if on RCA's "Gold Standard Series," GB-10477), 1975 ....$1.50-$3.00

NEIL DIAMOND:

Bang 547, "I Thank the Lord For the Night Time"/"The Long Way Home," 1967 ....$7.50-$15.00
(if second pressing, title corrected to "Thank The Lord For The Night Time"), 1967 ....$5.00-$10.00
Uni 55136, "Sweet Caroline (Good Times Never Seemed So Good)"/"Dig In," 1969 ....$3.00-$6.00
Columbia CNR-03345, "Heartlight" (one-sided pressing), 1982.....$2.50-$5.00

CELINE DION:

Showbizz C-334, "Ce n'était Qu'un Rêve"/(instrumental) (Canada only), 1981 ....$37.50-$75.00
(with picture sleeve, add), 1981....................$37.50-$75.00
Epic 34-73665, "Where Does My Heart Beat Now"/"(If There Was) Any Other Way," 1988....................$3.00-$6.00

DR. HOOK:

Capitol 4621, "Sharing The Night Together"/"You Make My Pants Want To Get Up And Dance," 1978....................$2.00-$4.00

THE DOOBIE BROTHERS:

Warner Bros. 7728, "China Grove"/"Evil Woman," 1973 ....$2.00-$4.00

THE DOORS:

Elektra 45615, "Light My Fire"/"The Crystal Ship"
(if first pressing, yellow-black label), 1967 ....$15.00-$30.00
(if second pressing, red-black-white label), 1967 ....$6.00-$12.00
45635, "Hello, I Love You, Won't You Tell Me Your Name?"/"Love Street," 1968....................$10.00-$20.00
(if second pressing, title shortened to "Hello I Love You"), 1968 ....$6.00-$12.00

THE EAGLES:

Asylum 45386, "Hotel California"/"Pretty Maids All In A Row," 1977 ....$2.00-$4.00

ENGLAND, DAN AND JOHN FORD COLEY:

Big Tree 16069, "I'd Really Love To See You Tonight"/"Not The Same," 1976 ....$2.00-$4.00

THE ELECTRIC LIGHT ORCHESTRA:

United Artists XW 729, "Evil Woman"/"10538 Overture (Live)," 1975 ....$2.00-$4.00

EVERY MOTHER'S SON:

MGM 13733, "Come On Down To My Boat"/"I Believe In You," 1967 ....**$5.00-$10.00**

SHELLEY FABARES:

Colpix 621, "Johnny Angel"/"Where's It Gonna Get Me," 1962 ....**$10.00-$20.00**
(with picture sleeve, add), 1962....................**$250.00-$500.00**
636, "Johnny Loves Me"/"I'm Growing Up," 1962....................**$10.00-$20.00**
(with picture sleeve, add), 1962....................**$60.00-$120.00**
721, "Football Season's Over"/"He Don't Love Me" (Jan Berry of Jan & Dean, producer), 1963....................**$50.00-$100.00**
Vee Jay 632, "I Know You'll Be There"/"Lost Summer Love," 1964 ....**$20.00-$40.00**

FABIAN:

Mono 45s
Chancellor 1029, "I'm a Man"/"Hypnotized," 1959....................**$10.00-$20.00**
(with picture sleeve that lists A-side as "I Am A Man," add), 1959 ....**$25.00-$50.00**
(with picture sleeve, title correctly spelled, add), 1959....................**$20.00-$40.00**
1033, "Turn Me Loose"/"Stop Thief!," 1959....................**$10.00-$20.00**
(with picture sleeve, add), 1959....................**$20.00-$40.00**
1037, "Tiger"/"Mighty Cold (To a Warm, Warm Heart)," 1959 ....**$10.00-$20.00**
(with picture sleeve, add), 1959....................**$20.00-$40.00**
Stereo 45s
Chancellor S-1029, "I'm a Man"/"Hypnotized," 1959....................**$25.00-$50.00**
S-1033, "Turn Me Loose"/"Stop Thief!," 1959....................**$25.00-$50.00**
S-1037, "Tiger"/"Mighty Cold (To a Warm, Warm Heart)," 1959 ....**$25.00-$50.00**

THE 5TH DIMENSION:

Soul City 752, "I'll Be Loving You Forever"/"Train, Keep On Moving," 1966 ....**$30.00-$60.00**
756, "Up-Up and Away"/"Which Way To Nowhere," 1967....................**$4.00-$8.00**

FIVE FOR FIGHTING:

Columbia 38-79661, "Superman (It's Not Easy)"/"America Town," 2000 ....**$4.00-$8.00**

FLEETWOOD MAC:

Reprise 1345, "Rhiannon (Will You Ever Win)"/"Sugar Daddy," 1976 ....**$2.00-$4.00**
Warner Bros. 8304, "Go Your Own Way"/"Silver Springs," 1976....**$4.00-$8.00**

DAN FOGELBERG:

Full Moon/Epic 50824, "Longer"/"Along the Road," 1980....................**$2.00-$4.00**
50961, "Same Old Lang Syne"/"Hearts and Crafts," 1980....................**$2.00-$4.00**
(with picture sleeve, add), 1980....................**$3.00-$6.00**

FOGHAT:

Bearsville 0306, "Slow Ride"/"Save Your Loving," 1975....................**$2.50-$5.00**

JOHN FRED AND HIS PLAYBOY BAND:

Paula 282, "Judy in Disguise (With Glasses)"/"When the Lights Go Out"
(if white label), 1967....................**$6.00-$12.00**
(if yellow label), 1967....................**$5.00-$10.00**
(if pink label, most common label variation), 1967....................**$4.00-$8.00**

THE BOBBY FULLER FOUR:

Exeter 124, "I Fought The Law"/"She's My Girl," 1964....................**$175.00-$350.00**
(if on Mustang 3014, B-side is "Little Annie Lou"), 1966....................**$7.50-$15.00**

ART GARFUNKEL:

Columbia 10190, "I Only Have Eyes For You"/"Looking For The Right One," 1975....................**$2.50-$5.00**

DAVID GATES:

Elektra 45450, "Goodbye Girl"/"Sunday Rider," 1977....................**$2.00-$4.00**
(with picture sleeve, add), 1977....................**$2.50-$5.00**

GRAND FUNK RAILROAD/GRAND FUNK:

Capitol 2877, "Closer To Home"/"Aimless Lady," 1970....................**$3.00-$6.00**

THE GUESS WHO:

Quality 1691, Chad Allan and the Expressions, "Shakin' All Over"/"Till We Kissed" 1965....................**$12.50-$25.00**
(if on Quality 1691, writing credits to Johnny Kidd, label credits band as "Guess Who?"), 1965....................**$10.00-$20.00**
(if on Quality 1691, "Chad Allan and the Expressions" and "Guess Who?" both listed on label), 1965....................**$7.50-$15.00**
Scepter 1295, "Shakin' All Over"/"Till We Kissed," 1965....................**$7.50-$15.00**
(if B-side is "Monkey in a Cage" by the Discotays), 1965....................**$15.00-$30.00**
RCA Victor 74-0102, "These Eyes"/"Lightfoot," 1969....................**$3.00-$6.00**

DARYL HALL AND JOHN OATES:

Atlantic 2993, "She's Gone"/"I'm Just A Kid (Don't Make Me Feel Like A Man)" (first pressing), 1973....................**$4.00-$8.00**
(if on Atlantic 3332, pressed after "Sara Smile" became a hit), 1976 ....**$2.00-$4.00**
RCA PB-10860, "Rich Girl"/"London Luck & Love," 1976....................**$2.00-$4.00**
(with picture sleeve, add), 1976....................**$4.00-$8.00**

HAMILTON, JOE FRANK AND REYNOLDS:

ABC Dunhill 4276, "Don't Pull Your Love"/"Funk-in-Wagnall," 1971 ....**$3.00-$6.00**

RICHARD HARRIS:

Dunhill 4134, "MacArthur Park"/"Didn't We," 1968....................**$4.00-$8.00**
(with special promotional issue sleeve, add), 1968....................**$7.50-$15.00**
(if on ABC/Dunhill 4134, second pressing), 1968....................**$3.00-$6.00**

THE HAUNTED:

Quality 1814, "1-2-5"/"8 O'Clock in the Morning," 1966....................**$10.00-$20.00**

RUPERT HOLMES:

Infinity 50035, "Escape (The Piña Colada Song)"/"Drop It," 1979 ....**$2.50-$5.00**
(if on MCA 50035), 1979....................**$2.00-$4.00**

BRIAN HYLAND:

Leader 805, "Itsy Bitsy Teeny Weeny Yellow Polka Dot Bikini"/"Don't Dilly Dally, Sally," 1960....................**$15.00-$30.00**
Kapp 342, "Itsy Bitsy Teeny Weeny Yellow Polka Dot Bikini"/"Don't Dilly Dally, Sally," 1960....................**$7.50-$15.00**
(with picture sleeve, add), 1960....................**$15.00-$30.00**
ABC-Paramount 10336, "Sealed with a Kiss"/"Summer Job," 1962 ....**$6.00-$12.00**
(with picture sleeve, add), 1962....................**$10.00-$20.00**

THE INTERNATIONAL SUBMARINE BAND:

Ascot 2218, "The Russians Are Coming"/"Truck Driving Man," 1966 ....**$7.50-$15.00**
(with picture sleeve, must have Ascot logo and catalog number, or it's a counterfeit sleeve), 1966....................**$25.00-$50.00**

MICHAEL JACKSON:

Epic 9-50742, "Don't Stop 'Til You Get Enough"/"I Can't Help It," 1979 ....**$2.00-$4.00**
34-03509, "Billie Jean"/"Can't Get Outta the Rain," 1983....................**$2.00-$4.00**
(if on Epic ENR-03575, no B-side), 1983....................**$7.50-$15.00**
34-78000, "Scream"/"Childhood," 1995....................**$1.50-$3.00**
34-79656, "You Rock My World" (same on both sides), 2001....................**$1.00-$2.00**
(with picture sleeve, add), 2001....................**$1.00-$2.00**

JAY AND THE AMERICANS:

United Artists 415, "She Cried"/"Dawning," 1962....................**$7.50-$15.00**
626, "Only in America"/"My Clair de Lune," 1963....................**$6.00-$12.00**
50475, "This Magic Moment"/"Since I Don't Have You," 1969..**$6.00-$12.00**

TOMMY JAMES AND THE SHONDELLS:

Snap 102, "Hanky Panky"/"Thunderbolt"
(if group listed as the "Shondells," no mention of Red Fox Records on the label), 1963....................**$40.00-$80.00**
(if group listed as the "Shondells," "Dist. by Red Fox Records, Pgh., Pa." on label), 1966....................**$15.00-$30.00**
(if on Red Fox 110, group is listed as "The Shondells"), 1966....**$20.00-$40.00**
(if on Roulette 4686), 1966....................**$5.00-$10.00**

THE JIVE BOMBERS:

Savoy 1508, "Bad Boy"/"When Your Hair Has Turned to Silver," 1957 ....**$12.50-$25.00**

BILLY JOEL:

Family Productions 0900, "She's Got A Way"/"Everybody Loves You Now," 1971....................**$12.50-$25.00**
Columbia 10646, "Just The Way You Are"/"Get It Right The First Time," 1977 ....**$2.50-$5.00**

ELTON JOHN:

DJM 70008, "Lady Samantha"/"All Across the Havens," 1969 ....**$150.00-$300.00**
Congress 6022, "Border Song"/"Bad Side of the Moon," 1970....**$25.00-$50.00**
MCA 40344, "Lucy In The Sky With Diamonds"/"One Day At A Time," 1974....................**$2.50-$5.00**
(with picture sleeve, add), 1974....................**$5.00-$10.00**
MCA 40000, "Crocodile Rock"/"Elderberry Wine," 1972....................**$3.00-$6.00**
Rocket 31456 8108-7, "Something About the Way You Look Tonight"/"Candle in the Wind 1997," 1997....................**$2.50-$5.00**

KANSAS:

Kirshner 4267, "Carry On Wayward Son"/"Questions of My Childhood," 1976 ...... **$2.50-$5.00**

k.d. lang:

Sire 18942, "Constant Craving"/"Season of Hollow Soul," 1992 ...... **$2.00-$4.00**

THE LETTERMEN:

Capitol 4658, "When I Fall In Love"/"Smile," 1961 ...... **$6.00-$12.00**
(with picture sleeve, add), 1961 ...... **$10.00-$20.00**
5649, "I Only Have Eyes For You"/"Love Letters," 1966 ...... **$4.00-$8.00**
(with picture sleeve, add), 1966 ...... **$6.00-$12.00**
2054, "Goin' Out of My Head—Can't Take My Eyes Off You"/"I Believe," 1967 ...... **$4.00-$8.00**

GARY LEWIS AND THE PLAYBOYS:

Liberty 55756, "This Diamond Ring"/"Hard to Find," 1964 ...... **$6.00-$12.00**
(if B-side is "Tijuana Wedding"), 1964 ...... **$5.00-$10.00**
55778, "Count Me In"/"Little Miss Go-Go," 1965 ...... **$5.00-$10.00**

JENNIFER LOPEZ:

Epic 34-79560, "Love Don't Cost a Thing" (same on both sides), 2001 ...... **$2.00-$4.00**
34-79662, "I'm Real"/"Love Don't Cost a Thing," 2001 ...... **$1.50-$3.00**

TRINI LOPEZ:

Reprise 20198, "If I Had a Hammer"/"Unchain My Heart," 1963 ...... **$6.00-$12.00**
0336, "Lemon Tree"/"Pretty Eyes," 1965 ...... **$5.00-$10.00**
(with picture sleeve, add), 1965 ...... **$7.50-$15.00**

LOVE:

Elektra 45603, "My Little Red Book"/"Message to Pretty," 1966 ...... **$5.00-$10.00**
45613, "Que Vida"/"Hey Joe," 1967 ...... **$25.00-$50.00**

THE LOVIN' SPOONFUL:

Kama Sutra 201, "Do You Believe In Magic"/"On The Road Again"
(if first pressing, orange-red label), 1965 ...... **$7.50-$15.00**
(if second pressing, yellow label, "Kama Sutra" in red), 1965 ...... **$5.00-$10.00**
(if third pressing, yellow label, "Kama Sutra" in black), 1965 ...... **$4.00-$8.00**

LYNYRD SKYNYRD:

Shade Tree 101, "Need All My Friends"/"Michelle" (300 copies, name spelled "Lynard Skynard" on label), 1971 ...... **$750.00-$1,500.00**
Sounds of the South 40258, "Sweet Home Alabama"/"Take Your Time," 1974 ...... **$4.00-$8.00**
MCA 40328, "Free Bird"/"Down South Jukin'," 1974 ...... **$2.50-$5.00**

MADONNA:

Sire 29841, "Everybody"/(instrumental), 1982 ...... **$10.00-$20.00**
(if promotional copy, "Everybody" on both sides), 1982 ...... **$5.00-$10.00**
29478, "Holiday"/"I Know It," 1983 ...... **$2.00-$4.00**
29534, "Borderline"/"Think of Me," 1984 ...... **$2.00-$4.00**
(with foldout picture sleeve, add), 1984 ...... **$40.00-$80.00**
29210, "Like A Virgin"/"Stay," 1984 ...... **$1.50-$3.00**
(with picture sleeve, add), 1984 ...... **$1.50-$3.00**
28591, "True Blue"/"Ain't No Big Deal," 1986 ...... **$1.50-$3.00**
(with picture sleeve, add), 1986 ...... **$1.50-$3.00**
(if on blue vinyl), 1986 ...... **$2.50-$5.00**
(with picture sleeve that says "Limited edition blue vinyl pressing," add), 1986 ...... **$2.50-$5.00**
22723, "Oh Father"/"Pray for Spanish Eyes," 1989 ...... **$1.50-$3.00**
(with picture sleeve, available only on promo copies), 1989 ...... **$75.00-$150.00**
Maverick 17244, "Frozen"/"Shanti-Ashtangi," 1998 ...... **$1.50-$3.00**
17206, "Ray of Light"/"Has To Be," 1998 ...... **$1.50-$3.00**

THE MAMAS AND THE PAPAS:

Dunhill 4020, "California Dreamin'"/"Somebody Groovy," 1966 ...... **$5.00-$10.00**
(with promo picture sleeve, add), 1966 ...... **$150.00-$300.00**

BARRY MANILOW:

Bell 45613, "Mandy"/"Something's Comin' Up," 1974 ...... **$2.50-$5.00**
Arista 0330, "Even Now"/"I Was A Fool (To Let You Go)," 1978 ...... **$2.00-$4.00**
(with picture sleeve, add), 1978 ...... **$2.00-$4.00**

THE MARSHALL TUCKER BAND:

Capricorn 0270, "Heard It In A Love Song"/"Life in a Song," 1977 ...... **$2.50-$5.00**

PAUL McCARTNEY AND WINGS:

Capitol 4175, "Venus and Mars Rock Show"/"Magneto and Titanium Man," 1975 ...... **$2.50-$5.00**
4504, "Girls School"/"Mull of Kintyre" (black label), 1977 ...... **$2.50-$5.00**
(if purple label, geared edge around label), 1978 ...... **$60.00-$120.00**
(with picture sleeve, add), 1977 ...... **$6.00-$12.00**
50291, "Freedom"/"From a Lover to a Friend," 2001 ...... **$2.50-$5.00**

THE McCOYS:

Bang 506, "Hang On Sloopy"/"I Can't Explain It," 1965 ...... **$7.50-$15.00**

MEAT LOAF:

Epic/Cleveland International 50613, "Two Out Of Three Ain't Bad"/"For Crying Out Loud":
(if "Two Out Of Three Ain't Bad" is only 3:50 long), 1978 ...... **$2.50-$5.00**
(if "Two Out Of Three Ain't Bad" is 5:12 in length), 1978 ...... **$3.00-$6.00**

JOHN MELLENCAMP:

MCA 40634, "American Dream"/"Oh, Pretty Woman" (as Johnny Cougar), 1976 ...... **$5.00-$10.00**
Riva 209, "Hurts So Good"/"Close Enough" (as John Cougar), 1982 ...... **$2.00-$4.00**
(with picture sleeve, add), 1982 ...... **$5.00-$10.00**
214, "Crumblin' Down"/"Golden Gates" (as John Cougar Mellencamp), 1983 **$2.00-$4.00**
(with picture sleeve, add), 1983 ...... **$2.50-$5.00**
Mercury 574244-7, "Key West Intermezzo (I Saw You First)"/"Just Another Day" (as John Mellencamp), 1997 ...... **$1.50-$3.00**

SERGIO MENDES AND BRASIL '66:

A&M 924, "The Look of Love"/"Like a Lover," 1968 ...... **$2.50-$5.00**
(with picture sleeve, add), 1968 ...... **$4.00-$8.00**

THE STEVE MILLER BAND:

Capitol 2156, "Roll With It"/"Sittin' in Circles," 1968 ...... **$6.00-$12.00**
(with picture sleeve, add), 1968 ...... **$12.50-$25.00**
3732, "The Joker"/"Something To Believe In," 1973 ...... **$2.50-$5.00**
4424, "Jet Airliner"/"Babes in the Wood," 1977 ...... **$2.00-$4.00**

HAYLEY MILLS:

Buena Vista 385, "Let's Get Together"/"Cobbler, Cobbler," 1961 ...... **$6.00-$12.00**
(with picture sleeve, add), 1961 ...... **$12.50-$25.00**

MOBY GRAPE:

Columbia 44172, "8:05"/"Mister Blues," 1967 ...... **$4.00-$8.00**
(with picture sleeve, add), 1967 ...... **$10.00-$20.00**

THE MONKEES:

Colgems 66-1001, "Last Train to Clarksville"/"Take A Giant Step," 1966 ...... **$7.50-$15.00**
(with picture sleeve, no mention of Monkees fan club, add), 1966 ...... **$15.00-$30.00**
(with picture sleeve, "Write the Monkees"), 1966 ...... **$10.00-$20.00**
66-1002, "I'm A Believer"/"(I'm Not Your) Stepping Stone," 1966 ...... **$7.50-$15.00**
(with picture sleeve, add), 1966 ...... **$15.00-$30.00**
66-1004, "A Little Bit Me, A Little Bit You"/"The Girl I Knew Somewhere," 1967 ...... **$7.50-$15.00**
66-1012, "Daydream Believer"/"Goin' Down," 1967 ...... **$7.50-$15.00**
(with picture sleeve, add), 1967 ...... **$15.00-$30.00**
66-5000, "Tear Drop City"/"A Man Without A Dream," 1969 ...... **$5.00-$10.00**
(with picture sleeve, add), 1969 ...... **$12.50-$25.00**

ALANIS MORISSETTE:

Lamor LMR 10-12, "Fate Stay With Me"/"Find the Right Man" (Canada only), 1986 ...... **$125.00-$250.00**
(with picture sleeve, add), 1986 ...... **$125.00-$250.00**
Maverick 17644, "You Learn"/"You Oughta Know" (Live Grammy Version), 1996 ...... **$2.00-$4.00**

MICHAEL MURPHEY:

Epic 50084, "Wildfire"/"Night Thunder," 1975 ...... **$2.50-$5.00**

ANNE MURRAY:

Capitol 2738, "Snowbird"/"Just Bidin' My Time," 1970 ...... **$3.00-$6.00**
4574, "You Needed Me"/"I Still Wish The Very Best For You," 1978 ...... **$2.00-$4.00**

RICK NELSON/RICKY NELSON:

Verve 10047, "I'm Walkin'"/"A Teenager's Romance"
(if orange-yellow label), 1957 ...... **$25.00-$50.00**
(if black-white label), 1957 ...... **$20.00-$40.00**
Imperial 5503, "Believe What You Say"/"My Bucket's Got a Hole in it"
(if red label), 1958 ...... **$25.00-$50.00**
(if black label), 1958 ...... **$15.00-$30.00**
(with picture sleeve, add), 1958 ...... **$35.00-$70.00**
5528, "Poor Little Fool"/"Don't Leave Me This Way," 1958 ...... **$15.00-$30.00**
5741, "Travelin' Man"/"Hello Mary Lou," 1961 ...... **$12.50-$25.00**
(if on red vinyl), 1961 ...... **$400.00-$800.00**
(with picture sleeve, add), 1961 ...... **$35.00-$70.00**

Decca 31533, "Fools Rush In"/"Down Home," 1963 .... **$7.50-$15.00**
(with picture sleeve, add), 1963 .... **$15.00-$30.00**
32980, "Garden Party"/"So Long Mama," 1972 .... **$5.00-$10.00**

OLIVIA NEWTON-JOHN:
MCA 40043, "Take Me Home, Country Roads"/"Sail Into Tomorrow," 1973 .... **$15.00-$30.00**
40280, "I Honestly Love You"/"Home Ain't Home Anymore," 1974 .... **$2.50-$5.00**

NRBQ:
Button 037, "Froggy Went a-Courtin'"/"Bless Your Beautiful Hide," 1975 .... **$25.00-$50.00**
Red Rooster 1001, "Ridin' in My Car"/"Do The Bump," 1977 .... **$5.00-$10.00**

THE OUTLAWS:
Arista 0213, "Green Grass and High Tides"/"Prisoner," 1976 .... **$2.50-$5.00**

PABLO CRUISE:
A&M 2048, "Love Will Find A Way"/"Always Be Together," 1978 **$2.00-$4.00**
(with picture sleeve, add), 1978 .... **$2.50-$5.00**

THE PARTRIDGE FAMILY:
Bell 910, "I Think I Love You"/"Somebody Wants to Love You," 1970 .... **$2.50-$5.00**
(with picture sleeve, add), 1970 .... **$3.00-$6.00**
45414, "Lookin' for a Good Time"/"Money Money," 1973 .... **$20.00-$40.00**
(with picture sleeve, add), 1973 .... **$20.00-$40.00**

PROCOL HARUM:
A&M 1389, "A Whiter Shade of Pale"/"Lime Street Blues," 1972 .. **$2.50-$5.00**
(with picture sleeve, add), 1972 .... **$2.50-$5.00**

SNOOKY PRYOR:
Parrot 807, "Crosstown Blues"/"I Want You For Myself," 1954 **$7.50-$1,500.00**
(if on red vinyl), 1954 .... **$1,250.00-$2,500.00**

GARY PUCKETT AND THE UNION GAP:
Columbia 44967, "This Girl Is A Woman Now"/"His Other Woman," 1969 .... **$3.00-$6.00**

QUEEN:
Elektra 45297, "Bohemian Rhapsody"/"I'm In Love With My Car"
(if label has a butterfly), 1975 .... **$4.00-$8.00**
(if label is red, a rare variation), 1976 .... **$5.00-$10.00**

THE YOUNG RASCALS/THE RASCALS:
Atlantic 2321, The Young Rascals, "Good Lovin'" /"Mustang Sally," 1966 .... **$7.50-$15.00**
2401, "Groovin'" /"Sueno," 1967 .... **$4.00-$8.00**
2493, The Rascals, "A Beautiful Morning"/"Rainy Day," 1968 .... **$3.00-$6.00**
(with picture sleeve, add), 1968 .... **$10.00-$20.00**
2537, "People Got To Be Free"/"My World," 1968 .... **$3.00-$6.00**
(with picture sleeve, add), 1968 .... **$6.00-$12.00**

THE RASPBERRIES:
Capitol 3348, "Go All the Way"/"With You In My Life," 1972 .... **$3.00-$6.00**
3946, "Overnight Sensation (Hit Record)"/"Hands on You," 1974 .... **$3.00-$6.00**

LOU REED:
RCA Victor 74-0887, "Walk on the Wild Side"/"Perfect Day," 1973 .... **$3.00-$6.00**
APBO-0238, "Sweet Jane"/"Lady Day," 1974 .... **$15.00-$30.00**

THE REFLECTIONS:
Golden World 9, "(Just Like) Romeo and Juliet"/"Can't You Tell By The Look In His Eyes," 1964 .... **$10.00-$20.00**

REO SPEEDWAGON:
Epic 10827, "Sophisticated Lady"/"Prison Women," 1972 .... **$6.00-$12.00**
50953, "Keep On Loving You"/"Follow My Heart," 1980 .... **$2.00-$4.00**

PAUL REVERE AND THE RAIDERS:
Columbia 43556, "Kicks"/"Shake It Up," 1966 .... **$5.00-$10.00**
(if "Kicks" on both sides, red vinyl promo), 1966 .... **$25.00-$50.00**

CLIFF RICHARD:
ABC-Paramount 10042, "Living Doll"/"Apron Strings," 1959 .... **$12.50-$25.00**
Rocket 40574, "Devil Woman"/"Love On (Shine On)," 1976 .... **$2.50-$5.00**

KENNY ROGERS:
Carlton 454, Kenneth Rogers, "That Crazy Feeling"/"We'll Always Have Each Other," 1958 .... **$50.00-$100.00**
(if credited to "Kenny Rogers"), 1958 .... **$50.00-$100.00**
Mercury 72545, "Here's That Rainy Day"/"Take Life in Stride," 1966 .... **$12.50-$25.00**

United Artists XW929, "Lucille"/"Till I Get It Right," 1976 .... **$2.00-$4.00**

MITCH RYDER AND THE DETROIT WHEELS:
New Voice 820, "Sock It To Me—Baby!"/"I Never Had It Better"
(if first version, lyric "feels like a punch" is mumbled and sounds obscene, most pressings with this lyric variation appear on multicolored labels), 1967 .... **$12.50-$25.00**
(if second version, lyric "hits me like a PUNCH!!" clearly audible, most pressings with this lyric variation appear on blue-labeled copies, both with printed labels and "sprayed on" labels), 1967 .... **$5.00-$10.00**

SAM THE SHAM AND THE PHARAOHS:
Dingo 001, "Haunted House"/"How Does a Cheating Woman Feel," 1964 .... **$100.00-$200.00**
MGM 13322, "Wooly Bully"/"Ain't Gonna Move," 1965 .... **$7.50-$15.00**

SEALS AND CROFTS:
T-A 188, "In Tune"/"Seldom's Sister," 1969 .... **$4.00-$8.00**
Warner Bros. 7606, "Summer Breeze"/"East of Ginger Tree," 1972 **$2.50-$5.00**

NEIL SEDAKA:
Rocket 40313, "Laughter in the Rain"/"Endlessly," 1974 .... **$2.00-$4.00**
40370, "The Immigrant"/"Hey Mister Sunshine"
(if the words "Dedicated to John Lennon" are printed on the label), 1975 .... **$5.00-$10.00**
(if John Lennon is not mentioned on the record), 1975 .... **$2.00-$4.00**

BOB SEGER:
Cameo 1966, "East Side Story"/"East Side Sound," 1966 .... **$12.50-$25.00**
465, "Chain Smokin'"/"Persecution Smith," 1967 .... **$12.50-$25.00**
Capitol 2297, "Ramblin' Gamblin' Man"/"Tales of Lucy Blue," 1968 .... **$6.00-$12.00**
4369, "Night Moves"/"Ship of Fools," 1976 .... **$2.00-$4.00**
4702, "Old Time Rock and Roll"/"Sunspot Baby," 1979 .... **$2.00-$4.00**
(with picture sleeve, add), 1979 .... **$3.00-$6.00**

THE SHANGRI-LA'S:
Red Bird 10-008, "Remember (Walkin' in the Sand)"/"It's Easier to Cry," 1964 .... **$12.50-$25.00**
10-014, "Leader of the Pack"/"What is Love," 1964 .... **$12.50-$25.00**
10-043, "I Can Never Go Home Anymore"/"Bull Dog," 1965 .. **$10.00-$20.00**
(if B-side is "Sophisticated Boom Boom"), 1965 .... **$15.00-$30.00**

BOBBY SHERMAN:
Decca 31672, "Man Overboard"/"You Make Me Happy," 1964 .... **$7.50-$15.00**
Metromedia 121, "Little Woman"/"One Too Many Mornings," 1969 .... **$2.50-$5.00**
(with picture sleeve, add), 1969 .... **$2.50-$5.00**
177, "Easy Come, Easy Go"/"Sounds Along the Way," 1970 .... **$2.50-$5.00**
(with picture sleeve, add), 1970 .... **$2.50-$5.00**

NANCY SINATRA:
Reprise 0432, "These Boots Are Made For Walkin'" /"The City Never Sleeps At Night," 1965 .... **$6.00-$12.00**
0461, "How Does That Grab You, Darlin'?"/"The Last of the Secret Agents," 1966 .... **$5.00-$10.00**
0620, "Lightning's Girl"/"Until It's Time For You To Go," 1967 .... **$5.00-$10.00**
(with picture sleeve, add), 1967 .... **$10.00-$20.00**

SMASHING PUMPKINS:
Sub Pop 90, "Tristessa"/"La Dolly Vita"
(if on pink vinyl, 4000 pressed), 1991 .... **$12.50-$25.00**
(if on black vinyl, 3,000 pressed), 1991 .... **$15.00-$30.00**
(if on red vinyl, 5 pressed), 1991 .... **$250.00-$500.00**
(if on grey vinyl, 50 pressed), 1991 .... **$60.00-$120.00**
(with picture sleeve, add), 1991 .... **$12.50-$25.00**
Virgin 38522, "1979"/"Bullet with Butterfly Wings," 1996 .... **$2.50-$5.00**
(with picture sleeve, add), 1996 .... **$2.50-$5.00**
(if on Virgin 38825, "For Jukeboxes Only!" on label), 2002 .... **$2.00-$4.00**

GRANT SMITH AND THE POWER:
Boo 681, "Keep On Running"/"Her Own Life," 1968 .... **$7.50-$15.00**

SONNY AND CHER:
Atco 6359, "I Got You Babe"/"It's Gonna Rain," 1965 .... **$6.00-$12.00**
Reprise 0309, "Baby Don't Go"/"Walkin' the Quetzal," 1964 .... **$10.00-$20.00**
(if on Reprise 0392, released after "I Got You Babe" became a big hit), 1965 .... **$7.50-$15.00**

SOUNDS OF OUR TIMES:
Capitol 2291, "Hey Jude"/"Harper Valley P.T.A." (writers' credit on A-side erroneously listed as "Paul Lennon—John McCartney"), 1968 .... **$10.00-$20.00**

BRITNEY SPEARS:
Jive 42545, "Baby One More Time" (same on both sides), 1999 ...... **$2.50-$5.00**
42653, "From The Bottom Of My Broken Heart"/"You Drive Me Crazy," 2000 .... **$2.50-$5.00**
42696, "Oops! I Did It Again" (same on both sides), 2000 .... **$2.50-$5.00**
42745, "Lucky" (same on both sides), 2000 .... **$2.00-$4.00**

RONNIE SPECTOR:
Epic 50374, "Say Goodbye to Hollywood"/"Baby Please Don't Go," 1977 .... **$5.00-$10.00**
(with picture sleeve, add), 1977 .... **$12.50-$25.00**
Columbia 07300, "Love on a Rooftop"/"Good Love is Hard to Find," 1987 .... **$2.00-$4.00**

BRUCE SPRINGSTEEN:
Columbia 45805, "Blinded By The Light"/"The Angel," 1972 .... **$250.00-$500.00**
(with picture sleeve, add), 1972 .... **$200.00-$400.00**
10209, "Born To Run"/"Meeting Across the River," 1975 .... **$10.00-$20.00**
11431, "Fade Away"/"Be True," 1981 .... **$2.00-$4.00**
(if B-side is erroneously listed as "To Be True"), 1981 .... **$12.50-$25.00**

THE STACCATOS:
Capitol 72453, "Half Past Midnight"/"Weatherman," 1967 .... **$20.00-$40.00**

RINGO STARR:
Atlantic 3412, "Drowning in the Sea of Love"/"Just A Dream," 1977 .... **$60.00-$120.00**
Portrait 70015, "Lipstick Traces (on a Cigarette)"/"Old Time Relovin'," 1978 .... **$7.50-$15.00**
Boardwalk NB7-11-130, "Wrack My Brain"/"Drumming Is My Madness," 1981 .... **$2.50-$5.00**
(with picture sleeve, add), 1981 .... **$2.50-$5.00**

STEELY DAN:
ABC 11323, "Dallas"/"Sail the Waterway" (neither track ever appeared on a US Steely Dan album), 1972 .... **$15.00-$30.00**
11352, "Reeling In The Years"/"Only A Fool Would Say That," 1973 .... **$2.00-$4.00**

CAT STEVENS:
A&M 1265, "Moon Shadow"/"I Think I See The Light," 1971 .... **$2.00-$4.00**
(with picture sleeve, add), 1971 .... **$2.00-$4.00**
2711, "Father and Son"/"Father and Son" (A&M 2711) (white label promo only), 1985 .... **$5.00-$10.00**

ROD STEWART:
Mercury 73224, "Maggie May"/"Reason To Believe," 1971 .... **$3.00-$6.00**
Warner Bros. 8724, "Da Ya Think I'm Sexy?"/"Scarred and Scared," 1978 .... **$2.00-$4.00**
(with picture sleeve, add), 1978 .... **$2.50-$5.00**

THE STITCH IN TYME:
Yorkville 45001, "Got To Get You Into My Life"/"Dry Your Eyes," 1966 .... **$7.50-$15.00**

STYX:
Wooden Nickel 65-0116, "Lady"/"You Better Ask," 1973 .... **$5.00-$10.00**
WB-10102, "Lady"/"Children of the Land," 1974 .... **$2.50-$5.00**

SUPERTRAMP:
A&M 2193, "Take The Long Way Home"/"Ruby," 1979 .... **$2.00-$4.00**
(with picture sleeve with yellow maze, add), 1979 .... **$2.00-$4.00**
(with picture sleeve with green maze, red maze, or any other color, add), 1979 **$2.50-$5.00**

SWEENEY, TODD:
London 2590, "Roxy Roller"/"The Kilt" (first pressing, Nick Gilder on vocals), 1976 .... **$4.00-$8.00**
(second pressing, London 5N-240, Clark Perry on vocals, B-side is "Rue de Chance"), 1976 .... **$10.00-$20.00**
(third pressing, London 5N-244, Bryan Adams on vocals, B-side is "Rue de Chance"), 1976 .... **$7.50-$15.00**

THE SWEET:
Paramount 0044, "All You'll Ever Get From Me"/"The Juicer," 1970 .... **$10.00-$20.00**
Bell 45251, "Little Willy"/"Man from Mecca," 1972 .... **$3.00-$6.00**
Capitol 4157, "Fox On The Run"/"Burn On the Flame," 1975 .... **$2.50-$5.00**

SYLVIA:
Jubilee 5093, Little Sylvia, "Drive, Daddy, Drive"/"I Found Somebody to Love," 1952 .... **$25.00-$50.00**
Vibration 521, "Pillow Talk"/"My Thing," 1973 .... **$3.00-$6.00**

JAMES TAYLOR:
Warner Bros. 7387, "Sweet Baby James"/"Suite for 20G," 1970 .... **$4.00-$8.00**
8109, "How Sweet It Is (To Be Loved By You)"/"Sarah Maria," 1975 .... **$2.50-$5.00**

10CC:
UK 49015, "Rubber Bullets"/"Waterfall," 1973 .... **$3.00-$6.00**

THIN LIZZY:
London 20076, "Whiskey in the Jar"/"Black Boys on the Corner," 1972 .... **$4.00-$8.00**
Mercury 73786, "The Boys Are Back In Town"/"Jailbreak," 1976 .... **$2.50-$5.00**

THREE DOG NIGHT:
ABC Dunhill 4272, "Joy To The World"/"I Can Hear You Calling," 1971 .... **$2.50-$5.00**

THE TREASURES:
Valor 4750, "Minor Chaos"/"Valley of the Broken Hearts," 1964 .... **$50.00-$100.00**
(if marbled vinyl), 1964 .... **$200.00-$400.00**
(if green vinyl), 1964 .... **$100.00-$200.00**

THE TURTLES:
White Whale 244, "Happy Together"/"Like the Seasons," 1967 ..... **$4.00-$8.00**
(with picture sleeve, add), 1967 .... **$10.00-$20.00**
251, "Guide for the Married Man"/"Think I'll Run Away," 1967 .... **$20.00-$40.00**
273, "The Story of Rock and Roll"/"Can't You Hear the Cows," 1968 .... **$4.00-$8.00**
(with picture sleeve, add), 1968 .... **$25.00-$50.00**

THE UGLY DUCKLINGS:
Yorktown 45001, "Nothin'"/"I Can Tell," 1967 .... **$25.00-$50.00**
YV-45013, "Gaslight"/"Rimb Nugget," 1967 .... **$25.00-$50.00**

THE ULTIMATE SPINACH:
MGM 14023, "(Just Like) Romeo and Juliet"/"Some Days You Just Can't Win," 1969 .... **$6.00-$12.00**

THE VELVET UNDERGROUND:
Verve 10427, "All Tomorrow's Parties"/"I'll Be Your Mirror," 1966 .... **$300.00-$600.00**
(if marked for promotional use only), 1966 .... **$150.00-$300.00**
(with rare picture sleeve, add), 1966 .... **$4,000.00-$8,000.00**

THE VIDEOS:
Casino 102, "Trickle, Trickle"/"Moonglow You Know"
(if "Casino" in shadow print, no playing cards, no mention of distribution by Gone Records), 1958 .... **$25.00-$50.00**
(if playing cards on label), 1958 .... **$10.00-$20.00**
(if "Casino" in normal print, no playing cards, no mention of distribution by Gone Records), 1958 .... **$15.00-$30.00**
(no playing cards, with distribution by Gone Records), 1961 .... **$12.50-$25.00**

THE VOGUES:
Blue Star 229, "You're The One"/"Some Words," 1965 .... **$12.50-$25.00**
(if on Co and Ce 229, major label debut), 1965 .... **$6.00-$12.00**
Reprise 0686, "Turn Around, Look At Me"/"Then," 1968 .... **$4.00-$8.00**

JOE WALSH:
Asylum 45493, "Life's Been Good"/"Theme From Boat Weirdos," 1978 .... **$2.00-$4.00**

WE FIVE:
A&M 770, "You Were On My Mind"/"Small World," 1965 .... **$6.00-$12.00**

EDGAR WINTER:
Epic 10945, "Frankenstein"/"Hangin' Around," 1973 .... **$4.00-$8.00**

GLENN YARBOROUGH:
RCA Victor 47-8498, "Baby The Rain Must Fall"/"I've Been To Town," 1965 .... **$5.00-$10.00**
(with picture sleeve, add), 1965 .... **$7.50-$15.00**

NEIL YOUNG:
Reprise 0785, "The Loner"/"Sugar Mountain," 1968 .... **$60.00-$120.00**
Reprise 1065, "Heart of Gold"/"Sugar Mountain"
(if no reference to "Harvest" album), 1971 .... **$2.00-$4.00**
(if "Harvest" album is mentioned on label), 1971 .... **$2.50-$5.00**

WARREN ZEVON:
Asylum 45472, "Werewolves of London"/"Roland the Headless Thompson Gunner," 1978 .... **$2.50-$5.00**

ZZ TOP:
London 220, "Tush"/"Blue Jean Blues," 1975 .... **$2.50-$5.00**
(with picture sleeve, add), 1975 .... **$4.00-$8.00**

Chapter 2

Bootlegs and Unauthorized Recording

History

They come with intriguing titles like *LiveR Than You'll Ever Be, Great White Wonder, Fire!* or *Alpha Omega.* The vinyl may contain live concert recordings, curious studio outtakes, or private rehearsal tracks. The sound quality ranges from surprisingly clear stereo to painfully muffled, bass-heavy monaural. The album covers might possess full-color cartoon drawings, or maybe a simple rubber-stamped white cover. And the labels themselves—Kornyphone, Trade Mark of Quality, Yellow Dog—might exude an appearance of authenticity, even with a wink-wink to those in the know.

Yet despite their appearance and content, these recordings are unauthorized releases of material that neither the artist nor the record company wanted the public to hear at that time, if at all. The only person receiving money for these recordings is an unknown third party with access to some recording sessions and a pressing plant.

Photo credit: From the collection of Michael Cumella.

Typical of many bootleg pressings is this Jimi Hendrix album, recorded live in Amsterdam and sold by TAKRL. Besides using a stock photograph of the Jimi Hendrix Experience, the bootlegger tried to dress up the cover with "Learn Guitar Now" advertisements that normally appear in comic books.

This is the world of bootleg records, where master tapes disappear from studio vaults, where concealed microphones capture a live concert; where rehearsal tapes originally designated for an artist's copyright protection, all appear in low-budget, illegally pressed, limited-edition albums and CDs. Besides bootleg records, there are also counterfeit or "pirate" pressings, which illegally duplicate an artist's catalog for resale; as well as "fantasy" pressings, where a 45 or LP is created resembling a purported release that never happened, or to create a picture sleeve for a 45 that never had one in its initial release.

While today's collectors associate bootleg recordings with copies of rock and roll performances from the 1960s, bootleg recordings can be traced back to the early 1900s, when Lionel Mapleson used an Edison cylinder recorder

Photo credit: From the collection of Harvey Gilman.

This pressing of Verdi's A Masked Ball, by a company called Classic Editions, touts performances by various Italian opera legends, including Maria Caniglia and Carlo Tagliabue. This opera was actually transcribed from a performance at New York's Metropolitan Opera House, with Daniza Ilitsch and Jan Peerce. Not only were some of the vocalists under contract to RCA Victor, but Classic Editions manufactured these discs at RCA's own custom pressing division, a major embarrassment to RCA.

Jolly Roger Records was formed in 1950, and like Classic Editions, had their product manufactured at RCA's custom pressing departments. These 10-inch LPs were the first jazz bootleg albums, and featured unreleased material from Benny Goodman, Billie Holiday, Louis Armstrong, and Jelly Roll Morton.

The original Dylan Great White Wonder *bootlegs were sold in a plain white cover, with the words "Great White Wonder" rubber-stamped on top. This pressing shown here is actually a reissue of the original boots, and is stamped on colored vinyl and contains a typewritten song list on the jacket.*

to capture performances of singers at the Metropolitan Opera House. In the late 1940s, companies like the Wagner-Nichols Home Recordist Guild recorded live classical and opera performances, also from the Metropolitan Opera House, that were broadcast over the ABC Radio Network. Another company, calling itself the "Golden Age of Opera," issued several bootleg albums of recordings taken from broadcast acetate safety transcription discs.

Jazz and blues fans also had bootleg performances to pick and choose from. Jolly Roger Records boldly issued early jazz, blues, and swing music on their bootleg label, releasing a series of 10-inch LPs with crudely drawn artwork. Even the name "Jolly Roger" flaunted the record company's piracy. The company shut down a year later, after Columbia Records and Louis Armstrong sued for invasion of property rights.

In the late 1960s, a blank-covered double-album set appeared in some Los Angeles record stores with the words "Great White Wonder" rubber-stamped on the cover. Customers who bought this mystery package discovered that the double-album set contained 24 unreleased tracks from Bob Dylan's career including recordings made with the Band at Big Pink; songs recorded with an acoustic guitar in a Minneapolis hotel, and a song dubbed from a television broadcast. *Great White Wonder* eventually spawned other Dylan bootlegs, with titles like *Troubled Troubadour, Waters of Oblivion,* and *Name That Tune* (a boot of a 1991 Dylan concert where the performer slurred through many of the songs), made by concert tapers who had access to a record pressing plant. Eventually Dylan and his label, Columbia, released many of the previously bootlegged songs as part of authorized releases, but the Dylan bootleg pressings continue to this day.

The Beatles have also been plagued with bootleg pressings, mostly containing rehearsal tapes, unreleased songs, and songs in varying forms of completion. The first Beatles bootlegs, collected in an album called *Kum Back*, were stereo tracks originally scheduled for an upcoming Beatles album tentatively titled *Get Back*. The recordings were originally transferred to an acetate by Glyn Johns, who had made several mixes of the tapes before the *Get Back* project was ultimately transferred to Phil Spector and became *Let It Be*. Somehow, the Glyn Johns acetates made their way to the Northeastern United States, where a series of vinyl pressings were illicitly made.

During the 1970s, other Beatles bootlegs appeared, including songs that were originally taped from live appearances on BBC radio, or from tape recorders that were smuggled into concerts. A series of 7-inch 45s on the Deccagone label chronicled the Beatles' original failed audition tapes for Decca Records; many of these Deccagone singles were released with colored vinyl and picture sleeves that depicted the Beatles in their much more successful Capitol/Parlophone runs. Nevertheless, the pressings are still bootlegs.

One of the arguments used for pressing bootleg recordings is that the fans deserve to hear an artist's collected work, even if the record company or the artist himself feels the material is unsuited for an official release. Other bootleg collectors believe that the release of some bootleg material might spur a record company to release full authorized versions. Some people study bootlegs, as a

Don't be fooled by the big Apple Records logo on the cover; this Get Back *album was never released as a legitimate Beatles pressing. This LP contains recordings from the Glyn Johns acetates, including a jam on the old Drifters classic "Save the Last Dance for Me," and some mumbling, guitar tuning and ruminations on the Beatles' recording techniques.*

One of the most tasteless bootlegs released, The Who Stampede, was transcribed from The Who's 1979 Cincinnati concert. Yes, that's the one where 11 people were trampled to death. Not only does the bootleg LP contain a pre-concert interview with Pete Townshend, as well as The Who's stage performances (along with some sing-alongs from the taper), the bootleggers shamelessly added a news broadcast audio clip at the end that described the injuries and deaths.

chance to see the creative process in action, to understand how some of our favorite recordings evolved.

Opponents of bootleg pressings cite that neither the artist nor his record company receives payment for these releases; that the unauthorized pressings actually compete in the marketplace with legitimate issued releases; that the artist has no control over a bootleg pressing of what might either be a subpar performance (poor crowd response, guitarist hit sour notes, lead singer performing with the flu) or a five-star performance that would be saved for a scheduled live album.

The consumer also has absolutely no idea how the recording was made. The recorded concerts advertised on the album jacket may not reflect where the concert actually took place—for example, many of the Beatles' bootleg concert albums were recorded at one concert, but were credited to another location. Concerts recorded at Los Angeles' Hollywood Bowl were advertised as being from New York's Shea Stadium; meanwhile, a Shea Stadium concert bootleg was called *Last Live Show*, possibly confusing listeners that this was either the Beatles' Candlestick Park concert, or perhaps their last live show atop the roof of Apple Studios. Even a bootleg pressing from the Beatles' Philadelphia concerts was sold as having taken place at the spurious "Whiskey Flats" concert hall!

Some bootlegs are notorious for their inclusion of concerts for which the performance was not the most noteworthy part of the show. During a Frank Zappa/ Mothers of Invention concert in Montreux, Switzerland, someone shot a flare gun into the ceiling of the performance hall, burning the place to the ground. The Montreux concert, besides inspiring the Deep Purple song "Smoke on the Water," eventually surfaced on a bootleg vinyl pressing called *Swiss Cheese/Fire!*

Some other bootleg pressings involve out-of-phase stereo, also known as "OOPS" or "phasing." In this instance, a mixing board is specially wired so that when a stereo record is fed into the board, all sound that is equal in both the left and right channels (in other words, the centered vocals) gets cancelled out. Depending on whether the original source was a true stereo song, rechanneled stereo, fake stereo, or poorly combined stereo (*i.e.*, singer in left channel, band in right), by running this song through a mixing board equipped with OOPS, you can create an entirely new version of a song. Monaural recordings become silent, as the sound waves are equal in both speakers. What some bootleggers will do is take a stereo record, *e.g.*, the Beatles or Stevie Wonder, record it using an OOPS filter, and then press it as a "new mix," then sell it to an unsuspecting buyer.

Another factor in the bootleg market is the existence of unauthorized compilations. In 1972, a company in New Jersey pressed a four-LP boxed set of Beatles hits, called the set *Alpha Omega*, and released it in both vinyl and 8-track configurations to the public. The songs' running order were neither chronologically nor thematically arranged, and, in fact, several solo Beatles' recordings were included in the set. The company pressed three volumes of their Beatles greatest hits package before production was shut down.

While there is some evidence that both John Lennon and

Mick Jagger were avid bootleg collectors, other artists, such as Frank Zappa, have taken a different tack towards these discs. Zappa, who complained vehemently that bootleggers could get his own recordings to store shelves faster than he could, acquired several bootleg albums and reissued them under his own label as twin 8-LP boxed sets called *Beat the Boots! (Vol. I and II)*.

An example of the originators out-booting the bootleggers occurred in 1981. Jaap Eggermont, the original drummer for the band Golden Earring, discovered that a bootleg 12-inch dance medley, "Let's Do It In the 80s," included the Shocking Blue's 1970 hit "Venus," for which Eggermont held a copyright, and was a major hit in Holland dance clubs. In an effort to make a legal version of the bootleg mix (and essentially make some money in the process), Eggermont hired studio musicians to replicate the medley. Adding a few Beatles songs into the mixture, he brought in studio singers Bas Muys, Hans Vermeuien, and Okkie Huysdens to replicate the Beatles' vocals. Eggermont's medley, credited to "Stars on 45," became a hit and spawned a medley craze throughout the early 80s.

Remix bootlegs first appeared in the late 1970s, when some club DJs mixed disco records, then recorded them for play in clubs. Sometimes a tape would disappear from the DJ's case, only to turn up as a quickly produced and easily purchasable bootleg 12-inch dance disc. While legitimate companies do exist that create mixes for club DJs on a subscription service, there are also bootleggers who make their own mixes.

Bruce Springsteen was very upset when he saw this album, "E Ticket," available in independent record stores—with early rough mixes of songs from his Born to Run *album.*

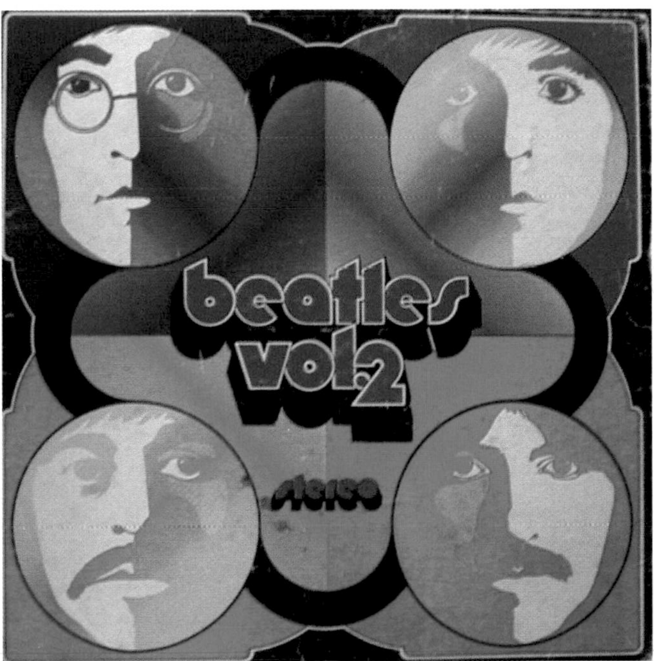

By the time this second volume of the Beatles' Alpha Omega bootleg series appeared in 1972, the bootleggers added solo songs like Paul McCartney's "Too Many People," George Harrison's "All Things Must Pass," and John Lennon's "Oh Yoko" to the 4-LP boxed set.

Web Pages

A listing of Bruce Springsteen bootleg vinyl pressings: http://www.springsteen.org.uk/bootin.htm

A listing of Beatles bootleg vinyl pressings and the history behind same: http://www.vex.net/~paulmac/beatles/history.html

The Web page for the Recording Industry Association of America, for more information on bootlegs and pirated recordings and their effect on legitimate album releases: http://www.riaa.com

The Bootleg Zone, a Web site that can help determine if your pressing is a bootleg and where that original recording came from: http://www.bootlegzone.com

Patrick's Disco and Funk page, containing information on dance bootlegs: http://home.wanadoo.nl/discopatrick/bootleg.htm

What To Look For

Those who collect bootlegs are often hardcore collectors who want every recording an artist or group ever created, every live performance, every unreleased hidden track. They're willing to put up with, in many cases, the muffled sound of a concealed microphone at a concert; the flat, tinny recording from a cassette tape; and minimalist packaging with low-grade graphics. It is also common for bootleg albums to have the same content, but different titles or running orders.

Be aware that the sale of bootleg albums is considered illegal, as they are unauthorized recordings that were pressed and sold without the consent or remuneration of the artist or his record company. Although this book does acknowledge and explain the existence of bootleg pressings and recordings, there will be no prices listed for them.

Books

Heylin, Clinton, *Bootleg: The Secret History of the Other Recording Industry*, St. Martin's Press, New York, 1994.

Some bootleg compilations, like Killed By Death *and* Powerpearls, *can help collectors of certain musical genres hear some of the rarest punk, garage, and power pop tracks.*

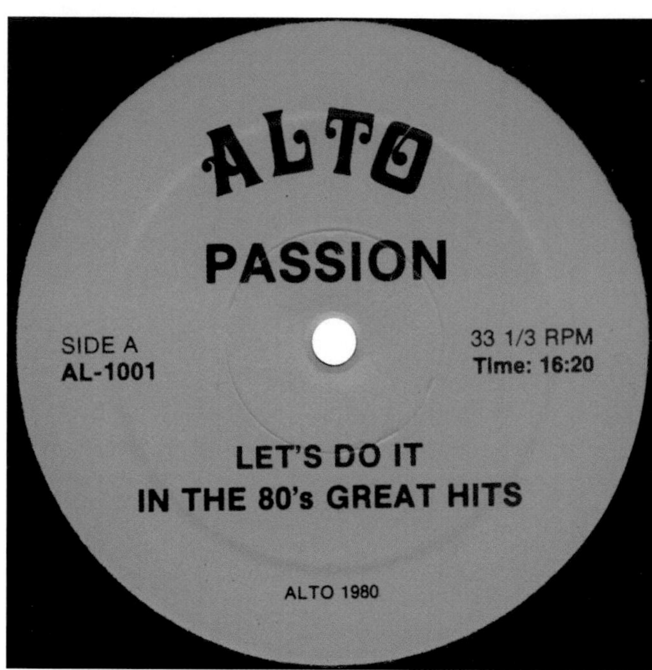

The medley 12-inch that Jaap Eggermont transformed into his "Stars on 45" legit group. Among the tracks spliced into this dance mix were Madness' "One Step Beyond," Neil Sedaka's "Breaking Up is Hard To Do," and Brian Hyland's "Itsy Bitsy Teeny Weenie Yellow Polkadot Bikini."

New York club DJ Mikey D'Merola's homemade "Bits and Pieces 1 and 2" mix tape, originally created for his club work, was pirated and released without his knowledge as the "Big Apple Mix, Volume 1," and credited to the mysterious "Ser and Duff."

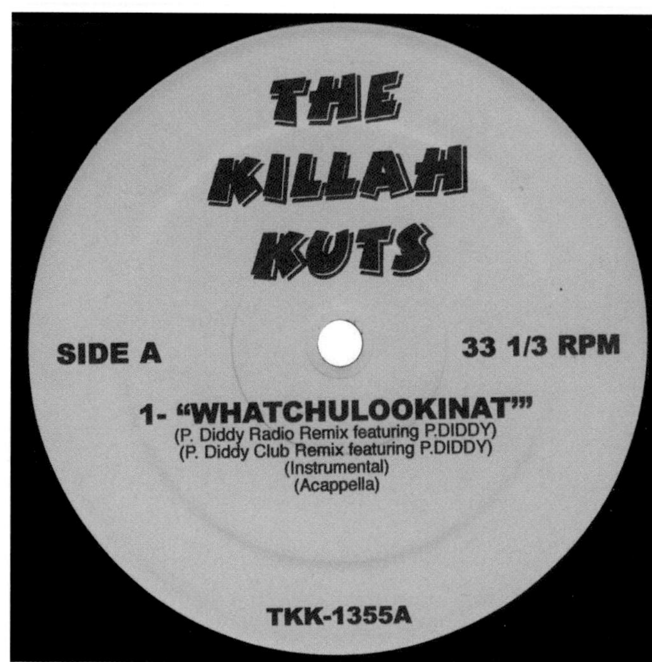

These "Killah Kuts" pressings of remixed hits of popular hip-hop and rap artists don't even mention the original vocalist or rapper on the cover. This pressing, for example, is a remix of Whitney Houston's "Whatchulookinat," with her name left off the label.

Chapter 3

Colored Vinyl

History

For over 100 years, record companies have pressed non-black records as special prizes for consumers, as collectible one-of-a-kind pressings, as a possible visual enticer to test a new song, or to delineate the musical style on the record. Colored vinyl records are one of the hottest music collectibles today, as colored vinyl essentially denotes to the consumer that the record is "special," and that the company made a conscious effort to change their methods of production for this release.

Although the earliest 78s were made of clear shellac, companies mixed charcoal, lampblack, byritis, and cotton flock with the shellac to create a deep black disc. Beginning in 1920, the Aeolian Company, a major manufacturer of musical instruments, pressed a line of reddish-brown

The earliest examples of colored-vinyl pressings were shellac mixed with aniline dyes to create a swirl or mottled effect. This process was most often used with celebratory or commemorative pressings, such as the two Aeolian-Vocalion pressings commemorating the end of the Great War, or the mottled red-black Pathé record celebrating Charles Lindbergh's successful solo flight across the Atlantic Ocean.
Clockwise from top: ***$60**, NM condition;* ***$500**, NM condition;* ***$100**, NM condition*

records under the Vocalion imprint, essentially distinguishing themselves from the more established labels of Victor and Columbia. They also produced two spectacular multicolor pressings to commemorate America's victory in the First World War. Aeolian-Vocalion continued to press reddish-brown records until 1924, when the company sold its record division to the Brunswick-Balke-Callender company.

It is theorized that the color compounds for non-black records in the 78-RPM era actually came from the mixture of shellac and aniline dyes. In fact, during the early years of cylinder and flat disc recordings, aniline dyes were employed to create the pink in Lambert cylinders and the blue in Edison Amberol cylinders.

After Aeolian-Vocalion discontinued their reddish pressings, other companies took up the rouge. Perfect Records, a budget-line label of the parent Pathé Frères Phonograph Corporation, provided chocolate-colored pressings to music lovers at 39 cents apiece, or three for a dollar. This lasted until 1931, when Perfect switched to black-colored discs. Other reddish shellacked 78s include releases on the Puretone label (1923-25) and the Domino label (1924-33). In the 1930s, Columbia issued a series of blue-shellacked discs. But despite their differences in shade and hue, colored vinyl pressings were only employed by their respective labels for a couple of years.

In 1949, when Columbia introduced the 12-inch, 33-1/3 RPM phonograph record, RCA Victor created their own 7-inch vinylite 45 RPM phonograph discs, which would play on their specially built RCA Victor phonographs. And in a tactic reminiscent of turn-of-the-century record companies of the 1900s, who pressed their records with spindle holes of different sizes to force customers to purchase that company's phonographs, RCA Victor's new records would have a 1-1/2" center hole—a perfect diameter for RCA Victor's new line of Victrola thick-spindled dropchanger phonographs.

RCA Victor even color-coded their pressings, to ensure that consumers who desired certain musical formats could find them by the color of the record's vinyl. The serial number prefixes were staggered, from 47- to 52-, with each number represented by a different colored vinyl. The 47- prefixes were black vinyl, for pop pressings. 48- prefixes were country music recordings, molded in green vinyl; 49- prefixes were part of RCA Victor's "Red Seal" line of classical pressings, and were naturally pressed on translucent red vinyl. The 50- prefixes were R&B songs, pressed on an orange-rose "cerise" vinyl; 51- prefixes had a light "sky blue" tint for international material; 52- prefixes had a deeper "midnight blue" color, suitable for "light classics." The WY- prefixes were pressed on opaque yellow vinyl, and were reserved for children's songs and stories. The colored vinyl experiment only lasted until 1950, although yellow-vinyl children's records were pressed until 1952, and the "Red Seal" classical line existed on red vinyl until 1953. Today, those colored vinyl pressings draw some collectors, especially the cerise recordings of Tampa Red, the Four Tunes, the Five Trumpets, and Jazz Gillum.

By the late 1940s, record companies used vinylite or polyvinyl chloride (PVC) for their "unbreakable" records. Most of these colored-vinyl pressings were made for the children's music market, such as this Voco Christmas record with red-yellow starburst vinyl patterns.

***$4**, VG condition*

So how are today's colored vinyl pressings made? Before records are pressed, PVC pellets arrive at the record plant. The pellets are melted down and poured between the record stampers. A few seconds later, a black vinyl record is made. But black is not the only color of PVC available for pressing. PVC is also available in shades of red, green, blue, white, gold, and clear. The careful mixture of each of these colors can create, when the PVC is melted, any color in the visual rainbow. Once the mixture is heated, it can come out looking like a frosty snow cone, it can come out in a pancake form and shaped like a hockey puck, or it can come out in noodle-like strips. The pressing agents keep records of every possible color formula, and can create enough of a color mixture so that the 50,000th pressing is as close to the same exact color as the first pressing.

A single color in a record is one thing, but some artists may want two or more colors in their pressings. A starburst pressing, for example, might require two melting machines, one for each separate color needed. Instead of the vinyl being processed as a flat disc, it is processed in noodle form, and the PVC noodles are placed on top of the stampers. Depending on how creative the stamping operators are, one can create starbursts, two-tone discs, or various other patterns.

Some colored-vinyl records are truly one of a kind—and that's often because only one copy was pressed. During the 1960s, some pressing plant employees made "after-hours" pressings—in effect, a single record or a few pressings here and there, made from whatever colored vinyl is left in the office, the pressing made after hours at an employee's

A rainbow of RCA Victor's first 45s, each one in a different color to appeal to different customers. The most collectible of these color-coded pressings are the rose-orange cerise R&B pressings (such as the Jazz Gillum "Signifying Woman" shown here), as well as green country pressings featuring Eddy Arnold. And while RCA Victor had no trouble making colored vinyl, they still had to iron out some kinks when printing information on the labels, especially on the cerise pressings, where age and fading have made most of the labels on that line nearly unreadable.

*Top row (L to R): **$5**, NM condition; **$50**, NM condition; **$5**, NM condition; **$80**, NM condition; bottom row (L to R): **$10**, NM condition; **$12.50**, VG+ condition; **$4**, VG+ condition*

whim. "After hours" vinyl pressings exist of Elvis Presley recordings, Rolling Stones albums, Ronettes 45s, and Bob Dylan albums. Most of these pressings were made at independent record plants by late-night employees. When these records do come to light, they sell for large sums of money at auctions. Because there is no way of knowing how many "after hours" pressings were made, or where they were pressed, an accurate inventory of their existence is impossible, and prices for these records are speculative at best.

Many colored vinyl releases were manufactured concomitant to the standard black-vinyl release. While the black-vinyl records were sold in stores, colored-vinyl pressings were often sent to disc jockeys in the hopes that a bright orange 45 might get played sooner than the 30th black vinyl 45 that appeared in the studio. During the 1960s, Columbia Records, along with their sister label Epic, pressed many of their biggest 45s in clear red vinyl, as special promotional records for radio stations. This means that red-vinyl 45s exist for such artists as Bob Dylan, the Dave Clark Five, Simon and Garfunkel, the Cyrkle, Paul Revere and the Raiders, and Donovan.

With few exceptions, virtually every colored vinyl 45 and LP is worth more than its black-vinyl counterpart. One of the reasons for this is because colored-vinyl records are pressed in smaller runs—it is harder to maintain the same color consistently throughout a print run, while black-vinyl records will always remain black from first pressing to last.

However, there are some instances where a black vinyl record is worth more than its colored vinyl counterpart. An example is Elvis Presley's album *Moody Blue*. Originally,

Cameo-Parkway Records often pressed a limited run of reddish-orange vinyl for radio stations or for special giveaways. Pressings like this orange vinyl of Chubby Checker's "Let's Twist Again" can sell for up to $100 in near-mint condition.

***$100**, NM condition*

Photo credit: Dylan LP originally from the collection of Charles Essmeier.

Two examples of "after hours" pressings. This red "Freewheelin' Bob Dylan" vinyl was made by a CBS factory worker in the 1970's, and is one of only two copies purported to exist. The splash vinyl Chopin 45 was also made after hours by an RCA Victor employee, most likely by using PVC pellets from RCA Victor's other colored-vinyl pressing projects.

*(L to R) speculative **$1,000** NM condition; speculative **$50**, NM condition*

the plan was to press blue vinyl copies for the first two months, then switch to black vinyl for the rest of the copies. Just as the record company changed over to black vinyl, Elvis Presley passed away. Immediately the company switched back to pressing blue-vinyl copies, ostensibly to provide Elvis Presley fans with a collectible souvenir. Today, collectors search out the rare black-vinyl pressings (and some green, red, and white test pressings that were even rarer), while the blue-vinyl pressings of that album only sell for a few dollars apiece.

In the 1990s, Sub Pop Records, a Seattle-based label, created a "Singles Club" subscription service. By spending $40 for a yearly fee (or $25 for six months), you were guaranteed to receive at least one new colored-vinyl Sub Pop 45 every month, a pressing of one of Seattle's new up-and-coming bands. The lineup for Sub Pop pressings reads like a who's who of alternative music. Imagine a record company lineup featuring Nirvana, the Smashing Pumpkins, Hole, the White Stripes, the Afghan Whigs, Fugazi, Mudhoney, Dinosaur Jr., the Velvet Monkeys, the Reverend Horton Heat, Sonic Youth, Urge Overkill, the Fastbacks, Shonen Knife, the John Spencer Blues Explosion, Ween, Combustible Edison, Green River—with specially licensed pressings by Cheap Trick and the Beach Boys, to top it all off. The first run of the Singles Club only lasted from 1988 to 1993. A second Sub Pop Singles Club began in 1997, ending in 2002.

Today, in an effort to bring back collectibility to current 45s, many reissue pressings are now on colored vinyl. Entire runs of Beatles singles, of Elvis Presley 45s, and of Phil Spector's Philles recordings have been pressed on colored vinyl, while the Sundazed label has reissued 1960s albums in colored vinyl. Although these records do not contain the same collectibility as the original pressings did, one can still hold these colored vinyl records up to a light, admire the colored light stream through the vinyl grooves, and say "cool, man."

Donovan's "Sunshine Superman" was one of many Columbia and Epic red-vinyl promotional pressings to help stimulate radio airplay. Naturally, any popular Columbia/Epic Top 10 hits in this format are more collectible than their black-vinyl counterparts.

***$30**, VG+ condition*

Two examples of colored vinyl from the Sub Pop Singles Clubs. The pink vinyl pressing was an early recording by the Smashing Pumpkins, and is one of the most collectible non-Nirvana, colored-vinyl pressings in the first run of the Sub Pop Singles Club. The red-white 45 by the White Stripes is one of the top jewels in the Sub Pop Singles Club's second run.

(L to R) ***$55****, NM condition;* ***$200****, NM condition*

What To Look For

Colored vinyl collecting is an easy collecting niche to get involved with; some people only collect red vinyl pressings (red is the most popular colored vinyl release), while others search for every possible hue in the spectrum.

Be aware that in the 1990s, many reissue companies have pressed colored-vinyl pressings of 1950s and 1960s popular songs. Some of these companies even issue their colored-vinyl product in boxed sets.

If you are unsure of whether a colored vinyl record exists as an original pressing or as a reproduction, examine the label carefully. For original pressings, the label artwork should be crisp and sharp; the letters should have sharp points, the lines should be straight. A reproduction may have rounded corners on the letters, or the lines might have small bulges in them, as if they were photocopied labels.

As a way of saying "thank you" for achieving their third straight multi-platinum album, the band Styx pressed a series of "platinum vinyl" copies of their Cornerstone *album for their Styx Armada fan club.*

$30*, NM condition*

Books

Neely, Tim, *Goldmine Price Guide to 45 RPM Records*, Krause Publications, Iola, WI, 2003.

Neely, Tim, *Goldmine Price Guide to Alternative Records*, Krause Publications, Iola, WI, 1996.

Web Pages

Erika Records is the country's largest producer of colored vinyl and picture discs: http://www.erikarecords.com

The Vinyl Underground, an online gallery of colored vinyl and picture discs: http://www.vinylunderground.net

FAYE ADAMS:

45s

Herald 416, "Shake a Hand"/"I've Got To Leave You," red vinyl, 1953 ....**$50.00-$100.00**

DUANE AND GREGG ALLMAN:

45s

Bold 200, "Morning Dew," same on both sides, promo, red vinyl, 1973 ....**$10.00-$20.00**

EDDY ARNOLD:

45s

RCA Victor 48-0001, "Bouquet of Roses"/"Texarkana Baby," green vinyl, 1949 ....**$25.00-$50.00**

(w/picture sleeve, add), 1949 ....**$40.00-$80.00**

48-0002, "Anytime"/"What A Fool I Was," green vinyl, 1949...**$25.00-$50.00**

48-0165, "The Lily Of the Valley"/"Evil, Tempt Me Not," green vinyl, 1950 ....**$25.00-$50.00**

PETER BEST:

45s

Mr. Maestro 712, "Casting My Spell"/"I'm Blue," blue vinyl, 1965 ....**$100.00-$200.00**

PAT BOONE:

LPs

Dot DLP-25270, Moonglow, blue vinyl, 1960....**$25.00-$50.00**

DAVID BOWIE:

45s

EMI America 8321, "Blue Jean"/"Dancing with the Big Boys," blue vinyl, 1984 ....**$4.00-$8.00**

THE BYRDS:

45s

Columbia 43271, "Mr. Tambourine Man," same on both sides, red vinyl, 1965 ....**$75.00-$150.00**

CHUBBY CHECKER:

45s

Parkway 811, "The Twist"/"Twistin' U.S.A."

(if on red vinyl), 1961....**$100.00-$200.00**

(if on yellow vinyl), 1961....**$75.00-$150.00**

824, "Let's Twist Again"/"Everything's Gonna Be Alright," orange vinyl, 1961 ....**$100.00-$200.00**

DAVE CLARK FIVE:

45s

Epic 9863, "Over and Over," same on both sides, promo, red vinyl, 1965 ....**$20.00-$40.00**

THE COMMODORES:

45s

Motown 1307, "Machine Gun" (stereo)/(mono), promo, red vinyl, 1974 ....**$2.50-$5.00**

1381, "Sweet Love" (stereo)/(mono), promo, yellow vinyl, 1976 ..**$7.50-$15.00**

PERRY COMO:

45s

RCA Victor 52-0071, "Ave Maria"/"The Lord's Prayer," blue vinyl, 1949 ....**$12.50-$25.00**

ARTHUR "BIG BOY" CRUDUP:

RCA Victor 50-0000, "That's All Right"/"Crudup's After Hours," cerise vinyl, 1949 ....**$200.00-$400.00**

50-0001, "Boy Friend Blues"/"Katie May," cerise vinyl, 1949 ..**$50.00-$100.00**

50-0032, "Hoodoo Lady Blues"/"Tired of Worry," cerise vinyl, 1949 ....**$50.00-$100.00**

50-0109, "My Baby Left Me"/"Anytime is the Right Time," cerise vinyl, 1951 ....**$75.00-$150.00**

DION:

LPs

Laurie LLP 2009, Runaround Sue, mono, exists in gold, green, and blue vinyl pressings, value is equal, 1961....**$400.00-$800.00**

FATS DOMINO:

45s

Imperial 45-5209, "How Long"/"Dreaming," red vinyl, 1952..**$150.00-$300.00**

45-5220, "Nobody Loves Me"/"Cheatin'," red vinyl, 1953.....**$150.00-$300.00**

45-5231, "Going to the River"/"Mardi Gras in New Orleans," red vinyl, 1953 ....**$250.00-$500.00**

X5407, "Blueberry Hill"/"Honey Chile," red vinyl, 1956........**$75.00-$150.00**

X5492, "Yes, My Darling"/"Don't You Know I Love You," red vinyl, 1958 ....**$75.00-$150.00**

THE DU DROPPERS:

45s

Red Robin 108, "Can't Do Sixty No More"/"Chain Me Baby (Blues of Desire)," red vinyl, 1952 ....**$250.00-$500.00**

BOB DYLAN:

45s

Columbia 43242, "Subterranean Homesick Blues," same on both sides, red vinyl, 1965 ....**$125.00-$250.00**

43346, "Like a Rolling Stone," same on both sides, red vinyl, 1965 ....**$100.00-$200.00**

THE EVERLY BROTHERS:

45s

Warner Bros. 5199, "Ebony Eyes"/"Walk Right Back," promo, gold vinyl, 1961 ....**$50.00-$100.00**

THE FIVE ROYALES:

45s

Apollo 441, "Courage to Love"/"You Know I Know," red vinyl, 1952 ....**$200.00-$400.00**

443, "Baby Don't Do It"/"Take All of Me," 1952 ....**$200.00-$400.00**

THE FOUR TUNES:

45s

RCA Victor 50-0008, "You're Heartless"/"Careless Love," cerise vinyl, 1949 ....**$100.00-$200.00**

50-0072, "There Goes My Heart"/"Am I Blue," cerise vinyl, 1950 ....**$75.00-$150.00**

50-0131, "May That Day Never Come"/"Carry Me Back to the Lone Prairie," cerise vinyl, 1951....**$75.00-$150.00**

ARETHA FRANKLIN:

45s

Arista 9028, "Jumpin' Jack Flash"/"Integrity," clear vinyl, 1986 ....**$2.50-$5.00**

BIG JOHN GREER:

45s

RCA Victor 50-0007, "Drinkin' Wine Spo-Dee-O-Dee"/"Long Tall Gal," cerise vinyl, 1949 ....**$35.00-$70.00**

50-0029, "If I Told You Once"/"I Found a Dream," 1949, cerise vinyl ....**$35.00-$70.00**

50-0051, "Rockin' Jenny Jones"/"I've Just Found Love," cerise vinyl, 1950 ....**$35.00-$70.00**

BILL HALEY AND THE COMETS:

45s

Essex 303, "Rock the Joint"/"Icy Heart," red vinyl, 1952 ...**$1,350.00-$1,800.00**

DARYL HALL AND JOHN OATES:

45s

RCA JR-14259, "Jingle Bell Rock from Daryl"/"Jingle Bell Rock from John," available in red and green vinyl, value is equal for both, 1985 ....**$5.00-$10.00**

THE IN-CROWD:

45s

Abnak 121, "Inside Out"/"Big Cities," promo on yellow vinyl, 1967 ....**$6.00-$12.00**

129, "Let's Take A Walk"/"Hangin' From Your Lovin' Tree," promo on yellow vinyl, 1968....**$6.00-$12.00**

JAN AND DEAN:

LPs

Sundazed LP-5022, Jan and Dean (The Dore Album), 2 LPs, colored vinyl, 1996 ....**$5.00-$10.00**

THE JAZZ CRUSADERS:

LPs

Pacific Jazz ST-43, Lookin' Ahead, stereo, yellow vinyl, 1962 ......**$30.00-$60.00**

JETHRO TULL:

45s

Chrysalis S7-18211, "Christmas Song"/"Skating Away on the Thin Ice of a New Day," green vinyl, 1994 ....**$2.50-$5.00**

LONNIE JOHNSON:

45s

Rama 9, "My Woman is Gone"/"Don't Make Me Cry, Baby," red vinyl, 1953 ....**$75.00-$150.00**

THE KINKS:

45s

Arista Sp-5, "Sleepwalker"/"All the Kids on the Street," promo on gold vinyl, 1977 .... **$5.00-$10.00**

KISS:

LPs

Mercury 522-647-1, Alive III, 2 LPs, pressed on red, white, blue, or black vinyl, value is equal, 1994 .... **$12.50-$25.00**

THE MAJESTICS:

45s

Jordan 1057, "Angel of Love"/"Searching for a New Love," yellow vinyl, 1961 .... **$150.00-$300.00**

BARBARA MANDRELL:

45s

MCA 57237, "Fast Lanes and Country Roads," same on both sides, yellow vinyl, 1985 .... **$5.00-$10.00**

DAVE MASON:

LPs

Blue Thumb BTS-19, Alone Together, multicolored splash vinyl

(if Blue Thumb logo), 1970 .... **$10.00-$20.00**

(if Blue Thumb logo, record misprinted as "All Together"), 1970 .... **$100.00-$200.00**

(if ABC logo), 1975 .... **$6.00-$12.00**

MADONNA:

LPs

Sire 25157, Like A Virgin, white vinyl, silver spine on jacket, 1984 .... **$30.00-$60.00**

(if white vinyl, cream spine), 1984 .... **$25.00-$50.00**

THE MOODY BLUES:

45s

Polydor 885201-7, "The Other Side of Life"/"The Spirit," blue vinyl, 1986 .... **$2.50-$5.00**

(w/specially designed picture sleeve, add), 1986 .... **$2.50-$5.00**

JOE MORRIS:

45s

Herald 420, "Travelin' Man"/"No, It Can't Be Done," red vinyl, 1954 .... **$40.00-$80.00**

RICK NELSON:

45s

Imperial 5545, "Lonesome Town"/"I Got A Feeling," red vinyl, 1958 .... **$300.00-$600.00**

5741, "Travelin' Man"/"Hello Mary Lou," red vinyl, 1961 .... **$400.00-$800.00**

5935, "Old Enough to Love"/"If You Can't Rock Me," red vinyl, 1963 .... **$250.00-$500.00**

5958, "A Long Vacation"/"Mad Mad World," red vinyl, 1963 .... **$150.00-$300.00**

WILLIE NELSON:

45s

Columbia AE7-1183, "Pretty Paper"/"Rudolph the Red Nosed Reindeer," red vinyl, 1979 .... **$12.50-$25.00**

NIRVANA:

45s

Sub Pop 73, "Silver"/"Dive"

(if blue vinyl, first 3,000 copies), 1990 .... **$20.00-$40.00**

(if clear pink-lavender vinyl), 1990 .... **$25.00-$50.00**

(w/fold-over picture sleeve, add), 1990 .... **$5.00-$10.00**

THE OAK RIDGE BOYS:

45s

MCA S45-17233, "When You Give It Away"/"The Voices of Rejoicing Love," promo, green vinyl, 1986 .... **$7.50-$15.00**

COLIN O'MOORE:

78s

Pathé 32272, "Like an Angel You Flew into Everyone's Heart" (Lindbergh)/ "Charlie is My Darling," mottled black-red pressing, 1928 .... **$30.00-$60.00**

THE ORIOLES:

45s

Jubilee 5051, "Baby, Please Don't Go"/"Don't Tell Her What's Happened To Me," red vinyl, 1951 .... **$1,500.00-$2,000.00**

5092, "Don't Cry Baby"/"See See Rider," red vinyl, 1952 .... **$750.00-$1,500.00**

5107, "I Miss You So"/"Till Ten," red vinyl, 1952 .... **$750.00-$1,500.00**

5108, "Teardrops On My Pillow"/"Hold Me, Thrill Me, Kiss Me," red vinyl, 1953 .... **$750.00-$1,500.00**

5120, "I Cover the Waterfront"/"One More Time," red vinyl, 1953 .... **$600.00-$1,200.00**

ORION:

45s

Sun 1148, "Remember Bethlehem," same on both sides, promo, yellow vinyl, 1979 .... **$5.00-$10.00**

1152, "It Ain't No Mystery," same on both sides, promo, yellow vinyl, 1980 .... **$5.00-$10.00**

1153, "Texas Tea," same on both sides, promo, yellow vinyl, 1980 .... **$5.00-$10.00**

PATTI PAGE:

45s

Mercury 5645, "Mister and Mississippi"/"These Things I Offer You," red vinyl, 1951 .... **$20.00-$40.00**

THE PARAMOURS:

45s

Moonglow 214, "That's All I Want Tonight"/"There She Goes," red vinyl, 1962 .... **$20.00-$40.00**

DOLLY PARTON:

45s

RCA JB-11296, "Heartbreaker," same on both sides, promo, red vinyl, 1978 .... **$5.00-$10.00**

JB-11420, "Baby I'm Burning," same on both sides, promo, red vinyl, 1979 .... **$5.00-$10.00**

JB-11705, "Great Balls of Fire," same on both sides, promo, red vinyl, 1979 .... **$5.00-$10.00**

JH-11926, "Starting Over Again," same on both sides, promo, green vinyl, 1980 .... **$6.00-$12.00**

JH-12133, "9 to 5," same on both sides, promo, blue vinyl, 1980 . **$7.50-$15.00**

PINK FLOYD:

LPs

Columbia C 64200, The Division Bell, blue vinyl, 1994 .... **$10.00-$20.00**

ELVIS PRESLEY:

45s

Collectables COL-0103, Elvis Presley, Elvis #1 Hit Singles Collection, 23 singles in box set, red vinyl—contains five Sun-labeled 45s on red vinyl, 2001 .... **$50.00-$100.00**

COL-0134, Elvis Hit Singles Collection Volume 2, 23 singles in box set, red vinyl, 2002 .... **$50.00-$100.00**

RCA DME1-1803, "King of the Whole Wide World"/"King Creole," test pressings on green, blue, white, and clear vinyl, value is equal for all pressings, 1997 .... **$200.00-$400.00**

(w/picture sleeve, add), 1997 .... **$4.00-$8.00**

LPs

RCA LSP-2426, Blue Hawaii, blue vinyl, 197? .... **$500.00-$1,000.00**

AFK1-2428, Moody Blue, clear blue vinyl, very common, 1977 .... **$5.00-$10.00**

(if on black vinyl, much rarer), 197 .... **$100.00-$200.00**

(if on any color other than clear blue or black, test pressing), 1977 .... **$1,000.00-$2,000.00**

RCA AFL1-5353, A Valentine Gift For You, red vinyl, 1985 .... **$10.00-$20.00**

AFL1-5418, Reconsider Baby, blue vinyl, 1985 .... **$10.00-$20.00**

AFL1-5430, Always On My Mind, purple vinyl, 1985 .... **$10.00-$20.00**

PRINCE:

45s

Warner Bros. 29286, "When Doves Cry"/"17 Days," purple vinyl, 1984 .... **$10.00-$20.00**

29174, "Purple Rain"/"God," purple vinyl, 1984 .... **$2.00-$4.00**

(w/plastic transparent picture sleeve, add), 1984 .... **$4.00-$8.00**

? AND THE MYSTERIANS:

LPs

Collectables COL 2004, ? and the Mysterians, Featuring 96 Tears, orange vinyl, tracks are re-recorded versions, not the originals, 1997 .... **$6.00-$12.00**

R.E.M.:

45s

Fan Club U-23518M, "Parade of the Wooden Soldiers"/"See No Evil," green vinyl, 1988 .... **$30.00-$60.00**

REM 2000, "Christmas Time (Is Here Again)"/"Hastings and Main"/"Take Seven," blue vinyl, 2000 .... **$5.00-$10.00**

EDDIE RABBITT:

45s

Elektra 378, "Song of Ireland," same on both sides, small spindle hole, green vinyl, 1978 .... **$7.50-$15.00**

BONNIE RAITT:

45s

Capitol S7-18039, "You"/"Sign of Falling," red vinyl, 1994 .... **$2.00-$4.00**

JIMMY REED:

45s

105, "I Found My Baby"/"Jimmy's Boogie," red vinyl, 1953 .. **$200.00-$400.00**

119, "You Don't Have To Go"/"Boogie in the Dark," red vinyl, 1954 .... **$150.00-$300.00**

JIM REEVES:

45s

Abbott 148, "Bimbo"/"Gypsy Heart," red vinyl, 1953 .... **$30.00-$60.00**

THE RESIDENTS:

45s

Ralph RZ 8422, "It's A Man's Man's Man's World"/"Safety is a Cootie Wootie," white vinyl, labels reversed—side A listed, but plays side B, 1984 .... **$10.00-$20.00**

(if labels are on correct sides), 1984 .... **$7.50-$15.00**

RZ 8622, "Kaw-Liga"/"Stars and Stripes Forever," white vinyl, 1986 .... **$5.00-$10.00**

PAUL REVERE AND THE RAIDERS:

45s

Columbia 43556, "Kicks," same on both sides, red vinyl, 1966 ..... **$25.00-$50.00**

43678, "Hungry," same on both sides, red vinyl, 1966 .... **$25.00-$50.00**

43810, "The Great Airplane Strike," same on both sides, red vinyl, 1966 .... **$25.00-$50.00**

THE RIP CHORDS:

45s

Columbia 42921, "Hey Little Cobra," same on both sides, yellow vinyl, 1963 .... **$25.00-$50.00**

THE ROVERS:

45s

Music City 750, "Why Oh-h"/"Ichi-Bon Tami Dachi," red vinyl, 1954 .... **$125.00-$250.00**

780, "Salute to Johnny Ace"/"Jadda," red vinyl, 1955 .... **$125.00-$250.00**

BILLY JOE ROYAL:

45s

Columbia 43305, "Down in the Boondocks," same on both sides, red vinyl, 1965 .... **$20.00-$40.00**

BOB SEGER:

45s

Capitol 4653, "We've Got Tonight," mono/stereo, promo, silver vinyl, 1978 .... **$5.00-$10.00**

SIMON AND GARFUNKEL:

45s

Columbia 43396, "The Sounds of Silence," same on both sides, red vinyl, 1965 .... **$25.00-$50.00**

43396, "The Sounds of Silence," acoustic version on one side (dead wax number ends with "1C"); electric version on other side (dead wax number ends with "1D"), red vinyl, 1965 .... **$30.00-$60.00**

43617, "I Am A Rock," same on both sides, red vinyl, 1966 ...... **$25.00-$50.00**

SMASHING PUMPKINS:

45s

Sub Pop 90, "Tristessa"/"La Dolly Vita," pink vinyl, 4000 pressed, 1991 .... **$27.50-$55.00**

(if above on red vinyl, 5 pressed), 1991 .... **$250.00-$500.00**

(if above on grey vinyl, 50 pressed), 1991 .... **$60.00-$120.00**

(w/picture sleeve, add), 1991 .... **$2.50-$5.00**

HANK SNOW:

45s

RCA Victor 48-0056, "Marriage Vow"/"The Star Spangled Waltz," green vinyl, 1949 .... **$20.00-$40.00**

48-0356, "The night I Stole Sammy Morgan's Gin"/"I Cried But My Tears Were Too Late," green vinyl, 1950 .... **$15.00-$30.00**

THE SONS OF THE PIONEERS:

45s

RCA Victor 48-0004, "Cool Water"/"Chant of the Wanderer," green vinyl, 1949 .... **$15.00-$30.00**

48-0005, "Tumbling Tumbleweeds"/"Everlasting Hills of Oklahoma," green vinyl, 1949 .... **$15.00-$30.00**

48-0183, "Cigareets, Whusky, and Wild, Wild Women"/"My Best To You," green vinyl, 1950 .... **$15.00-$30.00**

GEORGE STRAIT:

45s

MCA 53087, "All My Ex's Live in Texas," same on both sides, yellow vinyl, 1987 .... **$7.50-$15.00**

STYX:

LPs

A&M SP-3711, Cornerstone, platinum-colored vinyl, 1979 .... **$15.00-$30.00**

TAMPA RED:

45s

RCA Victor 50-0019, "Come On If You're Coming"/"When Things Go Wrong With You," cerise vinyl, 1950 .... **$60.00-$120.00**

50-0027, "It's a Brand New Boogie"/"Put Your Money Where Your Mouth Is," cerise vinyl, 1950 .... **$60.00-$120.00**

50-0094, "It's Good Like That"/"New Deal Blues," 1950 .... **$50.00-$100.00**

THE UNFORGETTABLES:

45s

Pamela 204, "Oh Wishing Well"/"Daddy Must Be a Man," blue vinyl, 1961 .... **$250.00-$500.00**

VOCALION CONCERT BAND:

78s

Aeolian-Vocalion 22024, "Allied National Airs"/"There's A Long, Long Trail (When You Come Back)" (by Criterion Quartet) (multicolored splash pressing), 1919 .... **$250.00-$500.00**

VOCALION MILITARY BAND:

78s

Aeolian-Vocalion 12000, "America and the Star Spangled Banner"/"Patriotic Medley" (red-white-blue pressing), 1918 .... **$50.00-$100.00**

SLIM WHITMAN:

45s

Imperial 8156, "Indian Love Call"/"China Doll," opaque red vinyl, 1952 .... **$25.00-$50.00**

YES:

45s

Atlantic 2854, "Roundabout," mono/stereo, yellow vinyl, 1972 .... **$50.00-$100.00**

Photo credit: Ultimix Records

For its 100th edition, the Ultimix series of club DJ remixes pressed their centennial set in colored vinyl. These mixes have sold for $50-$100 on the secondary market, and can command even higher prices if the discs contain a remix of the Beatles' greatest hits, or a compilation of top songs in a multi-mega-medley mix.

***$100**, NM condition*

Not only was the White Stripes album Elephant *released as a two-LP vinyl set, in keeping with the duo's consistent color schemes, one of the records was pressed on translucent red vinyl, the other on opaque white vinyl.*

***$25**, NM condition*

While radio stations and MTV played a clean version of Radiohead's hit song "Creep" (with lyrics like "You're so very special…") this green vinyl jukebox-only 45 of "Creep" contains the unexpurgated album cut.

***$4**, NM*

Perfect Records made the chocolate brown 78s as part of a budget-priced or "dime-store" product line. Many of these pressings have been overplayed by steel needles, so finding a decent copy with its original chocolate shine is tough.

***$5**, VG+ condition*

This red vinyl promotional pressing of Simon and Garfunkel's "The Sounds of Silence" is unique in that it contains the original 1964 acoustic version from their first album, Wednesday Morning, 3 A.M. *on one side—and the 1965 version, the #1 hit version enhanced with electric guitars, on the B-side.*

***$20**, Fair condition*

CHAPTER 4

PICTURE DISCS AND FLEXIDISCS

History

Instead of your standard-issue black vinyl or shellac recording, picture discs and flexidiscs offered a visually enticing alternative. Picture discs contained a photograph or artwork embedded directly into the record; while flexidiscs were printed on a sheet of pliable plastic or laminated cardboard. The collectibility of these unique pressings is directly proportional to the artist's popularity, the content of the product, or the image on the picture disc.

The first picture discs were made in the early 1930s, as RCA Victor released some special-edition picture discs of their top performers. These pressings, featuring black-and-white photographs encased in a shellac record, gave music lovers an instant collectible, as well as the opportunity to see their favorite artists—Jimmie Rodgers, Enrico Caruso, Paul Whiteman's Orchestra—on a playable disc.

Photo credit: From the collection of Kurt Nauck.

One of the many Vogue picture disc titles that were pressed between 1946 and 1947. Because of the uneven print run, while some Vogue titles are very common, others—like this pressing from Art Kassel and His Orchestra—are extremely rare, with possibly less than a dozen copies of "Queen for a Day" in existence.
***$5,000**, NM condition*

In 1946, the first all-picture-disc record label, Thomas Saffady's Vogue Picture Discs, was born. Saffady's company had perfected an automatic assembly-line process for constructing picture discs. Two paper color illustrations were placed on either side of an aluminum core. The illustrations and core were coated with clear vinylite polymer, and the grooves were stamped onto the final product. Unfortunately, initial sales were very poor—pretty picture records could not compensate for their high retail price. The company filed for bankruptcy a year into their existence, leaving a legacy of more than 75 colored vinyl titles, in a cross-section of various genres.

In the 1970s, some record companies pressed picture discs as a novelty—mostly the pictures replicated the front of the album cover—but their existence sparked a picture disc collecting craze. Most of the collectors who purchased picture discs in the late 1970s either hung them on the wall like fine art, or displayed them with plate stands to show their full-color glory. These discs were rarely played; many picture disc collectors at the time already had the black vinyl version of those albums, and played the picture disc maybe once to make sure the correct album was in the grooves.

Today's picture discs are more durable than their 78 RPM ancestors. The paper illustrations are now affixed to a polyvinyl chloride center disc, then sheets of mylar are placed over each picture, like the bread slices of a sandwich. The mylar-artwork-vinyl collage is then stamped by the pressing machines—and 45 seconds later, a picture disc is born.

While most picture discs feature album art found on the black vinyl albums, some discs contain rare band photos or specially modified art. Other picture discs contain interviews with the band or lead singer, and these interviews exist only in the picture-disc format.

Flexidiscs, also known as "soundsheets" or "pocket records," were first popularized in the 1930s as brown records called "Hits of the Week." The records were

The rock band Boston sold 17 million copies of their debut album. That title, like many of Columbia/Epic's million-selling rock titles, was reissued in the late 1970s on picture disc.

***$15**, NM condition*

Photo credit: Collection of Michael Cumella, from the Internet Museum of Flexi/Cardboard/Oddity Records.

In 1982, the Musicland retail chain offered special flexidiscs for customers who purchased Beatles records. The rarest of these were sold through Sam Goody stores, and can run as much as $25 in near-mint condition.

***$20**, NM condition*

pressed on a flexible plastic called Durium, and were sold for 5 cents apiece for a three-minute song at department stores and newsstands. While most of the titles on this line sell for a few dollars apiece at auction, one desirable pressing promotes a group called the Harlem Hot Chocolates—actually a pseudonym for Duke Ellington's orchestra!

By the 1950s, the Eva-Tone Company of Clearwater, Florida, developed a process that allowed records to be pressed on thin sheets of PVC plastic. These "soundsheets" could be affixed to a cardboard backing (allowing records to appear on the backs of cereal boxes or postcards), or could be distributed through magazines like *National Geographic, Goldmine,* or *Mad*.

Two flexidisc product lines appeared in the late 1960s, Hip-Pocket Records and Pocket Discs. Distributed by Philco, 1967's Hip-Pocket Records were designed for play on their new line of tiny phonographs, featured monaural versions of popular hits by The Doors, Sonny & Cher, Tommy James & the Shondells, and other artists. This product line produced 41 titles over a two-year period. In 1969, Americom produced a line of flexidiscs that could be purchasable through vending machines. Besides having artists like Aretha Franklin and Steppenwolf on their roster, Americom also was fortunate to acquire the rights to reproduce certain Beatles records in this line.

Today, flexidiscs are mostly used as a promotional tool, an attempt to entice the consumer to purchase a full-length album, or as a bonus giveaway after a customer has bought a new album. Flexidiscs are also commonly found as fan club premiums, offering fans of groups like the Beatles, R.E.M., or Pearl Jam a special treat at Christmastime.

The majority of picture discs are round, but some discs are irregularly shaped, in an effort to follow the picture disc's artwork. In this case, the record is pressed with the paper insert and the mylar sheets, but a 7-inch odd-shaped disc is pressed in a 12-inch format, then the record is cut

Photo credit: Collection of Michael Cumella, from the Internet Museum of Flexi/Cardboard/Oddity Records.

This Hip-Pocket pressing of the Doors' "Light My Fire" is hard to find, especially in an unopened condition.

***$40**, NM condition*

Photo credit: From the collection of Bruce Spizer.

In an effort to spread the Beatles' music to new locations, these "flexidiscs" could provide a Beatles fan with the group's latest Top 40 hits, all on unbreakable flexible PVC sheets.

***$300**, NM condition*

with a special pre-sculpted die, similar to a cookie cutter. This gives the illusion of a bigger-than-life 7-inch record, even though the grooves still spin in a circular pattern.

Even without a picture encased in its grooves, shaped records have also developed a collectible following. The perimeter of a shaped record will often follow the theme of the recorded content—a heart-shaped record for a love song is very common.

Another type of picture disc, the "laser-etched" album, also appeared in the late 1970s. Using special tools similar to those employed by engravers to make dollar bill pressing plates, the record lacquer is scraped or "etched" before the grooves are cut. The finished product is visually striking—when viewed in reflected light, the black vinyl contains rainbow-colored patterns which shimmer as the record spins on the turntable.

Many record collectors have mixed feelings about picture discs. These records are more likely to end up on a wall or display shelf than on a turntable—and if the mylar used to press the record was from thin sheets, the record itself will have a muffled sound when played. If a record company or pressing plant uses thicker mylar, however, the record will sound as clear as its vinyl counterpart.

Two examples of "shaped vinyl." Neil Young's triangular record replicates the artwork from his Re-Ac-Tor album. In 2000, Jimi Hendrix' "Star Spangled Banner" was pressed with die-cut stars, as the song plays in the inner groove.

*(L to R) **$250**, NM condition; **$100**, NM condition*

Photo credit: Hendrix Star Spangled Banner courtesy of Erika Records, Downey, Calif.

What To Look For

For most picture disc collectors, a clean vinyl image is key. Picture discs are one of the few record collectibles in which the visual appearance is more important than the sound on the grooves.

If you plan to display your records on a wall, don't just hang them up by putting a nail in the wall and slipping the record on through its spindle hole. These are works of art; a 12 x16-inch frame can be purchased at any art supply store or framing shop (if you bring the disc in, the framers can even create a customized matte to enhance your picture disc). Avoid hanging your picture disc on a wall that receives direct sunlight—the picture inside can fade in just a few years from direct sunshine.

Most picture discs were sold in 12-inch jackets, whose front covers were die-cut so that consumers could see the entire album in all its full-color glory. These jackets tend to wrinkle and split over time, with most of the splits occurring where the surface area between the seam and the die-cut circle is the thinnest. Those who want the jackets as well as the picture disc also look for jackets that have not been "notched" by the record company for discount sales. The discs themselves were stored inside clear plastic inner sleeves; if the record was improperly placed inside the jacket, the inner lining will wrinkle and tear.

As for flexidiscs, although they are very durable, be aware that if there are any dents, folds, creases, or bends in the flexidisc grooves, the needle will mistrack. Records that were once on the backs of cereal boxes are worth twice as much if they remained on the boxes. Hip-Pocket Records were sold in specially colored envelopes, and a record in that format must still be in the sealed, undamaged envelope to be considered near mint. Some artists recorded flexidiscs as tie-ins with food products or toys, and despite the novelty of these pressings, they may contain recordings that have never surfaced on compact disc.

Photo credit: Collection of Michael Cumella, from the Internet Museum of Flexi/Cardboard/Oddity Records

Although credited to the Beach Boys, this flexidisc is essentially a Brian Wilson leftover track from his solo album, and was only attainable if you bought a special Barbie® doll and playset.

***$15**, NM condition*

Books

Curry, Edgar L., *Vogue: The Picture Record (2nd Edition)*, self-published by the author, 1998, available through jancur@halcyon.com.

Web Pages

Erika Records of Downey, California, is America's largest producer of colored vinyl and picture discs. They can be reached at: http://www.erikarecords.com.

A history of flexible records, by Hans Koert, is available at this Web site: http://www.worldofgramophones.com/label1.html

The Internet Museum of Flexi/Cardboard/Oddity Records: http://www.wfmu.org/MACrec/

The Vinyl Underground, a gallery of picture discs and colored vinyl: http://www.vinylunderground.net/

A Picture Disc Collectors Club Web site: http://groups.yahoo.com/group/picturediscollectors/

ARTIST VG+ to NM

THE ARCHIES:

Cardboard 45s

Post cereal, features characters dancing on a yellow background, will play one of the following: "You Make Me Wanna Dance," "Catchin' Up On Fun," "Jingle Jangle," "Love Light," 1969 .... **$2.50-$5.00**

Post cereal, features characters holding a black ring in center of record, will play one of the following: "Archie's Party," "You Know I Love You," "Nursery Rhymes," "Jingle Jangle," 1969 .... **$2.50-$5.00**

Post cereal, features characters holding a black ring in center of record, will play one of the following: "You Make Me Wanna Dance," "Catching Up On Fun," "Jingle Jangle," "Love Light," 1969 .... **$2.50-$5.00**

Post cereal, features characters playing instruments, may play one of the following: "Everything's Archie," "Bang Shang-A-Lang," "Boys and Girls," "Hide and Seek," 1969 .... **$2.50-$5.00**

THE BEACH BOYS:

Flexidiscs

Eva-Tone 4439-0300, "Living Doll," blue flexidisc sold only w/Barbie® boxed set, 1987 .... **$7.50-$15.00**

THE BEATLES:

4-inch flexible Pocket-Discs

Apple-Americom 5715, "Yellow Submarine"/"Eleanor Rigby," 1969 .... **$1,500.00-$2,000.00**

2276/M-221, "Hey Jude"/"Revolution," 1969 .... **$150.00-$300.00**

2490/M-335, "Get Back"/"Don't Let Me Down," 1969 ...... **$500.00-$1,000.00**

2531/M-382, "The Ballad of John and Yoko"/"Old Brown Shoe," 1969 .... **$400.00-$800.00**

Eva-Tone 420826cs, "All My Loving"/"You've Got To Hide Your Love Away" (if from Musicland store), 1982 .... **$5.00-$10.00**

(if from Discount store), 1982 .... **$10.00-$20.00**

(if from Sam Goody store), 1982 .... **$12.50-$25.00**

830771X, "Till There Was You"/"Three Cool Cats," 1983 .... **$3.00-$6.00**

Picture Disc LPs

Capitol SEAX-11840, Sgt. Pepper's Lonely Hearts Club Band, deduct 25% if cover is notched or cut 1978 .... **$10.00-$20.00**

BLONDIE:

Picture Disc LPs

Chrysalis CHP 5001, Parallel Lines, 1979 .... **$12.50-$25.00**

BOBBY CALDWELL:

Picture Discs

Clouds HSS-1, "What You Won't Do For Love"/"Love Won't Wait," red vinyl, heart-shaped, 1979 .... **$10.00-$20.00**

BOSTON:

Picture Disc LPs

Epic E99 44188, Boston, 1978 .... **$7.50-$15.00**

THE CARS:

Picture Disc LPs

Elektra 5E-567, Shake It Up, "KMET-FM" stamped on back, 1981 .... **$25.00-$50.00**

5E-567, without radio station stamped on back, 1981 .... **$20.00-$40.00**

ELVIS COSTELLO AND THE ATTRACTIONS:

Picture Disc LPs

Columbia, no number, My Aim Is True/This Year's Model, promo-only picture disc w/one side dedicated to each album), 1978 .... **$25.00-$50.00**

PETER CRISS:

Picture Discs

Casablanca NBPIX-7122, Peter Criss, deduct 25% if cover is notched or cut, 1978 .... **$25.00-$50.00**

NEIL DIAMOND:

4-inch Flexible Record

Hip-Pocket HP-5, "Girl, You'll Be A Woman Soon"/"Cherry Cherry," 1967 .... **$7.50-$15.00**

HP-17, "You Got To Me"/"Solitary Man," 1967 .... **$7.50-$15.00**

Picture Disc LPs

Columbia 9C9-39915, Primitive, 1984 .... **$10.00-$20.00**

THE DOORS:

4-inch Flexible Record

Hip-Pocket HP-9, "Light My Fire"/"Break on Through," 1967 .. **$20.00-$40.00**

THE DOWN HOMERS:

10-inch 78 RPM Picture Discs

Vogue R736, "Out Where the West Winds Blow"/"Who's Gonna Kiss You When I'm Gone," 1946 .... **$40.00-$80.00**

R786, "Baby I Found Out All About You"/"Boogie Woogie Yodel" .... **$50.00-$100.00**

THE FIVE AMERICANS:

4-inch Flexible Record

Hip-Pocket HP-10, "Western Union"/"Sounds of Love," 1967... **$10.00-$20.00**

THE FOUR TOPS:

Cardboard 45s

Topps/Motown 5, "I Can't Help Myself," 1967 .... **$37.50-$75.00**

9, "Baby I Need Your Loving," 1967 .... **$37.50-$75.00**

ACE FREHLEY:

Picture Discs

Casablanca NBPIX-7121, Ace Frehley, deduct 25% if cover is notched or cut, 1978 .... **$25.00-$50.00**

CECIL GANT:

10-inch Picture Disc 78s

Gilt Edge 500, "I Wonder"/"Cecil's Boogie," red picture disc with different photo on each side, 1944 .... **$125.00-$250.00**

MARVIN GAYE:

Cardboard 45s

Topps/Motown 6, "How Sweet It Is," 1967 .... **$37.50-$75.00**

THE HAPPENINGS:

4-inch Flexible Record

Hip-Pocket HP-7, "Go Away Little Girl"/"See You in September," 1967 .... **$10.00-$20.00**

THE HARLEM HOT CHOCOLATES:

Flexible Record

Durium "Hit of the Week" 1045, "Sing You Sinners," 1931 .... **$20.00-$40.00**

THE JIMI HENDRIX EXPERIENCE:

12-inch Picture Discs

Capitol SPRO 11284, "The Star Spangled Banner" (same on both sides), blue-vinyl record w/eight die-cut stars in vinyl, 199? .... **$50.00-$100.00**

Experience Hendrix 13487, "Star Spangled Banner"/"Purple Haze," promo, 1999 .... **$7.50-$15.00**

Rhino RNDF-254, The Jimi Hendrix Interview, picture disc, 1982 .... **$12.50-$25.00**

MARY HOPKIN:

4-inch Flexible Pocket-Discs

Apple/Americom 1801P/M-238, "Those Were The Days"/"Turn, Turn, Turn," 1969 .... **$300.00-$600.00**

IRON MAIDEN:

Picture Discs LPs

Capitol SEAX-12219, The Number of the Beast, 1982 .... **$25.00-$50.00**

TOMMY JAMES AND THE SHONDELLS:

4-inch Flexible Record

Hip-Pocket HP-1, "I Think We're Alone Now"/"Mirage," 1967 ... **$7.50-$15.00**

HP-2, "Hanky Panky"/"Gettin' Together," 1967 .... **$7.50-$15.00**

ELTON JOHN:

Picture Disc LPs

MCA 14951, A Single Man, 1978 .... **$10.00-$20.00**

(if on MCA L33-1995, promo only), 1978 .... **$20.00-$40.00**

ART KASSEL AND HIS ORCHESTRA:

10-inch 78 RPM Picture Discs

Vogue R714, "Doodle Doo Doo"/"All I Do Is Wantcha," 1946 ... **$50.00-$75.00**

R723, "Wave To Me My Lady"/"You Won't Be Satisfied (Til You Break My Heart)," 1946 .... **$70.00-$140.00**

R734, "Sweetheart"/"A Little Consideration," 1946 .... **$40.00-$80.00**

R770, "The Whiffenpoof Song"/"If That Phone Ever Rings (And It's You)," 1946 .... **$35.00-$70.00**

R771, "If I Could be With You"/"Jeannine," 1946 .... **$40.00-$80.00**

R780, "Let's Get Married"/"Touch Me Not," 1946 .... **$30.00-$60.00**

R781, "Sooner or Later"/"I Love You (For Sentimental Reasons)," 1946 .... **$30.00-$60.00**

R784, "Queen for a Day"/"At the End of a Perfect Day," 1947 .... **$2,500.00-$5,000.00**

R785, "The Echo Said No"/"Mu Adobe Hacienda," 1947 .... **$70.00-$90.00**

KISS:

Picture Discs

Mercury 836-887-1, Smashes, Thrashes and Hits, 1988 .... **$12.50-$25.00**

JOHN LENNON AND THE PLASTIC ONO BAND:

4-inch Flexible Pocket-Discs

Apple/Americom 1809P/M-435, "Give Peace a Chance"/"Remember Love," 1969 .... **$375.00-$750.00**

LULU BELLE & SCOTTY:

10-inch 78 RPM Picture Discs

Vogue R718, "Some Sunday Mornin'"/"In the Dog House Now," 1946 .... $40.00-$80.00

R719, "Have I told You Lately That I Love You"/"I Get A Kick Out of Corn," 1946 .... $40.00-$80.00

R720, "Grandpa's Getting' Younger E'ry Day"/"Time Will Tell," 1946 .... $40.00-$80.00

MARTHA AND THE VANDELLAS:

Cardboard 45s

7, "Dancing In The Street," 1967 .... **$37.50-$75.00**

14, "Love Is Like A Heat Wave," 1967 .... **$37.50-$75.00**

THE MARVELETTES:

Cardboard 45s

Topps/Motown 12, "Please Mr. Postman," 1967 .... **$37.50-$75.00**

PAUL McCARTNEY AND WINGS:

Picture Disc LPs

Capitol SEAX-11901, Band on the Run, 1978 .... **$20.00-$40.00**

THE McCOYS:

4-inch Flexible Record

Hip-Pocket HP-6, "Fever"/"Hang on Sloopy," 1967 .... **$10.00-$20.00**

MEAT LOAF:

Picture Disc LPs

Epic E99 34974, Bat Out Of Hell, 1978 .... **$10.00-$20.00**

METALLICA:

Picture Disc LPs

Megaforce MRI 069, Kill 'Em All, numbered, 1983 .... **$40.00-$80.00**

(if picture disc is not numbered), 1983 .... **$20.00-$40.00**

THE MIRACLES:

Cardboard 45s

Topps/Motown 11, "Shop Around," 1967 .... **$37.50-$75.00**

THE MONKEES:

Cardboard 45s

Frosted Rice Krinkles, will play one of the following: "(Theme From) The Monkees," "Tear Drop City," "Papa Gene's Blues, "The Day We Fall In Love," 1969 .... **$3.00-$6.00**

Alpha Bits, will play one of the following: "Last Train To Clarksville," "I Wanna Be Free," "Forget That Girl," "Valleri," 1969 .... **$3.00-$6.00**

Honeycombs, will play one of the following: "I'm A Believer," "Pleasant Valley Sunday," "I'm Not Your Steppin' Stone," "Mary, Mary," 1969 .... **$3.00-$6.00**

PATSY MONTANA:

10-inch 78 RPM Picture Discs

Vogue R721, "When I Gets to Where I'm Goin'"/"You're Only in My Arms (To Cry on My Shoulder)," 1946 .... **$50.00-$100.00**

MUDHONEY:

Picture Disc LPs

Sub Pop 105 PD, Every Good Boy Deserves Fudge, 2,500 copies pressed, 1991 .... **$15.00-$30.00**

NATIONAL LAMPOON:

Picture Disc LPs

Label 21 PIC, That's Not Funny, That's Sick!, 1978 .... **$10.00-$20.00**

OZZY OSBOURNE:

Picture Disc LPs

Jet AS99 1372, Diary of a Madman, promo, 1981 .... **$20.00-$40.00**

THE ALAN PARSONS PROJECT:
Picture Disc LPs
Arista ALPD 8263, Vulture Culture, promo, 1985 .... **$12.50-$25.00**

WILSON PICKETT:
4-inch Flexible Record
Hip-Pocket HP-11, "Land of 1000 Dances"/"Midnight Hour," 1967 .... **$10.00-$20.00**

PINK FLOYD:
Picture Disc LPs
Capitol SEAX-11902, The Dark Side of the Moon, 1978 .... **$15.00-$30.00**

THE POLICE:
Picture Disc LPs
A&M SP-3730, Ghost in the Machine, picture disc that lights up when placed on turntable, reportedly only five copies produced, 1981 .... **$500.00-$1,000.00**

BILLY PRESTON:
4-inch Flexible Pocket-Discs
Apple/Americom 1808P/M-433, "That's The Way God Planned It"/"What About You," 1969 .... **$200.00-$400.00**

LEO REISMAN AND HIS ORCHESTRA:
10-inch 78-RPM Picture Discs
RCA Victor 17-4000, "Adorable"/"My First Love To Last," picture of Janet Gaynor on disc, 1933 .... **$75.00-$150.00**

JIMMIE RODGERS:
10-inch 78-RPM Picture Discs
Victor 18-6000, "Cowhand's Last Ride"/"Blue Yodel No. 12," 1933 .... **$300.00-$600.00**

THE ROLLING STONES:
Picture Disc LPs
Rolling Stones COC 39114, Still Life (American Concert 1981), 1982 .... **$20.00-$40.00**

MITCH RYDER AND THE DETROIT WHEELS:
4-inch Flexible Record
Hip-Pocket HP-4, "Jenny Take a Ride"/"Sock It To Me Baby," 1967 .... **$7.50-$15.00**

THE CHARLIE SHAVERS QUINTET:
10-inch 78-RPM Picture Discs
Vogue R754, "She's Funny That Way"/"Dizzy's Dilemma," 1947 **$25.00-$50.00**
R755, "Serenade to a Pair of Nylons"/"Broadjump," 1947 .... **$40.00-$80.00**
R756, "Musicomania"/"If I Had You," 1947 .... **$75.00-$150.00**

GENE SIMMONS:
Picture Discs
Casablanca NBPIX-7120, Gene Simmons, deduct 25% if cover is notched or cut, 1978 .... **$30.00-$60.00**

SONNY AND CHER:
4-inch Flexible Record
Hip-Pocket HP-8, "I Got You Babe"/"The Beat Goes On," 1967 .... **$12.50-$25.00**

SPLIT ENZ:
45s
A&M 2339, "One Step Ahead"/"In The Wars," laser etched, 1981 .... **$5.00-$10.00**
(with picture sleeve that mentions laser etching, add:), 1981 .... **$5.00-$10.00**
12-inch Singles
A&M SP-17157, "I Don't Wanna Dance"/"Hard Act To Follow"/"History Never Repeats," 1981 .... **$15.00-$30.00**
LPs
A&M SP-4822, True Colours, laser-etched vinyl, contains four different covers, value is same for each cover, 1980 .... $7.50-$15.00

PAUL STANLEY:
Picture Discs
Casablanca NBPIX-7120, Paul Stanley, deduct 25% if cover is notched or cut, 1978 .... **$30.00-$60.00**

STYX:
Picture Disc LPs
A&M PR-4724, Pieces of Eight, 1978 .... **$12.50-$25.00**

THE SUPREMES:
Cardboard 45s
Topps/Motown 1, "Baby Love," 1967 .... **$37.50-$75.00**
2, "Stop! In The Name Of Love," 1967 .... **$37.50-$75.00**
3, "Where Did Our Love Go," 1967 .... **$37.50-$75.00**
15, "Come See About Me," 1967 .... **$37.50-$75.00**
16, "My World Is Empty Without You," 1967 .... **$37.50-$75.00**

THE TEMPTATIONS:
Cardboard 45s
Topps/Motown 4, "My Girl," 1967 .... **$37.50-$75.00**
13, "The Way You Do The Things You Do," 1967 .... **$37.50-$75.00**

TOTO:
Picture Discs
Columbia PD-36813, Turn Back, promo, 1981 .... **$12.50-$25.00**
8C8 38685, "Africa"/"Rosanna," disc shaped like the African continent, 1983 .... **$10.00-$20.00**

PAUL WHITEMAN AND HIS ORCHESTRA:
10-inch 78-RPM Picture Discs
Victor 39000, "A Night with Paul Whiteman at the Biltmore" (Pt. 1)/(Pt. 2), 1932 .... **$200.00-$400.00**

STEVIE WONDER:
Cardboard 45s
Topps/Motown 8, "Fingertips Part 2," 1967 .... **$37.50-$75.00**
10, "Uptight (Everything's Alright)," 1967 .... **$37.50-$75.00**

NEIL YOUNG:
Picture Discs
Reprise 49895, "Southern Pacific"/"Motor City," triangle-shaped record, 1982 .... **$125.00-$250.00**

Janet Gaynor starred in the 1933 motion picture Adorable*; this picture disc was one of several titles RCA Victor pressed, and are very hard to find today.*
***$150**, NM condition*

"Hit of the Week" flexible records were a popular and cheap record line in the 1930s. The flexible polymer causes the record to bend and curl with age; this pressing by the Harlem Hot Chocolates is the prize of the series, as the group was actually Duke Ellington's orchestra under a pseudonym.
***$40**, NM condition*

Split Enz' 1979 True Colours *album was "laser-etched" with symbols and letters, which makes this record collectible both in America, and in the group's home country of New Zealand, where that album was released without laser etching. Other albums pressed in the "laser-etched" format include Styx's* Paradise Theater *and the soundtrack to* Superman II.

***$15** with jacket, NM condition*

Blondie's Parallel Lines *picture disc replicates the original album cover motif, a common trait for 1970s picture discs.*

***$25**, NM condition*

In 1969, kids could find Monkees records on the backs of cereal boxes. The white circle above Davy Jones' head contains a single digit number, corresponding to one of four songs listed on the label. Notice the absence of Peter Tork from the artwork; he had left the group a year earlier. Other artists who went the "cereal box" route included the Archies, the Jackson Five, and Bobby Sherman.

***$4**, Good condition*

Toto's 1983 hit "Africa" was pressed as a special African-shaped picture disc. The B-side of this disc plays Toto's other hit "Rosanna," and features a photograph of Rosanna Arquette.

***$10**, VG+ condition*

Chapter 5

Picture Sleeves

History

Picture sleeves have been part of record collecting ever since records were first pressed. Even some of the earliest 78s had special paper sleeves that advertised a label's singing roster, with crisp line drawings of such singers as Enrico Caruso, Jenny Lind, and Nellie Melba.

While most 45s were sold either in white paper sleeves or in "company sleeves," a select number of records were sold with a full-color picture of the artist, the band, or a representative drawing of the song's concept. These "picture sleeves" can often be as valuable—in some cases, even more valuable—than the records contained inside.

By their very nature and existence, paper sleeves were designed to catch a purchaser's eye at the record store; and act as a carrying pouch to guide the 45 safely home. Unfortunately, after that the picture sleeve would be subject to every sort of wear and tear—splits on the seams, tears and wrinkles at the sleeve's opening, ringwear around the artist's face, etc. Because many record collectors stored their 45s in the accompanying picture sleeve, not expecting the sleeve to increase in any value, finding picture sleeves in near-mint condition becomes more difficult with each year.

In many cases, a picture sleeve will be made only for radio stations and promotional use. Sometimes a record will become such a quick hit, that the record company will simply run out of picture sleeves and package the hot discs in whatever generic sleeves it can find. Sometimes boxes of unused picture sleeves will turn up in a warehouse; in fact, the picture sleeve for Bruce Springsteen's first hit, "Blinded By The Light," is so rare that many of the copies existing today were allegedly found in a CBS dumpster.

Photo credit: From the collection of Eric Schwartz

The Grateful Dead's early sleeves are extremely hard to find, and this one, for their live favorite "Dark Star," is tough to locate, especially in good condition.
***$500**, NM condition*

Photo credit: From the Collection of Val Shively.

The Ronettes only had three picture sleeves during their run at Philles Records, and each one can run up to $150 in near-mint condition.
***$150**, NM condition*

This picture sleeve for Connie Francis' single "Where the Boys Are" is collectible by not only Connie Francis' fans, but also for fans of beach party movies and cheesecake covers with beautiful women in swimsuits.

***$15**, VG+ condition*

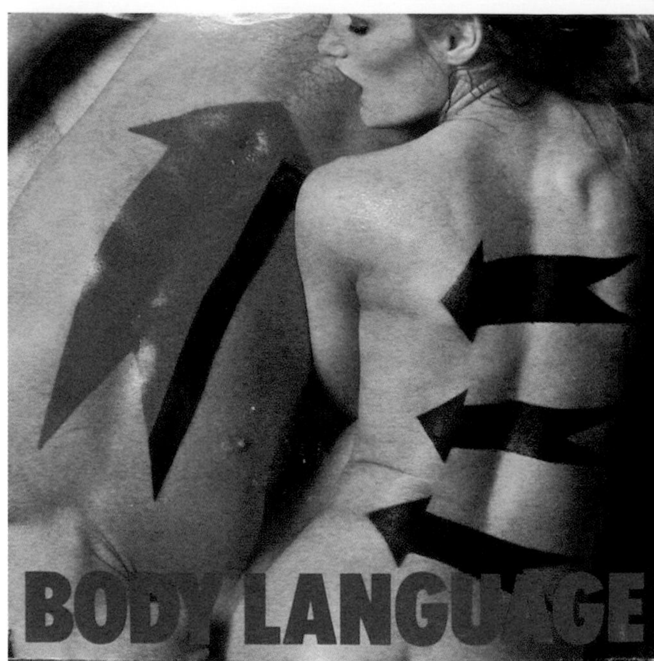

The sleeve for Queen's "Body Language" was yanked off the market because the cover showed a naked couple. The sleeve was replaced with a stark black sleeve, containing only the band's name and the song title.

***$15**, NM condition*

Not every picture sleeve is limited to a snazzy photo of the artist or group. Record companies have used many eye-catching tactics to make their records stand out, whether it includes foldout sleeves, label variations, or non-paper sleeves. Besides being a holder for the 45, picture sleeves often contained information on how to join an artist's fan club, what new releases were soon to be available, a concert tour schedule, or whether that artist would be appearing on a popular TV show.

Sometimes a record would be stored in a "foldout" picture sleeve, allowing the owner to get a bonus poster for their wall. Finding intact, near-mint copies of such foldout sleeves as Madonna's "Borderline," Duran Duran's "The Reflex" or the Grateful Dead's "Touch of Grey" has become more difficult, as these foldout sleeves may have tack holes in the corners (when they were put up on a bedroom wall), or the folds themselves may have split their seams (because the record was still stored inside). Some other picture sleeves were made of thin plastic, the same material used for bread bags. These sleeves tend to wrinkle easily, and the printed material on them can peel or scrape off quickly. Prince's "Purple Rain" and Kraftwerk's "Pocket Calculator" were stored in bread-bag sleeves. Other picture sleeves become rare collectibles because the content may have been changed—either the artwork was too salacious for initial release, or the band felt that a new cover was more appropriate for the music.

One of the benefits of picture sleeves is that, in the pre-video music age, it allowed fans to see pictures of up-and-coming new artists, or their favorite performers with a unique photograph available only for purchasers of a new 45. And if the previously unknown artist suddenly breaks through and becomes a superstar years later, those old picture sleeves can bring in some serious cash to that artist's new fans hoping to "discover" that artist's earliest material.

Records that aren't sold with picture sleeves are often sold in generic "company sleeves," artwork from a record label that can be used interchangeably with any 45 sold by that company. Some record companies, however, use "company sleeves" to promote other artists on the label, or to promote a certain artist's back catalog. Motown and Philadelphia International Records were two such labels that used their company sleeves to help sell other records within the organization.

As a young teenager, Alanis Morissette recorded two songs and had them pressed on the tiny Lamor label. Today, copies of these early pressings can bring up to $500 apiece—with $250 of that for the picture sleeve alone.

***$250**, NM condition*

To store your sleeves properly, first make sure they don't have records in them. This may sound odd—that the very item sleeves were designed to hold would do the most damage—but your records can be stored in inexpensive white paper sleeves. As for the colored picture sleeves, they can be stored in clear plastic sleeves, available through most equipment supply companies. Comic books also store non-PVC jackets, in which a 45 picture sleeve will fit nicely. Note that prices listed in this chapter are for picture sleeves only, with the record is worth more.

What To Look For

Picture sleeve storage is almost a Catch-22 situation. Optimally, you would want to store the record and the sleeve together. But the longer a record is stored in a picture sleeve, the more likely the sleeve will develop ring wear. If you want to collect picture sleeves, you should remove the record from the picture sleeve, storing the record in a white generic sleeve.

Glossy picture sleeves are very fragile; besides ring wear, they can also suffer from split seams, ridge cuts, and wrinkling. Sometimes the sleeve's internal glue may break down, causing the sleeve to come apart at the folds. And since these sleeves were made of paper, they tended to rip over time anyway.

Picture sleeves that were once owned by jukebox companies are rarely kept in good condition; sometimes the jukebox employees would cut a circular hole in the front of the sleeve, so they could reuse the sleeve for another record.

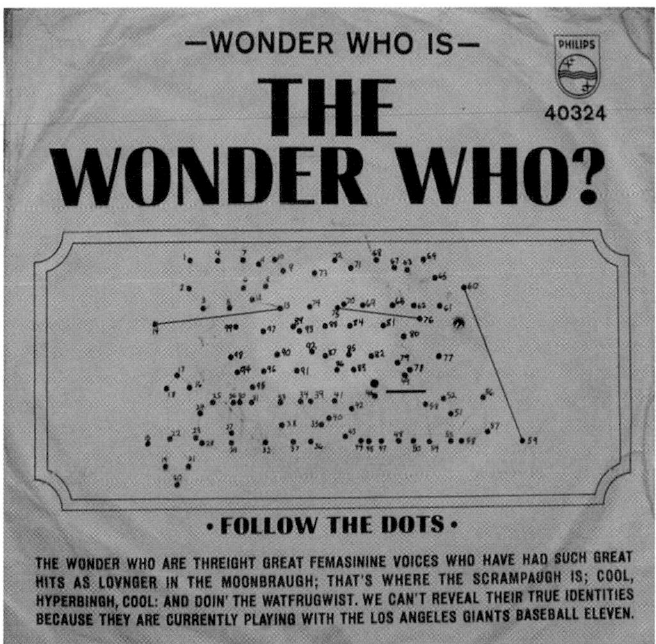

The "Wonder Who" covered Bob Dylan's "Don't Think Twice" and had a minor hit with it. This sleeve is often found with the "connect-the-dots" feature already filled in, revealing the phrase "We Are Your Favorites." Wonder if spelling out "We are really Frankie Valli and the Four Seasons" would have taken up too many dots.

***$20**, VG+ condition*

An example of an Atlantic company sleeve, with "floating heads" of the various artists on the Atlantic label at that time. Notice that while there are five members of the Clovers on the sleeve, the artwork for the Drifters features only their lead singer at the time, Clyde McPhatter.

*Company sleeve, **$4**, NM condition*

While most picture sleeves will have artwork from the original album, or a group shot of the band, some picture sleeves may contain original artwork that represents the song's lyrics. Although picture sleeves in the 1950s and 1960s contained shots of the artist, by the 1970s the sleeve was considered by many artists to be part of the whole musical experience, and care was taken with the picture sleeve artwork.

The most desirable picture sleeves are ones that are short-printed or were only available in a certain geographic area. Other rare sleeves include those that were for promotional use only, and those where something is edited out of the picture (early Beatles picture sleeves for "I Want To Hold Your Hand" show Paul McCartney with a cigarette in his fingers; when the sleeve was reissued for a 20th anniversary pressing, the cigarette was airbrushed out).

Please note that the prices listed below are only for the picture sleeves themselves; the value would certainly increase if the matching record was included.

Reference Books

Neely, Tim, *Goldmine Price Guide to 45 RPM Records*, Krause Publications, Iola, WI, 1999.

Szabla, Charles, *Goldmine 45 RPM Picture Sleeve Price Guide*, Krause Publications, Iola, WI, 1998.

Web Pages

You can see one-of-a-kind rare and unique Beatles picture sleeves at this site: http://www.rarebeatles.com

The cover artwork to Styx' "Come Sail Away" may give away the final secret of the song; but this unique artwork does not exist on any other Styx album or promotional material.

***$4**, VG+ condition*

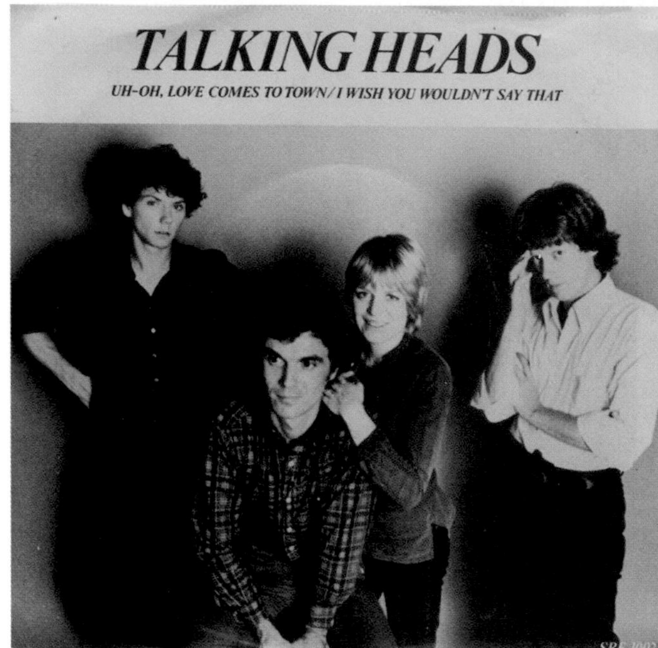

The standard artwork for most 1960s picture sleeves involved a stock photo of the artist or band, and the artist's name and song title in a white strip at the top of the sleeve. While this artwork style eventually disappeared, some examples still pop up, as in this early Talking Heads picture sleeve.

***$4**, VG+ condition*

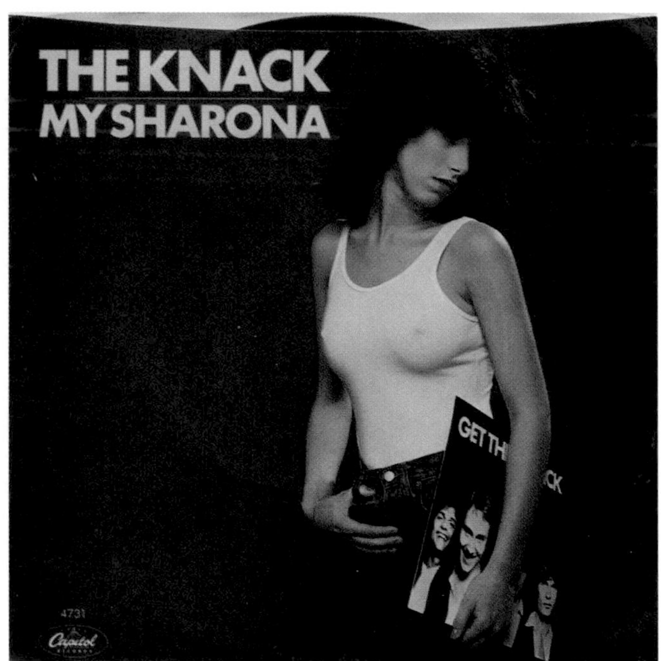

Because 45s from Capitol Records tended to have a geared edge around the label, the centers of these picture sleeves often suffer from ringwear. This 45 from the Knack's big hit "My Sharona" was most likely spared this fate by a collector who was as infatuated with the cover artwork as the song itself.

***$6**, NM condition*

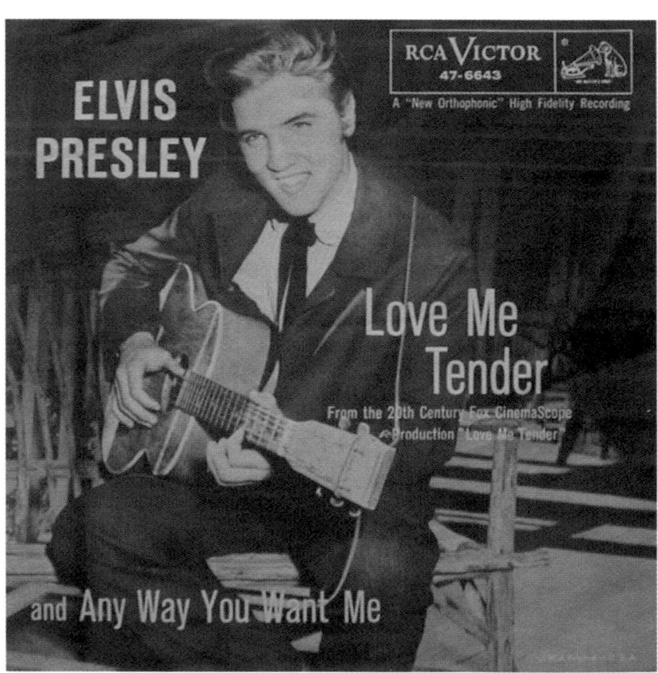

Nearly all of Elvis Presley's 45s were issued with some sort of picture sleeve. Most of them were pressed on glossy paper in full color; several of his earlier hits, including this sleeve for "Love Me Tender," were available only in a monochromatic or "spot color" format.

***$40**, NM condition*

ARTIST VG+ to NM

ANNETTE:
Disneyland F-102, "How Will I Know My Love"/"Don't Jump To Conclusions," 1958 .... $25.00-$50.00
Vista 354, "O Dio Mio"/"It Took Dreams," 1960 .... $15.00-$30.00
362, "Pineapple Princess"/"Luau Cha Cha Cha," 1960 .... $15.00-$30.00
433, "Muscle Beach Party"/"I Dream About Frankie," 1964 .... $15.00-$30.00

THE BEACH BOYS:
Capitol 4777, "Surfin' Safari"/"409," 1962 .... $40.00-$80.00
Brother 1001, "Heroes and Villains"/"You're Welcome" 1967 .... $50.00-$100.00
Capitol 5826, "Heroes and Villains" (printed in America, exported), 1967 .... $200.00-$400.00

THE BEATLES:
Capitol 5112, "I Want to Hold Your Hand"/"I Saw Her Standing There" (if die-cut opening, crops George Harrison's head in photo), 1964 .... $50.00-$100.00
(if straight-cut opening, show's all of George Harrison's head), 1964 .... $50.00-$100.00
(if giveaway from radio station WMCA, has picture of WMCA disc jockeys on reverse), 1964 .... $1,000.00-$2,000.00

CHUCK BERRY:
Chess 1898, "No Particular Place to Go"/"You Two" 1964 .... $25.00-$50.00
1943, "It Wasn't Me"/"Welcome Back Pretty Girl," 1965 .... $15.00-$30.00

DAVID BOWIE:
RCA APBO-0001, "Time"/"The Prettiest Star," 1973 .... $400.00-$800.00

JAMES BROWN:
King 5842, "Oh Baby Don't You Weep" (Pt. 1)/(Pt. 2), 1964 .... $12.50-$25.00
Scotti Bros. ZS4-05682, "Living in America" (Scotti Bros. ZS4-05682), 1985 .... $1.50-$3.00
(if marked "Demonstration Only—Not For Sale"), 1985 .... $2.00-$4.00

THE BYRDS:
Columbia 43271, "Mr. Tambourine Man"/"I Knew I'd Want You" (picture sleeve that promotes the Byrds' appearance on the TV show Hullabaloo), 1965 .... $150.00-$300.00
4-43578, "Eight Miles High"/"Why?" (Columbia 4-43578), 1966 .... $30.00-$60.00

FREDDY "BOOM BOOM" CANNON:
Swan 4043, "Way Down Yonder in New Orleans"/"Fractured," 1959 .... $15.00-$30.00

THE CARPENTERS:
A&M 1217, "We've Only Just Begun"/"All of My Life," 1970 .... $3.00-$6.00
2344, "Touch Me When We're Dancing"/"Because We Are In Love (The Wedding Song)," 1981 .... $2.00-$4.00

CHUBBY CHECKER:
Parkway 811, "The Twist"/"Twistin' U.S.A.," 1961 .... $12.50-$25.00

THE CLASH:
Epic 14-03061, "Should I Stay Or Should I Go?"/"First Night Back In London" (Ronald Reagan on sleeve), 1982 .... $6.00-$12.00
34-03457, "Should I Stay Or Should I Go?"/"Cool Confusion" (entire band on sleeve), 1983 .... $2.50-$5.00

ALICE COOPER:
Warner Bros. 7596, "School's Out"/"Gutter Cat," 1972 .... $5.00-$10.00

DICK DALE AND THE DEL-TONES:
Capitol 4963, "King of the Surf Guitar"/"Havah Nagilah," 1963 $40.00-$80.00

BOBBY DARIN:
Atco 6147, "Mack the Knife"/"Was There A Call For Me," 1959 .... $20.00-$40.00
6211, "Ave Maria"/"O Come All Ye Faithful," 1961 .... $80.00-$160.00

DEEP PURPLE:
Tetragrammaton 1603, "Hush"/"One More Rainy Day," 1968 .... $15.00-$30.00
1508, "Kentucky Woman"/"Hard Road," 1968 .... $7.50-$15.00

DEF LEPPARD:
Mercury 870298-7, "Pour Some Sugar On Me"/"Ring of Fire" (one of seven picture sleeves from the "Hysteria" album, if two more singles were released, one could arrange all nine sleeves into a mosaic of the original album cover), 1988 .... $1.50-$3.00

DION:
Laurie 3110, "Runaround Sue"/"Runaway Girl," 1961 .... $20.00-$40.00
3115, "The Wanderer"/"The Majestic," 1961 .... $20.00-$40.00
3123, "Lovers Who Wander"/"(I Was) Born to Cry," 1962 .... $20.00-$40.00

THE DOORS:
Elektra 45611, "Break On Through (To The Other Side)"/"End of the Night," 1966 .... $60.00-$120.00
45663, "Tell All the People"/"Easy Ride," 1969 .... $12.50-$25.00

THE ELECTRIC LIGHT ORCHESTRA:
United Artists XS 573, "Can't Get It Out of My Head"/"Illusions in G Major," 1974 .... $3.00-$6.00
Jet XW 1099, "Turn to Stone"/"Mister Kingdom," 1977 .... $4.00-$8.00

THE EVERLY BROTHERS:
Cadence 1337, "Wake Up Little Susie"/"Maybe Tomorrow," 1957 .... $125.00-$250.00
Warner Bros. 5151, "Cathy's Clown"/"Always It's You," 1960 .... $10.00-$20.00

THE FOUR SEASONS:
Philips 40211, "Rag Doll"/"Silence is Golden" (yellow or green sleeve, value is equal), 1964 .... $15.00-$30.00
40370, "Opus 17 (Don't You Worry 'Bout Me)"/"Beggar's Paradise," 1966 .... $12.50-$25.00

CONNIE FRANCIS:
MGM 12899, "Everybody's Somebody's Fool"/"Jealous of You," 1960 .... $10.00-$20.00
12971, "Where the Boys Are"/"No One," 1961 .... $10.00-$20.00

THE GRATEFUL DEAD:
Warner Bros. 7186, "Dark Star"/"Born Cross-Eyed," 1968 .... $250.00-$500.00
Arista 0383, "Good Lovin'"/"Stagger Lee," 1978 .... $300.00-$600.00
9606, "Touch of Grey"/"My Brother Esau" (foldout sleeve), 1987. $2.50-$5.00

BILL HALEY AND THE COMETS:
Decca 30314, "(You Hit The Wrong Note) Billy Goat"/"Rockin' Rollin' Rover," 1957 .... $60.00-$120.00

THE HASSLES:
United Artists 50215, "You've Got Me Hummin'"/"I'm Thinkin'," 1967 .... $10.00-$20.00

THE JIMI HENDRIX EXPERIENCE:
Reprise 0572, "Hey Joe"/"51st Anniversary," 1967 .... $500.00-$1,000.00

THE HOLLIES:
Imperial 66231, "On A Carousel"/"All the World Is Love," 1967 $15.00-$30.00
Epic 10180, "Carrie-Anne"/"Signs That Will Never Change," 1967 .... $7.50-$15.00

MICHAEL JACKSON:
Motown 1202, "I Wanna Be Where You Are"/"We Got A Good Thing Going," 1972 .... $5.00-$10.00
Epic 34-04026, "Human Nature"/"Baby Be Mine," 1983 .... $2.50-$5.00
(with "Demonstration - Not for Sale" on sleeve), 1983 .... $5.00-$10.00

JEFFERSON AIRPLANE:
RCA 5156-7-R, "White Rabbit"/"Plastic Fantastic Lover" (released in conjunction with the film Platoon), 1987 .... $2.50-$5.00

JOAN JETT AND THE BLACKHEARTS:
Boardwalk NB7-11-135, "I Love Rock and Roll"/"You Don't Know What You've Got," 1982 .... $5.00-$10.00

ELTON JOHN:
MCA 40344, "Lucy in the Sky with Diamonds"/"One Day at a Time," 1974 .... $5.00-$10.00

TOM JONES:
Parrot 9801, "Thunderball"/"Key to My Heart" (with dead female and spear gun), 1965 .... $10.00-$20.00
(if no spear gun or dead female on cover), 1965 .... $6.00-$12.00
40058, "She's A Lady"/"My Way," 1971 .... $4.00-$8.00

CAROLE KING:
Ode 66015, "It's Too Late"/"I Feel the Earth Move," 1971 .... $2.50-$5.00
66047, "Jazzman"/"You Go Your Way, I'll Go Mine," 1974 .... $3.00-$6.00
(if above on Ode 66101), 1974 .... $2.50-$5.00

KISS:
Casablanca 858, "Flaming Youth"/"God of Thunder," 1976 .... $30.00-$60.00

THE KNACK:
Capitol 4731, "My Sharona"/"Let Me Out," 1979 .... $3.00-$6.00
4822, "Baby Talks Dirty"/"End of the Game," 1980 .... $5.00-$10.00

BRENDA LEE:
Decca 30967, "Sweet Nothin's"/"Weep No More My Baby," 1959 .... $60.00-$120.00
31093, "I'm Sorry"/"That's All You Gotta Do," 1960 .... $25.00-$50.00

JERRY LEE LEWIS:
Sun 281, "Great Balls of Fire"/"You Win Again," 1957 .... **$40.00-$80.00**
296, "High School Confidential"/"Fools Like Me," 1958 .... **$40.00-$80.00**

LITTLE RICHARD:
Specialty 611, "Keep A Knockin'"/ "Can't Believe You Wanna Leave," 1957 .... **$30.00-$60.00**
624, "Good Golly, Miss Molly"/"Hey-Hey-Hey-Hey!," 1958... **$25.00-$50.00**

THE LOVIN' SPOONFUL:
Kama Sutra 208, "Daydream"/"Night Owl Blues," 1966 .... **$7.50-$15.00**
209, "Did You Ever Have to Make Up Your Mind"/"Didn't Want to Have to Do It," 1966 .... **$5.00-$10.00**

MADONNA:
Sire 29534, "Borderline"/"Think of Me" (foldout poster sleeve), 1984 .... **$40.00-$80.00**

THE MAMAS AND THE PAPAS:
Dunhill 4018, "Go Where You Wanna Go"/"Somebody Groovy," 1966 .... **$200.00-$400.00**
4020, "California Dreamin"/"Somebody Groovy" (promotional only), 1966 .... **$150.00-$300.00**
4083, "Creeque Alley"/"Did You Ever Want to Cry" (promotional only), 1967 .... **$20.00-$40.00**

JOHNNY MATHIS:
Columbia 4-40983, "Chances Are"/"The Twelfth of Never," 1957 .... **$10.00-$20.00**
41483, "Misty"/"The Story of Our Love," 1959 .... **$7.50-$15.00**

THE MONKEES:
Colgems 66-1001, "Last Train to Clarksville"/"Take A Giant Step"
(if no mention of Monkees fan club), 1966 .... **$15.00-$30.00**
(if on picture sleeve, "Write the Monkees"), 1966 .... **$10.00-$20.00**
66-1002, "I'm A Believer"/"(I'm Not Your) Stepping Stone" 1966 .... **$15.00-$30.00**
66-1012, "Daydream Believer"/"Goin' Down" 1967 .... **$15.00-$30.00**
66-5000, "Tear Drop City"/"A Man Without A Dream" 1969.. **$12.50-$25.00**
Arista 9505, "That Was Then, This is Now"/"(Theme From) The Monkees"
(with "Monkees" picture sleeve), 1986 .... **$5.00-$10.00**
(with "Mickey Dolenz and Peter Tork [Of The Monkees]" picture sleeve), 1986 .... **$1.50-$3.00**

ALANIS MORISSETTE:
Lamor LMR-10-12, "Fate Stay With Me"/"Find the Right Man," 1987 .... **$125.00-$250.00**

MÖTLEY CRÜE:
Leathur 001, "Stick To Your Guns"/"Toast of the Town," 1981. **$75.00-$150.00**

RICKY NELSON:
Imperial 5741, "Travelin' Man"/"Hello Mary Lou," 1961 .... **$35.00-$70.00**
5935, "Old Enough to Love"/"If You Can't Rock Me," 1963 .... **$20.00-$40.00**
Decca 31533, "String Along"/"Gypsy Woman," 1963 .... **$15.00-$30.00**

ROY ORBISON:
Monument 447, "Crying"/"Candy Man," 1961 .... **$20.00-$40.00**
806, "In Dreams"/"Shahdaroba," 1963 .... **$20.00-$40.00**
Virgin 99245, "You Got It," 1989 .... **$1.50-$3.00**

PEARL JAM:
Epic 78797, "Given to Fly"/"Leatherman," 1997 .... **$1.00-$2.00**
ES7 59252, "Bu$hleager"/"Down," 2002 .... **$2.50-$5.00**

CARL PERKINS:
Columbia 4-42514, "Hambone"/"Sister Twister," 1962 .... **$200.00-$400.00**

PINK FLOYD:
Tower 333, "Arnold Layne"/"Candy and a Currant Bun" (promotional only), 1967 .... **$350.00-$700.00**
356, "See Emily Play"/"Scarecrow" (promotional only), 1967 **$350.00-$700.00**
(if above, photo on sleeve), 1967 .... **$400.00-$800.00**
Columbia 11187, "Another Brick in the Wall (Pt. 2)"/"One of My Turns" 1980 **$4.00-$8.00**

ELVIS PRESLEY:
RCA Victor 47-6604, "Don't Be Cruel"/"Hound Dog"
(if "Hound Dog!" is listed above "Don't Be Cruel"), 1956 .... **$60.00-$120.00**
(if "Don't Be Cruel" is listed above "Hound Dog!"), 1956.... **$100.00-$$200.00**

PRINCE AND THE REVOLUTION:
Warner Bros. 29216, "Let's Go Crazy"/Prince with Sheila E., "Erotic City" 1984 .... **$4.00-$8.00**

QUEEN:
Elektra 45441, "We Will Rock You"/"We Are The Champions" 1977 .... **$5.00-$10.00**

47452, "Body Language"
(if first pressing, with a naked couple on cover), 1982 .... **$7.50-$15.00**
(if second pressing, white cover, B-side "Life is Real" listed), 1982 .... **$5.00-$10.00**

THE RAMONES:
Sire 734, "I Wanna Be Your Boyfriend"/"California Sun"/"I Don't Wanna Walk Around With You (Live)," 1976 .... **$7.00-$14.00**
1051, "Rock 'n Roll High School"/"Do You Wanna Dance," 1979 **$4.00-$8.00**

PAUL REVERE AND THE RAIDERS:
Columbia 44094, "Him or Me—What's It Gonna Be?"/"Legend of Paul Revere," 1967 .... **$5.00-$10.00**

THE RIGHTEOUS BROTHERS:
Philles 127, "Just Once in My Life"/"The Blues," 1965 .... **$15.00-$30.00**
Verve 10383, "(You're My) Soul and Inspiration"/"B Side Blues," 1966 .... **$15.00-$30.00**

THE RONETTES:
Philles 123, "Walkin' in the Rain"/"How Does It Feel," 1964 .... **$75.00-$150.00**
126, "Born To Be Together"/"Blues for Baby," 1965 .... **$75.00-$150.00**

RUSH:
Mercury 78019, "Tom Sawyer"/"Witch Hunt," 1981 .... **$12.50-$25.00**
76179, "New World Man"/"Vital Signs," 1982 .... **$7.50-$15.00**

SEALS AND CROFTS:
Warner Bros. 8190, "Get Closer"/"Don't Fall," 1976 .... **$10.00-$20.00**

NEIL SEDAKA:
RCA Victor 47-8046, "Breaking Up Is Hard To Do (As Long As I Live)," 1962 .... **$12.50-$25.00**

SIMON AND GARFUNKEL:
Columbia 4-44046, "At The Zoo," 1967 .... **$20.00-$40.00**
3-10230, "My Little Town"/Art Garfunkel, "Rag Doll"/Paul Simon, "You're Kind," 1975 .... **$2.50-$5.00**

SLY AND THE FAMILY STONE:
Epic 10407, "Everyday People"/"Sing a Simple Song," 1968 .... **$6.00-$12.00**
10450, "Stand"/"I Want to Take You Higher," 1969 .... **$6.00-$12.00**

THE SMASHING PUMPKINS:
Limited Potential LIMP 006, "I Am One"/"Not Worth Asking," 1990 .... **$60.00-$120.00**
Sub Pop 90, "Tristessa"/"La Dolly Vita," 1991 .... **$12.50-$25.00**

THE SMITHEREENS:
Enigma 75052, "Behind the Wall of Sleep"/"Blood and Roses," 1986 .... **$2.50-$5.00**

BRUCE SPRINGSTEEN:
Columbia 4-45805, "Blinded By The Light"/"The Angel," 1973 .... **$200.00-$400.00**

STYX:
A&M 1977, "Come Sail Away"/"Put Me On," 1977 .... **$3.00-$6.00**
2525, "Mr. Roboto"/"Snowblind," 1983 .... **$1.50-$3.00**

TALKING HEADS:
Sire 737, "Love Goes to a Building on Fire"/"New Feeling," 1977 .. **$4.00-$8.00**
1013, "Psycho Killer"/"Psycho Killer" (Acoustic), 1978 .... **$4.00-$8.00**
29565, "Burning Down the House"/"Get Wild—Wild Gravity," 1983 .... **$1.50-$3.00**

.38 SPECIAL:
A&M 2412, "Caught Up In You"/"Firestarter," 1982 .... **$2.00-$4.00**

THREE DOG NIGHT:
ABC Dunhill 4239, "Mama Told Me (Not To Come)"/"Rock and Roll Widow," 1970 .... **$6.00-$12.00**

THE TURTLES:
White Whale 244, "Happy Together"/"Like The Seasons," 1967 .... **$10.00-$20.00**
249, "She'd Rather Be With Me"/"The Walking Song," 1967 .... **$12.50-$25.00**

U2:
Island 49716, "I Will Follow"/"Out of Control (Live),," 1980..... **$12.50-$25.00**
(if promotional picture sleeve with tour dates), 1980 .... **$30.00-$60.00**

WHAM!
Columbia 38-04552, "Wake Me Up Before You Go-Go," 1984...... **$4.00-$8.00**

WHITESNAKE:
Geffen 28339-7, "Here I Go Again," 1984 .... **$2.00-$4.00**

THE VELVET UNDERGROUND:
Verve 10427, "All Tomorrow's Parties"/"I'll Be Your Mirror," 1966 .... **$4,000.00-$8,000.00**

Section 2

In The Mood—Popular Genres

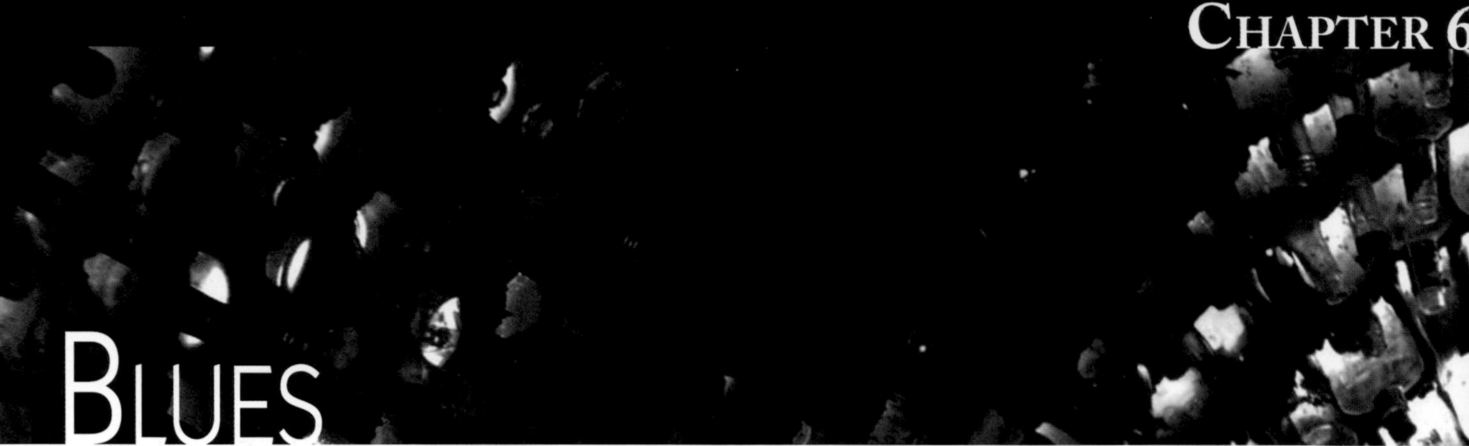

CHAPTER 6

BLUES

History

The sound of blues music can trace its lineage back over 150 years, from the songs of the slaves and the sharecroppers, to the road houses on the Mississippi delta and the clubs in the heart of Chicago. The blues not only was the forefather of rock and roll, its music has inspired the titles of rock groups and magazines. Over the years, rock's biggest stars have brought blues music back to public consciousness.

Although one might think of the blues as songs involving "my woman she done left me, all I've got are the strings on my guitar," the music of the blues is actually a passionate statement by the artist about his life, about the world in general, as told through his guitar, a harmonica, a piano, some drums, a bass—and his voice of a thousand emotions.

Describing the blues, however, is similar to asking someone to describe sports. There are different types of blues, depending on the region where the artist recorded, the instruments used, the era the recording was made, and whether the instruments used were electric or acoustic.

Some of the different genres of blues include the uptempo jump blues, featuring Louis Jordan and Wynonie Harris; piano blues, featuring the work of Professor Longhair and Otis Spann; country blues, such as Leadbelly and Mississippi John Hurt; and regional styles from places like Chicago (Big Bill Broonzy, Tampa Red and Howlin' Wolf), Texas (Lightnin' Hopkins and Blind Lemon Jefferson), and Memphis (B.B. King and Gus Cannon).

When looking for the most collectible blues artists of the pre-World War II era, three names often pop up—Robert Johnson, Blind Lemon Jefferson, and Charley Patton. While rumors of Johnson's guitar prowess have been embellished to the point where he traded his soul to Satan in exchange

Photo credit: Courtesy of the Tom Kelly Archives, St. Louis, Mo.

Although blues was a male-dominated genre, there were successful female singers. The "Mother of the Blues," Ma Rainey, recorded over 100 sides for Paramount, some of which are printed with her photograph on the label.

***$100**, NM condition*

Photo credit: Courtesy of the Tom Kelly Archives, St. Louis, Mo.

Robert Johnson's first recording for Vocalion, "Terraplane Blues," is among the easiest of his thirteen 78s to acquire—a slight consolation when one considers that near-mint copies of his records have sold for thousands of dollars.

***$6,000**, NM condition*

for his musical talent, the truth is that Johnson had played juke joints and clubs throughout Mississippi, Arkansas, and Texas for years, having learned his craft from a previously unrecorded country blues guitarist, Ike Zimmerman. Johnson's first recording for Vocalion, "Terraplane Blues," sold several thousand copies, a large amount for what was previously designated a "race" record. Johnson recorded eleven more records with Vocalion before dying in 1938 (according to legend, the hell hounds of Satan finally caught up to him; in reality, he died from complications after drinking contaminated whiskey, poisoned by a jealous ex-lover). Despite Johnson's brief recording career, his songs and musical style have been copied and studied by the Rolling Stones, Eric Clapton, and Steve Miller, just to name a few popular artists.

Texas-born country blues legend Blind Lemon Jefferson recorded over 100 sides in 24 months for the Paramount race label. Influenced by the guitar-plucking of Mexican flamenco guitarists, Jefferson incorporated a fast finger-plucking style into his blues recordings. While his early recordings were gospel songs under the pseudonym of "Elder J.C. Brown" or "Deacon L.J. Bates," Blind Lemon Jefferson eventually signed with Paramount and became one of the label's top stars. His legendary blues recordings included "See That My Grave is Kept Clean," "That Black Snake Moan," and "Match Box Blues," among others. Bob Dylan claimed him as an influence, and the group Jefferson Airplane allegedly was named after the legendary bluesman.

The recordings of Charley Patton, a Delta Blues guitarist and heavy influence on everybody from Son House and Robert Johnson to Jimi Hendrix, are extremely collectible—and finding near-mint copies of these pressings is almost impossible. The original masters disappeared when the Paramount record company went into bankruptcy; the surviving 78s have been heavily played and re-played, with needles that were never changed as frequently as one would have hoped, leaving hisses and scratches in most of those old pressings.

The post-World War II blues explosion occurred when southern black musicians, many of whose families toiled as sharecroppers, migrated north in search of jobs and new opportunities. Many of these musicians performed in Chicago clubs with such legends as Big Bill Broonzy, Washboard Sam, Earl Hooker, and the first Sonny Boy Williamson. And the best record label for Chicago blues at the time was the Chess family of labels—Chess, Checker, Aristocrat, Cadet, and Argo, all of which chronicled the birth of Chicago blues, rock and roll, and jazz.

In the late 1940s, brothers Leonard and Phil Chess owned a series of nightclubs and bar rooms, and many of these clubs played live blues music from artists who left sharecropping towns in Mississippi, Tennessee, and Alabama, moving north to Chicago for a new life. Since the Chess brothers felt that none of these musicians were being properly recorded, they formed their own label, Aristocrat, in 1947, and signed many of these artists to record for them.

Among the first—and most successful—of these blues artists on Aristocrat was McKinley Morganfield, known to millions of blues aficionados as Muddy Waters. Waters' classics, including "I'm Your Hoochie Coochie Man," "Rollin' Stone," "I Just Wanna Make Love To You," and "I

Photo credit: Courtesy of the Tom Kelly Archives, St. Louis, Mo.

Blind Lemon Jefferson's records are extremely collectible, and can range from $100 for a beat-up copy to over $500 for a near-mint pressing. This song, "See That My Grave Is Kept Clean," is one of many songs for which he is remembered.
***$600**, VG+ condition*

Photo credit: From the collection of John Tefteller.

How important was Muddy Waters' hit "Rollin' Stone?" It inspired Bob Dylan to write "Like a Rolling Stone," it inspired Mick Jagger and Keith Richards to name their group the Rolling Stones; it inspired one of the Temptations' biggest hits, "Papa was a Rolling Stone," and it inspired a magazine to which Dr. Hook and the Medicine Show aspired to appear on its cover.
***$400**, NM condition*

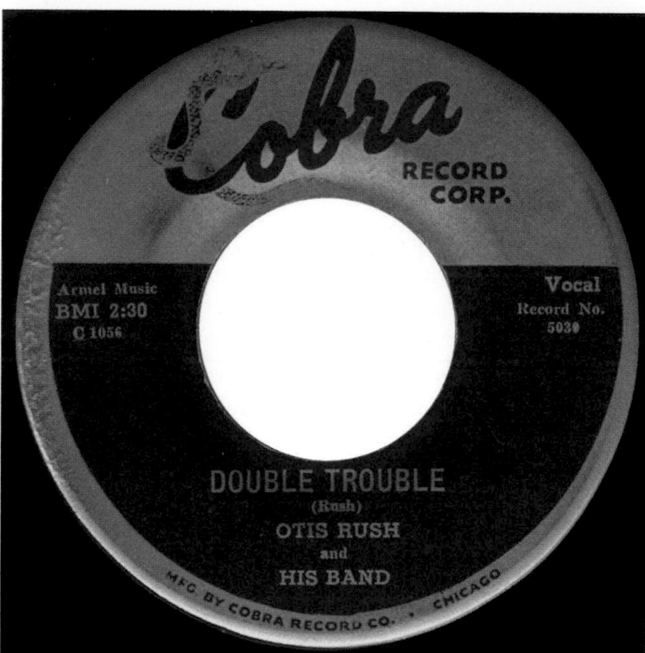

Otis Rush recorded several collectible blues sides for the Cobra label between 1956 and 1958. This Willie Dixon-penned song, "Double Trouble," inspired Stevie Ray Vaughan to rename his band Double Trouble, in honor of Rush's classic hit.
***$65**, NM condition*

Can't Be Satisfied," are blues masterpieces that influenced generations of musicians. "Rollin' Stone," for example, inspired Bob Dylan to write "Like A Rolling Stone." It also inspired Mick Jagger and Keith Richards to name their band the Rolling Stones. It further inspired the Temptations' urban classic "Papa Was a Rolling Stone," and a magazine for which Dr. Hook and the Medicine Show aspired to appear on its cover.

In 1951, Aristocrat was renamed Chess Records, and Muddy Waters' labelmates now included Howlin' Wolf, Little Walter, Sonny Boy Williamson, John Lee Hooker, and Al Hibbler. Chess also released a jump boogie track, "Rocket 88" by Jackie Brenston and his Delta Cats (Chess 1458), which some musicologists feel is the first true "rock and roll" record (actually, it was Ike Turner and his Kings of Rhythm on the track; the credited Brenston was one of Turner's saxophone players).

By the 1960s, British bands like the Rolling Stones, the Yardbirds, John Mayall's Bluesbreakers, Cream, and Led Zeppelin all embraced and incorporated the blues music of Muddy Waters, Willie Dixon, Howlin' Wolf, and Robert Johnson into classic rock songs. Many of these same British bands and artists invited surviving blues musicians to tour with them, introducing these legends to a new appreciative audience.

What To Look For

If you want to start your own blues music collection, your first decision should be whether you want to base your collection on vinyl releases or CDs. While compact disc reissues are less expensive than original vinyl releases, and through a respectable blues collection can exist with reissue CDs, many blues collectors search out the old vinyl recordings—the 78s, the 10-inch LPs, the albums pressed by small independent labels.

But if you plan to start your collection in vinyl, make sure you have lots of money and are not afraid to spend it. In many cases, there may be fewer copies of a specific blues 78 than there are fingers on your hands. 78s of the earliest blues legends—Charlie Patton, Blind Lemon Jefferson, and Robert Johnson—can command high prices, even if the vinyl is in less than fair condition. Even in the 1950s, original 45s and 78s of some blues artists, including Muddy Waters, Howlin' Wolf, John Lee Hooker, Lightnin' Hopkins, etc. are increasingly difficult to find, especially in good condition.

When the Chess studios in Chicago finally shut down in 1975, the new owners of the building threw out all the 78s and 45s that were left in the Chess storerooms. This means that thousands of Muddy Waters and Howlin' Wolf records are now in a Chicago landfill. While this may make a blues fan sing the blues, it also increases the rarity of the 45s and LPs that made it to the record stores and to private collections.

One logical fallacy among blues collectors is to equate a blues record's collectible price with its musical value. The rarity of some blues 78s, including some classic and seminal recordings, does warrant a higher value than today's LPs, but this does not mean the musical performance on these early discs are greater or lesser than today's current musical output.

Photo credit: Courtesy Last Vestige Music Store, Albany, N.Y.

This Lightnin' Hopkins album has been reissued several times; the inside label for this album can determine its value. A grey label is worth $50 in near-mint condition. If the label is black and has a silver "CROWN" on it, you have a $100 near-mint record. A multicolored logo, on the other hand, can only bring you $25 in near-mint condition.
***$50**, VG+ condition*

Books

Collis, John, *The Story of Chess Records*, Bloomsbury Publishing, New York, N.Y., 1998.

Brooks, Lonnie; Koda, Cub; Brooks, Wayne Baker, *Blues for Dummies*, IDG Books Worldwide, Foster City, CA, 1998.

Hansen, Barry, *Rhino's Cruise Through the Blues*, Miller Freeman Books, Los Angeles, CA, 2000.

Leigh, Keri, *Stevie Ray: Soul To Soul*, Taylor Publishing Company, Dallas, TX, 1993.

Patoski, Joe Nick and Crawford, Bill, *Stevie Ray Vaughan: Caught in the Crossfire*, Little, Brown, Boston, MA, 1993.

Web Pages

An online discography of various Paramount, OKeh, Vocalion and other blues 78s: *http://settlet.fateback.com*

The Blues Foundation: http://www.blues.org

A history of Muddy Waters: http://www.muddywaters.com

Both Sides Now: The Chess Story: http://www.bsnpubs.com/chesscheck.html

The Blue Flame Café, an interactive biographical encyclopedia of the great blues singers and singers of the blues: http://www.blueflamecafe.com

Usenet newsgroups: alt.music.blues, alt.fan.stevie-ray-vaughan, alt.fan.robert-cray

Museums

Blues & Legends Hall Of Fame Museum, 1021 Casino Center Drive, Robinsonville, MS, 38664, (901) 521-0086: http://www.bluesmuseum.org

Delta Blues Museum, PO Box 459, Clarksdale, MS, 38614, (662) 627-6820: http://www.deltabluesmuseum.org

The Blues Foundation, 49 Union Avenue, Memphis, TN, 38103.

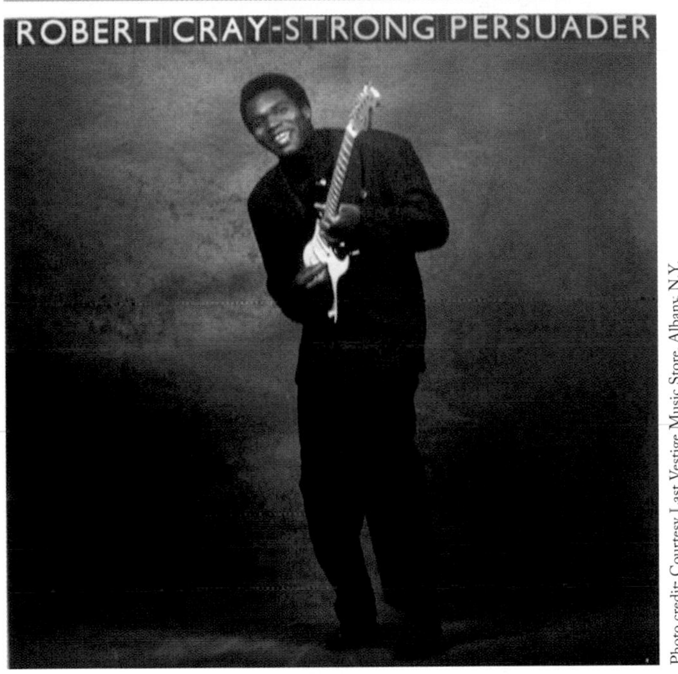

Photo credit: Courtesy Last Vestige Music Store, Albany, N.Y.

Robert Cray's first Top 40 hit, "Smoking Gun," appears on the Strong Persuader *album. Before this album, Cray spent 14 years on the road, backing up Albert Collins. You might have spotted him in the motion picture National Lampoon's Animal House; he's the bass player for Otis Day and the Knights.*
***$12**, NM condition*

This brown wax Paramount pressing of Alberta Hunter's "Chirpin' the Blues" features jazz legend Fletcher Henderson on the keyboards, making this record collectible for jazz lovers, blues lovers, and colored-vinyl collectors.
***$40**, NM condition*

ARTIST VG+ to NM

TEXAS ALEXANDER:

78s

OKeh 8673, "Tell Me Woman Blues"/"The Risin' Sun," 1929 .... **$80.00-$160.00**

BARBECUE BOB:

78s

Columbia 14331-D, "Chocolate to the Bone"/"Way Cross Georgia Blues," 1928 .... **$60.00-$120.00**

Columbia 14372-D, "Blind Pig Blues"/"Hurry and Bring It Back Home," 1928 .... **$40.00-$80.00**

THE BEALE STREET SHIEKS, FRANK STOKES & DAN SANE:

78s

Paramount 12518, "It's A Good Thing"/"You Shall," 1927 ...... **$125.00-$250.00**

12531, "Half Cup of Tea"/"Sweet to Mama," 1927 .... **$125.00-$250.00**

12552, "Mr. Crump Don't Like It"/"Blues in D," 1927 .... **$150.00-$300.00**

Although most of blues guitarist Stevie Ray Vaughan's albums are available at reasonable prices, this picture disc for his LP "Couldn't Stand the Weather" is an exception, with near-mint copies selling for as much as $150.
***$100**, VG+ NM condition*

Photo credit: Courtesy Last Vestige Music Store, Albany, NY

Koko Taylor's blues/R&B hit "Wang Dang Doodle" was written by Willie Dixon, who also sings background vocals on the song.
***$10**, NM condition*

TOMMIE BRADLEY:

78s

Champion 50050, "Adam and Eve"/"Pack Up Her Trunk Blues," 1935 .... **$150.00-$300.00**

JACKIE BRENSTON AND HIS DELTA CATS:

78s

Chess 1458, "Rocket 88"/"Come Back Where You Belong," 1949 .... **$150.00-$300.00**

1472, "Juiced"/"Independent Woman," 1951 .... **$100.00-$200.00**

45s

Chess 1458, "Rocket 88"/"Come Back Where You Belong," 1951 .... **$7,500.00-$10,000.00**

1469, "In My Real Gone Rocket"/"Tuckered Out," 1951 .... **$750.00-$1,000.00**

1472, "Juiced"/"Independent Woman," 1951 .... **$750.00-$1,000.00**

Federal 12283, "What Can It Be"/"Gonna Wait For My Chance," 1956 .... **$25.00-$50.00**

BIG BILL BROONZY:

45s

Mercury 8160, "You've Been Mistreating Me"/"I Stay Blue All the Time," 1951 .... **$15.00-$30.00**

Chess 1546, "Little City Woman"/"Lonesome," 1953 .... **$200.00-$400.00**

10-inch LPs

Dial LP-306, Blues Concert, 1952 .... **$250.00-$500.00**

Emarcy MG-26034, Folk Blues, 1954 .... **$100.00-$200.00**

ALBERT COLLINS:

45s

Great Scott 007, "Albert's Alley"/"Defrost," 1963 .... **$15.00-$30.00**

(if on Hallway 1913), 1963 .... **$6.00-$12.00**

LPs

TCF Hall 802, The Cool Sound of Albert Collins, 1965 .... **$150.00-$300.00**

Alligator AL-4743, Showdown! (also feat. Robert Cray and Johnny Copeland), 1985 .... **$5.00-$10.00**

IDA COX:

78s

Paramount 12053, "Any Woman's Blues"/"Blue Monday Blues," 1923 .... **$60.00-$120.00**

12085,"Mama Doo Shea Blues"/"Worried Mama Blues," 1924 .... **$70.00-$140.00**

WYNONIE HARRIS:

78s

Apollo 360, "Young Man's Blues"/"Straighten Him Out," 1945 .. **$15.00-$30.00**

JOHN LEE HOOKER (sometimes recorded under pseudonyms):

78s

Modern 20-627, "Sally May"/"Boogie Chillen," 1948 .... **$150.00-$300.00**

Chance 1108, John Lee Booker, "Miss Lorraine"/"Talkin' Boogie," 1951 .... **$250.00-$500.00**

1110, John Lee Booker, "Graveyard Blues"/"I Love to Boogie," 1952 .... **$250.00-$500.00**

Chess 1462, John Lee Booker, "Mad Man Blues"/"Boogie Now," 1951 .... **$100.00-$200.00**

1467, "Ramblin' By Myself"/"Leave My Wife Alone," 1951 ... **$75.00-$150.00**

LIGHTNIN' HOPKINS:

45s

Jax 315, "No Good Woman"/"Been a Bad Man" (red vinyl), 1953 .... **$150.00-$300.00**

318, "Automobile"/"Organ Blues" (red vinyl), 1953 .... **$150.00-$300.00**

321, "Contrary Mary"/"I'm Begging You" (red vinyl), 1953 ... **$150.00-$300.00**

THE HOKUM BOYS:

78s

Paramount 12777, "Caught Him Doing It"/"Better Cut That Out," 1929 .... **$70.00-$140.00**

12778, "Selling That Stuff"/Miller and Rodgers, "I Would if I Could," 1929 .... **$150.00-$300.00**

Vocalion 03156, "Caught Us Doing It"/"I Ain't Going That Way," 1936 .... **$40.00-$80.00**

HOWLIN' WOLF:

45s

Chess 1528, "Oh! Red"/"My Last Affair," 1952 .... **$350.00-$700.00**

1618, "Smoke Stack Lightning"/"You Can't Be Beat," 1956 ...... **$20.00-$40.00**

LPs

Chess LP-1434, Moanin' In The Moonlight, 1958 .... **$300.00-$600.00**

CH-60016, Howlin' Wolf a/k/a Chester Burnett (2 LPs), 1972 .... **$12.50-$25.00**

PAPA CHARLIE JACKSON:

78s

Paramount 12305, "Mama, Don't You Think I Know?"/"Hot Papa Blues," 1925 .... **$75.00-$150.00**

12320, "All I Want is a Spoonful"/"Maxwell Street Blues," 1925 .... **$50.00-$100.00**

BLIND LEMON JEFFERSON:

78s

OKeh 8455, "Black Snake Moan"/"Matchbox Blues," 1927 .... **$500.00-$1,000.00**

Paramount 12347, "Booster Blues"/"Dry Southern Blues," 1926 .... $500.00-$1,000.00
12493, "Weary Dog Blues"/"Hot Dogs," 1926 .... $500.00-$1,000.00
12650, "Piney Woods Mama Blues"/"Low Down Mojo Blues" (label has a portrait of Jefferson, record is designated as "Blind Lemon Jefferson Birthday Record"), 1928 .... $750.00-$1,500.00

LONNIE JOHNSON:

78s

OKeh 8340, "Baby You Don't Know My Mind"/"A Good Happy Home," 1926 .... $20.00-$40.00
8358, "Woman Changed My Life"/"Good Old Wagon," 1926 .... $30.00-$60.00
8537, "Kansas City Blues" (Pt. 1)/(Pt. 2), 1927 .... $20.00-$40.00

ROBERT JOHNSON:

78s

Vocalion 03416, "Kind Hearted Woman"/"Terraplane Blues," 1936 .... $3,000.00-$6,000.00
03445, "32-20 Blues"/"Last Fair Deal Gone Down," 1936 .... $4,000.00-$8,000.00
03475, "(I Believe I'll) Dust My Broom"/"Dead Shrimp Blues," 1936 .... $4,000.00-$8,000.00

Mono LPs

Columbia CL 1654, King of the Delta Blues Singers
(with red and black label, six eye logos), 1961 .... $250.00-$500.00
(with "Guaranteed High Fidelity" label), 1963 .... $25.00-$50.00
(with "360 Sound Mono" label), 1965 .... $12.50-$25.00
(with orange label, "Columbia" circling the edge), 1970 .... $6.00-$12.00
(with red label, "Columbia" in white on top, "Sony Music" under side numbers), 1998 .... $5.00-$10.00
(sticker on shrinkwrap says record was pressed on 180-gram vinyl), 2001 .... $7.50-$15.00

ALBERT KING:

45s

Parrot 798, "Bad Luck Blues"/"Be On Your Merry Way"
Bobbin 114, "Why Are You So Mean to Me"/"Ooh-Ee Baby," 1959 .... $12.50-$25.00

LPs

King 852, Big Blues, 1963 .... $250.00-$500.00
Atlantic SD 8213, King of the Blues Guitar, 1969 .... $12.50-$25.00
Stax ST-723, Born Under a Bad Sign, 1967 .... $40.00-$80.00
(if on Stax STS-723, stereo), 1967 .... $60.00-$120.00

B.B. KING:

78s

Bullet 309, "Miss Martha King"/"When Your Baby Packs Up and Goes," 1949 .... $500.00-$1,000.00
315, "Got the Blues"/"Take a Swing with Me," 1949 .... $350.00-$700.00
RPM 314, "Mistreated Woman"/"B.B. Boogie," 1950 .... $75.00-$150.00
339, "3 O'Clock Blues"/"That Ain't the Way to Do It," 1951 .. $60.00-$120.00

45s

RPM 339, "3 O'Clock Blues"/"That Ain't the Way To Do It," 1951 .... $450.00-$900.00
Bluesway 61032, "The Thrill Is Gone"/"You're Mean," 1969 .... $6.00-$12.00
(with picture sleeve, add), 1969 .... $10.00-$20.00

LPs

Crown CLP-8115, B.B. King Wails
(if on black label, mono, "Crown" is silver), 1959 .... $50.00-$100.00
(if on grey label, mono, "Crown" is black), 1963 .... $10.00-$20.00
(if on black label, mono, "Crown" is multicolored), 1960s .... $6.00-$12.00
(if on CST-147, rechanneled stereo, black vinyl), 1960 .... $6.00-$12.00
(if on CST-147, rechanneled stereo, red vinyl), 1960 .... $50.00-$100.00

FREDDIE KING:

45s

El-Bee 157, "Country Boy"/"That's What You Think," 1956 ... $200.00-$400.00
Federal 12384, "Have You Ever Loved a Woman"/"You've Got to Love Her with a Feeling," 1960 .... $20.00-$40.00
12450, "Takin' Care of Business"/"The Stumble," 1962 .... $10.00-$20.00

Mono LPs

King 762, Freddie King Sings the Blues, 1961 .... $125.00-$250.00
856, Freddie King Goes Surfin', 1963 .... $40.00-$80.00

LITTLE WALTER:

78s

Checker 758, "Juke"/"Can't Hold On Much Longer," 1952 .... $60.00-$120.00
767, "Don't Have to Hunt No More"/"Tonight with a Fool," 1953 .... $25.00-$50.00
786, "Lights Out"/"You're So Fine," 1953 .... $20.00-$40.00

MUDDY WATERS:

78s

Aristocrat 1305, "I Feel Like Going Home"/"I Can't Be Satisfied," 1948 .... $150.00-$300.00
Chess 1426, "Rollin' Stone"/"Walkin' Blues," 1950 .... $200.00-$400.00
1441, "Louisiana Blues"/"Evan's Shuffle," 1950 .... $75.00-$150.00

45s

Chess 1560, "I'm Your Hoochie Coochie Man"/"She's So Pretty" (some copies may say "You're So Pretty" or spell "Coochie" "Cooche" or "Kooche," value is equal), 1954 .... $50.00-$100.00
1602, "Manish Boy"/"Young Fashion Ways," 1955 .... $35.00-$70.00
1827, "Muddy Waters Twist"/"You Shook Me," 1962 .... $12.50-$25.00

LPs

Chess LP-1427, The Best of Muddy Waters
(if DJ white label promo), 1957 .... $1,000.00-$1,500.00
(if stock copy), 1957 .... $250.00-$500.00
(if reissue, catalog number CH-9255), 1987 .... $5.00-$10.00
LP-1444, Muddy Waters Sings Big Bill

MA RAINEY:

78s

Paramount 12083, "Moonshine Blues"/"Southern Blues," 1924 .. $25.00-$50.00
12098, "Dream Blues"/"Lost Wandering Blues," 1924 .... $50.00-$100.00
12200, "Ma Rainey's Mystery Record"/"Honey Where You Been So Long?," 1924 .... $20.00-$40.00
12508, "Dead Drunk Blues"/"Misery Blues," 1927 .... $50.00-$100.00

NOBLE SISSLE AND EUBIE BLAKE:

Edison Diamond Discs

51572, "Broken Busted Blues" / "You Ought to Know," 1925 ..... $20.00-$40.00

BESSIE SMITH:

78s

Columbia 13007-D, "Far Away Blues"/"I'm Going Back to My Used To Be," 1924 .... $60.00-$120.00
14056-D, "Reckless Blues"/"Sobbin' Hearted Blues," 1925 ...... $80.00-$160.00

STEVIE RAY VAUGHAN AND DOUBLE TROUBLE:

45s

Epic 04031, "Pride and Joy"/"Rude Mood," 1983 .... $2.50-$5.00

LPs

Epic BFE 38734, Texas Flood, 1983 .... $5.00-$10.00
FE 39304, Couldn't Stand the Weather, 1984 .... $5.00-$10.00
(if on Epic 838 39609, picture disc), 1984 .... $75.00-$150.00

Noble Sissle and Eubie Blake recorded this early piano blues record for Edison; Eubie Blake's life and career later became the subject of Eubie!*, a long running Broadway musical.*

$40, *NM condition*

Chapter 7

The British Invasion

History

Before 1964, very few British bands ever achieved North American success, and even those who did could only muster one top 40 hit. Lonnie Donegan, for example, may have inspired a generation of British "skiffle" bands, but his American chart career was limited to a cover of a blues song ("Rock Island Line") and a novelty track ("Does Your Chewing Gum Lose Its Flavour On the Bed Post Overnight"). Even Great Britain's most popular singer, Cliff Richard, couldn't crack the American-dominated pop scene.

After 1964, with the success of the Beatles and the Rolling Stones, suddenly the pop charts were flooded with British pop groups, self-contained rock bands and sultry female vocalists. It was as if somebody pulled most of the American pop hits off the radio, and replaced them with songs whose lead vocalist had a British accent.

Photo credit: From the collection of Boo's Blast from the Past.

Fans of the Dave Clark Five could only buy their American releases in mono or in poorly rechanneled stereo. Pressings with true stereo mixes didn't arrive in America until 1971.

***$20**, VG+ condition*

British pop and rock bands in the 1960s drew their influence by the American music they heard, whether it was the blues of Muddy Waters and Howlin' Wolf; or the Motown soul of the Marvelettes and the Temptations; or the rockabilly recordings from Charlie Feathers and Carl Perkins. American artists who toured England, such as Roy Orbison, Del Shannon, Buddy Holly, and Little Richard, were treated as incoming royalty. So when these British groups finally broke through and achieved their own success in North America, they were actually bringing the American music they heard back to the States.

Many of the British Invasion groups continued the Merseybeat sound of early Beatles records; it can be heard in the songs of the Dave Clark Five, of Gerry and the Pacemakers, and of Billy J. Kramer and the Dakotas. Others followed their own pop vein, including music-hall pop like Freddie and the Dreamers, Herman's Hermits, and Wayne Fontana and the Mindbenders, while rockers like the Kinks and the Who combined R&B and soul with two-chord fuzz guitar riffs. The "British Invasion" also included chanteuses like Petula Clark and Shirley Bassey, whose musical careers predated the Beatles—yet were able to ride the British Invasion into the American pop radio charts.

The initial effect of the British Invasion was that most of the popular American artists at the time were squeezed off the charts. Teen idols such as Bobby Rydell, Frankie Avalon, Fabian, and Connie Francis were surpassed by new teen idols from across the Atlantic Ocean. Doo-wop and vocal harmony groups like the Drifters and the Shirelles were also surpassed by the Brits. And whether the artists were from Manchester, Leeds, Sheffield, Stratford-on-Avon, London, or Liverpool, as long as they came from England, the record-buying community was happy enough.

In a situation eerily parallel to the old "cover songs" of the 1950s, where a white artist's "cover version" of a black artist's song would dominate the pop charts, American artists in the 1960s saw their pop songs get squeezed off the radio—in favor of a British artist's cover version of the same song. Earl-Jean's "I'm Into Something Good," for

While Lulu's "To Sir With Love" is a very common record, this six-song "Operator Pak" mini-album, specifically pressed for jukeboxes, is difficult to acquire. Near-mint copies should still have the tear-off jukebox strips.
***$30**, NM condition*

example, was nabbed by Herman's Hermits as their first American pop hit, and Bessie Banks' version of "Go Now" was quickly eclipsed by the Moody Blues' version.

On several occasions, an American record label would sign a British artist or group, only to acquire only a portion of that artist's catalog of hits. The Beatles went through this period, as their earliest hits were scattered among a series of small independent American labels; and many British groups and singers found that when the labels they recorded for in the United Kingdom did not have an American sister label, the songs were licensed to whichever record company was interested. The bulk of Freddie and the Dreamers' recorded output was on Mercury, but their biggest hit "I'm Telling You Now" was released on Capitol's Tower subsidiary. The Troggs' #1 hit "Wild Thing" was pressed by both the Atco and Fontana labels at the same time. These early pressings are extremely collectible, as they give music fans an idea of how the artists sounded before their worldwide success.

While this "dual record company" situation continued throughout the 1960s in America, the lion's share of British Invasion artists whose records were released in Canada appeared on Capitol's 72000 catalog series. Imagine a record company roster that included Gerry and the Pacemakers, the Animals, Freddie and the Dreamers, the Dave Clark Five, Billy J. Kramer and the Dakotas, Manfred Mann, the Hollies, Chad and Jeremy—and the Beatles, to top it all off.

During the 1960s, American record companies still pressed two types of albums per release; a monaural copy and a stereo copy. Unfortunately, trying to find true stereo copies of 1960s hits can be a difficult endeavor. Many of the 1960s stereo albums are either rechanneled or fake stereo—low notes in one channel, high notes in the other; or music in one channel, vocalists in the other. True stereo copies of songs by the Dave Clark Five, for example, were not released in America until the early 1970s.

Photo credit: From the collection of Val Shively.

Peter and Gordon had plenty of songwriting help for their pop hits. "I Go To Pieces" was written by Del Shannon; and their first Top 40 hit, "A World Without Love," was penned by John Lennon and Paul McCartney.
***$12**, NM condition*

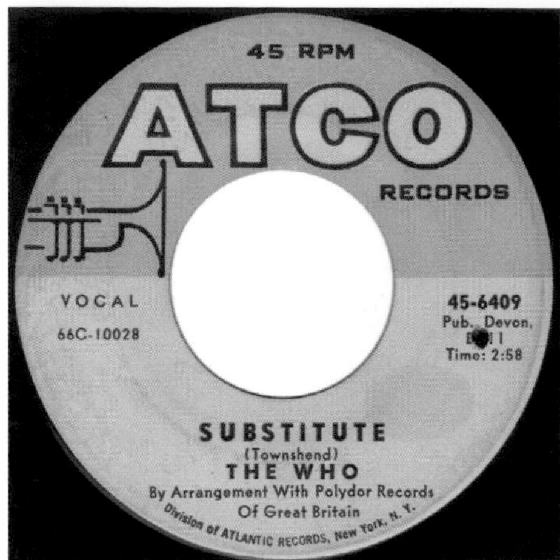

The Beatles were not the only British act to have their catalog spread over different record companies. Normally the Who's catalog would appear on Decca Records; this early song "Substitute" was originally pressed for Atco. Although the Dave Clark Five's biggest hits were released on Epic in America; their song "I Knew It All The Time" is only available on the Congress imprint. And the Kinks' earliest recording of "Long Tall Sally" appears only on the Cameo label; while the group's biggest hits appeared on Reprise.

(L to R) ***$25****, VG+ condition;* ***$10****, VG+ condition;* ***$600****, NM condition*

What To Look For

The most collectible releases by British Invasion artists are those records that actually predate the British Invasion—American releases from 1963 and earlier. Many of these records sold poorly upon their initial release, but when such artists became popular through the British Invasion, many fans avidly searched out those early American pressings.

A Capitol of Canada release by the Animals. This pressing contains the full-length version of "The House of the Rising Sun," whereas the American 45 has an edited version.

$20*, NM condition*

Some British acts did not have solid Top 40 hits until after the first British Invasion wave ended, in 1969. David Bowie's early work with the Lower Third is part of the selected price guide below; his later catalog can be found in other chapters.

A collectible subcategory of British Invasion records is produced by British producer Joe Meek. From his

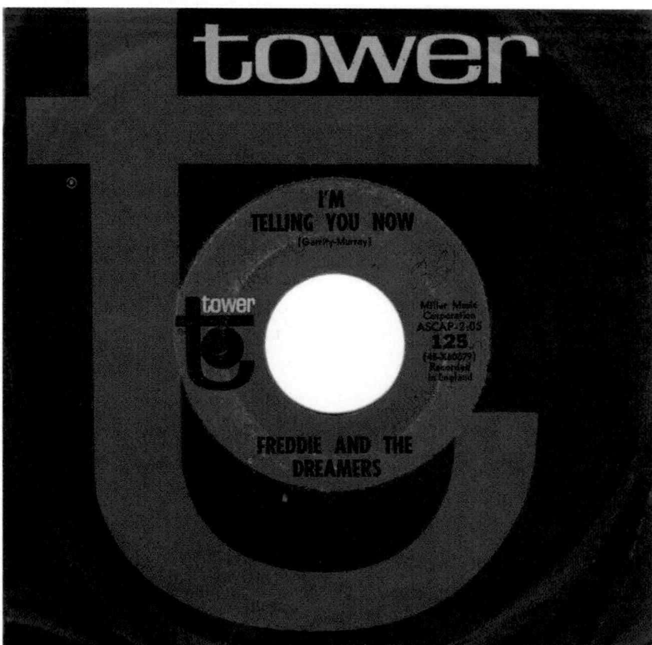

Half of Freddie and the Dreamers' American catalog was pressed for Mercury, but their biggest hit, "I'm Telling You Now," was released on Capitol's budget subsidiary Tower.

$10*, VG+ condition*

apartment studio, Meek's super-compressed pop songs, full of ghostly vocals and space-age sound effects, Meek was rock's first independent producer, leasing his tracks to various record companies. Even before the Beatles crashed American shores, Joe Meek's production of the Tornadoes' "Telstar" became a #1 hit. He would later produce UK and American hits for the Honeycombs, Heinz, Screaming Lord Sutch and the Blue Men, before taking his own life in 1967. Today, collectors actively search for Meek's American and British pressings, considering his work the product of a tortured genius.

Books

Neely, Tim; Thompson, Dave, *Goldmine British Invasion Record Price Guide*, Krause Publications, Iola, WI, 1997.

Web Pages

Peter and Gordon's official home page: http://www.peterandgordon.com

A fan-based home page for Freddie and the Dreamers: http://users.aol.com/bocad/freddie.htm

A fan-based home page for the Tremeloes: http://www.tremeloes.oldiemusic.de/english.html

Rod Argent and Colin Blunstone of the Zombies have built their own Web sites: http://www.rodargent.com, and http://www.colinblunstone.com

A discography of Capitol of Canada's 72000 series, containing nearly every British Invasion artist: http://www.capitol6000.com/protected/7200045s.htm

Usenet newsgroups: alt.fan.kinks, alt.rock-n-roll.classic, rec.music.rock-pop-r+b.1960s

Phil Spector may have had his monaural "Wall of Sound," but Joe Meek produced one of the most heavily processed and compressed singles of the 1960's in "Telstar." The 45 is very common; try to find the Tornadoes' two American LPs, each one is worth hundreds of dollars apiece.

***$5**, VG condition*

Two versions of David Bowie's hit "Space Oddity." The first American release of the song was on Bowie's record company Mercury, in a version edited for time. In 1970, Bowie's full-length version of "Space Oddity" was released by his new American record company RCA, where it became a hit.

*(L to R) **$25**, VG+ condition; **$6**, NM condition*

THE ANIMALS:

45s

MGM 13242, "Gonna Send You Back to Walker (Gonna Send You Back to Georgia)"/"Baby, Let Me Take You Home," 1964 ....**$7.50-$15.00**
13264, "The House of the Rising Sun"/"Talkin' About You," 1964 ....**$7.50-$15.00**
(with picture sleeve, add), 1964 ....**$15.00-$30.00**
Capitol of Canada 72121, "The House of the Rising Sun"/"Talkin' About You," features long version of A-side, 1964 ....**$10.00-$20.00**

Mono LPs

MGM E-264, The Animals, "The House of the Rising Sun" is edited 45 version, 1964 ....**$15.00-$30.00**
E-4281, The Animals On Tour, 1965 ....**$15.00-$30.00**

PETER BEST:

45s

Cameo 391, "Boys"/"Kansas City," 1965 ....**$20.00-$40.00**
(with picture sleeve, add), 1965 ....**$50.00-$100.00**
Happening 405, "If You Can't Get Her"/"Don't Play With Me," 1964 ....**$90.00-$180.00**

LPs

Savage BM-71, Best of the Beatles, legit copies have a white circle around Best's head, and white circle around "Savage," reproductions do not have white circles, 1966 ....**$100.00-$200.00**

DAVID BOWIE:

45s

Deram 85009, "Rubber Band"/"There Is a Happy Land," 1967 .**$50.00-$100.00**
85016, "Love You Till Tuesday"/"Did You Ever Have a Dream," 1967 ....**$50.00-$100.00**
Mercury 72949, "Space Oddity"/"Wild-Eyed Boy from Freecloud," 1969 ....
$25.00-$50.00
London 20079, "The Laughing Gnome"/"The Gospel According to Tony Day," 1973 ....**$25.00-$50.00**
RCA Victor 74-0876, "Space Oddity"/"The Man Who Sold the World," 1973.
$3.00-$6.00
(with picture sleeve, add), 1973 ....**$10.00-$20.00**

Mono LPs

Deram DE 16003, David Bowie, 1967 ....**$60.00-$120.00**

Stereo LPs

Deram DES 18003, David Bowie, 1967 ....**$75.00-$150.00**
Mercury SR 61246, Man of Words, Man of Music, 1969 ....**$75.00-$150.00**
SR 61325, The Man Who Sold the World (legit pressings have matrix numbers stamped in the runout groove area; counterfeits do not), 1970 ....**$20.00-$40.00**

CHAD AND JEREMY:

45s

World Artists 1021, "Yesterday's Gone"/"Lemon Tree," 1964........**$5.00-$10.00**
1027, "A Summer Song"/"No Tears for Johnny," 1964 ....**$5.00-$10.00**
1034, "Willow Weep for Me"/"If She Was Mine," 1964 ....**$5.00-$10.00**
(with picture sleeve, add), 1964 ....**$10.00-$20.00**

Mono LPs

World Artists WAM-2002, Yesterday's Gone, 1964 ....**$6.00-$12.00**
Columbia CL 2671, Of Cabbages and Kings, 1967 ....**$10.00-$20.00**

THE DAVE CLARK FIVE:

45s

Congress 212, "I Knew It All the Time"/"That's What I Said," 1964 ....**$10.00-$20.00**
(with picture sleeve, add), 1964 ....**$20.00-$40.00**
Epic 9656, "Glad All Over"/"I Know You," 1964 ....**$7.50-$15.00**
(with picture sleeve, add), 1964 ....**$10.00-$20.00**
9671, "Bits and Pieces"/"All of the Time," 1964 ....**$6.00-$12.00**
9704, "Because"/"Theme Without a Name," 1964 ....**$6.00-$12.00**
(with picture sleeve, add), 1964 ....**$10.00-$20.00**
9833, "Catch Us If You Can"/"On the Move," 1965 ....**$6.00-$12.00**
(with picture sleeve, add), 1965 ....**$10.00-$20.00**
Jubilee 5476, "Chaquita"/"In Your Heart," 1964 ....**$15.00-$30.00**
Laurie 3188, "I Walk the Line"/"First Love," 1963 ....**$25.00-$50.00**

7-inch Extended Plays:

Epic E 26185, The Dave Clark Five's Greatest Hits (contains "Over and Over," "Can't You See That She's Mine," "I Like It Like That," "Catch Us If You Can," "Because," "Glad All Over," 7-inch, 33-1/3 RPM, near-mint includes cover and jukebox strips), 1966 ....**$70.00-$140.00**

Mono LPs

Epic LN 24093, Glad All Over
(if first cover, group photo, no instruments), 1964 ....**$40.00-$80.00**
(if second cover, group photo, w/instruments), 1964 ....**$20.00-$40.00**
LN 24104, The Dave Clark Five Return, 1964 ....**$20.00-$40.00**
LN 24178, I Like It Like That, 1965 ....**$20.00-$40.00**

Stereo LPs (all before 1970 were rechanneled stereo, not true stereo)

Epic BN 26093, Glad All Over
(if first cover, group photo, no instruments), 1964 ....**$25.00-$50.00**
(if second cover, group photo, with instruments), 1964 ....**$15.00-$30.00**
BN 26104, The Dave Clark Five Return, 1964 ....**$15.00-$30.00**
BN 26162, Having a Wild Weekend, 1965 ....**$15.00-$30.00**
EG 30434, The Dave Clark Five, 2 LPs, all songs in true stereo, first pressings on yellow label, 1971 ....**$50.00-$100.00**
(second pressings, on orange label), 1973 ....**$40.00-$80.00**

PETULA CLARK:

45s

Coral 60971, "Song of the Mermaid"/"Tell Me Truly," 1953 ....**$12.50-$25.00**
Imperial 5655, "Now That I Need You"/"I Love a Violin," 1960 ....**$10.00-$20.00**
Laurie 3156, "I Will Follow Him"/"Darling Cheri," 1963 ....**$7.50-$15.00**
London 10510, "I'm Counting on You"/"Some Other World," 1962 ....**$7.50-$15.00**

Mono LPs

Imperial LP-9709, Pet Clark, 1959 ....**$40.00-$80.00**
LP-9281, Uptown with Petula Clark (reissue of LP-9709), 1965 ....**$10.00-$20.00**
Laurie LLP-2032, In Love!, 1965 ....**$7.50-$15.00**
Warner Bros. W 1590, Downtown, grey label, 1965 ....**$7.50-$15.00**
W 1598, I Know a Place, grey label, 1965 ....**$7.50-$15.00**
W 1630, My Love, 1966 ....**$5.00-$10.00**

THE SPENCER DAVIS GROUP:

45s

Fontana 1960, "I Can't Stand It"/"Midnight Train," 1964 ....**$7.50-$15.00**
Atco 6400, "Keep On Running"/"High Time Baby," 1966 ....**$7.50-$15.00**
United Artists 50108, "Gimme Some Lovin'"/"Blues in F," 1966 ..**$6.00-$12.00**
50144, "I'm a Man"/"Can't Get Enough of It," 1967 ....**$6.00-$12.00**

Mono LPs

United Artists UAL 3578, Gimme Some Lovin', 1967 ....**$25.00-$50.00**
UAL 3589, I'm a Man, 1967 ....**$20.00-$40.00**

DONOVAN:

45s

Hickory 1309, "Catch the Wind"/"Why Do You Treat Me Like You Do," 1965 ....**$7.50-$15.00**
Epic 10045, "Sunshine Superman"/"The Trip," 1966 ....**$5.00-$10.00**
(with picture sleeve, add), 1966 ....**$7.50-$15.00**
10098, "Mellow Yellow"/"Sunny South Kensington," 1966 ....**$5.00-$10.00**
(with picture sleeve, add), 1966 ....**$7.50-$15.00**
10434, "Atlantis"/"To Susan on the West Coast Waiting," 1969 ...**$4.00-$8.00**
(with picture sleeve, add), 1969 ....**$6.00-$12.00**

Mono LPs

Epic LN 24217, Sunshine Superman, 1966 ....**$15.00-$30.00**
LN 24239, Mellow Yellow, 1967 ....**$15.00-$30.00**
L2N 6071, A Gift from a Flower to a Garden (2 LPs, with portfolio of lyrics and drawings), 1967 ....**$25.00-$50.00**

MARIANNE FAITHFULL:

45s

London 9697, "As Tears Go By"/"Greensleeves," 1964 ....**$6.00-$12.00**
9802, "Go Away From My World"/"Oh Look Around You," 1965 ....**$5.00-$10.00**
(with picture sleeve, add), 1965 ....**$10.00-$20.00**
1022, "Sister Morphine"/"Something Better," 1969 ....**$50.00-$100.00**

Mono LPs

London LL 3423, Marianne Faithfull, 1965 ....**$10.00-$20.00**
LL 3482, Faithfull Forever, 1966 ....**$7.50-$15.00**

Stereo LPs

London PS 423, Marianne Faithfull, 1965 ....**$7.50-$15.00**
PS 452, Go Away From My World, 1965 ....**$7.50-$15.00**

FREDDIE AND THE DREAMERS:

45s

Capitol 5053, "I'm Telling You Now"/"What Have I Done to You," 1963 ....**$10.00-$20.00**

Tower 125, "I'm Telling You Now"/"What Have I Done to You," 1964 ....$7.50-$15.00
Mercury 72418, "Do the Freddie"/"Tell Me When," 1965 ....$5.00-$10.00

7-Inch Extended Plays

Mercury SRC-661, Pun Lovin' Freddie (contains "Thou Shalt Not Steal," "Funny Over You," "He Got What He Wanted," "I Fell In Love With Your Picture," "I Think of You," "Some Other Guy," jukebox mini-LP, value is for record, cover and title strips), 1965 ....$20.00-$40.00

Mono LPs

Mercury MG-21017, Freddie and the Dreamers, 1965 ....$12.50-$25.00
MG-21026, Do the Freddie, 1965 ....$10.00-$20.00
Tower T-5003, I'm Telling You Now, 1965 ....$12.50-$25.00

Stereo LPs

Mercury SR-61017, Freddie and the Dreamers, 1965 ....$10.00-$20.00
SR-61026, Do the Freddie, 1965 ....$12.50-$25.00
Tower ST-5003, I'm Telling You Now, 1965 ....$10.00-$20.00

GERRY AND THE PACEMAKERS:

45s

Laurie 3162, "How Do You Do It"/"Away From You, 1963 ....$10.00-$20.00
3251, "Don't Let the Sun Catch You Crying"/"Away from You," 1964 ....$7.50-$15.00
3284, "Ferry Across the Mersey"/"Pretend," 1965 ....$6.00-$12.00

Mono LPs

Laurie LLP-2024, Don't Let the Sun Catch You Crying, 1964 ....$15.00-$30.00
LLP-2031, Greatest Hits, 1965 ....$12.50-$25.00
United Artists UAL 3387, Ferry Cross the Mersey, 1965 ....$12.50-$25.00

HEINZ:

45s

London 9619, "Just Like Eddie"/"Don't You Knock on My Door," 1963 ....$7.50-$15.00
Tower 110, "Questions I Can't Answer"/"The Beating of My Heart," 1964 ....$10.00-$20.00
195, "Don't Worry Baby"/"Heart Full of Sorrow," 1966.............$15.00-$20.00

HERMAN'S HERMITS:

45s

MGM 13280, "I'm Into Something Good"/"Your Hand in Mine," 1964 ....$2.50-$5.00
13341, "Mrs. Brown You've Got a Lovely Daughter"/"I Gotta Dream On," 1965 ....$5.00-$10.00
(with picture sleeve, add), 1965 ....$7.50-$15.00
13681, "There's a Kind of Hush"/"No Milk Today," 1967 ....$4.00-$8.00
13681, "There's a Kind of Hush (All Over the World)"/"No Milk Today," 1967 ....$5.00-$10.00

Mono LPs

MGM E-4282, Introducing Herman's Hermits
(first version, with "Including Their Hit Single 'I'm Into Something Good'" on front cover), 1965 ....$12.50-$25.00
(second version, with sticker that says "Featuring 'Mrs. Brown You Have a Lovely Daughter'"), 1965 ....$10.00-$20.00
(third version, with sticker that says "Including "Mrs. Brown You've Got a Lovely Daughter'" on front cover), 1965 ....$7.50-$15.00
E-4295, Herman's Hermits on Tour, 1965 ....$6.00-$12.00

THE HOLLIES:

45s

Imperial 66026, "Just One Look"/"Keep Off That Friend of Mine," 1964 ....$10.00-$20.00
66134, "Look Through Any Window"/"So Lonely," 1965 ....$6.00-$12.00
66186, "Bus Stop"/"Don't Run and Hide," 1966...........................$6.00-$12.00
Epic 10180, "Carrie-Anne"/"Signs That Will Never Change," 1967 ....$4.00-$8.00
(with picture sleeve, add), 1967 ....$4.00-$8.00
10532, "He Ain't Heavy, He's My Brother"/"Cos You Like to Love Me," 1969 **$3.00-$6.00**

Mono LPs

Imperial LP-9265, Here I Go Again, black label with stars, 1964 ....$75.00-$150.00
(if black-pink label), 1964 ....$25.00-$50.00
Epic LN 24315, Evolution, 1967 ....$15.00-$30.00

Stereo LPs

Imperial LP-12265, Here I Go Again, black label with silver print, 1964 ....$50.00-$100.00
(if black-pink label), 1964 ....$15.00-$30.00
Epic BN 26315, Evolution, 1967 ....$12.50-$25.00

THE HONEYCOMBS:

45s

Interphon 7707, "Have I the Right?"/"Please Don't Pretend Again," 1964 ....$6.00-$12.00
7716, "Color Slide"/"That's the Way," 1965 ....$5.00-$10.00
(with picture sleeve listing A-side as "Colour Slide," add),

Mono LPs

Interphon IN-88001, Here Are the Honeycombs, 1964 ....$20.00-$40.00
Vee Jay IN-88001, Here Are the Honeycombs, 1964 ....$25.00-$50.00

Stereo LPs

Interphon IN-88001, Here Are the Honeycombs, 1964 ....$15.00-$30.00

JONATHAN KING:

45s

Parrot 9774, "Everyone's Gone to the Moon"/"Summer's Coming," 1965 ....$5.00-$10.00

Mono LPs

Parrot 61013, Jonathan King Or Then Again..., 1967 ....$20.00-$40.00

Stereo LPs

Parrot 71013, Jonathan King Or Then Again..., 1967 ....$25.00-$50.00

THE KINKS:

45s

Cameo 308, "Long Tall Sally"/"I Took My Baby Home," 1964 ....$300.00-$600.00
345, "Long Tall Sally"/"I Took My Baby Home," 1965 ....$150.00-$300.00
Reprise 0306, "You Really Got Me"/"It's All Right"
(first pressing, Reprise peach labels), 1964 ....$12.50-$25.00
(second pressing, orange brown labels), 1964 ....$7.50-$15.00

Mono LPs

Reprise R-6143, You Really Got Me, white label promo, 1965 $200.00-$400.00
R-6143, You Really Got Me, stock copy, 1965 ....$30.00-$60.00
R-6173, Kinda Kinks, white label promo, 1965 ....$100.00-$200.00
R-6173, Kinda Kinks, stock copy, 1965 ....$25.00-$50.00

BILLY J. KRAMER AND THE DAKOTAS:

45s

Imperial 66027, "Little Children"/"Bad to Me," 1964....................$6.00-$12.00
Liberty 55586, "Do You Want to Know a Secret"/"I'll Be On My Way" ....$15.00-$30.00
55567, "Bad to Me"/"Do You Want to Know a Secret," 1964 ....$12.50-$25.00

Mono LPs

Imperial LP 9267, Little Children, black label with stars, 1964 ....$25.00-$50.00
(if above, with black-pink label), 1964 ....$25.00-$50.00

Stereo LPs

Imperial LP 12-267, Little Children, black label with stars, 1964 $40.00-$80.00
(if above, with black-pink label), 1964 ....$20.00-$40.00

MANFRED MANN:

45s

Ascot 2151, "Hubble Bubble (Toil and Trouble)"/"I'm Your Kingpin," 1964 ....$100.00-$200.00
2157, "Do Wah Diddy Diddy"/"What You Gonna Do?," 1964...$7.50-$15.00

Mono LPs

Ascot AM-13015, The Manfred Mann Album, 1964..................$20.00-$40.00
AM-13021, My Little Red Book of Winners, 1965 ....$20.00-$40.00

THE MINDBENDERS:

45s

Fontana 1451, "A Groovy Kind of Love"/"Love Is Good," 1966 ...$6.00-$12.00

Mono LPs

Fontana MGF-27554, A Groovy Kind of Love
(with "Don't Cry No More"), 1966 ....$15.00-$30.00
(with "Ashes to Ashes"), 1966 ....$12.50-$25.00

Stereo LPs

Fontana SHE 67554, A Groovy Kind of Love
(with "Don't Cry No More"), 1966 ....$12.50-$25.00
(with "Ashes to Ashes"), 1966 ....$10.00-$20.00

THE MOODY BLUES:

45s

London 9726V, "Go Now!"/"It's Easy Child," orange-brown swirl label, may be promo only, 1965 ....$10.00-$20.00
London 9726, "Go Now!"/"Lose Your Money" (white-purple-blue label), 1965 ....$10.00-$20.00
(if on blue swirl label, "London" in white), 1965 ....$6.00-$12.00
(if on blue swirl label, "London" in black), 1965..............................$4.00-$8.00
(if on Sunrise label), 197? ....$3.00-$6.00

Deram 85023, "Nights in White Satin"/"Cities"
(if composer of "Nights in White Satin" is listed as "Redwave"), 1968 .... $5.00-$10.00
(if composer of "Nights in White Satin" is listed as "Justin Hayward"), 1968 .... $4.00-$8.00
(if composer of "Nights in White Satin" is listed as "Redwave-Hayward"), 1968 .... $4.00-$8.00
85028, "Tuesday Afternoon (Forever Afternoon)"/"Another Morning," 1968 .... $4.00-$8.00

Mono LPs

London LL 3428, Go Now-The Moody Blues #1, 1965 .... $25.00-$50.00
Deram DE 16012, Days of Future Passed, 1968 .... $125.00-$250.00

Stereo LPs

PS 428, Go Now-The Moody Blues #1, 1965 .... $20.00-$40.00
Deram DES 18012, Days of Future Passed, 1968 .... $10.00-$20.00
Deram 18017, In Search of the Lost Chord, gatefold cover, 1968 .... $10.00-$20.00

PETER AND GORDON:

45s

Capitol 5175, "A World Without Love"/"If I Were You," 1964 .... $6.00-$12.00
5335, "I Go to Pieces"/"Love Me, Baby," 1965 .... $6.00-$12.00
(with picture sleeve, add), 1965 .... $8.00-$16.00
5579, "Woman"/"Wrong from the Start" (A-side written by "Bernard Webb"), 1966 .... $6.00-$12.00
(if A-side listed as "A. Smith," actually written by Paul McCartney," 1966 .... $5.00-$10.00

Mono LPs

Capitol T 2115, A World Without Love, 1964 .... $10.00-$20.00
T 2220, I Don't Want to See You Again, 1964 .... $10.00-$20.00

DUSTY SPRINGFIELD:

45s

Philips 40162, "I Only Want to Be with You"/"Once Upon a Time," 1963 .... $6.00-$12.00
40207, "Wishin' and Hopin'"/"Do Re Mi (Forget About the Do and Think About Me)," 1964 .... $6.00-$12.00
40319, "I Just Don't Know What to Do with Myself"/"Some of Your Lovin," 1965 .... $5.00-$10.00
(with picture sleeve, add), 1965 .... $10.00-$20.00
40465, "The Look of Love"/"Give Me Time," 1967 .... $5.00-$10.00

Mono LPs

Philips PHM-200133, Stay Awhile, 1964 .... $15.00-$30.00
PHM-200156, Dusty, 1964 .... $15.00-$30.00

Stereo LPs

Philips PHS-600133, Stay Awhile, 1964 .... $20.00-$40.00
PHS-600256, The Look of Love, 1967 .... $15.00-$30.00
Atlantic SD 8214, Dusty in Memphis
(first pressings, purple-brown labels), 1969 .... $15.00-$30.00
(second pressings, green-red labels), 1969 .... $7.50-$15.00

THE WHO:

45s

Atco 6409, "Substitute"/"Waltz for a Pig," 1966 .... $25.00-$50.00
6509, "Substitute"/"Waltz for a Pig," 1967 .... $10.00-$20.00
Decca 31725, "I Can't Explain"/"Bald Headed Woman," 1965 .... $15.00-$30.00
32206, "I Can See For Miles"/"Mary-Anne with the Shaky Hands," 1967 .... $10.00-$20.00
32465, "Pinball Wizard"/"Dogs Part Two," 1969 .... $5.00-$10.00
(with picture sleeve, add), 1969 .... $10.00-$20.00

Mono LPs

Decca DL 4664, The Who Sing My Generation, 1966 .... $5000-$10.00
DL 4950, The Who Sell Out, 1967 .... $50.00-$100.00
(if white label promo, with songs in same order as stock copy), 1967 .... $100.00-$200.00
(if white label promo, side 1 banded for airplay, commercials gathered on one side), 1967 .... $150.00-$300.00

Stereo LPs

DL 74664, The Who Sing My Generation, 1966 .... $30.00-$60.00
DL 74950, The Who Sell Out, 1967 .... $25.00-$50.00
(if white label promo, with songs in same order as stock copy), 1967 .... $125.00-$250.00
(if white label promo, side 1 banded for airplay, commercials gathered on one side), 1967 .... $200.00-$400.00

THE YARDBIRDS:

45s

9709, "I Wish You Could"/"A Certain Girl," 1964 .... $20.00-$40.00
9709, "I Wish You Would"/"A Certain Girl," 1964 .... $25.00-$50.00
(with promo-only picture sleeve, add), 1964 .... $400.00-$800.00
9790, "For Your Love"/"Got to Hurry," 1965 .... $7.50-$15.00

Mono LPs

Epic LN 24167, For Your Love, white label promo, 1965 .... $200.00-$400.00
LN 24167, For Your Love, 1965 .... $150.00-$300.00
LN 24210, Over Under Sideways Down, white label promo, 1966 .... $200.00-$400.00
LN 24210, Over Under Sideways Down, 1966 .... $30.00-$60.00

Stereo LPs

Epic BN 26167, For Your Love, 1965 .... $100.00-$200.00
BN 26210, Over Under Sideways Down, 1966 .... $40.00-$80.00

THE ZOMBIES:

45s

Date 1604, "Time of the Season"/"I'll Call You Mine," 1968 .... $10.00-$20.00
1628, "Time of the Season"/"Friends of Mine," 1968 .... $6.00-$12.00
Parrot 9695, "She's Not There"/"You Make Me Feel So Good," 1964 .... $7.50-$15.00
9723, "Tell Her No"/"Leave Me Be," 1965 .... $7.50-$15.00
(with picture sleeve, add), 1965 .... $15.00-$30.00

A half-speed mastered edition of the Moody Blues' Days of Future Passed *album, containing the cleanest, warmest version of "Nights in White Satin" one will ever hear on vinyl.*
***$60**, NM condition*

Photo credit: Courtesy Last Vestige Music Store, Albany, N.Y.

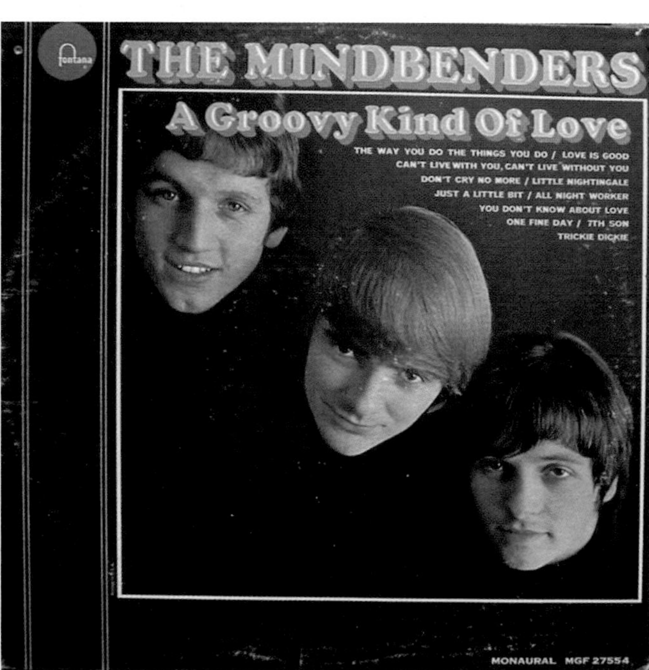

This album by the Mindbenders features their hit "A Groovy Kind of Love." First pressings of this album feature a song called "Don't Cry No More"; later pressings replace this song with "Ashes to Ashes."
***$10**, Good condition*

Chapter 8

Children's Records

History

There's a theory about record collecting that people start in the hobby when their parents give kids their very own 45s. Those records might have a label on them like Disneyland or Peter Pan or Cricket or Voco, yet as a kid we wouldn't pass these discs up for the world. These were the records we could play on the big phonograph when our parents were done listening to their Limelighters or Chad Mitchell Trio or "Sing Along With Mitch" albums. And we could sing along with the songs too—all the Disney songs like "Cruella De Vil" or "Zip-A-Dee-Doo-Dah," or the very same versions from the Cricket studios, as performed by studio musicians. Remember the General Electric Show 'n Tell Phonograph, a combination record player and filmstrip projector? How about Red Raven records, where you could place a mirrored topper on a detailed label and create your own movie?

In fact, for more than 100 years, children's records have provided more than just a musical diversion for adolescents. Even Thomas Edison, the inventor of the phonograph, tested his new creation by recording the nursery rhyme "Mary Had a Little Lamb," essentially dictating the first children's record.

The oldest collectible line of children's records are the sixteen "Bubble Books," initially produced by Harper and Brothers, and eventually distributed by both the Columbia and Victor record companies in the 1920s. Promoted as the "Book That Sings," Bubble Books contained nursery rhymes and sing-along songs, all encased in a bound folio with ornate colored illustrations. Depending on condition,

Photo credit: From the collection of Peter Muldavin.

Emerson produced a series of animal-themed songs and grommeted the records to colorful artworks. Several animal prints exist, as well as a record attached to a drawing of Uncle Sam.

***$200**, NM condition*

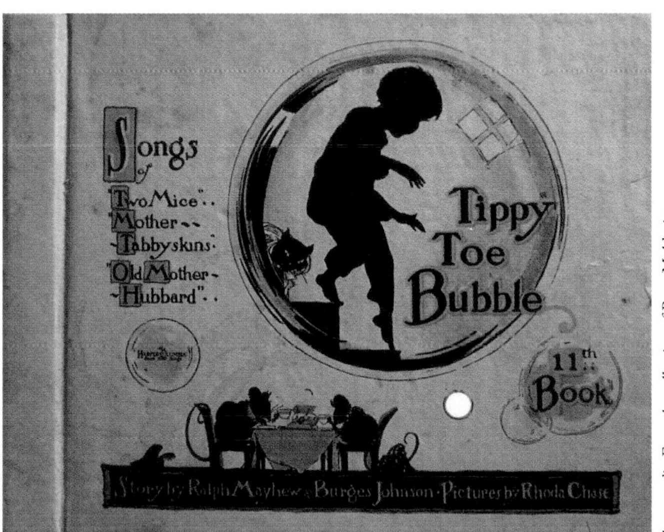

Photo credit: From the collection of Peter Muldavin.

Harper-Columbia's "Bubble Books" series contained three small 78s in a bound folio with nursery rhymes and stories. Near-mint copies must have all three records with no cracks or chips, and the book must have no signs of aging, tears or page rips.

***$30**, NM condition*

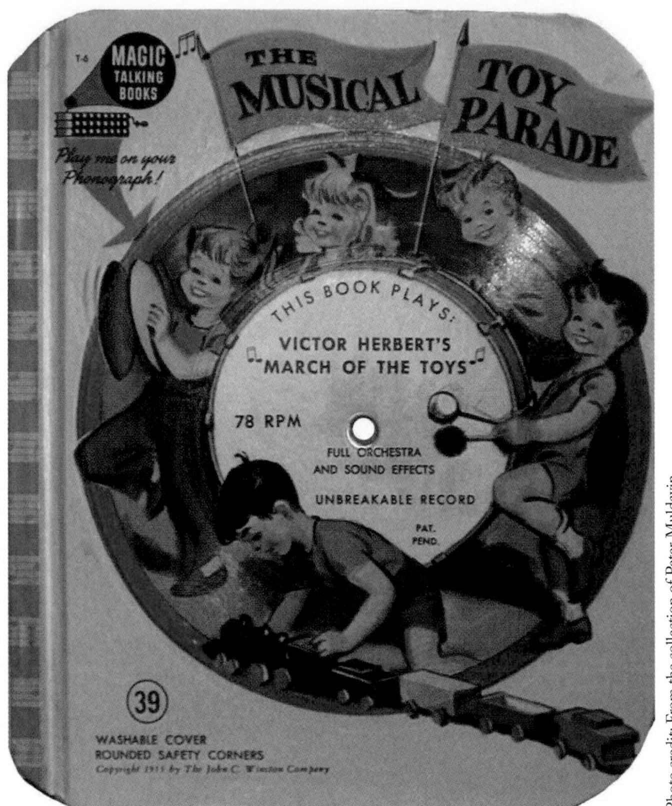

Photo credit: From the collection of Peter Muldavin.

This "Magic Talking Book" from 1935 has a spindle hole through the center of the book. After reading the text, a child can place the book directly on the phonograph and play the cover!

***$8**, NM condition*

these Bubble Books can sell for as much as $25-$40 to a children's record collector (the higher numbers, Bubble Books 14, 15 and 16, are harder to find).

The success of the Bubble Books spurred other record companies to create their own book-and-record sets for the youth market. Victor Emerson's record company produced a series of "Talking Books," essentially a small 78-RPM record attached to a die-cut artwork. Other children's records were essentially books that could be played on a turntable—the whole book had a center spindle hole, and you could play the book's cover on your phonograph.

In an effort to appeal to children both visually as well as sonically, many companies released their product in colored vinyl or on picture discs. Some record companies even attempted to "brand" their childrens' music line. RCA, for example, had a "Little Nipper" book-and-record series, featuring selections from Howdy Doody, Kukla Fran and Ollie, Captain Video, and the Walt Disney Studios (there was even a "Little Nipper" club, with a membership card and pinback buttons). During the 1940s and early 1950s, Capitol Records marked their covers with a Bozo the Clown logo (Capitol DBX-3056, a "Lady and the Tramp" book-and-record 78 with a Bozo logo, can fetch as much as $50 in near-mint condition). Columbia released over 100 titles as part of their "Playtime" series, mostly 6-inch and 7-inch 78-RPM discs. As an added treat, many of the "Book-And-Record" releases were narrated by popular Hollywood stars of the time, including James Stewart and Shirley Temple. Television show hosts of the 1950s, such as Paul Wing ("Mr. I. Magination"), Fran Allison ("Kukla, Fran and Ollie"), and Bob Keeshan ("Captain Kangaroo") also appear on vinyl, narrating stories for the youth audience.

In 1948, publisher Simon & Schuster launched their own children's label, Golden Records. Their 6-inch yellow-vinylite discs were available at department stores, where a child with a quarter could purchase a Golden Record. The early pressings featured narrated read-along renditions of the company's popular children's books, such as *The Poky Little Puppy*, with an audio notation to the children that when the puppy barks (arf arf), the kids could turn the page. At that

Photo credit: Bozo record, Peter Muldavin collection; Little Nipper pressing, author's collection.

Two examples of record company brand-name children's sets. Long before he was a TV star, Bozo was a cartoon character, voiced by Pinto Colvig on a series of Capitol 78s. Paul Wing, who worked on various children's record projects, is featured on this "Little Nipper" catalog title.

*(L to R) **$20**, NM condition; **$40**, NM condition*

Photo credit: From the collection of Peter Muldavin.

This rare "picture-play" pressing of "Over the Rainbow" originally sold for 29 cents; today, in its original shrink-wrap and red title banner, it can sell for $50 or more, depending on if the collector is into children's music, picture discs, or Wizard of Oz *memorabilia.*

With cellophane sleeve and banner, ***$50****, NM condition*

The first Red Raven records had laminated grooves on cardboard, with a metal ring around the outside of the disc. Later Red Raven discs were pressed on colored vinyl, with the reflective artwork printed on the label. You can see that this artwork is designed to be read in a mirror; unless this is a song about a cow that goes "oom."

$30*, VG+ condition*

same time, another record company, the Record Guild of America, pressed a line of picture discs that were sold in cellophane wrappers. Finding the records with the wrappers is nearly impossible today.

By the 1950s, some record companies added an extra dimension to a child's musical experience, by producing special records with attachable toppers, or picture sleeves with cutout characters. Red Raven Records, for example, added a circus tent-shaped mirrored topper to the phonograph spindle; kids could watch a reflected movie in the mirror as the record spun on the turntable.

In the 1960s, General Electric entered the children's music field. Their new line of phonographs featured, of all things, a built-in filmstrip projector, called the "Show 'n Tell Phonoviewer." Place the General Electric record on the turntable, slide the filmstrip into an adjoining hole under the tonearm, put the needle on the record, turn on the combination backlight/volume control, and if all went well, you saw a slide show—with accompanying narration and/or dialogue.

By 1970, there were a series of Walt Disney GE Phonoviewer discs, as well as licensed product from the *Captain Kangaroo* show, *Romper Room*, and the *Double Sixteen Company* of Wheaton, Illinois, who produced a series of "Sunday School" religious discs for the Show 'N Tell. General Electric also improved the design on the phonograph itself; adding such gee-whiz items as an AM radio and an analog clock. These players can sell for up to $50-$75 in near-mint condition, adding an extra $10-$20 for the AM radio or the clock.

Another music collectible that has recently gained new appreciation is the "school educational records" genre.

A General Electric Show 'N Tell Phonoviewer record-and-filmstrip phonograph folder from 1964, sold with a 7-inch 33-1/3 record, and with a miniature filmstrip encased in a white plastic sheath.

$5*, VG+ condition*

These records, usually played by third-grade teachers on a huge classroom turntable, were used by schools to reinforce concepts in reading, phonics, and foreign languages. One of the most collectible series of "school educational records" are the "Bremner Musical Multiplication Tables," originally custom-manufactured by RCA and sold to schools in 1956 to 1973. Each box of 5 to 6 discs contained a singalong chorus, as schoolkids sang their multiplication tables with voice actor Billy Leach. Also included in the boxed set were some flash cards, advertising for a book of phonics records, and testimonials from parents, teachers and principals about the discs.

It was not unusual for children's television shows to have a special tie-in with a purchasable phonograph record—both to increase the show profits, or for the benefit of a charitable or non-profit organization. In the 1950s, TV kiddie shows like *Howdy Doody* and *Winky Dink* issued records that today are highly collectible, both by children's music aficionados and classic TV collectors. Even RCA Victor's trademark dog Nipper was part of a 1950s TV series, as the record company sponsored the *Rootie Kazootie Show* (when RCA dropped their sponsorship, the "Nipper" dog on the show was renamed "Gala Poochie Pup").

By the 1960s and 1970s, with the advent of non-profit "public broadcasting" shows, childrens' records from shows like *Sesame Street*, *Mister Rogers' Neighborhood*, *The Electric Company*, and *Zoom* could be found in stores. While most of these pressings have not risen in collectible value over the years, an exception is made for pressings from the PBS series *The Electric Company*. Among the members of this show's ensemble cast were Bill Cosby, Morgan Freeman (as the suave "Easy Reader"), and Rita Moreno, whose trademark scream "Hey You Guy-y-y-ys!' started every broadcast.

Photo credit: From the collection of Peter Muldavin.

Winky Dink was a popular 1950s television character, narrated by game show host Jack Barry and voiced by Mae Questal (who also did the voice of Olive Oyl). This Decca 78 is a hot collectible, especially prized by TV nostalgia buffs.
***$40**, VG+ condition*

The soundtrack to the TV series The Electric Company *comes with some bonus inserts, including a "Crypto-Spectometer" as used by the peripatetic private investigator Fargo North, Decoder.*
***$30**, NM condition*

What To Look For

More than any other collectible format, picture sleeves are an extremely important part of collecting childrens' records. The fragile paper sleeves often had well-detailed, full-color artwork or images, and are much harder to find than the records they once held.

Collectible characters often dominate the children's record market, as licensed characters from Walt Disney, Warner Bros., Peanuts, Hanna-Barbera, Popeye, or Tarzan all have huge collecting fan bases. Characters that are part of a popular children's story can also bring high prices. Some collectors will search out all copies of stories like *The Little Engine That Could*, *The Poky Little Puppy*, *Tubby the Tuba*, or *Gossamer Wump*, no matter who is narrating or on what format the record is pressed.

Children's records that contain characters or stories from a television series or motion picture are more collectible when the actors or actresses performing the voices of the characters on screen also appear on the record. Some records exist with titles like "Songs From Mister Rogers' Neighborhood" or "Songs From The Great Disney Movies," but these records feature studio musicians and stock artwork, not the original performers that we all grew up with.

Condition is key—even though many children's records

Photo credit: Both records from the collection of Peter Muldavin.

Stars from the motion picture The Wizard of Oz *can be found narrating various 78-RPM childrens' records. Frank Morgan, who played Professor Marvel in the movie, narrates the story of Gossamer Wump, who wanted to play the triangle in the marching band. Meanwhile, Ray Bolger, famous for his role as the Scarecrow, voiced a series of Decca children's 78 titles, including "The Churkendoose" and "Max Mainspring, the Mechanical Man."*

(L to R) ***$60****, NM condition;* ***$75****, VG+ condition*

in the 1940s and 1950s were stamped "unbreakable," that didn't stop kids from writing on them with crayons or pens. And if the records were played on a cheap phonograph with a dull needle, that "unbreakable" record can sound awful when played on modern equipment. "Book and record" sets need to have BOTH the book and the record; if either of the two are missing, its collectible value is greatly diminished, and should only be bought if you need the book or the record to replace a poor or worn copy in your own collection.

Some children's records have special regional appeal, depending on whether a TV kiddie show host was popular only in his or her local viewing area (such as "Uncle Don" Carney in New York) or had a national television audience (like *Howdy Doody* or *Ding Dong School*).

Photo credit: From the collection of Peter Muldavin.

Children's radio show host Uncle Don Carney broadcast for many years from New York radio station WOR, and lent his name to a series of records and books, an example of which is seen here.

$20*, NM condition*

Web Pages

Peter Muldavin's Web site that features a history of children's records: http://www.kiddierekordking.com

A history of the Harper-Columbia Bubble Books is at http://home.att.net/~hula2/home.html

A discography of Warner Bros. cartoon characters on Capitol "Bozo-Approved" records: http://looney.toonzone.net/miscelooneyous/records

A discography of United Artists' "Tale Spinners for Children" series of 1960s children's LPs: http://www.artsreformation.com/talespinners/

Books

Murray, R. Michael, *The Golden Age of Walt Disney Records 1933-1988*, Antique Trader Books, Dubuque, Iowa, 1997.

101 DALMATIANS (original motion picture soundtrack):

LPs

Disneyland ST-1908, mono, 1960 .... **$12.50-$25.00**
ST-4903, mono, gatefold cover with pop-up scene in center, 1963 .... **$75.00-$150.00**
ST-3931, mono, 1965 .... **$20.00-$40.00**

ALICE IN WONDERLAND:

78s

Decca DA-376, "Alice in Wonderland," Ginger Rogers, narrator, 1944 .... **$12.50-$25.00**

LPs

Hanna-Barbera HBR-2051, The New Alice in Wonderland, or, What's a Nice kid Like You Doing in a Place Like This?, 1966 .... **$20.00-$40.00**

ATARI VIDEO GAME RECORDS:

LPs

Kid Stuff KSS-5029, A Pac-Man Christmas, 1980 .... **$7.50-$15.00**
KSS-5031, Missile Command, 1981 .... **$5.00-$10.00**
KSS 5033, Yars' Revenge, 1981 .... **$5.00-$10.00**

RAY BOLGER:

78s

Decca CU 102, "The Churkendoose," 1947 .... **$25.00-$50.00**
Decca 88052 K-16, "Max Mainspring, the Mechanical Man," 1950 .... **$50.00-$100.00**

BETTY BOOP:

7-inch 78

Durotone R-81, Betty Boop in "Peter and Wendy"/Betty Boop in "She Loves Him Not," 193? .... **$20.00-$40.00**

BOZO THE CLOWN:

78s

Capitol DAS-3046, Bozo Laughs, 1946 .... **$7.50-$15.00**
BBX65, Bozo and His Rocket Ship, 2 78s with book, 1947 .... **$10.00-$20.00**
DBS-84, Bozo Sings, 2 78s in gatefold sleeve, 1948 .... **$10.00-$20.00**
DBX-3076, Bozo on the Farm, 2 78s with book, 1950 .... **$10.00-$20.00**

BREMNER MUSICAL MULTIPLICATION TABLES:

RCA Custom boxed set, 6 7-inch 78-RPM discs, with flash cards and testimonials, 1956 .... **$15.00-$30.00**
RCA Custom boxed set, 5 7-inch 33-1/3-RPM discs, with flash cards and testimonials, 1956 .... **$10.00-$20.00**
Capitol Custom boxed set, 5 7-inch 33-1/3-RPM discs, with flash cards and testimonials, 1956 .... **$7.50-$15.00**

BUBBLE BOOKS:

7-inch 78s, three in booklet, made by Harper-Columbia (value is for all three single-sided records and the booklet)

The Bubble Book, 1917 .... **$15.00-$30.00**
The Second Bubble Book, 1917 .... **$15.00-$30.00**
The Third Bubble Book, 1918 .... **$15.00-$30.00**
4, The Animal Bubble Book, 1918 .... **$15.00-$30.00**
5, The Pie Party, 1919 .... **$15.00-$30.00**
6, The Pet Bubble Book, 1919 .... **$15.00-$30.00**
7, The Funny Froggy Bubble Book , 1919 .... **$15.00-$30.00**
8, Happy-Go-Lucky Bubble Book, 1919 .... **$15.00-$30.00**
9, The Merry Midget Bubble Book, 1919 .... **$15.00-$30.00**
10, The Little Mischief Bubble Book, 1920 .... **$15.00-$30.00**
11, Tippy Toe Bubble Book, 1920 .... **$15.00-$30.00**
12, The Gay Games Bubble Book, 1920 .... **$15.00-$30.00**
13, The Child's Garden of Verses, 1922 .... **$25.00-$50.00**
14, The Chimney Corner Bubble Book, 1922 .... **$25.00-$50.00**
15, The Robin and Wren Book (2 records, one single-sided and one double-sided), 1930 .... **$25.00-$50.00**
16, Higgledy Piggledy Bubble Book (2 records, one single-sided and one double-sided), 1930 .... **$25.00-$50.00**

Victor Bubble Book No. 1 (all Victor Bubble Books contain three double-sided 78s, and are reissues of the Harper-Columbia sets), 1924 .... **$20.00-$40.00**
Victor Bubble Book No. 2, 1924 .... **$20.00-$40.00**
Victor Bubble Book No. 3, 1924 .... **$20.00-$40.00**
Victor Bubble Book No. 4, 1924 .... **$20.00-$40.00**
Victor Bubble Book No. 5, 1924 .... **$20.00-$40.00**
Victor Bubble Book No. 6, 1924 .... **$20.00-$40.00**

THE BUNIN PUPPETS:

78s

Caravan C-22, Foodini's Trip to the Moon, 1949 .... **$30.00-$60.00**

CHARLOTTE'S WEB (original motion picture soundtrack):

LPs

Paramount PAS-1008, 1973 .... **$15.00-$30.00**

CINDERELLA (original motion picture soundtrack):

Decca DA-391, three 78s in folio, 1945 .... **$25.00-$50.00**
RCA Victor Y-399, two 78s in folio with booklet, 1950 .... **$25.00-$50.00**
Disneyland WDL-4007, mono, gatefold cover, 1957 .... **$100.00-$200.00**
1207, mono, white back cover with ads for nine other LPs, 1959 .... **$20.00-$40.00**
1207, mono, pink back cover, 1963 .... **$15.00-$30.00**
1207, mono, high gloss cover with prince putting glass slipper on Cinderella's foot, 1987 .... **$12.50-$25.00**

THE ELECTRIC COMPANY:

LPs

Warner Bros. 2636, The Electric Company (with booklet and "Fargo North, Decoder" Crypto-Spectometer), 1972 .... **$15.00-$30.00**
Sesame Street 22052, The Electric Company, 1974 .... **$7.50-$15.00**

FANTASIA (original motion picture soundtrack):

LPs

Disneyland WDX-101, 3 records, first issue, maroon labels, with 24-page booklet, 1957 .... **$30.00-$60.00**
Buena Vista WDX-101, 3 records, second issue, blue labels, with 24-page booklet, 1961 .... **$15.00-$30.00**
STER-101, stereo, 3 records, black and yellow rainbow labels, with 24-page booklet, 1961 .... **$20.00-$40.00**
101, stereo reissue, two records, no booklet, 1982 .... **$10.00-$20.00**
V-104, digitally re-recorded music track, 2 records, Mickey Mouse as Sorcerer's Apprentice on cover, 1982 .... **$12.50-$25.00**

GENERAL ELECTRIC SHOW 'N TELL PICTURESOUND DISCS

33-1/3 RPM, 7-inch, to be in mint condition, folder must contain both record and filmstrip; deduct 50% if either filmstrip or record is missing

Disney releases (contain a "WD" in prefix), 1969 .... **$5.00-$10.00**
Canon Bible Series (contains a "CBP" in prefix), 1966 .... **$4.00-$8.00**

GOLDILOCKS AND THE THREE BEARS:

78s

Capitol DB-121, Goldilocks and the Three Bears, Margaret O'Brien, narrator, 1948 .... **$5.00-$10.00**

This unique children's record was sold at the old Storytown amusement park in upstate New York in the 1960s. The park's "Ghost Town" attraction featured a daily showdown where the town's sheriff, Wild Windy Bill McKay, captured the bad guys.

With autograph, ***$10****, VG+ condition*

"Movie Wheels" contained a flexidisc, with a special rotating slideshow built into a cardboard casing. The packages featured several top cartoon characters from the early 1960s, including Huckleberry Hound, Yogi Bear, and Felix the Cat, and used the same voices from the cartoons.

***$25**, NM condition*

CAPTAIN KANGAROO:

LPs

Golden Records GLP26, Merry, Merry, Merry Christmas, 1958 .... **$6.00-$12.00**
GLP40, Introduces You to the Nutcracker Suite, 1959 .... **$6.00-$12.00**
GLP116, Captain Kangaroo Sings The Horse in the Striped Pajamas, 196? .... **$6.00-$12.00**
Everest LP-3043, Peter and the Wolf, 1960 .... **$7.50-$15.00**
Columbia/Harmony HL 9508, Captain Kangaroo's TV Party, 196? .... **$5.00-$10.00**
Chelsea CHL 701-2, Colors, 1976 .... **$5.00-$10.00**
Peter Pan 8067, Sings Songs of the Treasure House, 197? .... **$5.00-$10.00**

LADY AND THE TRAMP (original motion picture soundtrack):

Capitol DBX-3056, two 78s in booklet, "Bozo Approved," 1955 .. **$25.00-$50.00**
Decca DL 5557, 10-inch LP, 1955 .... **$30.00-$60.00**
DL 8462, mono 12-inch LP, 1957 .... **$35.00-$70.00**
Disneyland 3103, picture disc, 1981 .... **$15.00-$30.00**

LITTLE NIPPER SERIES:

78-RPM records in folio

RCA Victor Y-383, The Adventures Of Little Black Sambo, 1949 .... **$25.00-$50.00**
Y-385, Pinocchio, 1949 .... **$20.00-$40.00**
Y-397, Howdy Doody and the Air-O-Doodle, 1949 .... **$25.00-$50.00**
Y-414, Howdy Doody's Laughing Circus, 1949 .... **$20.00-$40.00**
Y-438, Winnie-the-Pooh No. 1, James Stewart, narrator, 1949 .. **$30.00-$60.00**
Y 446, It's Howdy Doody Time, 1951 .... **$30.00-$60.00**

LOONEY TUNES/MERRIE MELODIES:

10-inch 78s in folio

Capitol CC-64, Bugs Bunny Stories for Children, 1947 .... **$10.00-$20.00**
DBX-93, Bugs Bunny and the Tortoise (with book), 1948 .... **$12.50-$25.00**
DBX-3021, Bugs Bunny In Storyland, 1949 .... **$12.50-$25.00**
CAS-3074, Tweety Pie, 1950 .... **$10.00-$20.00**

FRANK LUTHER:

78s

RCA Victor 222, Winnie the Pooh Sings
(if picture disc), 1934 .... **$175.00-$350.00**
(if standard black 78), 1934 .... **$5.00-$10.00**
224-226, Walt Disney Presents Silly Symphonies (3, 78s, picture discs, with custom sleeves, value is for all three discs, one disc features Mickey Mouse and Minnie Mouse), 1933 .... **$1,250.00-$2,500.00**
Decca 23733, "The Cherry Scarecrow"/"My Raggedy Ann," 1946 .... **$5.00-$10.00**
23755, "Tired Old Horse"/"Coo Coo Clock," 1946 .... **$5.00-$10.00**
Decca Children's Series K-4, "Brumas the Roly Poly Bear"/"Pudgy the Whistling Piggy," 195? .... **$2.50-$5.00**

MAGIC TALKING BOOKS:

T-6, Musical Toy Parade, Victor Herbert's March of the Toys, cover of book can be played on phonograph, 1955 .... **$4.00-$8.00**
T-19, Davy Crockett and the Indians, Straight Shootin' Davy, cover of book can be played on phonograph, 1955 .... **$40.00-$50.00**

GROUCHO MARX:

78s

Young Peoples Records #YPR-719, "The Funniest Song in the World" (Pt. 1)/(Pt. 2), 1949 .... **$15.00-$30.00**

BILLY MAY:

78s

Capitol DCN-115, Rusty in Orchestraville, 3 78s in folio, 1946 .... **$15.00-$30.00**
DC-78, Sparky's Magic Piano, 3 78s in folio, 1947 .... **$15.00-$30.00**
DC-119, Sparky and the Magic Train, 3 78s in folio, 1947 .... **$15.00-$30.00**

FRANK MORGAN:

78s

Capitol ESA-3012, "Gossamer Wump" (Pt. 1)/(Pt. 2), 1949 .... **$30.00-$60.00**

MIGHTY MOUSE:

78s

RCA Bluebird BY-10, Mighty Mouse Saves Dinky, 1953 .... **$10.00-$20.00**
Little Golden Record R-217, The Mighty Mouse TV Theme Song, 1955 .... **$10.00-$20.00**

LPs

Lion L70115, Mighty Mouse Playhouse, 1959 .... **$10.00-$20.00**

PINOCCHIO (original motion picture soundtrack):

RCA Victor P-18, three 78s, light blue, die-cut cover, eight color picture panels on inner jacket and sleeves, 1940 .... **$75.00-$150.00**
P-18, second issue, cover not die-cut, no internal pictures, 194? .. **$37.50-$75.00**
Y-385, two 78s in folio, 1949 .... **$25.00-$50.00**
Decca A-110, four 78s, "Songs from Pinocchio," 1940 .... **$30.00-$60.00**
A-424, reissue, 1946 .... **$25.00-$50.00**
Disneyland WDL-4002, mono, 1956 .... **$125.00-$250.00**
DO-1202, second edition, 1959 .... **$15.00-$30.00**
DO-1202MO, third edition, 1963 .... **$10.00-$20.00**
ST-4905, gatefold cover with pop-up graphics, 1963 .... **$75.00-$150.00**
3012, picture disc, 1981 .... **$15.00-$30.00**

POPEYE THE SAILOR:

7-inch 78

Durotone Set 50, three records in cardboard box set, to be played with filmstrip 193? .... **$37.50-$75.00**

45s

Little Golden Record FF346, Jack Mercer, "I'm Popeye the Sailor Man"/The Sandpipers, "Scuffy the Tugboat," 1957 .... **$7.50-$15.00**
Cricket C-124, Captain Paul and his Seafarin' Band, "I'm Popeye the Sailor Man"/"I Wanna Be a Life Guard," 1958 .... **$5.00-$10.00**

LPs

Golden LP56, Popeye The Sailorman and His Friends, 196? .... **$7.50-$15.00**

MARY POPPINS (original motion picture soundtrack):

LPs

Buena Vista BV-4026, mono, gatefold cover, 1964 .... **$6.00-$12.00**
STER-4026, stereo, gatefold cover, 1964 .... **$7.50-$15.00**
STER-5005, stereo, reissue, no gatefold, 1973 .... **$5.00-$10.00**
RCA Victor COP-111, mono, gatefold cover, RCA Record Club edition, 1964 **$7.50-$15.00**
CSO-111, stereo, gatefold cover, RCA Record Club edition, 1964 .... **$10.00-$20.00**

RED RAVEN RECORDS:

78s

Red Raven M-1/M-2, "Tootles the Tug"/"The Little Red Engine," laminated cardboard with metal ring around outer edge, 1951 .... **$20.00-$40.00**
(if above, colored vinyl, no metal ring), 1956 .... **$5.00-$10.00**
M-7/M-8, "Sidewalks of New York"/"Bicycle Built for Two," colored vinyl, 1956 .... **$10.00-$20.00**
M-33/M-34, "Raggedy Ann"/"Raggedy Andy," colored vinyl, 1956 .... **$25.00-$50.00**

Red Raven mirrored topper, fits on center spindle, different styles
(manual changer, carousel with knob on top) .... **$75.00-$125.00**
(automatic changer, carousel with open hole) .... **$100.00-$150.00**

FRED ROGERS/MISTER ROGERS:

LPs

Small World 81053, Josephine the Short Necked Giraffe, 1968 .... **$6.00-$12.00**
Neighborhood MRN-8101, Won't You Be My Neighbor, 197? .... **$4.00-$8.00**
8102, Let's Be Together Today, 197? .... **$4.00-$8.00**
8103, You Are Special, 197? .... **$4.00-$8.00**
8104, A Place of Our Own, 197? .... **$4.00-$8.00**

SESAME STREET:

LPs

Columbia CR 21530, Sesame Street Original Cast, 1970 .... **$4.00-$8.00**
C-30387, The Year of Roosevelt Franklin, 1971 .... **$5.00-$10.00**
22067, My Name is Roosevelt Franklin, 1974 .... **$4.00-$8.00**
25516, A Sesame Street Christmas, 197? .... **$4.00-$8.00**
79007, The Stars Come Out on Sesame Street, 197? .... **$4.00-$8.00**
K-Tel KF 142, Sesame Street 25 Greatest Hits, 1975 .... **$10.00-$20.00**
Sesame Street 22104, Born to Add Rock and Roll, 1984 .... **$5.00-$10.00**

SONG OF THE SOUTH:

78s

Capitol CC-40, Johnny Mercer, "Tales of Uncle Remus," 1947 ... **$35.00-$70.00**

SNOW WHITE AND THE SEVEN DWARFS (original motion picture soundtrack):

RCA Victor J-8, three 78s in picture cover, Seven Dwarfs walking over log, value includes cover, 1937 .... **$125.00-$250.00**
Y-6, three 78s, reissue in envelope with parade of kings and clowns on cover, 1944 .... **$75.00-$150.00**
Y-17, three 78s, reissue in folio, Seven Dwarfs walking over log, 1949 .... **$25.00-$50.00**
Y-33, two 78s in folio, cover shows Snow White dancing, 1949 **$30.00-$60.00**
Decca A-368, four 78s in folio, pink cloudy cover with characters, 1940 .... **$30.00-$60.00**
Disneyland WDL-4005, mono, gatefold cover, 12-inch LP, 1956 .... **$100.00-$200.00**
DO-1201, mono, whirlpool-like designs on cover, 1959 .... **$25.00-$50.00**

It was not unusual for children's television shows to have a special tie-in with a purchasable phonograph record—both to increase the show profits or for the benefit of a charitable or non-profit organization. In the 1950s, TV kiddie shows like "Howdy Doody" *and* "Winky Dink" *isuued records that today are highly collectible both by children's music aficionados and classic TV collectors. Even RCA Victor's trademark dog Nipper was part of a 1950s TV series, as the record company sposored the* "Rootie Kazootie Show.""

***$20**, NM condition*

Photo credit: From the collection of Peter Muldavin

Groucho Marx recorded this children's record, "The Funniest Song in the World," in 1949. The 78-RPM and 45-RPM versions of this song split the five parts of the song over two sides of the record; a 33-1/3 LP version contains all five parts on one side, with the second side featuring four non-Groucho songs.

***$30**, NM condition*

3101, picture disc, 1961 .... **$15.00-$20.00**
1201, reissue of Disneyland WDL-4005 without gatefold, 1968 .... **$12.50-$25.00**
DQ-1201, high-gloss cover with photos on back, 1987 .... **$15.00-$30.00**
Buena Vista 102, three LPs, contains entire movie, available through mail order, 1975 .... **$25.00-$50.00**

TALKING BOOK by EMERSON:

Small 78s attached to picture

Emerson 21145, "I Am Your Uncle Sam," Uncle Sam grommeted to record, 1917 .... **$100.00-$200.00**
21457, "The Tiger," tiger grommeted to record, 1917 .... **$100.00-$200.00**

THE THREE STOOGES:

Mono LPs

Vocalion VL 3823, The Three Stooges Sing for Kids, 196? .... **$10.00-$20.00**

Stereo LPs

Vocalion VL 72823, The Three Stooges Sing for Kids, 196? .... **$12.50-$25.00**
Peter Pan 8098, The Three Stooges, 1970 .... **$12.50-$25.00**

TUBBY THE TUBA:

LPs

Cricket Play Hour Records CR 13, David Wayne Narrates "Tubby The Tuba" and "Adventures Of A Zoo," 1959 .... **$10.00-$20.00**
Disneyland ST-1928, Annette Funicello Narrates "Musical Story of Tubby the Tuba," 1963 .... **$15.00-$30.00**

WILLY WONKA AND THE CHOCOLATE FACTORY (original motion picture soundtrack):

LPs

Paramount PAS-6012, 1971 .... **$20.00-$40.00**
MCA 37124, reissue, 198? .... **$5.00-$10.00**

LORETTA YOUNG:

78s

Decca DA-399, "The Littlest Angel," 1945 .... **$12.50-$25.00**

Chapter 9

Country and Western

History

Country music grew from the small towns and southern farmlands, a mixture of violin or "fiddle songs" and Irish ballads. Today, it is one of the most popular and profitable forms of music, as artists from Garth Brooks to the Dixie Chicks have sold millions of 45s, albums, and CDs. And unlike most other popular music genres, for whom 45s and LPs almost disappeared in the 1990s, country music still continues to manufacture 45s for both the collector's market and for thousands of still-functioning jukeboxes.

The earliest recorded country music were "fiddle songs" from the 1920s. An A&R man from Victor Records, Ralph Peer, set up a portable recording studio in Bristol, Tennessee, and searched the town for new talent for his label. On August 1, 1927, Peer recorded two legends of country music—Jimmie Rodgers and the Carter Family—in a makeshift recording studio in a Bristol barn. From these recordings came the earliest sounds of country music.

With the birth of radio, country music was transported to millions of homes outside of country's rural base. The most popular radio show to feature country music, WSM's *Grand Ole Opry*, is still on the air today, and features every form of country music, from bluegrass to western bop, from contemporary country to old-time country gospel. WSM's first major success, Roy Acuff, was as popular among country music fans as Frank Sinatra was among pop music fans of the time. With hits like "The Great Speckle Bird," "The Precious Jewel," and "The Wabash Cannonball," Acuff performed with the Opry for over 50 years, and later headed a successful music publishing company.

But in the 1940s, the country music that most people

"The Happiest Girl in the Whole U.S.A." was originally turned down by Tanya Tucker, so the songwriter, Donna Fargo, recorded the song herself, and it became an international hit.

***$6**, VG+ condition*

Several department stores offered records as part of a purchasable product line. Victor Records, for example, pressed several recordings by the Carter Family on this collectible Montgomery Ward label.

***$35**, NM condition*

Roy Acuff was an extremely prolific country music artist, and his earliest recordings, including this OKeh 78 of "Wabash Cannon Ball," are not hard to find.

***$7.50**, VG+ condition*

Dusty Owens was part of WWVA's "Jamboree" radio broadcasts when his song "Hello Operator" was released. Because of the strength of the station's signal, which could reach Atlantic Canada on a clear night, country music fans thousands of miles away from the station's West Virginia studios could hear Owens' hit.

***$15**, VG+ condition*

heard came not from the south, but from the west—Hollywood, to be more precise. "Singing Cowboys" like Gene Autry and Roy Rogers starred in successful motion pictures and serials, and always stopped the bandits, kissed the girl, strummed on their guitar and sang "Back in the Saddle Again" or "Don't Fence Me In" or "Happy Trails" as they rode off into the sunset.

Country music benefited from various broadcast media, and radio was especially important to the genre's growth. During the 1930s, it seemed every major city from New York to Los Angeles had a station with a country music

Photo credit: From the collection of Ed Guy.

Before Hank Williams signed with MGM Records, his first sides were for the tiny Sterling label, and near-mint copies of these early titles can range from $500-800 apiece.

***$800**, NM condition*

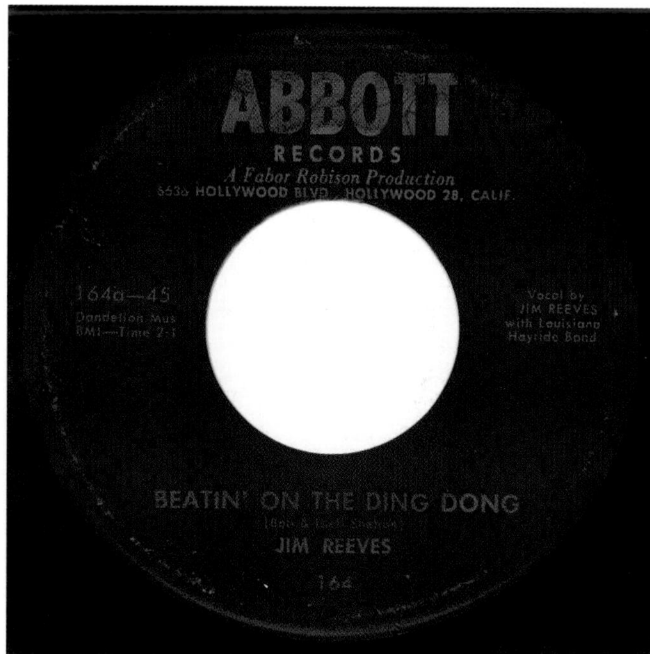

When Jim Reeves signed with RCA Victor, his later recordings, including "Four Walls" and "He'll Have to Go," are in a deeper, perfectly-dictated baritone voice. That's in direct contrast to his early pressings on Abbott Records, where he sang in a high-pitched "hillbilly" voice, with novelty titles like "Bimbo," "Mexican Joe," and "Beatin' on the Ding Dong."

***$20**, VG+ condition*

Three early recordings by country music's most legendary female voices. Loretta Lynn's first three 45s were recorded for Zero Records of Vancouver, B.C., and are extremely rare. Patsy Cline's "Walkin' After Midnight" was one of the last 78s pressed by Decca Records, and is one of her most collectible pressings. Dolly Parton has become one of the most successful and astute country music performers in the world; how ironic is it that her first country hit was called "Dumb Blonde?"

(L to R) ***$400**, NM condition;* ***$100**, NM condition;* ***$10**, NM condition*

variety program. WSM's *Grand Ole Opry,* there were the "Brush Creek Follies" at Kansas City's KMBC; the "Hoosier Hop" at Fort Wayne, Indiana's WOWO; the Wheeling, West Virginia "Saturday Night Jamboree" broadcast live over WWVA; and the "Iowa Barn Dance Frolic" at WHO in Des Moines. There was even a Dinner Bell Roundup broadcast from KXLA in Pasadena, California, as well as a Village Barn Dance broadcast from Greenwich Village in New York City. These radio programs and live simulcasts gave country music artists a chance to promote their records and concert appearances. By the end of the 1930s, there were over 600 daytime and evening country shows nationwide, catering to a combined audience of some 40 million listeners.

After World War II, the most popular country singer—in fact, one of the forefathers of rock and roll—was Hank Williams. From 1949 until the time of his death in 1953, Hank Williams dominated the country charts, with such #1 songs as "Lovesick Blues," "Cold Cold Heart," "Hey Good Lookin'," "Jambalaya (on the Bayou)," and "Your Cheating Heart." His songs were as tortured as his life; his emotive voice wrenched in doubt and sadness over the loves he lost and the ones he never had. At the height of his popularity, Williams made $1,000 a night in front of capacity crowds. But drugs and drink wrecked his marriages and ruined his career, eventually causing his death in 1953.

By the 1960s, a new type of country singer appeared—the "country crooner." With lush orchestrations and soothing background singers, artists like Eddy Arnold, Bill Anderson, and Jim Reeves were able to "cross over" from their traditional country fan base to the pop charts. Surprisingly, Jim Reeves has been able to maintain a presence on the pop music charts for more than 20 years after his death in a 1964 plane crash, thanks to the discovery of over 80 homemade demo recordings.

Female country singers have always been revered by their fans; whether it was the bigger-than-life personae of Dolly Parton, the heartfelt, emotive voice of Patsy Cline, or the down-to-earth success stories of Tammy Wynette and Loretta Lynn, these singers have captured the hearts of generations of their fans. For many female country music fans, these songs spoke to them personally—describing life as a mother or housewife, drawing strength to keep a family together—or summoning the strength to leave when the environment becomes too painful.

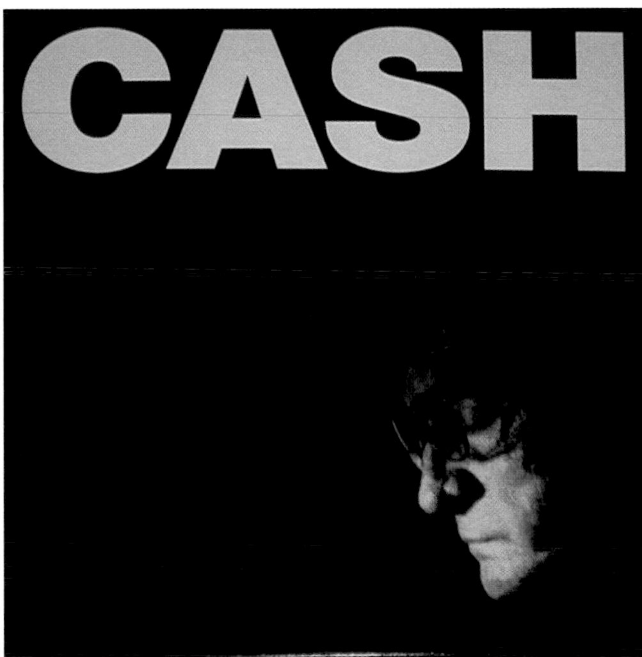

One of the true icons of country music, a rebel long before it was fashionable to be called such, the late Johnny Cash performed and recorded under his own terms. Even in the twilight of his years, Cash's album American IV: The Man Comes Around, *received major acclaim from rock and country music fans alike—and was also released on this double-LP vinyl album package.*

***$30**, NM condition*

While radio shows like the *Grand Ole Opry* helped spread country music throughout the 1920s and 1930s, television shows like *Hee Haw* promoted country music's biggest stars in the 1960s and 1970s. Hosted by country music singers Roy Clark and Buck Owens, *Hee Haw* brought together all facets of country music; every show had at least four musical numbers, two featuring a special "guest artist." And even though the humor was as corny as the Kornfield Kounty location of the show, the program did provide viewers with a reverent and honored approach to popular country music. *Hee Haw* also provided new exposure for established country singers Minnie Pearl, Grandpa Jones, and Archie Campbell.

In the 1970s, some artists broke away from traditional country music and created "outlaw country," or progressive country songs. They embraced new musical genres, and wrote songs incorporating more mature themes of love and loss. Many of these artists included Willie Nelson, Waylon Jennings, Jessi Colter, Merle Haggard, and Johnny Cash.

By the 1990s, as more country artists added music videos to their musical repertoire, the old country establishment was shaken up once more. Garth Brooks marketed his music to both country and rock and roll fans; Shania Twain combined her vocal abilities with her glamorous music videos. And new stars such as LeAnn Rimes, the Dixie Chicks, and Tim McGraw performed on that same *Grand Ole Opry* stage as did Roy Acuff and Eddy Arnold.

What To Look For

Major label country music 45s from the 1970s and 1980s are very easy to find, as are the albums from that same period. Vinyl items that are more difficult to locate are mono LPs from the 1960s, stereo LPs from the 1950s and 10-inch albums from the 1950s.

Many country artists originally had success on the pop charts; country singers Conway Twitty and Sonny James had pop hits in the early days of rock and roll. Because of this, some artists who had their biggest hits in the 1960s may have released a 45 or two in the 1950s. If these records are on small independent labels and received poor distribution upon their initial release, those records have a very high collectible value today.

While record companies abandoned vinyl 45s and LPs in the early 1990s, there have always been 45s for country music artists. Garth Brooks, in fact, has released all his singles on 7-inch vinyl, as have Trisha Yearwood, the Dixie Chicks, Shania Twain, and Alan Jackson. And vinyl LPs for many of these stars also exist—many record and tape clubs continued to make albums long after the major record companies stopped doing so.

Almost all of Garth Brooks' biggest hits—from "Friends in Low Places" to "The Thunder Rolls" to "The Dance"—were pressed on 45s as opposed to cassette singles or CD singles. Brooks' first few albums, including Ropin' the Wind, *were also available on vinyl, if you happened to buy them while a member of the Columbia Record and Tape Club.*

$6, *NM condition*

Shania Twain's hit "I'm Gonna Getcha Good!" was released on this jukebox-only 7-inch single. The A-side features the "country music" version of the song, while the B-side has a remixed "rock and roll" rendition.

$6, *NM condition*

Web Pages

Roughstock's Country Music history page: http://www.roughstock.com/country

The Country Music Association: http://www.cmaworld.com

TCM Radio, a Web site broadcasting traditional country music on the Internet, and hosted by country singer Dusty Owens: http://www.tcmradio.com

Hank Williams, Jr.'s home page: http://www.hankjr.com

Doc Williams' home page, where he chronicles his six decades as a country music performer: http://www.docwilliams.com

A history of the *Grand Ole Opry*, as well as other information, can be found at this site: http://www.grandoleopry.com

Information on *Jamboree USA*, a country music show from Wheeling, West Virginia, broadcast live over radio station WWVA, AM 1170: http://www.jamboreeusa.com

Usenet newsgroups: rec.music.country.old-time, rec.music.country.western, alt.music.country-classic

A discography of the releases of Vernon Dalhart, famous for his 1920s million-seller "The Prisoner's Song": http://www.geocities.com/robtmorca/vernon-dalhart.html

Museums

The Grand Ole Opry Museum, at 2802 Opryland Drive, Nashville, TN, 37214. (615) 889-3060.

Country Music Hall Of Fame® And Museum, A Division Of The Country Music Foundation®, 222 Fifth Avenue South, Nashville, TN, 37203, 1-800-852-6437: http://www.countrymusichalloffame.com

The Alabama Music Hall of Fame, whose honorees include Jimmie Rodgers and Tammy Wynette. U.S. Highway 72 West, Tuscumbia, Alabama. (800) 239-2643.

The International Bluegrass Music Museum, 207 East Second Street, Owensboro, KY, 42303, 1-888-MY-BANJO: http://www.bluegrass-museum.org

Jimmie Rodgers Museum, PO Box 4555, Meridan, MS, 39304, (601) 485-1808: http://www.jimmierodgers.com

Books

Neely, Tim, *Goldmine Country and Western Record Price Guide*, Krause Publications, Iola, WI, 2001.

Mason, Michael, Ed., *The Country Music Book*, Charles Scribner's Sons, New York, NY, 1985.

Osborne, Jerry, *The Official Price Guide to Country Music Records*, House of Collectibles/Ballantine Publishing, NY, 1996.

Whitburn, Joel, *Billboard Top Country Singles 1944-2001*, Record Research, Inc., Menomonee Falls, WI, 2002.

ARTIST VG+ to NM

ALABAMA:

45s

RCA PB-12008, "My Home's in Alabama"/"I Wanna Come Over," 1980 ....**$2.00-$4.00**

(with picture sleeve, add), 1980 ....**$3.00-$6.00**

LPs

Alabama ALA-78-9-01, The Alabama Band, 1978 ....**$200.00-$400.00**

EDDY ARNOLD:

45s

RCA Victor 47-8679, "Make the World Go Away"/"The Easy Way," 1965 ....**$4.00-$8.00**

(with picture sleeve, add), 1965 ....**$7.50-$15.00**

78s

Bluebird 33-0520, "The Cattle Call"/"Each Minute Seems Like A Million Years," 1945 ....**$30.00-$60.00**

LPs

RCA Victor LPM-3753, Lonely Again, mono, 1967 ....**$10.00-$20.00**

LSP-3753, same title, stereo, 1967 ....**$7.50-$15.00**

GENE AUTRY:

78s

Banner 32349, "That Silver Haired Daddy of Mine"/"Mississippi Valley Blues," 1931 ....**$35.00-$70.00**

ELTON BRITT:

78s

Bluebird B-9000, "There's A Star Spangled Banner Waving Somewhere"/"When the Roses Bloom Again," 1942 ....**$15.00-$30.00**

GARTH BROOKS:

45s

Capitol Nashville NR-44701, "The Dance"/"Two of a Kind, Workin' on a Full House," 1991 ....**$3.00-$6.00**

NR-44727, "The Thunder Rolls"/"Victim of the Game," 1991 ....**$3.00-$6.00**

LPs

Capitol Nashville C1-596330, Ropin' the Wind (vinyl available only through Columbia House), 1991 ....**$25.00-$50.00**

ARCHIE CAMPBELL:

LPs

Starday 167, Bedtime Stories for Adults, 1962 ....**$15.00-$30.00**

THE CARTER FAMILY:

78s

"Can the Circle Be Unbroken (By and By)"/"Glory to the Lamb"

(if on Perfect 13155, Oriola 8484, Banner 33465, Romeo 5484, Melotone 13432, or Conqueror 8529, value is equal), 1935 ....**$25.00-$50.00**

(if on Vocalion 03027, reissue), 1937 ....**$20.00-$40.00**

(if on OKeh 03027, reissue), 1940 ....**$15.00-$30.00**

(if on Columbia 37669, reissue), 1947 ....**$10.00-$20.00**

(if on Columbia 20268, reissue), 1948 ....**$10.00-$20.00**

LPs

Acme LP-2, In Memory of A.P. Carter, 1960 ....**$100.00-$200.00**

WILF CARTER:

78s

Bluebird 4966, "My Swiss Moonlight Lullaby"/"The Capture Of Albert Johnson," 1933 ....**$20.00-$40.00**

4600, "My Little Swiss and Me"/"I Long for Old Wyoming," 193?? ....**$15.00-$30.00**

4624, "Old Alberta Plains"/"Won't You Be the Same Old Pal," 193?? ....**$15.00-$30.00**

JOHNNY CASH:

45s

Sun 241, "I Walk The Line"/"Get Rhythm," 1956 ....**$20.00-$40.00**

283, "Ballad of a Teenage Queen"/"Big River," 1958 ....**$12.50-$25.00**

Columbia 42788, "Ring of Fire"/"I'd Still Be There," 1963............$5.00-$10.00
(if "Ring of Fire" is on both sides, red vinyl promo), 1963
....$20.00-$40.00

LPs

Sun SLP-1220, Johnny Cash With His Hot And Blue Guitar (mono), 1956
....$50.00-$100.00

Columbia CS 9827, Johnny Cash at San Quentin, 1969 ....$6.00-$12.00
(if on Columbia CQ 30961, quadraphonic), 1971 ....$10.00-$20.00

American 440 063 336-1, American IV: The Man Comes Around (2 LPs), 2003 ....$15.00-$30.00

ROY CLARK:

45s

Dot 17246, "Yesterday, When I Was Young"/"Just Another Man," 1969
....$2.50-$5.00

LPs

Capitol T 1780, The Lightning Fingers of Roy Clark (mono), 1962
....$10.00-$20.00
(if on Capitol ST 1780, stereo), 1962..$12.50-$25.00

PATSY CLINE:

45s

Decca 30221, "Walkin' After Midnight"/"A Poor Man's Roses (Or a Rich Man's Gold)," 1957 ....$10.00-$20.00
31317, "Crazy"/"Who Can I Count On," 1961 ....$6.00-$12.00

78s

Decca 30221, "Walkin' After Midnight"/"A Poor Man's Roses (Or a Rich Man's Gold)," 1957 ....$50.00-$100.00

LPs

Decca DL 8611, Patsy Cline (mono)
(if first pressing, black label with silver print), 1957................$50.00-$100.00
(if second pressing, black label with color bars), 1960...............$25.00-$50.00

BILLY "CRASH" CRADDOCK:

45s

ABC Dot 17659, "Broken Down in Tiny Pieces"/"Shake It Easy," 1976
....$2.00-$4.00

VERNON DALHART:

Cylinders

Edison 4954, "The Prisoner's Song," 1924...................................$15.00-$30.00

78s

Victor 19427, "The Prisoner's Song"/"Wreck of the Old '97" (A-side recorded for several different record companies), 1924..............................$10.00-$20.00

THE CHARLIE DANIELS BAND:

45s

Epic 50700, "The Devil Went Down To Georgia"/"Rainbow Ride," 1979
....$2.00-$4.00

LPs

Epic JE 35751, Million Mile Reflections, 1979 ....$5.00-$10.00
(if on Epic PE 35751, budget reissue), 198? ....$4.00-$8.00
(if on Mobile Fidelity 1-176, audiophile vinyl), 1984 ....$15.00-$30.00

THE DIXIE CHICKS:

45s

Monument 79352, "Goodbye Earl"/"Cowboy Take Me Away," 2000
....$2.00-$4.00

DAVE DUDLEY:

45s

Golden Wing 3020, "Six Days On The Road"/"I Feel A Cry Coming On" (label later changed name to Golden Ring), 1963..........................$6.00-$12.00

LPs

Golden Ring 110, Six Days on the Road, 1963...........................$25.00-$50.00

DALE EVANS:

78s

Majestic 11025, "Under a Texas Moon"/"His Hat Cost More Than Mine," 194?? ....$10.00-$20.00

THE EVERLY BROTHERS:

45s

Cadence 1315, "Bye Bye Love"/"I Wonder If I Care As Much," 1957
....$12.50-$25.00
1337, "Wake Up Little Susie"/"Maybe Tomorrow," 1957
....$15.00-$30.00
(with picture sleeve, add), 1957...$125.00-$250.00

DONNA FARGO:

LPs

Dot DLP-26000, The Happiest Girl in the Whole U.S.A., 1972
....$6.00-$12.00

LESTER FLATT AND EARL SCRUGGS:

45s

Columbia 21295, "Foggy Mountain Breakdown"/"You're Not a Drop in the Bucket," 1954 ....$10.00-$20.00

78s

Mercury 6247, "Foggy Mountain Breakdown"/"No Mother or Dad," 1950
....$10.00-$20.00

LPs

Columbia CL 1664, Songs of the Famous Carter Family (mono), 1961
....$10.00-$20.00
(if on Columbia CS 8464, stereo), 1961....................................$12.50-$25.00

TENNESSEE ERNIE FORD:

78s

Capitol 15430, "Country Junction"/"Philadelphia Lawyer," 1949 $10.00-$20.00

LEFTY FRIZZELL:

45s

Columbia 20739, "If You've Got The Money I've Got The Time"/"I Love You 1000 Ways," 1950..$20.00-$40.00

MERLE HAGGARD:

45s

Capitol 2626, "Okie from Muskogee"/"If I Had Left It Up To You," 1969
....$4.00-$8.00
(with picture sleeve, add), 1969..$4.00-$8.00

LPs

Capitol ST 638, A Tribute to the Best Damn Fiddle Player in the World (Or, My Salute to Bob Wills), 1970 ....$12.50-$25.00
(if on Capitol SN-16279, budget reissue), 1982..........................$4.00-$8.00

EMMYLOU HARRIS:

45s

Jubilee 5679, "I'll Be Your Baby Tonight"/"I'll Never Fall In Love Again," 1969
....$10.00-$20.00

HAWKSHAW HAWKINS:

45s

King 5712, "Lonesome 7-7203"/"Everything Has Changed," 1963
....$7.50-$15.00

HIGHWAY 101:

45s

Warner Bros. 27867, "Just Say Yes"/"I'll Be Missing You," 1988......$1.75-$3.00
(with picture sleeve, add), 1988..$2.00-$4.00

HOMER AND JETHRO:

LPs

RCA Victor LPM-1560, The Worst of Homer and Jethro (RCA Victor LPM-1560), 1958 ....$25.00-$50.00

FERLIN HUSKY:

45s

Capitol 4406, "Wings of a Dove"/"Next to Jimmy," 1960.............$6.00-$12.00

LPs

Capitol T 1280, Ferlin's Favorites (mono)
(if black label with rainbow perimeter, Capitol logo at left), 1960
....$20.00-$40.00
(if black label with rainbow perimeter, Capitol logo at top), 1962
....$12.50-$25.00

RED INGLE:

78s

Capitol 15045, "Cigareetes, Whuskey and Wild, Wild Women"/"Party Maude," 1948 ....$7.50-$15.00

WAYLON JENNINGS:

45s

Ramco 1997, "My World"/"Another Blue Day," 1968 ....$6.00-$12.00

RCA PB-10924, "Luckenbach, Texas (Back to the Basics of Love)"/"Belle of the Ball," 1977...$2.50-$5.00

CORKY JONES:

45s

Dixie 505, "Hot Dog"/"Rhythm and Booze" (later became Buck Owens), 1956
$200.00-$400.00

GEORGE JONES:

45s

Starday 202, "Why Baby Why"/"Season Of My Heart," 1955 ....$25.00-$50.00

Mercury 71406, "White Lightning"/"Long Time To Forget," 1959
....$7.50-$15.00

Epic 02526, "Still Doin' Time"/"Good Ones and Bad Ones," 1981
....$1.50-$3.00

LPs

Starday SLP-101, The Grand Ole Opry's New Star (mono), 1958 ....**$600.00-$1,200.00**

Mercury MG-20477, George Jones Sings White Lightning And Other Favorites (mono), 1959 ....**$75.00-$150.00**

GRANDPA JONES:

45s

Decca 30823, "The All-American Boy"/"Pickin' Time," 1959......**$10.00-$20.00**

78s

King 624, "Mountain Dew"/"My Darling's Not My Darling Anymore," 1947 ....**$12.50-$25.00**

LPs

King 554, Grandpa Jones Sings His Biggest Hits, 1958 ....**$50.00-$100.00**

BRENDA LEE:

45s

Decca 31309, "Fool #1"/"Anybody But Me," 1961....................**$7.50-$15.00**

JERRY LEE LEWIS:

45s

Smash 2186, "What's Made Milwaukee Famous (Has Made A Loser Out Of Me)"/"All the Good Is Gone," 1968....................**$5.00-$10.00**

LPs

Mercury SR-61366, Who's Gonna Play This Old Piano ... (Think About It Darlin'), 1972 ....**$7.50-$15.00**

LONZO AND OSCAR:

78s

RCA Victor 20-2563, "I'm My Own Grandpa"/"You Blacked My Blue Eyes Once Too Often," 1947....................**$12.50-$25.00**

LULU BELLE & SCOTTY:

78s

Melotone 6-06-53, "The Farmer's Daughter"/"Madam, I've Come to Marry You," 1936 ....**$12.50-$25.00**

LORETTA LYNN:

45s

Zero 107, "I'm A Honky Tonk Girl"/"Whispering Sea," 1960 ....**$250.00-$500.00**

112, "The Darkest Day"/"Gonna Pack My Troubles," 1961 ....**$200.00-$400.00**

Decca 32045, "Don't Come Home A-Drinkin' (With Lovin' On Your Mind)"/"A Saint To A Sinner," 1966....................**$5.00-$10.00**

MCA 52219, "Lyin', Cheatin', Woman Chasin', Honky Tonkin', Whiskey Drinkin' You"/"Star Light, Star Bright," 1983 ....**$2.00-$4.00**

LPs

Decca DL 75084, Your Squaw Is On The Warpath

(if first pressing, includes song "Barney"), 1969 ....**$20.00-$40.00**

(if second pressing, "Barney" is deleted), 1969 ....**$12.50-$25.00**

BARBARA MANDRELL:

LPs

ABC Dot DOSD-2067, Midnight Angel, 1976....................**$6.00-$12.00**

CLYDE McCOY:

78s

King 706, "Carolina Waltz"/"Red Roses Tied in Blue," 1948.......**$10.00-$20.00**

ROGER MILLER:

45s

Mercury 71212, "Poor Little John"/"My Fellow," 1957 ....**$12.50-$25.00**

Smash 1965, "King of the Road"/"Atta Boy Girl," 1965 ....**$6.00-$12.00**

LPs

Smash MGS-27049, Roger and Out (mono), 1964....................**$7.50-$15.00**

(if retitled "Dang Me/Chug-a-Lug," with the same catalog number), 196? ....**$6.00-$12.00**

Smash SRS-67049, Roger and Out (stereo), 1964....................**$10.00-$20.00**

(if retitled "Dang Me/Chug-a-Lug," with the same catalog number), 196? ....**$7.50-$15.00**

RONNIE MILSAP:

45s

Scepter 12127, "A Thousand Miles From Nowhere"/"When It Comes To My Baby," 1966....................**$6.00-$12.00**

RCA Victor PB-10976, "It Was Almost Like A Song"/"It Don't Hurt To Dream," 1977 ....**$2.00-$4.00**

Virgin 58853, "Time, Love and Money"/"Livin' on Love," 2000 ....**$1.50-$3.00**

LPs

RCA Victor APL1-0846, A Legend In My Time, 1975 ....**$7.50-$15.00**

(if on RCA Victor APD1-0846, quadraphonic), 1975 ....**$10.00-$20.00**

MONTANA SLIM:

78s

Bluebird B-6515, "My Swiss Moonlight Lullaby"/"Midnight, the Unconquered Outlaw," 1936 ....**$15.00-$30.00**

LPs

RCA Camden CAL-527, Wilf Carter/Montana Slim, 1958.......**$20.00-$40.00**

WILLIE NELSON:

45s

Belaire 107, "Night Life"/"Rainy Day Blues," 1963 ....**$15.00-$30.00**

(if pressed on colored vinyl), 1963....................**$30.00-$60.00**

Sarg 260, "A Storm Has Just Begun"/"When I Sing My Last Hillbilly Song," 196?....................**$25.00-$50.00**

Columbia 10176, "Blue Eyes Cryin' in the Rain"/"Bandera," 1975 ..**$2.50-$5.00**

LPs

Columbia PC 34482, Red Headed Stranger, 1975....................**$7.50-$15.00**

(if back cover has UPC bar code, reissue), 1979....................**$4.00-$8.00**

(if on Columbia HC 43482, half-speed mastered pressing), 1982 ....**$20.00-$40.00**

THE OAK RIDGE BOYS:

45s

Warner Bros. 5359, "This Ole House"/"Early in the Morning," 1963 ....**$10.00-$20.00**

MCA 51084, "Elvira"/"A Woman Like You," 1981....................**$2.00-$4.00**

BUCK OWENS:

45s

Capitol 5336, "I've Got A Tiger by the Tail"/"Cryin' Time," 1965 ....**$5.00-$10.00**

(with picture sleeve, add), 1965 ....**$7.50-$15.00**

LPs

Labrea 1017, Buck Owens (mono), 1961....................**$50.00-$100.00**

(if on Labrea 8017, stereo), 1961 ....**$75.00-$150.00**

BUCK OWENS AND RINGO STARR:

45s

Capitol B-44409, "Act Naturally"/"The Key's in the Mailbox," 1989 ....**$5.00-$10.00**

DUSTY OWENS:

45s

Columbia 4-21202, "Hello Operator"/"The Life You Want to Live," 1954 ....**$12.50-$25.00**

BRAD PAISLEY:

45s

Arista Nashville 13156, "Who Need Pictures"/"It Never Woulda Worked Out Anyway," 1999....................**$2.00-$4.00**

69152, "I'm Gonna Miss Her"/"I Wish You'd Stay," 2002 ....**$2.00-$4.00**

DOLLY PARTON:

45s

Gold Band 1086, "Puppy Love"/"Girl Left Alone," 1959........**$300.00-$600.00**

Monument 982, "Dumb Blonde"/"The Giving and the Taking," 1967 ....**$5.00-$10.00**

RCA Victor APBO-0145, "Jolene"/"You're So Beautiful Tonight," 1973 ....**$2.50-$5.00**

LPs

RCA Victor LPM-3949, Just Because I'm A Woman (mono), 1968 ....**$50.00-$100.00**

(if on RCA Victor LSP-3949, stereo, black label), 1968............**$15.00-$30.00**

(if on RCA Victor LSP-3949, stereo, orange label), 1968..........**$10.00-$20.00**

JOHNNY PAYCHECK:

45s

Epic 8-50469, "Take This Job And Shove It"/"Colorado Kool-Aid," 1977 ....**$4.00-$8.00**

WEBB PIERCE:

45s

Decca 9-28091, "That Heart Belongs To Me"/"So Used To Loving You," 1952 ....**$12.50-$25.00**

RAY PRICE:

45s

Columbia 21510, "Crazy Arms"/"You Done Me Wrong," 1956 ....**$7.50-$15.00**

45178, "For The Good Times"/"Grazin' in Greener Pastures," 1970 ....**$3.00-$6.00**

LPs

Columbia C 301016, For The Good Times, 1970....................**$6.00-$12.00**

(if on Columbia CQ 30106, quadraphonic), 1972 ....**$10.00-$20.00**

CHARLEY PRIDE:

45s

"Kiss An Angel Good Mornin'"/"No One Could Ever Take Me From You," 1971 .... **$3.00-$6.00**

JIM REEVES:

45s

Abbott 148, "Bimbo"/"Gypsy Heart," 1953 .... **$12.50-$25.00**
(if on red vinyl), 1953 .... **$30.00-$60.00**
RCA Victor 47-6625, "Bimbo"/"Penny Candy," 1956 .... **$10.00-$20.00**

LPs

Abbot LP-5001, Jim Reeves Sings (mono), 1956 .... **$1,500.00-$2,000.00**
RCA Victor LPM-1410, Bimbo (reissue of Abbott LP), 1957 .... **$100.00-$200.00**

LeANN RIMES:

45s

Curb 76959, "Blue"/"The Light In Your Eyes," 1996 .... **$2.00-$4.00**

TEX RITTER:

45s

Capitol 4567, "I Dreamed of a Hill-Billy Heaven"/"The Wind and the Tree," 1961 .... **$6.00-$12.00**

78s

Capitol 40114, "Deck of Cards"/"Rounded Up in Glory," 1948 .... **$10.00-$20.00**

CARSON ROBISON:

78s

Columbia 15548-D, "Ohio Prison Fire"/"Why Are the Young Folks So Thoughtless?," 1930 .... **$12.50-$25.00**
Clarion 5109-C, "Oklahoma Charley"/"Red River Valley," 1931 .... **$15.00-$30.00**

JIMMIE RODGERS:

78s

Victor 23574, "Moonlight and Skies"/"Jimmie Rodgers Visits the Carter Family," 1931 .... **$35.00-$70.00**
24456, "Blue Yodel No. 12"/"The Cowhand's Last Ride," 1933 .... **$125.00-$250.00**
(if on Victor 18-6000, picture disc), 1935 .... **$750.00-$1,500.00**

ROY ROGERS:

45s

RCA Victor 0008, "Don't Fence Me In"/"Roll On Texas Moon" (green vinyl), 1949 .... **$20.00-$40.00**

ARTHUR "GUITAR BOOGIE" SMITH:

78s

MGM 10229, "Banjo Boogie"/"Have a Little Fun," 1948 .... **$10.00-$20.00**
10441, "Cracker Boogie"/"One Little, Two Little, Three Little Times," 1949 .... **$10.00-$20.00**

HANK SNOW:

LPs

RCA Victor LPM-3471, Heartbreak Trail (mono), 1966 .... **$12.50-$25.00**
(if on RCA Victor LSP-3471, stereo), 1966 .... **$15.00-$30.00**

THE SONS OF THE PIONEERS:

45s

RCA Victor WBY-25, "Ballad of Davy Crockett"/"The Graveyard Filler of the West," 1955 .... **$15.00-$30.00**
(with picture sleeve, add), 1955 .... **$25.00-$50.00**

78s

Decca 5047, "Tumbling Tumbleweeds"/"Moonlight on the Prairie," 1934 .... **$15.00-$30.00**
5939, "Cool Water"/"So Long to the Red River Valley," 1941 .... **$12.50-$25.00**

LPs

RCA Victor LPM-2118, Cool Water (mono), 1960 .... **$12.50-$25.00**
(if on RCA Victor LSP-2118, stereo), 1960 .... **$15.00-$30.00**

SHANIA TWAIN:

45s

Mercury 856-488-7, "Whose Bed Have Your Boots Been Under?"/"Any Man of Mine," 1995 .... **$5.00-$10.00**
088 172 272, "I'm Gonna Getcha Good!" (2 versions), 2001 .... **$3.00-$6.00**

ERNEST TUBB:

78s

Bluebird B-6693, "The Passing of Jimmie Rodgers"/"Last Thoughts of Jimmie Rodgers," 1936 .... **$250.00-$500.00**
B-7000, "Since That Black Cat Crossed My Path"/"T.B. is Whipping Me," 1938 .... **$125.00-$250.00**
Decca 46144, "Have You Ever Been Lonely? (Have You Ever Been Blue)"/"Let's Say Goodbye Like We Said Hello," 1948 .... **$10.00-$20.00**

TANYA TUCKER:

45s

Columbia 45991, "Would You Lay With Me (In A Field Of Stone)"/"No Man's Land," 1974 .... **$2.50-$5.00**

LPs

Columbia KC 31742, Delta Dawn, 1972 .... **$7.50-$15.00**
(if on Columbia PC 31742, budget reissue), 198? .... **$4.00-$8.00**

PORTER WAGONER:

45s

RCA Victor 47-5086, "Takin' Chances"/"I Can't Live With You," 1952 .... **$15.00-$30.00**

LPs

RCA Victor LPM-2706, Y'all Come, 1963 .... **$12.50-$25.00**
(if on RCA Victor LSP-2650, stereo), 1963 .... **$15.00-$30.00**

THE WILBURN BROTHERS:

45s

Decca 30591, "Oo Bop Sha Boom"/"My Baby Ain't My Baby No More," 1958 .... **$15.00-$30.00**
31764, "I Had One Too Many"/"Left Out," 1965 .... **$5.00-$10.00**

LPs

Decca DL 4721, The Wilburn Brothers Show (mono), 1966 .... **$30.00-$60.00**
(if on Decca DL 74721, stereo, both records feature Loretta Lynn and Ernest Tubb), 1966 .... **$40.00-$80.00**

WILD COUNTRY:

LPs

LSI 0177, Deuces Wild (group later became Alabama), 1977 .... **$600.00-$1,200.00**

DOC WILLIAMS AND THE BORDER RIDERS:

78s

Wheeling 1001, "Beyond the Sunset"/"Bright Red Horizon" (exists with both red and blue labels, value is equal), 1949 .... **$20.00-$40.00**

HANK WILLIAMS:

45s

MGM 8010, "Lonesome Blues"/"Never Again," 1949 .... **$30.00-$60.00**
(if on MGM 10352, reissue), 1950 .... **$20.00-$40.00**
11000, "Hey, Good Lookin'"/"My Heart Would Know," 1951 .... **$15.00-$30.00**
11416, "Kaw-Liga"/"Your Cheatin' Heart," 1953 .... **$15.00-$30.00**

78s

Sterling 201, "Calling You"/"Never Again (Will I Knock On Your Door)," 1946 .... **$400.00-$800.00**
MGM 10171, "Honky Tonkin'"/"I'll Be a Bachelor Till I Die," 1948 .... **$25.00-$50.00**

LPs

MGM E-168, Moanin' the Blues (10-inch LP), 1952 .... **$200.00-$400.00**
(if on MGM E-3330, 12-inch LP, yellow label), 1956 .... **$50.00-$100.00**
(if on MGM E-3330, 12-inch LP, black label), 1960 .... **$20.00-$40.00**
MGM PRO-912, Reflections of Those Who Loved Him (3 LPs) (promo-only box set), 1975 .... **$125.00-$250.00**

HANK WILLIAMS, JR.:

45s

Elektra 47191, "All My Rowdy Friends (Have Settled Down)"/"Everytime I Hear That Song," 1981 .... **$2.50-$5.00**
Warner Bros. 29184, "All My Rowdy Friends Are Coming Over Tonight"/"Video Blues," 1984 .... **$2.00-$4.00**

LPs

MGM M3G-4988, Bocephus, 1974 .... **$6.00-$12.00**

TAMMY WYNETTE:

45s

Epic 10398, "Stand By Your Man"/"I Stayed Long Enough," 1968 .... **$5.00-$10.00**

LPs

Epic LN 24305, Your Good Girl's Gonna Go Bad (mono), 1967 .... **$15.00-$30.00**
(if on Epic BN 26305, stereo), 1967 .... **$10.00-$20.00**

TRISHA YEARWOOD:

45s

MCA 54076, "She's In Love With The Boy"/"Victim of the Game" (MCA 54076), 1991 .... **$4.00-$8.00**

DWIGHT YOAKAM:

LPs

Oak OR 2356, Guitars, Cadillacs, etc., etc. (six song EP, does not contain title track, black and white cover), 1984 .... **$400.00-$800.00**
Reprise 25372, Guitars, Cadillacs, etc., etc. (10-song LP, color cover), 1986 .... **$5.00-$10.00**

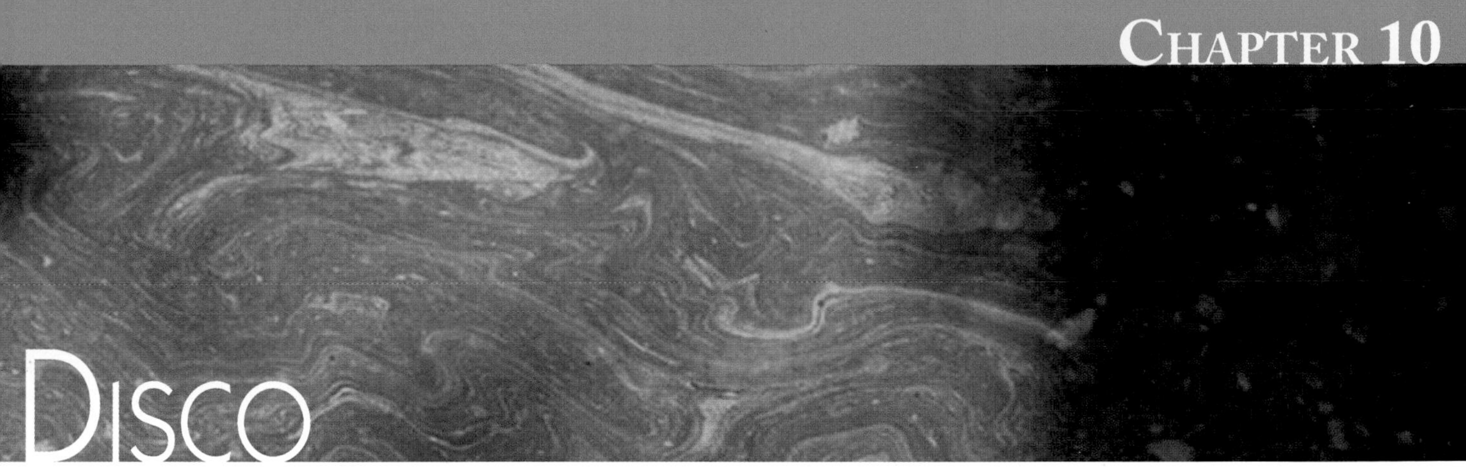

Chapter 10

Disco

History

The 1970s were the years of disco. It was the most successful dance music since the "Twist" records of the early 1960s—a studio orchestra draped over a syncopated 4/4 beat, with lyrical topics ranging from steamy sex to goofy double entendre.

This new music originally came from dance clubs, or "discotheques," in the early 1970s. Club DJs would play a mixture of funk music, salsa and popular dance songs, keeping the beat hot and the dance floor packed. The patrons boogied to James Brown's "Sex Machine," Eddie Kendricks' "Girl, You Need a Change of Mind," and Manu DiBango's "Soul Makossa," dancing to music at a time when AM stations were playing bubblegum music, and FM stations were hooked on album-oriented rock.

Disco music broke into the mainstream in 1974, as groups like Harold Melvin and the Blue Notes, MFSB and the O'Jays brought a new sound to the clubs—a pulsing beat, combined with a full orchestra and soulful lyrics, and extended mixes that seem to last as long as there was recording tape in the studio. Whether it was slow jams like Silver Convention's "Fly, Robin, Fly," or hot Florida salsa rhythms like K.C. and the Sunshine Band's "Get Down Tonight," or tease-me disco songs like Donna Summer's "Love To Love You Baby," or even funk-based disco like Parliament's "Tear The Roof Off The Sucker," disco was now a dominant force in 1970s music.

From Donna Summer's first song, where she purred "Love To Love You Baby" to a sultry beat, and throughout

Debbie Harry peers from the label of Blondie's 12-inch extended version of the hit "Heart of Glass."

***$15**, NM condition*

The title track for Donna Summer's "Love To Love You Baby" is over 16 minutes long, and takes up the entire first side of the LP.

***$8**, VG+ condition*

A promotional copy of Gloria Gaynor's "I Will Survive," which lasted eight minutes. Not every extended disco remix of the 1970s was available in stores; some were only provided to radio stations or mobile DJs.

***$7.50**, VG condition*

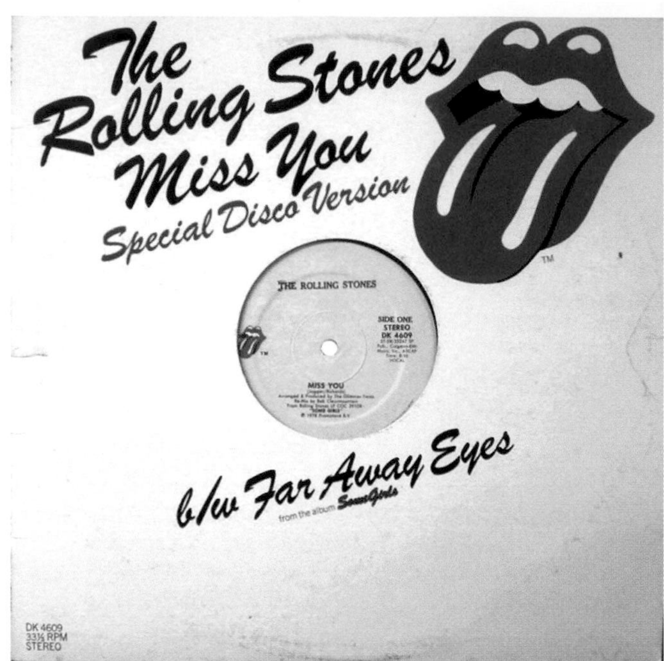

The disco movement was so popular in the late 1970s that almost every popular artist of the time released at least one disco record—including the Rolling Stones, as this "disco remix" version of their song "Miss You" shows.

***$6**, VG+ condition*

the disco music era, Summer was a multiplatinum performer whose every dance track was a "must-hear" in discos. Songs like "Hot Stuff," "Bad Girls," "On the Radio," and "I Feel Love" were not only disco smashes, they were also early successful forays into techno-pop and social commentary.

Disco also popularized a new recording format—the 12-inch disc. Also known as a "maxi-single" or "disco disc," 12-inch discs allowed club DJs to play extended versions of popular dance songs of the day. While Santa Esmerelda's version of the Animals' "Don't Let Me Be Misunderstood" only clocked in at 3:48 on radio, the 12-inch version was extended to over 20 minutes. Club DJs would memorize such minutiae as a song's beats per minute and musical key, then by using two turntables and an electronic cross-fader, they would synchronize the end of one disco song to the beginning of another, matching the beats and tempo in a seamless segue.

By 1978, the biggest-selling album of the year was the soundtrack to a film about the disco life, *Saturday Night Fever*. Among the many artists featured on this album were the Bee Gees, who had changed their image from syrupy balladeers to disco legends. And if the Bee Gees could do it, well so could—and did—the Rolling Stones ("Miss You"), the Kinks ("Wish I Could Fly Like Superman"), and Rod Stewart ("Da Ya Think I'm Sexy").

Late '70s disco music also featured thumping bass beats, and is probably one of the few musical styles (surf instrumental being another) where the bass guitarist has as much of a prominent role as a guitarist or pianist. Two perfect examples of bass-heavy disco include A Taste of Honey's "Boogie Oogie Oogie," and a million-selling disco groove called "Le Freak."

Chic, the group behind "Le Freak," parlayed the success of that song into a string of dance club/disco classics, including "Good Times" and "I Want Your Love." Two of the members of Chic, Nile Rodgers and Bernard Edwards, expanded upon their disco beginnings, becoming successful producers and songwriters for other artists. And one of Chic's classic tracks, "Good Times," became the soundtrack for early rap records like the Sugarhill Gang's "Rapper's Delight."

Donna Summer's home label, Casablanca, arguably had the biggest disco vocal group on its roster, the Village People. A six-man vocal group from New York City, the Village People would perform on stage dressed as construction workers, policemen, even an American Indian with full feathered headdress. Their songs "Macho Man," "In The Navy," and "Y.M.C.A." were huge radio hits, and while the Village People may have looked like cartoon characters to some people, to others the group's costumes and song lyrics reflected homosexual stereotypes in New York's Greenwich Village.

Eventually every group that recorded a song that made people dance were grouped into disco music, even if their sound came from another genre. One such group was K.C. and the Sunshine Band, who are grouped into the disco category simply because their music made people get up and shake their booties. The band's two main songwriters, Harry Wayne Casey and Richard Finch, produced other artists for TK Records, including "Rock Your Baby," a #1 pop and disco hit for George McCrae. When Casey and Finch formed the Sunshine Band, their earliest funk songs, "Queen of Clubs" and "Sound Your Funky Horn," became hits in England, and paved the way for American chart-topping hits like "That's The Way (I Like It)" and "I'm Your Boogie Man."

In 1979, disco music began its descent into oblivion. The music itself was now considered a suitable beat for children's music, as albums like "Sesame Street Fever" and "Mickey Mouse Disco" appeared in stores. Other forms of music, such as punk, new wave and arena rock, began to dominate the airwaves, taking away disco's radio base. Some radio stations stopped playing disco records, advertising their stations as "Bee Gee Free." In fact, much of the blame for disco's demise can be laid at the feet of record companies. In the late 1970s, record companies could press millions of copies of an artist's debut single, send them to stores—and if the stores didn't sell all the records, they could be returned for credit.

But what happened to all those 12-inch discs? Many of them clogged cutout bins for years. And if record collectors in 1979 didn't like disco, they would show their contempt to anybody who would listen. During a baseball doubleheader in Chicago, fans were asked to bring their disco records to the stadium for use in "Disco Demolition Night." After the first game of the doubleheader, thousands of disco records were strewn all over Comiskey Park—and blown up. (The second game of the doubleheader had to be forfeited because the field was now as unplayable as the chunks of vinyl littering the grass and base paths.)

The last remaining profitable disco labels were small independent companies like Prelude Records in New York City. Prelude's biggest disco group, "D" Train, may have been just the duo of Hubert Eaves III and James "D Train" Williams, but their keyboard-influenced disco-funk sound replicated what originally took a full orchestra to produce.

Even though disco was considered a "four-letter" word by music elitists, disco-themed songs still continued to fill dance floors and cross over to the pop charts. Many of these early 1980s disco songs were classified as "Hi-NRG"

Atlantic Records used a yellow label for their extended dance remixes, as opposed to their usual black-red artwork styles. In fact, this version of Chic's "Le Freak" isn't much longer or shorter than the group's original 7-inch 45 hit.

***$20**, NM condition*

Although K.C. and the Sunshine Band's recordings were more salsa than disco, it didn't stop the group from topping the charts with "That's The Way (I Like It)" and "Get Down Tonight," while rocking the floors with dance hits like "Sound Your Funky Horn," "Blow Your Whistle," and "Queen of Clubs."

***$3**, VG condition*

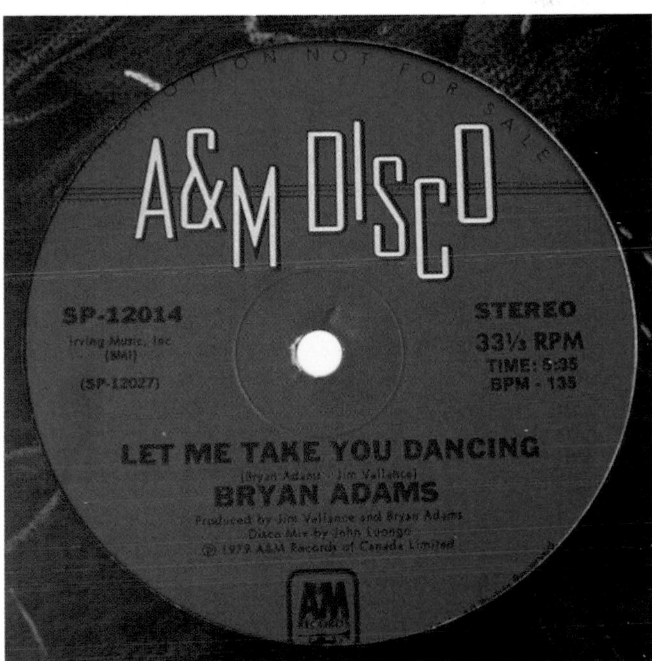

Bryan Adams' first solo record was this disco hit, "Let Me Take You Dancing," a song that remixer John Luongo turned from a simple rock song into a full-blown disco track. Despite its success, the song has never been reissued on any Bryan Adams CD.

***$30**, NM condition*

("high-energy") songs, and contained female vocalists cooing about the availability of male suitors. The biggest disco/dance songs of this era included Miquel Brown's "So Many Men, So Little Time" and the Weather Girls' "It's Raining Men."

The "disco sound" would sporadically appear over the next few years, but people were quick to call the new discs "dance records," trying to avoid the five-letter word as much as possible. Even when the band U2 recorded a song called "Discotheque," employed 1970s dance rhythms, and even dressed up in the music video as the Village People, the record itself was considered a poor seller for the band.

Taana Gardner's dance hit "Heartbeat" was later sampled by rapper Imi Kamoze as the song "Here Comes the Hotstepper."

***$8**, VG condition*

As the duo D Train, James "D-Train" Williams and Hubert Eaves III had a string of disco and dance hits, their biggest one being the classic "You're The One For Me." Notice that this Prelude 12-inch pressing says "45 RPM," making the record compatible with European 12-inch dance records, which also spun at 45 RPM.

***$15**, VG+ condition*

What To Look For

With the 1970s currently experiencing a kitschy revival period, people are hunting for original disco records once again. Disco 45s and LPs have very little collectible value (many titles are barely worth $10 with both vinyl and picture sleeve in near-mint condition), but 12-inch disco discs are especially prized. 12-inch discs often contained extended mixes that were not available on LP, and are currently not available on any CD reissue. Be aware that many 12-inch discs may contain "cue burn," caused when a disc jockey backspins a record to its beginning notes and holds it with his fingers, while the turntable spins underneath. Once the DJ releases his fingers on the vinyl, the record spins almost exactly to the beat (called "slip-cueing"). But since records weren't designed for a needle to travel anticlockwise on the groove, you may hear a slight hissing before the song's intro. That's cue burn.

Many of the original disco labels, such as TK, RSO, and Casablanca, no longer exist. Records may still be pressed with those company names on the label; in these cases, the trademark may have been licensed by another company, so double-check the fine print around the label's perimeter to see if the record is a first pressing or a reissue. Because

This France Joli jacket came with two identical records inside, to allow club DJs to "mix" the records together, creating new sounds and extending the action on the dance floor.

***$10**, Good condition*

disco music was only around for a few years, the colorful 12-inch company sleeves often remained consistent throughout disco's reign, with only an advertising sticker marking the difference between two artists using the same label. Company sleeves should be crisp and even; 12-inch covers are often subjected to seam splitting, heavy ringwear, and even magic marker graffiti (usually from a DJ scribbling beats-per-minute or personal information on the jacket).

Another rare and lesser-known disco item is the remix disc. Some DJs subscribed to companies like Rockpool, Disconet, and Ultimix, who would send them records filled with unique remixes of hot dance tracks. Although the companies specifically requested that their remix discs not be resold, some titles still surface today on the secondary collectors' market.

Books

Dannon, Frederic, *Hit Men: Power Brokers and Fast Money Inside The Music Business*, Vintage Books, New York, 1991.

Jones, Alan; Jussi, Kantonen, *Saturday Night Forever: The Story of Disco*, Mainstream Publishing, Great Britain, 1999.

Web Pages

Andrea Izzotti's 70s dance/disco page: http://www.70disco.com

Another fantastic disco page, this one from Sweden: http://www.disco-disco.com

A Casablanca Records discography: http://www.kissfaq.com/casa/

A page dedicated to the most famous disco of them all, New York's Studio 54: http://www.geocities.com/westhollywood/heights/5939

Vicki Sue Robinson's biggest hit "Turn The Beat Around" exists in an extended version on her album. The song first became a hit in England's "Northern Soul" dance clubs, and the buzz spread back to the states, where the track eventually hit #1 on the pop charts.

$8, VG condition

The bass line in A Taste of Honey's "Boogie Oogie Oogie" came from an instrumental jam session. The song later hit #1, and helped win the disco group a Grammy® award as Best New Artist.

With sleeve, $4, Good condition

ARTIST VG+ to NM

BRYAN ADAMS:

12-inch Singles

A&M SP-12014, "Let Me Take You Dancing"/(instrumental), 1979 ..... **$15.00-$30.00**

B.T. EXPRESS:

45s

Scepter 12395, "Do It (Till You're Satisfied)"/(long version), 1974 .. **$2.50-$5.00**

Roadshow 7001, "Express"/"Express" (long version), 1975 ..... **$2.00-$4.00**

12-inch Singles

Roadshow 233, "Can't Stop Groovin' Now, Wanna Do It Some More" (stereo)/(mono), 1976 ..... **$25.00-$50.00**

LPs

Roadshow 41001, Non-Stop, 1975 ..... **$6.00-$12.00**

CLAUDJA BARRY:

45s

Chrysalis 2313, "Boogie Woogie Dancin' Shoes"/"Love of the Hurtin' Kind," 1979 ..... **$2.50-$5.00**

12-inch Singles

Chrysalis CDS 2316, "Boogie Woogie Dancin' Shoes"/"Love of the Hurtin' Kind," 1979 ..... **$7.50-$15.00**

CDS 2389, "You Make Me Feel the Fire"/"Everybody Needs Love," 1980 ..... **$5.00-$10.00**

LPs

Chrysalis CHR 1232, Boogie Woogie Dancin' Shoes, 1979 .... **$6.00-$12.00**

THE BLACKBYRDS:

45s

736, "Walking in Rhythm"/"The Baby," 1975 .... **$2.00-$4.00**

LPs

Fantasy F-9472, Flying Start, 1974.......... **$7.50-$15.00**

(if on FPM-4004, quadraphonic), 1975 .... **$12.50-$25.00**

BLONDIE:

45s

Chrysalis 2295, "Heart of Glass"/"11:59," 1979 .... **$2.00-$4.00**

(with picture sleeve, add), 1979 .... **$2.00-$4.00**

12-inch Singles

CDS-2275, "Heart of Glass"/(instrumental), 1979 .... **$7.50-$15.00**

BOHANNON:

12-inch Singles

Mercury DS 2001, "Bohannon Disco Symphony"/"Andrea," 1977 .... **$7.50-$15.00**

Phase II AS 857, "Throw Down the Groove" (Pt. 1)/(Pt. 2), 1980 .... **$6.00-$12.00**

LPs

Dakar 6910, Keep On Dancing, 1973 .... **$6.00-$12.00**

76916, Insides Out, 1974 .... **$6.00-$12.00**

Mercury SRM-1-1159, Phase II, 1977 .... **$5.00-$10.00**

BRASS CONSTRUCTION:

12-inch Singles

United Artists SP-190, "Get Up"/"Starting Tomorrow," 1978 .... **$10.00-$20.00**

LPs

United Artists UA-LA545-G, Brass Construction, 1976 .... **$5.00-$10.00**

UA-LA677-G, Brass Construction II, 1976.......... **$5.00-$10.00**

LT-1060, Brass Construction 6, 1980 .... **$6.00-$12.00**

BRICK:

45s

Bang 727, "Dazz"/"Southern Sunset," 1976 .... **$2.50-$5.00**

LPs

Bang BLP-408, Good High (reproductions exist, beware of newly sealed copies), 1976.......... **$6.00-$12.00**

BLP-409, Brick, 1977 .... **$6.00-$12.00**

ALICIA BRIDGES:

45s

Polydor 14483, "I Love the Nightlife (Disco 'Round)"/"Self-Applause," 1978 .... **$2.00-$4.00**

12-inch Singles

Polydor PDD 503, "I Love the Nightlife (Disco 'Round)"/"City Rhythm," 1978 .... **$5.00-$10.00**

PR-12-6851, "I Love the Nightlife" (four versions, black vinyl), 1994 .... **$5.00-$10.00**

853705-1, "I Love the Nightlife" (four versions, pink vinyl), 1994 .... **$6.00-$12.00**

MARILYN CHAMBERS:

45s

Roulette 7206, "Benihana" (short)/(long), 1977 .... **$15.00-$30.00**

CHIC:

12-inch Singles

Atlantic DKSO 101, "Dance, Dance, Dance (Yowah, Yowsah, Yowsah)" (2 versions), 1977.......... **$10.00-$20.00**

DSKO 131, "Le Freak"/"Savoir Faire," picture disc, 1978.......... **$20.00-$40.00**

DK 4700, "Le Freak"/"Savoir Faire," 1978.......... **$10.00-$20.00**

LPs

Atlantic SD 19153, Chic, 1977 .... **$4.00-$8.00**

SD 19209, C'est Chic, 1978.......... **$4.00-$8.00**

SD 16011, Les Plus Grands Succes de Chic—Chic's Greatest Hits, 1979 .... **$4.00-$8.00**

CROWN HEIGHTS AFFAIR:

45s

De-Lite 1570, "Dreaming a Dream" (Pt. 1)/(Pt. 2), 1975.......... **$2.00-$4.00**

912, "Dance Lady Dance"/"Come Fly With Me," 1979.......... **$2.00-$4.00**

12-inch Singles

De-Lite DDS 582, "Do It the French Way"/"Sexy Ways," 1977 .... **$20.00-$40.00**

DDS 588, "Dancin'"/"Love Me," 1977 .... **$20.00-$40.00**

RICK DEES AND HIS CAST OF IDIOTS:

45s

RSO 857, "Disco Duck" (Pt. 1)/(Pt. 2), 1976 .... **$2.00-$4.00**

CARL DOUGLAS:

45s

20th Century 2140, "Kung Fu Fighting"/"Gamblin' Man," 1974 .... **$2.00-$4.00**

LPs

20th Century T-464, Kung Fu Fighting and Other Great Love Songs, 1974 .... **$6.00-$12.00**

CAROL DOUGLAS:

45s

Midland International MB-10113, "Doctor's Orders"/"Baby, Don't Let This Good Love Die," 1974 .... **$2.00-$4.00**

MB-10229, "Hurricane is Coming Tonight"/"I Fell In Love With You," 1975 .... **$2.00-$4.00**

12-inch Singles

Midsong International 13905, "Night Fever"/"You Come Into My Life," 1978 .... **$6.00-$12.00**

THE EMOTIONS:

45s

Columbia 3-10347, "Best of My Love"/"A Feeling Is," 1977.......... **$2.50-$5.00**

LPs

Columbia PC 34163, Flowers (reissues have bar code on the cover, deduct 10% from price if your copy has one), 1976 .... **$5.00-$10.00**

MARVIN GAYE:

45s

Tamla 54280, "Got To Give It Up (Pt. 1)"/(Pt. 2), 1977 .... **$2.00-$4.00**

(with picture sleeve, add), 1977 .... **$5.00-$10.00**

LPs

Tamla T7-352, Marvin Gaye Live at the London Palladium, 2 LPs, 1977 .... **$7.50-$15.00**

GLORIA GAYNOR:

45s

MGM 14748, "Never Can Say Goodbye"/"We Can Just Make It," 1974 .... **$2.00-$4.00**

Polydor 14508, "I Will Survive"/"Substitute," 1978 .... **$2.00-$4.00**

12-inch Singles

Polydor PD-D-512, "I Will Survive" (both sides), 1978 .... **$5.00-$10.00**

Silver Blue 220, "I Am What I Am (from "La Cage Aux Folles")/(dub mix), 1983 .... **$4.00-$8.00**

DARYL HALL AND JOHN OATES:

12-inch Singles

RCA PD-12358, "I Can't Go For That (No Can Do)"/"Unguarded Minute," 1981 .... **$6.00-$12.00**

PD-13428, "One on One (Club Mix)"/"I Can't Go For That (No Can Do)," 1983.......... **$6.00-$12.00**

HERBIE HANCOCK:

45s

Columbia 04054, "Rockit" (2 versions), 1983.......... **$2.50-$5.00**

12-inch Singles

Columbia 03978, "Rockit" (2 versions), 1983.......... **$5.00-$10.00**

04200, "Autodrive"/"Chameleon," 1983.......... **$3.00-$6.00**

04960, "Mega-Mix" (2 versions), 1984.......... **$4.00-$8.00**

HEATWAVE:

12-inch Singles

Epic 28-50371, "Boogie Nights"/"Too Hot to Handle," 1977 .... **$20.00-$20.00**

28-50541, "The Groove Line"/"Always and Forever," 1978 .... **$10.00-$20.00**

LPs

Epic PE 34761, Too Hot to Handle, first pressings with orange labels, 1977 .... **$5.00-$10.00**

JE 35260, Central Heating, 1978.......... **$5.00-$10.00**

HOT CHOCOLATE:

45s

Big Tree 16038, "Disco Queen"/"Makin' Music," 1975 .... **$2.50-$5.00**

16047, "You Sexy Thing"/"Amazing Skin Song," 1975 .... **$2.50-$5.00**

Infinity 50002, "Every 1's A Winner"/"Power of Love," 1978 .... **$2.00-$4.00**

LPs

Big Tree BT 89512, Hot Chocolate, 1975 .... **$5.00-$10.00**

Infinity INF-9002, Every 1's A Winner, 1978 .... **$5.00-$10.00**

THELMA HOUSTON:

45s

Tamla 54278, "Don't Leave Me This Way"/"Today Will Soon Be Yesterday," 1977 .... **$2.00-$4.00**

12-inch Singles

Motown 00053, "Ride to the Rainbow"/"Love Machine," 1979 ...... **$4.00-$8.00**

LPs

Tamla T7-358R1, The Devil In Me, 1977 .... **$5.00-$10.00**

THE INTRUDERS:

45s

Philadelphia International 3624, "I'll Always Love My Mama" (Pt. 1)/(Pt. 2), 1975 .... **$2.50-$5.00**

THE JACKSONS:

12-inch Singles

Epic ASD 523, "Blame it on the Boogie" (same on both sides), 1978 .... **$35.00-$70.00**

AS 551, "Shake Your Body (Down to the Ground)"/"Things I Do For You," 1978 .... **$15.00-$30.00**

28-50271, "Shake Your Body (Down to the Ground) (European Version)"/"That's What You Get (For Being Polite)," 1978 .... **$10.00-$20.00**

LPs

Epic PE 34229, The Jacksons (original pressings with orange labels), 1976 .... **$5.00-$10.00**

JE 34835, Goin' Places (original pressings with orange labels), 1977 .... **$5.00-$10.00**

K.C. AND THE SUNSHINE BAND:

45s

TK 1001, "Blow Your Whistle"/"I'm Going to Do Something Good To You," 1973 .... **$2.50-$5.00**

1009, "Get Down Tonight"/"You Don't Know," 1975 .... **$2.00-$4.00**

1015, "That's The Way (I Like It)"/"What Makes You Happy," 1975 .... **$2.00-$4.00**

1023, "Keep It Comin' Love"/"Baby I Love You," 1977 .... **$2.00-$4.00**

(with picture sleeve, add), 1977 .... **$2.50-$5.00**

12-inch Singles

Sunshine Sound 207, "Do You Wanna Go Party" (2 versions), 1979 .... **$4.00-$8.00**

LPs

TK 500, Do It Good, 1974 .... **$6.00-$12.00**

503, KC and the Sunshine Band, 1975 .... **$5.00-$10.00**

612, Greatest Hits, 1980 .... **$5.00-$10.00**

EDDIE KENDRICKS:

45s

Tamla 54230, "Girl, You Need A Change of Mind" (Pt. 1)/(Pt. 2), 1973 .... **$2.50-$5.00**

EVELYN "CHAMPAGNE" KING:

45s

RCA PB-11122, "Shame"/"Dancin', Dancin', Dancin'," 1977 .... **$2.50-$5.00**

PB-13273, "Love Come Down"/(instrumental), 1982 .... **$2.00-$4.00**

LIPPS, INC.:

45s

Casablanca 2233, "Funkytown"/"All Night Dancing," 1980 .... **$2.50-$5.00**

12-inch Singles

Casablanca 20207, "Funkytown" (single-sided), 1980 .... **$10.00-$20.00**

THE LOVE UNLIMITED ORCHESTRA:

45s

20th Century 2069, "Love's Theme"/"Sweet Moments," 1973 .... **$2.50-$5.00**

LPs

20th Century T-433, Rhapsody in White, 1974 .... **$5.00-$10.00**

CHERYL LYNN:

45s

Columbia 3-10808, "Got To Be Real"/"Come In From the Rain" (A-side 3:42), 1978 .... **$3.00-$6.00**

(if A-side of above is 5:10), 1978 .... **$2.50-$5.00**

3-10907, "Star Love"/"You're the One," 1979 .... **$2.50-$5.00**

12-inch Singles

Columbia 23-10869, "Got To Be Real"/"Star Love," 1978 .... **$7.50-$15.00**

LPs

Columbia JC 35486, Cheryl Lynn, 1978 .... **$5.00-$10.00**

VAN McCOY AND THE SOUL CITY SYMPHONY:

45s

Avco 4653, "The Hustle"/"Hey Girl, Come and Get It," 1975 .... **$2.00-$4.00**

12-inch Singles

H&L 2002, "Rhythms of the World"/"Soul Cha Cha"/"That's The Joint," 1976 .... **$10.00-$20.00**

LPs

Avco AV-69002, Love is the Answer, 1974 .... **$5.00-$10.00**

AV-69006, Disco Baby, 1975 .... **$5.00-$10.00**

GEORGE McCRAE:

45s

TK 1004, "Rock Your Baby" (Pt. 1)/(Pt. 2), 1974 .... **$2.50-$5.00**

12-inch Singles

TK 22, "Love in Motion"/"Givin' Back the Feeling," 1977 .... **$6.00-$12.00**

62, "Kiss Me (The Way I Like It)" (2 versions), 1977 .... **$6.00-$12.00**

LPs

TK 501, Rock Your Baby, 1974 .... **$5.00-$10.00**

GWEN McCRAE:

45s

Cat 1996, "Rockin' Chair"/"It Keeps On Raining," 1975 .... **$2.50-$5.00**

LPs

Cat 2603, Gwen McCrae, 1974 .... **$5.00-$10.00**

2605, Rockin' Chair, 1975 .... **$5.00-$10.00**

McFADDEN AND WHITEHEAD:

45s

Philadelphia International 3681, "Ain't No Stoppin' Us Now"/"I Got the Love," 1979 .... **$2.00-$4.00**

12-inch Singles

Philadelphia International 7365, "Ain't No Stoppin' Us Now"/"I Got the Love," 1979 .... **$6.00-$12.00**

HAROLD MELVIN AND THE BLUE NOTES:

45s

Philadelphia International 3533, "The Love I Lost" (Pt. 1)/(Pt. 2), 1973 .... **$2.50-$5.00**

3562, "Bad Luck" (Pt. 1)/(Pt. 2), 1975 .... **$2.50-$5.00**

LPs

Philadelphia International KZ 31648, Harold Melvin and the Blue Notes, 1972 .... **$6.00-$12.00**

PZ 34232, Collector's Item—All Their Greatest Hits!, 1976 .... **$6.00-$12.00**

THE MIRACLES:

45s

Tamla 54262, "Love Machine" (Pt. 1)/(Pt. 2), 1975 .... **$2.50-$5.00**

LPs

Tamla T6-339, City of Angels, 1975 .... **$6.00-$12.00**

WALTER MURPHY AND THE BIG APPLE BAND:

45s

Private Stock 45073, "A Fifth of Beethoven"/"California Strut," 1976 .... **$2.00-$4.00**

THE O'JAYS:

45s

Philadelphia International 3524, "Love Train"/"Who Am I," 1973 . **$2.50-$5.00**

3577, "I Love Music" (Pt. 1)/(Pt. 2), 1975 .... **$2.50-$5.00**

12-inch Singles

Philadelphia International 4Z8-3708, "Sing a Happy Song"/"Get On Out and Party," 1979 .... **$7.50-$15.00**

4Z8-3713, "I Love Music"/"Livin' For the Weekend," 1979 ...... **$12.50-$25.00**

LPs

Philadelphia International PZ 33807, no UPC code on back cover, 1975 .... **$5.00-$10.00**

PZ 34245, Message in the Music, 1976 .... **$5.00-$10.00**

ODYSSEY:

45s

RCA PB-11129, "Native New Yorker"/"Ever Lovin' Sam," 1977 .... **$2.00-$4.00**

12-inch Singles

RCA PD-11063, "Native New Yorker"/"Easy Come, Easy Go"/"Hold De Mota Down," 1977 .... **$10.00-$20.00**

PD-13341, "Together"/"Native New Yorker," 1982 .... **$5.00-$10.00**

LPs

RCA Victor APL1-2204, Odyssey, 1977 .... **$5.00-$10.00**

BONNIE POINTER:

45s

Motown 1451, "Free Me From My Freedom—Tie Me To A Tree (Handcuff Me)"/(instrumental)

(if on black vinyl), 1978 .... **$2.00-$4.00**

(if on red vinyl), 1978 .... **$4.00-$8.00**

(with picture sleeve, add), 1978 .... **$3.00-$6.00**

1459, "Heaven Must Have Sent You"/(instrumental), 1979 ....**$2.00-$4.00**

12-inch Singles

Motown M00020-D1, "Heaven Must Have Sent You" (2 versions), 1979 ....**$5.00-$10.00**

LPs

Motown M7-911R1, Bonnie Pointer, 1978 ....**$6.00-$12.00**

M7-929M1, Bonnie Pointer (same title, different album), 1979 ....**$5.00-$10.00**

LOU RAWLS:

45s

Philadelphia International 3592, "You'll Never Find Another Love Like Mine"/"Let's Fall in Love All Over Again," 1976 ....**$2.50-$5.00**

LPs

Philadelphia International PZ 33957, All Things In Time (first editions without UPC code on cover), 1976 ....**$5.00-$10.00**

THE RITCHIE FAMILY:

45s

20th Century 2218, "Brazil"/"Hot Trip," 1975 ....**$2.00-$4.00**

Marlin 3306, "The Best Disco in Town" (Pt. 1)/(Pt. 2), 1976 ....**$2.00-$4.00**

12-inch Singles

Casablanca NBD 20192, "Put Your Feet to the Beat"/"Bad Reputation," 1979 ....**$7.50-$15.00**

VICKI SUE ROBINSON:

45s

RCA PB-10562, "Turn the Beat Around"/"Lack of Respect," 1976 ....**$2.50-$5.00**

12-inch Singles

RCA PC-1507, "Turn the Beat Around"/"Hold Tight," 1979 ....**$6.00-$12.00**

LPs

RCA Victor APL1-1829, Vicki Sue Robinson, 1977 ....**$6.00-$12.00**

THE ROLLING STONES:

12-inch Singles

Rolling Stones DK 4609, "Miss You"/"Far Away Eyes"
(with standard Atlantic-Atco sleeve), 1978 ....**$5.00-$10.00**
(with custom Rolling Stones sleeve), 1978 ....**$6.00-$12.00**

THE SALSOUL ORCHESTRA:

45s

Salsoul 2002, "Salsoul Hustle" (Pt. 1)/(Pt. 2), 1975 ....**$2.50-$5.00**

2004, "Tangerine"/"Salsoul Hustle," 1975 ....**$2.50-$5.00**

12-inch Singles

Salsoul 358, "Deck the Halls"/"The Salsoul Christmas Suite," 1981 ....**$6.00-$12.00**

LPs

Salsoul SZS 5502, Nice 'n' Naasty, 1976 ....**$5.00-$10.00**

SHALAMAR:

45s

Soul Train SB-10885, "Uptown Festival" (Pt. 1)/(Pt. 2), 1977 ....**$2.50-$5.00**

Solar YB-11709, "The Second Time Around"/"Leave It All Up To Love," 1979 ....**$2.00-$4.00**

LPs

Soul Train BVL1-2289, Uptown Festival, 1977 ....**$7.50-$15.00**

Disco spawned dozens of one-hit wonders, including schoolteacher-turned-pop star Anita Ward, whose song "Ring My Bell" was a pop smash in 1979. There are two label variations on this record on Juana—a dark purplish label and this rarer white label with producer Frederick Knight's logo at the 3:00 position.

$5, NM condition

SILVER CONVENTION:

45s

Midland International MB-10339, "Fly Robin Fly"/"Chains of Love"
(if "Fly Robin Fly" is over 4 minutes long, matrix number 10339-A), 1975 ....**$3.00-$6.00**
(if "Fly Robin Fly" is 3:05 minutes long, matrix number 10339-Z), 1975 ....**$2.00-$4.00**

LPs

Midland International BKL1-1369, Silver Convention, 1976 ....**$5.00-$10.00**
(if on Midsong International BXL1-1369, reissue), 1978 ....**$4.00-$8.00**

ROD STEWART:

45s

Warner Bros. 8724, "Da Ya Think I'm Sexy?"/"Scarred and Scared," 1978 ....**$2.00-$4.00**
(with picture sleeve, add), 1978 ....**$2.50-$5.00**

DONNA SUMMER:

45s

Oasis 401 A/B, "Love to Love You Baby"/"Need-A-Man Blues" (A-side has different mix than the hit we know), 1975 ....**$6.00-$12.00**

401 AA/BB, "Love to Love You Baby" (2 versions), 1975 ....**$3.00-$6.00**

Casablanca 884, "Can't We Just Sit Down (And Talk It Over)"/"I Feel Love," 1977 ....**$3.00-$6.00**

884, "I Feel Love"/"Can't We Just Sit Down {And Talk It Over)"}"I Feel Love" listed as A-side), 1977 ....**$2.50-$5.00**

926, "Last Dance"/"With Your Love," 1978 ....**$2.00-$4.00**

12-inch Singles

Casablanca NBLP 7041, "Love to Love You Baby"/"Try Me, I Know We Can Make It," 1976 ....**$10.00-$20.00**

NBD-20104, "I Feel Love"/"Theme From The Deep (Deep, Down Inside)" (both songs on side 1, side 2 blank), 1977 ....**$10.00-$20.00**

NBD-20167, "Hot Stuff"/"Bad Girls" (both songs on side 1, side 2 blank), 1979 ....**$7.50-$15.00**

LPs

Oasis OCLP 5003, Love to Love You Baby (add 50% if poster included), 1975 ....**$6.00-$12.00**

Casablanca NBLP 7078, Once Upon a Time... (2 LPs), 1977 ....**$6.00-$12.00**

NBLP 7150, Bad Girls (2 LPs), 1979 ....**$6.00-$12.00**

NBLP 7191, On the Radio—Greatest Hits Vols. 1 and 2 (2 LPs), 1989 ....**$6.00-$12.00**

A TASTE OF HONEY:

45s

Capitol 4565, "Boogie Oogie Oogie"/"World Spin," 1978 ....**$2.00-$4.00**
(with picture sleeve, add), 1978 ....**$2.50-$5.00**

LPs

Capitol ST-11754, A Taste of Honey, 1978 ....**$5.00-$10.00**

THE TRAMMPS:

45s

Atlantic 3306, "That's Where the Happy People Go" (2 versions), 1975 ....**$2.50-$5.00**

3389, "Disco Inferno"/"You Touch My Hot Line," 1977 ....**$3.00-$6.00**
(with picture sleeve, add), 1977 ....**$4.00-$8.00**
(if B-side is "That's Where the Happy People Go"), 1978 ....**$2.50-$5.00**

LPs

Atlantic SD 18172, Where the Happy People Go, 1976 ....**$5.00-$10.00**

SD 19194, The Best of the Trammps, 1978 ....**$5.00-$10.00**

VILLAGE PEOPLE:

45s

Casablanca 922, "Macho Man"/"Key West," 1978 ....**$2.50-$5.00**

945, "Y.M.C.A."/"The Women," 1978 ....**$2.50-$5.00**

973, "In the Navy"/"Manhattan Woman," 1979 ....**$2.50-$5.00**
(with promo-only picture sleeve, add), 1979 ....**$10.00-$20.00**

LPs

Casablanca NBLP-7064, Village People, 1977 ....**$5.00-$10.00**

NBLP-7183, Live and Sleazy (2 LPs), 1979 ....**$6.00-$12.00**

BARRY WHITE:

45s

20th Century 2018, "I'm Gonna Love You Just a Little More Baby"/"Just a Little More Baby," 1973 ....**$2.50-$5.00**

2120, "Can't Get Enough of Your Love, Babe"/"Just Not Enough," 1974 ....**$2.50-$5.00**

2350, "It's Ecstasy When You Lay Down Next To Me"/"I Never Thought I'd Fall In Love With You," 1977 ....**$2.50-$5.00**

LPs

20th Century T-493, Barry White's Greatest Hits, 1975 ....**$5.00-$10.00**

Chapter 11

Doo-Wop

History

Doo-wop groups and music achieved their greatest popularity during the early years of rock and roll, from 1954 to 1963, and the doo-wop sound can still be heard in some of today's hits. Early doo-wop began in the 1950s, when high school friends would sing in assemblies and glee clubs by day, but at night, under the luminescent warmth of a street lamp, singers would blend their voices together, snapping their fingers for a drumbeat.

The earliest doo-wop groups were R&B acts from the 1950s, many of whom were influenced by the intricate harmonies of gospel choirs. Groups like the Ravens, the Orioles, the Dominoes, and the Crows had hits on the R&B charts, and made some inroads into the pop music field before their songs were "covered" by white vocal groups and artists. But by the mid-1950s, both white and black vocal harmony groups co-existed on the pop charts, all unified in doo-wop music.

The characteristics of doo-wop records include vocal harmony of three to seven singers, with vocal parts ranging from falsetto to bass. The lyrics are easy to hear and to understand—except maybe the nonsense syllables scatted throughout the verses, refrains, and bridges. Hundreds of doo-wop groups in major cities were offered record contracts and promises of fame and fortune. Many of these groups performed on rock and roll package tours, and groups like Dion and the Belmonts, Frankie Lymon and the Teenagers, the Moonglows, and the Del-Vikings found stardom. Other groups, such as the Platters, the Coasters,

Although the Medallions' song "The Letter" was not a major hit, it did contain this famous lyric, in which lead singer Vernon Green discusses "the pompitous of love." That lyric was later referenced by Steve Miller in his song "The Joker," and also became the subject of a motion picture, The Pompatus of Love.

***$30**, Good condition*

Photo credit: From the collection of Rodney Branham.

The success of the Del Vikings' hit "Come Go With Me" spurred Luniverse Records to release this album of early Del Vikings recordings, including an early version of "Come Go With Me."

***$500**, NM condition*

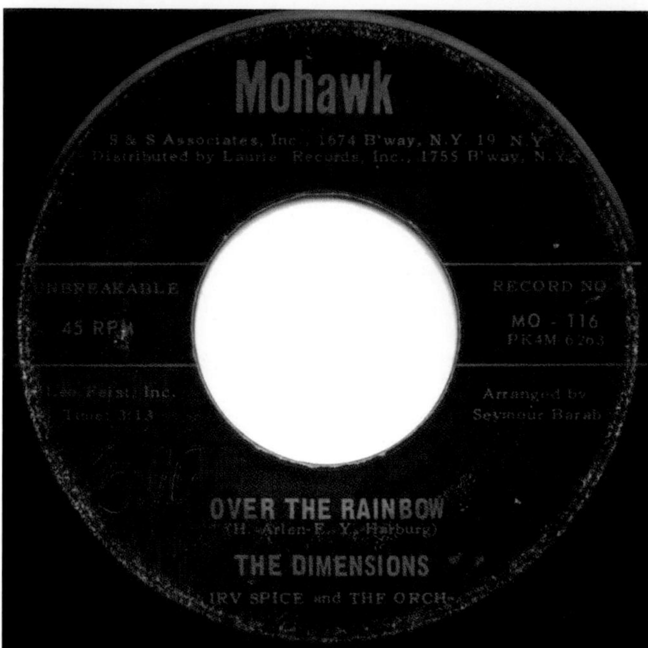

While other groups used "Over the Rainbow" to prove their vocalistic prowess, the Demensions actually turned their doo-wop version into a Top 40 hit. The record company, however, misprinted the group's name on this 45 as "The Dimensions."

***$4**, Fair*

The Diamonds took "Little Darlin'" to the top of the pop charts, but their rendition was a "cover version" originally recorded by Maurice Williams and the Gladiolas, on this hard-to-find 45.

***$60**, VG+ condition*

the Drifters, and the Four Seasons, rose from doo-wop backgrounds to offer their full vocal harmonies to the tapestry of rock and roll.

Doo-wop in the 1950s was an urban sound—its greatest popularity came from the groups in New York, Los Angeles, Philadelphia, Boston, and Pittsburgh, the men who sang on street corners, and the women who sang at assemblies and social functions. In these major cities, the music of the Jive Five, the Harptones, Lee Andrews and the Hearts, the Marcels, and the Chords survived and thrived. Legend has it that if two doo-wop groups ever met each other on the street corner, the groups might challenge each other to a musical duel, endeavoring to discover who could attach better harmonies to "Sunday Kind of Love" or "Somewhere Over the Rainbow," each group fiercely guarding their vocal territories as if they were streets of gold.

Interest in doo-wop groups and the music they sang has been augmented by the release of successful nostalgia films like *American Graffiti, The Five Heartbeats, Why do Fools Fall in Love, Looking for an Echo,* and *American Hot Wax*, as well as the Broadway show *Forever Plaid.* Today, thanks to successful CD box sets of classic and rare doo-wop music from labels like Rhino and Collectibles, fans are discovering—many for the first time—some of the most intricate vocal harmonies of the rock era.

Since the most popular doo-wop hits were pressed on millions of 45s and 78s, their value has not significantly risen. As a point of reference, the most common doo-wop records are the ones most often heard on oldies stations today. But for some doo-wop songs, especially those tracks that were not hits upon their original release, or those containing performances by early incarnations of doo-wop groups, collectors may spend thousands of dollars searching for near-mint copies of these extremely rare recordings.

Many doo-wop groups of the 1950s only recorded a couple of songs, not enough tracks for an album. But for those who did have enough material and time to record an album, these 12-inch LPs, with their low print runs, are very hard to find and are extremely collectible today. In the 1950s, the single release—either on 45 or on 78—was the most popular musical format; an album was recorded only so that a record company could cash in on the single's success.

One of the rarest doo-wop records in history is the Five Sharps' 1952 doo-wop song "Stormy Weather." The song begins with thunderstorm sound effects and a mournful piano intro, an aural concept that preceded Phil Spector's "wall of sound" work by a decade. The Sharps sang "Stormy Weather" in a slow, emotional yet impassioned manner, a classic doo-wop rendition of its time. Unfortunately, very few people have ever heard the song—the master tape for this song was lost years ago, and less than half a dozen copies of this song exist in 78 RPM format—and of those, one known copy is cracked (and sold in 2003 to a private collector for $19,000). Although theoretically a 45 should exist of the original "Stormy Weather," as Jubilee Records was pressing 45s of Sonny Til and the Orioles at that time, no legitimate 45s featuring that original pressing have surfaced in nearly 50 years. If a legitimate 45 of "Stormy Weather" ever appeared, the selling price could rival the rarest Elvis Presley or Beatles record.

Photo credit: From the collection of Kurt Nauck.

"Stormy Weather" by the Five Sharps, the Holy Grail of doo-wop record collecting. Although only four voices are heard on the record, the fifth "Sharp" is the group's pianist.

***$20,000**, VG condition*

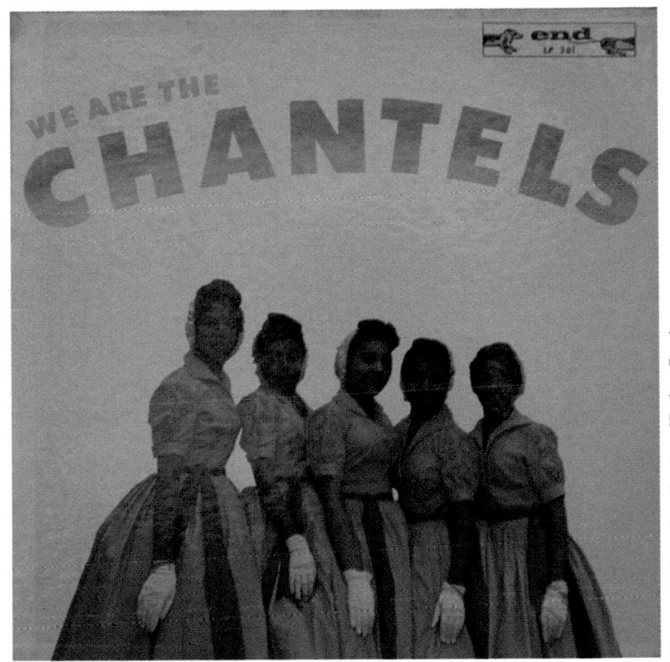

Photo credit: From the collection of Rodney Branham.

Arlene Smith and the Chantels recorded this LP after the success of their song "Maybe." The album appeared with two distinct cover variations—this one seen here is the first, and features the vocal quintet on the cover. Later pressings show two teenagers hunched over a jukebox.

***$1,500**, NM condition*

Photo credit: From the collection of Val Shively.

This 45 of "Stormy Weather" is actually a re-recording of the song, as performed by a different group of Five Sharps. The B-side is different, as well—the original version had the song "Sleepy Cowboy," while this 45s B-side is "Mammy Jammy."

***$12**, NM condition*

One of the early progenitors of doo-wop and jump blues, the "5" Royales recorded this highly collectible album on the Apollo label, before leaving for King Records in the early 1950s.

*With purple inner label, **$4,000** NM condition*

What To Look For

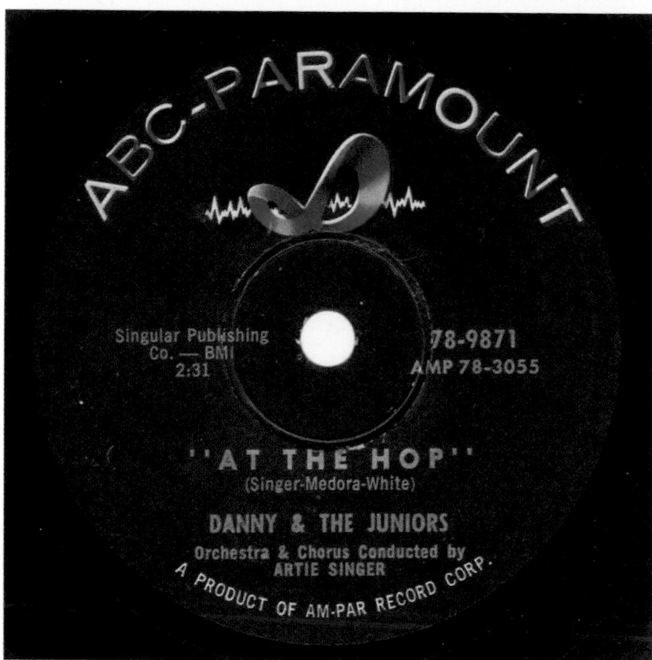

While Danny and the Juniors' 45s of "At the Hop" and "Rock and Roll is Here to Stay" are very easy to find, their late-issue 78s of those same titles can sell for hundreds of dollars.

***$120**, NM condition*

When they took the stage as an opening act at the Apollo Theater, Benjamin Nelson and the Crowns were an up-and-coming doo-wop group. Later that evening, they were signed by George Treadwell to become Ben E. King and the Drifters. This 45, recorded before they became the Drifters, is hard to find today.

***$40**, VG+ condition*

For doo-wop collectors, the most desirous recordings are songs that were pressed on small independent labels with poor distribution. Many doo-wop groups had their first release on a regional label, then were later picked up by a major label. Because of the low print runs by most independent labels, doo-wop pressings on these labels is much more desirable to collectors, even though both the minor and major labels may contain the exact same song.

Since the popularity of doo-wop music coincided with the rise of 45s and decline of 78s as a popular format, most collectors will look for a doo-wop group on 45 rather than 78, but will purchase a 78 if the song was never pressed on a 45. Doo-wop music existed during the last years of 78-RPM discs, and their value varies proportionately. Although doo-wop 78s garner a lesser price than the same song on a 45, things changed after 1958, when the major labels stopped offering 78s for sale. Some smaller labels continued pressing 78s, and in fact those late 1950s 10-inch artifacts are actually worth more than the simultaneous 45 recordings.

Although there are doo-wop collectors across North America, there are more doo-wop collectors in major metropolitan cities like New York, Boston, Los Angeles, Philadelphia, Baltimore, and Pittsburgh, partially because doo-wop was born on the street corners of these cities. In fact, more than any other musical genre, the collectible value of doo-wop records can vary from city to city—many doo-wop groups can command a higher price in their hometown.

Because of their high collectible value, some of the rarest doo-wop 45s have been bootlegged. Copies of the Five Keys' "Red Sails in the Sunset," the Royals' "Starting From Tonight," and the Clovers' "Yes Sir That's My Baby" exist both as legitimate pressings and as cheap bootlegs. Make sure you are working with a reputable dealer who is willing to offer a money-back guarantee if you are not satisfied with the record's authenticity.

By the same token, some record companies have re-issued classic 45s, many of whom have been "enhanced" (electronic stereo, additional instruments, even re-recorded vocals). The Penguins' "Earth Angel" exists in two versions—the first version with the Penguins' harmonies against a subdued musical background (on Dootone 348, B-side is "Hey Senorita"); the second version with the music almost drowning out the Penguins (on Mercury 70943, B-side is "Ice"). Doo-wop collectors often want the first version of any doo-wop record, and may acquire the second version only to complete a collection.

Books

Gribin, Dr. Anthony J.; and Dr. Matthew M. Schiff, *Doo Wop: The Forgotten Third of Rock and Roll*, Krause Publications, Iola, WI, 1992, ISBN: 0-87341-197-8.

Gribin, Dr. Anthony J.; and Dr. Matthew M. Schiff, *The Complete Book of Doo-Wop*, Krause Publications, Iola, WI, 2000, ISBN: 0-87341-829-8.

Groia, Phil, *They All Sang On The Corner*, Phillie Dee Enterprises, New Rochelle, NY, 1983.

Propes, Steve, *Those Oldies But Goodies: A Guide To 50s Record Collecting*, The MacMillan Company, New York, 1973.

Shannon, Bob; John Javna, *Behind the Hits: Inside Stories of Classic Pop and Rock and Roll*, Warner Books, New York, NY 1986. ISBN: 0-446-38171-3.

Web Pages

The Vocal Group Harmony Web site: http://www.vocal-harmony.com

The Platters' Web site: http://www.theplatters.com

Primarily A Cappella, a site dedicated to instrument-less vocalists and groups: http://www.singers.com

The Wanderer, the "First Oldies Site on the Net," has sections devoted to rare doo-wop and to other 1950s and 1960s music. http://www.wanderers.com/wanderer

Museums

The Vocal Group Hall of Fame and Museum, 98 East State Street, Sharon, PA 16146. 1-800-753-1648. http://www.vocalhalloffame.com

ARTIST — VG+ to NM

THE ANGELS:

45s

Caprice 107, "'Til"/"A Moment Ago," 1961 ... **$10.00-$20.00**

Smash 1834, "My Boyfriend's Back"/"(Leave Me) Now," 1963 ... **$8.00-$16.00**

1854, "I Adore Him"/"Thank You and Goodnight," 1963 ... **$7.50-$15.00**

(with picture sleeve, add), 1963 ... **$20.00-$40.00**

Mono **LPs**

Caprice LP 1001, ... And the Angels Sing, 1962 ... **$60.00-$120.00**

Smash MGS-27039, My Boyfriend's Back, 1963 ... **$20.00-$40.00**

Stereo **LPs**

Caprice SLP 1001, ... And the Angels Sing, 1962 ... **$100.00-$200.00**

Smash SRS-67039, My Boyfriend's Back, 1963 ... **$30.00-$60.00**

THE AQUATONES:

45s

Fargo 1001, "You"/"She's the One for Me," 1958 ... **$12.50-$25.00**

1002, "Say You'll Be Mine"/"So Fine," 1958 ... **$12.50-$25.00**

LPs

Fargo 3001, The Aquatones Sing, 1964 ... **$250.00-$500.00**

THE BOBBETTES:

45s

Atlantic 1144, "Mr. Lee"/"Look at the Stars," 1957 ... **$12.50-$25.00**

1194, "The Dream"/"Um Bow Bow," 1958 ... **$10.00-$20.00**

2069, "I Shot Mr. Lee"/"Untrue Love," 1960 ... **$15.00-$30.00**

End 1093, "Mr. Johnny Q"/"Teach Me Tonight," 1961 ... **$10.00-$20.00**

RCA Victor 47-8832, "I've Gotta Face the World"/"Having Fun," 1966 ... **$7.50-$15.00**

THE CADILLACS:

45s

Josie 769, "Wishing Well"/"I Want to Know About Love," 1954 ... **$250.00-$500.00**

778, "Widow Lady"/"Down the Road," 1955 ... **$100.00-$200.00**

785, "Speedoo"/"Let Me Explain," 1955 ... **$30.00-$60.00**

792, "Zoom"/"You Are," 1956 ... **$25.00-$50.00**

836, "Speedo Is Back"/"A' Looka Here," 1958 ... **$15.00-$30.00**

LPs

Jubilee JGM-1045, The Fabulous Cadillacs (blue label), 1957 .. **$200.00-$400.00**

(if flat black label), 1959 ... **$125.00-$250.00**

(if glossy black label), 1960 ... **$50.00-$100.00**

JGM-1089, The Crazy Cadillacs (flat black label), 1959 ... **$150.00-$300.00**

(if glossy black label), 1960 ... **$50.00-$100.00**

THE CHANTELS:

45s

End 1005, "Maybe"/"Come My Little Baby" (black label), 1957 ... **$40.00-$80.00**

(if on greyish white label), 1958 ... **$20.00-$40.00**

(if on multicolored label), 1959 ... **$10.00-$20.00**

1020, "I Love You So"/"How Could You Call It Off," 1958 ... **$20.00-$40.00**

1048, "I'm Confessin'"/"Goodbye to Love," 1959 ... **$12.50-$25.00**

Ludix 101, "Eternally"/"Swamp Water," 1963 ... **$10.00-$20.00**

78s

End 1005, "Maybe"/"Come, My Little Baby" (End 1005), 1958 ... **$60.00-$120.00**

LPs

End LP-301, We Are the Chantels

(if group photo on front cover, grey label, "11-17-58" in trail-off wax), 1958 ... **$1,000.00-$1,500.00**

(if jukebox on front cover, grey label, "11-17-58" in trail-off wax), 1959 ... **$200.00-$400.00**

(if jukebox on front cover, grey label, "1962" in trail-off wax), 1962 ... **$100.00-$200.00**

(if jukebox on front cover, multicolor label, "8-65" in trail-off wax), 1965 ... **$40.00-$80.00**

(if jukebox on front cover, grey label, "8-65" in trail-off wax), 1965 ... **$50.00-$100.00**

End LP-312, There's Our Song Again, 1962 ... **$60.00-$120.00**

Carlton LP-144, The Chantels On Tour/Look in My Eyes, 1962 ... **$100.00-$200.00**

THE CHEVRONS:

45s

Brent 7000, "That Comes With Love"/"Don't Be Heartless," 1959 ... **$25.00-$50.00**

7015, "Little Darlin'"/"Little Star," 1960 ... **$25.00-$50.00**

Time 1, "Come Go with Me"/"I'm in Love Again," 1960 ... **$20.00-$40.00**

LPs

Time T-10008, Sing-a-Long Rock & Roll, 1961 ... **$40.00-$80.00**

THE CHIFFONS:

45s

Laurie 3152, "He's So Fine"/"Oh My Love" (B-side may also be listed as "Oh My Lover," value is equal), 1963 ... **$10.00-$20.00**

3179, "One Fine Day"/"Why Am I So Shy," 1963 ... **$10.00-$20.00**

3340, "Sweet Talkin' Guy"/"Did You Ever Go Steady," 1966 ... **$7.50-$15.00**

3364, "My Boyfriend's Back"/"I Got Plenty of Nuttin'," 1966 ... **$5.00-$10.00**

3630, "My Sweet Lord"/"Main Nerve," 1975 ... **$5.00-$10.00**

Mono LPs

Laurie LLP-2018, He's So Fine, 1963 ... **$60.00-$120.00**

LLP-2020, One Fine Day, 1963 ... **$100.00-$200.00**

LLP-2036, Sweet Talkin' Guy, 1966 ... **$50.00-$100.00**

Stereo LPs

Laurie SLP-2036, Sweet Talkin' Guy, 1966 ... **$75.00-$150.00**

4001, Everything You Always Wanted to Hear by the Chiffons, 1975 ... **$10.00-$20.00**

THE CHORDS:

45s

Cat 104, "Sh-Boom"/"Little Maiden," 1954 ... **$30.00-$60.00**

104, "Sh-Boom"/"Cross Over the Bridge," 1954 ... **$60.00-$120.00**

112, "A Girl to Love"/"Hold Me Baby" (as "The Chordcats"), 1955 ... **$20.00-$40.00**

117, "Could It Be"/"Pretty Wild" (as "The Sh-Booms"), 1955 ... **$20.00-$40.00**

Atlantic 2074, "Blue Moon"/"Short Skirts" (as "The Sh-Booms"), 1960 ....$10.00-$20.00
Atco 6213, "Sh-Boom"/"Little Maiden" (as "The Sh-Booms"), 1961 ....$7.50-$15.00

THE CLEFTONES:

45s

Old Town 1011, "The Masquerade Is Over"/"My Dearest Darling," 1955 ....$250.00-$500.00
Gee 1000, "You Baby You"/"I Was Dreaming," 1955 ....$30.00-$60.00
1064, "Heart and Soul"/"How Do You Feel," 1961 ....$12.50-$25.00

Mono LPs

Gee GLP-705, Heart and Soul, 1961 ....$100.00-$200.00
GLP-707, For Sentimental Reasons, 1961 ....$125.00-$250.00

Stereo LPs

Gee SGLP-705, Heart and Soul, 1961 ....$250.00-$500.00
SGLP-707, For Sentimental Reasons, 1961 ....$600.00-$1,200.00

THE COASTERS:

45s

Atco 6064, "Down in Mexico"/"Turtle Dovin'," 1956 ....$40.00-$80.00
6087, "Searchin'"/"Young Blood" (maroon label), 1957 ....$35.00-$70.00
(if on white-yellow label), 1957 ....$12.50-$25.00
6116, "Yakety Yak"/"Zing Went the Strings of My Heart," 1958 ....$12.50-$25.00
6132, "Charlie Brown"/"Three Cool Cats," 1959 ....$12.50-$25.00
6146, "Poison Ivy"/"I'm a Hog for You," 1959 ....$10.00-$20.00

Stereo 45s

Atco SD-45-6132, "Charlie Brown"/"Three Cool Cats" (blue label, silver print, "Stereo" under the "O" of Atco), 1959 ....$30.00-$60.00

Mono LPs

Atco 33-101, The Coasters (yellow "harp" label), 1958 ....$150.00-$300.00
(if gold-blue label), 196? ....$30.00-$60.00
Atco 33-123, One By One (yellow "harp" label), 1960 ....$75.00-$150.00
(if gold-grey label), 196? ....$30.00-$60.00

Stereo LPs

Atco SD-33-123, One By One (yellow "harp" label), 1960 ....$200.00-$400.00
(if purple-brown label), 196? ....$75.00-$150.00

THE CRESTS:

45s

Joyce 103, "My Juanita"/"Sweetest One" (if label is spelled "joYce"), 1957 ....$150.00-$300.00
(if label is spelled "Joyce"), 1959 ....$25.00-$50.00
Coed 501, "Pretty Little Angel"/"I Thank the Moon" ("Coed" in red print), 1958 ....$75.00-$150.00
(if "Coed" in red-black print), 1958 ....$20.00-$40.00
506, "16 Candles"/"Beside You," 1958 ....$15.00-$30.00
515, "The Angels Listened In"/"I Thank the Moon," 1959 ....$15.00-$30.00
Times Square 2, "No One to Love"/"Wish She Was Mine" (red vinyl), 1962 ....$10.00-$20.00

LPs

Coed LPC-901, The Crests Sing All Biggies (yellow label, black print), 1960 ....$200.00-$400.00
(if red label), 1960 ....$100.00-$200.00

THE CROWS:

45s

Rama 5, "Gee"/"I Love You So" (blue label, black vinyl), 1953 ....$35.00-$70.00
(if blue label, red vinyl), 1953 ....$200.00-$400.00
(if red label, black vinyl), 1955 ....$15.00-$30.00
Rama 10, "Heartbreaker"/"Call a Doctor" (black vinyl), 1953 ....$200.00-$400.00
(if black vinyl, label credits as "The Jewels"), 1953 ....$300.00-$600.00
(if black vinyl, "The Jewels" on one side, "The Crows" on the other), 1953 ....$300.00-$600.00
(if red vinyl), 1953 ....$400.00-$800.00
(if red vinyl, label credits as "The Jewels"), 1953 ....$800.00-$1,200.00

DANNY AND THE JUNIORS:

45s

Singular 711, "At The Hop"/"Sometimes" (blue label, machine-stamped in dead wax, record begins with a "count-in," no mention of Artie Singer on label), 1957 ....$500.00-$1,000.00
(if blue label, machine-stamped in dead wax, record begins with a "count-in," "Orchestra Directed by Artie Singer" credit—any Singular records with black labels, or with out the audio "count-in" may be reproductions), 1957 ....$500.00-$1,000.00

ABC-Paramount 9871, "At The Hop"/"Sometimes (When I'm All Alone)," 1957 ....$15.00-$30.00
9888, "Rock And Roll Is Here to Stay"/"School Boy Romance," 1958 ....$15.00-$30.00
Swan 4060, "Twistin' U.S.A."/"A Thousand Miles Away," 1960 ...$10.00-$20.00

7-inch EPs

ABC-Paramount EP-11, At the Hop (contains "At The Hop"/"School Boy Romance"/"Rock And Roll Is Here To Stay"/"Sometimes (When I'm All Alone)," value is for record and jacket), 1958 ....$750.00-$1,500.00

78s

ABC-Paramount 9871, "At the Hop"/"Sometimes When I'm All Alone," 1957 ....$60.00-$120.00
9888, "Rock and Roll Is Here To Stay"/"School Boy Romance," 1958 ....$100.00-$200.00

THE DEL VIKINGS:

45s

Fee Bee 205, "Come Go with Me"/"How Can I Find True Love" (orange label, one side has bee, other side doesn't), 1957 ....$125.00-$250.00
(if orange label, bee on top) 1957 ....$250.00-$500.00
(if orange label, no bee), 1961 ....$15.00-$30.00
205, "Come Go with Me"/"Whispering Bells," 1964 ....$10.00-$20.00
214, "Whispering Bells"/"Don't Be a Fool," 1957 ....$200.00-$400.00
Dot 15538, "Come Go with Me"/"How Can I Find True Love," 1957 ....$15.00-$30.00
15592, "Whispering Bells"/"Don't Be a Fool," 1957 ....$15.00-$30.00
16092, "Come Go with Me"/"How Can I Find True Love," 1960 ....$10.00-$20.00
Luniverse 106, "Somewhere Over the Rainbow"/"Hey, Senorita," 1957 ....$50.00-$100.00

78s

Fee Bee 205, "Come Go With Me"/"How Can I Find True Love," 1957 ....$75.00-$150.00
Dot 15538, "Come Go With Me"/"How Can I Find True Love," 1957 ....$25.00-$50.00

LPs

Luniverse LP-1000, Come Go with the Del Vikings (originals have eight tracks and cover is composed of slicks), 1957 ....$250.00-$500.00
Mercury MG-20314, They Sing—They Swing, 1957 ....$150.00-$300.00
Dot DLP-6885, Come Go with Me (mono), 1966 ....$100.00-$200.00
DLP-25685, Come Go with Me (rechanneled stereo), 1966 ..$75.00-$150.00

THE DREAMLOVERS:

45s

Len 1006, "Take It from a Fool"/"For the First Time," 1958 ...$100.00-$200.00
Heritage 102, "When We Get Married"/"Just Because," 1961 ....$10.00-$20.00
107, "Zoom, Zoom, Zoom"/"While We Were Dancing," 1962 ...$7.50-$15.00

THE DUPREES:

45s

Coed 569, "You Belong to Me"/"Take Me As I Am," 1962 ....$10.00-$20.00
587, "(It's No) Sin"/"The Sand and the Sea," 1964 ....$7.50-$15.00

LPs

Coed LPC-905, You Belong to Me, 1962 ....$150.00-$300.00
LPC-906, Have You Heard, 1963 ....$100.00-$200.00

THE FIVE KEYS:

45s

Aladdin 3099, "The Glory of Love"/"Hucklebuck with Jimmy," 1951 ....$500.00-$1,000.00
3127, "Red Sails in the Sunset"/"Be Anything, But Be Mine," 1952 ....$4,500.00-$6,000.00
3190, "These Foolish Things"/"Lonesome Old Story," 1953 ....$2,000.00-$4,000.00
3245, "Deep in My Heart"/"How Do You Expect Me to Get It," 1954 ....$400.00-$800.00
Capitol F-2945, "Ling, Ting, Tong"/"I'm Alone," 1954 ....$20.00-$40.00
F-3392, "She's the Most"/"I Dreamt I Dwelt in Heaven" (if regular large hole), 1956 ....$20.00-$40.00
(if small hole), 1956 ....$35.00-$70.00

7-inch EPs

Capitol EAP 1-572, The Five Keys on Stage! Volume 1 (contains "Ling Ting Tong"/"I'm Alone"/"Close Your Eyes"/"Doggone It, You Did It" value is for record and jacket)
(if on the cover, the far left singer's thumb is sticking out at crotch level), 1957 ....$100.00-$200.00
(if on the cover, the far left singer's thumb is airbrushed off), 1957 ....$125.00-$250.00

78s

Aladdin 3099, "The Glory of Love"/"Hucklebuck With Jimmy," 1951 ....$100.00-$200.00

LPs

Aladdin LP-806, The Best of the Five Keys (bootlegs are titled "On the Town"), 1956....................$1,500.00-$2,000.00

Capitol T 828, The Five Keys On Stage!

(if on the cover, the far left singer's thumb is sticking out at crotch level), 1957 ....$150.00-$300.00

(if on the cover, the far left singer's thumb is airbrushed off), 1957 ....$250.00-$500.00

THE FIVE SATINS:

45s

Standord 200, "In the Still of the Nite"/"The Jones Girl," 1956 ....$600.00-$900.00

(if "Produced by Martin Kuegell" on label), 1956....................$1,500.00-$2,000.00

Ember 1005, "In the Still of the Nite"/"The Jones Girl" (red label, "6106A" in the trail-off vinyl), 1956 ....$100.00-$200.00

(if red label, "E-1005" in the trail-off vinyl), 1956....................$15.00-$30.00

(if red label, "E-2105-45" in the trail-off vinyl), 1956 ....$25.00-$50.00

(if multi-color "logs" label), 1959 ....$20.00-$40.00

1005, "I'll Remember (In the Still of the Nite)"/"The Jones Girl" (red label), 1956....................$15.00-$30.00

(if multi-color "logs" label, reads "Special Demand Release"), 1959 ....$25.00-$50.00

(if multi-color "logs" label, no reference to "Special Demand Release"), 1959 ....$15.00-$30.00

1005, "In the Still of the Night 'I'll Remember"/"The Jones Girl" (black label, white logo, red flames at left), 1961 ....$15.00-$30.00

THE FIVE SHARPS:

45s

Jubilee 5478, "Stormy Weather"/"Mammy Jammy" (second version by group who would later become the Videos), 1964....................$6.00-$12.00

78s

Jubilee 5104, "Stormy Weather"/"Sleepy Cowboy" (a 45 of this record, if it existed with a blue-pink label, has never been found), 1953 ....$18,750.00-$25,000.00

THE FLEETWOODS:

45s

Dolphin 1, "Come Softly to Me"/"I Care So Much," 1959....................$12.50-$25.00

Liberty 55188, "Come Softly to Me"/"I Care So Much," 1959 ...$12.50-$25.00

Dolton 5, "Mr. Blue"/"You Mean Everything to Me," 1959 ....$10.00-$20.00

40, "Tragedy"/"Little Miss Sad One," 1961 ....$7.50-$15.00

Stereo 45s

Liberty 77188, "Come Softly to Me"/"I Care So Much," 1959 ...$25.00-$50.00

Dolton S-3, "Graduation's Here"/"Oh Lord, Let It Be," 1959.....$25.00-$50.00

Mono LPs

Dolton BLP-2001, Mr. Blue (pale blue label, dolphins on top), 1959 ....$40.00-$80.00

(if dark label, logo at left, reissue), 1963 ....$10.00-$20.00

BLP-2018, The Fleetwoods' Greatest Hits, 1962....................$12.50-$25.00

Stereo LPs

Dolton BST-8001, Mr. Blue (pale blue label, dolphins on top), 1959 ....$50.00-$100.00

(if dark label, logo at left, reissue), 1963 ....$12.50-$25.00

BST-8020, The Fleetwoods Sings for Lovers by Night, 1963....$20.00-$40.00

THE FOUR LOVERS:

45s

Epic 9255, "My Life for Your Love"/"Pucker Up," 1957....$1,000.00-$2,000.00

RCA Victor 47-6518, "You're the Apple of My Eye"/"The Girl of My Dreams," 1956....................$20.00-$40.00

LPs

RCA Victor LPM-1317, Joyride, 1956 ....$350.00-$700.00

THE FOUR SEASONS:

45s

Vee Jay 456, "Sherry"/"I've Cried Before" (oval logo, rainbow perimeter), 1962 ....$12.50-$25.00

485, "Walk Like a Man"/"Lucky Ladybug," 1963....................$7.50-$15.00

Philips 40211, "Rag Doll"/"Silence Is Golden" (black label), 1964 ....$7.50-$15.00

40370, "Opus 17 (Don't You Worry 'Bout Me)"/"Beggar's Paradise," 1966 ....$5.00-$10.00

Warner Bros. 8122, "Who Loves You"/"Who Loves You (Disco Version)," 1975 ....$2.50-$5.00

8168, "December, 1963 (Oh, What a Night)"/"Slip Away," 1975 ..$2.50-$5.00

Mono LPs

Vee Jay LP-1053, Sherry & 11 Others, 1962 ....$20.00-$40.00

Philips PHM 200124, Dawn (Go Away) and 11 Other Great Songs, 1964 ....$10.00-$20.00

200150, All the Song Hits of the Four Seasons, 1964....................$10.00-$20.00

Stereo LPs

Vee Jay SR-1053, Sherry & 11 Others, 1962 ....$30.00-$60.00

Philips PHS 600124, Dawn (Go Away) and 11 Other Great Songs, 1964 ....$12.50-$25.00

THE HARPTONES:

45s

Bruce 101, "A Sunday Kind of Love"/"I'll Never Tell"

(if "Bruce" in block lettering), 1953....................$40.00-$80.00

(if "Bruce" in script lettering), 1953 ....$2,000.00-$3,000.00

102, "My Memories of You"/"It Was Just for Laughs," 1954 ....$100.00-$200.00

102, "My Memories of You"/"The Laughs on You" (same B-side, different title), 1954....................$60.00-$120.00

78s

Bruce 101, "Sunday Kind of Love"/"I'll Never Tell," 1953 ....$60.00-$120.00

THE IMPALAS:

45s

Cub 9022, "Sorry (I Ran All The Way Home)"/"Fool, Fool, Fool," 1959 ....$10.00-$20.00

(if A-side titled "I Ran All The Way Home," original title), 1959 ....$30.00-$60.00

Mono LPs

Cub 8003, Sorry (I Ran All the Way Home), 1959 ....$200.00-$400.00

Stereo LPs

Cub S-8003, Sorry (I Ran All the Way Home), 1959....................$300.00-$600.00

THE JIVE FIVE:

45s

Beltone 1006, "My True Story"/"When I Was Single," 1961.......$15.00-$30.00

2024, "What Time Is It?"/"Beggin' You Please," 1962....................$10.00-$20.00

LITTLE ANTHONY AND THE IMPERIALS:

45s

End 1060, "Shimmy, Shimmy, Ko-Ko Bop"/"I'm Still in Love with You," 1959 ....$15.00-$30.00

1067, "My Empty Room"/"Bayou, Bayou, Baby," 1960....................$7.50-$15.00

1128, "Hurt So Bad"/"Reputation," 1965 ....$5.00-$10.00

(with picture sleeve, add), 1965....................$20.00-$40.00

Mono LPs

DCP DCL-3801, I'm On the Outside Looking In, 1964 ....$12.50-$25.00

Stereo LPs

DCP DCS-6801, I'm On the Outside Looking In, 1964....................$15.00-$30.00

DCS-6808, Goin' Out of My Head, 1965 ....$15.00-$30.00

FRANKIE LYMON AND THE TEENAGERS:

45s

Gee 1002, "Why Do Fools Fall in Love"/"Please Be Mine"

(if red-black label, vocal solo on B-side), 1956....................$15.00-$30.00

(if red-black label, vocal duet on B-side), 1956....................$25.00-$50.00

(if red-gold label), 1956 ....$40.00-$80.00

(if white label, "Gee Records" at top, B-side is "My Girl"), 1958 ....$12.50-$25.00

(if grey label, "Gee Records" at bottom, label credit is "The Teenagers Featuring Frankie Lymon"), 1959....................$7.50-$15.00

1018, "I Promise to Remember"/"Who Can Explain," 1956 ....$15.00-$30.00

1026, "I'm Not a Juvenile Delinquent"/"Baby Baby," 1957 ....$15.00-$30.00

78s

Gee 1002, "Why Do Fools Fall In Love"/"Please Be Mine," 1955 ....$25.00-$50.00

LPs

Gee GLP-701, The Teenagers featuring Frankie Lymon

(if red label, first pressings), 1956....................$250.00-$500.00

(if gray label), 1961 ....$75.00-$150.00

(if white label, thin vinyl), 197?....................$6.00-$12.00

THE MARCELS:

45s

Colpix 186, "Blue Moon"/"Goodbye to Love," 1961....................$15.00-$30.00

(with picture sleeve, add), 1961....................$30.00-$60.00

612, "Heartaches"/"My Love for You," 1961....................$12.50-$25.00

(with picture sleeve, add), 1961....................$50.00-$100.00

LPs

Colpix CP-416, Blue Moon (gold label), 1961 ....**$175.00-$350.00**

(if blue label), 1963 ....**$60.00-$120.00**

THE MIDNIGHTERS:

45s

Federal 12169, "Work With Me Annie"/"Until I Die"
(if silver top label, credit "The Midnighters (Formerly Known as the Royals),"
1954 ....**$50.00-$100.00**

(if all green label, credit "The Midnighters (Formerly Known as the Royals),"
1954 ....**$20.00-$40.00**

12195, "Annie Had a Baby"/"She's the One," 1954 ....**$30.00-$60.00**

12227, "It's Love Baby (24 Hours a Day)"/"Looka Here," 1955
....**$30.00-$60.00**

10-inch LPs

Federal 295-90, Their Greatest Hits, 1954 ....**$6,000.00-$8,000.00**

12-inch LPs

Federal 5411, Their Greatest Hits (yellow cover), 1955
....**$500.00-$1,000.00**

(if red cover), 1955 ....**$750.00-$1,500.00**

THE MOONGLOWS:

45s

Chance 1147, "Baby Please"/"Whistle My Love," 1953 ....**$500.00-$1,000.00**

(if on red vinyl), 1953...**$2,250.00-$3,000.00**

1152, "Secret Love"/"Real Gone Mama" (yellow-black label), 1954
....**$500.00-$1,000.00**

(if silver-blue label), 1954 ....**$750.00-$1,500.00**

1161, "My Gal"/"219 Train," 1954.....................................**$3,750.00-$5,000.00**

Chess 1581, "Sincerely"/"Tempting" (if blue label, silver top), 1954
....**$30.00-$60.00**

1589, "Most of All"/"She's Gone" (blue label, silver top), 1955
....**$30.00-$60.00**

LPs

Chess LP 1430, Look! It's the Moonglows, 1959 ....**$250.00-$500.00**

1471, The Best of Bobby Lester & the Moonglows (black label), 1962
....**$150.00-$300.00**

(if blue-to-white label), 1966...**$25.00-$50.00**

(if on Chess CH-9193, reissue), 1987 ....**$6.00-$12.00**

THE ORIOLES:

45s

Jubilee 5000, "It's Too Soon to Know"/"Barbara Lee," 1951
....**$2,000.00-$4,000.00**

5017, "What Are You Doing New Year's Eve"/"Lonely Christmas," 1951
....**$400.00-$800.00**

(with picture sleeve produced three years later, add), 1954
....**$500.00-$1,000.00**

5122, "Crying in the Chapel"/"Don't You Think I Ought to Know," 1953
....**$40.00-$80.00**

THE ORLONS:

45s

Cameo 198, "I'll Be True"/"Heart Darling Angel," 1961 ....**$25.00-$50.00**

218, "The Wah-Watusi"/"Holiday Hill," 1962 ....**$10.00-$20.00**

231, "Don't Hang Up"/"The Conservative," 1962 ....**$10.00-$20.00**

(with picture sleeve, add), 1962...**$20.00-$40.00**

243, "South Street"/"Them Terrible Boots," 1963.....................**$10.00-$20.00**

(with picture sleeve, add;), 1963 ....**$20.00-$40.00**

LPs

Cameo C 1020, The Wah-Watusi, 1962......................................**$30.00-$60.00**

1041, South Street, 1963...**$30.00-$60.00**

THE PARAGONS:

45s

Musicraft 1102, "Wedding Bells"/"Blue Velvet," 1960.................**$12.50-$25.00**

Tap 500, "If"/"Hey Baby," 1961 ....**$25.00-$50.00**

504, "These Are the Things I Love"/"If You Love Me," 1961
....**$20.00-$40.00**

THE PENGUINS:

45s

Dootone 348, "Earth Angel"/"Hey Senorita" (first pressings, glossy red labels),
1954 ....**$75.00-$150.00**

(if on black label), 1955...**$15.00-$30.00**

(if on blue label), 1955 ....**$20.00-$40.00**

(if on maroon label), 1955 ....**$25.00-$50.00**

LPs

Dootone DTL-204, The Best Vocal Groups...Rhythm and Blues (include several groups, including the Medallions, Don Julian and the Meadowlarks, and the Dootones—full maroon label), 1957 ....**$750.00-$1,500.00**

(if on glossy maroon label), 195?...**$250.00-$500.00**

(if on Dooto DTL-204, blue-yellow label), 1959 ....**$100.00-$200.00**

(if on Dooto DTL-204, black label, gold-orange-blue ring), 196?
....**$50.00-$100.00**

THE RAYS:

45s

XYZ 102, "Silhouettes"/"Daddy Cool" (blue label), 1957 ....**$30.00-$60.00**

(if grey label), 1957 ....**$100.00-$200.00**

607, "Magic Moon"/"Louie Hoo Hoo" (red label), 1960 ....**$12.50-$25.00**

(if blue label), 1960 ....**$20.00-$40.00**

Cameo 117, "Silhouettes"/"Daddy Cool," 1957 ....**$12.50-$25.00**

133, "Rags to Riches"/"The Man Above," 1958 ....**$15.00-$30.00**

THE RIVINGTONS:

45s

Liberty 55427, "Papa-Oom-Mow-Mow"/"Deep Water," 1962
....**$12.50-$25.00**

55513, "Kickapoo Joy Juice"/"My Reward," 1962 ....**$7.50-$15.00**

55528, "Mama-Oom-Mow-Mow"/"Waiting," 1962 ....**$7.50-$15.00**

55553, "The Bird's the Word"/"I'm Losing My Grip," 1963......**$10.00-$20.00**

RUBEN AND THE JETS:

45s

Verve 10362, "Jelly Roll Gum Drop"/"Any Way the Wind Blows," 1968
....**$75.00-$150.00**

10632, "Jelly Roll Gum Drop"/"Deseri," 1968.........................**$75.00-$150.00**

LPs

Mercury SRM-1-659, For Real, 1973..**$7.50-$15.00**

SRM-1-694, Con Safos, 1974 ....**$6.00-$12.00**

THE SKYLINERS:

45s

Calico 103/4, "Since I Don't Have You"/"One Night, One Night," 1959
....**$25.00-$50.00**

106, "This I Swear"/"Tomorrow," 1959 ....**$15.00-$30.00**

Motown 1046, "Since I Fell for You"/"I'd Die" (two copies exist, both test pressings), 1963 ....**$1,500.00-$2,000.00**

THE SOLITAIRES:

45s

Old Town 1000, "Blue Valentine"/"Wonder Boy," 1954...........**$200.00-$400.00**

(if red vinyl), 1954...**$750.00-$1,500.00**

1006/7, "Please Remember My Heart"/"South of the Border," 1954
....**$350.00-$700.00**

(if red vinyl), 1954 ....**$2,000.00-$3,000.00**

1032, "Give Me One More Chance"/"Nothing Like a Little Love," 1956
....**$100.00-$200.00**

1071, "Light a Candle in the Chapel"/"Helpless," 1959 ....**$20.00-$40.00**

THE SPANIELS:

45s

Chance 1141, "Baby It's You"/"Bounce," 1953 ....**$250.00-$500.00**

(if red vinyl), 1953..**$1,000.00-$2,000.00**

Vee Jay 101, "Baby It's You"/"Bounce" (maroon label), 1953
....**$400.00-$800.00**

(if red vinyl), 1953...**$2,250.00-$4,500.00**

(if black vinyl, black label), 1961 ....**$20.00-$40.00**

78s

Vee Jay 107, "Goodnight, Sweetheart, Goodnight"/"You Don't Move Me,"
1954 ....**$40.00-$80.00**

LPs

Vee Jay LP-1002, Goodnite, It's Time to Go (maroon label, group pictured on cover), 1958 ....**$300.00-$600.00**

(if black label, dogs on cover), 1961 ....**$100.00-$200.00**

(if flimsy vinyl, 1980s issue), 198? ....**$6.00-$12.00**

THE TYMES:

45s

Parkway 871, "So In Love"/"Roscoe James McClain," 1963 ....**$12.50-$25.00**

871, "So Much In Love"/"Roscoe James McClain," 1963 ....**$7.50-$15.00**

(with picture sleeve, add), 1963...**$15.00-$30.00**

884, "Wonderful! Wonderful!"/"Come with Me to the Sea," 1963
....**$7.50-$15.00**

(with picture sleeve, add), 1963...**$12.50-$25.00**

MAURICE WILLIAMS AND THE ZODIACS:

45s

Cole 100, "Golly Gee"/"'I' Town," 1959 ....**$25.00-$50.00**

Herald 552, "Stay"/"Do You Believe," 1960 ....**$10.00-$20.00**

CHAPTER 12

FUNK

History

Funk music is hard-edged dance music designed to get your rump off the couch and boogie. With its thick, jumpy baselines, rhythmic drums, trumpet blasts, and call-and-response vocals, funk is a harder-edged version of soul music—or a danceable version of rock, the choice is yours. While collectors want to acquire recordings by the most popular funk artists—James Brown, Parliament/Funkadelic, Rick James, and Prince—there is also a strong desire for short-pressed, independent 45s with killer funk breaks, as well as soundtracks from 1970s "blaxploitation" films like *Dolemite*, *Truck Turner*, and *Shaft*.

More than any other musical genre, funk music brought the electric bass guitar to the forefront of the band. Bass guitarists, who formerly plucked their instruments in virtual anonymity, now slapped, and thumped, and pounded those strings with reckless abandon and fervor. By the 1970s, the next generation of funk-based artists would now layer their musical compositions around their bass player's thick, bouncing instrumental riffs.

James Brown may be the "Godfather of Soul," but he was also the tree of life from which all funk grows. While his ballads "Try Me" and "Please, Please, Please" were pure soul, he added a bass-heavy melody to his recordings, punctuating certain breaks in the song with drum solos and horn riffs. While with King Records, he recorded tracks like "Papa's Got A Brand New Bag," "I Got You (I Feel Good)," "Cold Sweat," and "Mother Popcorn," songs which catapulted Brown across all radio and racial barriers.

Rudy Ray Moore took Dolemite, his character from a series of stag albums, and made him a success on the big screen. This soundtrack album to the film Dolemite *is packed with funky grooves and jams, while Moore makes a cameo appearance at the end of the record.*

***$75**, VG+ condition*

James Brown's "Please, Please, Please" was a hit when he recorded it on the Federal label; when he moved to King Records, the title was re-released, eventually selling a million copies.

***$40**, NM condition*

Not only are James Brown's funk grooves collectible, but so are records that he produced for other artists, including this track by Vicki Anderson.

***$20**, VG+ condition*

In order to maximize the acoustical punch and sonic quality of this 12-inch disc for Parliament's "Theme from the Black Hole," the record was pressed with two songs on the A-side, and no songs for the B-side—in other words, the B-side is essentially a grooveless black hole.

***$20**, NM condition*

When Sly and the Family Stone's Greatest Hits *was originally released, the only mixes available for three of the songs—"Hot Fun In The Summertime," "Everybody Is A Star," and "Thank You (Falettinme Be Mice Elf Agin)"—were in rechanneled stereo. Six months later, the missing full stereo master tapes for those three songs turned up, and they were used on the quadraphonic version of* Greatest Hits.

***$100**, NM condition*

He brought funk music to black and white fans alike, and Brown's Famous Flames backup band laid down such a funky beat that concert theaters they performed in became dance clubs that night.

By 1971, James Brown disbanded the Famous Flames, and formed the JB's with former Famous Flame Jimmy Nolen, and new additions Maceo Parker, St. Clair Pinckney, and Fred Wesley. He also left King Records, the label for which he had recorded his greatest hits, and signed a long-term deal with Polydor. He also created a new record label, People Records, so that Polydor could distribute recordings by Lyn Collins and Donald Byrd.

Many of the ex-Famous Flames joined up with George Clinton's Parliament/Funkadelic operation. Clinton's funk band evolved from the Parliaments, a doo-wop group who had a Top 20 hit in 1967 on Revilot, "(I Wanna) Testify." In 1969, when a contract dispute took Clinton's right to call his group the "Parliaments" away from him, he renamed the band Funkadelic and signed with Westbound Records (and eventually to Warner Bros. in the mid-1970s). A year later, when he regained the rights to the name "Parliaments," he rechristened his band Parliament and signed them to a competing record company, Invictus (that version of Clinton's band moved to Casablanca in 1976). The two Clinton funk bands continued until 1980, when another legal wrangling took the names Parliament and Funkadelic away from him. Undaunted, he signed with Capitol Records as a solo artist, and released the funk hits "Atomic Dog" and "Loopzilla," backing himself with the "P-Funk All-Stars."

Other groups mixed funk with a Latin beat (War), while some bands expanded on the call-and-response vocals of James Brown and Parliament-Funkadelic (such as the Ohio Players, Con Funk Shun). Bands like Tower of Power and Charles Wright and the Watts 103rd Street Rhythm Band brought West Coast urban funk to radio; groups like the Brothers Johnson, the Gap Band, and Cameo incorporated funk into slick, polished productions that captured millions of fans. Sylvester Stewart, a former disc jockey and songwriter, mixed funk with psychedelia—his creation, Sly and the Family Stone, commandeered radios with funk and dance anthems like "Dance to the Music," "Thank You (Falletinme Be Mice Elf Agin)," and "Everyday People."

By the 1980s, Prince Rogers Nelson mixed funky bass lines with synthesizer riffs and off-the-wall lyrical subject matter. His early songs like "I Wanna Be Your Lover," "Dirty Mind," and "Controversy" paved the way for the success of his albums *1999* and *Purple Rain*. During his career, Prince found time to produce another funk band, The Time; an all-girl trio, Vanity 6 (later renamed Apollonia 6 when the group switched lead singers), and an all-instrumental crew, Madhouse. He also wrote music for the films *Under the Cherry Moon* and *Graffiti Bridge* (he also starred in both), and recorded songs to promote the film *Batman*.

Prince's funky 45 "Delirious" is a very common title, but this picture sleeve—which unfolds to reveal a poster and calendar—is hard to find, especially in good condition.

***$25**, sleeve in VG condition*

What To Look For

Interestingly, the funk records that are most difficult to find are not James Brown's early issues, or Prince's promotional picture sleeves, or quadraphonic Sly and the Family Stone LPs. Hardcore funk collectors actively search for grooves from small, independent record labels and artists who may have printed only a few hundred copies, but whose funky groove is as strong as any major-label issue. Titles like "Sagittarius Black" by Timothy McNealy, "Funky Chick" by the Majestics, and "Hung Up" by Salt are enough to make collectors shell out hundreds of dollars for the copies.

Other collectors want killer funk grooves as samples for their own remixes. Common tracks like Funkadelic's "(not just) Knee Deep" and James Brown's "Funky Drummer" have been found in dozens of songs, either replicated by house musicians or transferred directly from old vinyl. Some funk tracks have even made their way into commercials—the Majestics' "Funky Chick" was later used in a series of KFC ads!

Be aware that any pressings on the "Funk 45" label are reproductions of original rare recordings, manufactured so that funk fans could enjoy these grooves at a reduced price.

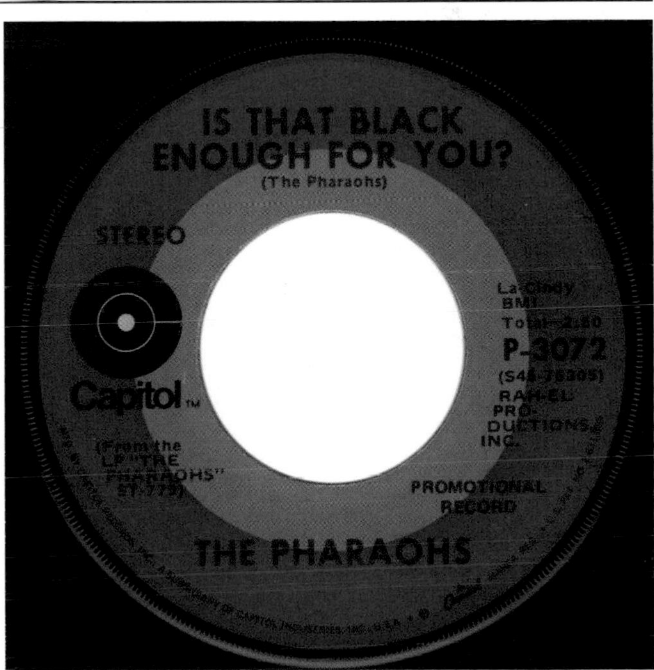

While the A-side of this 45 by the Pharaohs, a slow jam remake of the Miracles' "Tracks of My Tears" was promoted as the A-side, funk collectors search high and low for this record because of its killer B-side, "Is That Black Enough For You?," in which the band smokes through three minutes of funky drums and horns.

***$150**, NM condition*

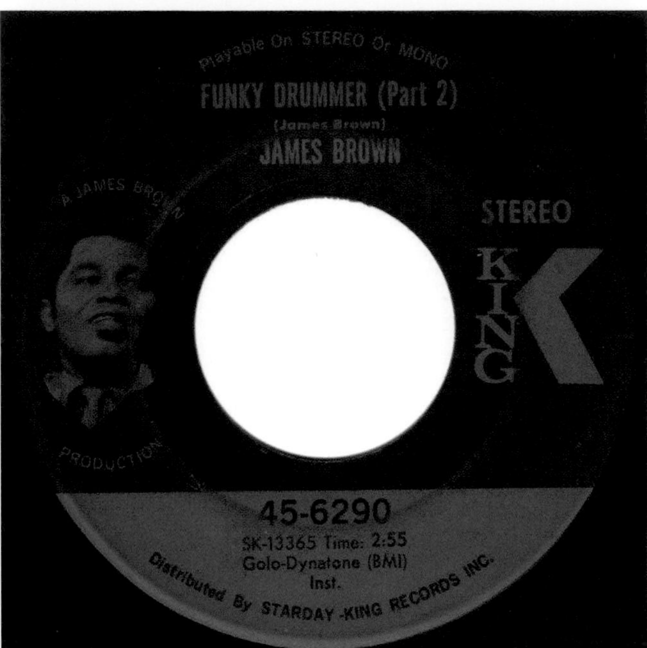

In an interview with Goldmine *magazine, Grandmaster Flash said he once practiced his turntable remixing craft with records like James Brown's "Funky Drummer," remixing the last fifteen seconds of the B-side into extended jams at his Bronx neighborhood B-boy parties.*

$4, *Good condition*

Museums

Memphis Rock 'N' Soul Museum, 145 Lt. George W. Lee Avenue, Memphis, TN 38103, (901) 543-0800: http://www.memphisrocknsoul.org

Funk music in Washington, D.C., morphed into "go-go" music, with bands like Trouble Funk, E.U., and Chuck Brown & the Soul Searchers taking their 10-15 member bands and 15-20 minute live jams to packed clubs throughout the Potomac Basin.

$4, *VG condition*

Books

Manship, John, *Manship's USA Rare Soul 45 RPM Concise Price Guide*, John Manship Press, London, 2003.

Whitburn, Joel, *Top R&B Singles 1942-1995*, Record Research Inc., Menomonee Falls, WI, 1996.

Whitburn, Joel, *Top R&B Albums 1965-1998*, Record Research Inc., Menomonee Falls, WI, 1999.

Ward, Ed; Geoffrey Stokes; Ken Tucker, *Rock of Ages: The Rolling Stone History of Rock and Roll*, Rolling Stone Press, Summit Books, Simon & Schuster, New York, 1986.

Web Pages

A major Web site for rare funk, including sound files: http://www.funk45s.com

A Web site for deep funk grooves, along with a streaming radio show: http://www.deepfunk.org

NPG Online Ltd., Prince's official site: http://www.npgonlineltd.com

A fan page devoted to James Brown: http://www.funky-stuff.com

A home page with plenty of funk biographies: http://www.soul-patrol.com/funk

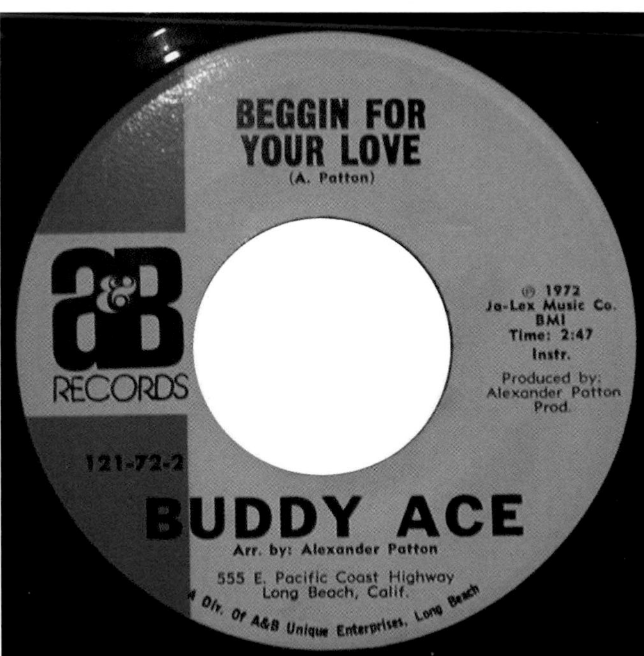

Buddy Ace was a Texas blues singer with a couple of minor R&B hits on the Duke label to his credit. Today, rare gems like the 45 shown here have become prized acquisitions by funk collectors.

$150, *NM condition*

BUDDY ACE:

45s

A&B Records 121-72, "(I'm Just a Beggar) Beggin' For Your Love"/"Beggin' For Your Love," 1972 ....**$75.00-$150.00**

VICKI ANDERSON:

45s

Smash 1985, "I Love You"/"Nobody Cares," 1965 ....**$5.00-$10.00**
Fontana 1527, "Never, Never Let You Go (Part 1)"/"Never, Never Let You Go (Part 2)," 1965 ....**$6.00-$12.00**
King 6091, "Think" (with James Brown)/"Nobody Cares," 1967 ....**$5.00-$10.00**
6152, "You've Got the Power" (with James Brown)/"What the World Needs Now Is Love," 1968 ....**$5.00-$10.00**

JAMES BARNES AND THE AGENTS:

45s

Golden Hit 102, "Good & Funky"/The Funky Four Plus, "The Bomb," 1968 ....**$50.00-$100.00**

CHUCK BROWN AND THE SOUL SEARCHERS:

45s

Source 40967, "Bustin' Loose" (Pt. 1)/(Pt. 2), 1979 ....**$3.00-$6.00**

JAMES BROWN:

45s

Federal 12258, "Please, Please, Please"/"Why Do You Do Me?," 1956 ....**$20.00-$40.00**
12337, "Try Me"/"Tell Me What I Did Wrong," 1958....................**$15.00-$30.00**
12361, "Don't Let It Happen to Me"/"Good Good Lovin'," 1959 ....**$10.00-$20.00**
12369, "I'll Go Crazy"/"I Know It's True," 1960 ....**$10.00-$20.00**
King 5614, "Night Train"/"Why Does Everything Happen to Me," 1962 ....**$7.50-$15.00**
5853, "Please, Please, Please"/"In the Wee Wee Hours," 1964.....**$7.50-$15.00**
5999, "Papa's Got a Brand New Bag Part I"/"Papa's Got a Brand New Bag Part II," 1965 ....**$7.50-$15.00**
6015, "I Got You (I Feel Good)"/"I Can't Help It (I Just Do, Do, Do)," 1965 ....**$7.50-$15.00**

Stereo 45s

Federal S-12352, "I've Got to Change"/"It Hurts to Tell You," 1959 ....**$25.00-$50.00**
S-12361, "Don't Let It Happen to Me"/"Good Good Lovin'," 1959 ....**$25.00-$50.00**

7-inch EPs

King EP-430, Please, Please, Please (contains "Please, Please, Please"/"That's When I Lost My Heart"/"Try Me"/"Tell Me What I Did Wrong," value is for record and jacket) 1959 ....**$300.00-$600.00**

Mono LPs

King 610, Please Please Please
(if "woman's and man's legs" cover, "King" on label is two inches wide), 1958 ....**$600.00-$1,200.00**
(if "woman's and man's legs" cover, "King" on label is three inches wide), 1961 ....**$500.00-$1,000.00**
683, Think!
(if "baby" cover, "King" on label is two inches wide), 1960...**$450.00-$900.00**
(if "baby" cover, "King" on label is three inches wide), 1961 ....**$300.00-$600.00**
(if James Brown photo on cover, "crownless" King label), 1963 ....**$50.00-$100.00**
(if James Brown photo on cover, "crown" King label), 1966 .....**$25.00-$50.00**
826, Live at the Apollo
(if other King albums on back cover, "crownless" King label), 1963 ....**$75.00-$150.00**
(if custom back cover, "crownless" King label), 1963 ....**$100.00-$200.00**
(if white label promo, banded for airplay), 1963 ....**$400.00-$800.00**
(if "crown" King label), 1966 ....**$25.00-$50.00**
Smash MGS-27072, James Brown Plays James Brown—Today & Yesterday, 1965 ....**$15.00-$30.00**

Stereo LPs

King KS-826, Live at the Apollo
(if other King albums on back cover, "crownless" King label), 1963 ....**$100.00-$200.00**
(if custom back cover, "crownless" King label), 1963 ....**$150.00-$300.00**
(if "crown" King label), 1966 ....**$35.00-$70.00**
LPS-946, I Got You (I Feel Good)
(if "crown" King label), 1966 ....**$25.00-$50.00**
(if "crownless" King label), 1966 ....**$75.00-$150.00**
KS-1020, Cold Sweat, 1967....................**$35.00-$70.00**
KSD-1110, Sho Is Funky Down Here, 1971 ....**$20.00-$40.00**
Smash SRS-67058, Out of Sight, 1965 ....**$75.00-$150.00**
SRS-67072, James Brown Plays James Brown—Today & Yesterday, 1965 ....**$20.00-$40.00**
Polydor PD2-3007, The Payback (2 LPs), 1973 ....**$25.00-$50.00**
PD-2-9001, Hell (2 LPs), 1974....................**$40.00-$80.00**
PD-1-6042, Sex Machine Today, 1975....................**$20.00-$40.00**
PD-1-6181, Take a Look at Those Cakes, 1978 ....**$15.00-$30.00**

CAMEO:

45s

Chocolate City 001, "Find My Way"/"Good Company," 1975 ....**$2.50-$5.00**
019, "I Just Want to Be"/"The Rock," 1979....................**$2.00-$4.00**
3225, "Freaky Dancin'" /"Better Days," 1981....................**$2.00-$4.00**
Atlanta Artists 812054-7, "Style"/"Enjoy Your Life," 1983.............**$1.50-$3.00**

12-inch Singles

Chocolate City CCD 20005, "Rigor Mortis (Disco Mix 6:14)"/"(Mono Mix 3:12)," 1977 ....**$20.00-$40.00**
Atlanta Artists 812053-1, "Style" (two versions), 1983 ....**$6.00-$12.00**
884933-1, "Word Up" (3 versions)/"Urban Warrior," 1986 ....**$5.00-$10.00**
870587-1, "You Make Me Work" (3 versions)/"DKWIG," 1988 ....**$4.00-$8.00**

LPs

Chocolate City CCLP 2003, Cardiac Arrest, 1977....................**$6.00-$12.00**
CCLP 2019, Knights of the Sound Table, 1981 ....**$6.00-$12.00**
Atlanta Artists 830265-1, Word Up!, 1986....................**$5.00-$10.00**

GEORGE CLINTON:

45s

Capitol B-5160, "Loopzilla"/"Pot Sharing Tots," 1982 ....**$2.00-$4.00**
B-5201, "Atomic Dog"/(instrumental), 1983....................**$2.00-$4.00**
(with picture sleeve, add), 1983....................**$3.00-$6.00**

12-inch Singles

Capitol V-8544, "Atomic Dog" (Album Version) (Single Version), 1982 ....**$12.50-$25.00**
V-8603, "Atomic Dog" (Atomic Mix Long Version) (instrumental), 1984 ....**$7.50-$15.00**

LPs

Capitol ST-12246, Computer Games, 1982 ....**$5.00-$10.00**
ST-12308, You Shouldn't-Nuf Bit Fish, 1984....................**$5.00-$10.00**
Warner Bros. 25887, George Clinton Presents Our Gang Funky, 1988 ....**$5.00-$10.00**

LYN COLLINS, THE FEMALE PREACHER:

45s

King 6373, "Wheels of Life"/"Just Won't Do Right," 1971.............**$4.00-$8.00**
People 608, "Think (About It)"/"Ain't No Sunshine," 1972...........**$5.00-$10.00**
641, "Rock Me Again & Again & Again & Again & Again & Again"/"You Can't Love Me If You Don't Respect Me," 1974....................**$3.00-$6.00**

FUNKADELIC:

45s

Westbound 158, "I Got a Thing, You Got a Thing, Everybody's Got a Thing"/"Fish, Chips and Sweat," 1970 ....**$5.00-$10.00**
175, "You and Your Folks, Me and My Folks"/"Funky Dollar Bill," 1971 ....**$5.00-$10.00**
Warner Bros. 8618, "One Nation Under a Groove (Part 1)"/"One Nation Under a Groove (Part 2)," 1978 ....**$2.50-$5.00**
(with picture sleeve, add), 1978....................**$2.50-$5.00**
49040, "(Not Just) Knee Deep — Part 1"/"(Not Just) Knee Deep — Part 2," 1979 ....**$2.50-$5.00**

LPs

Westbound 1001, Standing on the Verge of Getting It On, 1974 ....**$25.00-$50.00**
(if on Westbound 208, reissue), 1975....................**$12.50-$25.00**
(if on Westbound 1001, with bar code), 1991 ....**$7.50-$15.00**

ISAAC HAYES:

45s

Brunswick 55258, "Sweet Temptation"/"Laura," 1964 ....**$5.00-$10.00**
Enterprise 9038, "Theme from Shaft"/"Cafe Regio's," 1971 ....**$2.50-$5.00**
9085, "Wonderful"/"Someone Made You for Me," 1974 ....**$2.50-$5.00**

Mono LPs
Enterprise E-100, Presenting Isaac Hayes, 1968 **$20.00-$40.00**
Stereo LPs
Enterprise ES-100, Presenting Isaac Hayes, 1968 **$15.00-$30.00**
ENS-1001, Hot Buttered Soul, 1969 **$10.00-$20.00**
ENS-5002, Shaft (2 LPs), 1971 **$10.00-$20.00**
ENS-7507, Truck Turner (2 LPs), 1974 **$7.50-$15.00**
ABC/HBS D-874, Chocolate Chip, 1975 **$7.50-$15.00**

RICK JAMES:

45s
A&M 1615, "Funkin' Around"/"My Mama," 1974 **$12.50-$25.00**
Gordy 7156, "You & I"/"Hollywood," 1978 **$2.50-$5.00**
7197, "Give It to Me Baby"/"Don't Give Up on Love," 1981 **$2.00-$4.00**
7205, "Super Freak (Part 1)"/"Super Freak (Part 2)," 1981 **$2.00-$4.00**
12-inch Singles
Motown 981, "You and I" (same on both sides), 1978 **$5.00-$10.00**
4511, "Cold Blooded"/(instrumental), 1983 **$3.00-$6.00**
LPs
Gordy G7-981, Come Get It!, 1978 **$5.00-$10.00**
G8-1002, Street Songs, 1981 **$4.00-$8.00**
6043 GL, Cold Blooded, 1983 **$4.00-$8.00**
Reprise 25659, Wonderful, 1988 **$5.00-$10.00**

KOOL & THE GANG:

45s
De-Lite 534, "Funky Man"/"1, 2, 3, 4, 5, 6, 7, 8," 1970 **$3.00-$6.00**
559, "Jungle Boogie"/"North, South, East, West," 1973 **$2.50-$5.00**
LPs
De-Lite 2003, Kool and the Gang, 1969 **$12.50-$25.00**
2016, Spirit of the Boogie, 1975 **$5.00-$10.00**
9513, Ladies Night, 1979 **$5.00-$10.00**

THE OHIO PLAYERS:

45s
Tangerine 978, "Neighbors"/"A Thing Called Love," 1967 **$6.00-$12.00**
Westbound 214, "Funky Worm"/"Paint Me," 1973 **$3.00-$6.00**
Mercury 73643, "Fire"/"Together," 1974 **$2.50-$5.00**
73814, "Who'd She Coo?"/"Bi-Centennial," 1976 **$2.50-$5.00**
LPs
Westbound 2015, Pain, 1972 **$10.00-$20.00**
2017, Pleasure, 1973 **$10.00-$20.00**
Trip 8029, First Impression, 1972 **$6.00-$12.00**
Mercury SRM-1-705, Skin Tight (red label), 1974 **$6.00-$12.00**
(if skyline of Chicago on label), 1974 **$5.00-$10.00**
SRM-1-1038, Honey, 1975 **$5.00-$10.00**

THE PARLIAMENTS:

45s
Len 101, "Don't Need You Anymore"/"Honey, Take Me Home With You," 1958 **$40.00-$80.00**
Revilot 207, "(I Wanna) Testify"/"I Can Feel the Ice Melting," 1967 **$7.50-$15.00**

PARLIAMENT:

45s
Invictus 9077, "I Call My Baby Pussy Cat"/"Little Ole Country Boy," 1970 **$5.00-$10.00**
9095, "Breakdown"/"Little Ole Country Boy," 1971 **$5.00-$10.00**
Casablanca 0013, "Up for the Down Stroke"/"Presence of a Brain," 1974 **$3.00-$6.00**
(if on either Casablanca 0104 or 803), 1974 **$2.50-$5.00**
856, "Tear the Roof Off the Sucker (Give Up the Funk)"/"P-Funk" (blue "Bogart" label), 1956 **$2.50-$5.00**
LPs
Invictus ST-7302, Osmium, 1970 **$50.00-$100.00**
Casablanca NBLP 9003, Up for the Down Stroke (Warner Bros. distribution), 1974 **$25.00-$50.00**
(if no mention of Warner Bros. distribution, later pressing), 1974 **$20.00-$40.00**
NBLP 7022, Mothership Connection, 1976 **$15.00-$30.00**
7195, Gloryhallastoopid (Or Pin the Tale on the Funky), 1979 **$15.00-$30.00**

PRINCE:

45s
Warner Bros. 8619, "Soft and Wet"/"So Blue," 1978 **$15.00-$30.00**
49050, "I Wanna Be Your Lover"/"My Love Is Forever," 1979 **$5.00-$10.00**
(if white label promo, "I Wanna Be Your Lover" stereo/mono pressing), 1979 **$7.50-$15.00**
(if white label promo, "My Love is Forever" stereo/mono pressing), 1979 **$10.00-$20.00**
(with picture sleeve for "My Love is Forever," withdrawn when its flipside "I Wanna Be Your Lover" became the hit), 1979 **$40.00-$80.00**
49638, "Dirty Mind"/"When We're Dancing Close and Slow," 1980 **$7.50-$15.00**
29746, "Little Red Corvette"/"All the Critics Love U in New York," 1983 **$2.50-$5.00**
29503, "Delirious"/"Horny Toad" (A-side listed at 3:56), 1983 **$3.00-$6.00**
(with foldout picture sleeve, add), 1983 **$25.00-$50.00**
Paisley Park 29052, "Paisley Park"/"She's Always In My Hair" (picture sleeve only, never issued in America in this coupling), 1985 **$250.00-$500.00**
12-inch Singles
Custom pressing, Catalog No. JUN 7, "Gett Off (Approx: Damn Near 10 Min.)"/(B-side blank) (1500 copies made), 1991 **$100.00-$200.00**
Warner Bros. DWBS 50028, "Let's Work" (Dance Remix, Long Version 8:02)"/"Gotta Stop (Messin' About)" (2:55), 1982 **$30.00-$60.00**
20170, "Let's Pretend We're Married (7:20)"/"Irresistible Bitch (4:11)," 1983 **$10.00-$20.00**
20246, "Let's Go Crazy (Special Dance Mix 7:35)"/"Erotic City (7:24)," 1984 **$5.00-$10.00**
Paisley Park 20442, "Kiss (Extended Version 7:16)"/"Love or $ (Extended Version)," 1986 **$6.00-$12.00**
20727, "U Got the Look" (2 versions)/"Housequake" (2 versions), 1987 **$7.50-$15.00**
40138, "Gett Off" (several versions), 1991 **$5.00-$10.00**
LPs
Warner Bros. 25110, Purple Rain (with poster), 1984 **$5.00-$10.00**
(if on purple vinyl, with poster), 1984 **$25.00-$50.00**
Paisley Park 25677, The Black Album (withdrawn prior to release, some copies escaped, numerous counterfeits exist on other labels and on colored vinyl, 1987 **$1,000.00-$2,000.00**
(if entire album on two 45 RPM 12-inch records), 1987 **$1,500.00-$3,000.00**
(if on Warner Bros. PRO-A-7330, promo), 1994 **$25.00-$50.00**
(if on Warner Bros. 45793, peach vinyl, 1,000 copies), 1994 **$50.00-$100.00**
(if on Warner Bros. 45793, white vinyl, 300 numbered copies in gold on the label, numbered from 051-350), 1994 **$100.00-$200.00**
(if on Warner Bros. 45793, grey marbled vinyl, 50 copies), 1994 **$250.00-$500.00**
Arista 14624, Rave Un2 the Joy Fantastic (2 LPs), 1999 **$6.00-$12.00**
NPG/Bellmark 72514, The Rainbow Children, 2001 **$12.50-$25.00**

SLY AND THE FAMILY STONE:

45s
Loadstone 9351, "I Ain't Got Nobody"/"I Can't Turn You Loose," 1967 **$10.00-$20.00**
Epic 10256, "Dance to the Music"/"Let Me Hear It from You," 1967 **$5.00-$10.00**
10450, "Stand!"/"I Want to Take You Higher," 1969 **$5.00-$10.00**
(with picture sleeve, add), 1969 **$6.00-$12.00**
10497, "Thank You (Falettinme Be Mice Elf Agin)"/"Everybody Is a Star," 1969 **$3.00-$6.00**
(with picture sleeve, add), 1969 **$5.00-$10.00**
Mono LPs
Epic LN 24324, A Whole New Thing, 1967 **$10.00-$20.00**
LN 24371, Dance to the Music, 1968 **$20.00-$40.00**
Stereo LPs
Epic BN 26324, A Whole New Thing, 1967 **$10.00-$20.00**
BN 26371, Dance to the Music, 1968 **$7.50-$15.00**
KE 30325, Sly and the Family Stone's Greatest Hits (yellow label, gatefold cover), 1970 **$6.00-$12.00**
(if on Epic EQ 30325, quadraphonic pressing, with alternate mixes of "Hot Fun in the Summertime," "Thank You," and "Everybody Is a Star"), 1971 **$50.00-$100.00**
KE 30986, There's a Riot Goin' On (yellow label, gatefold cover), 1971 **$6.00-$12.00**

TROUBLE FUNK:

45s
D.E.T.T. 1001, "Trouble Funk Express"/(instrumental), 1983 **$4.00-$8.00**
12-inch LPs
JAMTU 101, "Pump Me Up"/"Get Down With Your Get Down"/"Super Grit"/"Drop the Bomb"/"Get Down With Your Get Down" (instrumental), 1982 **$10.00-$20.00**

Heavy Metal

History

What we know today as "heavy metal" music began in the mid-1960s. Rock bands increased the volume and the fuzz pedal on their guitars, mixing old blues licks with the new PA systems, resulting in thicker and heavier—and louder—live shows and records.

The earliest "heavy metal" excursions include remakes of pop and rock songs, like Blue Cheer's "Summertime Blues" and Vanilla Fudge's "You Keep Me Hanging On." Other original pre-metal recordings included Iron Butterfly's "In-A-Gadda-Da-Vida" and Steppenwolf's "Born To Be Wild," where the lyrics "heavy metal thunder" first gave the new musical genre a name.

In England, the hard chords and thumping bass led to bands like Led Zeppelin and Deep Purple. As well, the heavy blues bands took classic blues songs from such artists as Muddy Waters and Howlin' Wolf, and played them with as much volume as humanly possible. Before long, the musical sonic boom included bands like Black Sabbath and Uriah Heep, who had evolved from the progressive rock genre, mixed in some psychedelia and classical music, and added killer guitar licks to a new powerful sound.

Meanwhile, American "hard rock" acts like Aerosmith and Ted Nugent added more R&B and boogie to their sonic palate. Over-the-top theatrics were added by KISS and Alice Cooper, who wanted their fans to both see and hear a heavy metal experience. In fact, most heavy metal albums of the time were a mélange of loud rock tracks, fuzz-drenched boogie songs, and even a power ballad or two.

Iron Butterfly's "In-A-Gadda-Da-Vida" is available on this 45, but to get the full, extended version, complete with drum solo, one has to purchase the album as well.

***$10**, NM condition*

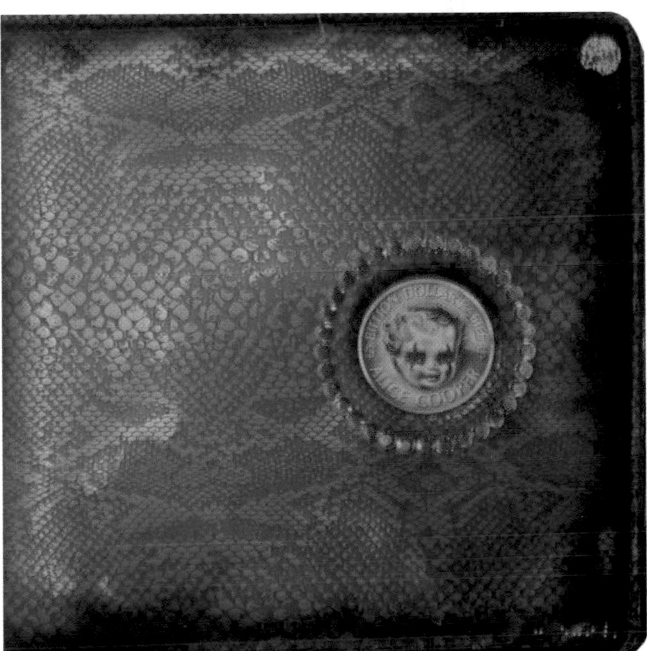

Alice Cooper's album Billion Dollar Babies *spawned the hit "No More Mr. Nice Guy," as well as some seminal rock-metal tracks like "Generation Landslide." It is a common album to find today, its low collectible price not reflecting its high quality of rock.*

***$4**, VG condition*

Featuring some songs from their album Hot in the Shade, *as well as an original demo of their early songs "Strutter" and "Deuce,"* FIRST KISS Last Licks *was a promotional album limited to only 800 copies—and is the only album to feature the members of KISS both with and without their trademark facepaint.*

***$100**, NM condition*

Legendary heavy metal guitarist Yngwie Malmsteen recorded a couple of albums with the band Alcatrazz. Their first LP, No Parole from Rock 'n' Roll, *was only printed for a few weeks before the record company folded.*

***$20**, VG+ condition*

In terms of total sales and marketability, the most popular metal band of the 1970s was KISS. With their kabuki face paint, studded leather costumes, and a pyrotechnic stage show, KISS' thunder-crunching, fist-pounding rock songs captured the ears of millions of fans. Formed in 1973 by New Yorkers Gene Simmons and Paul Stanley, with Peter Criss and Ace Frehley joining after answering newspaper ads, KISS adopted a larger-than-life persona, their face paint changing them from mild-mannered musicians to full-fledged superhero rockers.

But in the 1980s, American groups would begin to dominate not only heavy metal sales, but pop and rock sales as well. Groups like Mötley Crüe, Quiet Riot, Twisted Sister, and Bon Jovi became multi-platinum superstars, as they mixed punk and pop with heavy metal sounds of the 1970s. Not to be outdone, European groups like Def Leppard, Motorhead, Judas Priest, and the Scorpions also became worldwide metal sensations.

Eventually copycat metal groups appeared, groups who tried to emulate the 1980s metal bands for their own successes. Some of these groups included Guns N' Roses, Poison, Ratt, Warrant, Cinderella, Winger, and L.A. Guns. Many of these groups were also called "hair bands" because of their poufed-out hairstyles and androgynous wardrobes.

The popularity of hair metal bands waned in the early 1990s with the arrival of grunge. Bands like Nirvana, Alice in Chains, Soundgarden, and Rage Against the Machine, with their raw musical style and stripped-down appearances, broke new ground in hard rock music. Other groups embraced a type of heavy metal music called "speed metal," which involved songs with a faster tempo and darker lyrics. The first "speed metal" groups were essentially Judas Priest, Venom, and Motorhead, who would later be followed by the "Big Four" of thrash: Metallica, Anthrax, Megadeth, and Slayer.

One of the main perceptions by people who don't like heavy metal music is that the artists and their songs are either satanic or have a devil-worshipping agenda. Allegedly some records can be played backwards to reveal satanic messages, while other artists do indeed use pentagrams or demonic artwork on their covers. Because of this, some have claimed that heavy metal music is a tool used by the devil to command teenagers to kill their parents or themselves. Of course, if backwards messages actually worked, if some heavy metal band recorded "get a job, pay your bills, respect animals" into a backward message on their songs...who knows?

Today's hardcore/metal/punk/hip-hop mélange bands owe a tremendous debt to their heavy metal forefathers. Alice Cooper, for example, shocked audiences long before Marilyn Manson was born. The Insane Clown Posse's face paint was pioneered by KISS a generation ago. And the sonic noise of Korn and Limp Bizkit have their lineage in Black Sabbath, Motorhead, and Slayer.

Beginning with their own homegrown pressings on the Roadster label, Manilla Road were one of the first proponents of "Epic Metal," with songs inspired by Viking legends and Edgar Allen Poe short stories. Their albums are extremely collectible and hard to find today.

***$100**, NM condition*

Taking their name from a verse in the Bible (Isaiah 53:5, "By his stripes we are healed"), the Christian heavy metal band Stryper developed a strong following in the late 1980s.

***$7**, NM condition*

What To Look For

If a heavy metal music collector has a choice between an American, European, or Japanese pressing, they will often choose the import rather than the domestic product. Imported metal albums often are pressed on cleaner vinyl, and may contain bonus tracks or alternate mixes than the American pressings. Also, some metal albums exist on vinyl only as Japanese or German imports, as the American record company may have stopped making albums for their entire stable of artists.

Although Atlantic Records never released a stock copy of Led Zeppelin's opus "Stairway to Heaven" on a 45, it did release some promotional 45s for radio station use. This 45 came from a special 20th-anniversary promotional package, which contains a foldout popup sleeve that replicates the Zeppelin IV artwork, a 45 and a CD, each with "Stairway to Heaven" on them.

*With sleeve, CD, **$100**, NM condition*

Iron Maiden's headbanging character Eddie has appeared on almost all the group's album covers. On "Flight of Icarus," Eddie appears on one of the few picture sleeves for an Iron Maiden 45.

***$10** VG+ condition sleeve*

That being said, the rarer American copies of heavy metal records often come from tiny independent labels, or from short-printed albums that may have been taken off the market for a controversial lyric or album cover. The most collectible heavy metal albums are 1980s independent label pressings, many of which feature an entire album of brain-crunching metal, without compromise or posture. Some of these independent pressings may exist in runs of less than 500 copies. Traditional "power" metal or "progressive" metal is in; hair bands, thrash, or "death" metal are out.

With regard to KISS albums, be aware that thousands of KISS albums from the late 1970s, including the band's four simultaneous solo albums, may have a notched cover. KISS may have sold millions of records, but sometimes their record company over-estimated sales and printed more albums than were sold. These discs eventually made their way to the "cutout bin" of the record store, where they were sold for less than cost. Deduct 75% of a KISS album's near-mint value if the record cover is notched or cut.

First pressings of Led Zeppelin's "Immigrant Song" contain this cryptic message, "Do What Thou Wilt Shall Be the Whole of the Law." The phrase, which has been digitally enhanced for this photograph, was later deleted from subsequent pressings of the 45.

***$15**, VG condition*

Metallica's anthem "One" came with this picture sleeve. Many heavy metal collectors also collect picture sleeves from a metal band, as the artwork is not often replicated on any of the group's albums or CDs.

***$5**, NM condition picture sleeve*

Books

Popoff, Martin, *The Collector's Guide to Heavy Metal*, CG Publishing, Inc., Burlington, Ontario, 1997.

Popoff, Martin, *Goldmine Heavy Metal Record Price Guide*, Krause Publications, Iola, WI, 1999.

Strong, Martin C., *The Great Metal Discography*, Canongate Books, Edinburgh, Great Britain, 1998.

Eddy, Chuck, *Stairway To Hell: The 500 Best Heavy Metal Albums In The Universe*, Da Capo Press, NY, 1998.

Lendt, C.K., *Kiss and Sell: The Making Of A Supergroup*, Billboard Books, Watson-Guptill Publications, BPI Communications, New York, NY, 1997.

Shannon, Tom, *Goldmine KISS Collectibles Price Guide*, Krause Publications, Iola, WI, 2000.

Sherman, Dale, *Black Diamond II: The Illustrated Collector's Guide To Kiss*, CB Publishing, Toronto 1997.

Web Pages

Addicted to Metal, a home page devoted to heavy metal music: http://www.atmetal.com

The Ring of Zeppelin, a list of fan-based pages devoted to Led Zeppelin: http://www.crickrock.com/cgi-bin/webring/list.pl?ringid=zepring

KISS' home page: http://www.kissonline.com

Pantera's home page: http://www.pantera.com

The official Iron Maiden Web site: http://www.ironmaiden.com

Usenet newsgroups: alt.music.judas-priest, alt.music.led-zeppelin

ARTIST — VG+ to NM

AC/DC:

45s

Atco 7068, "High Voltage"/"It's A Long Way To The Top," 1976 ... $4.00-$8.00
Atlantic 3787, "Back in Black"/"What Do You Do For Money Honey," 1980 ... $2.00-$4.00

LPs

Atlantic LAAS-001, Live at the Atlantic Studios, 1977 ... $30.00-$60.00
SD 19244, Highway to Hell, 1979 ... $5.00-$10.00
SD 16033, Dirty Deeds Done Dirt Cheap, 1981 ... $5.00-$10.00
SD 16018, Back in Black, 1980 ... $5.00-$10.00
Epic 90643, AC/DC (16 LPs), 2003 ... $100.00-$200.00

AEROSMITH:

45s

Columbia 45894, "Dream On"/"Somebody" (A-side remixed, edited), 1973 ... $3.00-$6.00
10278, "Dream On"/"Somebody" (A-side full-length), 1975 ... $2.50-$5.00
10449, "Walk This Way"/"Uncle Salty," 1976 ... $2.50-$5.00

LPs

Columbia KC 32847, Get Your Wings, 1974 ... $6.00-$12.00
(if on Columbia KCQ 32847, quadraphonic), 1974 ... $12.50-$25.00
A3S 187, Pure Gold From Rock 'n' Roll's Golden Boys (compilation from Aerosmith's first three LPs), 1976 ... $25.00-$50.00
Geffen GHS 24162, Permanent Vacation, 1987 ... $5.00-$10.00

ALCATRAZZ:

LPs

Rocshire 22016, No Parole from Rock 'n' Roll, 1983 ... $12.50-$25.00
Capitol ST-12385, Disturbing the Peace, 1985 ... $10.00-$20.00
ST-12477, Dangerous Games, 1986 ... $10.00-$20.00

ALICE IN CHAINS:

LPs

Sony C257804, Sap/Jar of Flies (2 LPs), 1994 ... $10.00-$20.00

ANGEL OF MERCY:

LPs

The Record Company AM87001, The Avatar, 1987 ... $150.00-$300.00

AUTOGRAPH:

45s

RCA PB-13953, "Turn Up the Radio"/"Thrill of Love," 1984 ... $2.00-$4.00
(with picture sleeve, add), 1984 ... $3.00-$6.00

LPs

RCA Victor AFL1-5423, Sign In Please, 1984 ... $4.00-$8.00
AFL1-7009, That's the Stuff, 1985 ... $4.00-$8.00

BLACK SABBATH:

45s

Warner Bros. 7437, "Paranoid"/"Wizard," 1970 ... $5.00-$10.00
7530, "Iron Man"/"Electric Funeral," 1971 ... $4.00-$8.00
7764, "Sabbath, Bloody Sabbath"/"Changes," 1973 ... $4.00-$8.00
7802, "Iron Man"/"Electric Funeral," 1974 ... $4.00-$8.00

LPs

Warner Bros. WS 1871, Black Sabbath (if first pressing, on green label), 1970 ... $7.50-$15.00
(if on "Burbank" label with palm trees), 1973 ... $5.00-$10.00
(if on white or tan label), 1979 ... $4.00-$8.00
1887, Paranoid (if first pressing, on green label), 1971 ... $7.50-$15.00
(if on "Burbank" label with palm trees), 1973 ... $5.00-$10.00
(if on Warner Bros. WS4 1887, quadraphonic pressing), 1974 ... $15.00-$30.00

BLUE CHEER:

45s

Philips 40516, "Summertime Blues"/"Out of Focus" (Philips 40516), 1968 ... $6.00-$12.00
(with picture sleeve, add), 1968 ... $12.50-$25.00

LPs

Philips PHM200264, Vincebus Eruptum (mono), 1968 ... $40.00-$80.00
(if on Philips PHS 600264, stereo), 1968 ... $20.00-$40.00
PHS 600278, Outsideinside, 1968 ... $20.00-$40.00
PHS 600305, New! Improved! Blue Cheer, 1969 ... $20.00-$40.00

BLUE OYSTER CULT:

45s

Columbia 3-10384, "(Don't Fear) The Reaper"/"Tattoo Vampire," 1976 ... $3.00-$6.00
3-10697, "Godzilla"/"Nosferatu," 1978 ... $2.50-$5.00

LPs

Columbia PC 36164, Agents of Fortune
(if original gatefold, no bar code on cover), 1976 ... $5.00-$10.00
(if on Columbia PC 36164, budget reissue with bar code), 198? ... $4.00-$8.00

BON JOVI:

45s

Mercury 818309-7, "Runaway"/"Love Lies," 1984 ... $2.00-$4.00
(with picture sleeve, add), 1984 ... $3.00-$6.00
Island 314-562801-7, "It's My Life"/"Next 100 Years," 2000 ... $2.00-$4.00

LPs

Mercury 814982-1, Bon Jovi, 1984 ... $4.00-$8.00
830264-1, Slippery When Wet, 1986 ... $4.00-$8.00
(if on Mercury 830822-1, picture disc), 1986 ... $7.50-$15.00

THE CHERRY BOMBZ:

LPs

PVC 5913, 100 Degrees in the Shade, 1986 ... $6.50-$13.00

ALICE COOPER:

45s

Straight 101, "Reflected"/"Living," 1969 ... $150.00-$300.00
Warner Bros. 7596, "School's Out"/"Gutter Cat," 1972 ... $2.50-$5.00
(with picture sleeve, add), 1972 ... $5.00-$10.00
7691, "No More Mr. Nice Guy"/"Raped and Freezin'," 1973 ... $2.50-$5.00

LPs

Straight ST51501, Pretties For You (yellow label), 1969 ... $75.00-$150.00
(if on Straight ST51501, white label promo), 1969 ... $100.00-$200.00
(if on Straight ST51501, pink label), 1970 ... $30.00-$60.00
Warner Bros. BS 2685, Billion Dollar Babies (green "WB" label), 1973 ... $6.00-$12.00
(if on Warner Bros. BS4 2685, quadraphonic), 1974 ... $12.50-$25.00

DEEP PURPLE:

45s

Tetragrammaton 1503, "Hush"/"One More Rainy Day," 1968 ... $6.00-$12.00
(with picture sleeve, add), 1968 ... $15.00-$30.00
7710, "Smoke on the Water" (Edited Version—Studio)/"Smoke on the Water" (Edited Version—Live), 1973 ... $2.50-$5.00

LPs

Tetragrammon T131, Concerto for Group and Orchestra, 1970 ... $150.00-$300.00
(if on Warner Bros. WS 1860), 1970 ... $6.00-$12.00
Warner Bros. BS 2607, Machine Head
(if green label), 1972 ... $6.00-$12.00
(if "Burbank" labels with palm trees), 1973 ... $5.00-$10.00
(if on Warner Bros. BS4 2607, quadraphonic), 1974 ... $12.50-$25.00

DEF LEPPARD:

45s

Mercury 811-215-7, "Photograph"/"Action, Not Words"
(if on Chicago skyline label), 1983 ... $2.50-$5.00
(if on black label), 1983 ... $2.00-$4.00
(with picture sleeve, add), 1983 ... $5.00-$10.00
870298-7, "Pour Some Sugar on Me"/"Ring of Fire," 1988 ... $1.50-$3.00
(with picture sleeve, add), 1988 ... $1.50-$3.00
870402-7, "Love Bites"/"Billy's Got a Gun," 1988 ... $1.50-$3.00
(with picture sleeve, add), 1988 ... $1.50-$3.00

LPs

Mercury SRM-1-3828, On Through the Night (Chicago skyline label), 1980 ... $6.00-$12.00
SRM-1-4021, High 'n' Dry (Chicago skyline label), 1981 ... $6.00-$12.00
(if on Mercury 811836-1, adds "Me & My Wine"), 1984 ... $4.00-$8.00
810308, Pyromania, 1983 ... $2.00-$4.00

RONNIE JAMES DIO:

LPs

Jove J-108, Dio at Domino's (500 copies pressed), 1963 ... $200.00-$400.00

DOKKEN:

12-inch Singles

Elektra ED 5124, "In My Dreams" (2 versions), 1985 ... $4.00-$8.00

LPs

Elektra 60290, Breakin' The Chains, 1981 ... $2.00-$4.00

GIRLSCHOOL:

LPs

Mercury SRM 14066, Screaming Blue Murder, 1982 **$4.25-$8.50**

GUNS N' ROSES:

45s

Geffen 27759, "Welcome To The Jungle"/"Mr. Brownstone," 1988 **$2.00-$4.00**

(with picture sleeve, add), 1988 **$2.00-$4.00**

LPs

Uzi Suicide USR 001, Live?!*@ Like a Suicide, 1986 **$60.00-$120.00**

Geffen XXXG24148, Appetite for Destruction ("rape" cover), 1988 **$25.00-$50.00**

(if on Geffen G24148, "cross" cover), 1988 **$4.00-$8.00**

24415, Use Your Illusion I (2 LPs), 1991 **$10.00-$20.00**

24420, Use Your Illusion II (2 LPs), 1991 **$10.00-$20.00**

IRON BUTTERFLY:

45s

Atco 6606, "In-A-Gadda-Da-Vida"/"Iron Butterfly Theme" (Atco 6606), 1968 **$5.00-$10.00**

Mono LPs

Atco 33-227, Heavy, 1967 **$15.00-$30.00**

33-250, In-A-Gadda-Da-Vida, 1968 **$25.00-$50.00**

Stereo LPs

Atco SD-33-227, Heavy (brown-purple label), 1967 **$12.50-$25.00**

(if yellow label), 1969 **$7.50-$15.00**

SD-33-250, In-A-Gadda-Da-Vida (brown-purple label), 1968 **$12.50-$25.00**

(if yellow label), 1969 **$7.50-$15.00**

(if any other later Atco label), 197? **$5.00-$10.00**

IRON MAIDEN:

45s

Capitol B-5248, "Flight of Icarus"/"I've The Fire," 1983 **$5.00-$10.00**

LPs

Capitol ST-12202, The Number of the Beast, 1982 **$4.00-$8.00**

(if on Capitol SEAX-12219, picture disc), 1982 **$25.00-$50.00**

ST-12274, Piece of Mind, 1983 **$4.00-$8.00**

(if on Capitol SEAX-12306, picture disc), 1983 **$30.00-$60.00**

SJ-12321, Powerslave, 1984 **$4.00-$8.00**

SABB-12241, Live After Death (2 LPs), 1985 **$5.00-$10.00**

JUDAS PRIEST:

45s

Columbia 11000, "Rock Forever"/"The Green Manalishi (With the Two-Pronged Crown)," 1979 **$2.00-$4.00**

11308, "Living After Midnight"/"Metal Gods," 1980 **$2.00-$4.00**

LPs

Janus JXS-7019, Sad Wings of Destiny, 1976 **$12.50-$25.00**

Columbia AS99 1543, Screaming for Vengeance (picture disc)

(if disc plays correct album on both sides), 1982 **$10.00-$20.00**

(if disc actually plays Neil Diamond's "Heartlight" but has Judas Priest picture disc artwork), 1982 **$15.00-$30.00**

KISS:

45s

Casablanca 0004, "Love Theme From KISS"/"Nothin' To Lose," 1974 **$6.00-$12.00**

850, "Rock and Roll All Nite (live)"/"Rock and Roll All Nite (studio)," 1975 **$5.00-$10.00**

858, "Flaming Youth"/"God of Thunder," 1976 **$5.00-$10.00**

(with picture sleeve, add), 1976 **$30.00-$60.00**

863, "Detroit Rock City"/"Beth" (Casablanca 863) ("Detroit Rock City" is listed as A-side), 1976 **$5.00-$10.00**

863, "Beth"/"Detroit Rock City" (Casablanca 863) ("Beth" is listed as A-side), 1976 **$2.50-$5.00**

2365, "I Love It Loud"/"Danger" (Casablanca 2365), 1982 **$2.50-$5.00**

(with picture sleeve, add), 1982 **$10.00-$20.00**

LPs

Casablanca NB 9001, Kiss (does not contain the song "Kissin' Time"), 1974 **$40.00-$80.00**

(if on Casablanca NBLP 7001, contains the song "Kissin' Time"), 1974 **$15.00-$30.00**

NBLP 7020, Alive! (2 LPs) (dark blue "Bogart" label), 1975 **$20.00-$40.00**

(if above is on tan Casablanca "camels" label, no motion picture cameras or "Filmworks" reference), 1976 **$10.00-$20.00**

NBLP 7037, Love Gun (mint copy must contain inserted cardboard gun), 1977 **$20.00-$40.00**

Mercury 792-1, First Kiss, Last Licks (Mercury 792-1) (white label promo sampler), 1990 **$50.00-$100.00**

LED ZEPPELIN:

45s

Atlantic 2690, "Whole Lotta Love" (3:12)/"Living Loving Maid (She's Just a Woman)," 1969 **$7.50-$15.00**

2690, "Whole Lotta Love" (5:33)/"Living Loving Maid (She's Just a Woman)," 1969 **$10.00-$20.00**

2777, "Immigrant Song"/"Hey, Hey, What Can I Do" (if "Do What Thou Wilt Shalt Be the Whole of the Law" written in dead wax near label), 1970 **$12.50-$25.00**

(if phrase not written in dead wax), 1971 **$7.50-$15.00**

(if smaller, bolder type, Warner Communications logo in perimeter of label), 1977 **$2.50-$5.00**

Atlantic PR 175, "Stairway To Heaven" (mono/stereo) (promo only), 1972 **$50.00-$100.00**

(with promo picture sleeve, add), 1972 **$125.00-$250.00**

(if on Atlantic PR 269, both sides in stereo), 1973 **$25.00-$50.00**

(if on Atlantic PR 4424, 20th anniversary promo pack with foldout popup sleeve, 45 and single-song CD), 1992 **$50.00-$100.00**

LPs

Atlantic 7208, Led Zeppelin (album also known as Led Zeppelin IV, Runes or Zoso)

(if on Atlantic 7208, mono, white label promo only), 1971 **$150.00-$300.00**

(if on Atlantic SD 7208, stereo, white label promo), 1971 **$75.00-$150.00**

(if on Atlantic SD 7208, stereo, "1841 Broadway" address on label), 1971 **$6.00-$12.00**

(if on Atlantic SMAS-94019, Capitol Record Club), 1972 **$20.00-$40.00**

(if on Atlantic SD 7208, stereo, "75 Rockefeller Plaza" address on label), 1974 **$5.00-$10.00**

(if on Atlantic SD 19129, reissue), 1977 **$4.00-$8.00**

(if on Atlantic SD 7208, Classic Records reissue on audiophile vinyl), 2000 **$12.50-$25.00**

MAHOGANY RUSH:

45s

Nine 369, "Buddy"/"All In Your Mind," 1973 **$4.00-$8.00**

LPs

Nine 936, Maxoom, 1973 **$25.00-$50.00**

20th Century T-451, Child of the Novelty, 1974 **$12.50-$25.00**

Columbia PC 34190, Mahogany Rush IV (no bar code on back), 1976 **$7.50-$15.00**

(with bar code on back cover), 198? **$4.00-$8.00**

YNGWIE MALMSTEEN:

LPs

Polydor 825324, Yngwie Malmsteen's Rising Force, 1985 **$2.50-$5.00**

MANILLA ROAD:

LPs

Roadster MR 1001, Invasion, 1980 **$50.00-$100.00**

MR 1002, Metal, 1982 **$50.00-$100.00**

MR 1003, Crystal Logic, 1983 **$25.00-$50.00**

MEGADETH:

45s

Capitol S7-57798, "Symphony of Destruction"/"Breakpoint" (label misspells band name as "Megadeath"), 1992 **$4.00-$8.00**

LPs

Capitol 48148, So Far, So Good... So What!, 1988 **$2.75-$5.50**

(if on picture disc), 1988 **$12.50-$25.00**

METALLICA:

45s

Elektra 69329, "One"/"The Prince," 1988 **$2.50-$5.00**

(with picture sleeve, add), 1988 **$2.50-$5.00**

LPs

Megaforce MRI 169, Kill 'Em All, 1983 **$15.00-$30.00**

(if on picture disc, numbered limited edition version, same catalog number), 1983 **$40.00-$80.00**

(if on picture disc, un-numbered version, same catalog number), 1983 **$20.00-$40.00**

MRI 769, Ride the Lightning, 1984 **$15.00-$30.00**

Elektra 60812, ...And Justice for All (2 LPs), 1988 **$10.00-$20.00**

61113, Metallica (2 LPs), 1991 **$20.00-$40.00**

61923, Load (2 LPs), 1996 **$7.50-$15.00**

62299, Garage Inc. (3 LPs), 1998 **$10.00-$20.00**

MONTROSE:

LPs

Warner Bros. BS 2740, Montrose, 1974 .... **$6.00-$12.00**
BS 2823, Paper Money, 1974 .... **$6.00-$12.00**
BS 2892, Warner Bros. Presents Montrose!, 1975 .... **$6.00-$12.00**
BS 2963, Jump On It, 1976 .... **$6.00-$12.00**

MÖTLEY CRÜE:

45s

Leathur 001, "Stick To Your Guns"/"Toast of the Town," 1981 ... **$40.00-$80.00**
(with picture sleeve, add), 1981 .... **$75.00-$150.00**

LPs

Leathur LR 123, Too Fast For Love
(if first pressing, white lettering on cover), 1981 .... **$150.00-$300.00**
(if second pressing, red lettering on cover), 1981 .... **$75.00-$150.00**
(if on Elektra 60174, deletes the song "Stick To Your Guns"), 1981 .... **$2.25-$4.50**
Elektra 60289, Shout at the Devil, 1982 .... **$4.00-$8.00**
60418, Theatre of Pain, 1985 .... **$4.00-$8.00**
60725, Girls, Girls, Girls, 1987 .... **$4.00-$8.00**
60829, Dr. Feelgood, 1989 .... **$5.00-$10.00**

MÖTORHEAD:

LPs

Mercury SRM-1-4011, Ace of Spades, 1980 .... **$5.00-$10.00**
Island 90233, No Remorse (2 LPs), 1984 .... **$6.00-$12.00**
(if leather album jacket), 1984 .... **$15.00-$30.00**

MOUNTAIN:

45s

Windfall 532, "Mississippi Queen"/"The Laird," 1970 .... **$4.00-$8.00**

LPs

Windfall 4501, Mountain Climbing!, 1970 .... **$7.50-$15.00**
5500, Nantucket Sleighride (with inserts), 1971 .... **$7.50-$15.00**

NINE INCH NAILS:

LPs

Nothing/TVT/Interscope PR 5509, The Downward Spiral ("Halo Eight") (2 LPs, vinyl is promo only), 1994 .... **$25.00-$50.00**
Nothing/Interscope 490473, The Fragile ("Halo Fourteen") (3 LPs), 1999 .... **$20.00-$40.00**
490744, Things Falling Apart ("Halo Sixteen") (2 LPs), 2000 ..... **$7.50-$15.00**

TED NUGENT:

45s

Epic 50425, "Cat Scratch Fever"/"Wang Dang Sweet Poontang," 1977 .... **$2.50-$5.00**

LPs

Epic FE 36000, State of Shock, 1979 .... **$5.00-$10.00**
(if on Epic AS99-607, promo-only picture disc), 1979 .... **$20.00-$40.00**
(if on Epic PE 36000, budget reissue), 198? .... **$4.00-$8.00**

OZZY OSBOURNE:

45s

Jet 02079, "Crazy Train"/"Steal Away (The Night)," 1981 .... **$2.50-$5.00**
(if on CBS Associated 07168, studio and live versions of "Crazy Train"), 1987 .... **$1.50-$3.00**

LPs

Jet FZ 37492, Diary of a Madman, 1981 .... **$2.50-$5.00**
(if on Epic AS99 1372, picture disc, promo only), 1981 .... **$14.00-$28.00**

PANTERA:

LPs

Metal Magic MMR 1984, Projects in the Jungle (with fan club insert), 1984 .... **$37.50-$75.00**
(if on yellow vinyl), 1984 .... **$37.50-$75.00**

POISON:

LPs

Capitol/Enigma C1-48493, Open Up and Say...Ahh!, 1988 .... **$4.00-$8.00**
(if album cover features fully visible woman's tongue, not cropped, no large black bars on top or bottom of cover), 1988 .... **$6.00-$12.00**
Capitol ST512523, Look What The Cat Dragged In, 1986 .... **$2.25-$4.50**

QUEENSRYCHE:

LPs

EMI 48640, Operation: Mindcrime, 1988 .... **$2.25-$4.50**
(if on EMI SPRO1436, picture disc), 1988 .... **$22.50-$45.00**

RAGE AGAINST THE MACHINE:

45s

Epic 74927, "Bullet in the Head"/"Darkness," 1993 .... **$2.50-$5.00**
(with picture sleeve, add), 1993 .... **$2.50-$5.00**

LPs

Epic E 57523, Evil Empire, 1996 .... **$5.00-$10.00**

RAINBOW:

45s

Polydor 14290, Blackmore's Rainbow, "Snake Charmer"/"Man on the Silver Mountain," 1975 .... **$3.00-$6.00**
Mercury 76146, "Stone Cold"/"Rock Fever," 1982 .... **$2.00-$4.00**
(with picture sleeve, add), 1982 .... **$2.50-$5.00**

LPs

Oyster OY-1-1601, Rainbow Rising, 1976 .... **$6.00-$12.00**
(if on Polydor 823655-1, reissue), 1985 .... **$4.00-$8.00**

RATT:

LPs

Atlantic 81257, Invasion of Your Privacy, 1985 .... **$2.25-$4.50**

SAXON:

LPs

Carrere 37679, Strong Arm of the Law, 1980 .... **$3.50-$7.00**

SCORPIONS:

LPs

Billingsgate 1004, Lonesome Crow, 1974 .... **$15.00-$30.00**
Mercury 814981-1, Love at First Sting
(if first pressing, with man and woman on cover), 1984 .... **$5.00-$10.00**
(if second pressing, with band on cover), 1984 .... **$6.00-$12.00**

SLAYER:

LPs

Metal Blade 71034, Show No Mercy, 1983 .... **$4.25-$8.50**
(if on Metal Blade 72214, picture disc), 1987 .... **$12.50-$25.00**

SOUNDGARDEN:

LPs

A&M 31454 0198 1, Superunknown (2 LPs) (available on gold, blue, or clear vinyl, value is equal), 1994 .... **$7.50-$15.00**

STARZ:

45s

Capitol 4399, "Cherry Baby"/"Rock Six Times," 1977 .... **$2.00-$4.00**
(if on yellow vinyl), 1977 .... **$6.00-$12.00**

LPs

Capitol ST 11617, Violation, 1977 .... **$5.00-$10.00**
(if on yellow vinyl, promo only), 1977 .... **$10.00-$20.00**

STEPPENWOLF:

45s

ABC Dunhill 4138, "Born To Be Wild"/"Everybody's Next One," 1968 .... **$4.00-$8.00**

LPs

ABC Dunhill DS-50029, Steppenwolf, 1968 .... **$10.00-$20.00**
DS-50037, The Second (white border on cover), 1968 .... **$15.00-$30.00**
(if chrome border on cover), 1968 .... **$12.50-$25.00**

STRYPER:

LPs

Enigma E 1064, The Yellow and Black Attack, 1986 .... **$3.50-$7.00**
(if on Enigma ST73207, blue or yellow vinyl, round cover), 1986 .... **$10.00-$20.00**

TYGERS OF PAN TANG:

LPs

MCA 5235, Spellbound, 1981 .... **$6.00-$12.00**
5237, The Cage, 1982 .... **$6.00-$12.00**

UFO:

LPs

Rare Earth RS 624, UFO 1, 1971 .... **$12.50-$25.00**
Chrysalis PV 41307, The Wild, The Willing and the Innocent, 1983 .... **$4.00-$8.00**

VAN HALEN:

LPs

Warner Bros. 23985, 1984, 1984 .... **$2.25-$4.50**
(if promo copy, pressed on Quiex II vinyl), 1984 .... **$12.50-$25.00**
1W-26594, For Unlawful Carnal Knowledge (vinyl only available through Columbia House), 1991 .... **$10.00-$20.00**

WARGASM:

LPs

Profile PRO 1254, Why Play Around?, 1988 .... **$3.75-$7.50**

WHITE ZOMBIE:

LPs

Geffen 24802, Astro Creep 2000 (purple vinyl), 1995 .... **$11.50-$23.00**

CHAPTER 14

JAZZ

History

"Jazz music" covers such diverse musical styles as bebop, hard bop, fusion, free form, New Orleans jazz, Midwestern jazz—even traditional Dixieland and "new age" recordings have been grouped into the jazz definition. There are rare jazz recordings whose existence harkens back to the earliest shellac 78s. There are record companies whose very names—Blue Note, Fantasy, Prestige—are synonymous with the world of jazz. And the collectibility of these treasures has not diminished to this day.

Jazz is also one of the few musical genres where collectors search for not only a particular musical style, but also how a particular musical instrument is used in that style. There are jazz saxophone fans who search for recordings by Coleman Hawkins, John Coltrane, Charlie "Yardbird" Parker, and Cannonball Adderly. Jazz trumpet collectors will gravitate towards the works of Louis Armstrong, Bix Beiderbecke, Miles Davis, and Dizzy Gillespie. Keyboard enthusiasts will search out the early recordings of Earl "Fatha" Hines, Fats Waller, Thelonious Monk, Dave Brubeck, and Vince Guaraldi.

Even the voice itself has become a powerful jazz instrument, as collectors of music by Bessie Smith, Ethel Waters, Connee Boswell, or Billie Holiday will attest. Vocalists could sing the lyrics as written; they could "scat" the melody with vocal and lyrical gymnastics, or a trio or quartet could blend their voices in synchronicity with the featured instruments or orchestra. There are also popular "vocalese" performers, artists who use their vocal skills to replace a trumpet solo, adding lyrics that match perfectly with the music and theme.

Photo credit: Courtesy of Russell Shor and Mark Berresford, VJM's Jazz and Blues Mart.

Louis Armstrong was a 23-year-old cornetist when he traveled from New Orleans to Chicago, recording some sides with King Oliver's Creole Jazz Band. Very few of these fragile 78s have survived to this day. This pressing of "Zulus Ball" sold at auction in 2002 for $32,000.00, the highest price ever paid for a 78-RPM record.

$32,000

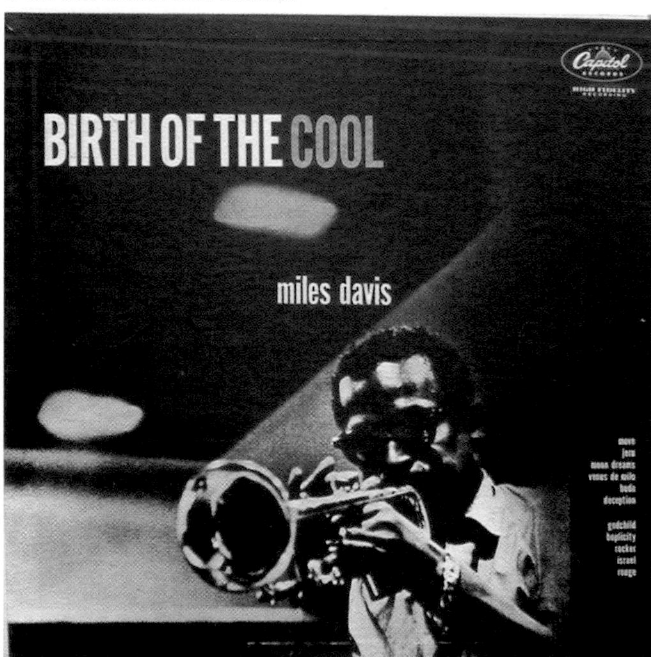

After his years recording with Charlie Parker, Miles Davis brought together several of the best jazz musicians, including John Lewis, Gerry Mulligan, Max Roach, and Kai Winding. The 78s recorded from that session were later compiled into the album Birth of the Cool, *one of the most influential modern jazz albums ever.*

***$75**, VG+ condition (1956 pressing)*

The first vinyl collaboration by Dave Lambert, Jon Hendricks, and Annie Ross was a collection of Count Basie standards, in which the trio replicated the bandleader's instruments with their own voices. Sing a Song of Basie *influenced a generation of "vocalese" jazz artists, including the Hi-Lo's, Eddie Jefferson, King Pleasure, and the Manhattan Transfer.*

***$50**, NM condition*

The Original Dixieland "Jass" Band's "Livery Stable Blues," a sprightly Dixieland foxtrot in which the instruments replicate animal sounds, is regarded as the first successful jazz recording ever preserved on a record.

***$10**, Fair condition*

The first jazz sounds came from New Orleans, a multicultural melting pot where blues, spirituals, Dixieland, and ragtime could be heard from Storyville to the French Quarter. Such New Orleans jazz proponents include Jelly Roll Morton, Kid Ory, Sidney Bechet, and the legendary Buddy Bolden. By the 1920s, thousands of African-Americans migrated north to industrial cities like Chicago, Detroit, and Pittsburgh, where factory jobs were plentiful. Chicago became a hotbed for jazz music in the 1920s, as Louis Armstrong, Joe "King" Oliver, and Bix Beiderbecke helped jazz to evolve.

Jazz music survived the Depression-era 1930s, evolving into "big band" music. Orchestras and combos crisscrossed America, performing in clubs, halls, and arenas, spreading jazz as a new musical message. Fletcher Henderson's big band included, at various times, Coleman Hawkins and Louis Armstrong. Paul Whiteman's big band included Jack Teagarden and Bix Biederbecke. Cab Calloway brought excitement to the stage with every "hi-de-ho," while Lionel Hampton held double duty as vibraphonist and conductor in his own orchestra.

By 1945, saxophonist Charlie Parker and trumpeter Dizzy Gillespie created new jazz sounds from New York. With its high-spirited melodies and daring orchestrations, this new form of jazz music, known as "bebop," found new popularity in New York's smoky jazz clubs. Besides Parker and Gillespie, other bebop legends include Coleman Hawkins, Buddy Rich, Thelonious Monk, and Sonny Stitt.

Bebop itself eventually split into two different musical styles—Cool Jazz and Hard Bop. West Coast cool jazz was sweeter and mellower, its sound a mixture of bebop and swing, along with classical music from Claude Debussy and George Gershwin. Among the proponents of cool jazz were Miles Davis, whose early 78s were collected into the seminal album *Birth of the Cool*; Dave Brubeck, whose experiments with time signatures created the masterpiece *Take Five*; and Shorty Rogers, whose albums *Portrait of*

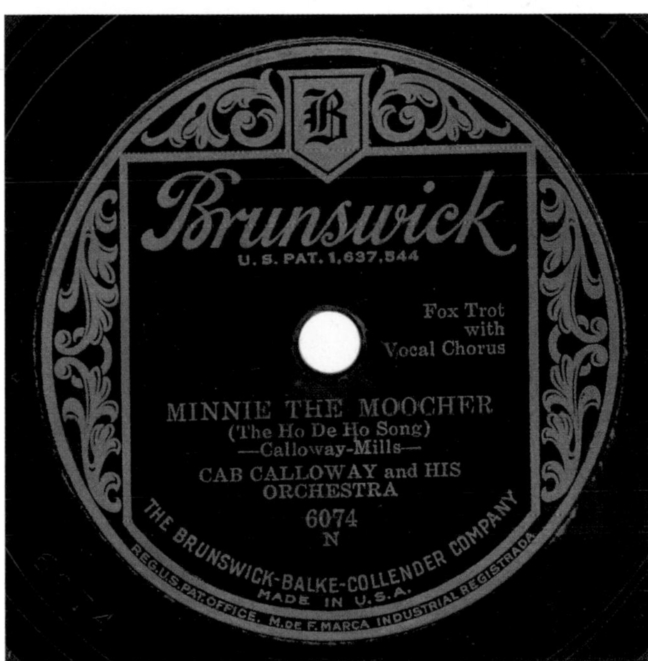

Cab Calloway's "Minnie the Moocher," one of the most popular songs of its era, was later made into an animated short film starring Betty Boop. Calloway later performed the song in the 1980s motion picture The Cotton Club.

***$20**, NM condition*

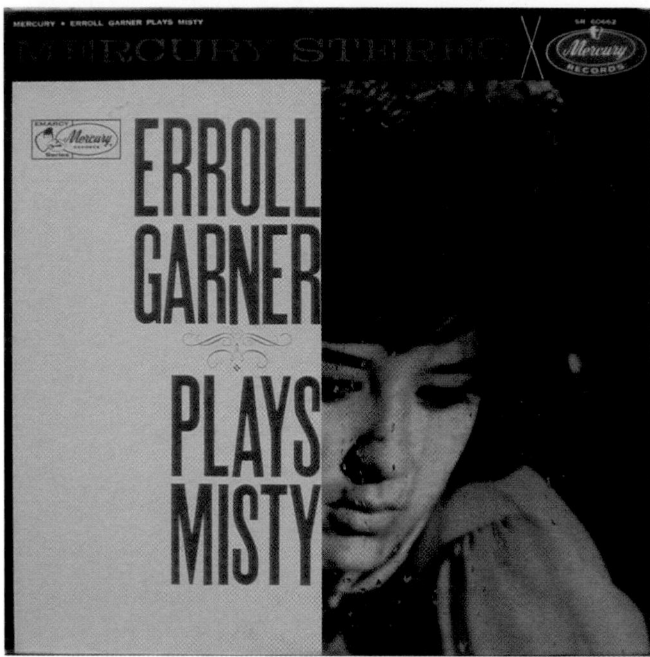

The song "Misty" has been covered by hundreds of artists, from Johnny Mathis to Ray Stevens, and was also the thematic subject of a Clint Eastwood motion picture, Play Misty For Me. *Its composer, jazz pianist Erroll Garner, was so talented that he once recorded three albums' worth of music in a single day—all in first takes.*

***$20**, NM condition (1962 pressing)*

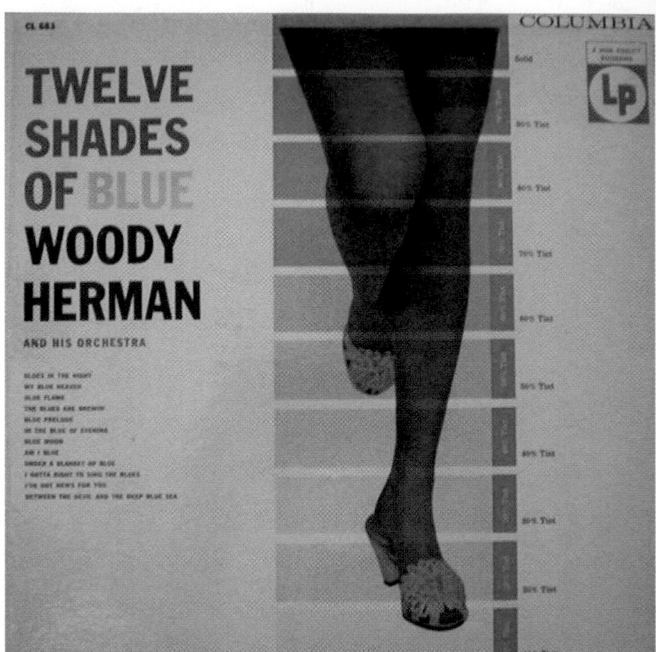

Woody Herman led several "Herds" of big bands in his performing career. A collection of bound 78s with the color "blue" either in the song titles or as part of the theme, Eight Shades of Blue, *was later released in 1955, with four additional tracks, as—naturally—*Twelve Shades of Blue.

***$30**, NM condition*

Shorty and *The Shorty Rogers Quintet* are staples of cool jazz libraries. Hard bop was not as mellow as cool jazz, but it did have more emotion and passion, its musicians turning their New York City life experiences into powerful musical excursions. Legends of hard bop include Art Blakey and his Jazz Messengers, Dexter Gordon, Clifford Brown, and Sonny Rollins.

By the 1960s, jazz evolved into "free jazz," with the soaring sax solos of John Coltrane, the intricate "harmolodics" of Ornette Coleman, and the intergalactic adventures of Sun Ra and his various Arkestras. The 1970s brought a mixture of jazz to rock and roll, creating "fusion." Proponents of this style of jazz music include Chick Corea and Return to Forever; Pat Metheny, Keith Jarrett, Weather Report, and Herbie Hancock.

An offshoot of free jazz became "new age" music. This form of jazz music involves lighter, calmer musical excursions, relaxing the mind and freeing the soul. The label most associated with new age music is Windham Hill Records. Windham Hill has featured eclectic jazz and new age releases by such artists as William Ackerman, Michael Hedges, Alex DeGrassi, and Shadowfax. Windham Hill's most successful artist has been pianist George Winston, whose album *December* has become a holiday perennial since its release in 1982.

George Winston incorporated the themes and styles of other famous and legendary jazz pianists, such as Vince Guaraldi and Erroll Garner, into his album December, *an excursion into the music and emotions of the holiday season. First pressings of this album feature the title embossed in raised letters on the album cover; second pressings have the title printed on the cover itself.*

***$10**, VG+ condition*

What To Look For

More than any other musical style, the price of collectible jazz has fluctuated greatly. One collector I spoke with even suggested that to get the most accurate prices for rare jazz, you should go to Tokyo for a week, visit the collectible jazz shops, write down the prices in yen, then convert those figures to U.S. dollars. That being said, the works of many of the original masters are still highly collectible—including first pressings of albums by Charlie Parker, John Coltrane, and Sun Ra.

Because of the prolific output of many jazz artists, many of their albums appear as budget-line reissues. These reissues are great to listen to and enjoy, while your early pressings of the same title stay safe on the shelves.

Between 1948 and 1955, many record companies pressed 10-inch albums as a standard format. Eventually the 12-inch album became the dominant format for multi-song recordings, but the original 10-inch discs have leaped in value, commanding anywhere from $60 to $500 for near-mint examples of legendary jazz performances.

The Blue Note record label is one of the most desirous jazz labels, with a rich history of recorded sound. However, many jazz collectors will want the first pressings of a Blue Note album, and to properly determine that the Blue Note disc you own is either an original or a reissue, one needs to examine the record's paper label.

1950s up to 1956—Blue Note albums are pressed with a deep groove that actually penetrates the paper label to the vinyl below.

1956—The label cites Blue Note's address as Lexington Avenue.

1957—The label cites Blue Note's address as West 63rd Street.

1963—The label now says Blue Note's address is New York, USA.

1960s—The label acknowledges Blue Note's affiliation with Liberty Records.

1984—Blue Note labels now say that Blue Note is "The Finest in Jazz Since 1939."

Photo credit: From the collection of David Beckett, WWPV-FM, Burlington, VT.

Sun Ra's loyal fans actively search for his entire catalog, including both his major label recordings on Savoy and Impulse!, and his independent pressings on the Saturn label, such as the one shown above.

***$150**, VG condition*

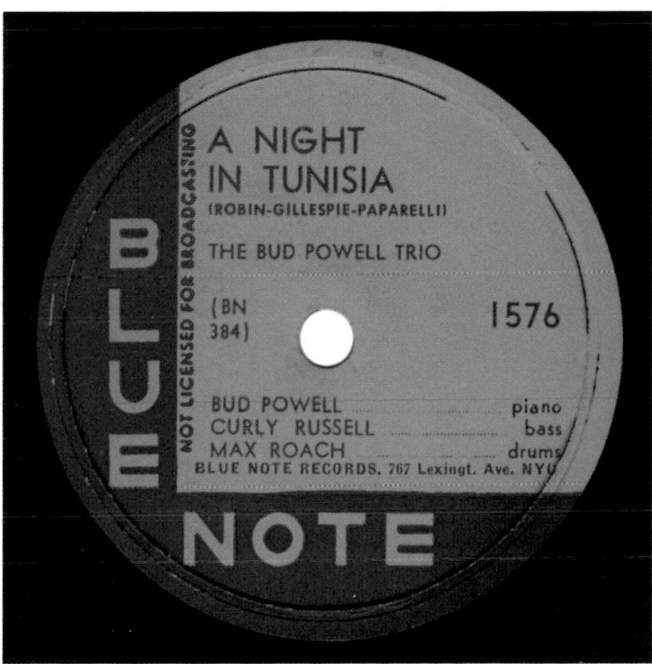

The "deep groove" around a label's inner perimeter can be found on most early Blue Note pressings, including this 78 from The Bud Powell Trio.

***$12**, VG+ condition*

Books

Neely, Tim, *Goldmine Jazz Album Price Guide*, Krause Publications, Iola, WI, 2000.

Sutro, Dirk, *Jazz for Dummies*, IDG Books Worldwide, Foster City, CA, 1998.

Ward, Geoffrey C.; Ken Burns, *Jazz: A History of America's Music*, Knopf, NY, 2000.

Kofsky, Frank, *Black Nationalism and the Revolution in Music*, Pathfinder Press, New York, NY, 1970. Contains insightful interviews and essays on the life of John Coltrane and the jazz culture of the 1940s and 1950s.

Web Pages

Blue Note Records, the legendary jazz label: http://www.bluenote.com

For the history of jazz before 1930, visit this page: http://www.redhotjazz.com

A Web page devoted to Louis Armstrong: http://www.satchmo.com

A Web page devoted to the music and careers of John Coltrane and McCoy Tyner: http://www.jazz.route66.net

A complete discography of the music of Sun Ra, available at this site: http://www.dpo.uab.edu/~moudry/discintr.htm

Usenet newsgroups: rec.music.bluenote, rec.music.makers.jazz, tw.bbs.music.jazz

Museums

American Jazz Museum, 18th and Vine Streets, Kansas City, MO, (816) 474-8463. http://www.americanjazzmuseum.com

Graystone International Jazz Museum and Hall of Fame, 249 Washington Boulevard, Suite 201, Detroit, Michigan 48226, (313) 963-3813: http://hometown.aol.com/gjazzmuseu/front.html

Louisiana State Museum New Orleans Jazz Exhibition, Old U.S. Mint, 400 Esplanade Avenue, New Orleans, Louisiana 70116, 1-800-568-6968: http://lsm.crt.state.la.us

ARTIST — VG+ to NM

CANNONBALL ADDERLY:

45s

Blue Note 1737, "Autumn Leaves" (Pt. 1)/(Pt. 2), 1959 .... **$5.00-$10.00**
Capitol 5798, "Mercy, Mercy, Mercy"/"Games," 1966 .... **$3.50-$7.00**

Stereo LPs

Blue Note BST-1595, Somethin' Else
(if deep groove pressed into label), 1959 .... **$50.00-$100.00**
(if West 63rd Street address on label), 1959 .... **$37.50-$75.00**
(if New York USA address on label), 1963 .... **$10.00-$20.00**
(if on Blue Note BST-81595, "A Division of Liberty Records" on label), 1966 .... **$7.50-$15.00**
(if on Blue Note BM-LA169-F, reissue), 1973 .... **$5.00-$10.00**
(if on Blue Note LT-169, reissue), 1981 .... **$5.00-$10.00**
(if on Blue Note BST-81595, stereo, "The Finest in Jazz Since 1939" on label), 1984 .... **$5.00-$10.00**
(if on Blue Note B1-46338, audiophile reissue), 1997 .... **$10.00-$20.00**
(if on Blue Note BST-81595, Classic Records reissue), 199? .... **$12.50-$25.00**

LOUIS ARMSTRONG:

45s

Decca 29102, "Basin Street Blues" (Pt. 1)/(Pt. 2), 1954 .... **$7.50-$15.00**
Kapp 573, "Hello Dolly!"/"A Lot Of Lovin' To Do," 1964 .... **$3.00-$6.00**
(with picture sleeve, add), 1964 .... **$5.00-$10.00**

78s

OKeh 8535, "Savoy Blues"/"Hotter Than That," 1927 .... **$15.00-$30.00**
Columbia 2606-D, "All of Me"/"Home," 1931 .... **$10.00-$20.00**
Victor 24200, "Hobo You Can't Ride This Train"/"That's My Home," 1932 .... **$10.00-$20.00**

10-inch LPs

Brunswick BL 58004, Armstrong Classics, 1950 .... **$50.00-$100.00**
Decca DL 5509, Louis Armstrong and the Mills Brothers, 1954 **$30.00-$60.00**

Mono LPs

Decca DX 155, Satchmo, A Musical Autobiography (4 LPs, black labels, silver print), 1956 .... **$50.00-$100.00**
(if black labels with color bars, reissue), 1960 .... **$20.00-$40.00**

Stereo LPs

Verve MGVS-6101, I've Got the World on a String, 1960 .... **$20.00-$40.00**
Buena Vista BF-4044, Disney Swings the Satchmo Way, 1968 ... **$20.00-$40.00**

COUNT BASIE:

45s

RCA Victor 47-2990, "Did You See Jackie Robinson Hit That Ball?"/"Shoutin' Blues," 1949 .... **$20.00-$40.00**
Clef 89070, "Blee Blop Blues"/"Small Hotel," 1953 .... **$7.50-$15.00**
Roulette 4124, "Jumpin' at the Woodside"/"Rusty Dusty Blues," 1958 .... **$5.00-$10.00**

10-inch LPs

Clef MCG-120, Count Basie and His Orchestra Collates, 1953 .... **$100.00-$200.00**
EmArcy MG-26023, Jazz Royalty, 1954 .... **$35.00-$70.00**

Mono LPs

Columbia CL 901, Blues By Basie, 1956 .... **$20.00-$40.00**
Brunswick BL 54012, Count Basie, 1957 .... **$20.00-$40.00**

Stereo LPs

Roulette SR 52003, Basie, 1958 .... **$15.00-$30.00**
(if on red vinyl), 1958 .... **$50.00-$100.00**
ABC S-570, Basie's Swingin'—Voices Singin', 1966 .... **$12.50-$25.00**

SIDNEY BECHET:

10-inch LPs

Blue Note BLP-7001, Sidney Bechet's Blue Note Jazz Men, 1950 .... **$200.00-$400.00**
BLP-7002, Jazz Classics, Volume 1, 1950 .... **$125.00-$250.00**
Atlantic ALS-118, Sidney Bechet Solos, 1952 .... **$60.00-$120.00**

Mono LPs

Atlantic 1206, Sidney Bechet Duets (with Muggsy Spanier), 1956 .... **$40.00-$80.00**
Blue Note BLP-1201, Jazz Classics, Volume 1
(if first pressings, with deep groove on label), 1955 .... **$75.00-$150.00**
(if regular edition, Lexington Ave. address on label), 1955 ...... **$50.00-$100.00**
RCA Victor LPV-510, Bechet of New Orleans, 1965 .... **$10.00-$20.00**
LPV-535, Blue Bechet, 1966 .... **$10.00-$20.00**

ART BLAKEY AND THE JAZZ MESSENGERS:

10-inch LPs

Blue Note BLP-5037, A Night at Birdland, Volume 1, 1954 .... **$150.00-$300.00**
BLP-5038, A Night at Birdland, Volume 2, 1954 .... **$150.00-$300.00**
EmArcy MG-26030, Blakey, 1954 .... **$125.00-$250.00**

Mono LPs

Blue Note BLP-1507, At the Café Bohemia, Volume 1
(if "deep groove" indentation on label), 1956 .... **$75.00-$150.00**
(if regular version, Lexington Ave. address on label), 1956 ...... **$50.00-$100.00**
Jubilee JLP-1049, Cu-Bop, 1958 .... **$40.00-$80.00**

Stereo LPs

Blue Note BST-4003, Art Blakey and the Jazz Messengers
(if "deep groove" indentation on label), 1959 .... **$50.00-$100.00**
(if regular version, W. 63rd St. address on label), 1959 .... **$40.00-$80.00**
(if "New York, U.S.A." address on label), 1963 .... **$10.00-$20.00**
Impulse! AS-7, Art Blakey!!!! Jazz Messengers!!!!, 1961 .... **$20.00-$40.00**
(if on ABC Impulse! AS-7, reissue), 1968 .... **$6.00-$12.00**

CLIFFORD BROWN:

10-inch LPs

Blue Note BLP-5032, New Star on the Horizon, 1953 .... **$250.00-$500.00**
BLP-5047, Clifford Brown Quartet, 1954 .... **$250.00-$500.00**
Pacific Jazz PJLP-19, The Clifford Brown Ensemble, 1955 ... **$150.00-$300.00**

Mono LPs

EmArcy MG-36005, Clifford Brown with Strings, 1955 .... **$60.00-$120.00**
Blue Note BLP-1526, Clifford Brown Memorial Album
(if deep groove indentation in label), 1956 .... **$100.00-$200.00**
(if regular edition, Lexington Ave. address on label), 1956 ...... **$75.00-$150.00**
(if "New York, U.S.A." address on label), 196? .... **$12.50-$25.00**
(if W. 63rd St. address on label), 196? .... **$25.00-$50.00**

DAVE BRUBECK:

45s

Fantasy 524, "Stardust"/"Lulu's Back in Town," 1953 .... **$7.50-$15.00**
Columbia 41479, "Take Five"/"Blue Rondo A La Turk," 1960 ...... **$6.00-$12.00**

10-inch LPs

Fantasy 3-1, Dave Brubeck Trio, 1951 .... **$75.00-$150.00**
3-3, Dave Brubeck Octet, 1951 .... **$75.00-$150.00**

CAB CALLOWAY:

78s

Brunswick 6209, "Kickin' the Gong Around"/"Between the Devil and the Deep Blue Sea," 1931 .... **$7.50-$15.00**
6511, "Minnie the Moocher"/"Kickin' the Gong Around," 1931 .... **$10.00-$20.00**
OKeh 6391, "St. James Infirmary"/"You Are The One In My Heart," 1941 .... **$7.50-$15.00**

10-inch LPs

Brunswick 58101, Cab Calloway, 1954 .... **$50.00-$100.00**

12-inch LPs

RCA Victor LPM-2021, Hi De Hi De Ho (mono), 1958 .... **$15.00-$30.00**
(if on LSP-2021, stereo), 1958 .... **$20.00-$40.00**

JOHN COLTRANE:

45s

Impulse! 203, "Easy to Remember"/"Greensleeves," 1961 .... **$5.00-$10.00**
Prestige 267, "Stardust"/"Love Thy Neighbor," 1961 .... **$6.00-$12.00**

Mono LPs

Blue Note BLP-1577, Blue Train
(if deep groove indentation in label), 1957.............................. **$75.00-$150.00**
(if regular version, W. 63rd St., NYC address on label), 1957 .... **$50.00-$100.00**
(if New York, USA address on label), 196? .... **$15.00-$30.00**

Stereo LPs

Blue Note BST-1577, Blue Train
(if deep groove indentation in label), 1959.............................. **$60.00-$120.00**
(if regular version, W. 63rd St., NYC address on label), 1959 .... **$40.00-$80.00**
(if New York, USA address on label), 196? .... **$12.50-$25.00**
Atlantic SD 1354, Coltrane Jazz (green-blue label, white fan logo), 1960 .... **$15.00-$30.00**
(if green-blue label, black fan logo), 1962 .... **$7.50-$15.00**
(if red-green label), 1969.. **$6.00-$12.00**
Atlantic/Rhino R1-71984, The Heavyweight Champion: The Complete Atlantic Recordings (12 LPs, boxed set, liner notes, 150-gram vinyl pressings), 1995 .... **$125.00-$250.00**
R1-71984, The Heavyweight Champion: The Complete Atlantic Recordings (Year 2000 Second Edition) (12 LPs, 1,500 copies, numbered boxed sets, 180-gram vinyl pressings 2000 .... **$100.00-$200.00**

MILES DAVIS:

45s

Capitol F1221, "Venus de Milo"/"Darn That Dream," 1950 .... **$12.50-$25.00**
Columbia 42057, "It Ain't Necessarily So"/"All Blues," 1961......... **$6.00-$12.00**
42069, "I Loves You, Porgy"/"It Ain't Necessarily So," 1961 .... **$6.00-$12.00**

10-inch LPs

Blue Note BLP-5013, Miles Davis (Young Man with a Horn), 1952 .... **$150.00-$300.00**
BLP-5022, Miles Davis, Vol. 2, 1953.................................. **$150.00-$300.00**
Capitol H 489, Jeru, 1954 .... **$125.00-$250.00**

Mono LPs

Capitol T 762, Birth of the Cool, 1956...................................... **$75.00-$150.00**
Capitol T 1974, Birth of the Cool (reissue), 1963........................ **$15.00-$30.00**
Columbia CL 949, 'Round About Midnight (six "eye" logos on label), 1957 .... **$25.00-$50.00**
(if "Guaranteed High Fidelity" on label), 1963 .... **$12.50-$25.00**
(if "Mono" on label), 1965.. **$10.00-$20.00**

Stereo LPs

Columbia CS 8163, Kind of Blue
(if six "eye" logos on label), 1959 .... **$60.00-$120.00**
(if "360 Sound Stereo" in black on label), 1963 .... **$12.50-$25.00**
(if "360 Sound Stereo" in white on label), 1965 .... **$10.00-$20.00**
(if orange label), 1971 .... **$6.00-$12.00**
(if on Columbia KCS 8163, reissue), 1974.................................... **$5.00-$10.00**
(if on Columbia PC 8163, reissue), 1977 .... **$4.00-$8.00**
(if reissue, 2 LPs, second LP contains side 1 remastered at correct slower speed, distributed by Classic Records), 1997 .... **$35.00-$70.00**

KENNY DREW:

10-inch LPs

Blue Note BLP-5023, Introducing the Kenny Drew Trio, 1953 .... **$200.00-$400.00**
Norgran MGM-29, The Ideation of Kenny Drew, 1954.......... **$125.00-$250.00**

Mono LPs

Blue Note BLP-4059, Undercurrent
(if "W. 63rd St." address on label), 1961....................................... **$40.00-$80.00**
(if "New York, USA" address on label), 1964............................. **$12.50-$25.00**
Norgran MGN-1002, Progressive Piano, 1954........................ **$100.00-$200.00**

Stereo LPs

Blue Note BST-84059, Undercurrent
(if "W. 63rd St." address on label), 1961....................................... **$40.00-$80.00**
(if "New York, USA" address on label), 1964............................. **$12.50-$25.00**
Riverside RLP-1112, Pal Joey, 1959 .... **$20.00-$40.00**

DUKE ELLINGTON:

45s

RCA Victor 47-2955, "The Sidewalks Of New York"/"Don't Get Around Much Anymore," 1949 .... **$10.00-$20.00**
Capitol F2458, "Satin Doll"/"Without A Song," 1953 .... **$6.00-$12.00**

10-inch LPs

Columbia CL 6024, Mood Ellington, 1949.............................. **$50.00-$100.00**
CL 6073, Liberian Suite, 1949 .... **$50.00-$100.00**
RCA Victor WPT-11, Duke Ellington, 1951 .... **$50.00-$100.00**

Mono LPs

Bethlehem BCP-60, Historically Speaking, The Duke, 1956 .... **$30.00-$60.00**
Columbia Masterworks ML 4639, Ellington Uptown (blue or green label with gold print), 1951.. **$50.00-$100.00**
Columbia CL 830, Hi-Fi Ellington Uptown, 1956 .... **$20.00-$40.00**
(if red label, "Guaranteed High Fidelity" or "360 Sound Mono"), 1963 .... **$7.50-$15.00**
Decca DL 9241, Duke Ellington, Volume 2 — Hot in Harlem (black label, silver print), 1959 .... **$20.00-$40.00**
(if black label, with color bars), 1961.. **$12.50-$25.00**
Smithsonian Collection P6-15079, An Explosion of Genius 1938-1940 (6 LPs), 1976 .... **$25.00-$50.00**
Mosaic MQ8-160, The Complete Capitol Recordings of Duke Ellington (8 LPs), 1997 .... **$75.00-$150.00**

MAYNARD FERGUSON:

10-inch LPs

EmArcy MG-26017, Maynard Ferguson's Hollywood Party, 1954 .... **$50.00-$100.00**
MG-26024, Dimensions, 1954.. **$50.00-$100.00**

ELLA FITZGERALD:

45s

Decca 27634, "Do You Really Love Me"/"Even As You and I," 1951 .... **$10.00-$20.00**
Verve 2002, "It's Only a Man"/"Too Young for the Blues," 1956 .... **$6.00-$12.00**

10-inch LPs

Decca DL 5084, Souvenir Album, 1950 .... **$60.00-$120.00**
DL 5300, Ella Fitzgerald Sings Gershwin Songs, 1951........... **$60.00-$120.00**

Mono LPs

Verve MGV-4010-4, Ella Fitzgerald Sings the Duke Ellington Song Book (4 LPs), 1957.. **$75.00-$150.00**

Stereo LPs

Verve V6-4053, Clap Hands, Here Comes Charley, 1962 .... **$75.00-$150.00**
V6-4061, Ella and Basie!, 1963.. **$12.50-$25.00**
Atlantic SD 1631, Ella Loves Cole, 1972 .... **$6.00-$12.00**

ERROLL GARNER:

10-inch LPs

Dial LP-205, Erroll Garner, Volume 1, 1950........................... **$100.00-$200.00**
Blue Note BLP-5007, Overture to Dawn, Volume 1, 1952 .... **$100.00-$200.00**

Mono LPs

Columbia CL 1141, Encores in Hi-Fi, 1958 .... **$15.00-$30.00**
Mercury MG-20662, Erroll Garner Plays Misty, 1962................. **$7.50-$15.00**

Stereo LPs

Mercury SR 60662, Erroll Garner Plays Misty
(if black label with all silver print), 1962.................................... **$10.00-$20.00**
(if red label, "MERCURY" in all caps at top), 1965 .... **$6.00-$12.00**
(if Chicago skyline label), 1975 .... **$5.00-$10.00**
(if black label with neon "mercury" logo), 1983............................. **$4.00-$8.00**

STAN GETZ:

45s

Verve 10322, "The Girl From Ipanema"/"Corcovado" (with Astrid Gilberto), 1964 .... **$5.00-$10.00**

10-inch LPs

Savoy MG-9004, New Sounds in Modern Music, 1951 .... **$150.00-$300.00**

Prestige PRLP-102, Stan Getz and the Tenor Sax Stars, 1951 **$100.00-$200.00**

Roost R-407, Jazz at Storyville, 1952 .... **$75.00-$150.00**

Mono LPs

Modern MLP-1202, Groovin' High, 1956 .... **$75.00-$150.00**

DIZZY GILLESPIE:

10-inch LPs

Atlantic ALR-138, Dizzy Gillespie, 1952 .... **$200.00-$400.00**

Blue Note BLP-5017, Horn of Plenty, 1953 .... **$150.00-$300.00**

Contemporary C-2504, Dizzy in Paris, 1953 .... **$100.00-$200.00**

Mono LPs

RCA Victor LJM-1009, Dizzier and Dizzier, 1954 .... **$60.00-$120.00**

Philips PHM 200106, Dizzy Gillespie and the Double Six of Paris, 1963 .... **$10.00-$20.00**

Stereo LPs

Verve MGVS-6023, Dizzy Gillespie at Newport, 1960 .... **$30.00-$60.00**

MGVS-6047, Have Trumpet, Will Excite, 1960 .... **$30.00-$60.00**

VINCE GUARALDI:

45s

Fantasy 563, "Cast Your Fate to the Wind"/"Samba de Orpheus," 1962 .... **$5.00-$10.00**

593, "Linus & Lucy"/"Oh, Good Grief," 1964 .... **$10.00-$20.00**

Mono LPs

Fantasy 3337, Jazz Impressions of Black Orpheus (Cast Your Fate to the Wind)

(if black vinyl, red label, flexible vinyl), 1962 .... **$7.50-$15.00**

(if black vinyl, red label, non-flexible thick vinyl), 1962 .... **$12.50-$25.00**

(if red vinyl), 1962 .... **$20.00-$40.00**

LIONEL HAMPTON:

10-inch LPs

Decca DL 5230, Boogie Woogie, 1950 .... **$40.00-$80.00**

RCA Victor LPT-18, A Treasury of Immortal Performances, 1951 .... **$50.00-$100.00**

Clef MGC-142, The Lionel Hampton Quartet, 1953 .... **$60.00-$120.00**

Blue Note BLP-5046, Rockin' and Groovin', 1954 .... **$150.00-$300.00**

Mono LPs

Epic LN 3190, Apollo Hall Concert 1954, 1955 .... **$25.00-$50.00**

Jazztone J-1238, The Fabulous Lionel Hampton and His All-Stars, 1957 .... **$20.00-$40.00**

Stereo LPs

Decca DL 74194, The Original Star Dust, 1962 .... **$10.00-$20.00**

HERBIE HANCOCK:

Mono LPs

Blue Note BLP-4195, Maiden Voyage, 1965 .... **$17.50-$35.00**

Stereo LPs

Blue Note BST-84195, Maiden Voyage (if New York, USA address on label), 1965 .... **$17.50-$35.00**

(if "A Division of United Artists" on label), 197? .... **$6.00-$12.00**

(if "The Finest in Jazz Since 1939," reissue), 1985 .... **$5.00-$10.00**

Columbia KC 32371, Head Hunters, 1973 .... **$6.00-$12.00**

(if on Columbia PC 32371, reissue), 197? .... **$4.00-$8.00**

(if on Columbia CQ 32371, quadraphonic pressing), 1973 .... **$12.50-$25.00**

COLEMAN HAWKINS:

10-inch LPs

EmArcy MG-26013, The Bean, 1954 .... **$100.00-$200.00**

Savoy MG-15039, The Hawk Talks, 1954 .... **$100.00-$200.00**

Capitol H 327, Classics in Jazz, 1952 .... **$125.00-$250.00**

WOODY HERMAN:

10-inch LPs

Columbia CL 6026, Sequence in Jazz, 1949 .... **$35.00-$70.00**

Coral CRL 56005, Blue Prelude, 1950 .... **$35.00-$70.00**

Capitol H 324, Classics in Jazz, 1952 .... **$35.00-$70.00**

Mono LPs

Columbia CL 592, The Three Herds (maroon label, gold print), 1955 .... **$25.00-$50.00**

(if red-black label with six "eye" logos), 1956 .... **$15.00-$30.00**

CL 683, Twelve Shades of Blue, 1956 .... **$15.00-$30.00**

Everest LPBR-5003, The Herd Rides Again, 1958 .... **$15.00-$30.00**

BILLIE HOLIDAY:

45s

Mercury 89064, "Stormy Weather"/"Tenderly," 1953 .... **$10.00-$20.00**

10-inch LPs

Columbia CL 6129, Billie Holiday Sings, 1950 .... **$100.00-$200.00**

Decca DL 5345, Lover Man, 1951 .... **$100.00-$200.00**

Mono LPs

Columbia CL 637, Lady Day (maroon label, gold print), 1954 .... **$35.00-$70.00**

(red-black label, six "eye" logos), 1956 .... **$20.00-$40.00**

(red "Guaranteed High Fidelity" or "360 Sound" label), 1962 .... **$7.50-$15.00**

(orange label), 197? .... **$6.00-$12.00**

Clef MGC-721, Lady Sings the Blues, 1956 .... **$60.00-$120.00**

Mobile Fidelity 1-247, Body and Soul (audiophile vinyl), 1996 .... **$60.00-$120.00**

LAMBERT, HENDRICKS AND ROSS:

Mono LPs

ABC-Paramount ABC-223, Sing a Song of Basie, 1958 .... **$25.00-$50.00**

Columbia CL 1403, The Hottest New Group in Jazz (black-red label with six "eye" logos), 1959 .... **$15.00-$30.00**

Stereo LPs

ABC-Paramount ABCS-223, Sing a Song of Basie, 1958 .... **$25.00-$50.00**

Columbia CS 8198, The Hottest New Group in Jazz (black-red label, six "eye" logos), 1959 .... **$20.00-$40.00**

(if red label, "360 Sound Stereo" at bottom), 1963 .... **$10.00-$20.00**

CS 8310, Lambert, Hendricks and Ross Sing Ellington (black-red label, six "eye" logos), 1960 .... **$20.00-$40.00**

(if red label, "360 Sound Stereo" at bottom), 1963 .... **$10.00-$20.00**

MANHATTAN TRANSFER:

45s

Atlantic 3292, "Operator"/"Tuxedo Junction," 1975 .... **$2.50-$5.00**

3491, "Four Brothers"/"It's Not the Spotlight," 1978 .... **$2.50-$5.00**

3636, "Birdland"/"Shaker Song," 1979 .... **$2.50-$5.00**

89533, "Ray's Rockhouse"/"Another Life in Tunisia," 1985 .... **$2.00-$4.00**

LPs

Atlantic SD 18133, The Manhattan Transfer, 1975 .... **$5.00-$10.00**

SD 19258, Extensions, 1979 .... **$5.00-$10.00**

81266, Vocalese, 1985 .... **$5.00-$10.00**

CHARLES MINGUS:

10-inch LPs

Savoy MG-15050, Charlie Mingus, 1955 .... **$100.00-$200.00**

Mono LPs

Bethlehem BCP-65, The Jazz Experiment of Charlie Mingus, 1956 .... **$50.00-$100.00**

BCP-6026, A Modern Jazz Symposium of Jazz and Poetry, 1958 .... **$50.00-$100.00**

THELONIOUS MONK:

10-inch LPs

Prestige PRLP-142, Thelonious Monk Trio, 1953 .... **$100.00-$200.00**

PRLP-166, Thelonious Monk Quintet with Sonny Rollins and Julius Watkins, 1953 .... **$100.00-$200.00**

Mono LPs

Blue Note BLP-1510, Genius of Modern Music, Vol. 1 (with deep groove inside label), 1956 .... **$100.00-$200.00**

(if regular edition, Lexington Ave. address on label), 1956 .... **$75.00-$150.00**

(with "New York, USA" address on label), 1963 .... **$12.50-$25.00**

Stereo LPs

Riverside RLP 1101, Monk's Music (black label with reel and microphone logo), 1959 .... **$20.00-$40.00**

RLP 1133, Misterioso, 1958 .... **$25.00-$50.00**

Analogue Productions AP-37, The Riverside Tenor Sessions (7 LPs), 1999 .... **$125.00-$250.00**

JAMES MOODY:

10-inch LPs

Blue Note BLP-5005, James Moody with Strings, 1952 .... **$150.00-$300.00**

EmArcy MG-26040, Moodsville, 1954 .... **$75.00-$150.00**

Prestige PRLP-157, Moody in France, 1953 .... **$75.00-$150.00**

Mono LPs

Argo LP-613, Moody's Mood for Love, 1957 .... **$20.00-$40.00**

EmArcy MG-36031, The Moody Story, 1955 .... **$50.00-$100.00**

Stereo LPs

Argo LPS-637, Last Train from Overbrook, 1959 .... **$15.00-$30.00**

LPS-648, James Moody, 1959 .... **$15.00-$30.00**

LPS-666, Hey! It's James Moody, 1960 .... **$20.00-$40.00**

CHARLIE PARKER:

10-inch LPs

Dial LP-201, Charlie Parker Quintet, 1949 **$400.00-$800.00**
LP-207, Charlie Parker Sextet, 1949 **$400.00-$800.00**
Savoy MG-9000, Charlie Parker, 1950 **$250.00-$500.00**
MG-9001, Charlie Parker, Volume 2, 1951 **$250.00-$500.00**
Birdland 425, A Night at Carnegie Hall, 1956 **$150.00-$300.00**

Mono LPs

Dial LP-901, The Bird Blows the Blues, 1950 **$300.00-$600.00**
LP-904, Alternate Masters, 1951 **$300.00-$600.00**
Clef MGC-646, The Magnificent Charlie Parker, 1955 **$200.00-$400.00**
Blue Note BT-85108, Charlie Parker at Storyville, 198? **$6.00-$12.00**

BUDDY RICH:

45s

Pacific Jazz 88139, "Norwegian Wood"/"Monitor Theme," 1967 **$2.50-$5.00**
88145, "Mercy, Mercy, Mercy"/"Big Mama Cass," 1968 **$3.00-$6.00**

78s

V-Disc 775, "Budella" (with Ella Fitzgerald), 1946 **$20.00-$40.00**

10-inch LPs

Norgran MGN-26, Buddy Rich Swingin', 1954 **$60.00-$120.00**

Mono LPs

Norgran MGN-1031, Sing and Swing with Buddy Rich, 1955 **$40.00-$80.00**

Stereo LPs

Pacific Jazz ST-20113, Swingin' New Big Band, 1966 **$10.00-$20.00**
Verve V6-8471, Burnin' Beat, 1962 **$15.00-$30.00**

SUN RA:

LPs

Saturn SRLP-0216, Super-Sonic Jazz
(if blank cover), 1957 **$75.00-$150.00**
(if silkscreened cover), 1957 **$150.00-$300.00**
(if purple "keyboard" cover), 1958 **$75.00-$150.00**
(if blue or green cover), 1965 **$25.00-$50.00**
(if on Saturn LP-204, Chicago address on label), 1968 **$25.00-$50.00**
ESR-1970, My Brother the Wind, 1970 **$20.00-$40.00**
IHNY-165, Sun Ra and His Arkestra Featuring Pharoah Sanders and Black Harold, 1976 **$20.00-$40.00**

MA RAINEY:

10-inch LPs

Riverside RLP-1003, Ma Rainey, Vol. 1, 1953 **$125.00-$250.00**
RLP-1016, Ma Rainey, Vol. 2, 1953 **$125.00-$250.00**
RLP-1045, Ma Rainey, Vol. 3, 1954 **$125.00-$250.00**

Mono LPs

Riverside RLP 12-108, Ma Rainey, 1955 **$100.00-$200.00**
RLP 12-137, Broken Hearted Blues, 1956 **$50.00-$100.00**

MAX ROACH:

10-inch LPs

Debut DLP-13, Max Roach Quartet Featuring Hank Mobley, 1954 **$150.00-$300.00**

Mono LPs

EmArcy MG-36098, Max Roach + 4, 1957 **$50.00-$100.00**
MG-36108, Jazz in 3/4 Time, 1957 **$40.00-$80.00**
Atlantic 1435, Max Roach Trio Featuring the Legendary Hasaan, 1965 **$10.00-$20.00**

Stereo LPs

EmArcy SR-80002, Jazz in 3/4 Time, 1959 **$30.00-$60.00**
SR-80010, Max Roach Plus Four At Newport, 1959 **$25.00-$50.00**
Impulse! AS-8, Percussion Bitter Sweet, 1961 **$20.00-$40.00**

GEORGE SHEARING:

45s

MGM 10763, "When Your Lover Has Gone"/"Carnegie Horizons," 1950 **$10.00-$20.00**

Mono LPs

MGM E-3122, An Evening with Shearing, 1955 **$15.00-$30.00**

Stereo LPs

Capitol ST 1187, George Shearing On Stage (if black label with rainbow perimeter, logo on left), 1959 **$12.50-$25.00**
(if black label with rainbow perimeter, logo on top), 1962 **$10.00-$20.00**
Mosaic MQ7-157, The Complete Capitol Live Recordings of George Shearing (7 LPs), 199? **$60.00-$120.00**

SPIRO GYRA:

Stereo LPs

Infinity INF-9004, Morning Dance, 1979 **$6.00-$12.00**
(if on Nautilus NR-9, audiophile vinyl), 1979 **$20.00-$40.00**
(if on MCA 37148, reissue), 198? **$4.00-$8.00**

ART TATUM:

10-inch LPs

Dial LP-206, Art Tatum Trio, 1950 **$125.00-$250.00**
Decca DL 5086, Art Tatum Piano Solos, 1950 **$60.00-$120.00**
Remington 2, Tatum Piano, 1950 **$50.00-$100.00**

Mono LPs

Clef MGC-612, The Genius of Art Tatum #1, 1954 **$40.00-$80.00**
MGC-613, The Genius of Art Tatum #2, 1954 **$40.00-$80.00**

Stereo LPs

Columbia CS 9655, Piano Starts Here (red "360 Sound" on label), 1968 **$10.00-$20.00**
Pablo 2625703, The Tatum Solo Masterpieces (13 LPs), 1974 **$50.00-$100.00**

SARAH VAUGHAN:

45s

Columbia 4-39873, "Sinner or Saint"/"Mighty Lonesome Feeling," 1952 **$10.00-$20.00**
Atlantic 1012, "It Might As Well Be Spring"/"You Go to My Head," 1953 **$50.00-$100.00**
Mercury 71477, "Broken-Hearted Melody"/"Misty," 1959 **$6.00-$12.00**

10-inch LPs

MGM E-165, Tenderly, 1950 **$60.00-$120.00**
EmArcy MG-26005, Images, 1954 **$40.00-$80.00**
Mercury MG-25188, Divine Sarah, 1955 **$50.00-$100.00**

Mono LPs

EmArcy MG-36004, Sarah Vaughan, 1955 **$40.00-$80.00**
MG-36058, In the Land of Hi-Fi, 1956 **$40.00-$80.00**
Roulette R 52082, You're Mine, 1962 **$12.50-$25.00**

Stereo LPs

Mercury SR-60110, The Magic of Sarah Vaughan, 1959 **$20.00-$40.00**
Roulette SR 52082, You're Mine, 1962 **$15.00-$30.00**
(if on red vinyl), 1962 **$30.00-$60.00**

FATS WALLER:

10-inch LPs

RCA Victor LPT-8, Fats Waller 1934-42, 1951 **$75.00-$150.00**
LPT-14, Fats Waller Favorites, 1951 **$75.00-$150.00**

Mono LPs

RCA Victor LPT-1001, Fats Waller Plays and Sings, 1954 **$40.00-$80.00**
LPM-1246, Ain't Misbehavin', 1956 **$25.00-$50.00**

PAUL WHITEMAN:

45s

Capitol F 1668, "Travelin' Light"/"The General Jumped at Dawn" (reissue from 1942), 1951 **$10.00-$20.00**

10-inch LPs

"X" Records LVA-3040, Paul Whiteman's Orchestra Featuring Bix Beiderbecke, 1955 **$40.00-$80.00**

Louis Armstrong recorded as a sideman, as a featured performer, and as the head of his own orchestra for over half a century. This 78 of "All of Me" was recorded during an era where Columbia Records pressed their records on blue-tinted shellac, and is not easy to find.

***$20**, NM condition*

Chapter 15

Northern Soul

History

Coined by reporter Dave Godin in a September 1971 edition of Blues and Soul magazine, "Northern Soul" is both a musical style—a pulsing Motown-like beat, with the horns and lyrics of a Chicago blues club or a Memphis roadhouse—as well as a musical fad, as British club DJs searched for rare, exclusive dance songs they could play in their own clubs for the "punters" on the dance floor.

The first club catering to this type of rare soul music was the Twisted Wheel Club of Manchester. It was also one of the first venues to offer R&B music as an all-night dance party (also known as "Nighters" or "All-Nighters"). The music played at the Twisted Wheel Club were moderate soul hits in the UK, but either because of poor distribution or poor sales, there were so few of these pressings in existence that the records instantly became collector's items to those who heard them at the club.

By the time the Twisted Wheel closed down in 1970, almost every northern England city and town had their own R&B club—the Catacombs, the Junction, the Golden Torch, to name a few. And their DJs made dance hits out of "newies," records that missed hit status the first time around, but were now played alongside classic "oldies." This mixture of "flyers" (fast songs) and "stompers" (heavy beat) became known as "Northern Soul."

In the 1970s, the most famous Northern Soul clubs were the Wigan Casino and the Blackpool Mecca. The Blackpool Mecca DJs played 1960s soul, as recorded only by black artists. The Wigan Casino, led by DJ Russ Winstanley, would play black and white artists, oldies, newies, and "current" songs, all in a credo of "if it's danceable, play it."

Photo credit: From the collection of Val Shively.

Although Al Wilson's biggest hit in America was the balad "Show and Tell," this early recording of "The Snake" has been a Northern Soul club-filler for years.

$8, *NM condition*

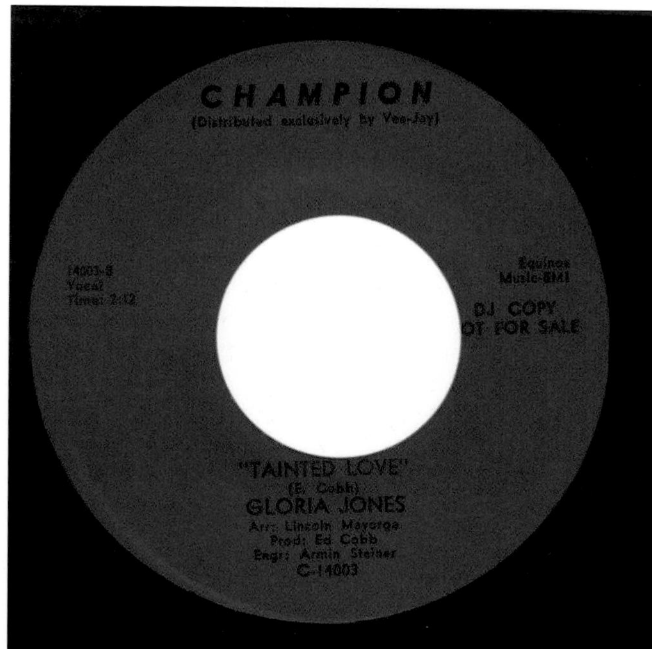

After Gloria Jones' song "Tainted Love" became a big hit for the British techno-pop duo Soft Cell, they went back to the Northern Soul club scene for their next hit, a cover of Judy Street's "What!"

$5, *Poor condition (off-center hole)*

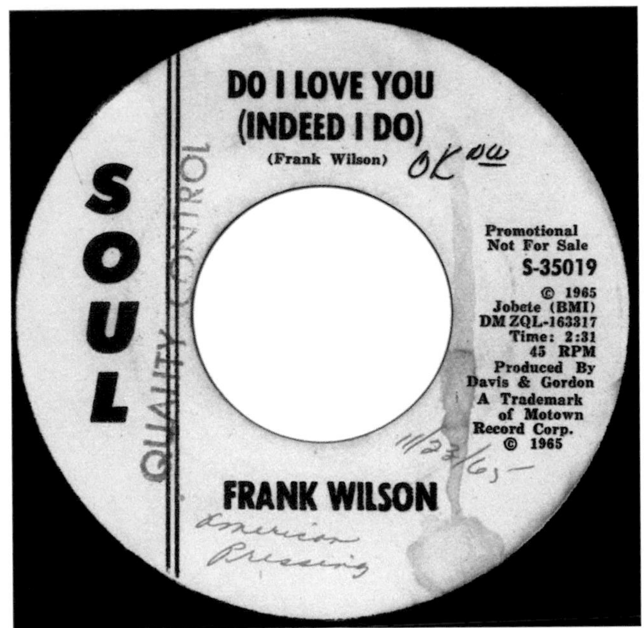

Photo credit: Frank Wilson 45 from the collection of Kev Roberts.

Even with its stain and handwritten "American Pressing" on the label, this 45 of Frank Wilson's "Do I Love You (Indeed I Do)" sold at auction for £15,000 (approximately $23,000.00 US), the highest sum ever paid for a Northern Soul record. The Eddie Foster version seen here is a bootleg pressing, containing the same audio track as the Frank Wilson 45.

Far left record **$23,000**

By the mid-1970s, the current crop of British "Northern Soul" 45s had dried up, forcing DJs to search through American 45s for their top dance records. As the DJs kept searching for "exclusives," records that could pack the floor at their club and nowhere else, high prices were paid for hard-to-find soul grooves. Many of these songs found a second life in the clubs, as British pop groups remade their favorite Northern Soul songs as Top 40 hits of their own. For example, in 1981, the British synth-pop duo Soft Cell copied Gloria Jones' "Tainted Love," a Northern Soul staple.

The rarest Northern Soul record, in fact one of the rarest records of all time, is Frank Wilson's "Do I Love You (Indeed I Do)"/"Sweeter as the Days Go By." Promotional test copies of this uptempo song were pressed, but at the last minute Motown president Berry Gordy pulled the record off the market—and then re-issued "Do I Love You" with Wilson's voice replaced by a female singer on the Motown roster, Chris Clark. The test copies stayed locked in the Motown vault until the early 1970s, when Northern Soul collector/DJ Simon Soussan acquired one of the promotional pressings. Soussan brought the record back to England and played it in his dance club, where it became a heavily-requested hit. To add to the demand for the song, bootleg copies of "Do I Love You" started appearing in stores, with a phony label and performing credits awarded to singer Eddie Foster. A second pressing of "Do I Love You" was auctioned in 1999, selling for over $15,000 to another Northern Soul collector, Kenny Burrell—legend says that after he bought the record, he took it to a club and actually played it!

Northern Soul clubs have turned forgotten tracks into major worldwide hits. Smokey Robinson and the Miracles' 1967 album track "The Tears of a Clown" became a huge floor-packer in Northern Soul clubs, so much so that in 1970 Motown released the song as a commercially available 45—and watched it soar to #1 worldwide. Other tracks that first broke on Northern Soul dance floors, later to become major hits, include Vicki Sue Robinson's "Turn the Beat Around," Tavares' "Heaven Must Be Missing An Angel," and Esther Phillips' "What A Difference A Day Makes."

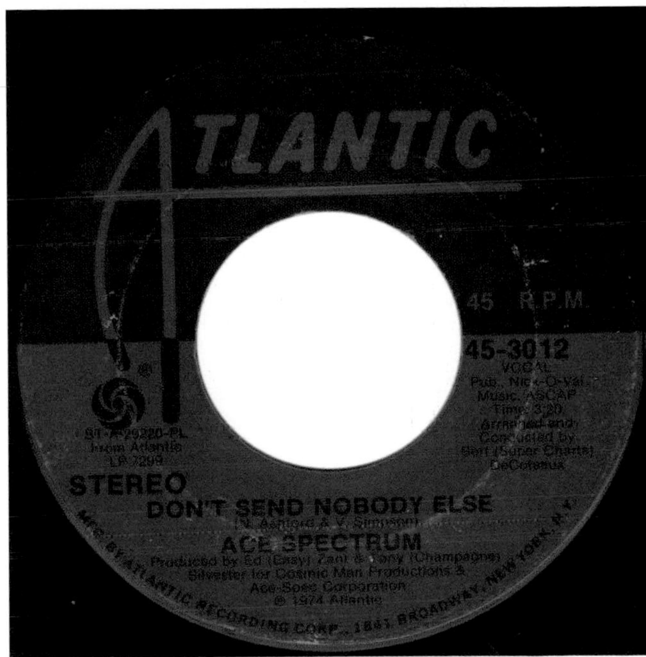

The vocal harmony group Ace Spectrum had a Top 40 R&B hit with "Don't Send Nobody Else." Today, a clean pressing of that song is a hot-selling Northern Soul 45.

***$17**, Good condition*

What To Look For

Northern Soul music is still a hot collectible, as 1970s minor hits like Ace Spectrum's "Don't Send Nobody Else" and Major Lance's "Ain't No Soul (Left In These Old Shoes)" are now selling for upwards of $50 for clean copies.

There are many distinct factors that determine a Northern Soul record—a raw 1960s soul record, with an early Motownish beat and Chicago blues horn section. Most of these records were never hits in their own right, either in America or in the UK—but to club DJs looking for rare, exclusive soul they could play in their clubs, these records were just the treat.

Northern Soul collectors are most desirous of white label promo copies of both American and UK 45s. Many of the British 45s will have a gigantic "A" on the front label. The British demo pressings may have a plastic removable center adapter, this must remain in the record or its collectible value is considerably diminished. Some Northern Soul records may have white mailing stickers pasted over the labels—this was a common practice among club DJs, in an attempt to keep rival DJs from seeing the record, finding out who's singing on it, and getting a copy for their own club.

Don't be afraid to ask questions from a dealer if they say a record is "Northern Soul" and you're unfamiliar with the title or song. Don't be fooled into purchasing a record just because someone marked it as a "Northern Soul" title. Northern Soul music is driven by 45s—rarely do Northern Soul collectors hunt out albums, unless it contains that rare track they have not been able to find on a 45.

Collectors who want to appreciate the music, without having to spend hundreds or thousands of dollars for rare Northern Soul titles, can rest assured that many of the top genre hits have been pressed on reissue labels like Soul Supply/Goldmine, Ace/Kent, Westside, and Rhino.

An example of a Northern Soul hit being found on the "B" side of a Top 40 A-side, Chubby Checker's minor cover of Freddie and the Dreamers' "Do the Freddie" was on the flip of this Northern Soul smash, "At The Discotheque." Northern Soul hits on Cameo-Parkway have not been reissued on CD yet, making these platters all the more precious.

***$10**, VG condition*

Books

Roberts, Kev, *The Northern Soul Top 500*, Goldmine/ Soul Supply Ltd., Todmorden, U.K., 2000.

Manship, John, *Manship's Northern Soul & Motown 45 RPM Price Guide*, 2nd Edition, London, 2003.

Winstanley, Russ; Nowell, David, *Soul Survivors: The Wigan Casino Story*, Robson Books, London, 1996.

McKenna, Pete, *Nightshift: Personal Recollections Of Growing Up In And Around The Casino Soul Club*, Empress Hall, Wigan, Sept. 1973 to Dec. 1981, S.T. Publishing, Dunoon, U.K., 1996.

Guralnick, Peter, *Sweet Soul Music: Rhythm & Blues & the Southern Dream of Freedom*, HarperTrade, NY, 1986.

Web Pages

Northern soul collector and historian Kev Roberts' Web site: http://www.kevroberts.com

The Night Owl Club, a Web page devoted to Northern Soul music and culture: http://www.nightowlclub.com.

The Northern Soul Web ring, a listing of dozens of sites dedicated to "keeping the faith," can be accessed through this site: http://www.soul-source.co.uk/welcome.htm

An excellent essay by Paul Wynne comparing Northern Soul collectors with archeologists: http://homepage.ntlworld.com/paul.wynne/NS/

Nick Crocker's Northern Soul page, a good starting point for anyone looking for Northern Soul history and images: http://www.soulsurfin.co.uk

An online radio station that streams Northern Soul classics, http://www.classicgoldam.com

Another online radio station with Northern Soul tracks: http://www.solarradio.com

Candy and the Kisses' hit "The 81" was based on a popular Philadelphia dance. Co-written by Kenny Gamble and Jerry Ross, and similar in sound to Martha and the Vandellas' track "In My Lonely Room," "The 81" also features keyboardist Leon Huff on the orchestral track. Gamble and Huff would later form a successful songwriting partnership, which evolved into Philadelphia International Records, the hitmaking soul label of the 1970s.

***$20**, NM condition*

The O'Jays would become soul superstars in the 1970s, but their 1960s dance tracks and ballads have been Northern Soul staples for years. Especially prized are their early recordings on the Neptune label, years before their first Philadelphia International hits.

***$8**, NM condition*

Photo credit: From the collection of Kev Roberts.

Frankie Karl and the Chevrons' song "You Should 'O Held On," was a regional hit in Philadelphia, but when Congress Records picked up the disc for national distribution, they renamed the Chevrons as the 7th Avenue Aviators. No matter—the song was a flop in its initial release, but has since become a Northern Soul classic.

***$400**, NM condition*

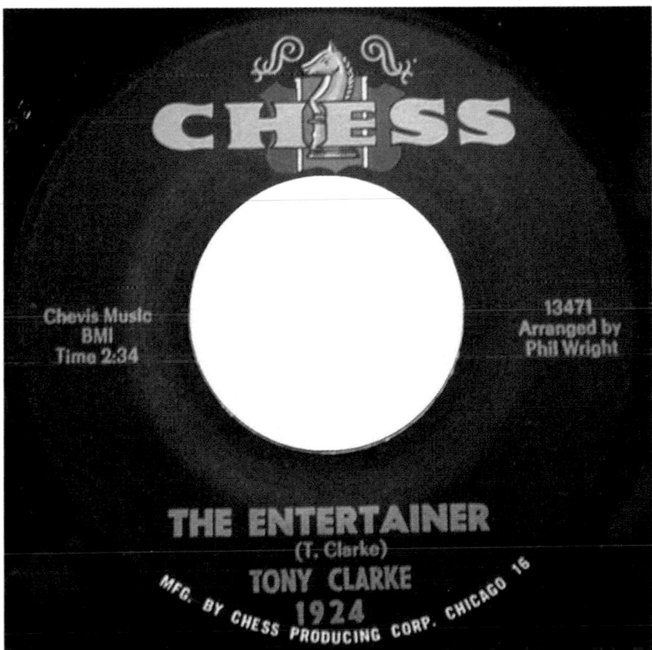

Photo credit: From the collection of Val Shively.

Tony Clarke's "The Entertainer" was a slower Northern Soul song, as well as a Top 10 soul hit in America.

***$20**, NM condition*

ACE SPECTRUM:
Atlantic 3012, "Don't Send Nobody Else"/"Don't Let Me Be Lonely Tonight," 1974 .... **$25.00-$50.00**

GENE ANDERSON:
Nu-Tone RCR-65-01, "Do You Love Me Baby"/"Tell Me That You Love Me," 196? .... **$75.00-$150.00**

YVONNE BAKER:
Parkway 140, "You Didn't Say A Word"/"To Prove My Love Is True," 1967 .... **$50.00-$100.00**

ARNOLD BLAIR:
Gemigo 0504, "Trying to Get Next to You" (stereo)/(mono), 1975 .... **$40.00-$80.00**

TERRY CALLIER:
Cadet 5623, "Look At Me Now"/"You Goin' Miss Your Candy Man," 1963 .... **$150.00-$300.00**

CANDY AND THE KISSES:
Cameo 336, "The 81"/"Two Happy People," 1964 .... **$10.00-$20.00**

NOLAN CHANCE:
Bunky 161, "Just Like the Weather"/(B-side unknown), 1965 .... **$600.00-$1,200.00**
Constellation 161, "Just Like the Weather"/"Don't Use Me," 1965 .... **$60.00-$120.00**

CHUBBY CHECKER:
Parkway 949, "Let's Freddie"/"At The Discotheque," 1965 .... **$10.00-$20.00**
965, "You Just Don't Know"/"Two hearts Make One Love," 1965 .... **$200.00-$400.00**

CHRIS CLARK:
VIP 25038, "Love's Gone Bad"/"Put Yourself In My Place," 1965 .... **$7.50-$15.00**
(if above A-side is misspelled "Love's Gone Mad"), 1965 .... **$30.00-$60.00**

THE CONTOURS:
Gordy 7005, "Do You Love Me"/"Move Mr. Man," 1962 .... **$10.00-$20.00**
7052, "Just a Little Misunderstanding"/"Determination," 1965 .... **$6.00-$12.00**

THE DELICATES:
Soultown 101, "He Gave Me Love"/"Stop Shoving Me Around," 196? .... **$35.00-$70.00**

TROY DODDS:
El Camino 701, "The Real Thing"/"Try My Love," 196? .... **$450.00-$900.00**

THE DRIFTERS:
Atlantic 2746, "You Got to Pay Your Dues"/"Black Silk," 1970 .... **$5.00-$10.00**

THE FALCONS:
Big Wheel 1972, "Good Good Feeling"/"Love You Like You Never Been Loved Before," 1966 .... **$90.00-$180.00**

THE FANTASTIC FOUR:
Ric-Tic 113, "Can't Stop Looking For My Baby" (Pt. 1)/(Pt. 2), 1966 .... **$100.00-$200.00**
121, "Can't Stop Looking For My Baby"/"Just the Lonely," 1967 .... **$90.00-$180.00**
Soul 35072, "On the Brighter Side of a Blue World"/"I'm Gonna Hurry On," 1970 .... **$6.00-$12.00**

THE FLAMINGOS:
Philips 40347, "The Boogaloo Party"/"The Nearness of You," 1965 .... **$7.50-$15.00**

EDDIE FOSTER:
In 6311, "I Will Wait"/"I Never Knew," 196? .... **$125.00-$250.00**

CORNELL GUNTER:
Together 101, "Love In My Heart"/"Down In Mexico," 196? .... **$100.00-$200.00**

ROY HAMILTON:
Epic 5-9538, "Earthquake"/"I Am," 1962 .... **$37.50-$75.00**

PATRICE HOLLOWAY:
Capitol 5778, "Love and Desire"/"Ecstacy," 1967 .... **$30.00-$60.00**

LINDA HOPKINS:
Brunswick 55256, "Tortured"/"Slight Case of Love," 1963 .... **$5.00-$10.00**

THE IN-BETWEENS:
Blue Onion 105, "She's Walkin' Down the Street"/"Just Friends," 196? .... **$10.00-$20.00**

GLORIA JONES:
Champion 14003, "Tainted Love"/"My Bad Boy's Coming Home," 1964 .... **$10.00-$20.00**

JOHNNY JONES AND THE KING CASUALS:
Brunswick 55389, "Purple Haze"/"Horsing Around," 1968 .... **$10.00-$20.00**

FRANKIE KARL AND THE CHEVRONS:
Philtown 105, "You Should 'O Held On"/"Boy Next Door," 1967 .... **$200.00-$400.00**
Congress 255, above titles same, credited to 7th Avenue Aviators, 1967 .... **$100.00-$200.00**

MAJOR LANCE:
OKeh 7175, "The Monkey Time"/"Mama Didn't Know," 1963 .... **$7.50-$15.00**
7284, "You Don't Want Me No More"/"Wait Till I Get You In Your Arms," 1967 .... **$25.00-$50.00**

BARBARA McNAIR:
Motown 1087, "You're Gonna Love My Baby"/"Touch of Time," 1965 .... **$12.50-$25.00**

TONY MIDDLETON:
MGM 13493, "Don't Ever Leave Me"/"To The Ends Of The Earth," 1966 .... **$20.00-$40.00**

REVEREND GEORGE MORTON:
HI-Q 915F-1335, "This Is My Story"/"Wade in the Water," 196? .... **$125.00-$250.00**

THE NATURAL FOUR:
ABC 11253, "Hurt"/"I Thought You Were Mine," 1969 .... **$12.50-$25.00**

GERRI REID:
Sla-Mon 304, "No Fool No More"/"Out In the Cold," 196? .... **$45.00-$90.00**

THE SAPPHIRES:
ABC-Paramount 10639, "Gee I'm Sorry, Baby"/"Gotta Have Your Love," 1965 .... **$7.50-$15.00**

THE SEVEN SOULS:
OKeh 7289, "I Still Love You"/"I'm No Stranger," 1967 .... **$200.00-$400.00**

BOBBY SHEEN:
Capitol 5672, "Doctor Love"/"Sweet Sweet Love," 1966 .... **$35.00-$70.00**

THE SHOWMEN:
Minit 643, "The Wrong Girl"/"Fate Planned It This Way," 1962 .... **$40.00-$80.00**

THE SOUL BROTHERS SIX:
Atlantic 2406, "I'll Be Loving You"/"Some Kind Of Wonderful," 1966 .... **$45.00-$90.00**

JACKIE AND THE STARLITES:
Mascot 131, "I'll Burn Your Letters"/"Walking From School," 196? .... **$12.50-$25.00**

THE TAMS:
ABC-Paramount 10573, "Hey Girl Don't Bother Me"/"Take Away," 1964 .... **$6.00-$12.00**

R. DEAN TAYLOR:
V.I.P. 25042, "There's a Ghost in My House"/"Don't Fool Around," 1966 .... **$12.50-$25.00**

EARL VAN DYKE AND THE SOUL BROTHERS:
Soul 35009, "All For You"/"Too Many Fish in the Sea," 1965 .... **$400.00-$800.00**

EARL VAN DYKE AND THE MOTOWN BRASS:
Soul 35028, "6 x 6"/"There Is No Greater Love," 1967 .... **$10.00-$20.00**

THE VIBRATIONS:
Epic 10418, "Because You're Mine"/"I Took An Overdose," 1968 .... **$10.00-$20.00**

KIM WESTON:
Tamla 54106, "A Little More Love"/"Go Ahead And Laugh," 1964 .... **$50.00-$100.00**
Gordy 7050, "Helpless"/"A Love Like Yours (Doesn't Come Knockin' Every Day)," 1966 .... **$10.00-$20.00**

FRANK WILSON:
Soul 35019, "Sweeter as the Days Go By"/"Do I Love You (Indeed I Do)," 1966 .... **$15,000.00-$20,000.00**

CHUCK WRIGHT:
Ember 1091, "The Palm of Your Hand"/"Don't Play That Song," 1963 .... **$45.00-$90.00**

Chapter 16

Progressive Rock

History

Progressive rock, also known as "prog-rock" or "art-rock," evolved in the late 1960s as artists began to base their music not just on their rock and roll pioneers, but on those who came before—classical composers like Beethoven, Handel, and Bach. The term "progressive rock" can be interpreted as rock music evolving, or "progressing," from its present state. Songs might encompass far-reaching concepts of jealousy, passion, history, or fantasy. Non-traditional rock instruments may be added to the mix, such as violins, cellos, piccolos, harpsichords, Theremins, bassoons, or early synthesizers.

Prog-rock songs were not limited to a three-minute 45—some releases in this genre easily top ten to fifteen minutes. Mike Oldfield's prog-rock classic *Tubular Bells* album contains two 20+ minute songs, one for each side of the disc. Some prog-rock groups experiment with the standard 4/4 beat, as groups like Pink Floyd and Rush have released songs in different time signatures.

Another form of progressive rock came from early synthesizer experiments. For these bands, their influences were the early tonal experiments of John Cage and Karlheinz Stockhausen, who generated electronic sound in a new sonic symphony. In 1968, Robert Moog created the Moog synthesizer, an instrument capable of creating whole new musical landscapes from an electronic piano keyboard. Some of the earliest artists and groups to incorporate synthesizers and other electronic instruments into their music include Kraftwerk, Tangerine Dream, and Jean-Michael Jarre. These groups, created musical masterpieces like *Autobahn*, *Phaedra,* and *Oxygene*.

A pioneer in progressive rock, the band Genesis must have been pleasantly surprised to discover that their American debut was initially released on ABC's Impulse! jazz label, as seen here.

***$30**, NM condition*

Photo credit: From the Collection of Jim Wright.

While the bulk of Rush's catalog is easy to acquire, just try finding this rare Canadian 45—it's their first single ever, with only 1,000 copies pressed.

***$500**, NM condition*

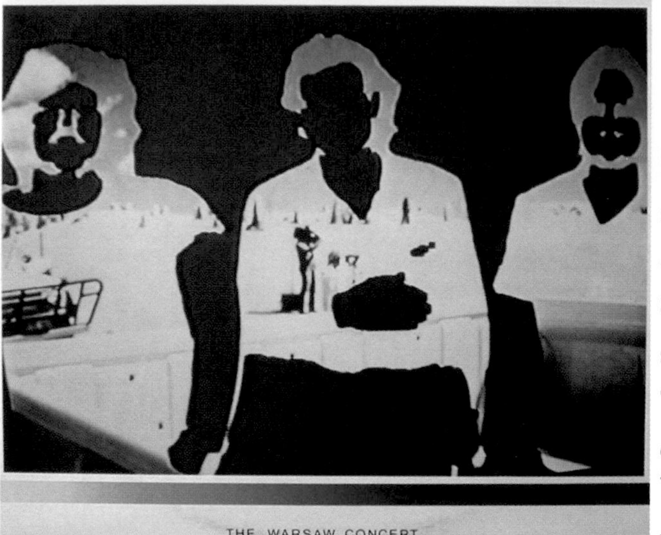

Photo credit: Courtesy Last Vestige Music Store, Albany, N.Y.

Whereas Kraftwerk experimented with dance rhythms on their albums, Tangerine Dream used their synthesizers to create spectacular aural landscapes.
***$8**, Good condition*

The first incarnation of Renaissance featured ex-Yardbirds member Keith Relf, and was a folk-rock band. Renaissance's second lineup included lead singer Annie Haslam, with her three-octave vocal range.
***$12**, NM condition*

Progressive rock has also been labeled "art-rock," but while prog-rock allows for more jazz and classical improvisation, "art-rock" leans toward the gothic and mystical, incorporating demons, wizards, and dragons into their compositions. Progressive rock bands arguably have the most loyal fan bases, almost rivaling the Grateful Dead in terms of fan devotion. Even if an act like Renaissance or Jethro Tull has not released an album in years (or if they have released some albums, yet the radio stations have ignored the new LP in favor of classic "oldies" tracks), they could still pack an arena or theater nearly on word of mouth alone.

The introduction of classical music and traditional instruments into a rock and roll band sometimes had an unexpected side effect—because these artists and groups were experimenting with the blending of different musical genres, some of these bands were thought to be the Beatles, working under a pseudonym. The most famous example of this occurred when the Canadian prog-rock quartet Klaatu released their debut album in 1976. Although the disc sold poorly, a rumor circulated that this band was actually the Beatles in disguise. There was plenty of circumstantial evidence to back this theory up—didn't Ringo Starr's album "Goodnight Vienna" feature a photograph of the Klaatu robot from *The Day The Earth Stood Still?* Klaatu's LP suddenly became a hot seller, until it was discovered that the band actually hailed from Canada, not Liverpool.

Photo credit: Courtesy Last Vestige Music Store, Albany, N.Y.

Klaatu's debut album featured the song "Calling Occupants of Interplanetary Craft," which was recorded by the Carpenters as a Top 40 hit.
***$7.50**, VG condition*

What To Look For

Some progressive rock artists did release 45s, but album tracks like "Autobahn" and "Tubular Bells" paled when heavily edited down to a 3-minute 45. In many cases, though, an artist's earliest releases on 45s do have some collectible value—but these recordings are few and far between.

The cleaner a progressive rock album sounds, the more collectible it becomes. While the standard album pressing does contain a collectible value, collectors will search for audiophile or quadraphonic pressings if they exist.

Photo credit: From the Collection of Val Shively.

This white label promo for the Jethro Tull song "Hymn 43" features not only the artwork of two record companies—Reprise and Chrysalis—but also a small photo of the album "Hymn 43" came from Aqualung.

$5, NM condition

Many prog-rock albums sold quite well upon their initial release, as artists like Genesis, Yes, Gentle Giant, and Jethro Tull had successful chart runs. Some records, however, were overpressed, and today can turn up with notch marks or drill holes on the cover. These pressings, which were sold in closeout stores or in $1.99 bargain bins, should only sell for about 50% to 75% of the value of an unnotched copy.

A drill-hole in the upper-right corner denotes this pressing of Gentle Giant's The Missing Piece *as a cutout, meaning the record company pressed more copies than actually sold, and are disposing of the leftovers at bargain prices.*

$5, Good condition

Books

Neely, Tim, *Goldmine Record Album Price Guide*, Krause Publications, Iola, WI, 1999.

Neely, Tim, *Goldmine Price Guide to Alternative Records*, Krause Publications, Iola, WI, 1996.

Web Pages

A progressive rock home page, with links to many bands: http://www.progrock.com

Kraftwerk home page, with Flash and Quicktime movies based on their most popular compositions: http://www.kraftwerk.com

The home page of former Renaissance singer Annie Haslam: http://www.annie-haslam.com

Pink Floyd's home page: http://www.pinkfloyd-co.com

Tangerine Dream's home page: http://www.tangerinedream.de

Usenet newsgroups: alt.music.jethro-tull

Photo credit: Courtesy Last Vestige Music Store, Albany, N.Y.

Former Jethro Tull guitarist Mick Abrahams formed his own progressive rock group Blodwyn Pig. The group recorded some albums in the 1970s, but were not able to equal or surpass Jethro Tull's success and longevity.
***$15**, NM condition*

This early experimental progressive album brought together four of the top electronic music composers, including a pre-"Switched-on Bach" Wendy Carlos.
***$75**, NM condition*

ARTIST VG+ to NM

BLODWYN PIG

45s

A&M 1158, "Dear Jill"/"Summer Day," 1969 .... **$3.00-$6.00**

LPs

A&M SP-4210, Ahead Rings Out, 1969 .... **$7.50-$15.00**
SP-4243, Getting to This, 1970 .... **$7.50-$15.00**

WENDY CARLOS:

LPs

Columbia Masterworks 7194, Switched-On Bach
(first cover, Bach sitting, cover quickly replaced, grey label with "360 Sound Stereo"), 1968 .... **$25.00-$50.00**
(second cover, Bach standing, no artist credit, grey label, "360 Sound Stereo"), 1968 .... **$7.50-$15.00**
(third cover, Bach standing, "Walter Carlos" on cover, orange Columbia logos, no "360 Sound Stereo"), 1970 .... **$6.00-$12.00**
(fourth cover, Bach standing, "Wendy Carlos" properly credited on cover, bar code on back cover), 198?? .... **$7.50-$15.00**
CBS Masterworks FM 44567, Peter And The Wolf (w/"Weird Al" Yankovic), 1988 .... **$75.00-$150.00**

EMERSON, LAKE AND PALMER

45s

Cotillion 44106, "Lucky Man"/"Knife's Edge," 1971 .... **$3.00-$6.00**
44131, "A Time and a Place"/"Stone of Years," 1971 .... **$2.50-$5.00**
Manticore 2003, "Still You Turn Me On"/"Brain Salad Surgery," 1973 .... **$2.50-$5.00**
(with picture sleeve, add), 1973 .... **$5.00-$10.00**
Atlantic 3398, "Fanfare for the Common Man"/"Brain Salad Surgery," 1977 .... **$2.50-$5.00**
3555, "All I Want Is You"/"Tiger in a Spotlight," 1979 .... **$2.50-$5.00**
3641, "Peter Gunn Theme"/"Tiger in a Spotlight," 1980 .... **$2.50-$5.00**

LPs

Cotillion ELP 66666, Pictures at an Exhibition, 1971 .... **$6.00-$12.00**
SD 9040, Emerson, Lake and Palmer, 1971 .... **$6.00-$12.00**
SD 9900, Tarkus, 1971 .... **$6.00-$12.00**
SD 9903, Trilogy, 1972 .... **$6.00-$12.00**
SMAS 94773, Trilogy (Capitol Record Club Edition), 1972 .... **$7.50-$15.00**
Manticore ELP 66669, Brain Salad Surgery, 1973 .... **$6.00-$12.00**
SD-3-200, Welcome Back, My Friends, to the Show That Never Ends, Ladies and Gentlemen (3 LPs), 1974 .... **$10.00-$20.00**
(if any above are on Atlantic, reissues), 1977 .... **$4.00-$8.00**
Atlantic SD 19211, Love Beach, 1978 .... **$5.00-$10.00**
SD 19255, Emerson, Lake and Palmer In Concert, 1979 .... **$5.00-$10.00**
SD 19283, The Best of Emerson, Lake and Palmer, 1980 .... **$5.00-$10.00**
Mobile Fidelity 1-031, Pictures at an Exhibition (audiophile), 1980 .... **$15.00-$30.00**
1-203, Tarkus (audiophile), 1994 .... **$12.50-$25.00**
1-218, Trilogy (audiophile), 1994 .... **$20.00-$40.00**

GENESIS:

45s

Parrot 3018, "Silent Sun"/"That's Me"
(if stock copy with black label, green-yellow bird on label), 1968 .... **$200.00-$400.00**
(if promo copy, orange label, black bird), 1968 .... **$50.00-$100.00**
Charisma 103, "Watcher of the Skies"/"Willow Farm," 1973 .... **$25.00-$50.00**
26002, "I Know What I Like"/"Twilight Ale House," 1973 .... **$20.00-$40.00**
Atco 7013, "The Lamb Lies Down on Broadway"/"Counting Out Time," 1975 **$10.00-$20.00**
7050, "Entangled"/"Ripples," 1976 .... **$5.00-$10.00**
7076, "Your Own Special Way"/"In That Quiet Earth," 1977 .... **$5.00-$10.00**
Atlantic 3474, "Follow You Follow Me"/"Inside and Out," 1978 .... **$2.00-$4.00**
3511, Go West Young Man (In the Motherlode)"/"Scene from a Night's Dream," 1978 .... **$2.00-$4.00**
3662, "Misunderstanding"/"Behind the Lines," 1980 .... **$2.00-$4.00**
(with picture sleeve, add), 1980 .... **$2.50-$5.00**
3751, "Turn It On Again"/"Evidence of Autumn," 1980 .... **$2.00-$4.00**
3858, "No Reply At All"/"Heaven Love My Life," 1981 .... **$2.00-$4.00**
3891, "Abacab"/"Who Dnnnit?," 1982 .... **$2.00-$4.00**
(with picture sleeve, add), 1982 .... **$2.00-$4.00**
4025, "Man on the Corner"/"Submarine," 1982 .... **$2.00-$4.00**
(with picture sleeve, add), 1982 .... **$2.00-$4.00**
4053, "Paperlate"/"You Might Recall," 1982 .... **$2.00-$4.00**

LPs

ABC Impulse! ASD-9205, Trespass, 1971 .... **$15.00-$30.00**
ABC X-816, Trespass, 1971 .... **$6.00-$12.00**
Charisma CAS-1052, Nursery Cryme, 1971 .... **$7.50-$15.00**
(if Classic Records audiophile reissue), 2000 .... **$12.50-$25.00**
CAS-1058, Foxtrot, 1972 .... **$7.50-$15.00**
(if Classic Records audiophile reissue), 2001 .... **$12.50-$25.00**
CAS-6060, Selling England by the Pound, 1973 .... **$7.50-$15.00**
(if Classic Records audiophile reissue), 2001 .... **$12.50-$25.00**

CA 2701, Nursery Cryme/Foxtrot (2 LPs), 1976 ....$7.50-$15.00
London PS 643, From Genesis to Revelation, 1974 ....$10.00-$20.00
LC-50006, In the Beginning, 1977 ....$6.00-$12.00
Atco 2-401, The Lamb Lies Down on Broadway (2 LPs, yellow label), 1974
....$7.50-$15.00
36-129, A Trick of the Tail, 1976..$6.00-$12.00
36-144, Wind & Wuthering, 1977 ....$6.00-$12.00
Atlantic 2-9002, Seconds Out (2 LPs), 1977 ....$6.00-$12.00
19173, ...and then there were three, 1978 ....$5.00-$10.00
16014, Duke, 1980...$5.00-$10.00
19313, Abacab (four different colored covers, value is equal), 1981
....$5.00-$10.00
SD 2-2000, Three Sides Live (2 LPs), 1982 ....$6.00-$12.00
80116, Genesis, 1983 ....$4.00-$8.00
81641, Invisible Touch, 1986 ....$4.00-$8.00

GENTLE GIANT

45s

Capitol 4484, "Cogs in Cogs"/"I'm Turning Around," 1977
....$2.50-$5.00

LPs

Vertigo VE-1005, Acquiring the Taste, 1971 ....$7.50-$15.00
Columbia KC 31649, Three Friends, 1972 ....$6.00-$12.00
KC 32022, Octopus, 1973...$6.00-$12.00
Capitol ST-11337, The Power and the Glory, 1974 ....$5.00-$10.00
ST-11428, Free Hand, 1975 ....$5.00-$10.00
ST-11532, Interview, 1976 ....$5.00-$10.00
SKBB-11592, The Official "Live" Gentle Giant- Playing the Fool (2 LPs), 1977 ....$6.00-$12.00
SST 11696, The Missing Piece, 1977 ....$5.00-$10.00
SW-11813, Giant for a Day, 1978...$5.00-$10.00
(if any of the above Capitol issues with an "SN" prefix, reissue), 1980
....$4.00-$8.00

JETHRO TULL:

45s

Reprise 0815, "Love Story"/"Song for Jeffrey," possibly promo only, 1969
....$7.50-$15.00
0845, "Living in the Past"/"Driving Song," possibly promo only, 1969
....$10.00-$20.00
0886, "Reasons for Waiting"/"Sweet Dream," 1970.....................$7.50-$15.00
0899, "Teacher"/"Witch's Promise," 1970 ....$7.50-$15.00
0927, "Inside"/"Time for Everything," 1970 ....$2.50-$5.00
1024, "Hymn 43"/"Mother Goose," 1971 ....$2.50-$5.00
1054, "Locomotive Breath"/"Wind-Up," 1971 ....$2.50-$5.00
Chrysalis 2006, "Living in the Past"/"Christmas Song," 1972
....$3.00-$6.00
2012, "A Passion Play (Edit #9)"/"A Passion Play (Edit #8)," 1973
....$3.00-$6.00
2017, "A Passion Play (Edit #6)"/"A Passion Play (Edit #10)," 1973
....$2.50-$5.00
2101, "Bungle in the Jungle"/"Back Door Angels," 1974.................$2.50-$5.00
(with picture sleeve, add), 1974...$5.00-$10.00
2103, "Skating Away (On the Thin Ice of a New Day)"/"Sealion," 1975
....$2.50-$5.00
2110, "Locomotive Breath"/"Fat Man," 1975 ....$2.50-$5.00
2114, "Too Old to Rock and Roll, Too Young to Die"/"Bad Eyed and Loveless," 1976 ....$2.50-$5.00
2135, "The Whistler"/"Strip Cartoon," 1977 ....$2.50-$5.00
2387, "Home"/"Warm Sporran," 1979..$2.50-$5.00
2613, "Fallen on Hard Times"/"Pussy Willow," 1982 ....$2.00-$4.00
43172, "Steel Monkey"/"Down at the End of Your Road," 1987
....$2.00-$4.00
S7-18211, "Christmas Song"/"Skating Away on the Thin Ice of a New Day," green vinyl, 1994..$2.50-$5.00

LPs

Reprise MS 2035, Aqualung, 1971 ....$7.50-$15.00
MS 2072, Thick as a Brick, 1972 ....$7.50-$15.00
2MS 2106, Living in the Past, two-record set with booklet, sleeves attached to booklet, 1972 ....$12.50-$25.00
RS 6360, Stand Up, two-tone orange label, "r" and "W7" logos on label, band "stands up" when gatefold cover is opened, 1969 ....$10.00-$20.00
CHR 1003, Thick as a Brick
(if green label, "3300 Warner Blvd." address), 1973 ....$6.00-$12.00
(if blue label, New York address), 1977 ....$5.00-$10.00
CHR 1040, A Passion Play
(if green label, "3300 Warner Blvd." address), 1973 ....$6.00-$12.00
(if blue label, New York address), 1977 ....$5.00-$10.00
CHR 1041, This Was
(if green label, "3300 Warner Blvd." address), 1973 ....$6.00-$12.00
(if blue label, New York address), 1977 ....$5.00-$10.00
PRO 623, The Jethro Tull Radio Show, promo, 1975 ....$25.00-$50.00
CHR 1044, Aqualung
(if green label, "3300 Warner Blvd." address), 1973 ....$5.00-$10.00
(if blue label, New York address), 1977 ....$5.00-$10.00
(if on CH4 1044, quadraphonic pressing), 1974.............................$20.00-$40.00
CHR 1238, Stormwatch, 1979 ....$5.00-$10.00
CHR 1301, A, 1980..$5.00-$10.00
V5X 41653, 20 Years of Jethro Tull, 5 LPs, 1988 ....$40.00-$80.00
VX2 41655, 20 Years of Jethro Tull, 2 LPs, abridged version of above, 1989
....$12.50-$25.00
DCC Compact Classics LPZ 2033, Aqualung, audiophile pressing, 1997
....$50.00-$100.00
Mobile Fidelity 1-061, Aqualung, audiophile pressing, 1980
....$35.00-$70.00

KLAATU:

45s

Island 011, "California Jam"/"Doctor Marvello," 1975 ....$5.00-$10.00
Capitol 4377, "Calling Occupants"/"Doctor Marvello," 1976
....$4.00-$8.00
4412, "Calling Occupants"/"Sub-Rosa Subway," 1977.....................$2.50-$5.00
4516, "Around the Universe in 80 Days"/"We're Off You Know," 1977
....$2.50-$5.00
4627, "Dear Christine"/"Older," 1978 ....$2.50-$5.00

LPs

Capitol ST-11542, Klaatu, 1976 ....$7.50-$15.00
ST-11633, Hope, 1977 ....$6.00-$12.00
SW-11836, Sir Army Suit, 1978..$6.00-$12.00
ST-12080, Endangered Species, 1980 ....$6.00-$12.00
(if above with an "SN" prefix, 1980 reissue), 1980 ....$4.00-$8.00

KRAFTWERK:

45s

Vertigo 203, "Autobahn"/"Morgan Spaziergance," 1975 ....$4.00-$8.00
Capitol 4211, "Radioactivity"/"Antenna," 1976....................................$2.50-$5.00
(with picture sleeve, add:, 1976 ....$4.00-$8.00
4460, "Trans-Europe Express"/"Franz Schubert," 1977.........................$2.50-$5.00
4620, "Neon Lights"/"The Robots," 1978 ....$2.50-$5.00
Warner Bros. 49795, "Computer Love"/"Numbers," 1981 ....$1.50-$3.00
49723, "Pocket Calculator"/"Denkatu," 1981..$1.50-$3.00
(if on yellow vinyl), 1981 ....$2.50-$5.00
(with plastic picture sleeve for yellow vinyl pressing, add), 1981
....$2.50-$5.00
29342, "Tour de France" (2 versions), 1984...$1.50-$3.00
29532, "Musique Non-Stop" (2 versions), 1986 ....$1.00-$2.00
(with picture sleeve, add), 1986..$1.00-$2.00
28441, "The Telephone Call"/"Der Telefon Anruf," 1987 ....$1.50-$3.00
(with picture sleeve, add), 1987..$1.50-$3.00

12-inch Singles

Capitol 8502, "Showroom Dummies"/"Les Mannequins," 1977
....$10.00-$20.00
8526, "Neon Lights"/"The Model," 1978 ....$12.50-$25.00
Warner Bros. PRO-A-951, "Pocket Calculator"/"Denkatu," 1981
....$6.00-$12.00
20549, "Musique Non Stop" (2 versions), 1986.......................................$4.00-$8.00

LPs

Vertigo VEL-2003, Autobahn, 1974...$10.00-$20.00
VE-2006, Ralf & Florian, 1976 ....$8.00-$16.00
Mercury SRM-1-2704, Autobahn, 1977 ....$7.50-$15.00
Capitol ST-11457, Radio-Activity, 1975 ....$8.00-$16.00
SW 11603, Trans-Europe Express, 1977 ....$8.00-$16.00
SW-11728, The Man-Machine, 1978..$8.00-$16.00
(if above Capitol releases with "SN" prefix, 1980s reissue), 198?
....$5.00-$10.00
Warner Bros. 3459, Computer World, 1981 ....$5.00-$10.00
25525, Electric Café, 1986..$6.00-$12.00
Elektra 60869, The Mix, 2 LPs, 1991 ....$6.00-$12.00

MIKE OLDFIELD:

45s

Virgin 55100, "Tubular Bells (Now the Original Theme from the Movie "The Exorcist")"/"Tubular Bells," 1973 ....$4.00-$8.00

PR 196, "Tubular Bells Excerpts" (six edits, promo only), 1974 ....$12.50-$25.00
PR 199, "Tubular Bells" (promo, same on both sides?), 1974.....$12.50-$25.00
PR 223, "Hergest Ridge" (promo, two different edits?), 1974 ....$10.00-$20.00
Virgin/Epic 14-02877, "Family Man"/"Mount Teide," 1982 ....$3.00-$6.00
Virgin 99402, "Magic Touch"/"Wind Chimes Part 1," 1987 ....$2.00-$4.00
(with picture sleeve, add), 1987 ....$2.00-$4.00

10-inch Singles

Virgin PR 361, "Guilty"/"North Star"/"Platinum Finale," 1979 ....$50.00-$100.00

LPs

Virgin VR-13-105, Tubular Bells, 1973 ....$7.50-$15.00
(if on QR 13-105, quadraphonic), 1974....................$12.50-$25.00
VR 13-115, The Orchestral Tubular Bells, 1979 ....$5.00-$10.00
PZ 34116, Tubular Bells, 1976....................$6.00-$12.00
VR 13135, Tubular Bells, 1979 ....$5.00-$10.00
VR 13143, Airborn (2 LPs, US-only pressing), 1980....................$7.50-$15.00
90591, The Killing Fields, 1987....................$5.00-$10.00
91270, Earth Moving, 1990....................$6.00-$12.00

RENAISSANCE:

45s

Capitol 3487, "Prologue"/"Spare Some Love," 1972 ....$4.00-$8.00
3715, "Carpet of the Sun"/"Bound for Infinity," 1973....................$4.00-$8.00
Sire 714, "Mother Russia"/"I Think of You," 1974 ....$3.00-$6.00
728, "Carpet of the Sun"/"Kiev," 1976 ....$3.00-$6.00
740, "Midas Man"/"Captive Heart," 1977....................$3.00-$6.00
1022, "Northern Lights"/"Opening Out," 1978....................$2.50-$5.00
1041, "Northern Lights"/"Opening Out," 1979....................$2.50-$5.00
49041, "Forever Changing"/"Jekyll and Hyde," 1979....................$2.50-$5.00
IRS 9904, "Remember"/"Bon Jour Swan Song," 1982 ....$2.50-$5.00
9914, "Richard IX"/(B-side unknown), 1982....................$2.50-$5.00

LPs

Elektra EKS-74068, Renaissance (first incarnation of group, with Keith Relf), 1969 ....$15.00-$30.00
Capitol SMAS-11116, Prologue, 1972 ....$7.50-$15.00
ST-11216, Ashes Are Burning, 1973....................$7.50-$15.00
Sire SAS-7502, Turn of the Cards, 1974....................$6.00-$12.00
SASD-7510, Scheherazade and Other Stories, 1975 ....$6.00-$12.00
SACD-3902, Live at Carnegie Hall, 2 LPs, 1976....................$7.50-$15.00
7526, Novella, 1977 ....$6.00-$12.00
(if any of the above Sire releases have "SR" prefix, 1977 reissue), 1977 ....$5.00-$10.00
SRK 6049, A Song for All Seasons, 1978....................$6.00-$12.00
SRK 6068, Azure d'Or, 1979 ....$6.00-$12.00
IRS SP-70019, Camera Camera, 1981 ....$5.00-$10.00
SP-70033, Time Line, 1983....................$5.00-$10.00
Mobile Fidelity 1-099, Scheherazade and Other Stories, audiophile pressing, 1982 ....$25.00-$50.00

RUSH:

45s

Moon MN 001, "Not Fade Away"/"You Can't Fight It," 1973 ....$250.00-$500.00
(if stamped "Not for Sale" in red on the label), 1973....................$200.00-$400.00
73623, "Finding My Way"/"Need Some Love," 1974....................$25.00-$50.00
73623, "Finding My Way (mono)/(stereo) (promo), 1974 ....$20.00-$40.00
73647, "In the Mood"/"What You're Doing," 1974....................$12.50-$25.00
73681, "Anthem"/"Fly by Night," 1975....................$5.00-$10.00
73737, "Bastille Day"/"Lakeside Park," 1975....................$5.00-$10.00
73803, "Lessons"/"Twilight Zone," 1976....................$5.00-$10.00
73873, "Fly by Night-In the Mood"/"Something for Nothing," 1976 ....$5.00-$10.00
73912, "Making Memories"/"Temples of Syrinx," 1977 ....$5.00-$10.00
73958, "Closer to the Heart"/"Madrigal," 1977....................$5.00-$10.00
73990, "Anthem"/"Fly by Night," 1978....................$5.00-$10.00
74051, "The Trees"/"Circumstances," 1979 ....$5.00-$10.00
76044, "The Spirit of Radio"/"Circumstances," 1980....................$5.00-$10.00
76060, "Entre Nous"/"Different Strings," 1980 ....$5.00-$10.00
(with picture sleeve, add), 1981....................$12.50-$25.00
76124, "Closer to the Head"/"Freewill," 1981....................$4.00-$8.00
76179, "New World Man"/"Vital Signs," 1982....................$7.50-$15.00
76196, "Countdown"/"Subdivision," 1982 ....$5.00-$10.00
880050-7, "Body Electric"/"Between the Wheels," 1984....................$4.00-$8.00
884191-7, "The Big Money"/"Red Sector A," 1985....................$4.00-$8.00
(with picture sleeve, add), 1985....................$7.50-$15.00
888891-7, "Time Stand Still"/"High Water," 1987....................$3.00-$6.00
(with picture sleeve, add), 1987....................$5.00-$10.00

LPs

Mercury MK-32, Everything Your Listener Ever Wanted to Hear by Rush (promo), 1975....................$50.00-$100.00
MK-185, Rush 'N Roulette (six-grooved EP, record plays one of six songs, depending on where the stylus starts), 1981 ....$50.00-$100.00
SRM-1-1011, Rush, 1974 ....$5.00-$10.00
SRM-1-1023, Fly by Night, 1975 ....$5.00-$10.00
SRM-1-1046, Caress of Steel, 1975 ....$5.00-$10.00
SRM-1-1079, 2112, 1976....................$5.00-$10.00
SRM-2-7508, All the World's a Stage (2 LPs), 1976 ....$6.00-$12.00
SRM-1-1184, A Farewell to Kings, 1977 ....$5.00-$10.00
SRP-1-1300, Hemispheres (picture disc), 1979....................$20.00-$40.00
SRM-1-3743, Hemispheres, 1978....................$5.00-$10.00
SRM-3-9200, Archives, 1978....................$10.00-$20.00
SRM-1-4001, Permanent Waves, 1980 ....$5.00-$10.00
SRM-1-4013, Moving Pictures, 1981 ....$5.00-$10.00
SRM-2-7001, Exit. Stage Left (2 LPs), 1981....................$6.00-$12.00
SRM-1-4063, Signals, 1982 ....$5.00-$10.00
818476-1, Grace Under Pressure, 1984 ....$5.00-$10.00
(if any of the above have Mercury catalog numbers 822541-822550, 1985 reissue), 1985 ....$4.00-$8.00
(if any of the above have Mercury catalog numbers 822551-822553, multi-record 1985 reissue), 1985 ....$5.00-$10.00
826098-1, Power Windows, 1985....................$5.00-$10.00
832464-1, Hold Your Fire, 1987 ....$5.00-$10.00
836346-1, A Show of Hands (2 LPs), 1988....................$6.00-$12.00
Atlantic 82040, Presto, 1989 ....$10.00-$20.00

TANGERINE DREAM:

45s

MCA 40740, "Betrayal (Sorcerer's Theme)"/"Grind," 1977 ....$5.00-$10.00
Virgin 9516, "Moonlight (Part 2)"/"Coldwater Canyon (Part 2)," 1977 ....$5.00-$10.00

12-inch Singles

Relativity EMC 8044, "Streethawk (2 versions)"/"Tiergarten," 1985 ....$10.00-$20.00

LPs

Virgin VR 13-108, Phaedra, 1974....................$7.50-$15.00
VR 13-116, Rubycon, 1975 ....$7.50-$15.00
PZ 34427, Stratosfear, 1976....................$7.50-$15.00
PZG 35014, Encore (2 LPs), 1977 ....$10.00-$20.00
Elektra 5E-521, Thief, 1981 ....$5.00-$10.00
5E-557, Exit, 1981....................$5.00-$10.00
EMI America ST-17141, Flashpoint, 1984....................$5.00-$10.00
Private Music 2042-1-P, Optical Race, 1988 ....$7.50-$15.00
2047-1-P, Miracle Mile, 1989....................$7.50-$15.00
2057-1-P, Lily on the Beach, 1989 ....$7.50-$15.00
Relativity EMC 8043, Le Pare, 1989....................$6.00-$12.00
EMC 8045, Poland (2 LPs), 198? ....$7.50-$15.00
86561 8068, Electronic Meditation, 1986....................$6.00-$12.00
86561 8069, Alpha Centauri, 1986....................$6.00-$12.00
86561 8070, Zeit (2 LPs), 1986 ....$7.50-$15.00
86561 8071, Atam (2 LPs), 1986 ....$6.00-$12.00

URIAH HEEP:

45s

Mercury 73103, "Gypsy"/"Real Turned On," 1970 ....$4.00-$8.00
73174, "High Priestess"/(B-side unknown), 1970....................$5.00-$10.00
76177, "That's the Way It Is"/"Son of a Bitch," 1982....................$2.00-$4.00
Warner Bros. 7738, "Stealin'"/"Sunshine," 1973 ....$2.50-$5.00
Chrysalis 2274, "Come Back to Me"/"Love or Nothing," 1978.......$2.00-$4.00

LPs

Mercury SR-61294, Uriah Heep, 1970 ....$6.00-$12.00
SR-61319, Salisbury, 1970....................$6.00-$12.00
SRM-1-614, Look at Yourself, 1971....................$5.00-$10.00
SRM-2-7503, Uriah Heep Live (2 LPs), 1973 ....$6.00-$12.00
Warner Bros. BS 2724, Sweet Freedom, 1973....................$5.00-$10.00
W 2800, Wonderworld, 1974 ....$5.00-$10.00
BS 2869, Return to Fantasy, 1975....................$5.00-$10.00
Chrysalis CHR 1204, Fallen Angel, 1978....................$5.00-$10.00
Mercury, SRM-1-4057, Abominog, 1982....................$4.00-$8.00
812313-1, Head First, 1983 ....$4.00-$8.00
Columbia BFC 40132, Equator, 1985....................$4.00-$8.00

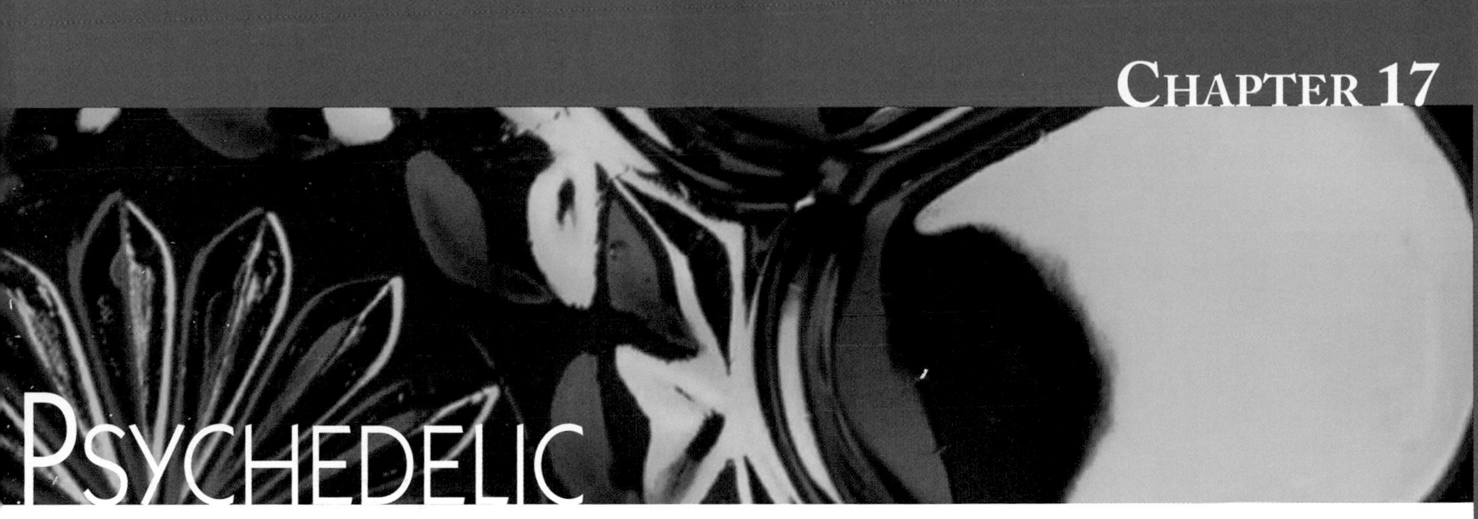

Chapter 17

Psychedelic

History

The 1960s were a time of turbulent change. Musicians and songwriters discovered such hallucinogenic drugs as cannibis sativa (marijuana) and lysergic acid diethylamide (LSD), and attempted to integrate their psychotropic excursions with their musical creations. Many artists incorporated non-traditional musical instruments into the standard rock combo, using sitars, Theremins, and synthesizers to create previously unrealized sonic visions—as if the notes and sounds could be seen and felt. From San Francisco to Austin, Texas, from London to New York City, whether listeners tuned in, turned on, freaked out or dropped out, rock and roll took a mind-altering twist.

Psychedelic rock was one of the first genres to explore the possibilities of the recording studio, to capture performances that could not be reproduced in a live concert setting. One could add such simple things as an echo or reverb to a master tape, or multitrack several voices or instruments to create an otherworldly experience. It was also one of the first rock genres to break from the three-minute pop single format, as songs might fill six or seven minutes (or even an entire side) on an LP. Psychedelic rock also allowed liberal interpretation of the lyrics—in Jefferson Airplane's "White Rabbit," was Grace Slick singing about the characters from Alice in Wonderland, or was the song an allegory to a bad trip? Could "Lucy in the Sky with Diamonds" be a coded reference to LSD?

Bands like the Jefferson Airplane and the Grateful Dead were part of the San Francisco countercultural movement,

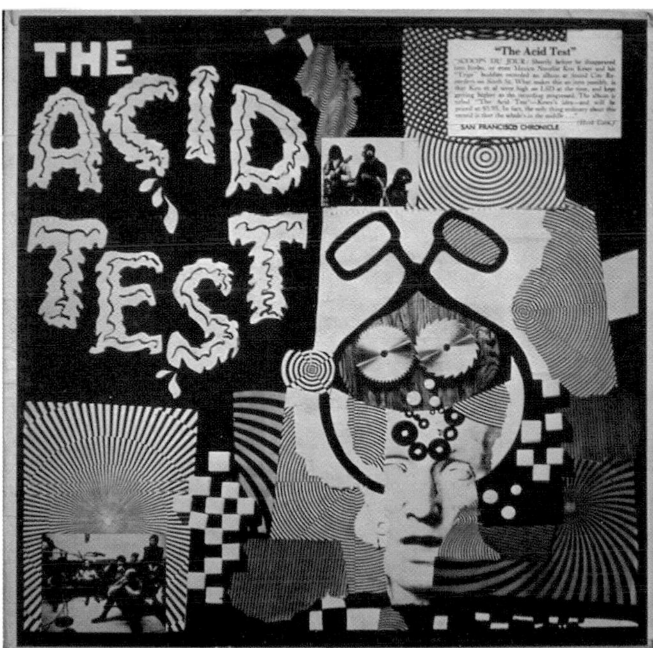

Ken Kesey, the "Merry Prankster" whose LSD experiments helped fuel the psychedelic movement, recorded this album in October 1966, at San Francisco State College. The entire album was culled from 36 hours of Kesey and his friends during an acid test. The Grateful Dead are part of this LP; they can be heard playing in the background.

***$300**, NM condition*

Photo credit: From the collection of Val Shively.

Was the Byrds' "Eight Miles High" a reference to a bad airplane flight, or a hidden meaning to a different type of "high?" This perceptive ambiguity helped fuel multiple interpretations of various psychedelic songs, including this pop hit.

***$60**, NM picture sleeve*

Photo credit: From the Collection of Eric Schwartz.

Counterfeits of this early Grateful Dead 45, on the tiny Scorpio label, have surfaced. Originals will have "Commercial Records" engraved in the dead wax; bootlegs will not.

***$1,000**, NM condition*

"You're Gonna Miss Me," the Thirteenth Floor Elevators' biggest psych hit, originally appeared on other labels, including Contact and Hanna-Barbera. The owner of International Artists, Loren Rogers, had a famous brother—country singer Kenny Rogers—who also recorded a psychedelic hit, "Just Dropped In (To See What Condition My Condition Was In)."

***$20**, NM condition*

as albums like *Surrealistic Pillow* and *Anthem of the Sun* introduced America to the San Francisco "Summer of Love" countercultural movement. In an earlier incarnation, the Grateful Dead were the band of choice for Ken Kesey's Acid Tests, a series of then-legal experimentations with LSD in San Francisco; to this day, the Grateful Dead have developed a loyal and dedicated following throughout the Bay Area—and around the world.

Psychedelic rock was also on the rise in Austin, Texas, where the Thirteenth Floor Elevators incorporated drug trips into their musical oeuvre. With lead singer Roky Erickson's mewling vocals and songs like "You're Gonna Miss Me" and "Roller Coaster," that embodied the aftereffects of a psychotropic drug trip, the Thirteenth Floor Elevators evolved from their garage band roots to one of the unsung heroes of the psychedelic rock movement.

Psychedelic rock also found a voice in other cities, as Pink Floyd's original pop singles "Arnold Layne" and "See Emily Play" were three-minute psychedelic pop shots that only gave a hint of the sonic excursions that would follow. In New York, the Velvet Underground set the seeds for psychedelic rock and early punk and new wave, working with Andy Warhol as his house band. The Doors, whose psychedelic excursions include "Riders on the Storm," "Light My Fire," and "Break On Through to the Other Side," took their name from a poem by William Blake, "When the doors of perception are cleansed, man will see things as they truly are, infinite."

First pressings of The Doors' final album with Morrison's living participation, L.A. Woman, *contain rounded corners and a transparent colored background in the jacket; later pressings have a standard cardboard cover.*

***$12.50**, Fair condition*

What To Look For

Among the more popular psychedelic artists, their rarest titles are often their first albums or 45s, or albums that might have a limited edition cover. Some artists have had songs removed from albums because references to drugs were either implied—or overt. Tracks like the Rolling Stones' "Stoned" (an instrumental) and the Jefferson Airplane's "Runnin' Round This World" were withdrawn from circulation, making those pressings that contain the banned songs instant collectibles.

The rarest psychedelic recordings are from independent rock bands and groups whose music came out on tiny regional labels. Groups like Graced Lightning, The Painted Ship, and Poobah could turn on crowds with mind-expanding rock and roll, and their few songs that appeared on vinyl have become treasured collectibles.

Poobah, a psych-rock trio from Youngstown, Ohio, released this album in 1973, its cover artwork reminiscent of the Fabulously Furry Freak Brothers cartoon.

***$150**, Fair condition*

Web Pages

The Dead (formerly the Grateful Dead) home page: http://www.dead.net

Vernon Joynson's online psych discography, "Fuzz Acid and Flowers," http://www.borderlinebooks.com/us6070s/fuzz.html

A home page devoted to fans of the Byrds: http://www.lyon.edu/webdata/users/kadler/public_html/rmcguinn

A tribute site to the Velvet Underground: http://www.velvetunderground.com

Frank Zappa's home page: http://www.zappa.com

Books

DeRogatis, Jim, *Turn On Your Mind: Four Decades of Great Psychedelic Rock*, Hal Leonard Corporation, Milwaukee, WI, 2003.

Trager, Oliver, *The American Book of the Dead: The Definitive Grateful Dead Encyclopedia*, Fireside/Simon and Schuster Inc., New York, NY, 1997.

The first Pink Floyd 45s were issued on Capitol Records' subsidiary label Tower. Songs like "Arnold Layne" and "See Emily Play" did not crack through to pop listeners, and copies of the original 45s are hard to find today.

***$200**, NM condition*

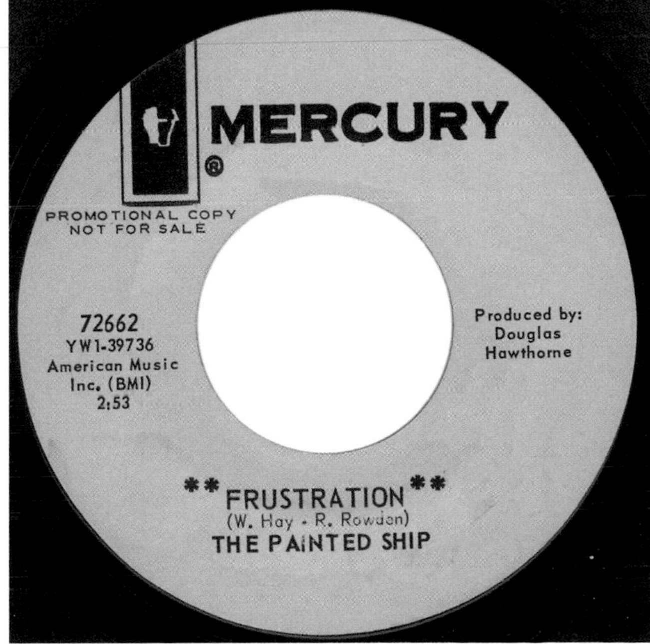

This collectible 45 by the Vancouver psych-rock band The Painted Ship is one of only two singles the group ever released, and their only title to be released in America.

***$100**, NM condition*

SYD BARRETT:

LPs

Harvest SABB-11314, The Madcap Laughs/Barrett (2 LPs), 1974 .... **$12.50-$25.00**

BLUE CHEER:

45s

Philips 40516, "Summertime Blues"/"Out of Focus" (Philips 40516), 1968 .... **$6.00-$12.00**
(with picture sleeve, add), 1968 .... **$12.50-$25.00**

LPs

Philips PHM200264, Vincebus Eruptum (mono), 1968 .... **$40.00-$80.00**
(if on Philips PHS 600264, stereo), 1968 .... **$20.00-$40.00**
PHS 600278, Outsideinside, 1968 .... **$20.00-$40.00**
PHS 600305, New! Improved! Blue Cheer, 1969 .... **$20.00-$40.00**

THE BYRDS:

45s

Columbia 43271, "Mr. Tambourine Man"/"I Knew I'd Want You," 1965 .... **$7.50-$15.00**
(if red vinyl promo), 1965 .... **$75.00-$150.00**
(with promotional sleeve, promoting the Byrds' appearance on the TV show Hullabaloo), 1965 .... **$150.00-$300.00**
43578, "Eight Miles High"/"Why," 1966 .... **$6.00-$12.00**
(with picture sleeve, add), 1966 .... **$30.00-$60.00**
43702, "5D (Fifth Dimension)"/"Captain Soul," 1966 .... **$6.00-$12.00**
43766, "Mr. Spaceman"/"What's Happening," 1966 .... **$6.00-$12.00**

Mono LPs

Columbia CL 2372, Mr. Tambourine Man (with "Guaranteed High Fidelity" on label), 1966 .... **$15.00-$30.00**
(if "360 Sound Mono" on label), 1966 .... **$15.00-$30.00**
CL 2549, Fifth Dimension (5D), 1966 .... **$15.00-$30.00**
CL 2642, Younger than Yesterday, 1967 .... **$15.00-$30.00**

Stereo LPs

Columbia CS 9172, Mr. Tambourine Man (red label, "360 Sound" in black), 1965 .... **$20.00-$40.00**
(if red label, "360 Sound" in white), 1966 .... **$12.50-$25.00**
(if orange label), 1971 .... **$5.00-$10.00**
(if on Columbia PC 9172, budget reissue), 198? .... **$4.00-$8.00**
CS 9349, Fifth Dimension (5D) (red "360 Sound" label), 1966 .... **$12.50-$25.00**
(if orange label), 1971 .... **$5.00-$10.00**
(if on Columbia PC 9349, budget reissue), 198? .... **$4.00-$8.00**

CAPTAIN BEEFHEART:

Mono LPs

Buddah BDM-1001, Safe as Milk, 1967 .... **$50.00-$100.00**

Stereo LPs

Buddah BDS-5001, Safe as Milk, 1967 .... **$30.00-$60.00**
(if on Buddah 5063, reissue), 1969 .... **$12.50-$25.00**
Straight 2 STS-1053, Trout Mask Replica (2 LPs), 1969 .... **$125.00-$250.00**
(if on Straight 2MS 2027, jacket still has catalog number 1053), 1969 .... **$30.00-$60.00**

DONOVAN:

45s

Hickory 1309, "Catch the Wind"/"Why Do You Treat Me Like You Do," 1965 .... **$7.50-$15.00**
Epic 10045, "Sunshine Superman"/"The Trip," 1966 .... **$5.00-$10.00**
(with picture sleeve, add), 1966 .... **$7.50-$15.00**
10098, "Mellow Yellow"/"Sunny South Kensington," 1966 .... **$5.00-$10.00**
(with picture sleeve, add), 1966 .... **$7.50-$15.00**
10434, "Atlantis"/"To Susan on the West Coast Waiting," 1969 .... **$4.00-$8.00**
(with picture sleeve, add), 1969 .... **$6.00-$12.00**

Mono LPs

Epic LN 24217, Sunshine Superman, 1966 .... **$15.00-$30.00**
LN 24239, Mellow Yellow, 1967 .... **$15.00-$30.00**
L2N 6071, A Gift from a Flower to a Garden (2 LPs, with portfolio of lyrics and drawings), 1967 .... **$25.00-$50.00**

Stereo LPs

Epic BN 26217, Sunshine Superman, 1966 .... **$7.50-$15.00**
BN 26239, Mellow Yellow, 1967 .... **$7.50-$15.00**
B2N 171, A Gift from a Flower to a Garden (2 LPs, with portfolio of lyrics and drawings), 1967 .... **$12.50-$25.00**
BN 26420, Hurdy Gurdy Man, 1968 .... **$6.00-$12.00**

THE DOORS:

45s

Elektra 45611, "Break On Through (to the Other Side)"/"End of the Night" (yellow-black label), 1966 .... **$15.00-$30.00**
(if red-black-white label), 1967 .... **$10.00-$20.00**
(if red-black-pink label), 1967 .... **$10.00-$20.00**
(with picture sleeve, add), 1966 .... **$60.00-$120.00**
45615, "Light My Fire"/"The Crystal Ship"
(if first pressing, yellow-black label), 1967 .... **$15.00-$30.00**
(if second pressing, red-black-white label), 1967 .... **$6.00-$12.00**
45635, "Hello, I Love You, Won't You Tell Me Your Name?"/"Love Street," 1968 .... **$10.00-$20.00**
(if second pressing, title shortened to "Hello I Love You"), 1968 .... **$6.00-$12.00**
45726, "Love Her Madly"/"(You Need Meat) Don't Go No Further," 1971 .... **$4.00-$8.00**

Mono LPs

Elektra EKL-4007, The Doors, 1967 .... **$100.00-$200.00**
EKL-4014, Strange Days, 1967 .... **$300.00-$600.00**
EKL-4024, Waiting for the Sun, 1968 .... **$500.00-$1,000.00**

Stereo LPs

Elektra EKS-74007, The Doors (brown labels), 1967 .... **$25.00-$50.00**
(if red label with large "E"), 1969 .... **$7.50-$15.00**
(if butterfly labels), 1971 .... **$6.00-$12.00**
(if red label with Warner Communications logo in lower right), 1980 .... **$5.00-$10.00**
(if red-black labels), 1967 .... **$20.00-$40.00**
EKS-75011, L.A. Woman (with plastic cover, yellow inner sleeve, photo of Jim Morrison on a cross), 1971 .... **$25.00-$50.00**
(with standard cover, butterfly label), 197? .... **$6.00-$12.00**
(if red label, Warner Communications logo in lower right), 1980 .... **$5.00-$10.00**
(if red-black label), 1983 .... **$4.00-$8.00**

THE ELECTRIC PRUNES:

45s

Reprise 0473, "Ain't It Hard"/"Little Olive," 1966 .... **$20.00-$40.00**
0532, "I Had Too Much to Dream Last Night"/"Lovin'," 1966 .... **$10.00-$20.00**
0564, "Get Me to the World On Time"/"Are You Lovin' Me," 1967 .... **$12.50-$25.00**

Mono LPs

Reprise R-6248, The Electric Prunes, 1967 .... **$25.00-$50.00**
R-6262, Underground, 1967 .... **$25.00-$50.00**
R-6275, Mass in F Minor, 1967 .... **$20.00-$40.00**

Stereo LPs

Reprise RS-6248, The Electric Prunes, 1967 .... **$20.00-$40.00**
RS-6262, Underground, 1967 .... **$20.00-$40.00**
RS-6275, Mass in F Minor, 1967 .... **$15.00-$30.00**
RS-6316, Release of an Oath, 1968 .... **$15.00-$30.00**
RS-6342, Just Good Rock 'n Roll, 1969 .... **$15.00-$30.00**

THE GRATEFUL DEAD:

45s

Scorpio 201, "Stealin'"/"Don't Ease Me In" (counterfeits exist; originals have "Commercial Records" in the dead wax), 1966 .... **$500.00-$1,000.00**
Warner Bros. 7186, "Dark Star"/"Born Cross-Eyed," 1968 .... **$12.50-$25.00**
(with picture sleeve, add), 1968 .... **$250.00-$500.00**
7667, "Sugar Magnolia"/"Mr. Charlie," 1972 .... **$6.00-$12.00**
Grateful Dead Records XW-718, "The Music Never Stopped"/"Help On The Way," 1975 .... **$7.50-$15.00**

Mono LPs

Warner Bros. W 1689, The Grateful Dead, 1967 .... **$100.00-$200.00**

Stereo LPs

Warner Bros. WS 1689, The Grateful Dead (gold label), 1967 .... **$40.00-$80.00**
(if green label, "W7" logo), 1968 .... **$12.50-$25.00**
(if green label, "WB" logo), 1970 .... **$7.50-$15.00**
(if "Burbank" label with palm trees), 1973 .... **$6.00-$12.00**
(if white or tan stock label), 1979 .... **$4.00-$8.00**
WS 1749, Anthem of the Sun (green label, "W7" logo), 1968 .... **$15.00-$30.00**
(if on green label, "WB" logo, purple cover), 1970 .... **$7.50-$15.00**
(if on green label, "WB" logo, white background on cover, album has been remixed), 197? .... **$25.00-$50.00**
(if on "Burbank" label with palm trees), 1973 .... **$6.00-$12.00**
(if on white or tan stock label), 1979 .... **$4.00-$8.00**

WS 1689, Workingman's Dead
(if on green label, "WB" logo, textured cover with back cover slick upside down), 1970 .... $12.50-$25.00
(if on "Burbank" label with palm trees, standard cover, back cover right side up), 1973 .... $6.00-$12.00
(if on white or tan stock label), 1979 .... $4.00-$8.00

GRACED LIGHTNING:

45s

Wildwood 1-A, "Silver Lining"/"Lard," 1975 .... $12.50-$25.00

LPs

Golden Voice Studios, no catalog number, The Graced Lightning Side, 1975 .... $250.00-$500.00

THE INCREDIBLE STRING BAND:

45s

Elektra 45696, "This Moment"/"Big Ted," 1970 .... $4.00-$8.00

Mono LPs

Elektra EKM-322, The Incredible String Band, 1967 .... $15.00-$30.00
EKM-4010, The 5,000 Spirits, 1967 .... $15.00-$30.00

Stereo LPs

Elektra EKS-7322, The Incredible String Band (brown label), 1967 .... $10.00-$20.00
(if butterfly label), 1971 .... $6.00-$12.00
EKS-74010, The 5,000 Spirits (brown label), 1967 .... $10.00-$20.00
(if red label, large "E"), 1969 .... $7.50-$15.00
(if on butterfly label), 1971 .... $6.00-$12.00
EKS-74057, Changing Horses (red label, large "E"), 1969 .... $7.50-$15.00
(if butterfly label), 1971 .... $6.00-$12.00

IRON BUTTERFLY:

45s

Atco 6606, "In-A-Gadda-Da-Vida"/"Iron Butterfly Theme," 1968 .... $5.00-$10.00

Mono LPs

Atco 33-227, Heavy, 1967 .... $15.00-$30.00
33-250, In-A-Gadda-Da-Vida, 1968 .... $25.00-$50.00

Stereo LPs

Atco SD-33-227, Heavy (brown-purple label), 1967 .... $12.50-$25.00
(if yellow label), 1969 .... $7.50-$15.00
SD-33-250, In-A-Gadda-Da-Vida (brown-purple label), 1968 .... $12.50-$25.00
(if yellow label), 1969 .... $7.50-$15.00
(if any other later Atco label), 197? .... $5.00-$10.00

JEFFERSON AIRPLANE:

45s

RCA Victor 47-8769, "It's No Secret"/"Runnin' Round This World," 1966 .... $7.50-$15.00
47-9140, "Somebody to Love"/"She Has Funny Cars," 1967 .... $7.50-$15.00
47-9248, "White Rabbit"/"Plastic Fantastic Lover," 1967 .... $7.50-$15.00
(if on Grunt JB-10988, "White Rabbit" on both sides, mono/stereo, white vinyl), 1978 .... $15.00-$30.00
(if on RCA 5156-7-R, "White Rabbit"/"Plastic Fantastic Lover"), 1987 .... $2.50-$5.00
(with picture sleeve for above, released in conjunction with the movie Platoon), 1987 .... $2.50-$5.00

Mono LPs

RCA Victor LPM-3584, Jefferson Airplane Takes Off!
(if first version, with "Runnin' Round This World" as last song on side 1—must be played to verify, covers will list the song whether or not it's on the record), 1966 .... $2,250.00-$3,000.00
(if second version, no "Runnin' Round This World," and questionable lyrics in "Let Me In" and "Run Around," must be heard to confirm), 1966 .... $500.00-$1,000.00
(if third version, no "Runnin' Round This World," edited lyrics in "Let Me In" and "Run Around," all later pressings follow this pressing), 1966 .... $12.50-$25.00
LPM-3766, Surrealistic Pillow, 1967 .... $30.00-$60.00

Stereo LPs

RCA Victor LSP-3584, Jefferson Airplane Takes Off!
(if first version, with "Runnin' Round This World" as last song on side 1—must be played to verify, covers will list the song whether or not it's on the record), 1966 .... $3,000.00-$5,000.00
(if second version, no "Runnin' Round This World," and questionable lyrics in "Let Me In" and "Run Around," must be heard to confirm), 1966 .... $900.00-$1,800.00
(if third version, no "Runnin' Round This World," edited lyrics in "Let Me In" and "Run Around," all later pressings follow this pressing), 1966 .... $12.50-$25.00
(if orange label), 1969 .... $6.00-$12.00
(if tan label), 1975 .... $5.00-$10.00
(if on RCA Victor AYL1-3739, reissue), 1980 .... $4.00-$8.00
LSP-3766, Surrealistic Pillow (black label, dog and gramophone on top of label), 1967 .... $15.00-$30.00
(if orange label), 1969 .... $6.00-$12.00
(if tan label), 1975 .... $5.00-$12.00
(if on RCA Victor AYL1-3738, reissue), 1980 .... $4.00-$8.00

PAUL KANTNER/JEFFERSON STARSHIP:

LPs

RCA Victor LSP-4448, Blows Against the Empire, 1970 .... $7.50-$15.00
(if on clear vinyl promo), 1970 .... $75.00-$100.00
(if on RCA AYL1-3868, budget reissue), 1981 .... $4.00-$8.00

KEN KESEY:

LPs

Sound City 27690, The Acid Test, 1967 .... $150.00-$300.00

MOBY GRAPE:

45s

Columbia 44172, "8:05"/"Mister Blues," 1967 .... $4.00-$8.00
(with picture sleeve, add), 1967 .... $10.00-$20.00

THE PAINTED SHIP:

45s

Mercury 72662, "Frustration"/"Little White Lies," 1966 .... $50.00-$100.00
London 17351, "Frustration"/"Little White Lies" (Canadian pressing), 1966 .... $75.00-$150.00
17354, "And She Said Yes"/"Audience Reaction" (Canadian pressing), 1966 .... $100.00-$200.00

PEARLS BEFORE SWINE:

45s

ESP-Disk 4554, "Morning Song"/"Drop Out," 1967 .... $20.00-$40.00
Reprise 0873, "If You Don't Want To"/"These Things Too," 1969 .. $6.00-$12.00

Mono LPs

ESP-Disk 1054, One Nation Under Ground, 1967 .... $25.00-$50.00

Stereo LPs

ESP-Disk 1054, One Nation Under Ground (black-white cover), 1967 .... $25.00-$50.00
(if sepia-tone cover with no border, or with white border, value is equal), 1967 .... $25.00-$50.00
(if full-color cover), 1968 .... $15.00-$30.00
Reprise RS 6467, Beautiful Lies You Could Live In, 1971 .... $20.00-$40.00

PINK FLOYD:

45s

Tower 333, "Arnold Layne"/"Candy and a Currant Bun," 1967 .... $100.00-$200.00
(with picture sleeve, only issued with promo copies, add), 1967 .... $350.00-$700.00
356, "See Emily Play"/"Scarecrow," 1967 .... $100.00-$200.00
(with title picture sleeve, only issued with promo copies, add), 1967 .... $350.00-$700.00
(with photo picture sleeve, only issued with promo copies, add), 1967 .... $400.00-$800.00
Harvest 3609, "Money"/"Any Colour You Like," 1973 .... $7.50-$15.00
P-3609, "Money" (Edited Mono)/"Money" (Edited Stereo) (promo), 1973 .... $10.00-$20.00
SPRO-6669, "Money" (Censored Edited Mono)/"Money" (Censored Edited Stereo) (should also have a note from the record company telling radio stations to disregard the first promo), 1973 .... $7.50-$15.00

Mono LPs

Tower T 5093, Pink Floyd (The Piper at the Gates of Dawn), 1967 .... $125.00-$250.00

Stereo LPs

Tower ST 5093, Pink Floyd (The Piper at the Gates of Dawn) (orange label), 1967 .... $40.00-$80.00
(if multicolored striped label), 1968 .... $20.00-$40.00
Harvest SMAS-832, Meddle, 1971 .... $7.50-$15.00
ST-11078, Obscured by Clouds, 1972 .... $7.50-$15.00
SMAS-11163, The Dark Side of the Moon, 1973 .... $6.00-$12.00
(if record contains poster and two stickers), 1973 .... $12.50-$25.00
(if on Mobile Fidelity 1-017, audiophile pressing), 1980 .... $25.00-$50.00
(if on Mobile Fidelity MFQR-017, "Ultra High Quality Recording" in box), 1982 .... $150.00-$300.00

THE PRETTY THINGS:

Mono LPs

Fontana MGF-27544, The Pretty Things, 1965 .... **$40.00-$80.00**

Stereo LPs

Fontana SRF-67544, The Pretty Things, 1965 .... **$40.00-$80.00**
Rare Earth RS 506, S.F. Sorrow (rounded cover at top), 1969 ..... **$25.00-$50.00**
(if standard-shaped square cover), 1969 .... **$10.00-$20.00**
RS 515, Parachute, 1970 .... **$10.00-$20.00**

THE RED CRAYOLA:

Mono LPs

International Artists 2, Parable of the Arable Land, 1968 .... **$50.00-$100.00**

Stereo LPs

International Artists 2, Parable of the Arable Land, 1968 .... **$30.00-$60.00**
7, God Bless the Red Crayola, 1968 .... **$30.00-$60.00**
(if above titles have "Masterfonics" in the trail-off vinyl, reissues), 1979 .... **$7.50-$15.00**

SAGITTARIUS:

45s

Columbia 44163, "My World Fell Down"/"Libra," 1967 .... **$5.00-$10.00**
Together 105, "In My Room"/"Navajo Girl," 1969 .... **$5.00-$10.00**
122, "I Can Still See Your Face"/"I Guess the Lord Must Be in New York City," 1969 .... **$5.00-$10.00**

LPs

Columbia CS 9644, Present Tense, 1968 .... **$15.00-$30.00**
Together STT-1002, The Blue Marble (with two bonus photos), 1969 .... **$25.00-$50.00**

THE SOFT MACHINE:

45s

Probe 452, "Joy of a Toy"/"Why Are We Sleeping," 1969 .... **$5.00-$10.00**

LPs

Probe CPLP-4500, The Soft Machine (if cover has moving parts), 1968 .... **$20.00-$40.00**
(if regular cover), 1969 .... **$10.00-$20.00**
CLPLP-4505, The Soft Machine, Vol. 2, 1969 .... **$12.50-$25.00**
Columbia G 30339, Third (2 LPs), 1970 .... **$7.50-$15.00**
C 30754, Fourth, 1971 .... **$6.00-$12.00**

THE THIRTEENTH FLOOR ELEVATORS:

45s

Hanna-Barbera 492, "You're Gonna Miss Me"/"Tried to Hide," 1966 .... **$100.00-$200.00**
Contact 5269, "You're Gonna Miss Me"/"Tried to Hide," 1966 .... **$50.00-$100.00**
International Artists 107, "You're Gonna Miss Me"/"Tried to Hide" (if yellow-green label), 1967 .... **$10.00-$20.00**
(if blue label), 1967 .... **$15.00-$30.00**
111, "Reverberation (Doubt)"/"Fire Engine," 1967 .... **$10.00-$20.00**
113, "Before You Accuse Me"/"Levitation," 1968 .... **$10.00-$20.00**
121, "Baby Blue"/"She Lives," 1968 .... **$10.00-$20.00**
122, "Slip Inside This House"/"Splash 1," 1968 .... **$10.00-$20.00**
126, "May the Circle Remain Unbroken"/"I'm Gonna Love You Too," 1968 .... **$10.00-$20.00**
130, "Livin' On"/"Scarlet and Gold," 1969 .... **$20.00-$40.00**

Mono LPs

International Artists 1, Psychedelic Sounds (green-yellow label), 1967 .... **$125.00-$250.00**
(if all-yellow label), 1968 .... **$75.00-$150.00**
5, Easter Everywhere (mono is promo only), 1968 .... **$200.00-$400.00**

Stereo LPs

International Artists 1, Psychedelic Sounds (all-yellow label), 1968 .... **$75.00-$150.00**
(if aqua-blue label), 1968 .... **$100.00-$200.00**
5, Easter Everywhere, 1968 .... **$75.00-$150.00**
8, 13th Floor Elevators Live, 1968 .... **$50.00-$100.00**
9, Bull of the Woods, 1968 .... **$40.00-$80.00**
(if any of the above, "Masterfonics" in the trail-off vinyl, reissue), 1979 .... **$12.50-$25.00**

TOMORROW:

LPs

Sire SES-97912, Tomorrow, 1968 .... **$30.00-$60.00**

THE VELVET UNDERGROUND:

45s

Verve 10427, "All Tomorrow's Parties"/"I'll Be Your Mirror," 1966 .... **$300.00-$600.00**
(if marked for promotional use only), 1966 .... **$150.00-$300.00**
(with rare picture sleeve, add), 1966 .... **$4,000.00-$8,000.00**

Mono LPs

Verve V-5008, The Velvet Underground and Nico
(if first version, cover has peel-off banana peel, band framed by male torso), 1967 .... **$150.00-$300.00**
(if second version, cover has peel-off banana, torso obscured by a sticker), 1967 .... **$150.00-$300.00**
(if third version, peel-off banana, no torso on cover), 1967 .... **$100.00-$200.00**

Stereo LPs

Verve V6-5008, The Velvet Underground and Nico
(if first version, cover has peel-off banana peel, band framed by male torso), 1967 .... **$100.00-$200.00**
(if second version, cover has peel-off banana, torso obscured by a sticker), 1967 .... **$100.00-$200.00**
(if third version, peel-off banana, no torso on cover), 1967 .... **$75.00-$150.00**
(if fourth version, banana can not be peeled off), 1968 .... **$50.00-$100.00**
(if on Verve 823290-1, reissue, 1985 .... **$6.00-$12.00**

FRANK ZAPPA/MOTHERS OF INVENTION:

Mono LPs

Verve V-5005-2, Freak Out! (2 LPs)
(if blurb on inside gatefold on how to get a map of "freak out hot spots" in L.A.), 1966 .... **$100.00-$200.00**
(if no blurb inside, second cover version), 1966 .... **$75.00-$150.00**
(if white label promo), 1966 .... **$200.00-$400.00**
V-5013, Absolutely Free, 1967 .... **$60.00-$120.00**
(if white label promo), 1967 .... **$100.00-$200.00**
5045, We're Only in It for the Money (with sheet of cutouts), 1968 .... **$75.00-$150.00**
(if white label promo), 1968 .... **$150.00-$300.00**

Stereo LPs

Verve V6-5005-2, Freak Out! (2 LPs)
(if blurb on inside gatefold on how to get a map of "freak out hot spots" in L.A.), 1966 .... **$150.00-$300.00**
(if no blurb inside, second cover version), 1966 .... **$30.00-$60.00**
(if yellow label promo), 1966 .... **$150.00-$300.00**
V6-5013, Absolutely Free, 1967 .... **$30.00-$60.00**
V6-5045, We're Only in It for the Money (with sheet of cutouts), 1968 .... **$30.00-$60.00**
(if censored version, the songs "Who Needs the Peace Corps?" and "Let's Make the Water Turn Black" have lyrics deleted), 1968 .... **$75.00-$150.00**
V6-5074, The XXXX of the Mothers, 1969 .... **$25.00-$50.00**
(if yellow label promo), 1969 .... **$75.00-$100.00**

Frank Zappa and the Mothers of Invention may not be totally classified as part of psychedelic rock—their background owed more to Edgard Varèse than Timothy Leary—but they sure took a healthy swing at it on their album We're Only In It For The Money.

***$75**, VG+ condition*

Chapter 18

Punk

History

There are two schools of thought as to the beginning of punk music. Some say that punk was born in London, as disaffected teens rebelled against glam music and disco, creating their own sound and having the attitude that nothing is sacred. Others claim that the powerful sound was nurtured at a New York City club called CBGB's, where bands like the Ramones and Television played to loyal and rabid crowds. Some argue convincingly that early 1970s groups like the Stooges, the MC5, and the New York Dolls were the forefathers of punk music.

The first punk group to achieve worldwide fame were the Sex Pistols. Led by lead singer Johnny Rotten, the Pistols were confrontational in interviews, taunted the audiences, and played three-chord rock like it was their last breath of life. Their first UK singles, on EMI and A&M respectively, were quickly pulled from shelves because of their material; the band finally signed with Virgin UK, who released their anti-monarchy song "God Save The Queen" during Queen Elizabeth's 50th birthday celebration. The Pistols toured America, and broke up after that tour ended.

The Sex Pistols may have been the first punk band to achieve fame and fortune, but they were not the last. Before long, punk groups were appearing throughout England, including groups like the Clash, Siouxie and the Banshees, X-Ray Spex, and the Buzzcocks.

Over time, many of these British punk groups dabbled in other musical formats and styles. The Clash, for example, recorded several songs with ska and reggae influences, including covering the Equals' ska hit "Police on My Back." By the early 1980s, they recorded songs that showed their appreciation for rap music ("The Magnificent Seven") and dance music ("Rock the Casbah").

Although the most famous proponents of punk music came from England, the American punk scene had its own stars, many of which recorded collectible singles and albums. Early American punk bands included Iggy and the Stooges, the Ramones, and the MC5, all of which still have a loyal following today. Many other American punk recordings were on small labels like SST, Alternative Tentacles, or Ism, and the lyrics were more vulgar than their British counterparts. Such groups included the Dead Kennedys, Black Flag, the Minutemen, X, and the Butthole Surfers. The prices listed are for American pressings only.

Just as the value of garage records have increased due to some titles' inclusion in compilation albums like *Nuggets*, the bootleg reissue series *Killed By Death* has been a boon for collectors seeking rare independent punk pressings. *Killed By Death*, along with other bootleg reissue series like *Powerpearls*, gives punk fans the opportunity to hear small independent punk recordings from the 1970s and 1980s, at an affordable price. It also has boosted the value of these independent 45s and LPs. compilation as a badge of honor.

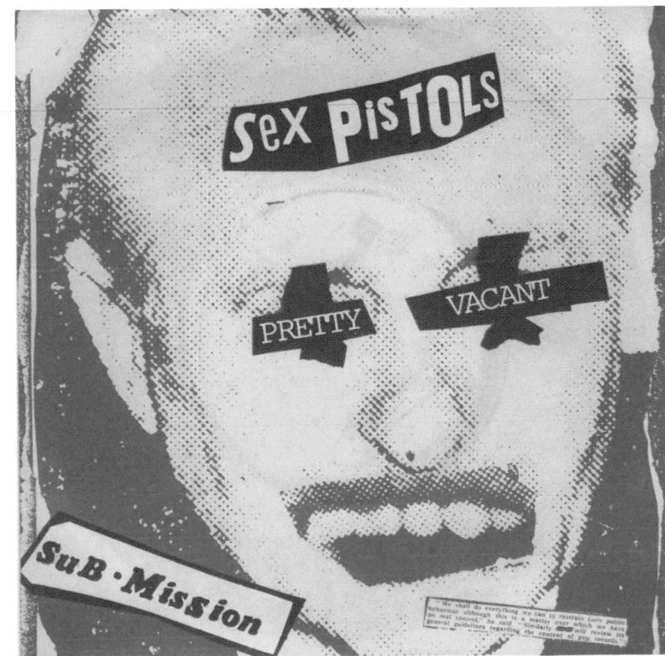

Although the album Never Mind the Bollocks Here's the Sex Pistols *was released in America, Warner Bros. chose to promote the song "Pretty Vacant" as the Sex Pistols' first—and only—American 45. It also came with a custom picture sleeve, as seen here.*

***$30**, NM record and sleeve*

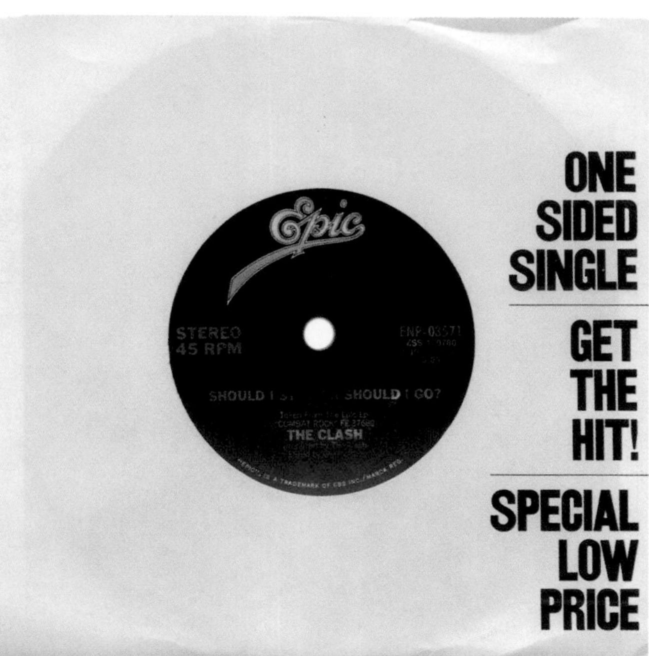

The Clash's song "Should I Stay or Should I Go" was issued several times in America, eventually acquiring three different B-sides during its releases. This version was released as part of a budget line of single-sided 45s, with no playable B-side.

$4, *VG+ condition*

Photo credit: Courtesy Last Vestige Music Store, Albany, N.Y.

Undoubtedly the most vocal American punk band, the Dead Kennedys tested the boundaries of free speech and moral standards in almost every song they ever performed.

$12, *NM condition*

This early Ramones promo 45 features "Blitzkreig Bop" in all its sonic monaural ambiance. In 2003, the street corner of CBGB's, the New York City club where the Ramones played for many years, was renamed "Joey Ramone Place" in honor of the group's late lead singer and songwriter.

$20, *VG condition*

London, Ontario's high princes of glam punk, '63 Monroe, appeared on several underground punk compilations, eventually driving up the collectible value of their small independent albums. This 1985 LP, Stinkin' Out the Joint, *features their punk covers of Herman's Hermits' "I'm Henry VIII, I Am" and Johnny Horton's "The Battle of New Orleans."*

$50, *NM condition*

What To Look For

With British punk bands, the UK pressings are more desirable to punk collectors than the American releases, unless the American album has different tracks or a different running order (some copies of the Sex Pistols' *Never Mind the Bullocks* and the Clash's *The Clash* fall into this category). Sex Pistols collectors, for example, are more interested in finding the rare UK 7-inch pressings of "Anarchy in the U.K." on EMI (UK), and of "God Save The Queen" on A&M (UK). As for American releases, some punk labels like SST and Alternative Tentacles have actually kept their artists' records in print for years, meaning the discs and songs are as easily obtainable today as they were 20 years ago.

The rare items in this genre are radio and promotional pressings, as well as 10-inch "gimmick" releases. The records of one punk group, the Misfits, have sold for as much as $350 in near-mint condition. Many of their records were pressed on colored vinyl, in very small print runs (some as low as 16 copies!). Because of this, many Misfits records have been counterfeited, so check with a reputable dealer who is an expert in alternative/punk music.

Even though the lyrics on this record reference old 70s shows like "Fridays," "That's Incredible" and "Quincy," Black Flag's "TV Party" has remained in print well into the 1990s. It also appeared, with new lyrics, on the soundtrack album for the film Repo Man, *along with other punk bands like Suicidal Tendencies and the Plugz.*

***$7.50**, VG condition*

At first glance, this looks like a rare Misfits 7-inch EP. In fact, it was recorded by "The Misfits"—an Albany, New York punk band from 1981 who chose that name independently of the Glenn Danzig-helmed punk group. Eventually the Albany Misfits renamed themselves as "The Tragics," and copies of this EP were restickered with the band's new name.

***$100**, NM condition*

Books

Neely, Tim, *Goldmine Price Guide to Alternative Records*, Krause Publications, Iola, WI, 1996.

Southern, Terry, *Virgin: A History of Virgin Records*, A Publishing Company, Axminster, Devon, England, 1996.

McNeil, Legs; and Gillian McCann, *Please Kill Me: The Uncensored History of Punk*, Penguin, NY, 1996.

Web Pages

House of the Rising Punk, a directory of punk Web sites from around the world: *http://www.punkrock.org*

A page for the Misfits: *http://www.misfits.com*

A U.S. punk and hardcore discography can be found at this site: http://www.fuzzlogic.com/flex/

Photo credit: Courtesy Last Vestige Music Store, Albany, N.Y.

Wendy O. Williams and the Plasmatics may have been the first group—punk or otherwise—to incorporate chainsaws and shaving cream as musical instruments. They lasted long enough to have this one major-label release; their other recordings were on independent labels.

***$15**, NM condition*

Australia's punk music scene was dominated by The Saints, The Celibate Rifles, and Radio Birdman, a punk group from Sydney who packed a hard stream of metal, punk and pop into their worldwide debut album, Radios Appear. *The album contains their most notable surf-punk hit, "Aloha Steve and Danno," as well as a Stooges cover, "T.V. Eye."*

***$15**, NM condition*

Photo credit: Courtesy Last Vestige Music Store, Albany, N.Y.

This Meat Puppets album contains a bonus 10-inch disc. The value of the record increases if the 10-inch disc is inside, and if an identifying DJ sticker is on the front cover.

***$24**, NM condition*

The Meatmen's live album, We're The Meatmen and You Suck!!! *is collectible as much for its lyrical content (one of the least offensive songs on the album is a Beatles tribute song, "One Down Three to Go"), as it is a parody of punk music and what it stands for.*

***$25**, NM condition*

GG ALLIN:

LPs

Orange, catalog # unknown, Always Was, Is and Always Shall Be, 1980 ....**$50.00-$100.00**
(if on Black & Blue 006053-X, reissue), 1985 ....**$25.00-$50.00**
Blood, catalog # unknown, Eat My Fuc (with hand-decorated plain cover), 198? ....**$25.00-$50.00**
(if on Black & Blue, catalog # unknown, reissue), 1988 ....**$6.00-$12.00**

BAD BRAINS:

45s

Bad Brains 001, "Pay to Cum"/"Stay Close to Me" (black vinyl, first pressings), 1980 ....**$20.00-$40.00**
(with picture sleeve and lyric insert—reissues have photocopies of the picture sleeve—add), 1980 ....**$20.00-$40.00**

LPs

PVC 8917, Rock for Light, 1983 ....**$7.50-$15.00**
Caroline CAROL-1375, Quickness, 1989 ....**$6.00-$12.00**
Victory VR 64, The Omega Sessions (10-inch LP), 1997 ....**$5.00-$10.00**

BAD RELIGION:

45s

Sympathy For The Record Industry SFTRI 158, "Atomic Garden" (B-side etched), 1991 ....**$2.00-$4.00**
(with picture sleeve, add), 1991 ....**$2.00-$4.00**

7-inch EPs

Epitaph 1072, Bad Religion (contains "Bad Religion"/"Politics"/"Sensory Overload"/"Slaves"/"Drastic Actions"/"World War III," red vinyl, if the word "SUFFER" is on the label, it's a bootleg; value is for record and jacket), 1981 ....**$100.00-$200.00**

LPs

Epitaph EPI-BRLP-1, How Could Hell Be Any Worse? (with lyric sheet, increase value if personal notes or band member autographs on the inner sleeves), 1982 ....**$15.00-$30.00**
(if on Epitaph 86407, reissue), 1989 ....**$6.00-$12.00**
Epitaph 86404, Suffer, 1988 ....**$6.00-$12.00**

BLACK FLAG:

45s

SST/Unicorn 95006, "TV Party"/"I've Got to Run"/"My Rules," 1981 ....**$7.50-$15.00**

LPs

SST 015, Everything Went Black (2 LPs), 1982 ....**$7.50-$15.00**
021, The First Four Years, 1983 ....**$6.00-$12.00**

THE BUTTHOLE SURFERS:

45s

Capitol S7-19200, "Pepper"/"Birds," 1996 ....**$2.00-$4.00**
S7-19253, "Cough Syrup"/"Jingle of a Dog's Collar," 1996 ....**$2.00-$4.00**

LPs

Alternative Tentacles VIRUS 32, Butthole Surfers, 1983 ....**$12.50-$25.00**
(if same catalog number, album titled "Brown Reason to Live," brown swirl vinyl), 1983 ....**$10.00-$20.00**
Touch & Go 5, Psychic...Powerless...Another Man's Sac (clear vinyl), 1985 ....**$10.00-$20.00**
(if on black vinyl, reissue), 1985 ....**$5.00-$10.00**

THE BUZZCOCKS:

45s

I.R.S. 9001, "Everybody's Happy Nowadays"/"Why Can't I Touch It," 1979 ....**$3.00-$6.00**
(with picture sleeve, add), 1979 ....**$3.00-$6.00**
9010, "I Believe"/"Something's Gone Wrong Again," 1980 ....**$2.50-$5.00**
(with picture sleeve, add), 1980 ....**$2.50-$5.00**

LPs

I.R.S. SP-001, Singles Going Steady, 1979 ....**$7.50-$15.00**
(if on I.R.S. SP-75001, reissue), 1981 ....**$5.00-$10.00**
SP-009, A Different Kind of Tension, 1980 ....**$7.50-$15.00**
(if on I.R.S. SP-75009, reissue), 1981 ....**$5.00-$10.00**

THE CLASH:

45s

Epic 9-50738, "I Fought the Law"/"White Man in Hammersmith Palais," 1979 ....**$5.00-$10.00**
9-50851, "Train in Vain (Stand By Me)"/"London Calling," 1980 ....**$2.50-$5.00**
14-03006, "Should I Stay or Should I Go"/"Inoculated City," 1982 ....**$4.00-$8.00**
14-03034, "Should I Stay or Should I Go"/"First Night Back in London," 1982 ....**$4.00-$8.00**
34-03245, "Rock the Casbah"/"Long Time Jerk," 1982 ....**$2.00-$4.00**

12-inch Singles

Epic 49-02036, "The Magnificent Dance"/"The Magnificent Seven"/"The Call Up"/"The Cool Out," 1981 ....**$7.50-$15.00**
49-02662, "This Is Radio Clash"/"Radio Clash"/"Outside Broadcast"/"Radio 5," 1981 ....**$5.00-$10.00**
49-03144, "Rock the Casbah"/"Mustapha Dance," 1982 ....**$7.50-$15.00**

10-inch LPs

Epic Nu-Disk 4E 36846, Black Market Clash, 1980 ....**$7.50-$15.00**

12-inch LPs

Epic JE 36060, The Clash, 1979 ....**$7.50-$15.00**
E2 36329, London Calling (2 LPs), 1979 ....**$7.50-$15.00**
E3X 37037, Sandinista! (3 LPs), 1981 ....**$10.00-$20.00**

THE CRAMPS:

45s

Vengeance 666, "Surfin' Bird"/"The Way I Walk," 1978 ....**$25.00-$50.00**
(with picture sleeve, add), 1978 ....**$30.00-$60.00**
668, "Human Fly"/"Domino," 1978 ....**$25.00-$50.00**
(with picture sleeve, add), 1978 ....**$30.00-$60.00**
I.R.S. 9014, "Garbage Man"/"Drug Train," 1980 ....**$10.00-$20.00**
(with picture sleeve, add), 1980 ....**$10.00-$20.00**
9021, "Goo Goo Muck"/"She Said," 1981 ....**$7.50-$15.00**

LPs

I.R.S. SP-007, Songs the Lord Taught Us, 1980 ....**$10.00-$20.00**
SP-70016, Psychedelic Jungle, 1981 ....**$10.00-$20.00**
SP-70042, Bad Music for Bad People, 1984 ....**$7.50-$15.00**

THE DAMNED:

45s

I.R.S. 9022, "Dr. Jeckyl and Mr. Hyde"/"Looking at You (Live)," 1981 ....**$4.00-$8.00**

LPs

I.R.S. SP-70012, The Black Album, 1980 ....**$6.00-$12.00**
Frontier 1003, Damned Damned Damned (US release of 1970s UK songs), 1987 ....**$6.00-$12.00**
MCA 2-8024, Light at the End of the Tunnel (2 LPs), 1988 ....**$7.50-$15.00**

THE DEAD BOYS:

45s

Sire 1004, "Sonic Reducer"/"Down In Flames," 1977 ....**$6.00-$12.00**
1029, "Tell Me"/"Not Anymore"/"Ain't Nothin' To Do," 1978 ....**$7.50-$15.00**

LPs

Sire SR-6038, Young, Loud & Snotty, 1977 ....**$10.00-$20.00**
SRK-6054, We Have Come For Your Children, 1978 ....**$10.00-$20.00**

THE DEAD KENNEDYS:

45s

Alternative Tentacles AT-95-41, "California Uber Alles"/"The Man With The Dogs," 1979 ....**$10.00-$20.00**
(if on Optional Music OPT-2), 1979 ....**$6.00-$12.00**
I.R.S./Faulty 9016, "Holiday in Cambodia"/"Policetruck," 1980 ....**$5.00-$10.00**
(with picture sleeve, add), 1980 ....**$5.00-$10.00**
Alternative Tentacles VIRUS 2, "Too Drunk to Fuck"/"The Prey," 1981 ....**$4.00-$8.00**
(with picture sleeve and lyric insert, add), 1981 ....**$4.00-$8.00**

LPs

Alternative Tentacles VIRUS 27, Plastic Surgery Disasters, 1982 ....**$6.00-$12.00**
VIRUS 45, Frankenchrist (with H.R. Giger poster insert), 1985 ....**$5.00-$10.00**
VIRUS 57, Give Me Convenience or Give Me Death, 1987 ....**$5.00-$10.00**

THE DICKIES:

45s

A&M 2225, "Nights In White Satin"/"Manny, Moe and Jack," 1980 ....**$5.00-$10.00**
(with picture sleeve [sleeve withdrawn because it showed Dickies in KKK robes], add), 1980 ....**$25.00-$50.00**

LPs

A&M SP-4742, The Incredible Shrinking Dickies (if first pressing on yellow vinyl), 1979 ....**$10.00-$20.00**
(if second pressing on black vinyl), 1979 ....**$7.50-$15.00**

FEAR:

45s

Criminal Records, no number, "I Love Livin' In The City"/"Now You're Dead," 1978 .... **$125.00-$250.00**
(with picture sleeve, add), 1978 .... **$125.00-$250.00**

LPs

Slash SR 111, The Record, 1982 .... **$10.00-$20.00**
(if on Slash 23933, reissue), 1982 .... **$5.00-$10.00**
Restless 72039, More Beer, 1985 .... **$7.50-$15.00**

THE GERMS:

45s

Slash 101, "Lexicon Devil"/"Circle One"/"No God," 1978 .... **$10.00-$20.00**
(with picture sleeve, add), 1978 .... **$10.00-$20.00**

LPs

Mohawk SCALP-001, Recorded Live at the Whiskey, June, 1977
(if numbered edition with sticker, first pressing), 1981 .... **$25.00-$50.00**
(if unnumbered edition, with sticker, second pressing), 1981 .... **$10.00-$20.00**
Slash SR-103, (GI), 1981 .... **$7.50-$15.00**

GREEN DAY:

45s

Reprise 17941, "Basket Case"/"When I Come Around," 1995 .... **$1.50-$3.00**

LPs

Lookout 22, 39/Smooth, 1990 .... **$5.00-$10.00**
46, Kerplunk, 1992 .... **$5.00-$10.00**
Reprise 44529, Dookie (black vinyl), 1994 .... **$7.50-$15.00**
(if on clear green vinyl, plain white cover, promo), 1994 .... **$17.50-$35.00**
(if on opaque green-white vinyl, promo), 1994 .... **$15.00-$30.00**
(if on pink vinyl, stock reissue), 1995 .... **$5.00-$10.00**

IGGY AND THE STOOGES:

45s

Siamese 001, "I Got a Right"/"Gimme Some Skin," 1977 .... **$12.50-$25.00**
(if second pressing, "Siamese" in fake Asian lettering with iguana logo), 1977 .... **$5.00-$10.00**

LPs

Elektra EKS 74051, The Stooges (red label pressing), 1969 .... **$25.00-$50.00**
EKS 74101, Fun House (red label pressing), 1970 .... **$25.00-$50.00**
Columbia KC 32111, Raw Power, 1973 .... **$25.00-$50.00**

THE INJECTIONS:

45s

Radio Active 04, "Prison Walls"/"Lies," 1980 .... **$100.00-$200.00**

IRON CROSS:

7-inch EPs

Skinflint/Dischord 1 (8 1/2), Skinhead Glory (green vinyl), 1982 .... **$30.00-$60.00**
(if on black vinyl), 1982 .... **$10.00-$20.00**
(with picture sleeve, add), 1982 .... **$10.00-$20.00**

ISM:

45s

S.I.N. 003, "I Think I Love You"/"A7," 1983 .... **$10.00-$20.00**

LPs

S.I.N. 004, A Diet for the Worms, 1983 .... **$75.00-$150.00**

JANE'S ADDICTION:

LPs

Triple X 51004, Jane's Addiction, 1987 .... **$7.50-$15.00**
Warner Bros. 25993, "Ritual de lo Habitual" (with drawing on cover), 1990 .... **$6.00-$12.00**
(if second cover, all white with text of First Amendment), 1990 .... **$5.00-$10.00**

L7:

45s

Sub Pop 58, "Shove"/"Packin' a Rod" (green vinyl, 1,200 pressed), 1990 .... **$10.00-$20.00**

LPs

Epitaph 86401, L7, 1988 .... **$25.00-$50.00**

THE LEWD:

45s

Scratched 101, "Kill Yourself"/"Trash Can Baby"/"Pay or Die," 1978 .... **$18.75-$37.50**
(with picture sleeve, add), 1978 .... **$18.75-$37.50**

LPs

ICI CF 200, American Wino, 1982 .... **$20.00-$40.00**

THE MC5:

45s

A-Square 333, "Looking at You"/"Borderline," 1967 .... **$40.00-$80.00**
(with picture sleeve, add), 1967 .... **$20.00-$40.00**
Elektra 45648, "Kick Out the Jams"/"Motor City is Burning," 1969 .... **$10.00-$20.00**
(if on Elektra MC5-1, given away at Fillmore East concert, December 1968, with alternate take of A-side), 1968 .... **$20.00-$40.00**

LPs

Elektra EKS-74042, Kick Out The Jams
(if gatefold jacket, contains John Sinclair liner notes, brownish Elektra label), 1969 .... **$25.00-$50.00**
(all other editions), 1969 .... **$10.00-$20.00**

THE MEAT PUPPETS:

LPs

SST 009, Meat Puppets, 1982 .... **$7.50-$15.00**
London 828 484-1, Too High to Die (if bonus 10-inch record is inside and DJ sticker is on jacket, double listed price), 1994 .... **$6.00-$12.00**

THE MEATMEN:

LPs

Touch N Go TGLP 001, We're The Meatmen... And You Suck, 198? .... **$12.50-$25.00**

THE MINUTEMEN:

45s

SST PSST E58, "Courage"/"What Is It?"/"Stories," 1985 .... **$4.00-$8.00**
(with rubberstamped picture sleeve, add), 1985 .... **$6.00-$12.00**

LPs

SST 004, The Punch Line (white labels), 1981 .... **$10.00-$20.00**
028, Double Nickels on the Dime (2 LPs), 1984 .... **$6.00-$12.00**
068, Ballot Result (2 LPs), 1987 .... **$6.00-$12.00**

THE MISFITS:

45s

Blank A 101, "Cough Cool"/"She" (500 copies), 1977 .... **$75.00-$150.00**
(with picture sleeve, add), 1977 .... **$75.00-$150.00**
Plan 9 PL 1009, "Horror Business"/"Teenagers from Mars"/"Children in Heat"
(if on yellow vinyl, 5000 copies pressed), 1979 .... **$30.00-$60.00**
(if on black vinyl, 25 copies pressed), 1979 .... **$100.00-$200.00**
(with picture sleeve and insert, add), 1979 .... **$50.00-$100.00**
(with picture sleeve only, add), 1979 .... **$25.00-$50.00**

LPs

Plan 9 PL9-06, Legacy of Brutality (if pressed on pink vinyl, 16 copies pressed), 1986 .... **$50.00-$100.00**
(if pressed on white vinyl, 500 copies pressed), 1986 .... **$12.50-$25.00**
(if pressed on red vinyl, 500 copies pressed), 1986 .... **$12.50-$25.00**
(if pressed on black vinyl), 1986 .... **$6.00-$12.00**
PL9-09, Misfits, 1988 .... **$6.00-$12.00**

THE MISFITS (Albany, New York, punk band, different from above):

7-inch EP

Black & White Wreckchords 110018, Mommi I'm a Misfit (value is for record and sleeve), 1981 .... **$50.00-$100.00**

THE MUMMIES:

45s

Estrus ES 79, "Out of Our Tree"/"Tall Cool One" (red vinyl), 1991 .... **$18.75-$37.50**
(if black vinyl), 1991 .... **$6.25-$12.50**
(with picture sleeve, add), 1991 .... **$6.25-$12.50**

THE NEW YORK DOLLS:

45s

Mercury 73414, "Trash"/"Personality Crisis," 1973 .... **$30.00-$60.00**
(with picture sleeve, add), 1973 .... **$7.50-$15.00**
73478, "Stranded in the Jungle"/"Who Are the Mystery Girls," 1974 .... **$7.50-$15.00**

LPs

Mercury SRM-1-675, New York Dolls, 1973 .... **$10.00-$20.00**
SRM-1-1001, In Too Much Too Soon, 1974 .... **$10.00-$20.00**

THE NUNS:

45s

415 Records S-0001, "Savage"/"Decadent Jew"/"Suicide Child," 1978 .... **$10.00-$20.00**
(with picture sleeve, add), 1978 .... **$10.00-$20.00**

LPs
Bomp! 4010, The Nuns, 1980 .... **$6.00-$12.00**

THE PAGANS:

45s
Bona Fide 7004, "Don't Leave Me"/"Real World" (red vinyl), 1987
.... **$10.00-$20.00**
(with poster foldout picture sleeve, add), 1987 .... **$10.00-$20.00**

THE PLASMATICS:

45s
Vice Squad VS 101/102, "Butcher Baby"/"Fast Food Service"/"Concrete Shoes" (red vinyl), 1978 .... **$10.00-$20.00**
(with picture sleeve, add), 1978 .... **$10.00-$20.00**
LPs
Vice Squad VS 105/106, Meet the Plasmatics, 1979
.... **$12.50-$25.00**
Stiff USE-11, Beyond the Valley of 1984, 1981 .... **$12.50-$25.00**

PUBLIC IMAGE, LTD.:

LPs
Island 2WX 3288, Second Edition, 1980 .... **$9.00-$18.00**
Elektra 60365, This Is What You Want ... This Is What You Get, 1984
.... **$5.00-$10.00**

THE QUEERS:

7-inch EPs
Doheny, no number, The Queers, 1982 .... **$60.00-$120.00**
(with handwritten picture sleeve, add), 1982 .... **$20.00-$40.00**
LPs
Shakin' Street 010, Grow Up (only 100-150 copies were ever made from a proposed 500-copy print run), 198? .... **$100.00-$200.00**

THE RAMONES:

45s
Sire 725, "Blitzkrieg Bop"/"Havana Affair," 1976 .... **$20.00-$40.00**
1008, "Rockaway Beach"/"Locket Love," 1977 .... **$2.00-$4.00**
(with picture sleeve, add), 1977 .... **$4.00-$8.00**
27663, "I Wanna Be Sedated"/"I Wanna Be Sedated (Ramones on 45 Mega-Mix)," 1988 .... **$2.00-$4.00**
(with picture sleeve, add), 1988 .... **$2.00-$4.00**
RSO 1055, "I Wanna Be Sedated"/"The Return of Jackie and Judy," 1980
.... **$2.50-$5.00**
LPs
Sire SASD-7520, Ramones (first copies distributed by ABC), 1976
.... **$12.50-$25.00**
(if on Sire SR 6020, distributed by Warner Bros., reissue), 1978
.... **$9.00-$18.00**
SASD-7528, Ramones Leave Home (distributed by ABC, has the song "Cabrona Not Glue"), 1977 .... **$25.00-$50.00**
(if distributed by ABC, has the song "Sheena Is A Punk Rocker"), 1977
.... **$12.50-$25.00**
(if distributed by Warner Bros., has the song "Sheena is a Punk Rocker"), 1978 .... **$9.00-$18.00**
SRK 6077, End of the Century, 1980 .... **$7.50-$15.00**

THE ROTTERS:

45s
Rotten TR 002, "Sit on My Face Stevie Nicks"/"Amputee," 1978
.... **$7.50-$15.00**
(with picture sleeve, add), 1978 .... **$12.50-$25.00**
Rotten TR 003, "Sink the Whales (Buy Japanese Goods)"/"Disco Queen," 1979 .... **$12.50-$25.00**

THE SAINTS:

45s
Sire 1005, "(I'm) Stranded"/"No Time," 1977 .... **$7.50-$15.00**
(with picture sleeve, add), 1977 .... **$3.50-$7.00**
LPs
Sire SR 6039, (I'm) Stranded, 1977 .... **$7.50-$15.00**
SRK 6055, Eternally Yours, 1978 .... **$7.50-$15.00**

SEX PISTOLS:

45s
Warner Bros. 8516, "Pretty Vacant"/"Sub-Mission," 1978 .... **$10.00-$20.00**
(with picture sleeve, add), 1978 .... **$5.00-$10.00**
LPs
Warner Bros. BSK 3147, Never Mind the Bollocks Here's the Sex Pistols (with sticker, "Contains Sub-Mission"), 1978 .... **$15.00-$30.00**
(if any other version with custom label), 1978 .... **$12.50-$25.00**
(with white WB labels), 1978 .... **$5.00-$10.00**

SIOUXIE AND THE BANSHEES:

45s
Polydor 14561, "Hong Kong Garden"/"Overground," 1979 .... **$20.00-$40.00**
LPs
Polydor PD1-6207, The Scream, 1978 .... **$15.00-$30.00**
PVC 7921, Kaleidoscope, 1980 .... **$10.00-$20.00**
Geffen GEF 24387, Superstition, 1991 .... **$6.00-$12.00**
GEF 24630, The Rapture, 1995 .... **$6.00-$12.00**

'63 MONROE:

45s
Savvy 003, "Henry the Eighth"/"Soup to Nuts," 1983 .... **$10.00-$20.00**
(with picture sleeve, add), 1983 .... **$10.00-$20.00**
LPs
Nardem 005, N.F.G., 1981 .... **$25.00-$50.00**
Savvy 85051, Stinkin' Out the Joint, 1985 .... **$25.00-$50.00**

SONIC YOUTH:

45s
Forced Exposure 001, "Making the Nature Scene"/"I Killed Christgau With My Big Fuckin' Dick"
(if test pressing, 25 made with special sleeve), 1984 .... **$60.00-$120.00**
(if multi-color sleeve with live band shot on rear, only issued with the test pressings, add), 1984 .... **$60.00-$120.00**
(if regular release), 1984 .... **$25.00-$50.00**
(with black and white picture sleeve, add), 1984 .... **$25.00-$50.00**
LPs
Neutral N-1, Sonic Youth, 1982 .... **$25.00-$50.00**

THE STAINS:

45s
Radical, no number, "John Wayne Was a Nazi"/"Born to Die," 1980
.... **$15.00-$30.00**
(with picture sleeve, add), 1980 .... **$15.00-$30.00**

SUICIDAL TENDENCIES:

LPs
Frontier 4604-1-L, Suicidal Tendencies, 1983 .... **$7.50-$15.00**
Epic FE 44288, How Will I Laugh Tomorrow/Feel Like Shit ... Déjà vu, 1989
.... **$5.00-$10.00**

TOXIC REASONS:

45s
Benit 4057, "War Hero"/"Somebody Help Me," 1980 .... **$25.00-$50.00**
(with picture sleeve, add), 1980 .... **$25.00-$50.00**
Risky NX 5232, "Ghost Town"/"Killer"/"Noise Boys," 1981
.... **$12.50-$25.00**
(with picture sleeve, add), 1981 .... **$12.50-$25.00**

THE VAINS:

7-inch EPs
No Threes 004, You Cannot Deny Terror (value is for record and jacket), 1980
.... **$30.00-$60.00**

WENDY O. WILLIAMS:

45s
Passport PB-6034, W.O.W., 1984 .... **$6.00-$12.00**
Profile PAL 1230, Maggots: The Record, 1987 .... **$7.50-$15.00**

X:

45s
Dangerhouse D-88, "Adult Books"/"We're Desperate," 1978 .... **$20.00-$40.00**
(with folded picture sleeve in plastic bag, add), 1978 .... **$20.00-$40.00**
Elektra 69885, "Blue Spark"/"Dancing with Tears in My Eyes," 1982
.... **$6.00-$12.00**
(with picture sleeve, add), 1982 .... **$6.00-$12.00**
LPs
Slash SR-104, Los Angeles, 1980 .... **$7.50-$15.00**
(if on Slash 23930, reissue), 1983 .... **$5.00-$10.00**
Elektra 60150, Under the Big Black Sun, 1982 .... **$6.00-$12.00**
60492, See How We Are, 1987 .... **$5.00-$10.00**

X-TERMINATORS:

45s
Radio Active 1, "Microwave Radiation"/"Occasional Lay," 1978
.... **$30.00-$60.00**

THE ZERO BOYS:

7-inch EPs
Z-Disk, catalog number unknown, Livin' in the 80s, 1980 .... **$37.50-$75.00**
(with picture sleeve, add), 1980 .... **$37.50-$75.00**
LPs
Nimrod 001, Vicious Circle, 1982 .... **$10.00-$20.00**

Chapter 19

Rap/Hip-Hop

History

Rap music and hip-hop music evolved from a myriad of sources. It was doo-wop music without the melody. It was a double-dutch rope-skipping chant without the rope. It was the original poetry and social commentary of the Last Poets and Gil Scott-Heron, and later evolved, with the addition of turntables, rhymes, and samples, into one of the most dominant musical styles in contemporary music.

New York City's urban neighborhoods produced the first rap stars in the 1970s—a posse of three to six rapid-fire poets ("Emcees" or "MC's"), with the instrumentation and beats provided by the group's turntable expert, who would play instrumental snippets on a pair of phonographs, controlling the sound output with a modified mixing board. By the mid-1970s, the Bronx rap scene included Afrika Bambaataa and the SoulSonic Force, Kool Herc, Kurtis Blow, Grandmaster Flash and the Furious Five, and DJ Hollywood. Even so, for years the only way somebody could hear the earliest rappers and remixers, such as the Fantastic Romantic 5's Grand Wizard Theodore or the Cold Crush Brothers' Grandmaster Caz, was on homemade cassettes recorded during these rap bands' legendary battles.

Some early rap recordings were actually released on major labels, as DJ Hollywood's "Shock, Shock the House" and Kurtis Blow's "The Breaks" became moderate R&B hits. Rap also made early appearances in pop music, either through established artists like Blondie (who referenced Grandmaster Flash in "Rapture") or through novelty studio acts like the Afternoon Delights ("General Hospi-Tale," a rapping history of the soap opera *General Hospital*).

Gil Scott-Heron was one of the progenitors of rap music, and records like "Johannesburg," "The Bottle," and "The Revolution Will Not Be Televised" reflect his strong lyrical content and sense of moral outrage.

***$8**, NM condition*

Originally existing on brittle cassette tapes, the original 1970s DJ/MC battles between the Cold Crush Brothers (led by Grandmaster Kaz) and the Fantastic Romantic 5 (with Grandwizard Theodore) have now been commercially released on a series of double-LP sets.

***$40**, NM condition*

Kurtis Blow was one of the first rappers to receive a contract with a major label, and songs like "The Breaks" and "Basketball" are still staples in rap history.
***$3**, VG condition*

The Sugarhill Gang's "Rapper's Delight" 12-inch dance record featured the rhythm track from Chic's "Good Times," as well as references to the Bar-Kays, the New York Knicks, and Superman—all stretched out over a 15-minute jam.
***$30**, NM condition*

In 1979, Sugar Hill Records released the first million-selling rap single, the Sugarhill Gang's "Rapper's Delight." The 15-minute long track featured the vocal interpolations of rappers Henry Jackson, Guy O'Brien, and Michael Wright (or, respectively, "Big Bank Hank," "Master Gee," and "Wonder Mike"), as they rapped about everything from women at the nightclubs, terrible food at a friend's house, and how Big Bank Hank could steal Lois Lane away from Superman. The success of that song spurred record company representatives on a feeding frenzy through the Bronx, looking for rap artists and groups that could give their label that same success.

In the early 1980s, the predominant rap theme was the prowess—lyrically, physically, and sexually—of the rappers behind the microphone, and the party-all-night, call-and-response exchange between them and the audience. But in 1983, Grandmaster Flash and the Furious Five's "The Message" changed all that. With its lyrics of inner-city slums, poverty, urban desolation, and despair, "The Message" has been hailed as one of the most important records—rap or otherwise—in music history. It projected Grandmaster Flash and the Furious Five to the rap forefront, and proved to the music world that rap was more than just party music.

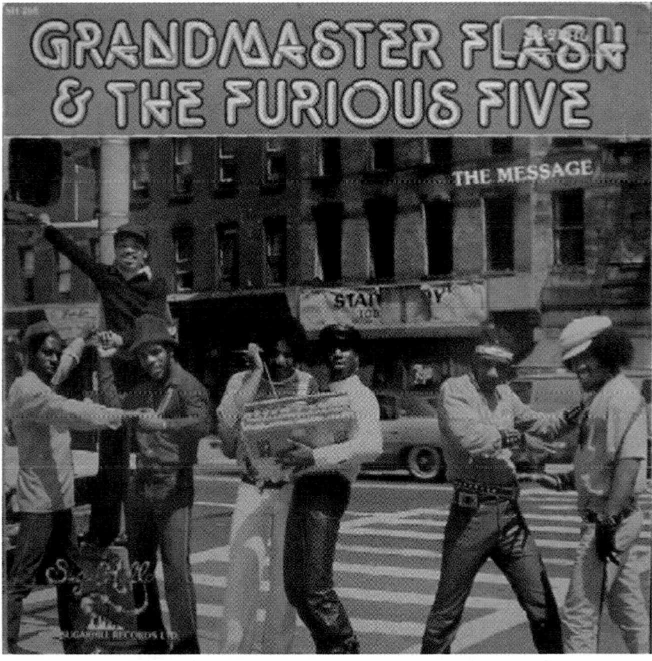

Grandmaster Flash and the Furious Five's "The Message" became a worldwide hit, spawning this album and changing the face of rap music forever.
***$20**, NM condition*

That hard-edged rap evolved when two other New York City-based rap troupes—Run-D.M.C. and Public Enemy—took the stage. Run-D.M.C. was one of the first rap groups to embrace rock music as part of rap. Their first single, "Rock Box," had screaming guitars throughout the song, and their hit songs "King of Rock" and "Jam-Master Jammin'" continued this trend. In 1986, Run-D.M.C. collaborated with Steven Tyler and Joe Perry of Aerosmith for a new rap-meets-rock version of the Aerosmith classic "Walk This Way," which became a Top 10 rock, pop, and soul hit.

Public Enemy, on the other hand, made rap political. Their raps included the imagery of Martin Luther King and Malcolm X, layered over funk and electronic rhythms, creating a rap concept that was part funk, part hip-hop, part social commentary, and part shock. With songs like

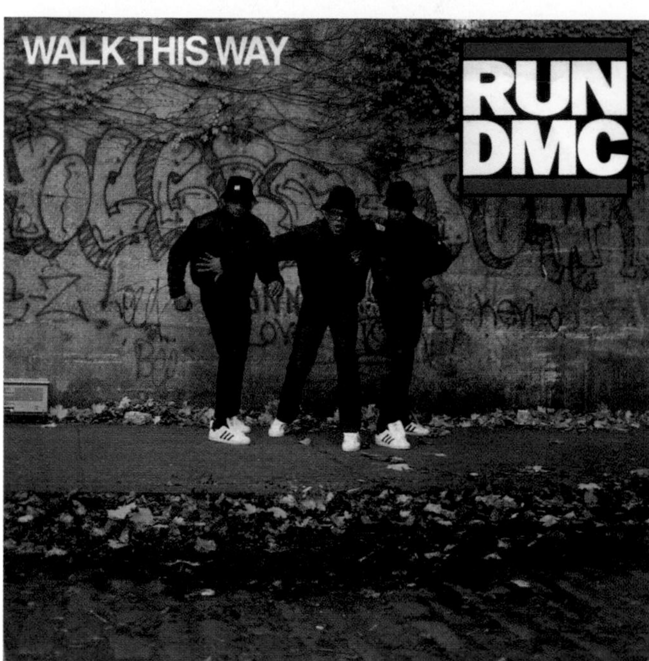

One could argue that the appearance of Steven Tyler and Joe Perry on Run-D.M.C.'s cover of "Walk This Way" propelled the rap trio to superstardom; an argument could also be made that Run-D.M.C.'s remake of the 1970s hit helped rejuvenate Aerosmith's career.

***$4** for NM sleeve*

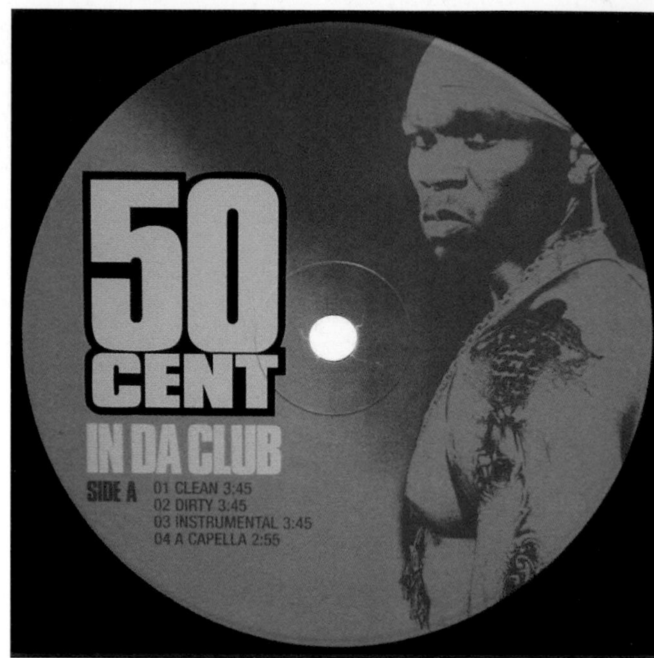

Rapper 50 Cent peers from the side of the label of his 12-inch vinyl pressing of "At Da Club." Even though rap is available on compact disc, 12-inch vinyl singles are still pressed in high numbers, for all the club and mobile DJs. Notice this disc contains "clean" and "dirty" lyrics, as well as instrumental and a cappella versions, the main ingredients for which DJs can create their own mixes.

***$10**, NM condition*

"Fight the Power," "911 Is A Joke," and "Night of the Living Baseheads," Public Enemy's Chuck D issued a rallying call to all disaffected youth to stand up and fight for their rights.

By the late 1980s, rap groups such as N.W.A. and the Wu-Tang Clan gave birth to "gangsta rap," which extolled the dilemmas and pleasures of inner-city "thug life." Eventually N.W.A. splintered into separate successful rap acts and groups, including Dr. Dre, Easy-E and Ice Cube, each influencing rap in their own way.

But, by the early 1990s, rap feuds between "West Coast" rappers (which included Dr. Dre, Snoop Doggy Dogg, and Tupac Shakur) and "East Coast" rappers (the Wu-Tang Clan, Notorious B.I.G., and producer Sean "Puff Daddy" Combs) escalated from attacks on each others' albums to verbal sparring at awards shows. The feud eventually culminated with the shooting deaths of rappers Tupac Shakur and the Notorious B.I.G., both of whose murderers have never been found.

Rap itself has continued to evolve to this day, as rap artists experiment with blues (Arrested Development), psychedelia (De La Soul), rock and hard funk (LL Cool J), and Caribbean and Third World polyrhythms (the Fugees). Rap lyrics have even evolved, whether through their meter (the ultra-quick raps of Bone-Thugs-n-Harmony's "Tha Crossroads") or their content (Snoop Doggy Dogg's "Murder Was The Case").

Rap music has also been at the forefront of major censorship issues. When the rap group 2 Live Crew released their album *As Nasty As They Wanna Be*, the lyrical content was so full of sex and adult themes—their Top 40 single "Me So Horny" was on this album—that a Florida record store owner was arrested and served jail time for selling a copy of the album to a minor, the first time in American history of an arrest and conviction for selling music. 2 Live Crew eventually endured a series of obscenity trials in Florida, both for their album and their live performances, and eventually turned the entire experience into another Top 40 single, "Banned in the U.S.A."

While African-American men have dominated the rap music scene, white male rappers (the Beastie Boys, Third Bass, Vanilla Ice, Eminem), and female rappers (Queen Latifah, the Sequence, Salt-n-Pepa), have broken the mold. Rap music has even re-embraced its early Jamaican "toasting" heritage, where Jamaican rappers would "toast" over dub versions of reggae hits. Today, artists like Shabba Ranks, Sean Paul, and Shaggy have had rap-reggae hits like "Boombastic," "Give Me The Light," and "It Wasn't Me."

What To Look For

Early recordings by rap artists are very hard to come by, especially in good condition. Many of these records were pressed on small labels, with print runs tailored more for sales throughout New York City. Between 1976 and 1984, some of the most desirable East Coast rap labels included Sugarhill, Streetwise, Sutra, Sunnyview, Tommy Boy, Profile, Def Jam, and Prelude. Groups like the Fat Boys, the Beastie Boys, the Sugarhill Gang, Run-D.M.C., and Spoonie Gee, recorded early hits on these labels.

The more common rap hits are readily available on 12-inch dance discs, although some reproductions exist. Some repressings even re-create the original label art from record companies that have long since folded. In many cases, the reissue labels have a silver or brown background; most New York City, old-school rap records, have multicolored labels, while their promo copies have a white background.

Also collectible are house records with extended remixes, which allow DJs to segue songs with similar beat patterns or tempos together in an effort to keep the dance floor packed. House music evolved from the Chicago club scene in the mid-1980s, as artists like Farley "Jackmaster" Funk and Frankie Knuckles, along with DJ Ron Hardy, got their remixes on the radio, helping the sound expand to new listeners and music lovers.

While many rap 45s exist, their value is very low in comparison to rap albums and 12-inch discs. Because of the space limitations of a 45, most 7-9 minute rap songs were trimmed down to 4-5 minutes on a 45, and many of the single edits were haphazard or jarring.

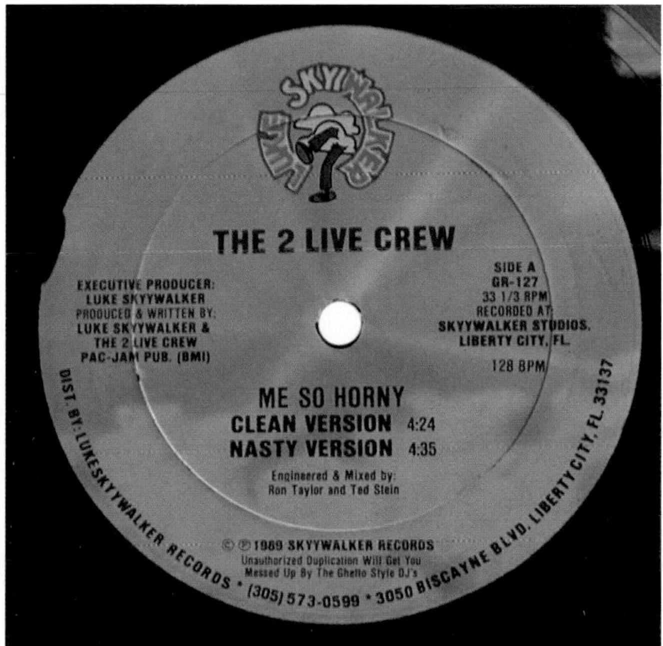

Not only did the 2 Live Crew have to battle censorship and First Amendment rights throughout their career, they also had to change the name of their record label to Luke Records after director George Lucas claimed the original label name constituted copyright infringement on his Star Wars character of Luke Skywalker. ***$12**, NM condition*

The Big Prizes

Rap stars' first discs, before they ever became hip-hop superstars, are highly desirable. From these discs, you can hear the original incarnations of a group—how the rappers in the posse interacted and bounced lyrics off each other; what the lyrical concepts were, and how they would eventually be recycled for future hits. In Grandmaster Flash and the Furious Five's seminal hit "The Message," rapper Melle Mel recites a stanza about "A child is born with no state of mind/blind to the ways of mankind..." That rap originally appeared on the group's first 12-inch on the Enjoy label, "Superrappin," long before the group became famous.

Books

Brewster, Bill, and Broughton, Frank, *Last Night a DJ Saved My Life: The History of the Disc Jockey*, Headline Book Pub., London, 1999.

Gregory, Hugh, *Soul Music A-Z*, Da Capo Press, New York, N.Y., 1995.

Toop, David, *Rap Attack 2: African Rap to Global Hip Hop*, Pluto Press, London, England, 1984.

Web Pages

A Web page devoted to old school rap: http://www.geocities.com/~tothebeat/

A dissertation by Professors Steven Best and Douglas Kellner on the history of rap and its racial and social ramifications: http://utminers.utep.edu/best/rap.htm

Grandmaster Flash's Web page: http://www.grandmasterflash.com

A history of rap and hip-hop, its major players and influences, can be found at this site: http://www.zulunation.com

Public Enemy's Web page: http://www.publicenemy.com

A site containing interviews with rap stars and hip-hop artists: http://www.hip-hop.com

Def Jam Records' home page, home to LL Cool J, Public Enemy, and the early recordings of the Beastie Boys: http://www.defjam.com

Eminem's Web page: http://www.eminem.com

Phil Cheeseman's history of house music was originally published in DJ Magazine; a copy of the article can be found on this Web site: http://music.hyperreal.org/library/history_of_house.html

Before Eminem hooked up with Dr. Dre, he was a struggling young rap artist, selling his own custom-pressed 12-inch discs at shows. His first LP, Infinite, was sold in a plain black album jacket. His next vinyl disc, The Slim Shady EP, features songs that would eventually appear on Eminem's major label releases. Both records were only pressed in limited runs—some sources say as low as 500 copies.

***$40**, NM condition*

In 1973, Michael Viner and some studio musicians, calling themselves "The Incredible Bongo Band," recorded a series of bongo-beated top 40 remakes. One of those tracks, a remake of Jorgen Ingemann's instrumental "Apache," has been sampled and rapped over by hundreds of artists—Grandmaster Flash used snippets of it in his seminal collage "The Adventures of Grandmaster Flash on the Wheels of Steel," and the Sugarhill Gang rapped their own version of "Apache," using the Bongo Band's orchestrations.

***$80**, NM condition*

ARTIST — VG+ to NM

AFRIKA BAMBAATAA AND THE SOULSONIC FORCE:

45s

Tommy Boy 823, "Planet Rock"/(Instrumental)
(if orange label, first pressing), 1982 .... **$6.00-$12.00**
(if blue-white label, second pressing), 1982 .... **$3.00-$6.00**
831, "Looking for the Perfect Beat"/(instrumental), 1982 .... **$3.00-$6.00**
Capitol B-44163, "Reckless" (same on both sides), 1988 .... **$2.00-$4.00**
(with picture sleeve, add), 1988 .... **$2.00-$4.00**

12-inch Singles

Winley, cat # unknown, "Zulu Nation Throwdown" (2 versions), 1980 .... **$100.00-$200.00**
Tommy Boy TB 821, "Jazzy Sensation" (3 versions), 1983 .... **$30.00-$60.00**
TB 823, "Planet Rock" (with bonus beats and instrumental), 1983 .... **$25.00-$50.00**
TB 831, "Looking for the Perfect Beat" (with bonus beats and instrumental), 1982 .... **$20.00-$40.00**
TB 839, "Renegades of Funk"/(instrumental), 1984 .... **$15.00-$30.00**
TB 847, "Unity" (6 versions), 1984 .... **$15.00-$30.00**
Capitol V-15739, "Reckless" (2 versions)/"Mind, Body & Soul" (3 versions), 1988 .... **$4.00-$8.00**
V-15385, "Shout It Out" (3 versions)/"Tell Me When You Need It Again," 1988 .... **$3.00-$6.00**

LPs

Tommy Boy TBLP-1007, Planet Rock—The Album, 1986 .... **$7.50-$15.00**
TBLP-1008, Beware (The Funk Is Everywhere), 1986 .... **$7.50-$15.00**
Capitol C1-90157, The Light, 1988 .... **$6.00-$12.00**

ROB BASE AND D.J. EZ-ROCK:

45s

Profile 5186, "It Takes Two"/(instrumental), 1988 .... **$3.00-$6.00**
5239, "Get On the Dance Floor"/"Keep It Going Now," 1988 .... **$1.50-$3.00**

12-inch Singles

Profile 7186, "It Takes Two"/(instrumental), 1988 .... **$7.50-$15.00**
7239, "Get On the Dance Floor" (4 versions)/"Keep It Going Now" (Hardcore Remix), 1988 .... **$3.50-$7.00**
7247, "Joy and Pain" (4 versions), 1989 .... **$4.00-$8.00**
Rampage 670168, "Diamonds" (several versions), 2000 .... **$3.00-$6.00**

THE BEASTIE BOYS:

45s

38-06595, "(You Gotta) Fight for Your Right (To Party!)"/"Paul Revere," 1987 .... **$3.00-$6.00**
Capitol B-44454, "Hey Ladies"/"Shake Your Rump," 1989 .... **$2.50-$5.00**
(if on Capitol 7PRO-79698, promo), 1989 .... **$5.00-$10.00**
B-44472, "Shadrach"/"And What You Give Is What You Get," 1989 .... **$3.00-$6.00**
S7-19973, "Intergalactic"/"Peanut Butter & Jelly," 1998 .... **$2.00-$4.00**

7-inch EPs

Rat Cage MOTR 21, "Polly Wog Stew" (eight songs, value is for record and jacket), 1982 .... **$20.00-$40.00**

12-inch Singles

Rat Cage 026, "Cookypuss" (four songs), 1983 .... **$20.00-$40.00**
Def Jam DJ 002, "Rock Hard"/"Beastie Groove"/"The Party's Getting Rough"/"Beastie Groove" (Instrumental) (withdrawn from market because of an unauthorized sample of AC/DC's "Back in Black" in "Rock Hard," brown label, brown Def Jam jacket), 1985 .... **$50.00-$100.00**

LPs

Def Jam BFC 40238, Licensed to Ill, 1986 .... **$7.50-$15.00**
(if second pressing, "02" added to back cover UPC code), 1986 .... **$5.00-$10.00**
Capitol C1-91743, Paul's Boutique
(if single gatefold edition), 1989 .... **$6.00-$12.00**
(if multi-gatefold edition, jacket is C1-92844, catalog number on album is same as above), 1989 .... **$10.00-$20.00**
Capitol C1-37716, Hello Nasty (2 LPs), 1998 .... **$7.50-$15.00**
C1-22940, The Sounds of Science (4 LPs), 2000 .... **$60.00-$120.00**
Grand Royal GR 061, Hello Nasty (2 LPs, yellow vinyl), 1998 .... **$10.00-$20.00**

KURTIS BLOW:

45s

Mercury DJ 562, "Christmas Rappin' Part 1"/"Christmas Rappin' Part 2," 1979 .... **$5.00-$10.00**
76075, "The Breaks" (Part 1)/(Part 2), 1980 .... **$3.00-$6.00**
76112, "Way Out West"/"Starlife," 1981 .... **$3.00-$6.00**

880408-7, "Basketball"/"One-Two-Five," 1984 ....**$3.00-$6.00**
881529-7, "Basketball"/Ralph MacDonald, "(It's) The Game," 1985 ....**$3.00-$6.00**
562559-7, "Christmas Rappin'" (8:11 version)/"Christmas Rappin' (Do It Yourself version)", 1999............................**$2.00-$4.00**

12-inch Singles:
Mercury MDS-4009, "Christmas Rappin'"/"Christmas Rappin' (Do It Yourself)," 1979............................**$10.00-$20.00**
MDS-4010, "The Breaks" (Vocal 7:14)/(Instrumental 5:52), 1980 ....**$10.00-$20.00**
880170-1, "8 Million Stories" (with Run-D.M.C.)/"A.J. Scratch," 1984 ....**$7.50-$15.00**
884079-1, "America"/"A.J. Meets Davy DMX," 1985............................**$6.00-$12.00**

LPs
Mercury SRM-1-3854, Kurtis Blow, 1980............................**$6.00-$12.00**
SRM-1-4020, Deuce, 1981............................**$5.00-$10.00**
826141-1, America, 1985............................**$5.00-$10.00**

BUSTA RHYMES:

12-inch Singles
EastWest ED 5882, "Live to Regret" (3 versions), 1996............**$10.00-$20.00**
Elektra ED 5820, "Woo-Hah!! Got You All in Check" (4 versions)/ "Everything Remains Raw," 1996............................**$7.50-$15.00**
67087, "Fire" (3 versions)/"Bladow" (3 versions), 2000............................**$4.00-$8.00**
J Records 21061, "Break Ya Neck" (4 versions), 2001............................**$4.00-$8.00**

LPs
Elektra ED 61742, The Coming (2 LPs), 1996............................**$7.50-$15.00**
62211, E.L.E. (Extinction Level Event) (2 LPs), 1998 ....**$7.50-$15.00**
J Records 20009, Genesis (2 LPs), 2001............................**$10.00-$20.00**

THE COLD CRUSH BROTHERS:

LPs
Slammin' 71257-1, DJ Charlie Chase Presents the Cold Crush Brothers vs. the Fantastic Romantic 5 (2 LPs), 2000............................**$20.00-$40.00**

DE LA SOUL:

12-inch Singles
Tommy Boy TB 917, "Jenifa (Taught Me)"/"Skip 2 My Loop"/"Potholes in My Lawn"/(two instrumentals), 1988............................**$10.00-$20.00**
TB 926, "Me Myself and I" (4 versions)/"Ain't Hip to Be Labeled a Hippie"/ "What's More"/"Brainwashed Follower" (second side of disc is "trick-tracked," two parallel grooves on record), 1989............................**$10.00-$20.00**
TB 990, "A Roller Skating Jam Named 'Saturdays'" (7 versions), 1991 ....**$6.00-$12.00**

LPs
Tommy Boy TB 1019, 3 Feet High and Rising
(if single LP), 1989............................**$10.00-$20.00**
(if two-disc set), 2001............................**$7.50-$15.00**
TB 1029, De La Soul Is Dead, 1991............................**$10.00-$20.00**
(if promotional 2-record set), 1991............................**$12.50-$25.00**

DIGITAL UNDERGROUND:

12-inch Singles
Tommy Boy TB 932, "Doowutchyalike" (4 versions)/"Hip Hop Doll" (2 versions), 1989............................**$6.00-$12.00**
TB 944, "The Humpty Dance" (3 versions), 1989............................**$5.00-$10.00**
TB 993, "Kiss You Back" (4 versions), 1991............................**$6.00-$12.00**

LPs
Tommy Boy TB 1026, Sex Packets, 1990............................**$6.00-$12.00**
TB-1045, Sons of the P., 1991............................**$6.00-$12.00**
Jake INT2-92061, Who Got the Gravy? (2 LPs), 1998............................**$7.50-$15.00**

DR. DRE:

12-inch Singles
Death Row/Interscope 53829, "Dre Day"/"Puffin' on Blunts"/"One Eight Seven," 1993............................**$7.50-$15.00**
Aftermath INT8P-6766, "Forgot About Dre" (several versions), 2000 ....**$7.50-$15.00**
497333, "The Next Episode" (several versions), 2000............................**$6.00-$12.00**

LPs
Death Row P1-50611, The Chronic, 1993............................**$7.50-$15.00**
Aftermath 490486, 2001 (2 LPs), 1999............................**$7.50-$15.00**
490571, 2001: Instrumentals (2 LPs), 2000............................**$10.00-$20.00**

EMINEM:

12-inch Singles
Aftermath 95040, "My Name Is" (4 versions), 1999............................**$10.00-$20.00**
97097, "Guilty Conscience (5 versions)/"I'm Shady" (3 versions), 1999 ....**$6.00-$12.00**
Shady 497815-1, "Lose Yourself" (several versions), 2002............................**$6.00-$12.00**

LPs
WEB Entertainment WEB 714V, Infinite, 1997............................**$20.00-$40.00**
EMM-2003, The Slim Shady EP, 1998,............................**$20.00-$40.00**
Aftermath 90287, The Slim Shady LP (2 LPs), 1999............................**$12.50-$25.00**
490629-1, The Marshall Mathers LP (2 LPs), 2000............................**$10.00-$20.00**
493290-1, The Eminem Show (2 LPs), 2002............................**$10.00-$20.00**

FATBACK:

45s
Spring 199, "King Tim III (Personality Jock)"/"You're My Candy Sweet," 1979 ....**$3.00-$6.00**

12-inch Singles
Spring 402, "King Tim III (Personality Jock)"/"You're My Candy Sweet," 1979 ....**$5.00-$10.00**

LPs
Spring 6718, Fired Up 'N' Kickin', 1978............................**$5.00-$10.00**
6721, Bright Lites, Big City, 1979............................**$5.00-$10.00**

50 CENT:

12-inch Singles
Interscope 497856, "In Da Club" (several mixes), 2003............................**$5.00-$10.00**

LPs
Interscope 493544-1, Get Rich or Die Tryin' (2 LPs), 2003............................**$7.50-$15.00**

GRANDMASTER FLASH AND THE FURIOUS FIVE:

12-inch Singles
Enjoy 6001, "Superrappin'" (2 versions), 1979............................**$150.00-$300.00**
Sugar Hill SH 549, "Freedom" (2 versions), 1980............................**$10.00-$20.00**
SH 555, "The Birthday Party" (2 versions), 1981............................**$7.50-$15.00**
SH 557, "The Adventures of Grandmaster Flash on the Wheels of Steel"/ "The Party Mix," 1981............................**$20.00-$40.00**
SH 584, "The Message" (2 versions), 1982............................**$7.50-$15.00**
Elektra 66908, "Girls Love the Way He Spins"/"Larry's Dance Theme" (2 versions), 1985............................**$7.50-$15.00**
66777, "Gold" (5 versions), 1988............................**$7.50-$15.00**

LPs
Sugar Hill SH 268, The Message, 1982............................**$10.00-$20.00**
(reissued in 2000 by Rhino, check for Rhino decal on back cover)
SH 9121, Greatest Messages, 1984............................**$10.00-$20.00**
Elektra 6389, They Said It Couldn't Be Done, 1985............................**$6.00-$12.00**
60769, On the Strength, 1988............................**$6.00-$12.00**

MC HAMMER:

45s
Bustin' 1987-7, "Let's Get It Started"/(instrumental), 1987............................**$10.00-$20.00**
Capitol B-44229, "Let's Get It Started"/(instrumental), 1988 ....**$1.50-$3.00**
B-44290, "Turn This Mutha Out"/"Ring'Em," 1989............................**$1.50-$3.00**
7PRO-79072, "U Can't Touch This" (promo, same on both sides), 1990 ....**$7.50-$15.00**
S7-57700, "2 Legit to Quit" (Long)/"2 Legit to Quit" (short), 1992 ....**$2.00-$4.00**
Giant 18218, "Pumps & a Bump" (Radio Edit)/"Pumps & a Bump" (album version), 1994............................**$1.50-$3.00**

12-inch Singles
Bustin' BR 003, "Cold Go MC Hammer" (2 versions), 1987 ....**$7.50-$15.00**
1987-3, "Let's Get It Started" (2 versions), 1987............................**$7.50-$15.00**
Capitol V-15411, "Let's Get It Started" (3 versions), 1988............................**$4.00-$8.00**
V-15571, "U Can't Touch This" (3 versions)/"Dancin' Machine" (2 versions), 1991............................**$5.00-$10.00**
V-15791, "2 Legit 2 Quit" (2 versions)/"Addams Groove" (instrumental), 1991............................**$4.00-$8.00**
Giant 41260, "Pumps & a Bump" (2 versions)/"It's All Good" (2 versions), 1994............................**$4.00-$8.00**
41473, "Don't Stop" (4 versions), 1994............................**$4.00-$8.00**

LPs
Bustin' BR-LP-001, Feel My Power, 1987............................**$12.50-$25.00**
Capitol C1-90924, Let's Get It Started, 1988............................**$5.00-$10.00**
C1-92857, Please Hammer, Don't Hurt 'Em, 1990............................**$7.50-$15.00**
C1-98151, Too Legit to Quit (2 LPs), 1991............................**$7.50-$15.00**
Giant PRO-A-6798, The Funky Headhunter (2 LPs, promo on vinyl), 1994 ....**$7.50-$15.00**

THE INCREDIBLE BONGO BAND:

LPs
Pride 0028, Bongo Rock (reissues exist that look almost like the original), 1973 ....**$40.00-$80.00**

6010, The Return of the Incredible Bongo Band, 1974..............**$10.00-$20.00**

DJ JAZZY JEFF AND THE FRESH PRINCE:

45s

Jive 1099-7, "Parents Just Don't Understand"/(instrumental), 1988 ....**$1.50-$3.00**

(with picture sleeve, add), 1988....................**$1.50-$3.00**

1147-7, "Girls Ain't Nothin' But Trouble"/"Brand New Funk," 1988 ....**$1.50-$3.00**

(with picture sleeve, add), 1988....................**$1.50-$3.00**

1282-7, "I Think I Can Beat Mike Tyson"/(instrumental), 1989 ...**$1.50-$3.00**

(with picture sleeve, add), 1989....................**$1.50-$3.00**

12-inch Singles

Word Up WD-001, "Girls Ain't Nothing But Trouble" (4 versions), 1985 ....**$6.00-$12.00**

WD-002, "Guys Ain't Nothing But Trouble" (same on both sides), 1985 ....**$7.50-$15.00**

WD-003, "Just One of Those Days" (same on both sides), 1985..**$7.50-$15.00**

Jive 1092-1, "Parents Just Don't Understand" (4 mixes), 1988..........**$4.00-$8.00**

1146-1, "Girls Ain't Nothin' But Trouble" (3 mixes)/"Brand New Funk" (4 mixes), 1988....................**$3.00-$6.00**

LPs

Word Up WDLP-0001, Rock the House, 1985 ....**$12.50-$25.00**

Jive 1091-1-J, He's the D.J., I'm the Rapper (2 LPs), 1988 ....**$6.00-$12.00**

(if cover contains a disclaimer for "Nightmare On My Street," scarce pressing), 1988....................**$8.00-$16.00**

1188-1-J, And in This Corner..., 1989 ....**$5.00-$10.00**

THE JUNGLE BROTHERS:

12-inch Singles

Warlock/Idlers WAR 022, "I'll House You" (6 versions), 1989 ....**$15.00-$30.00**

LL COOL J:

45s

Def Jam 38-05665, "I Can't Live Without My Radio"/"I Can Give You More," 1985 ....**$1.50-$3.00**

38-07120, "I'm Bad"/"Get Down," 1987 ....**$2.00-$4.00**

38-07679, "Going Back to Cali"/"Jack the Ripper," 1988..............**$1.50-$3.00**

(with picture sleeve, add), 1988....................**$2.00-$4.00**

38-73609, "Mama Said Knock You Out"/"Around the Way Girl," 1991 ....**$2.00-$4.00**

12-inch Singles

Def Jam 44-05291, "I Can Give You More" (2 versions)/"I Can't Live Without My Radio," 1985 ....**$7.50-$15.00**

44-06799, "I'm Bad (4:40)"/"Get Down," 1987....................**$7.50-$15.00**

44-07563, "Going Back to Cali"/"Jack the Ripper," 1987............**$7.50-$15.00**

44-73703, "Mama Said Knock You Out" (7 versions), 1991 ....**$6.00-$12.00**

568081-1, "Phenomenon" (3 versions)/"Hot Hot Hot" (3 versions), 1997 ....**$5.00-$10.00**

LPs

Def Jam FC 40239, Radio, 1985....................**$6.00-$12.00**

FC 40793, Bigger and Deffer, 1987....................**$6.00-$12.00**

FC 46888, Mama Said Knock You Out, 1990....................**$7.50-$15.00**

539186-1, Phenomenon (2 LPs), 1997....................**$7.50-$15.00**

546819-1, G.O.A.T. Featuring James T. Smith the Greatest of All Time (2 LPs), 2000....................**$7.50-$15.00**

THE LAST POETS:

45s

Douglas ADS-8, "O.D."/"Black Thighs," 1971 ....**$7.50-$15.00**

(with picture sleeve, add), 1971....................**$15.00-$30.00**

Blue Thumb 216, "Tribute to Orabi"/"Bird's Word," 1972.............**$6.00-$12.00**

LPs

Douglas 3, The Last Poets, 1970 ....**$25.00-$50.00**

Z 30583, This Is Madness, 1971 ....**$25.00-$50.00**

Z 30811, The Last Poets, 1971....................**$20.00-$40.00**

Blue Thumb BT-39, Chastisement, 1972....................**$15.00-$30.00**

LIL' KIM:

45s

Undeas/Queen Bee 7-84770, "No Matter What They Say"/"Single Black Female," 2000....................**$1.50-$3.00**

12-inch Singles

Undeas/Big Beat DMD 95574, "Not Tonight" (2 versions)/"Drugs" (2 versions)/"Crush on You" (2 versions), 1997....................**$5.00-$10.00**

Undeas/Queen Bee 84703, "No Matter What They Say" (4 versions), 2000 ....**$4.00-$8.00**

85032, "How Many Licks" (4 versions), 2000 ....**$4.00-$8.00**

LPs

Undeas 92733, Hard Core (2 LPs), 1996 ....**$10.00-$20.00**

92840, The Notorious K.I.M. (2 LPs), 2000 ....**$7.50-$15.00**

MALCOLM X:

12-inch Singles

Tommy Boy TB 840, "No Sell Out" (2 versions), 1983....................**$6.00-$12.00**

M/A/R/R/S:

12-inch Singles

4th & B'Way 452, "Pump Up the Volume" (4 versions)/"Anitina," 1987 ....**$4.00-$8.00**

NAUGHTY BY NATURE:

12-inch Singles

Tommy Boy TB 988, "O.P.P." (2 versions)"/"Wickedest Man Alive," 1991 ....**$6.00-$12.00**

TB 999, "Everything's Gonna Be Alright" (3 versions)/"O.P.P." (Live), 1991 ....**$5.00-$10.00**

TB 554, "Hip Hop Hooray" (3 versions)/"The Hood Comes First" (2 versions), 1993 ....**$6.00-$12.00**

LPs

Tommy Boy TBLP-1051, Naughty By Nature, 1991....................**$7.50-$15.00**

TBLP-1069, 19 Naughty III, 1993 ....**$10.00-$20.00**

TBLP-1111, Poverty's Paradise, 1995....................**$6.00-$12.00**

TBLP-1310, Nature's Finest: Naughty by Nature's Greatest Hits, 1999 ....**$7.50-$15.00**

Arista 19047, Nineteen Naughty Nine—Nature's Fury (2 LPs), 1999 ....**$10.00-$20.00**

NEWCLEUS:

12-inch Singles

Sunnyview SUN 408, "Jam On Revenge (The Wikki-Wikki Song)" (2 versions), 1984....................**$7.50-$15.00**

SUN 411, "Jam On It" (2 versions), 1984 ....**$7.50-$15.00**

SUN 427, "Let's Jam" (2 versions), 1985 ....**$5.00-$10.00**

LPs

Sunnyview SUN 4901, Jam On Revenge, 1984 ....**$10.00-$20.00**

N.W.A.:

45s

Ruthless 7206, "Express Yourself"/"Straight Outta Compton," 1989 ....**$5.00-$10.00**

(with picture sleeve, add), 1989....................**$5.00-$10.00**

12-inch Singles

Ruthless MRC 1034, "Panic Zone"/"Dope Man" (2 versions)/"B-Ball" (2 versions), 1987....................**$20.00-$40.00**

7263, "Gangsta Gangsta" (2 versions)/"Something Like That"/"Quiet on Tha Set"/"Something 2 Dance 2," 1989....................**$12.50-$25.00**

Priority SPRO 81104, "Express Yourself" (3 versions)/"Straight Outta Compton" (3 versions), 1998 ....**$10.00-$20.00**

LPs

Ruthless MRC 1057, N.W.A. and the Posse, 1987....................**$12.50-$25.00**

57102, Straight Outta Compton, 1989....................**$10.00-$20.00**

57126, Efil4zaggin, 1991 ....**$10.00-$20.00**

50561, Greatest Hits (2 LPs), 1996 ....**$7.50-$15.00**

OUTKAST:

12-inch Singles

LaFace 24067, "Player's Ball" (4 versions), 1994....................**$7.50-$15.00**

24525, "Ms. Jackson" (2 versions)/"Sole Sunday" (Radio Mix) (instrumental), 2000....................**$6.00-$12.00**

Arista 55883, "The Way You Move" (3 versions)/"Hey Ya" (2 versions), 2003 ....**$6.00-$12.00**

LPs

LaFace 26029, Atliens, 1996....................**$7.50-$15.00**

26053, Aquemini (2 LPs), 1998....................**$7.50-$15.00**

(if on LaFace 6153, 3 LPs, censored version), 1998....................**$10.00-$20.00**

26072, Stankonia (2 LPs), 2000....................**$7.50-$15.00**

P.M. DAWN:

12-inch Singles

Gee Street 866095-1, "Set Adrift on Memory Bliss" (2 versions)/"A Watcher's Point of View" (3 versions), 1991 ....**$4.00-$8.00**

862475-1, "The Ways of the Wind" (4 versions), 1993 ....**$4.00-$8.00**

LPs

Gee Street PRLP-6768-1, The Bliss Album...? (2 LPs, vinyl is promo only), 1993 ....**$10.00-$20.00**

524147-1, Jesus Wept (2 LPs), 1995 .... $10.00-$20.00

PUBLIC ENEMY:

45s

Def Jam 38-07222, "You're Gonna Get Yours"/"Miuzi Weighs a Ton," 1987 .... $3.00-$6.00

(with picture sleeve, add), 1987 .... $3.00-$6.00

38-08072, "Night of the Living Baseheads"/"Cold Lampin' With Flavor," 1988 .... $2.50-$5.00

(with picture sleeve, add), 1988 .... $3.00-$6.00

Motown 1972, "Fight the Power"/(Flavor Flav Meets Spike Lee Version), 1989 .... $2.50-$5.00

12-inch Singles

Def Jam 44-06719, "Public Enemy #1" (2 versions)/"Timebomb"/"Son of Public Enemy" (Flavor Whop version), 1987 .... $6.00-$12.00

44-06861, "You're Gonna Get Yours" (2 versions)/"Miuzi Weighs a Ton"/ "Rebel Without a Pause" (2 versions), 1987 .... $7.50-$15.00

44-73179, "911 Is a Joke" (2 versions)/"Revolutionary Generation" (2 versions), 1990 .... $6.00-$12.00

42-74487, "Hazy Shade of Criminal" (3 versions)/"Tie Goes to the Runner" (2 versions), 1992 .... $6.00-$12.00

LPs

Def Jam BFC 40658, Yo! Bum Rush the Show, 1987 .... $6.00-$12.00

BFW 44303, It Takes a Nation of Millions to Hold Us Back, 1988 .... $6.00-$12.00

C 45413, Fear of a Black Planet, 1990 .... $6.00-$12.00

C2 53014, Greatest Misses (2 LPs), 1993 .... $7.50-$15.00

Atomic Pop 0001, There's a Poison Goin' On (2 LPs, red vinyl), 1999 .... $12.50-$25.00

RUN-D.M.C.:

45s

Profile 5019, "It's Like That"/"It's Like That" (instrumental), 1983 .... $2.50-$5.00

5045, "Rock Box"/"Rock Box" (dub version), 1984 .... $2.50-$5.00

5112, "Walk This Way"/"King of Rock," 1986 .... $2.00-$4.00

(with picture sleeve, add), 1986 .... $2.00-$4.00

5202, "Run's House"/"Beats to the Rhyme," 1988 .... $2.00-$4.00

(with picture sleeve, add), 1988 .... $2.00-$4.00

12-inch Singles

Profile PRO-7019, "It's Like That"/"Sucker M.C.'s," 1983 .... $15.00-$30.00

PRO-7045, "Rock Box" (vocal dub version) (dub version)

(if original on tan label), 1984 .... $12.50-$25.00

(if reissue on black label), 1995 .... $6.00-$12.00

PRO-7079, "Here We Go (album version) (Live at the Funhouse)

(if original on tan label), 1985 .... $12.50-$25.00

(if reissue on black label), 1995 .... $6.00-$12.00

PRO-7112, "Walk This Way" (vocal)/(instrumental)

(if original, tan label, picture cover), 1986 .... $12.50-$25.00

(if reissue on black label), 1995 .... $6.00-$12.00

(if on Arista/Profile 17421, reissue), 2000 .... $4.00-$8.00

LPs

Profile PRO-1202, Run-D.M.C., 1984 .... $6.00-$12.00

PRO-1205, King of Rock, 1985 .... $6.00-$12.00

PRO-1217, Raising Hell (cover exists in two different color schemes, value is equal for either), 1986 .... $6.00-$12.00

PRO-1265, Tougher Than Leather, 1988 .... $6.00-$12.00

Arista 16400, Crown Royal (2 LPs), 2001 .... $7.50-$15.00

SALT-N-PEPA:

45s

Next Plateau KF 315, "Tramp"/"Push It," 1987 .... $5.00-$10.00

(if "Push It" is on both sides), 1987 .... $2.50-$5.00

KF 319, "Shake Your Thang"/"Spinderella's Not a Fella (But a Girl D.J.)," 1988 .... $1.50-$3.00

(with picture sleeve, add), 1988 .... $1.50-$3.00

London 850346, "Ain't Nuthin' But a She Thing (album version)"/remix), 1995. **$1.50-$3.00**

857356-7, "Shoop"/"Whatta Man," 1994 .... $1.50-$3.00

12-inch Singles

Pop Art PA 1413, Super Nature, "The Show Stoppa" (3 versions), 1985 .... $7.50-$15.00

Next Plateau NP 50063, "Tramp" (3 versions)/"Push It" (2 versions)/"Idle Chatter," 1987 .... $5.00-$10.00

NP 50157, "Let's Talk About Sex" (3 versions)/"Swift," 1991 .... $5.00-$10.00

857315-1, "Shoop" (4 versions)/"Emphatically No"/"AIDS P.S.A.," 1993 .... $4.00-$8.00

LPs

Next Plateau PL 1011, A Salt with a Deadly Pepa, 1988 .... $6.00-$12.00

PL 1019, Blacks' Magic, 1989 .... $6.00-$12.00

London/Red Ant 828959-1, Brand New (2 LPs), 1997 .... $6.00-$12.00

GIL SCOTT-HERON:

45s

Flying Dutchman FD-26011, "The Revolution Will Not Be Televised"/"Home is Where the Hatred Is," 1974 .... $4.00-$8.00

Arista 0117, "Superman (Ain't No Such Thing As…)"/"We Beg Your Pardon America," 1975 .... $2.50-$5.00

0647, "'B' Movie"/"(B-side unknown), 1981 .... $2.00-$4.00

LPs

Flying Dutchman FD-10143, Pieces of a Man, 1971 .... $10.00-$20.00

BLD1-0613, The Revolution Will Not Be Televised, 1974 .... $10.00-$20.00

Arista AL 8248, The Best of Gil Scott-Heron, 1984 .... $5.00-$10.00

TUPAC SHAKUR/2PAC:

12-inch Singles

Interscope INT8P-6489, "Changes" (several versions), 1998 .... $4.00-$8.00

INT8P-6508, "God Bless the Dead" (2 versions)/"Troublesome '96" (2 versions), 1999 .... $5.00-$10.00

LPs

Interscope 91767, 2Pacalypse Now, 1991 .... $7.50-$15.00

92399, Me Against the World (2 LPs), 1995 .... $10.00-$20.00

Death Row/Interscope 524204-1, All Eyez on Me (4 LPs), 1996 .... $15.00-$30.00

Amaru/Jive 41628, R U Still Down? (Remember Me) (3 LPs), 1997 .... $12.50-$25.00

Restless 72737, Strictly 4 My N.I.G.G.A.Z. (2 LPs, vinyl issue of 1993 CD issue), 1998 .... $7.50-$15.00

THE SUGAR HILL GANG:

45s

Sugar Hill 752, "Rapper's Delight" (4:55)/(6:30) (promo only on 45), 1979 .... $12.50-$25.00

755, "Here I Am"/"Rapper's Delight," 1980 .... $7.50-$15.00

774, "Apache"/"Rapper's Delight," 1981 .... $5.00-$10.00

12-inch Singles

Sugar Hill SH 542, "Rapper's Delight" (Long 15:00)/(Short 6:30), 1979 .... $15.00-$30.00

553, "8th Wonder"/"Sugar Hill Groove," 1980 .... $12.50-$25.00

567, "Apache"/(instrumental), 1981 .... $12.50-$25.00

524, "Rapper's Delight" (Hip Hop Remix 4:00)/(7:00)/"Hot Hot Summer Day," 1987 .... $6.00-$12.00

LPs

Sugar Hill SH 245, Sugar Hill Gang, 1980 .... $10.00-$20.00

SH 249, 8th Wonder, 1981 .... $7.50-$15.00

SH 9206, Livin' in the Fast Lane, 1984 .... $6.00-$12.00

THE 2 LIVE CREW:

45s

Luke Skyywalker LS-113, "Me So Horny" (same on both sides, promo), 1989 .... $7.50-$15.00

Luke 98915, "Banned in the U.S.A."/(instrumental), 1990 .... $2.50-$5.00

12-inch Singles

GR 117, "Do Wah Diddy" (Remix Radio)/"I Can't Go for That," 1988 .... $4.00-$8.00

GR 127, "Me So Horny" (2 versions)/"Get the F--- Out of My House" (3 versions), 1989 .... $6.00-$12.00

LPs

Luke Skyywalker XR-100, The 2 Live Crew Is What We Are, 1987 .... $7.50-$15.00

XR-107, As Nasty As They Wanna Be (2 LPs), 1989 .... $7.50-$15.00

XR-108, As Clean As They Wanna Be, 1989 .... $7.50-$15.00

Luke 122, Greatest Hits (2 LPs), 1992 .... $10.00-$20.00

TIMEZONE:

12-inch Singles

Celluloid CEL 176, "World Destruction" (2 versions), 1984 .... $5.00-$10.00

UTFO:

45s

Select 1182, "Roxanne, Roxanne"/"Roxanne with UTFO," "The Real Roxanne," 1985 .... $4.00-$8.00

LPs

Select 21614, UTFO, 1985 .... $12.50-$25.00

Chapter 20

Rhythm and Blues/Soul

History

Arthur Conley said it as clearly as anyone. "Do you like good music, that sweet soul music? As long as it's swingin, oh yeah, oh yeah." Rhythm and blues music, and later soul music, grew from major metropolitan urban areas—Chicago, Detroit, New Orleans, Memphis, Philadelphia, New York City, Los Angeles, St. Louis, and hundreds of other places where soul music absorbed the local influences of music and culture and life, to become the soundtrack of generations.

Today's soul music evolved from many sources. One can listen to a Scott Joplin ragtime piece, or to the gospel compositions of Thomas A. Dorsey, and hear the earliest fragments of soul. Or listen to some of the best jazz and big band groups—Duke Ellington and John Coltrane, Count Basie and Louis Armstrong, and Coleman Hawkins and Charlie Parker, to name only a few.

By the 1940s, "rhythm and blues" music evolved from gospel, jazz, and an uptempo big band sound called "jump blues." R&B artists like Louis Jordan, Ruth Brown, and LaVern Baker took the blues, added horns and drums, and sang over the instruments with fire and thrusts, as if they were shouting above the music to the audience in the back rows.

Eventually R&B groups like the Ravens, the Dominoes, the Royals, the Crows, and the Orioles blended their gospel-edged melodies with intricate choruses, creating doo-wop music. By the mid-1950s, R&B music (along with rockabilly and doo-wop) formed the holy trinity of rock and roll. Rock

This 10-inch LP of Billy Ward and his Dominoes contains their major hits, including "Sixty Minute Man" and "Have Mercy Baby." It's also one of the rarest 10-inch LPs, R&B or otherwise, in existence today, and its collectible value—as much as $6,000 in near-mint condition—reflects this.

***$6,000** NM condition*

Ruth Brown was one of the first successful artists for Atlantic Records, a haven for soul music in the 1950s, whose roster would include the Drifters, the Clovers, LaVern Baker, and Ray Charles. This was her first full-length album with Atlantic, and near-mint copies with a black label can sell for up to $200.

***$200**, NM condition*

Photo credit: From the collection of Scott Primeau.

Between 1953 and 1976, over twenty different men have recorded as "The Drifters." This pressing of "Dance With Me" is one of the last 78s made by Atlantic Records, and features a Drifters lineup that includes lead singer Ben E. King.

***$300**, VG+ condition*

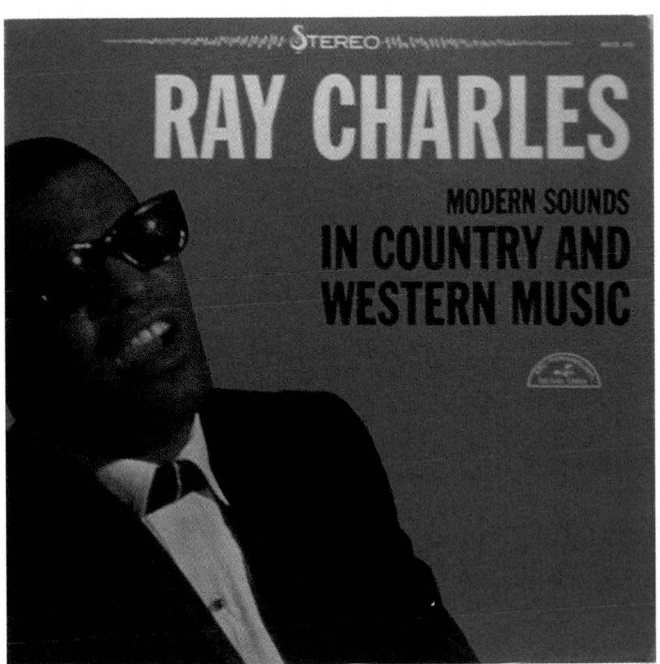

No other artist was as adept in blending gospel, country music, rhythm and blues, jazz, and pop as could the late Ray Charles. His albums for ABC-Paramount allowed him a freedom to experiment and reinterpret musical styles, resulting in million-selling albums like Modern Sounds in Country and Western Music.

***$30**, NM condition*

and roll also afforded artists such as Chuck Berry, Little Richard, and Sam Cooke a new avenue to spread rhythm & blues music to previously untapped audiences. Groups such as the Drifters, the Platters, and the Coasters achieved massive popularity with both white and black audiences; their songs were played on every radio station; they performed on every major TV variety show.

Many other R&B vocal groups made inroads into the pop music field, before their songs were "covered" by white vocal groups and artists. It was not unusual for an R&B artist or group to discover that their own song had been re-recorded by a white artist or group, and was racing up the charts while their own version struggled to find airplay. Many white artists recorded these "cover" records, which essentially allowed a songwriter to have his or her composition played on more radio stations and in more jukeboxes. Cover songs were not a common occurrence—in fact, up until the 1950s, the same song could be recorded and released by several artists, in many cases the competing versions appeared on the pop charts simultaneously. But, in the 1950s, with more teenagers listening to R&B and rock 'n roll music, the idea of clean-cut Pat Boone covering Little Richard's "Tutti-Fruitti," or Georgia Gibbs' version of the Royals' "Work With Me Annie" as a sanitized "Dance With Me Henry," was hard to take.

That being said, many R&B artists were able to "cross over" the unwritten-yet-enforced musical color barrier, as teenagers eventually eschewed the pale imitations and purchased instead the soulful originators. Ray Charles, "The Genius," recorded a series of R&B classics for Atlantic, including "Hallelujah I Love Her So" and "Rockhouse," as well as his soul-meets-gospel, call-and-response classic "What'd I Say." Charles would later move to ABC Records and continue his soul classics with "Hit The Road Jack" and "Unchain My Heart." His album *Modern Sounds in Country and Western Music* became one of the biggest-selling albums of 1962, as Charles took classic country songs like "I Can't Stop Loving You" and "You Don't Know Me," and brought them to life with his own soulful arrangements.

James Brown, "The Godfather of Soul," started his career as a gospel singer. The gospel group Brown joined, the Flames, were signed by Federal Records, and recorded the heartwrenching "Please, Please, Please" as "James Brown and the Famous Flames." A series of soul ballads and uptempo numbers followed, including "Try Me," "Think," and "Night Train." One of the crowning achievements in Brown's career was the release of a 1962 live album that captured all the energy and excitement of a James Brown concert. The album, *Live at the Apollo*, sold millions of copies and inspired a generation of performers, who listened to that album and tried to replicate Brown's moves.

The story of Jackie Wilson's career is both bitter and sweet. After initial hits with "Reet Petite" and "Lonely Teardrops," Wilson spent the next ten years recording in every musical style from pop to opera, at the request of his record company Brunswick. He earned the nickname "Mr. Excitement," as his talent and charisma would create pop hits like "Doggin' Around," "Baby Workout," and "(Your Love Keeps Lifting Me) Higher and Higher," despite all the overly lush orchestrations and banal background singers fostered upon him by Brunswick. Sadly, while on stage in a New Jersey club in 1975, Wilson was felled by a stroke, and

This rare 7-inch EP, pressed especially for jukeboxes, features several tracks from James Brown's Live at the Apollo *album.*

***$50**, NM condition*

Photo credit: Album courtesy Last Vestige Music Store, Albany, N.Y.

The greatest tribute to Jackie Wilson's musical legacy is that he was able to rise above the syrupy musical arrangements and overwrought choruses, producing soul masterpieces on 45 and LP.

***$25**, VG+ condition*

died in a nursing home eight years later. His musical legacy, however, lives on in such singer-dancer-entertainers as Michael Jackson and Al Green.

While the Motown musical hit factory was working overtime in Detroit, which is covered later in this book, another record company proved that soul music could still be made in the deep South. Originally formed in the 1950s as Satellite Records, Stax/Volt Records was the home of Otis Redding, the Staple Singers, Rufus Thomas, Sam & Dave, and the Dramatics, all of whom produced hits. Backing up the singers at Stax/Volt was its house band, Booker T. and the M.G.'s, creating the "Memphis Soul" sound—heavy on horns, with plenty of jazz and blues mixed in.

By the early 1970s, soul music found a new epicenter in Philadelphia. Songwriters-producers Kenny Gamble and Leon Huff created a new sound that mixed soul music with funk and classical overtones. Dubbed "The Sound of Philadelphia," Gamble and Huff's Philadelphia International Records made superstars out of the O'Jays, Harold Melvin and the Blue Notes, the Intruders, the Three Degrees, Billy Paul, and the People's Choice. Philadelphia International's house band, MFSB, even had hits of their own with "Love is the Message" and the theme from Soul Train, "TSOP (The Sound of Philadelphia)."

Other cities produced groups with soulful sounds—the Tavares brothers from Boston; the Chi-Lites from Chicago, the Commodores from Alabama and the Gap Band from Atlanta. In Los Angeles, Barry White turned his sensual bass voice into a series of love ballads and dance grooves. Archie Bell and the Drells dominated the Houston club scene before breaking through nationwide. Artists like Curtis Mayfield and Isaac Hayes created funky soundtracks

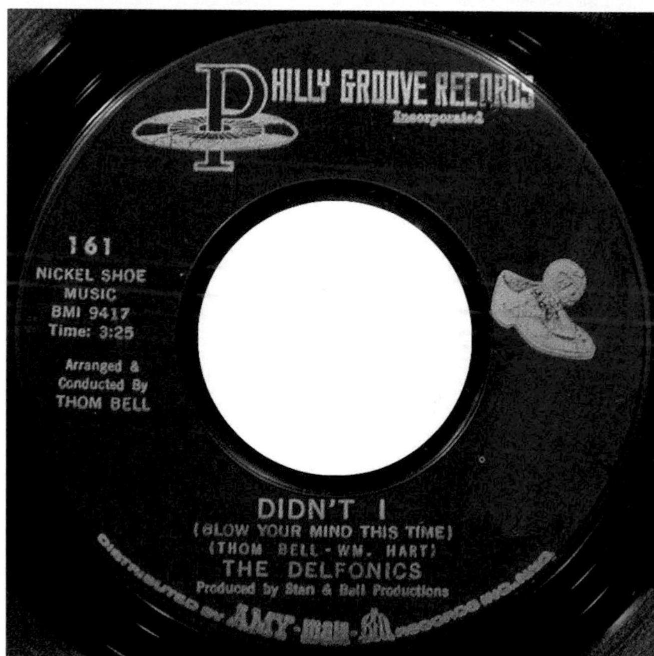

While he worked with Kenny Gamble and Leon Huff at Philadelphia International Records, producer-songwriter Thom Bell created aural soul symphonies for other artists, including the Delfonics, the Stylistics, Blue Magic, and the Spinners. In fact, when interviewed after their appearance on the Ed Sullivan show, members of the Jackson Five cited the Delfonics as one of their major influences.

***$7.50**, VG+ condition*

for films like "Superfly" and "Shaft," which became radio hits of their own. In these cities, the sound of soul music represented the strengths and struggles of the urban communities. Tavares sang sweet ballads like "Check It Out," and dance tracks like "Heaven Must Be Missing An Angel."

While the Chi-Lites sang sweet soul ballads like "Oh Girl" and "Have You Seen Her," they also sang "(For God's Sake) Give More Power to the People."

Soul music in the 1980s was now influenced by other musical styles, including funk, rap, and dance. Sexy male singers like Luther Vandross, Teddy Pendergrass, Babyface, and Kashif could melt hearts like ice in July. Meanwhile, singers like Anita Baker, Phyllis Hyman, Jennifer Holliday, and Whitney Houston showed they could also use every inch of their vocal cords to create powerful recordings like "Sweet Love," "And I Am Telling You I'm Not Going," and "Don't Wanna Change the World." Today's soul artists continue to mine the musical gems of the past, to create their own masterpieces. Alicia Keys mixes soul music with classical themes of Chopin and Bach. Lauryn Hill, and India. Arie take their inspirations from the soul hits of the 70s and 80s. Rappers continually mine classic R&B/soul grooves for rhythm tracks—James Brown's "Funky Drummer," for example, has arguably been sampled by more up-and-coming rappers than has any other classic track.

What To Look For

A good rule of thumb to follow when collecting R&B and soul records is—the older the record is, the higher its collectible value. For example, early R&B and soul records from the Five Keys, the Orioles, and Ruth Brown are hard to find, and the few surviving copies that have survived sell for very high prices. Conversely, most major label 45s and LPs from the 1970s are easily and readily available, and their collectible value has not risen. This is not to say that 1970s music is better or worse than 1950s music; but it is much easier to find a "million-selling" copy of the O'Jays' "Back Stabbers" than it is to find the group's early King recordings.

R&B albums from the 1950s are very rare—but near-mint condition 10-inch LPs can return thousands of dollars. As for 1970s albums, the rarer and more collectible albums are quadraphonic releases or half-speed mastered audiophile pressings, because of these formats' low print run.

Among collectible vocal R&B groups of the 1950s, keep an eye out for recordings by the Five Keys. This group's early 78s and 45s on Aladdin can command high prices, as can some of their early recordings on Capitol. Of special note is the album *The Five Keys On Stage!*, their first Capitol album. On the front cover, the group is posed with their hands spread out, as if they were sustaining a harmonic chord. But the right hand of the singer on the far left is in such a position that...well...Capitol eventually reissued the album with the offending "digit" airbrushed away, but that second pressing is actually rarer than the first!

Books

Gregory, Hugh, *Soul Music A-Z* (Revised Edition), Da Capo Press, Inc., New York, NY, 1995.

Graff, Gary, Freedom du Lac, Josh, McFarlon, Jim, Eds., *MusicHound R&B: The Essential Album Guide*, Visible Ink Press, Detroit, Mich., 1998.

Whitburn, Joel, *Top R&B Singles 1942-1995*, Record Research, Inc., Menomonee Falls, Wisconsin, 1996.

Museums:

Georgia Music Hall Of Fame, P.O. Box 870, Macon, Georgia 31202, 1-800-GA-ROCKS: http://www.gamusichall.com

Stax Museum Of American Soul Music, 870 East McLemore, Memphis, Tennessee 38106, (901) 942-7685: http://www.soulsvilleusa.com

Web Pages

A page devoted to classic soul recordings: *http://www.soul-patrol.com/soul*

A fan-created Web site devoted to Aretha Franklin: *http://ntfp.globalserve.net/ebutler*

The Ray Charles home page: *http://www.raycharles.com*

The Philadelphia International home page, containing information on Gamble-Huff produced soul songs of the 1970s: *http://www.phillyinternational.com*

Not to be confused with the comic book superhero quartet of the same name, the Fantastic Four were a Detroit R&B vocal group whose first release, "The Whole World is a Stage," was their biggest hit. This Fantastic Four later recorded for Berry Gordy's subsidiary label Soul, as well as the Westbound label in the 1970s.
***$7.50**, VG+ condition*

The Five Keys On Stage *album is a prime example why photographers should be aware of any misinterpretable background information in a photograph. The first album cover shows lead singer Rudy West's thumb sticking out parallel with his trousers, which might give the illusion of—well—you know.*

***$300**, NM condition*

Capitol retouched the photos to remove West's thumb, and reprinted the covers, not only for the mono and stereo LP jackets, but also for the concomitant EP jackets that were also released at that time.

***$500**, NM condition*

ARTIST | **VG+ to NM**

ASHFORD AND SIMPSON:

45s

Warner Bros. 8870, "Found a Cure"/"You Always Could," 1979......**$2.00-$4.00**
Capitol B-5397, "Solid"/"Solid" (dub version), 1984........................**$1.50-$3.00**

LPs

Warner Bros. BSK 3219, Is It Still Good to Ya, 1978....................**$5.00-$10.00**
Capitol ST-11282, High Rise, 1983..**$4.00-$8.00**

LAVERN BAKER:

45s

King 4556, "Trying"/Todd Rhodes, "Snuff Dipper," 1952............**$25.00-$50.00**
Atlantic 1047, "Tweedlee Dee"/"Tomorrow Night," 1954...........**$20.00-$40.00**
1116, "Jim Dandy"/"Tra La La," 1956...**$12.50-$25.00**
2167, "See See Rider"/"The Story of My Love," 1962.................**$6.00-$12.00**

LPs

Atlantic 8002, LaVern (black label), 1956...............................**$125.00-$250.00**
(with red-purple label, "fan" logo in white), 1960.......................**$15.00-$30.00**
(with red-purple label, "fan" logo in black), 1963.......................**$10.00-$20.00**

HANK BALLARD AND THE MIDNIGHTERS:

45s

King 5171, "Teardrops on Your Letter"/"The Twist," 1959..........**$15.00-$30.00**
5341, "Finger Poppin' Time"/"I Love You, I Love You So-o-o," 1960
....**$12.50-$25.00**
5400, "Let's Go, Let's Go, Let's Go"/"You'd Forgive Me," 1960**$12.50-$25.00**

LPs

King 618, Singin' and Swingin', 1959.......................................**$125.00-$250.00**

ARCHIE BELL AND THE DRELLS:

45s

Ovide 228, "Tighten Up"/"Dog Eat Dog," 1967.........................**$15.00-$30.00**
Atlantic 2478, "Tighten Up"/"Dog Eat Dog," 1968......................**$6.00-$12.00**
2478, "Tighten Up"/"Tighten Up—Pt. 2," 1968............................**$4.00-$8.00**

LPs

Atlantic 8181, Tighten Up (mono), 1968....................................**$25.00-$50.00**
(if on Atlantic SD 8181, stereo), 1968.......................................**$15.00-$30.00**

GEORGE BENSON:

45s

Groove 0024, "It Should Have Been Me #2"/"She Makes Me Mad," 1954
....**$20.00-$40.00**
Columbia 43684, "Summertime"/"Ain't That Peculiar," 1966.........**$5.00-$10.00**
Warner Bros. 8209, "This Masquerade"/"Lady," 1976......................**$2.50-$5.00**

LPs

Warner Bros. BS 2919, Breezin'
(if no mention of "This Masquerade" on front cover), 1976.........**$7.50-$15.00**
(if "Contains This Masquerade" on front cover), 1976.................**$5.00-$10.00**
Mobile Fidelity 1-011, Breezin' (audiophile vinyl), 1979.............**$30.00-$60.00**

BROOK BENTON:

45s

Mercury 71394, "It's Just a Matter of Time"/"Hurtin' Inside," 1959
....**$7.50-$15.00**
Cotillion 44057, "Rainy Night in Georgia"/"Where Do You Go From Here," 1969...**$5.00-$10.00**

78s

Mercury 71394, "It's Just a Matter of Time"/"Hurtin' Inside," 1959
....**$50.00-$100.00**

BOBBY BLAND/BOBBY "BLUE" BLAND:

45s

Duke 105, "Lovin' Blues"/"I.O.U. Blues," 1952........................**$150.00-$300.00**
332, "I Pity the Fool"/"Close to You," 1961..............................**$10.00-$20.00**
344, "Turn On Your Love Light"/"You're the One (That I Need)," 1961
....**$10.00-$20.00**

78s

Duke 705, "Lovin' Blues"/"I.O.U. Blues," 1952...........................**$30.00-$60.00**
303, "Wishing Well"/"I'm Not Ashamed" (his last 78), 1959
....**$125.00-$250.00**

LPs

Duke DLP-74, Two Steps from the Blues (purple-yellow label), 1961
....**$125.00-$250.00**
(if orange label, red vinyl), 1962..**$125.00-$250.00**
(if orange label, black vinyl), 1962...**$50.00-$100.00**

BLUE MAGIC:

45s

Atco 6961, "Sideshow"/"Just Don't Want to Be Lonely," 1974........**$3.00-$6.00**

LPs

Atco SD 7038, Blue Magic, 1974...**$6.00-$12.00**

BOOKER T. AND THE MG'S:

45s

Volt 102, "Green Onions"/"Behave Yourself," 1962.....................**$15.00-$30.00**

Stax 127, "Green Onions"/"Behave Yourself" (gray label), 1962 ....$10.00-$20.00
(if blue label), 1962 ....$8.00-$16.00
211, "Hip-Hug-Her"/"Summertime," 1967 ....$5.00-$10.00

Mono LPs

Stax ST-701, Green Onions, 1962 ....$35.00-$70.00
ST-713, In the Christmas Spirit (fingers and piano keys cover), 1966 ....$200.00-$400.00
(if cover has Santa Claus on it), 1967 ....$100.00-$200.00

Stereo LPs

Stax STS-713, In the Christmas Spirit (fingers and piano keys cover), 1966 ....$200.00-$400.00
(if cover has Santa Claus on it), 1967 ....$100.00-$200.00
STS-717, Hip-Hug-Her, 1967 ....$25.00-$50.00

JAMES BROWN:

45s

Federal 12258, "Please, Please, Please"/"Why Do You Do Me?," 1956 ....$20.00-$40.00
12337, "Try Me"/"Tell Me What I Did Wrong," 1958 ....$15.00-$30.00
King 5614, "Night Train"/"Why Does Everything Happen to Me," 1962 ....$7.50-$15.00
5853, "Please, Please, Please"/"In the Wee Wee Hours," 1964 ....$7.50-$15.00
5999, "Papa's Got a Brand New Bag Part I"/"Papa's Got a Brand New Bag Part II," 1965 ....$7.50-$15.00
6015, "I Got You (I Feel Good)"/"I Can't Help It (I Just Do, Do, Do)," 1965 ....$7.50-$15.00

Mono LPs

King 826, Live at the Apollo
(if other King albums on back cover, "crownless" King label), 1963 ....$75.00-$150.00
(if custom back cover, "crownless" King label), 1963 ....$100.00-$200.00
(if white label promo, banded for airplay), 1963 ....$400.00-$800.00
(if "crown" King label), 1966 ....$25.00-$50.00

Stereo LPs

King KS-826, Live at the Apollo
(if other King albums on back cover, "crownless" King label), 1963 ....$100.00-$200.00
(if custom back cover, "crownless" King label), 1963 ....$150.00-$300.00
(if "crown" King label), 1966 ....$35.00-$70.00
PD-1-6042, Sex Machine Today, 1975 ....$20.00-$40.00

RUTH BROWN:

45s

Atlantic 919, "Teardrops From My Eyes"/"Am I Making the Same Mistake," 1950 ....$200.00-$400.00
986, "(Mama) He Treats Your Daughter Mean"/"R.B. Blues," 1953 ....$30.00-$60.00
1077, "Love has Joined Us Together"/"I Gotta Have You" (duet with Clyde McPhatter), 1955 ....$15.00-$30.00

78s

Atlantic 879, "It's Raining"/"So Long," 1949 ....$25.00-$50.00
(if red vinyl promo, white label with red print), 1949 ....$250.00-$500.00
919, "Teardrops From My Eyes"/"Am I Making the Same Mistake," 1950 ....$30.00-$60.00

JERRY BUTLER:

45s

Abner 1024, "Lost"/"One By One," 1959 ....$15.00-$30.00
Vee Jay 354, "He Will Break Your Heart"/"Thanks To You," 1960 ....$10.00-$20.00
Mercury 72850, "Hey, Western Union Man"/"Just Can't Forget About You," 1968 ....$4.00-$8.00
72898, "Only the Strong Survive"/"Just Because I Really Love You," 1969 ....$4.00-$8.00

LPs

Abner R-2001, Jerry Butler, Esq., 1959 ....$200.00-$400.00
Vee Jay LP-1027, Jerry Butler, Esq., 1960 ....$75.00-$150.00
LP-1029, He Will Break Your Heart, 1960 ....$40.00-$80.00
Mercury SR-61198, The Ice Man Cometh, 1968 ....$7.50-$15.00

GENE CHANDLER:

45s

Vee Jay 416, "Duke of Earl"/"Kissin' in the Kitchen," 1961 ....$12.50-$25.00
(if later pressing, song credited to "The Duke of Earl"), 1962 ....$10.00-$20.00
Mercury 73083, "Groovy Situation"/"Not the Marrying Kind," 1970 ....$3.00-$6.00

Mono LPs

Vee Jay LP-1040, The Duke of Earl, 1962 ....$60.00-$120.00
(if on Vee Jay SR-1040, cover says stereo, record plays mono, black label, "VJ" in brackets), 196? ....$25.00-$50.00
Brunswick BL 54124, The Girl Don't Care, 1967 ....$12.50-$25.00

RAY CHARLES:

45s

Swing Time 250, "Baby, Let Me Hold Your Hand"/"Lonely Boy," 1951 ....$250.00-$500.00
Atlantic 976, "Roll With Me Baby"/"The Midnight Hour," 1952 ....$250.00-$500.00
2031, "What'd I Say" (Pt. 1)/"What'd I Say" (Pt. 2), 1959 ....$10.00-$20.00
ABC-Paramount 10330, "I Can't Stop Loving You"/"Born to Lose," 1962 ....$7.50-$15.00
ABC 11090, "Eleanor Rigby"/"Understanding," 1968 ....$4.00-$8.00

78s

Swing Time 217, "See See Rider"/"What Have I Done," 1949 ...$20.00-$40.00
Atlantic 976, "Roll With Me Baby"/"The Midnight Hour," 1952 ....$35.00-$70.00
2031, "What'd I Say" (Pt. 1)/"What'd I Say" (Pt. 2) (his last 78), 1959 ....$200.00-$400.00

Mono LPs

Atlantic 1289, Ray Charles at Newport (black label), 1958 ....$25.00-$50.00
(if red-white label, white fan logo at right), 1960 ....$12.50-$25.00
(if red-white label, black fan logo at right), 1962 ....$10.00-$20.00
ABC-Paramount 410, Modern Sounds in Country and Western Music, 1962 ....$12.50-$25.00

Stereo LPs

ABC-Paramount S-410, Modern Sounds in Country and Western Music, 1962 ....$15.00-$30.00
S-465, Ingredients in a Recipe for Soul, 1963 ....$12.50-$25.00
DCC Compact Classics, Greatest Country and Western Hits (audiophile pressing), 1995 ....$50.00-$100.00

THE CHI-LITES:

LPs

Brunswick BL 754170, (For God's Sake) Give More Power to the People, 1971 ....$12.50-$25.00

THE CLOVERS:

45s

Atlantic 934, "Don't You Know I Love You"/"Skylark," 1951 ....$500.00-$1,000.00
1083, "Devil or Angel"/"Hey, Doll Baby" (yellow label, no pinwheel), 1956 ....$100.00-$200.00
(if red label, no pinwheel), 1956 ....$20.00-$40.00
(if red label, no pinwheel, red vinyl), 1956 ....$3,000.00-$4,000.00

78s

Atlantic 934, "Don't You Know I Love You"/"Skylark," 1951 ....$50.00-$100.00
1083, "Devil or Angel"/"Hey, Doll Baby," 1956 ....$20.00-$40.00

LPs

Atlantic 1248, The Clovers, 1956 ....$300.00-$600.00
(if on Atlantic 8009, reissue), 1957 ....$200.00-$400.00
(if on Atlantic 8009, white "bullseye" label), 1960 ....$150.00-$300.00
(if on Atlantic 8009, red-white label), 1961 ....$100.00-$200.00

THE COASTERS:

45s

Atco 6087, "Searchin'"/"Young Blood" (maroon label), 1957 ....$35.00-$70.00
(if white-yellow label), 1957 ....$12.50-$25.00
6132, "Charlie Brown"/"Three Cool Cats," 1959 ....$12.50-$25.00

NAT "KING" COLE:

45s

Capitol F1010, "Mona Lisa"/"The Greatest Inventor (Of Them All)," 1950 ....$7.50-$15.00
F2610, "Lover Come Back to Me"/"That's All," 1953 ....$5.00-$10.00
4804, "Ramblin' Rose"/"Good Times," 1962 ....$6.00-$12.00
(with picture sleeve, add), 1962 ....$10.00-$20.00

78s

Excelsior 00102/3, "Vom, Vim, Veedle"/"All For You," 1943 ....$25.00-$50.00
Capitol 1010, "Mona Lisa"/"The Greatest Inventor (Of Them All)," 1950 ....$4.00-$8.00
2212, "Because You're Mine"/"I'm Never Satisfied," 1952 ....$4.00-$8.00

10-inch LPs

Capitol H 8, The King Cole Trio, 1950 ....$50.00-$100.00
H 213, Harvest of Hits, 1950 ....$35.00-$70.00

Mono LPs

W 689, The Piano Style of Nat King Cole (turquoise label), 1956 .... **$20.00-$40.00**
(if black label with rainbow perimeter, "Capitol" at left), 1958... **$15.00-$30.00**
(if black label with rainbow perimeter, "Capitol" at top), 1962... **$10.00-$20.00**

Stereo LPs

Capitol SWCL 1613, The Nat King Cole Story (3 LPs), 1961.... **$15.00-$30.00**

SAM COOKE:

45s

Keen 34013, "You Send Me"/"Summertime" (black label), 1957 .... **$12.50-$25.00**
(if on Keen 3-4013, multicolored label, different catalog number, reissue), 195? .... **$10.00-$20.00**
82112, "Wonderful World"/"Along the Navajo Trail," 1960 ...... **$10.00-$20.00**
RCA Victor 47-7783, "Chain Gang"/"I Fall in Love Every Day," 1960 .... **$7.50-$15.00**
(with picture sleeve, add), 1960 .... **$12.50-$25.00**
47-7883, "Cupid"/"Farewell, My Darling," 1961 .... **$7.50-$15.00**
(with picture sleeve, add), 1961 .... **$12.50-$25.00**

Mono LPs

Keen A-2001, Sam Cooke, 1958 .... **$100.00-$200.00**
RCA Victor LPM-2555, Twistin' the Night Away, 1962 .... **$20.00-$40.00**

THE DELLS:

45s

Vee Jay 204, "Oh What a Nite"/"Jo-Jo," 1956 .... **$60.00-$120.00**
338, "Oh What a Nite"/"I Wanna Go Home," 1960 .... **$10.00-$20.00**
Cadet 5649, "Oh What a Night"/"Believe Me," 1969 .... **$3.00-$6.00**

LPs

Vee Jay LP 1010, Oh What a Nite (maroon label), 1959 .... **$400.00-$800.00**
(if black label with rainbow perimeter), 1961 .... **$150.00-$300.00**
(if late 1980s reissue, "Trade Mark Reg." on label), 198? .... **$5.00-$10.00**
Cadet LPS-824, The Dells Greatest Hits, 1969 .... **$25.00-$50.00**

THE DRAMATICS:

45s

Volt 4058, "Whatcha See is Whatcha Get"/"Thankful for Your Love," 1971 .... **$4.00-$8.00**
4075, "In the Rain"/"Good Soul Music," 1972 .... **$4.00-$8.00**

LPs

Volt VOS-6018, Whatcha See is Whatcha Get, 1972 .... **$12.50-$25.00**

THE DRIFTERS:

45s

Atlantic 1006, "Money Honey"/"The Way I Feel," 1953 .... **$40.00-$80.00**
2025, "There Goes My Baby"/"Oh My Love," 1959 .... **$12.50-$25.00**
2182, "On Broadway"/"Let the Music Play," 1963 .... **$7.50-$15.00**
2237, "Under the Boardwalk"/"I Don't Want to Go On Without You," 1964 .... **$7.50-$15.00**

78s

Atlantic 1006, "Money Honey"/"The Way I Feel," 1953 .... **$25.00-$50.00**
2025, "There Goes My Baby"/"Oh My Love," 1959 .... **$200.00-$400.00**
2040, "Dance With Me"/"(If You Cry) True Love, True Love" (last 78 by this group), 1959 .... **$250.00-$500.00**

Mono LPs

Atlantic 8022, Rockin' and Driftin' (black label), 1958 .... **$300.00-$600.00**
(if white "bullseye" label), 1958 .... **$250.00-$500.00**
(if red-purple label, white "fan" logo at right), 1953 .... **$20.00-$40.00**

Stereo LPs

Atlantic SD 8099, Under the Boardwalk (black and white photo of group on cover), 1964 .... **$60.00-$120.00**
(if color photo of group on cover), 1964 .... **$30.00-$60.00**

EARTH, WIND AND FIRE:

45s

Columbia 3-10090, "Shining Star"/"Yearnin', Learnin'," 1975 .... **$2.50-$5.00**
(with picture sleeve, add), 1975 .... **$5.00-$10.00**
3-10688, "Fantasy"/"Runnin'," 1978 .... **$2.50-$5.00**

Stereo LPs

Columbia PG 33694, Gratitude (2 LPs), 1975 .... **$7.50-$15.00**
(with bar code on back cover, reissue), 198? .... **$4.00-$8.00**

Quadraphonic LPs

Columbia CQ 32194, Head to the Sky, 1973 .... **$10.00-$20.00**
CQ 32712, Open Our Eyes, 1974 .... **$10.00-$20.00**

THE FANTASTIC FOUR:

45s

Ric-Tic 113, "Can't Stop Looking For My Baby" (Pt. 1)/(Pt. 2), 1966 .... **$100.00-$200.00**
122, "The Whole World Is A Stage"/"Ain't Love Wonderful," 1967 .... **$7.50-$15.00**
Soul 35072, "On the Brighter Side of a Blue World"/"I'm Gonna Hurry On," 1970 .... **$6.00-$12.00**

THE 5TH DIMENSION:

45s

Soul City 752, "I'll Be Loving You Forever"/"Train, Keep On Moving," 1966 .... **$30.00-$60.00**
756, "Up, Up and Away"/"Which Way to Nowhere," 1967 .... **$4.00-$8.00**
772, "Aquarius/Let the Sunshine In (The Flesh Failures)"/"Don'tcha Hear Me Callin' To Ya," 1969 .... **$4.00-$8.00**
(if yellow vinyl promo), 1969 .... **$7.50-$15.00**
(with picture sleeve, add), 1969 .... **$4.00-$8.00**

THE FIVE KEYS:

45s

Aladdin 3099, "The Glory of Love"/"Hucklebuck with Jimmy," 1951 .... **$500.00-$1,000.00**
3127, "Red Sails in the Sunset"/"Be Anything, But Be Mine," 1952 .... **$4,500.00-$6,000.00**
3245, "Deep in My Heart"/"How Do You Expect Me to Get It," 1954 .... **$400.00-$800.00**
Capitol F-2945, "Ling, Ting, Tong"/"I'm Alone," 1954 .... **$20.00-$40.00**
F-3392, "She's the Most"/"I Dreamt I Dwelt in Heaven" (if regular large hole), 1956 .... **$20.00-$40.00**
(if small hole), 1956 .... **$35.00-$70.00**

THE FOUR TOPS:

45s

Grady 012, "If Only I Had Known"/(unknown) (credited to the "Four Aims"), 1956 .... **$300.00-$600.00**
Motown 1062, "Baby I Need Your Loving"/"Call On Me," 1964 .. **$7.50-$15.00**
ABC Dunhill 4339, "Ain't No Woman (Like the One I've Got)"/"The Good Lord Knows," 1973 .... **$2.50-$5.00**
Casablanca 2338, "When She Was My Girl"/"Something to Remember," 1981 .... **$2.00-$4.00**

LPs

ABC Dunhill DSX-50129, Keeper of the Castle, 1972 .... **$6.00-$12.00**
Motown M9-809A3, Anthology (3 LPs), 1974 .... **$10.00-$20.00**

ARETHA FRANKLIN:

45s

Checker 941, "Precious Lord" (Pt. 1)/(Pt. 2), 1960 .... **$7.50-$15.00**
Atlantic 2403, "Respect"/"Dr. Feelgood," 1967 .... **$5.00-$10.00**
2464, "Chain of Fools"/"Prove It," 1967 .... **$5.00-$10.00**
Arista 9354, "Freeway of Love"/"Until You Say You Love Me," 1985 .... **$1.50-$3.00**
(if on pink vinyl promo, "Freeway of Love" on both sides), 1985 .... **$10.00-$20.00**
(with picture sleeve, add), 1985 .... **$1.50-$3.00**

Mono LPs

Checker 10009, Songs of Faith (with Aretha sitting at the piano), 1965 .... **$250.00-$500.00**
10009, Gospel Soul (retitled from above), 1967 .... **$10.00-$20.00**
Atlantic 8176, Aretha: Lady Soul, 1968 .... **$15.00-$30.00**

Stereo LPs

Atlantic SD-8176, Aretha: Lady Soul (green-blue label), 1968 ... **$10.00-$20.00**
(if on green-red label), 1969 .... **$6.00-$12.00**

THE FRIENDS OF DISTINCTION:

45s

RCA Victor 74-0107, "Grazing in the Grass"/"I Really Hope You Do," 1969 .... **$3.00-$6.00**
74-0319, "Love or Let Me Be Lonely"/"This Generation," 1970 .. **$3.00-$6.00**

MARVIN GAYE:

45s

Tamla 54068, "Stubborn Kind of Fellow"/"It Hurts Me Too," 1962 .... **$15.00-$30.00**
54176, "I Heard It Through The Grapevine"/"You're What's Happening (In The World Today)," 1968 .... **$5.00-$10.00**
Columbia 38-03302, "Sexual Healing"/(instrumental), 1982 .... **$2.00-$4.00**
(if on Columbia CNR-03344, single-sided release), 1982 .... **$3.00-$6.00**

LPs

Tamla TS 258, How Sweet It Is To Be Loved By You, 1965 .... **$25.00-$50.00**
TS 285, I Heard It Through the Grapevine, 1969 .... **$10.00-$20.00**
TS 310, What's Going On, 1971 .... **$7.50-$15.00**
Columbia FC 38197, Midnight Love, 1982 .... **$5.00-$10.00**
(if on Columbia PC 38197, reissue), 1986 .... **$4.00-$8.00**

THE INTRUDERS:

45s

Gamble 201, "(We'll Be) United"/"Up and Down the Ladder," 1966 ....**$5.00-$10.00**

214, "Cowboys to Girls"/"Turn the Hands of Time," 1968 ....**$5.00-$10.00**

Philadelphia International 3624, "I'll Always Love My Mama" (Pt. 1)/(Pt. 2), 1977 ....**$2.50-$5.00**

MICHAEL JACKSON:

45s

Motown 1202, "I Wanna Be Where You Are"/"We Got A Good Thing Going," 1972 ....**$2.50-$5.00**

(with picture sleeve, add), 1972 ....**$5.00-$10.00**

Epic 9-50742, "Don't Stop 'Til You Get Enough"/"I Can't Help It," 1979 ....**$2.00-$4.00**

34-03509, "Billie Jean"/"Can't Get Outta the Rain," 1983 ....**$2.00-$4.00**

(if on Epic ENR-03575, single-sided budget release), 1983 ....**$7.50-$15.00**

34 79656, "You Rock My World" (same on both sides), 2001 ....**$1.00-$2.00**

(with picture sleeve, add), 2001 ....**$1.00-$2.00**

LPs

Motown M 755, Ben (if Michael Jackson only on cover), 1972.....**$7.50-$15.00**

(if Michael Jackson and rats on cover), 1972 ....**$30.00-$60.00**

Epic QE 38112, Thriller, 1982 ....**$4.00-$8.00**

(if on Epic 8E8 38867, picture disc), 1983....................**$10.00-$20.00**

(if on Epic HE 48112, half-speed mastered edition), 1982 ....**$20.00-$40.00**

ER 59000, HIStory: Past, Present and Future—Book 1 (3 LPs), 1995 ....**$10.00-$20.00**

CHAKA KHAN:

45s

Warner Bros 8683, "I'm Every Woman"/"Woman in a Man's World" (Burbank palm trees label), 1978....................**$4.00-$8.00**

(if tan label), 1978....................**$2.50-$5.00**

29195, "I Feel For You"/"Chinatown," 1984 ....**$2.00-$4.00**

(with picture sleeve, add), 1984....................**$2.00-$4.00**

LPs

Warner Bros. 25162, I Feel For You, 1984 ....**$5.00-$10.00**

GLADYS KNIGHT AND THE PIPS:

45s

Huntom 2510, "Every Beat of My Heat"/"Room in Your Heart," 1961 ....**$250.00-$500.00**

Vee Jay 386, "Every Beat of My Heart"/"Room In Your heart," 1961 ....**$10.00-$20.00**

Soul 35039, "I Heard It Through the Grapevine"/"It's Time To Go Now," 1967 ....**$5.00-$10.00**

Buddah 383, "Midnight Train to Georgia"/"Window Raising Granny," 1973 ....**$2.50-$5.00**

LPs

Fury 1003, Letter Full of Tears, 1962....................**$250.00-$500.00**

Soul SS 731, If I Were Your Woman, 1971....................**$7.50-$15.00**

Buddah BDS 5141, Imagination, 1973 ....**$6.00-$12.00**

RAMSEY LEWIS:

45s

Cadet 5506, "The 'In' Crowd"/"Since I Fell For You," 1966 ....**$3.00-$6.00**

5541, "Wade in the Water"/"Ain't That Peculiar," 1966....................**$4.00-$8.00**

Columbia 10103, "Sun Goddess"/"Jungle Strut," 1975 ....**$2.50-$5.00**

Stereo LPs

Cadet LPS-671, The Ramsey Lewis Trio in Chicago, 1966...........**$7.50-$15.00**

Columbia KC 33194, Sun Goddess, 1974....................**$5.00-$10.00**

DARLENE LOVE:

45s

Philles 111, "(Today I Met) The Boy I'm Gonna Marry"/"My Heart Beat a Little Bit Faster," 1963 ....**$15.00-$30.00**

111, "(Today I Met) The Boy I'm Gonna Marry"/"Playing for Keeps," 1963 ....**$10.00-$20.00**

123, "Stumble and Fall"/"(He's A) Quiet Guy" (yellow-red label stock copy), 1964....................**$400.00-$800.00**

(if promo, yellow-red label, "D.J. Copy Not for Sale" on label), 1964 ....**$150.00-$300.00**

HAROLD MELVIN AND THE BLUE NOTES:

45s

Landa 703, "Get Out (And Let Me Cry)"/"You May Not Love Me" (credited to "The Blue Notes"), 1964....................**$8.00-$16.00**

Philadelphia International 3520, "If You Don't Know Me By Now"/"Let Me Into Your World," 1972....................**$2.50-$5.00**

3562, "Bad Luck" (Pt. 1)/(Pt. 2), 1975 ....**$2.50-$5.00**

LPs

Philadelphia International KZ 32407, Black & Blue, 1973 ....**$6.00-$12.00**

Quadraphonic LPs

Philadelphia International ZQ 32407, Black & Blue, 1973 ....**$10.00-$20.00**

PZQ 33808, Wake Up Everybody, 1975....................**$10.00-$20.00**

THE MIDNIGHTERS:

10-inch LPs

Federal 295-90, Their Greatest Hits, 1954 ....**$6,000.00-$8,000.00**

Mono LPs

Federal 541, Their Greatest Hits (red cover), 1955................**$750.00-$1,500.00**

(if yellow cover), 1955 ....**$500.00-$1,000.00**

THE MILLS BROTHERS:

78s

Brunswick 6197, "Tiger Rag"/"Nobody's Sweetheart," 1931 ....**$15.00-$30.00**

6625, "Smoke Rings"/"My Honey's Loving Arms," 1933..........**$15.00-$30.00**

Decca 4187, "Lazy River"/"627 Stomp," 1942 ....**$6.00-$12.00**

18318, "Paper Doll"/"I'll Be Around," 1942 ....**$5.00-$10.00**

10-inch LPs

Decca DL 5102, Souvenir Album, 1950 ....**$25.00-$50.00**

DL 5516, Four Boys and a Guitar, 1954....................**$25.00-$50.00**

Mono LPs

Dot DLP 3103, Mmmm, the Mills Brothers, 1958 ....**$10.00-$20.00**

DLP-3565, Gems by the Mills Brothers, 1964....................**$6.00-$12.00**

THE MOMENTS/RAY, GOODMAN AND BROWN:

45s

Hog 1000, "Baby I Want You"/(B-side unknown) (as "The Moments"), 196? ....**$1,000.00-$2,000.00**

Stang 5012, "Love on a Two-Way Street"/"I Won't Do Anything" (as "The Moments"), 1970 ....**$4.00-$8.00**

Polydor 2033, "Special Lady"/"Deja Vu" (as "Ray, Goodman and Brown"), 1979 ....**$2.50-$5.00**

LPs

Stang ST-1006, The Moments Live at the New York State Womans Prison, 1971 ....**$12.50-$25.00**

Polydor PD-106240, Ray, Goodman & Brown, 1979....................**$5.00-$10.00**

THE MOONGLOWS:

45s

Chance 1147, "Baby Please"/"Whistle My Love," 1953 ....**$500.00-$1,000.00**

(if red vinyl), 1953....................**$2,250.00-$3,000.00**

Chess 1581, "Sincerely"/"Tempting," 1954 ....**$30.00-$60.00**

1705, "Ten Commandments of Love"/"Mean Old Blues" (as "Harvey and the Moonglows"), 1958....................**$15.00-$30.00**

78s

Champagne 7500, "I Just Can't Tell No Lie"/"I've Been Your Dog (Ever Since I've Been Your Man)," 1952 ....**$500.00-$1,000.00**

Chance 1147, "Baby Please"/"Whistle My Love," 1953 ....**$150.00-$300.00**

Chess 1581, "Sincerely"/"Tempting," 1954 ....**$25.00-$50.00**

Mono LPs

Chess LP 1430, Look! It's the Moonglows, 1959 ....**$250.00-$500.00**

(if on Chess CH-9193, reissue), 1987....................**$6.00-$12.00**

THE O'JAYS:

45s

King 5377, "The Story of My Heart"/"(Do The) Wiggle" (credited to "The Mascots"), 1960....................**$60.00-$120.00**

Neptune 22, "Deeper (In Love with You)"/"I've Got the Groove," 1970 ....**$4.00-$8.00**

Philadelphia International 3517, "Back Stabbers"/"Sunshine," 1972 ....**$2.50-$5.00**

3524, "Love Train"/"Who Am I," 1973 ....**$2.50-$5.00**

LPs

Imperial LP-12290, Comin' Through, 1965 ....**$25.00-$50.00**

Philadelphia International KZ 32408, Ship Ahoy, 1973 ....**$5.00-$10.00**

THE ORIOLES:

45s

Jubilee 5000, "It's Too Soon to Know"/"Barbara Lee," 1951 ....**$2,000.00-$4,000.00**

5017, "What Are You Doing New Year's Eve?"/"Lonely Christmas," 1951 ....**$400.00-$800.00**

(with picture sleeve produced three years later, add), 1954 ....**$500.00-$1,000.00**

5122, "Crying in the Chapel"/"Don't You Think I Ought to Know," 1953 ....**$40.00-$80.00**

5172, "Runaround"/"Count Your Blessings Instead of Sheep," 1954 ....**$25.00-$50.00**

5363, "Tell Me So"/"At Night" (credited to "Sonny Til and the Orioles"), 1959 ..... **$7.50-$15.00**

78s

It's a Natural 5000, "It's Too Soon to Know"/"Barbara Lee," 1948 ..... **$150.00-$300.00**

Jubilee 5000, "It's Too Soon to Know"/"Barbara Lee," 1948 ..... **$75.00-$150.00**

5108, "Teardrops on My Pillow"/"Hold Me, Thrill Me, Kiss Me," 1953 ..... **$50.00-$100.00**

5122, "Crying in the Chapel"/"Don't You Think I Ought to Know," 1953 ..... **$30.00-$60.00**

THE ORLONS:

45s

Cameo 231, "Don't Hang Up"/"The Conservative," 1962 ..... **$10.00-$20.00**

(with picture sleeve, add), 1962 ..... **$20.00-$40.00**

243, "South Street"/"Them Terrible Boots," 1963 ..... **$10.00-$20.00**

(with picture sleeve, add), 1963 ..... **$20.00-$40.00**

LPs

Cameo C 1041, South Street, 1963 ..... **$30.00-$60.00**

C 1061, The Orlons' Biggest Hits, 1964 ..... **$25.00-$50.00**

WILSON PICKETT:

45s

Double L 713, "If You Need Me"/"Baby Call On Me," 1963 ..... **$10.00-$20.00**

Atlantic 2320, "634-5789 (Soulsville, U.S.A.)"/"That's a Man's Way," 1966 ..... **$7.50-$15.00**

2365, "Mustang Sally"/"Three Time Loser," 1966 ..... **$7.50-$15.00**

Mono LPs

Atlantic 8114, In the Midnight Hour, 1965 ..... **$20.00-$40.00**

8136, The Wicked Pickett, 1967 ..... **$20.00-$40.00**

Stereo LPs

Double L SDL-8300, It's Too Late, 1963 ..... **$35.00-$70.00**

Atlantic SD 8136, The Wicked Pickett, 1967 ..... **$15.00-$30.00**

SD 8215, Hey Jude, 1969 ..... **$10.00-$20.00**

THE POINTER SISTERS:

45s

Atlantic 2845, "Don't Try to Take the Fifth"/"Tulsa County," 1971 ..... **$10.00-$20.00**

Blue Thumb 229, "Yes We Can Can"/"Jada," 1973 ..... **$3.00-$6.00**

Planet 45901, "Fire"/"Love is Like a Rolling Stone," 1978 ..... **$2.00-$4.00**

(with picture sleeve, add), 1978 ..... **$3.00-$6.00**

LPs

Blue Thumb BTS-48, The Pointer Sisters, 1973 ..... **$6.00-$12.00**

Planet 60203, Pointer Sisters' Greatest Hits, 1982 ..... **$5.00-$10.00**

LLOYD PRICE:

45s

ABC Paramount 9972, "Stagger Lee"/"You Need Love," 1958 ..... **$10.00-$20.00**

10018, "Personality"/"Have You Ever Had the Blues," 1959 ..... **$10.00-$20.00**

OTIS REDDING:

45s

Orbit 135, "Shout Bamalama"/"Fat Girl," 1961 ..... **$150.00-$300.00**

Volt 141, "Try a Little Tenderness"/"I'm Sick Y'All," 1966 ..... **$7.50-$15.00**

157, "(Sittin' On) The Dock of the Bay"/"Sweet Lorene" (if black-red label), 1968 ..... **$6.00-$12.00**

(if multicolor label), 1968 ..... **$5.00-$10.00**

Mono LPs

Atco 33-161, Pain in My Heart, 1964 ..... **$125.00-$250.00**

Volt 411, The Great Otis Redding Sings Soul Ballads, 1965 ..... **$45.00-$90.00**

Stereo LPs

Volt S-412, Otis Blue/Otis Redding Sings Soul, 1965 ..... **$25.00-$50.00**

S-419, The Dock of the Bay, 1968 ..... **$15.00-$30.00**

RUFUS FEATURING CHAKA KHAN:

45s

Epic 10691, "Read All About It"/"Brand New Day," 1971 ..... **$6.00-$12.00**

(with picture sleeve, add), 1971 ..... **$10.00-$20.00**

12010, "Tell Me Something Good"/"Smokin' Room," 1974 ..... **$2.50-$5.00**

12149, "Sweet Thing"/"Circles," 1975 ..... **$2.50-$5.00**

LPs

ABC X-783, Rufus, 1973 ..... **$5.00-$10.00**

D-909, Rufus Featuring Chaka Khan, 1975 ..... **$5.00-$10.00**

SAM AND DAVE:

45s

Stax 189, "Hold On! I'm a-Comin'"/"I Got Everything I Need," 1966 ..... **$7.50-$15.00**

231, "Soul Man"/"May I Baby," 1967 ..... **$6.00-$12.00**

Mono LPs

Stax ST-708, Hold On, I'm Comin', 1966 ..... **$20.00-$40.00**

ST-725, Soul Men, 1967 ..... **$15.00-$30.00**

Stereo LPs

Stax STS-708, Hold On, I'm Comin', 1966 ..... **$25.00-$50.00**

Atlantic SD 8205, I Thank You, 1968 ..... **$12.50-$25.00**

DEE DEE SHARP:

45s

Cameo 212, "Mashed Potato Time"/"Set My Heart at Ease," 1962 ..... **$10.00-$20.00**

274, "Wild!"/"Why Dontcha Ask Me?," 1963 ..... **$7.50-$15.00**

(with picture sleeve, add), 1963 ..... **$12.50-$25.00**

Philadelphia International 3638, "I Believe in Love"/"Just As Long As I Know You're Mine" (as "Dee Dee Sharp Gamble"), 1978 ..... **$2.50-$5.00**

Mono LPs

Cameo C-1018, It's Mashed Potato Time, 1962 ..... **$30.00-$60.00**

C-1027, All the Hits, 1962 ..... **$20.00-$40.00**

Stereo LPs

Cameo SC-1027, All the Hits, 1962 ..... **$25.00-$50.00**

Philadelphia International PZ 33839, Happy 'Bout the Whole Thing, 1976 ..... **$5.00-$10.00**

THE SPINNERS:

45s

Motown 1155, "In My Diary"/"(She's Gonna Love Me) At Sundown," 1969 ..... **$7.50-$1,500.00**

V.I.P. 25050, "In My Diary"/"(She's Gonna Love Me) At Sundown," 1969 ..... **$12.50-$25.00**

25057, "It's A Shame"/"Together We Can Make Such Sweet Music," 1970 ..... **$6.00-$12.00**

Atlantic 3355, "The Rubberband Man"/"Now That We're Together," 1976 ..... **$2.50-$5.00**

LPs

V.I.P. 405, 2nd Time Around, 1970 ..... **$20.00-$40.00**

Atlantic SD 7296, Mighty Love, 1974 ..... **$6.00-$12.00**

THE THREE DEGREES:

45s

Swan 4224, "Close Your Eyes"/"Gotta Draw the Line," 1965 ..... **$6.00-$12.00**

Neptune 23, "Reflections of Yesterday"/"What I See," 1970 ..... **$3.00-$6.00**

LPs

Roulette SR-42050, Maybe, 1970 ..... **$20.00-$40.00**

Philadelphia International KZ 32406, The Three Degrees, 1974 ..... **$6.00-$12.00**

IKE AND TINA TURNER:

45s

Sue 730, "A Fool in Love"/"The Way You Love Me," 1960 ..... **$15.00-$30.00**

Philles 131, "River Deep—Mountain High"/"I'll Keep You Happy," 1966 ..... **$10.00-$20.00**

Liberty 56216, "Proud Mary"/"Funkier Than a Mosquito's Tweeter," 1970 ..... **$3.00-$6.00**

LPs

Sue LP 2001, The Soul of Ike and Tina Turner, 1961 ..... **$200.00-$400.00**

LP 2003, Ike and Tina Turner's Kings of Rhythm Dance, 1962 ..... **$200.00-$400.00**

Philles PHLP 4011, River Deep—Mountain High (no cover printed, value is for record only), 1967 ..... **$4,000.00-$8,000.00**

United Artists UA-LA180-F, Nutbush City Limits, 1973 ..... **$6.00-$12.00**

BILLY WARD AND THE DOMINOES:

45s

Federal 12022AA, "Sixty Minute Man"/"I Can't Escape From You," 1951 ..... **$250.00-$500.00**

12068AA, "Have Mercy Baby"/"Deep Sea Blues," 1952 ..... **$125.00-$250.00**

12114, "The Bells"/"Pedal Pushin' Papa," 1952 ..... **$100.00-$200.00**

JACKIE WILSON:

45s

Brunswick 9-55024, "Reet Petite (The Finest Girl You Ever Want to Meet)"/"By the Light of the Silvery Moon," 1957 ..... **$15.00-$30.00**

Stereo LPs

Brunswick BL 754050, So Much (black label), 1960 ..... **$75.00-$150.00**

(if black label with rainbow bars), 1964 ..... **$12.50-$25.00**

CHAPTER 21

ROCK AND ROLL: THE EARLY YEARS

History

There will always be arguments on the first true "rock and roll" record. Arguments can be made for the jump boogie song "Rocket 88," recorded by Ike Turner's Kings of Rhythm (and credited to "Jackie Brenston and his Delta Cats") at Sam Phillips' Sun Studios and released on Chess Records, as the first "rock and roll" record. Others cite Bill Haley and His Comets' "(We're Gonna) Rock Around The Clock" for this honor, as it was the first "rock and roll" record to hit #1 on the Billboard charts. There are also some claims for the Chords' "Sh-Boom," Little Richard's "Tutti-Frutti," and Elvis Presley's "Heartbreak Hotel" as the first rock and roll record. All of these songs could take credit as the first rock and roll song, and so could many more.

No matter which song was first, the undeniable fact is that rock and roll music, a genre blending rhythm and blues music with country-western twang and pop sensibility, took the 1950s by storm and continues, in a myriad of formats and styles, to this day. Between 1955 and 1959, rock and roll music was at its first great creative period. Artists used different musical styles—country and western music mixed with rhythm and blues, thick soul blended with musical sincerity—and created sounds and melodies and rhythms no one had ever heard before.

In Texas, Bill Haley and His Comets took their western bop music nationwide with their teen dance classic "(We're Gonna) Rock Around The Clock." Buddy Holly and the Crickets followed the Comets out of Texas, and entered an

Photo credit: Courtesy of the Tom Kelly Archives, St. Louis, Mo.

*Although credited to Jackie Brenston and his Delta Cats, "Rocket 88" was actually performed by Ike Turner and his Kings of Rhythm. On an original 45, this record would certainly fetch $10,000.00 on the open market; this 78 is more affordable, relatively speaking, at **$300.00**.*

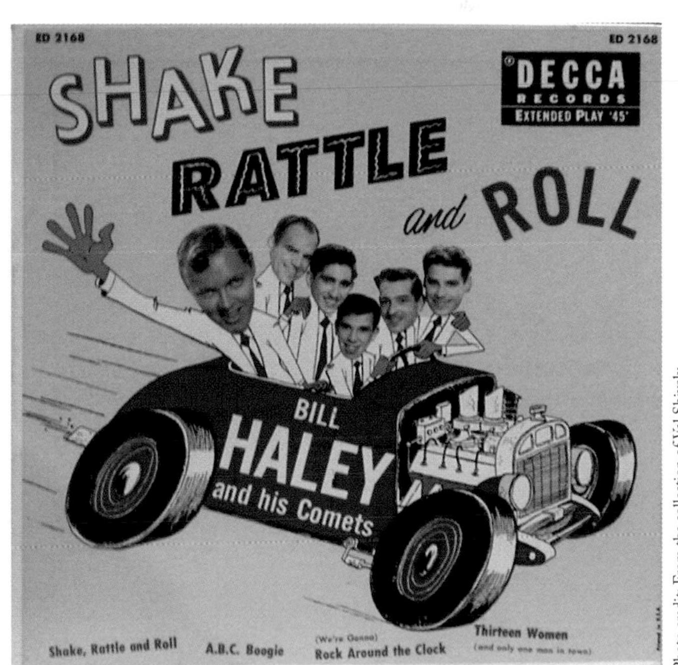

Photo credit: From the collection of Val Shively.

Bill Haley and His Comets' early recordings were available on several different formats, including this four-song EP, of which two of the songs—"Rock Around the Clock" and "Shake, Rattle and Roll"—are among Haley's most famous recordings.

***$120**, NM condition*

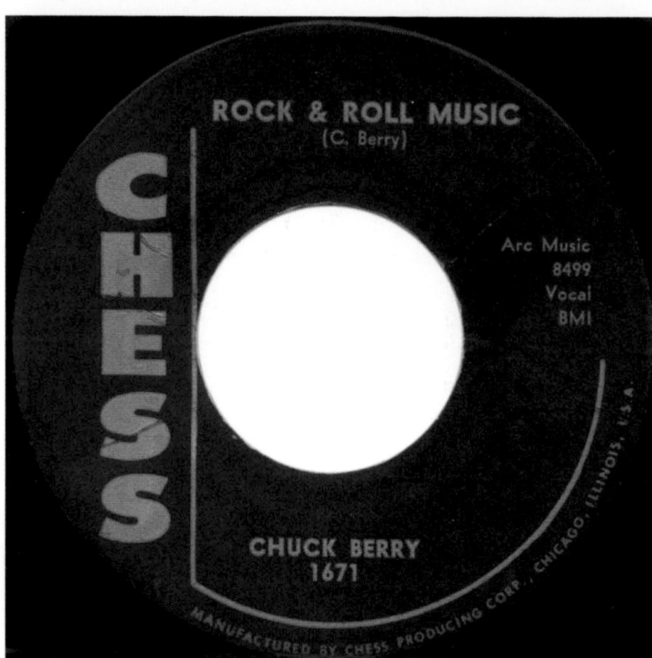

Among Chuck Berry's greatest hits is "Rock and Roll Music," a song that would be covered by both the Beach Boys and the Beatles.

***$10**, Good condition*

international spotlight. Meanwhile, Elvis Presley had shaken up Memphis and was on his way to conquering the world, and following him from the south were Jerry Lee Lewis, Carl Perkins, and the Everly Brothers.

In Chicago, the Chess/Checker labels had two of the most successful influences in the early rock and roll era—Chuck Berry on Chess, and Bo Diddley on Checker. Diddley, born Hubert Elias McDaniel, created the famous "Bo Diddley Beat," a clap-and-clap-and-clap-and-space-and-clap-clap rhythmic track featured in his hit "Bo Diddley," and later used by Buddy Holly, the Rolling Stones, George Michael and others. Meanwhile, Chuck Berry mixed the blues and intricate lyrics with his electric guitar, writing songs like "Johnny B. Goode" and "Sweet Little Sixteen," and influencing musicians on both sides of the Atlantic Ocean.

Other cities began to add their sound to the rock and roll fabric. In New Orleans, Fats Domino created a series of musical rock piano songs still being emulated by Louisiana musicians today. Other New Orleans artists added jazz and Dixieland music to their own R&B and boogie-woogie music, creating music that was perfect for parties or for passion. Also recording in New Orleans, but originally from Macon, George, was "Little Richard" Penniman. Little Richard was one of the most charismatic performers in the early rock era, with his high-coiffed pompadour, mascara, and face powder, but there was no denying his musical talent and the influences it provided. He brought high energy soul to the rock mix, and his songs "Tutti-Fruitti" and "Long Tall Sally" blasted from the nation's jukeboxes and radios.

There has been some argument that rock and roll and 45 RPM records came in at the same time. This is not correct. The 45 was created by RCA Records in 1948, and there were swing, blues, and contemporary recordings made in that format. In fact, by the mid-1950s—the beginning years of rock and roll—the 45 and the 78 RPM records were pressed in nearly equal amounts by both major and minor record companies. However, the cost-effectiveness of pressing a thin yet durable 45 eventually outweighed pressing bulky, fragile 78s, and as the 1950s drew to a close,

Photo credit: 78 photograph courtesy Scott Primeau, Primeau Music, London, Ont; 45 photograph from the collection of the author.

The New York City vocal duo of Tommy Graph and Jerry Landis had a minor hit with the song "Hey Schoolgirl." It was also released on a 78, in which the duo's real names, Paul Simon and Art Garfunkel, were listed on the writer credits.

*(L to R) **$35**, VG+ condition; **$75**, NM condition*

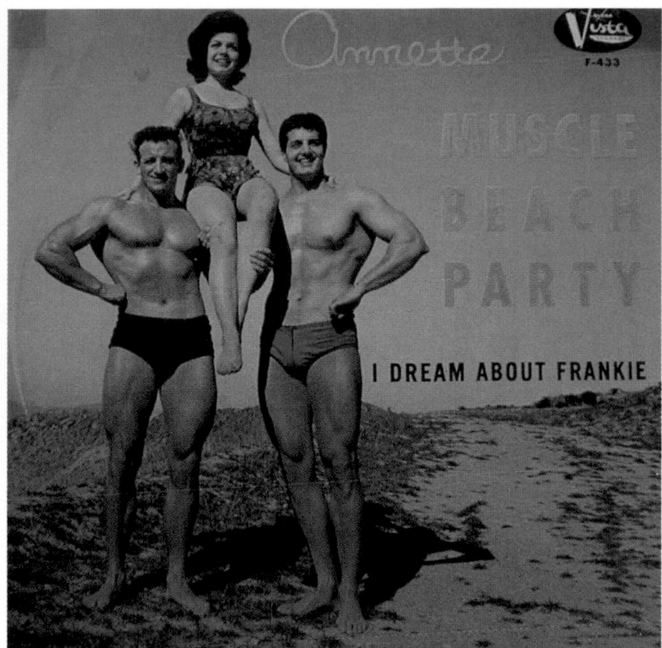

The most popular Mouseketeer of all time, Annette Funicello's albums, 45s and picture sleeves have remained collectible for over 40 years. This picture sleeve, promoting her appearance in the movie Muscle Beach Party, can be worth up to $30 in near-mint condition.

***$30** for NM sleeve*

This Chubby Checker greatest hits album includes a removable poster and stickers. Surprisingly, Checker's hit songs have never been commercially released on compact disc, nor have any songs from his labelmates Dee Dee Sharp, Bobby Rydell, the Orlons, or the Tymes—making Cameo-Parkway records increase in collectible value over the years.

***$30**, NM condition*

10-inch 78s disappeared as a viable listening alternative.

The first period of rock and roll nearly ended in 1959, as a series of events derailed some careers and ultimately ended others. Elvis Presley was drafted and served in the Army, away from his loyal fans. Jerry Lee Lewis married his 13-year-old cousin, and the negative publicity from the incestuous relationship destroyed his career. A plane crash took the lives of Buddy Holly, Ritchie Valens, and the Big Bopper. Chuck Berry spent time in jail; Little Richard ended his career and followed the path of the Lord.

The music that filled the void was ultimately provided by "teen idols," non-threatening singers whose good looks and adequate singing ability helped sell millions of singles and albums. Many of these teen idols came from smaller record companies like Chancellor, Swan and Parkway, although ABC-Paramount did have Paul Anka, and RCA Victor had Neil Sedaka. While male teen idols remain collectible to this day, mostly their 45 RPM picture sleeves, female teen idols draw the highest collectible prices. 45s and LPs by Annette Funicello, Hayley Mills, and Shelley Fabares can command premium values, especially if the album covers and picture sleeves are in top condition.

Although many of the early legends of rock and roll had disappeared, others came to hold the torch high. Freddy "Boom Boom" Cannon, for example, rocked out on almost every song he recorded in the 1960s. Del Shannon's "Runaway" was the first in a series of upbeat rockers with downbeat lyrics. Chubby Checker turned a simple dance, the Twist, into a national dance sensation. And Roy Orbison's impassioned, heartwrenching vocals on songs like "Only the Lonely" and "Crying" made him one of the top stars of the early 1960s.

Just as big band and swing music had regular radio broadcasts by its biggest stars, rock and roll benefited from several local and national televised music shows, the most popular of which was *American Bandstand*. First hosted by

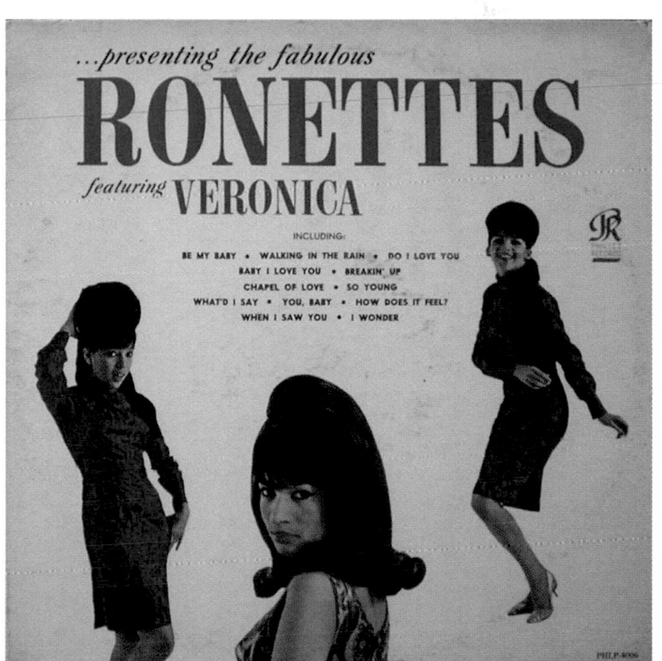

Photo credit: Courtesy Last Vestige Music Store, Albany, N.Y.

A perfect example of the effectiveness of Phil Spector's "Wall of Sound" production techniques can be found on this rare Ronettes album. Among the many hits on this LP are such strong tracks as "Be My Baby," "Baby I Love You," and "Walkin' in the Rain."

***$200**, Good condition*

Bob Horn, and later Dick Clark, millions of kids dreamed of appearing on the popular dance show, watching famous performers on the Bandstand stage, dancing to the latest songs, and even participating in the legendary "rate-a-record" survey, in which nearly every song had a great beat and you could dance to it.

During the early 1960s, producer Phil Spector created a series of pop songs that combined the talents of top songwriters with a "Wall of Sound," a multitracked symphony of strings, guitars, drums, and piano, all modeled to accentuate the vocalist, the lyrics and the melody. What Spector called "little symphonies for the kids" were classic pop tracks from Brill Building songwriters, mixed with Spector's aural orchestrations. Records by Spector's top stars—The Ronettes, The Crystals, Darlene Love, Bobb B. Soxx and the Blue Jeans, and later The Righteous Brothers, are still as influential and important as the day they were first recorded and released.

Although the overall description of these genres is "fifties" music, music from as late as 1963 is grouped into this collection, as the arrival of the Beatles changed the musical landscape forever. Many artists who had hits on a constant basis in the 1950s and early 1960s were suddenly squeezed off the radio in favor of British singers and bands. Even *American Bandstand* moved in 1964 from its daily broadcasts in Philadelphia to a Saturday-only show in Los Angeles.

What To Look For

While well-played 45s can still be found in big cardboard boxes at the flea market or church sale, near-mint copies of 1950s records are becoming harder to find with every passing year.

Records were often removed from their picture sleeves, so that the sleeve could be tacked to a bedroom wall or trimmed for a scrapbook. This makes picture sleeves from the 1950s very difficult to find, and extremely collectible in near-mint condition.

In the late 1950s and early 1960s, some record companies experimented with specially produced stereo 45s. These special 45s had smaller print runs, and actually contain true stereo recordings with proper microphone placement and sound separation, as opposed to rechanneled or "fake" stereo, where the singer is in one speaker and the music is in the other.

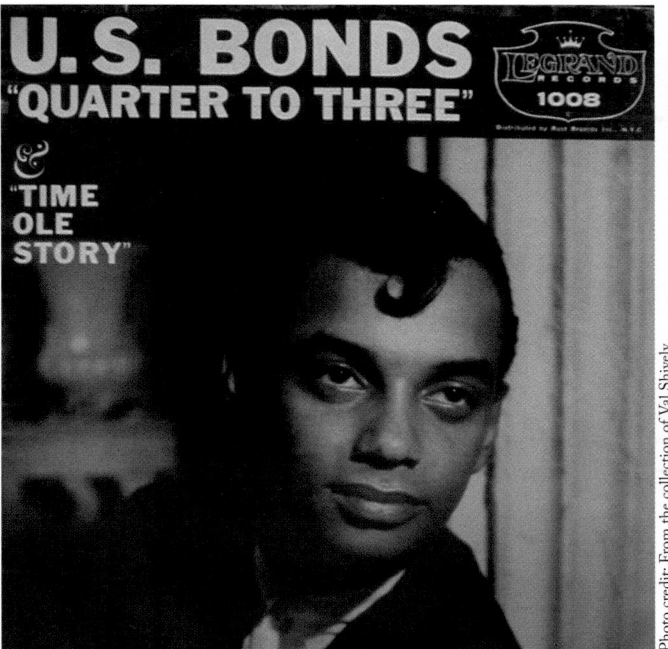

Photo credit: From the collection of Val Shively.

The producer of Gary Anderson's records suggested he rename himself "U.S. Bonds," to convince DJs to add a promotional service announcement to their patter (as in, "That was Quarter to Three, by [or buy] U.S. Bonds.") Anderson's later releases were credited as "Gary U.S. Bonds," the name he is known by today.
***$40**, for NM sleeve*

Books

Neely, Tim, *Goldmine Price Guide to 45 RPM Records*, Krause Publications, Iola, WI, 1999.

Whitburn, Joel, *Top Pop Singles 1955-1996*, Record Research, Inc., Menomonee Falls, WI, 1997.

Tobler, John, *The Buddy Holly Story*, Beaufort Books, N.Y., 1979.

Jackson, John A., *American Bandstand: Dick Clark and the Making of a Rock 'n' Roll Empire*, Oxford University Press, New York, NY, 1997.

Ribowski, Mark, *Phil Spector: He's A Rebel*, Cooper Square Press, NY, 2000.

Spector, Ronnie, with Waldron, Vince, *Be My Baby: How I Survived Mascara, Miniskirts, and Madness or My Life as a Fabulous Ronette*, Harmony Books/Crown Publishers, Inc., New York, NY, 1990.

Museums:

Rock And Roll Hall Of Fame And Museum, One Key Plaza, Cleveland, OH, 44114, (216) 781-7625: http://www.rockhall.com

Web Pages

Chubby Checker's home page: http://chubbychecker.com

Chuck Berry's home page: http://www.chuckberry.com

The official Jerry Lee Lewis home page: http://www.jerryleelewis.net

A fan page devoted to the career of Fats Domino: http://www.fortunecity.com/tinpan/costello/472

Roy Orbison's official Web site: http://www.orbison.com

Usenet newsgroups: rec.music.rock-pop-r+b.1950s

Mark Landwehr's Phil Spector Label Gallery, which contains a complete run of Philles records: http://www.toltbbs.com/~msland/Spector/PSindex.htm

Freddy Cannon's biggest hit, "Palisades Park," was a former B-side that several radio DJs "flipped over" to discover as a hit. What's even more remarkable is that the songwriter, Chuck Barris, later created such early reality TV fare as The Newlywed Game *and* The Gong Show.

***$8**, VG condition*

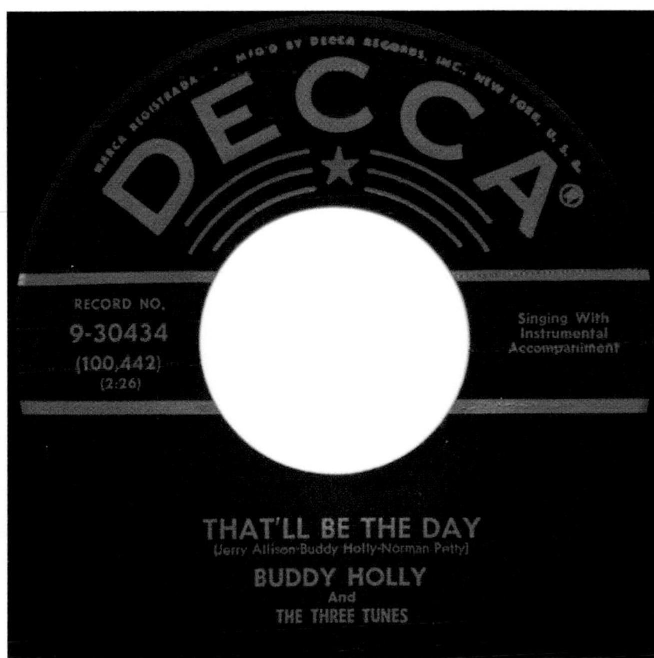

Buddy Holly's "That'll Be The Day" was originally recorded for Decca with his group, the Crickets, being rechristened "The Three Tunes." This version is an entirely different mix than the hit version that would eventually be released on Brunswick a year later.

***$250**, NM condition*

Photo credit: From the collection of Val Shively.

Roy Orbison's picture sleeves are getting harder and harder to find. Here's one for his song "Crying"—a second picture sleeve for "Crying" would appear in the late 1980s, when he re-recorded the song as a duet with k.d. lang.

***$30**, for VG+ sleeve*

PAUL ANKA:

45s

ABC-Paramount 9831, "Diana"/"Don't Gamble with Love," 1957 .... **$10.00-$20.00**

10082, "Puppy Love"/"Adam and Eve," 1960 .... **$7.50-$15.00**

(with picture sleeve, add), 1960.......... **$12.50-$25.00**

Stereo 45s

ABC-Paramount S-10011, "I Miss You So"/"Late Last Night," 1959 .... **$25.00-$50.00**

S-10040, "Put Your Head on My Shoulder"/"Don't Ever Leave Me," 1959 .... **$25.00-$50.00**

Mono LPs

ABC-Paramount 240, Paul Anka, 1958.......... **$25.00-$50.00**

347, Paul Anka Swings for Young Lovers, 1960 .... **$15.00-$30.00**

Stereo LPs

ABC-Paramount S-296, My Heart Sings, 1959 .... **$25.00-$50.00**

S-353, Anka at the Copa, 1960.......... **$20.00-$40.00**

ANNETTE:

45s

Buena Vista 349, "First Name Initial"/"My Heart Became of Age," 1959 .... **$7.50-$15.00**

(with picture sleeve, add), 1959.......... **$15.00-$30.00**

414, "Teenage Wedding"/"Walkin' and Talkin'," 1962.......... **$10.00-$20.00**

(with rare picture sleeve, add), 1962.......... **$300.00-$600.00**

433, "Muscle Beach Party"/"I Dream About Frankie," 1964 .... **$7.50-$15.00**

(with picture sleeve, add), 1964.......... **$15.00-$30.00**

Mono LPs

Buena Vista BV-3301, Annette, 1959.......... **$60.00-$120.00**

BV-3312, The Story of My Teens, 1962.......... **$37.50-$75.00**

Stereo LPs

Buena Vista STER-3314, Muscle Beach Party, 1963 .... **$75.00-$150.00**

STER-3320, Annette on Campus, 1964 .... **$50.00-$100.00**

FRANKIE AVALON:

45s

Chancellor 1011, "Dede Dinah"/"Ooh La La," 1958.......... **$7.50-$15.00**

1031, "Venus"/"I'm Broke," 1959 .... **$10.00-$20.00**

(with picture sleeve, add), 1959.......... **$20.00-$40.00**

Stereo 45s

Chancellor S-1031, "Venus"/"I'm Broke," 1959 .... **$20.00-$40.00**

S-1045, "Why"/"Swingin' on a Rainbow," 1959.......... **$20.00-$40.00**

Mono LPs

Chancellor CHL 5001, Frankie Avalon (pink label), 1958 .... **$25.00-$50.00**

(if black label), 1959.......... **$20.00-$40.00**

CHLX 5004, Swingin' on a Rainbow, 1959.......... **$20.00-$40.00**

Stereo LPs

Chancellor CHLXS 5004, Swingin' on a Rainbow, 1959.......... **$25.00-$50.00**

CHLS 5027, You're Mine, 1962 .... **$20.00-$40.00**

CHUCK BERRY:

45s

Chess 1604, "Maybellene"/"Wee Wee Hours," 1955.......... **$25.00-$50.00**

1626, "Roll Over Beethoven"/"Drifting Heart," 1956.......... **$25.00-$50.00**

1671, "Rock & Roll Music"/"Blue Feeling," 1957 .... **$15.00-$30.00**

1691, "Johnny B. Goode"/"Around and Around," 1958 .... **$15.00-$30.00**

1729, "Back in the U.S.A."/"Memphis Tennessee," 1959.......... **$15.00-$30.00**

78s

Chess 1604, "Maybelline"/"Wee Wee Hours," 1955 .... **$35.00-$70.00**

1747, "Too Pooped to Pop"/"Let It Rock," 1960 .... **$500.00-$1,000.00**

LPs

Chess LP-1426, After School Session, 1958.......... **$100.00-$200.00**

LP-1432, One Dozen Berrys, 1958 .... **$100.00-$200.00**

LP-1435, Chuck Berry Is On Top, 1959 .... **$90.00-$180.00**

THE BIG BOPPER:

45s

D Records 1008, "Chantilly Lace"/"The Purple People Eater Meets the Witch Doctor," 1958 .... **$125.00-$250.00**

Mercury 71219, "Beggar to a King"/"Crazy Blue" (credited to Jape Richardson), 1957 .... **$30.00-$60.00**

71343, "Chantilly Lace"/"The Purple People Eater Meets the Witch Doctor," 1958.......... **$10.00-$20.00**

LPs

Mercury MG-20402, Chantilly Lace (black label), 1959.......... **$250.00-$500.00**

(if red label with black, or black and white Mercury logo at top), 1964 .... **$100.00-$200.00**

(if red label with twelve Mercury logos around perimeter of label), 196? .... **$12.50-$25.00**

(if Chicago Skyline label), 1975 .... **$7.50-$15.00**

GARY "U.S." BONDS:

45s

Legrand 1003, "New Orleans"/"Please Forgive Me," 1960 .... **$7.50-$15.00**

(if purple label, artist is "By-U.S. Bonds"), 1960 .... **$10.00-$20.00**

1008, "Quarter to Three"/"Time Ole Story" (gold-red label, "U.S. Bonds"), 1961.......... **$7.50-$15.00**

(if purple label, "U.S. Bonds"), 1961 .... **$20.00-$40.00**

(with picture sleeve, add), 1961.......... **$20.00-$40.00**

1009, "School Is Out"/"One Million Years" (listed as "Gary U.S. Bonds"), 1961.......... **$7.50-$15.00**

(if artist is "U.S. Bonds," last 45 on Legrand labeled without the word "Gary"), 1961.......... **$10.00-$20.00**

LPs

Legrand LLP-3001, Dance 'Til Quarter to Three, 1961 .... **$50.00-$100.00**

LLP-3002, Twist Up Calypso, 1962 .... **$35.00-$70.00**

FREDDY "BOOM BOOM" CANNON:

45s

Swan 4031, "Tallahassee Lassie"/"You Know," 1959 .... **$10.00-$20.00**

4043, "Way Down Yonder in New Orleans"/"Fractured," 1959 .... **$10.00-$20.00**

(with picture sleeve, add), 1959.......... **$15.00-$30.00**

4106, "Palisades Park"/"June, July and August," 1962 .... **$8.00-$16.00**

Mono LPs

Swan LP-502, The Explosive! Freddy Cannon, 1960.......... **$60.00-$120.00**

LP-507, Freddy Cannon at Palisades Park, 1962.......... **$75.00-$150.00**

Stereo LPs

Swan LPS-502, The Explosive! Freddy Cannon, 1960.......... **$150.00-$300.00**

CHUBBY CHECKER:

45s

Parkway 804, "The Class"/"Schooldays, Oh Schooldays," 1959.... **$15.00-$30.00**

811, "The Twist"/"Toot" (first pressings, white label, blue print), 1960 .... **$15.00-$30.00**

(second pressings, orange label with black print), 1960 .... **$10.00-$20.00**

811, "The Twist"/"Twistin' U.S.A.," 1961 .... **$7.50-$15.00**

(if promo copy, yellow vinyl), 1961 .... **$75.00-$150.00**

(if promo vinyl, red vinyl), 1961.......... **$100.00-$200.00**

(with picture sleeve, add), 1961.......... **$12.50-$25.00**

824, "Let's Twist Again"/"Everything's Gonna Be Alright," 1961 .... **$7.50-$15.00**

(if on orange vinyl), 1961.......... **$100.00-$200.00**

(with picture sleeve, add), 1961.......... **$12.50-$25.00**

Mono LPs

Parkway P 7001, Twist with Chubby Checker (orange label), 1960 .... **$20.00-$40.00**

(if orange-yellow label), 1962.......... **$15.00-$30.00**

7004, Let's Twist Again (orange label), 1961 .... **$20.00-$40.00**

(if orange-yellow label), 1962 .... **$15.00-$30.00**

Stereo LPs

Parkway SP 7009, For Teen Twisters Only, 1962 .... **$20.00-$40.00**

SP 7022, Chubby Checker's Biggest Hits, 1962 .... **$15.00-$30.00**

JIMMY CLANTON:

45s

Ace 546, "Just a Dream"/"You Aim to Please," 1958.......... **$10.00-$20.00**

575, "Go, Jimmy, Go"/"I Trusted You" (white label), 1959.......... **$10.00-$20.00**

(if purple label), 1959 .... **$12.50-$25.00**

(with picture sleeve, add), 1959.......... **$15.00-$30.00**

DEE CLARK:

45s

Falcon 1009, "Oh Little Girl"/"Wondering," 1958 .... **$20.00-$40.00**

Abner 1029, "Hey Little Girl"/"If It Wasn't for Love," 1959 .... **$12.50-$25.00**

(with picture sleeve, add), 1959.......... **$20.00-$40.00**

Mono LPs

Abner LP-2000, Dee Clark, 1959.......... **$60.00-$120.00**

LP-2002, How About That, 1960.......... **$40.00-$80.00**

Stereo LPs

Abner SR-2000, Dee Clark, 1959.......... **$175.00-$350.00**

Abner SR-2002, How About That, 1960 .... **$60.00-$120.00**

EDDIE COCHRAN:

45s

Liberty 55112, "Twenty Flight Rock"/"Cradle Baby," 1957.......**$75.00-$150.00**
55144, "Summertime Blues"/"Live Again," 1958.......................**$15.00-$30.00**
55166, "C'mon Everybody"/"Don't Ever Let Me Go," 1958.....**$15.00-$30.00**

78s

Liberty 55144, "Summertime Blues"/"Live Again," 1958........**$250.00-$500.00**

LPs

Liberty LRP-3061, Singin' to My Baby (green label), 1957.....**$400.00-$800.00**
(if black label, reissue) 1960...**$150.00-$300.00**
LRP-3220, Never to Be Forgotten, 1962...............................**$50.00-$100.00**

THE CRICKETS:

45s

Brunswick 55009, "That'll Be the Day"/"I'm Lookin' for Someone to Love," 1957...............**$25.00-$50.00**
55035, "Oh, Boy!"/"Not Fade Away," 1957................................**$25.00-$50.00**
55053, "Maybe Baby"/"Tell Me How," 1958...............................**$25.00-$50.00**
Liberty 55392, "He's Old Enough to Know Better"/"I'm Feeling Better," 1961 ....**$12.50-$25.00**

78s

Brunswick 55009, "That'll Be The Day"/"I'm Lookin' for Someone to Love," 1957...............**$75.00-$150.00**

EPs

Brunswick EB 71036, The Chirping Crickets (contains "I'm Looking for Someone to Love"/"That'll Be the Day"/"Not Fade Away"/"Oh! Boy," value is for record and jacket), 1957.......................................**$300.00-$600.00**
EB 71038, The Sound of the Crickets (contains "Maybe Baby"/"Rock Me My Baby"/"Send Me Some Lovin'"/"Tell Me How," value is for record and jacket), 1958...**$250.00-$500.00**

LPs

Brunswick BL 54038, The "Chirping" Crickets
(if textured cover), 1957...**$400.00-$800.00**
(if regular cover), 1958..**$300.00-$600.00**
Coral CRL 57320, In Style with the Crickets, 1960...............**$100.00-$200.00**

THE CRYSTALS:

45s

Philles 106, "He's a Rebel"/"I Love You Eddie"
(if orange label), 1962..**$30.00-$60.00**
(if light blue label), 1962..**$20.00-$40.00**
(if yellow-red label, reissue), 1964.................................**$12.50-$25.00**
112, "Da Doo Ron Ron (When He Walked Me Home)"/"Git' It," 1963 ....**$15.00-$30.00**
115, "Then He Kissed Me"/"Brother Julius" (light blue label), 1963 ....**$20.00-$40.00**
(if yellow-red label), 1963..**$12.50-$25.00**

LPs

Philles PHLP-4000, Twist Uptown, 1962...............................**$300.00-$600.00**
PHLP-4001, He's a Rebel, 1963...**$300.00-$600.00**

DALE AND GRACE:

Michelle 921, "I'm Leaving It Up To You"/"That's What I Like," 1963 ....**$12.50-$25.00**
Montel 921, "I'm Leaving It Up To You"/"That's What I Like About You," 1963 ....**$6.00-$12.00**

LPs

Michelle 100, I'm Leaving It Up To You, 1964.........................**$75.00-$150.00**
Montel 100, I'm Leaving It Up to You, 1964............................**$75.00-$150.00**

BOBBY DAY:

45s

Class 211, "Little Bitty Pretty One"/"When the Swallows Come Back to Capistrano," 1957..............................**$12.50-$25.00**
229, "Rock-N Robin"/"Over and Over," 1958.........................**$15.00-$30.00**
RCA Victor 47-8196, "Buzz Buzz Buzz"/"Pretty Little Girl Next Door," 1963 ....**$5.00-$10.00**

JOEY DEE AND THE STARLITERS:

45s

Little 813/4, "Lorraine"/"The Girl I Walk to School," 1958....**$200.00-$400.00**
Roulette 4401, "Peppermint Twist—Part 1"/"Peppermint Twist—Part 2," 1961 ....**$8.00-$16.00**
4416, "Shout—Part 1"/"Shout—Part 2," 1962.........................**$7.50-$15.00**
(with picture sleeve, add), 1962..**$12.50-$25.00**

Mono LPs

Roulette R-25166, Doin' the Twist at the Peppermint Lounge, 1961 ....**$20.00-$40.00**
R-25171, All the World Is Twistin', 1962..............................**$15.00-$30.00**
S 503, The Peppermint Twisters, 1962..................................**$12.50-$25.00**

Stereo LPs

Roulette SR-25166, Doin' the Twist at the Peppermint Lounge, 1961 ....**$25.00-$50.00**
Roulette SR-25171, All the World Is Twistin', 1962...................**$20.00-$40.00**
Roulette SR-25173, Back at the Peppermint Lounge — Twistin', 1962 ....**$20.00-$40.00**

BO DIDDLEY:

45s

Checker 814, "Bo Diddley"/"I'm a Man," 1955........................**$25.00-$50.00**
931, "Say Man"/"Clock Strikes Twelve," 1959.........................**$15.00-$30.00**
(with picture sleeve, add), 1959...**$200.00-$400.00**

78s

Checker 814, "Bo Diddley"/"I'm A Man," 1955........................**$30.00-$60.00**
931, "Say Man"/"Clock Strikes Twelve," 1959.........................**$60.00-$120.00**

LPs

Checker LP 1431, Bo Diddley, 1958..**$75.00-$150.00**
LP 2974, Have Guitar, Will Travel, 1960..................................**$75.00-$150.00**
LP 2977, Bo Diddley Is a Gunslinger, 1961...............................**$75.00-$150.00**

FATS DOMINO:

45s

Imperial 45-5058, "The Fat Man"/"Detroit City Blues" (blue-label "script" logo, pressed around 1952, counterfeits exist), 1950..................**$1,000.00-$2,000.00**
45-5209, "How Long"/"Dreaming," 1952...................................**$40.00-$80.00**
(if on red vinyl), 1952...**$150.00-$300.00**
X5369, "Poor Me"/"I Can't Go On," 1955..................................**$12.50-$25.00**
X5407, "Blueberry Hill"/"Honey Chile" (black vinyl, red label), 1956 ....**$12.50-$25.00**
(if red vinyl), 1956..**$75.00-$150.00**
(if black vinyl, black label, reissue), 1957..............................**$7.50-$15.00**
X5417, "Blue Monday"/"What's the Reason I'm Not Pleasing You," 1957 ....**$12.50-$25.00**

78s

Imperial 5407, "Blueberry Hill"/"Honey Chile," 1956.................**$15.00-$30.00**

Mono LPs

Imperial LP-9004, Rock and Rollin' with Fats Domino (maroon label), 1956 ....**$75.00-$150.00**
(if black label, stars on top), 1958..**$40.00-$80.00**
(if black-pink label), 1964...**$12.50-$25.00**
(if black-green label), 1967..**$10.00-$20.00**
LP-9040, This Is Fats (maroon label), 1957..............................**$75.00-$150.00**
(if black label, stars on top), 1958..**$40.00-$80.00**
(if black-pink label), 1964...**$12.50-$25.00**
(if black-green label), 1967..**$10.00-$20.00**

Stereo LPs

Imperial LP-12066, A Lot of Dominos (black label, silver on top), 1961 ....**$75.00-$150.00**
(if black-pink label), 1964...**$20.00-$40.00**
(if black-green label), 1967..**$12.50-$25.00**
ABC-Paramount S 455, Here Comes... Fats Domino, 1963.......**$12.50-$25.00**

THE EVERLY BROTHERS:

45s

Cadence 1337, "Wake Up Little Susie"/"Maybe Tomorrow," 1957 ....**$15.00-$30.00**
(with picture sleeve, add), 1957...**$125.00-$250.00**
1348, "All I Have to Do Is Dream"/"Claudette," 1958...............**$12.50-$25.00**
(with red-black label reissue, scarcer than original), 1961 ....**$10.00-$20.00**
Warner Bros. 5151, "Cathy's Clown"/"Always It's You" (pink label), 1960 ....**$10.00-$20.00**
(if second pressing, red labels with arrows), 1960.........................**$7.50-$15.00**
(if gold vinyl, promo pressing), 1960......................................**$50.00-$100.00**

78s

Cadence 1337, "Wake Up Little Susie"/"Maybe Tomorrow," 1957 ....**$30.00-$60.00**

Mono LPs

Cadence CLP-3003, The Everly Brothers (maroon label, metronome logo), 1958...............**$50.00-$100.00**
(if red label, black border on label), 1962.................................**$30.00-$60.00**
CLP-3016, Songs Our Daddy Taught Us (maroon label, metronome logo), 1958...............**$50.00-$100.00**
(if red label, black border on label), 1962.................................**$30.00-$60.00**
Warner Bros. W 1381, It's Everly Time!, 1960.............................**$15.00-$30.00**
W 1418, Both Sides of an Evening, 1961.......................................**$15.00-$30.00**

Stereo LPs

Cadence CLP-25040, The Fabulous Style of the Everly Brothers (maroon label, metronome logo), 1960 .... **$60.00-$120.00**
(if red label, black border on label), 1962 .... **$30.00-$60.00**
Warner Bros. WS 1381, It's Everly Time!, 1960 .... **$20.00-$40.00**
WS 1418, Both Sides of an Evening, 1961 .... **$20.00-$40.00**

FABIAN:

45s

Chancellor 1033, "Turn Me Loose"/"Stop Thief!," 1959 .... **$10.00-$20.00**
(with picture sleeve, add), 1959 .... **$20.00-$40.00**
1037, "Tiger"/"Mighty Cold (To a Warm, Warm Heart)," 1959 .... **$10.00-$20.00**

Stereo 45s

Chancellor S-1029, "I'm a Man"/"Hypnotized," 1959 .... **$25.00-$50.00**
S-1044, "Hound Dog Man"/"This Friendly World," 1959 .... **$25.00-$50.00**

Mono LPs

Chancellor CHL-5003, Hold That Tiger! (pink label), 1959 .... **$50.00-$100.00**
(if black label), 1959 .... **$25.00-$50.00**
CHL-5012, The Good Old Summertime, 1960 .... **$25.00-$50.00**

Stereo LPs

Chancellor CHLS-5003, Hold That Tiger! (pink label), 1959 .... **$75.00-$150.00**
(if black label), 1959 .... **$37.50-$75.00**

THE FENDERMEN:

45s

Cuca 1003, "Mule Skinner Blues"/"Torture," 1960 .... **$100.00-$200.00**
Soma 1137, "Mule Skinner Blues"/"Torture," 1960 .... **$12.50-$25.00**

LPs

Soma MG-1240, Mule Skinner Blues, 1960 .... **$600.00-$1,200.00**
(if on blue vinyl), 1960 .... **$3,000.00-$4,000.00**

BILL HALEY AND HIS COMETS:

45s

Decca 29124, "(We're Gonna) Rock Around the Clock"/"Thirteen Women (And Only One Man in Town)"
(if lines on either side of "Decca"), 1954 .... **$30.00-$60.00**
(with star under "Decca"), 1955 .... **$10.00-$20.00**

7-inch EPs

Decca ED 2168, Shake, Rattle and Roll (contains "Shake, Rattle and Roll"/"A.B.C. Boogie"/"(We're Gonna) Rock Around the Clock"/"Thirteen Women (And Only One Man in Town)," value is for record and jacket), 1954 .... **$60.00-$120.00**

78s

Decca 29124, "(We're Gonna) Rock Around the Clock"/"Thirteen Women (And Only One Man In Town)"
(if black label, gold print, "Decca Personality Series"), 1955 .... **$60.00-$120.00**
(if black label, silver print, star under "Decca"), 1955 .... **$20.00-$40.00**

Mono LPs

Essex LP 202, Rock with Bill Haley and the Comets, 1955 .... **$250.00-$500.00**
Decca DL-5560, Shake, Rattle and Roll (10-inch record), 1955 .... **$400.00-$800.00**
DL 8225, Rock Around the Clock (all black label, silver print), 1955 .... **$75.00-$150.00**
DL 8345, Rock 'n Roll Stage Show, 1956 .... **$75.00-$150.00**

BUDDY HOLLY:

45s

Decca 29854, "Blue Days, Black Nights"/"Love Me" (with star under "Decca"), 1956 .... **$150.00-$300.00**
(with lines on either side of "Decca"), 1956 .... **$300.00-$600.00**
(if pink label, promo), 1956 .... **$200.00-$400.00**
34034, "That'll Be the Day"/"Rock Around with Ollie Vee" (with star under "Decca"), 1957 .... **$125.00-$250.00**
(with lines on either side of "Decca"), 1957 .... **$200.00-$400.00**
(if pink label, promo), 1957 .... **$125.00-$250.00**
Coral 61852, "Words of Love"/"Mailman, Bring Me No More Blues," 1957 .... **$250.00-$400.00**
61885, "Peggy Sue"/"Everyday" (orange label), 1957 .... **$25.00-$50.00**
(if black color bars label), 196? .... **$12.50-$25.00**
62074, "It Doesn't Matter Anymore"/"Raining in My Heart," 1959 .... **$20.00-$40.00**
62134, "Peggy Sue Got Married"/"Crying, Waiting, Hoping," 1959 .... **$30.00-$60.00**
62210, "True Love Ways"/"That Makes It Tough," 1960 .... **$25.00-$50.00**

LPs

Decca DL 8207, That'll Be the Day (black label, silver print), 1958 .... **$750.00-$1,500.00**
(if black label, with color bars), 1961 .... **$150.00-$300.00**
Coral CRL 57210, Buddy Holly (maroon label), 1958 .... **$200.00-$400.00**
(if black label with color bars), 1964 .... **$50.00-$100.00**

THE ISLEY BROTHERS:

45s

RCA Victor 47-7588, "Shout" (Part 1)/"Shout" (Part 2), 1959 .... **$15.00-$30.00**
Wand 124, "Twist and Shout"/"Spanish Twist," 1962 .... **$10.00-$20.00**

Stereo 45s

RCA Victor 61-7588, "Shout" (Part 1)/"Shout" (Part 2), 1959 .... **$30.00-$60.00**

Mono LPs

RCA Victor LPM-2156, Shout! ("Long Play" on label), 1959 .... **$60.00-$120.00**
Wand WD-653, Twist & Shout, 1962 .... **$40.00-$80.00**

Stereo LPs

RCA Victor LSP-2156, Shout! ("Living Stereo" on label), 1959 .... **$100.00-$200.00**
Wand WDS-653, Twist & Shout, 1962 .... **$50.00-$100.00**

LITTLE RICHARD:

45s

Specialty 561, "Tutti-Frutti"/"I'm Just a Lonely Guy," 1955 .... **$25.00-$50.00**
572, "Long Tall Sally"/"Slippin' and Slidin' (Peepin' and Hidin')," 1956 .... **$20.00-$40.00**
606, "Jenny, Jenny"/"Miss Ann," 1957 .... **$20.00-$40.00**
(with picture sleeve, add), 1957 .... **$30.00-$60.00**

78s

Specialty 561, "Tutti-Frutti"/"I'm Just A Lonely Guy," 1955 .... **$25.00-$50.00**

LPs

Specialty SP-2100, Here's Little Richard (thick vinyl), 1957 .... **$100.00-$200.00**
SP-2103, Little Richard (if front cover photo occupies the entire cover), 1958 .... **$75.00-$150.00**
(if front cover photo partially obscured by black triangle at upper left, thick vinyl), 196? .... **$50.00-$100.00**
(if reissue, thin vinyl), 197? .... **$10.00-$20.00**

GENE McDANIELS:

45s

Liberty 55308, "A Hundred Pounds of Clay"/"Take a Chance on Love," 1961 .... **$8.00-$16.00**
55405, "Chip Chip"/"Another Tear Falls," 1962 .... **$7.50-$15.00**

Stereo LPs

Liberty LST-7146, In Times Like These, 1960 .... **$20.00-$40.00**
(if on blue vinyl), 1960 .... **$100.00-$200.00**

THE MYSTICS:

45s

Laurie 3028, "Hushabye"/"Adam and Eve," 1959 .... **$15.00-$30.00**
3104, "Sunday Kind of Love"/"Darling I Know How," 1961 .... **$15.00-$30.00**

Stereo 45s

Laurie S-3028, "Hushabye"/"Adam and Eve," 1959 .... **$60.00-$120.00**

ROY ORBISON:

45s

Je-Wel 101, "Ooby Dooby"/"Tryin' to Get to You" (credited to "The Teen Kings," name mispelled "Oribson"), 1956 .... **$2,750.00-$4,000.00**
(if Orbison's name spelled correctly), 1956 .... **$2,750.00-$4,000.00**
Sun 242, "Ooby Dooby"/"Go! Go! Go!," 1956 .... **$50.00-$100.00**
251, "Rockhouse"/"You're My Baby," 1956 .... **$30.00-$60.00**
Monument 421, "Only the Lonely (Know the Way I Feel)"/"Here Comes That Song Again," 1960 .... **$12.50-$25.00**
467, "Leah"/"Workin' for the Man," 1962 .... **$10.00-$20.00**
(with picture sleeve, add), 1962 .... **$20.00-$40.00**
806, "In Dreams"/"Shahdaroba," 1963 .... **$10.00-$20.00**
(with picture sleeve, add), 1963 .... **$20.00-$40.00**
851, "Pretty Woman"/"Yo Te Amo Maria," 1964 .... **$15.00-$30.00**
(if A-side is retitled "Oh, Pretty Woman"), 1964 .... **$10.00-$20.00**

Mono LPs

Monument M-4002, Lonely and Blue, 1961 .... **$75.00-$150.00**
4007, Crying, 1962 .... **$60.00-$120.00**
MLP-8003, In Dreams (white-rainbow label), 1963 .... **$25.00-$50.00**
(if on green-gold label, reissue), 1964 .... **$15.00-$30.00**

Stereo LPs

Monument SM-14002, Lonely and Blue, 1961 .... **$300.00-$600.00**
SM-14007, Crying, 1962 .... **$300.00-$600.00**
SLP-18003, In Dreams (white-rainbow label), 1963 .... **$50.00-$100.00**
(if on green-gold label, reissue), 1964 .... **$25.00-$50.00**

THE PLATTERS:

45s

Federal 12164, "I'll Cry When You're Gone"/"I Need You All the Time," 1954 ....**$500.00-$1,000.00**

12244, "Only You (And You Alone)"/"You Made Me Cry," 1955 ....**$150.00-$300.00**

Mercury 70633, "Only You (And You Alone)"/"Bark, Battle and Ball" (pink label), 1955 ....**$25.00-$50.00**

(if black label), 1955 ....**$20.00-$40.00**

70753, "The Great Pretender"/"I'm Just a Dancing Partner" (maroon label), 1955 ....**$20.00-$40.00**

(if black label), 1955 ....**$10.00-$20.00**

71289, "Twilight Time"/"Out of My Mind," 1958 ....**$12.50-$25.00**

71383, "Smoke Gets In Your Eyes"/"No Matter What You Are" (blue label), 1958 ....**$15.00-$30.00**

(if black label), 1958 ....**$15.00-$30.00**

7-inch EPs

Federal EP-378, The Platters Sing For Only You (contains "Only You [And You Alone]"/"I Need You All The Time"/"Tell the World"/"Give Thanks," value is for record and jacket), 1956 ....**$400.00-$800.00**

Mercury EP 1-3336, The Platters (contains "My Prayer"/"Have Mercy"/"On My Word of Honor"/"I'm Sorry," value is for record and jacket), 1957 ....**$40.00-$80.00**

EP 1-3393, Twilight Time (contains "Twilight Time"/"For the First Time"/ "Don't Blame Me"/"But Not Like You," value is for record and jacket), 1958 ....**$40.00-$80.00**

Mono LPs

Federal 549, The Platters, 1957 ....**$800.00-$1,600.00**

King 651, The Platters, 1959 ....**$400.00-$800.00**

Mercury MG-20146, The Platters, 1956 ....**$50.00-$100.00**

Mercury MG-20298, The Flying Platters, 1957 ....**$50.00-$100.00**

Stereo LPs

Mercury SR-60043, The Flying Platters Around the World, 1959 ....**$25.00-$50.00**

SR-60087, Remember When?, 1959 ....**$25.00-$50.00**

THE RONETTES:

45s

Colpix 601, "I Want a Boy"/"Sweet Sixteen" (as "Ronnie and the Relatives"), 1961 ....**$50.00-$100.00**

Philles 116, "Be My Baby"/"Tedesco and Pittman," 1963 ....**$15.00-$30.00**

118, "Baby I Love You"/"Miss Joan and Mr. Sam," 1963 ....**$15.00-$30.00**

Mono LPs

Philles PHLP-4006, Presenting the Fabulous Ronettes Featuring Veronica (blue-black label), 1964 ....**$400.00-$800.00**

(if yellow-red label), 1964 ....**$200.00-$400.00**

Stereo LPs

Philles PHLP-ST-4006, Presenting the Fabulous Ronettes Featuring Veronica, 1965 ....**$300.00-$600.00**

NEIL SEDAKA:

45s

RCA Victor 47-7408, "The Diary"/"No Vacancy," 1958 ....**$10.00-$20.00**

(if white label promo, Sedaka's photo on label), 1958 ....**$20.00-$40.00**

47-7781, "You Mean Everything to Me"/"Run Samson Run," 1960 ....**$7.50-$15.00**

(with picture sleeve, add), 1960 ....**$12.50-$25.00**

47-7829, "Calendar Girl"/"The Same Old Fool," 1960 ....**$7.50-$15.00**

(with picture sleeve, add), 1960 ....**$12.50-$25.00**

47-8046, "Breaking Up Is Hard to Do"/"As Long As I Live," 1962 ....**$7.50-$15.00**

(with picture sleeve, add):, 1962 ....**$12.50-$25.00**

Mono LPs

RCA Victor LPM-2035, Neil Sedaka, 1959 ....**$30.00-$60.00**

LPM-2421, Little Devil and His Other Hits, 1961 ....**$25.00-$50.00**

Stereo LPs

RCA Victor LSP-2035, Neil Sedaka, 1959 ....**$50.00-$100.00**

LSP-2421, Little Devil and His Other Hits, 1961 ....**$30.00-$60.00**

DEL SHANNON:

45s

Big Top 3067, "Runaway"/"Jody," 1961 ....**$15.00-$30.00**

3075, "Hats Off to Larry"/"Don't Gild the Lily, Lily," 1961 ....**$12.50-$25.00**

3131, "Little Town Flirt"/"The Wamboo," 1962 ....**$12.50-$25.00**

Amy 915, "Keep Searchin' (We'll Follow the Sun)"/"Broken Promises," 1964 ....**$8.00-$16.00**

Mono LPs

Big Top 12-1303, Runaway, 1961 ....**$150.00-$300.00**

12-1308, Little Town Flirt, 1963 ....**$75.00-$150.00**

Stereo LPs

Big Top 12-1303, Runaway, 1961 ....**$800.00-$1,600.00**

12-1308, Little Town Flirt, 1963 ....**$750.00-$1,500.00**

(if one side is mono and one side is stereo, should be played to identify), 1963 ....**$75.00-$150.00**

Amy S-8003, Handy Man, 1964 ....**$40.00-$80.00**

TOM AND JERRY:

45s

Big 613, "Hey Schoolgirl"/"Dancing Wild," 1957 ....**$25.00-$50.00**

78s

Big 613, "Hey Schoolgirl"/"Dancing Wild," 1957 ....**$37.50-$75.00**

RITCHIE VALENS:

45s

Del-Fi 4106, "Come On, Let's Go"/"Framed," 1958 ....**$40.00-$80.00**

Del-Fi 4110, "Donna"/"La Bamba" (if blue/green/black label, with circles), 1958 ....**$35.00-$70.00**

(if green label), 1958 ....**$20.00-$40.00**

(if light blue label), 1958 ....**$15.00-$30.00**

LPs

Del-Fi DFLP 1201, Ritchie Valens (black label, "Diamonds" border), 1959 ....**$75.00-$150.00**

(if blue label, black border), 1959 ....**$125.00-$250.00**

DFLP 1214, In Concert at Pacoima Jr. High, 1960 ....**$125.00-$250.00**

BOBBY VINTON:

45s

Alpine 50, "First Impression"/"You'll Never Forget," 1959 ....**$15.00-$30.00**

Diamond 121, "I Love You the Way You Are"/Chuck and Johnny, "You're My Girl," 1962 ....**$10.00-$20.00**

Epic 9509, "Roses Are Red (My Love)"/"You and I," 1962 ....**$6.00-$12.00**

(two variations of picture sleeve exist, Vinton looking straight ahead with chin in hand, or looking toward lower right corner, value is equal, add), 1962 ....**$7.50-$15.00**

9593, "Blue on Blue"/"Those Little Things," 1963 ....**$6.00-$12.00**

(with picture sleeve, add), 1963 ....**$7.50-$15.00**

9614, "Blue Velvet"/"Is There a Place (Where I Can Go)," 1963..**$6.00-$12.00**

(with picture sleeve, add), 1963 ....**$7.50-$15.00**

Mono LPs

Epic LN 3727, Dancing at the Hop, 1961 ....**$15.00-$30.00**

LN 3780, Young Man with a Big Band, 1961 ....**$15.00-$30.00**

LN 24068, Blue On Blue, 1963 ....**$12.50-$25.00**

(if on blue vinyl, promo), 1963 ....**$75.00-$150.00**

Stereo LPs

Epic BN 579, Dancing at the Hop, 1961 ....**$25.00-$50.00**

597, Young Man with a Big Band, 1961 ....**$25.00-$50.00**

JACKIE WILSON:

45s

Brunswick 9-55024, "Reet Petite (The Finest Girl You Ever Want to Meet)"/ "By the Light of the Silvery Moon," 1957 $15.00-$30.00

9-55105, "Lonely Teardrops"/"In the Blue of Evening," 1958 ....**$15.00-$30.00**

55166, "Night"/"Doggin' Around" (orange label), 1960 ....**$7.50-$15.00**

(if on rare maroon label), 1960 ....**$20.00-$40.00**

(if on black label with rainbow arrow, reissue), 196? ....**$5.00-$10.00**

55239, "Baby Workout"/"I'm Going Crazy," 1963 ....**$10.00-$20.00**

55277, "Danny Boy"/"Soul Time," 1965 ....**$4.00-$8.00**

78s

Brunswick 55105, "Lonely Teardrops"/"In The Blue of the Evening," 1958 ....**$150.00-$300.00**

Mono LPs

Brunswick BL 54045, Lonely Teardrops (all black label), 1959 ....**$75.00-$150.00**

(if black label with color bars), 1964 ....**$12.50-$25.00**

BL 54105, Body and Soul (all black label), 1962 ....**$25.00-$50.00**

(if black label with color bars), 1964 ....**$10.00-$20.00**

BL 54110, Baby Workout (all black label), 1963 ....**$25.00-$50.00**

(if black label with color bars), 1964 ....**$10.00-$20.00**

Stereo LPs

Brunswick BL 754050, So Much (all black label), 1960 ....**$75.00-$150.00**

(if black label with color bars), 1964 ....**$12.50-$25.00**

BL 754105, Body and Soul (all black label), 1962 ....**$40.00-$80.00**

(if black label with color bars), 1964 ....**$12.50-$25.00**

CHAPTER 22

ROCKABILLY

History

As its name suggests, "Rockabilly" is a hybrid of rock and roll and hillbilly music. As musicians played blues and gospel music with an uptempo rocking beat, rockabilly music rose from the clubs and honkytonks throughout the South, and became one of the building blocks of modern rock and roll.

The most famous haven for rockabilly music was Sun Studios in Memphis, Tennessee, where studio owner Sam Phillips cultivated rockabilly artists like Elvis Presley, Carl Perkins, and Charlie Feathers on his Sun label. Rockabilly music also evolved in Texas, where Bill Haley and Buddy Holly's early hits, "Rock Around The Clock" and "That'll Be The Day" are rockabilly classics, even though the artists themselves called the music "western bop." At the same time, artists like Gene Vincent, Eddie Cochran, and Wanda Jackson garnered major label contracts with rockabilly smashes like "Summertime Blues," "Let's Have A Party," and "Be-Bop-A-Lula."

Although Elvis Presley's rockabilly output (his five singles on Sun and his early RCA recordings) are very collectible, one of the most collectible "pure rockabilly" artists is Charlie Feathers. Feathers, who mixed bluegrass music into his own version of rockabilly, recorded some singles on the Sun label, as well as for Sam Phillips' "Flip" subsidiary label. Even though his records did not have the same success as other rockabilly artists, Feathers finally received his due in the 1970s. While touring England, his live performances inspired a new generation of British rockabilly musicians, who today spend thousands of dollars for Feathers' 1950s recordings.

In July 1956, the Johnny Burnette Trio—Johnny Burnette,

Rockabilly legend Jerry Lee Lewis was one of the few artists for which Sun Records made picture sleeves of his 45s, as can be seen from this "High School Confidential" sleeve.

***$80**, NM condition*

Photo credit: From the collection of Phil Schwartz, Keystone Record Collectors Club.

Charlie Feathers recorded for several independent companies, and his Meteor recording of "Tongue-Tied Jill" is difficult to find, in either a 45 or 78-RPM format.

***$400**, NM condition*

Photo credit: From the collection of Phil Schwartz, Keystone Record Collectors Club.

A rare 78-RPM pressing of the Johnny Burnette Trio's "Train Kept A-Rollin'." When the Trio's records were repressed on a British LP in the 1970s, it spurred a rockabilly craze in the UK, paving the way for artists like the Stray Cats and Shakin' Stevens.

***$400**, NM condition*

Photo credit: From the collection of Phil Schwartz, Keystone Record Collectors Club.

Eddie Cochran's hits "Summertime Blues" and "C'mon Everybody" dominated the pop charts, but his song "Twenty Flight Rock" is a seminal rockabilly classic. Legend has it that Paul McCartney first impressed John Lennon by knowing all the chords and words to "Twenty Flight Rock."

***$150**, NM condition*

his brother Dorsey Burnette, and friend Paul Burlison—entered Nashville record producer Owen Bradley's studios, and within days the rockabilly trio cranked out some of the hottest and smokiest rockabilly classics, including "Train Kept A-Rollin'" and "Rock Billy Boogie." Legend has it that the Johnny Burnette Trio had the opportunity to sign with either Coral Records or Capitol Records—when they chose Coral, Capitol signed another rockabilly artist, Gene Vincent, instead.

As popular as rockabilly was in America, especially in the South, rockabilly was even more popular in Great Britain. There, several rockabilly artists toured the United Kingdom to screaming legions of fans—and their musical performances influenced hundreds of British musicians to play guitars like their American musical heroes. England was also the location of rockabilly's greatest tragedy, when a 1960 car crash killed rockabilly singer Eddie Cochran and severely injured Gene Vincent.

The initial rockabilly wave lasted from 1954 to 1959. Over the years, there have been bursts of rockabilly music from time to time, as artists incorporated the slap-back bass and reverb sound of those early rockabilly hits, or, like the Stray Cats and the Rev. Horton Heat, took in the entire atmosphere of late 1950s rock and style.

Books

Morrison, Craig, *Go Cat Go: Rockabilly Music and Its Makers,* University of Illinois Press, Chicago, IL, 1998.

Floyd, John, *Sun Records: An Oral History,* Avon Books, NY, 1998.

What To Look For

Rockabilly records are highly collectible. In fact, almost anything rockabilly pioneer Charlie Feathers ever recorded is extremely desirous by rockabilly collectors. Record collectors would prefer the original 45s, but will pay top dollar for old 78s recorded in 1957 or later, when such pressings are rare. Albums by rockabilly artists are also collectible, both for their rarity and their historical value. Gene Vincent's early albums can sell for as much as $2,000 in near-mint condition, and Wanda Jackson's *Rockin' with Wanda* can sell for three figures even in VG condition.

Web Pages

Terry Gordon's Rockin' Country Style home page, with listings of hundreds of rockabilly songs and artists: http://rcs.law.emory.edu/rcs/index.htm

The Rockabilly Hall of Fame Web site: http://www.rockabillyhall.com

A site featuring published articles on rockabilly artists: http://www.rockabilly.net

Usenet newsgroup: alt.music.rockabilly

Museums

The Buddy Holly Center, 1801 Avenue G, Lubbock, TX, 79401, (806) 767-2686: http://www.buddyhollycenter.org

The Rockabilly Hall of Fame, 211 College Street, Burns, TN, 37029. (615) 740-ROCK.

In the late 1950s, Mercury Records laminated their album covers with a shiny adhesive film. After exposure to years of sunlight and atmosphere, that film can frost and cloud the image below, as can be seen on the outer edges of this album by rockabilly piano player Chuck Miller. By the way, this Chuck Miller is not related in any way to this book's author.

***$30**, Fair condition*

Like most Sub Pop 45s, this release by modern rockabilly guitarist Rev. Horton Heat was pressed on colored vinyl—in this case, a blue-white vinyl mixture.

***$9**, NM condition*

Photo credit: From the collection of Phil Schwartz, Keystone Record Collectors Club.

Rockabilly artists from West Texas include famous groups like Buddy Holly and the Crickets, and the Teen Kings (with Roy Orbison). Also included in this mix is Sonny West (sometimes spelled "Sonee West"), whose song "Rock-Ola Ruby" was released on the tiny Texas label Nor-Va-Jak, before West signed a contract with Atlantic Records.

***$150**, NM condition*

Independent rockabilly artists recorded for regional labels, with some copies having a small print run of 500-1,000 copies. Lenny and the Star Chiefs, from Buffalo, N.Y., recorded two singles in 1959 before fading into obscurity—and collectibility.

***$20**, VG condition*

ARTIST VG+ to NM

SONNY BURGESS:

45s

Sun 247, "Red Headed Woman"/"We Wanna Boogie," 1956 ......**$75.00-$150.00**

304, "Thunderbird"/"Itchy," 1958 ......**$15.00-$30.00**

Phillips International 3551, "Sadie's Back in Town"/"Kiss Goodnight," 1960 ......**$15.00-$30.00**

JOHNNY BURNETTE:

45s

Von 1006, "You're Undecided"/"Go, Mule, Go," 1954 ......**$2,250.00-$3,000.00**

Coral 61719, "The Train Kept a-Rollin'"/"Honey Hush," 1956 ......**$125.00-$250.00**

61918, "Rock Billy Boogie"/"If You Want It Enough," 1957 ......**$150.00-$300.00**

Liberty 55222, "Settin' the Woods on Fire"/"Kentucky Waltz," 1959 ......**$10.00-$20.00**

78s

Coral 61675, "Midnight Train"/"Oh Baby Babe," 1956 ......**$200.00-$400.00**

61719, "The Train Kept a-Rollin'"/"Honey Hush," 1956 ......**$200.00-$400.00**

Mono LPs

Coral CRL 57080, Johnny Burnette & the Rock 'N' Roll Trio (maroon Coral labels, machine-stamped numbers in trail-off vinyl, printing on jacket's spine, "Printed in U.S.A." in lower right of back cover, must have all this information or it is a reproduction), 1956 ......**$4,000.00-$6,000.00**

Liberty LRP-3179, Dreamin', 1960 ......**$20.00-$40.00**

JOHNNY AND DORSEY BURNETTE/THE BURNETTE BROTHERS:

45s

Imperial 5509, "Warm Love"/"My Honey," 1958 ......**$50.00-$100.00**

Coral 62190, "Blues Stay Away from Me"/"Midnight Train," 1960 ......**$100.00-$200.00**

Reprise 20153, "It Don't Take Much"/"Hey Sue," 1963 ......**$10.00-$20.00**

JOHNNY CASH:

Sun 241, "I Walk the Line"/"Get Rhythm," 1956 ......**$20.00-$40.00**

283, "Ballad of a Teenage Queen"/"Big River," 1958 ......**$12.50-$25.00**

Columbia 42788, "Ring of Fire"/"I'd Still Be There," 1963 ......**$5.00-$10.00**

(with picture sleeve, add), 1963 ......**$15.00-$30.00**

(if red vinyl promo, "Ring of Fire" on both sides), 1963 ......**$20.00-$40.00**

43206, "Orange Blossom Special"/"All of God's Children Ain't Free," 1965 ......**$4.00-$8.00**

78s

Sun 241, " I Walk The Line"/"Get Rhythm," 1956 ......**$12.50-$25.00**

258, "Train of Love"/"There You Go," 1956 ......**$15.00-$30.00**

Mono LPs

Sun SLP-1220, Johnny Cash with His Hot and Blue Guitar, 1956 ......**$50.00-$100.00**

SLP 1235, The Songs That Made Him Famous, 1958 ......**$50.00-$100.00**

Stereo LPs

Sun SLP-1220, Johnny Cash with His Hot and Blue Guitar (front cover says "STEREO," rechanneled reissue), 196? ......**$10.00-$20.00**

EDDIE COCHRAN:

45s

Crest 1026, "Skinny Jim"/"Half Loved," 1956 ......**$150.00-$300.00**

Liberty 55070, "Mean When I'm Mad"/"One Kiss," 1957 ......**$15.00-$30.00**

(with picture sleeve, add), 1957 ......**$1,000.00-$1,500.00**

55112, "Twenty Flight Rock"/"Cradle Baby," 1957 ......**$75.00-$150.00**

55144, "Summertime Blues"/"Live Again," 1958 ......**$15.00-$30.00**

55166, "C'mon Everybody"/"Don't Ever Let Me Go," 1958 ......**$15.00-$30.00**

LPs

Liberty LRP-3061, Singin' To My Baby (green label), 1957 ......**$400.00-$800.00**

(if on black label), 1960 ......**$150.00-$30.00**

LRP-3172, Eddie Cochran (12 of his Biggest Hits), 1960 ......**$60.00-$120.00**

THE CRICKETS:

45s

Brunswick 55009, "That'll Be the Day"/"I'm Lookin' for Someone to Love," 1957 ......**$25.00-$50.00**

55035, "Oh, Boy!"/"Not Fade Away," 1957 ......**$25.00-$50.00**

Liberty 55392, "He's Old Enough to Know Better"/"I'm Feeling Better," 1961 ......**$12.50-$25.00**

LPs

Brunswick BL 54038, The "Chirping" Crickets

(if textured cover), 1957 ......**$400.00-$800.00**

(if regular cover), 1958 ......**$300.00-$600.00**

Coral CRL 57320, In Style with the Crickets, 1960 ......**$100.00-$200.00**

CHARLIE FEATHERS:

45s

Flip 503, "I've Been Deceived"/"Peeping Eyes," 1955 ......**$250.00-$500.00**

Sun 231, "Defrost Your Heart"/"Wedding Gown of White," 1956 ......**$400.00-$600.00**

503, "I've Been Deceived"/"Peeping Eyes," 1956 ......**$400.00-$600.00**

Meteor 5032, "Tongue-Tied Jill"/"Get With It" (on black label), 1956 ......**$200.00-$400.00**

(if on red label), 1956 ......**$1,000.00-$1,500.00**

King 4971, "Can't Hardly Stand It"/"Everybody's Lovin' My Baby," 1956 ......**$300.00-$600.00**

4997, "One Hand Loose"/"Bottle to the Baby," 1956 ......**$250.00-$500.00**

5022, "Nobody's Woman"/"When You Decide," 1957 ......**$200.00-$400.00**

King 5043, "When You Come Around"/"Too Much Alike," 1957 ......**$200.00-$400.00**

Wal-May 101, "Dinky John"/"South of Chicago," 1960 ......**$100.00-$200.00**

Kay 1001, "Jungle Fever"/"Why Don't You," 1960 ......**$100.00-$200.00**

Memphis 103, "Wild, Wild Party"/"Today and Tomorrow," 1961 ......**$50.00-$100.00**

Holiday Inn 114, "Deep Elm Blues"/"Nobody's Darling," 1962 ......**$100.00-$200.00**

EDDIE FONTAINE:

45s

Jalo 102, "Where is Da Woman"/"It Ain't Gonna Happen No More," 1956 ......**$40.00-$80.00**

Sunbeam 105, "Nothin' Shakin' (But the leaves on the Trees)"/"Oh, Wonderful Night," 1958 ......**$20.00-$40.00**

Argo 5309, "Nothin' Shakin'"/"Don't Ya Know", 1958 ......**$12.50-$25.00**

BILL HALEY AND HIS COMETS:

45s

Essex 321, "Crazy Man, Crazy"/"Whatcha Gonna Do," 1953 ......**$30.00-$60.00**

Decca 29124, "(We're Gonna) Rock Around the Clock"/"Thirteen Women (And Only One Man in Town)"

(if lines on either side of "Decca"), 1954 ......**$30.00-$60.00**

(with star under "Decca"), 1955 ......**$10.00-$20.00**

29791, "See You Later, Alligator"/"The Paper Boy (On Main Street, U.S.A.)," 1956 ......**$12.50-$25.00**

30148, "Don't Knock the Rock"/"Choo Choo Ch'Boogie," 1956 ......**$12.50-$25.00**

Mono LPs

Essex LP 202, Rock with Bill Haley and the Comets, 1955 ......**$250.00-$500.00**

Decca DL-5560, Shake, Rattle and Roll (10-inch record), 1955 ......**$400.00-$800.00**

DL 8225, Rock Around the Clock (all black label, silver print), 1955 ......**$75.00-$150.00**

DL 8345, Rock 'n Roll Stage Show, 1956 ......**$75.00-$150.00**

DALE HAWKINS:

45s

Checker 863, "Susie-Q"/"Don't Treat Me This Way," 1957 ......**$25.00-$50.00**

923, "Ain't That Lovin' You Baby"/"My Dream," 1959 ......**$12.50-$25.00**

944, "Poor Little Rhode Island"/"Every Little Girl," 1960 ......**$10.00-$20.00**

(with picture sleeve, add), 1960 ......**$150.00-$300.00**

LPs

Chess LP-1429, Oh! Susie-Q, 1958 ......**$1,000.00-$1,500.00**

BUDDY HOLLY:

45s

Decca 29854, "Blue Days, Black Nights"/"Love Me" (with star under "Decca"), 1956 ......**$150.00-$300.00**

(with lines on either side of "Decca"), 1956 ......**$300.00-$600.00**

(if pink label, promo), 1956 ......**$200.00-$400.00**

34034, "That'll Be the Day"/"Rock Around with Ollie Vee" (with star under "Decca"), 1957 ......**$125.00-$250.00**

(with lines on either side of "Decca"), 1957 ......**$200.00-$400.00**

(if pink label, promo), 1957 ......**$125.00-$250.00**

Coral 61852, "Words of Love"/"Mailman, Bring Me No More Blues," 1957 ......**$250.00-$400.00**

61885, "Peggy Sue"/"Everyday" (orange label), 1957 ......**$25.00-$50.00**

LPs

Decca DL 8207, That'll Be the Day (black label, silver print), 1958 ....**$750.00-$1,500.00**

(if black label, with color bars), 1961 ....**$150.00-$300.00**

WANDA JACKSON:

45s

Capitol 4397, "Let's Have a Party"/"Cool Love," 1960 ....**$20.00-$40.00**

Mono LPs

Capitol T 1384, Rockin' with Wanda

(if black label with rainbow perimeter, Capitol logo at left), 1960 ....**$200.00-$400.00**

(if gold "Star Line" label), 1962 ....**$125.00-$250.00**

(if black "Star Line" label), 1963 ....**$75.00-$150.00**

SLEEPY LABEEF:

45s

Wayside 1654, "Tore Up"/"Lonely" (as Tommy LaBeff), 1959 **$150.00-$300.00**

Starday 292, "I'm Through"/"All Alone" (as Sleepy LaBeff), 1960 ....**$75.00-$150.00**

Crescent 102, "Turn Me Loose"/"Ridin' Fence" (as Sleepy LaBeff), 1961 ....**$100.00-$200.00**

Picture 1937, "Ride On Josephine"/"Lonely" (as Sleepy LaBeff), 1961 ....**$75.00-$150.00**

Sun 1137, "Good Rockin' Boogie" (Part 1)/"Good Rockin' Boogie" (Part 2), 1978 ....**$2.00-$4.00**

LENNY AND THE STAR CHIEFS:

45s

Performance 502, "My Queen and Me"/"Warpath," 1959 ....**$20.00-$40.00**

JERRY LEE LEWIS:

45s

Sun 259, "Crazy Arms"/"End of the Road"

(if credited to "Jerry Lee Lewis and his Pumping Piano"), 1957 ....**$25.00-$50.00**

(if credited to "Jerry Lee Lewis," 1957 ....**$50.00-$100.00**

267, "Whole Lot of Shakin' Going On"/"It'll Be Me," 1957 .....**$20.00-$40.00**

281, "Great Balls of Fire"/"You Win Again," 1957 ....**$20.00-$40.00**

(with picture sleeve, add), 1957 ....**$40.00-$80.00**

296, "High School Confidential"/"Fools Like Me," 1958 ....**$15.00-$30.00**

(with picture sleeve, add), 1958 ....**$40.00-$80.00**

Smash 1930, "High Heel Sneakers"/"You Went Back on Your Word," 1964 ....**$7.50-$15.00**

2122, "Turn On Your Love Light"/"Shotgun Man," 1967 ....**$6.00-$12.00**

2244, "She Even Woke Me Up to Say Goodbye"/"Echoes," 1969 ....**$5.00-$10.00**

78s

Sun 259, "Crazy Arms"/"End of the Road," 1957 ....**$150.00-$300.00**

267, "Whole Lot of Shakin' Goin' On"/"It'll Be Me," 1957 ....**$100.00-$200.00**

281, "Great Balls of Fire"/"You Win Again," 1957 ....**$100.00-$200.00**

288, "Breathless"/"Down the Line," 1958 ....**$100.00-$200.00**

LPs

Sun LP-102, Original Golden Hits — Volume 1, 1969 ....**$7.50-$15.00**

LP-103, Original Golden Hits — Volume 2, 1969 ....**$7.50-$15.00**

Mercury SRM-1-637, The "Killer" Rocks On, 1972 ....**$7.50-$15.00**

SRM-1-690, Southern Roots — Back Home to Memphis, 1973 ....**$7.50-$15.00**

CHUCK MILLER:

45s

Capitol F2700, "The Pucker-Nut Free"/"After All," 1954 ....**$10.00-$20.00**

Mercury 70627, "The House of Blue Lights"/"Can't Help Wonderin'," 1955 ....**$10.00-$20.00**

71001, "The Auctioneer"/"Baby Doll," 1956 ....**$7.50-$15.00**

Mono LPs

Mercury MG-20195, After Hours, 1956 ....**$40.00-$80.00**

ROY ORBISON:

45s

Je-Wel 101, "Ooby Dooby"/"Tryin' to Get to You" (credited to "The Teen Kings," name misspelled "Oribson"), 1956 ....**$2,750.00-$4,000.00**

(if Orbison's name spelled correctly), 1956 ....**$2,750.00-$4,000.00**

Sun 242, "Ooby Dooby"/"Go! Go! Go!," 1956 ....**$50.00-$100.00**

251, "Rockhouse"/"You're My Baby," 1956 ....**$30.00-$60.00**

Monument 421, "Only the Lonely (Know the Way I Feel)"/"Here Comes That Song Again," 1960 ....**$12.50-$25.00**

Mono LPs

Monument M-4002, Lonely and Blue, 1961 ....**$75.00-$150.00**

4007, Crying, 1962 ....**$60.00-$120.00**

Stereo LPs

Monument SM-14002, Lonely and Blue, 1961 ....**$300.00-$600.00**

SLP-18003, In Dreams (white-rainbow label), 1963 ....**$50.00-$100.00**

(if on green-gold label, reissue), 1964 ....**$25.00-$50.00**

CARL PERKINS:

45s

Sun 234, "Blue Suede Shoes"/"Honey Don't!," 1956 ....**$30.00-$60.00**

243, "Boppin' the Blues"/"All Mama's Children," 1956 ....**$20.00-$40.00**

261, "Matchbox"/"Your True Love," 1957 ....**$15.00-$30.00**

Columbia 41131, "Pink Pedal Pushers"/"Jive After Five," 1958...**$15.00-$30.00**

(with picture sleeve, add), 1958 ....**$60.00-$120.00**

42405, "Hollywood City"/"The Fool I Used to Be," 1962 ....**$12.50-$25.00**

78s

234, "Blue Suede Shoes"/"Honey Don't!," 1956 ....**$20.00-$40.00**

243, "Boppin' the Blues"/"All Mama's Children," 1956 ....**$20.00-$40.00**

LPs

Sun SLP-1225, The Dance Album of Carl Perkins, 1957 .....**$600.00-$1,200.00**

SLP-1225, Teen Beat — The Best of Carl Perkins, 1961 ....**$250.00-$500.00**

REVEREND HORTON HEAT:

45s

Sub Pop 96, "Psychobilly Freakout"/"Baby You Know Who," 1990 ....**$3.00-$6.00**

(if on blue vinyl), 1990 ....**$4.50-$9.00**

(with foldover sleeve, add), 1990 ....**$3.00-$6.00**

BILLY LEE RILEY:

45s

Sun 245, "Trouble Bound"/"Rock with Me, Baby," 1956 ....**$60.00-$120.00**

260, "Flying Saucers Rock and Roll"/"I Want You Baby," 1957 ....**$50.00-$100.00**

Brunswick 55085, "Rockin' on the Moon"/"Is That All to the Ball," 1958 ....**$100.00-$200.00**

Mono LPs

Mercury MG-20965, Big Harmonica Special, 1964 ....**$10.00-$20.00**

GNP Crescendo GNP-2020, Billy Lee Riley, 1966 ....**$7.50-$15.00**

Stereo LPs

Mercury SR-60965, Big Harmonica Special, 1964 ....**$12.50-$25.00**

GNP Crescendo GNPS-2020, Billy Lee Riley, 1966 ....**$10.00-$20.00**

THE STRAY CATS:

45s

EMI America 8132, "Rock This Town"/"You Can't Hurry Love," 1982 ....**$1.50-$3.00**

(with picture sleeve, add), 1982 ....**$1.50-$3.00**

LPs

EMI America ST-17070, Built for Speed, 1982 ....**$6.00-$12.00**

SO-17102, Rant 'n Rave with the Stray Cats, 1983 ....**$5.00-$10.00**

GENE VINCENT:

45s

Capitol F3450, "Be-Bop-a-Lula"/"Woman Love" (small Capitol logo), 1956 ....**$25.00-$50.00**

(with large Capitol logo, any white label with blue vinyl pressings are counterfeits), 1956 ....**$35.00-$70.00**

F3530, "Race with the Devil"/"Gonna Back Up, Baby," 1956 ....**$20.00-$40.00**

F3558, "Bluejean Bop"/"Who Slapped John," 1956 ....**$20.00-$40.00**

Playground 100, "Story of the Rockers"/"Pickin' Poppies," 1968 ....**$100.00-$200.00**

LPs

Capitol T 764, Bluejean Bop!

(if turquoise label, stock copy), 1957 ....**$200.00-$400.00**

(if black label promo), 1957 ....**$500.00-$1,000.00**

(if yellow label promo), 1957 ....**$500.00-$1,000.00**

T 970, Gene Vincent and the Blue Caps

(if turquoise label stock copy), 1958 ....**$200.00-$400.00**

(if yellow label promo), 1958 ....**$500.00-$1,000.00**

(if black label promo), 1958 ....**$500.00-$1,000.00**

SONNY WEST:

45s

Atlantic 1174, "Rave On!"/"Call on Cupid," 1958 ....**$20.00-$40.00**

Nor-Va-Jak 1956, "Rock-Ola Ruby"/"Sweet Rockin' Baby" (misspelled "Sonee West"), 1959 ....**$50.00-$100.00**

78s

Nor-Va-Jak 1956, "Rock-Ola Ruby"/"Sweet Rockin' Baby" (misspelled "Sonee West"), 1959 ....**$75.00-$150.00**

History

Surf music, with its twangy guitar or bass guitar lead, sometimes combined with tightly woven vocal harmonies, began in the late 1950s. Instrumental surf music, best represented by artists such as Duane Eddy, Dick Dale and the Del-Tones, and the Ventures; and with songs like "Pipeline" by the Chantay's and "Wipe Out" by the Surfaris, captured the energy of the original "extreme" sport.

Vocal surf music added doo-wop lyrics about cars, girls, the beach, surfing, swimming—in short, having a good time at the Southern California shorelines. The Beach Boys and Jan and Dean crafted car song masterpieces ("Little Deuce Coupe," "409," "Little Old Lady from Pasadena"), as well as beach songs ("Surfin' U.S.A." and "Surf City"), and introspective pop songs about teen life ("In My Room," "A Surfer's Dream"). Other vocal surf groups include the Tigers ("GeeTO Tiger"), Ronny and the Daytonas ("GTO"), the Rip Chords ("Hey Little Cobra") and the Sunrays ("Andrea").

Several surf music records can be traced back to the creative pen of Brian Wilson. Besides helping out on several Jan and Dean classics, he also wrote and produced songs for The Honeys, an all-girl surf music trio. Wilson also helped the Beach Boys evolve into more experimental and exponential recordings, writing songs like "Good Vibrations" and "Wouldn't It Be Nice," as well as concept albums like the seminal *Pet Sounds*.

Surf music has made a small comeback, especially in movies and on television. Biopics of Jan and Dean and of

Photo credit: Courtesy Last Vestige Music Store, Albany, N.Y.

Duane Eddy's first album came with several cover variations. This one, with the record title in red and green print, was part of the second print run; titles with white print are part of the first print run, while a standing Duane Eddy represents the third and subsequent pressings.

***$50**, VG+ condition*

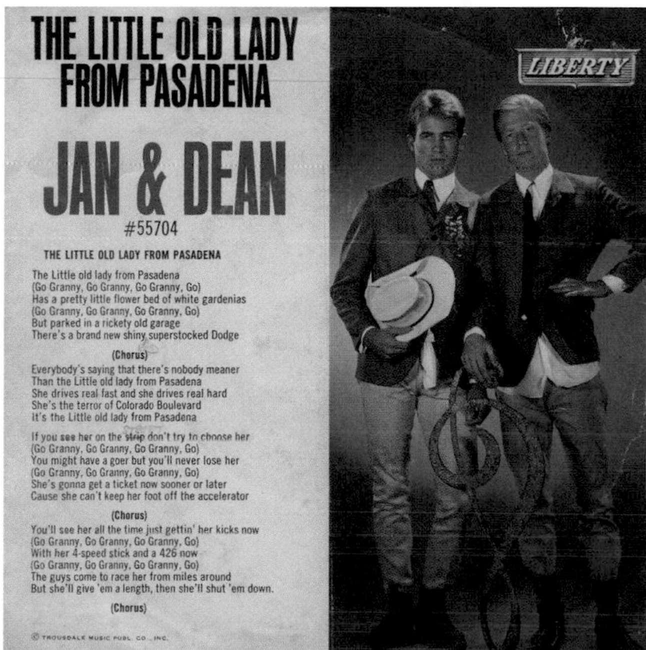

Jan Berry and Dean Torrance take the old car salesman anecdote about a used car driven by a "little old lady from Pasadena," and turned it into a surf-rock classic. This picture sleeve is much harder to find than the original 45 it once held.

***$7.50**, VG+ condition*

the Beach Boys were ratings-winners when they aired on TV, the Ventures' theme from "Hawaii Five-O" became their most recognized hit since "Walk—Don't Run," and Dick Dale's instrumental "Miserlou" was prominently featured in the film *Pulp Fiction*.

Surf music should not be confused with "Beach" music, the predominant dance music of the Carolinas. Beach music, like Northern Soul in England, involves danceable songs by both popular and unknown artists of the 1960s. Some pop/soul/rock groups whose music also can be classified as "beach music" include Spanky and Our Gang, Jay and the Techniques, and General Johnson.

Almost all the early Capitol 45s by the Beach Boys had picture sleeves of one form or another. This sleeve for "Help Me, Rhonda" is not difficult to locate.

***$40**, NM condition*

One of Dick Dale's earliest pressings, on his own custom "Del-Tone" label, before he joined Capitol Records. His Del-Tone catalog was later absorbed by Capitol, and several of his early surf guitar classics were reissued with new Capitol catalog numbers.

***$20**, NM condition*

Photo credit: From the Collection of Val Shively

What To Look For

Surf music has been reissued on countless CDs and greatest hits packages. Finding 45s is not hard, but finding the accompanying picture sleeves in near-mint condition is extremely tough. This is especially true of sleeves from the Beach Boys, Jan and Dean, and the Honeys.

The Ventures have released more albums than any instrumental group in the rock era, and have new titles available even today. Their earliest albums, which were recorded for the Blue Horizon and Dolton labels, are very collectible. Make sure if you do purchase a Ventures album that contains "Walk—Don't Run," that it contains the original version, as the group re-recorded the track in 1964 for use in a motion picture of the same name.

The lion's share of the Beach Boys' catalog exists on major labels like Capitol and Reprise, as well as their own custom label Brother. A series of recordings they made before signing with Capitol exist and have been regularly reissued by low-budget labels (these albums include the Beach Boys' first recording, "Surfin'," as well as an a capella version of "Surfer Girl"). Although the original 45 pressings of these tracks on the "X" and Candix labels are rare and collectible, pressings on other labels do not have this same collectible value.

Because the Ventures' first Dolton album, Walk Don't Run, *was recorded so quickly, the real Ventures couldn't stick around for the cover photograph—so both male and female models were used for the cover art.*

***$40**, VG+ condition*

Books

Blair, John, *The Illustrated Discography of Surf Music 1961-1965* (3rd Ed.), Popular Culture, Ann Arbor, Mich., 1995.

Dalley, Robert J., *Surfin' Guitars: Instrumental Surf Bands of the Sixties* (2nd Ed.), Popular Culture, Ann Arbor, Mich., 1996.

Web Pages

The Tsunami Soul Surf Music Page, with many links to other surf music home pages: http://www.oberlin.edu/~serials/Surf.html

The official home page for Dick Dale and the Del-Tones: http://www.dickdale.com

The Ventures' home page: http://www.theventures.com

An unofficial site for Beach Boys fans, with links to other pages: http://www.beachboys.com

Usenet newsgroups: rec.music.artists.beach-boys, alt.music.beach-boys

The Tigers' "GeeTO Tiger!" comes with different picture sleeves—this more common sleeve features the band around a '65 Pontiac GTO. A much-rarer sleeve actually features the car, with a tiger-skin rug draped over the car hood.
***$100**, for NM sleeve*

After the success of The Surfaris' "Wipe Out," the group made several "Hit City" albums for Decca, each one featuring surf renditions of popular songs of the day.
***$50**, NM condition*

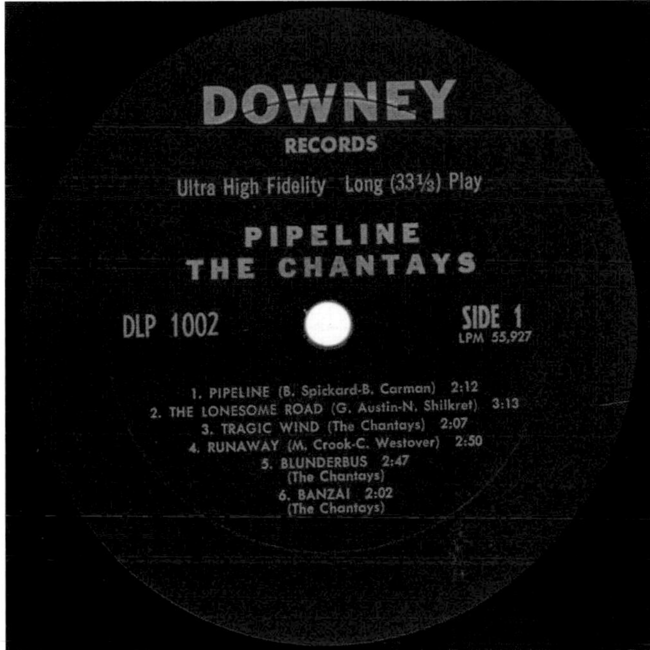

The most collectible surf records are those that were initially released on tiny independent labels—containing hits that eventually moved on to national distribution. Before "Pipeline," a hit by the Chantays, received major distribution through Dot Records, the song was originally released on Downey Records, owned by future talk show host Morton Downey, Jr.
***$220**, NM condition*

THE BEACH BOYS:

45s

X Records 301, "Surfin'"/"Luau," 1961 .... **$500.00-$1,000.00**
Candix 301, "Surfin'"/"Luau"
(if label says "Distributed by Era Record Sales, Inc."), 1961
.... **$100.00-$200.00**
(if no mention of Era Records on label), 1961 .... **$150.00-$300.00**
(if on Candix 331, reissue), 1962.. **$100.00-$200.00**
Capitol 4777, "Surfin' Safari"/"409," 1962 .... **$12.50-$25.00**
(with picture sleeve, add), 1962 .... **$40.00-$80.00**
4932, "Surfin' U.S A"/"Shut Down"
(if "Surfin' U.S.A." written by Brian Wilson), 1963..................... **$12.50-$25.00**
(if "Surfin' U.S.A." written by Chuck Berry), 1963 .... **$12.50-$25.00**
5009, "Surfer Girl"/"Little Deuce Coupe," 1963......................... **$12.50-$25.00**
5069, "Be True to Your School"/"In My Room," 1963.............. **$12.50-$25.00**
5118, "Fun, Fun, Fun"/"Why Do Fools Fall in Love"
(if A-side credited only to Brian Wilson), 1964 .... **$12.50-$25.00**
(if A-side credited to Brian Wilson and Mike Love), 1964 .... **$10.00-$20.00**
(with picture sleeve, add), 1964.. **$20.00-$40.00**
5174, "I Get Around"/"Don't Worry Baby" (first pressing, orange-yellow swirl label), 1964.. **$12.50-$25.00**
(with picture sleeve, add), 1964.. **$20.00-$40.00**
5395, "Help Me, Rhonda"/"Kiss Me, Baby," 1965 .... **$12.50-$25.00**
(with picture sleeve, add), 1965.. **$20.00-$40.00**
5561, "Barbara Ann"/"Girl Don't Tell Me," 1965......................... **$10.00-$20.00**
(with picture sleeve, glossy finish), 1965 .... **$75.00-$150.00**
(with picture sleeve, non-glossy finish), 1965 .... **$100.00-$200.00**
5602, "Sloop John B"/"You're So Good to Me," 1966............... **$10.00-$20.00**
(with picture sleeve, add), 1966.. **$15.00-$30.00**
5676, "Good Vibrations"/"Let's Go Away for Awhile," 1966 .... **$10.00-$20.00**
(with picture sleeve, add), 1966.. **$15.00-$30.00**
Brother 1001, "Heroes and Villains"/"You're Welcome," 1967....... **$6.00-$12.00**
(with picture sleeve, add), 1967.. **$50.00-$100.00**
Brother/Reprise 0894, "Add Some Music to Your Day"/"Susie Cincinnati," 1970 .... **$4.00-$8.00**
0998, "Cool, Cool Water"/"Forever," 1971 .... **$40.00-$80.00**
1325, "Sail On Sailor"/"Only With You," 1975 .... **$4.00-$8.00**
1336, "Wouldn't It Be Nice"/"Caroline, No," 1975 .... **$6.00-$12.00**
1354, "Rock and Roll Music"/"The TM Song," 1976 .... **$2.00-$4.00**
FBI 7701, "East Meets West"/"Rhapsody," 1986 .... **$10.00-$20.00**
Elektra 69385, "Kokomo"/Little Richard, "Tutti-Frutti," 1988........ **$1.50-$3.00**
Sub Pop 363, "I Just Wasn't Made for These Times"/"Wouldn't It Be Nice"/ "Here Today," 1996 .... **$2.50-$5.00**
(with folded cardboard picture sleeve, add), 1996 .... **$2.50-$5.00**

Mono LPs

Capitol T 1808, Surfin' Safari, 1962 .... **$20.00-$40.00**
T 1890, Surfin' U.S.A., 1963 .... **$20.00-$40.00**
T 1981, Surfer Girl, 1963 .... **$20.00-$40.00**
T 1998, Little Deuce Coupe, 1963 .... **$20.00-$40.00**
T 2458, Pet Sounds, 1966 .... **$20.00-$40.00**
T 2859, Wild Honey, 1967 .... **$20.00-$40.00**
Brother T 9001, Smiley Smile, 1967 .... **$20.00-$40.00**
(if Barry Turnbull is mentioned on back cover), 1967............... **$15.00-$30.00**
MS 2197, Pet Sounds, 1974 .... **$10.00-$20.00**
DCC Compact Classics LPZ-2006, Pet Sounds, 1995............. **$60.00-$120.00**

Stereo LPs

Asylum R 113793, Surf's Up (RCA Record Club edition, pressed with incorrect labels), 1972.. **$75.00-$150.00**
MS 2118, Holland (with bonus EP, "Mount Vernon and Fairway," in picture sleve), 1973.. **$7.50-$15.00**
(if white label promo), 1973.. **$20.00-$40.00**
(if test pressing contains "We Got Love," later deleted), 1973
.... **$250.00-$500.00**
Capitol DT 1808, Surfin' Safari
(with both "Capitol Full Dimensional Stereo" and "Duophonic" on cover), 1962 .... **$40.00-$80.00**
(if only "Duophonic" on cover), 1962... **$12.50-$25.00**
ST 1890, Surfin' U.S.A., 1963 .... **$25.00-$50.00**
ST 2110, All Summer Long
(with "Don't Break Down" on cover), 1964............................. **$25.00-$50.00**
(with "Don't Back Down" on cover), 1964 .... **$15.00-$30.00**
ST 2164, The Beach Boys' Christmas Album, 1964.................. **$25.00-$50.00**
DT 2458, Pet Sounds, 1966 .... **$15.00-$30.00**
ST 2859, Wild Honey, 1967 .... **$10.00-$20.00**
SVBB-11307, Endless Summer (2 LPs with poster, orange labels), 1974
.... **$10.00-$20.00**
SVBB-11384, Spirit of America (2 LPs, orange labels, "Capitol" on bottom), 1975 .... **$7.50-$15.00**
Caribou JZ 35752, L A. (Light Album), 1979 .... **$5.00-$10.00**
Mobile Fidelity 1-116, Surfer Girl (audiophile pressing), 1984
.... **$15.00-$30.00**

THE CHALLENGERS:

45s

Vault 900, "Bull Dog"/"Torquay," 1963 .... **$10.00-$20.00**
910, "Hot Rod Hootenanny"/"Maybellene," 1964.................... **$15.00-$30.00**
GNP Crescendo 362, "The Man from U.N.C.L.E."/"The Streets of London,"

Mono LPs

Vault LP-100, Surfbeat 1963, 1963 .... **$25.00-$50.00**
LP-101, Lloyd Thaxton Goes Surfin' with the Challengers, 1963
.... **$30.00-$60.00**
(if title changed to "Surfin' with the Challengers"), 1963......... **$25.00-$50.00**
GNP Crescendo GNP-2010, The Challengers at the Teenage Fair, 1965
.... **$10.00-$20.00**
GNP-2018, The Man from U.N.C.L.E., 1965 .... **$10.00-$20.00**

Stereo LPs

Vault VS-100, Surfbeat 1963
(if black vinyl), 1963 .... **$40.00-$80.00**
(if orange, red or yellow vinyl), 1963 .... **$125.00-$250.00**
VS-101, Lloyd Thaxton Goes Surfin' with the Challengers
(if black vinyl), 1963 .... **$50.00-$100.00**
(if orange, red, blue or yellow vinyl), 1963 .... **$125.00-$250.00**
GNP Crescendo GNPS-2010, The Challengers at the Teenage Fair, 1965
.... **$12.50-$25.00**

THE CHANTAYS:

45s

Downey 104, "Pipeline"/"Move It," 1963.................................... **$30.00-$60.00**
108, "Monsoon"/"Scotch Heights," 1963 .... **$15.00-$30.00**
Dot 116440, "Pipeline"/"Move It," 1963...................................... **$12.50-$25.00**
(if on Dot 145, reissue), 1966 .... **$4.00-$8.00**
16492, "Monsoon"/"Scotch Heights," 1963 .... **$10.00-$20.00**

Mono LPs

Downey DLP-1002, Pipeline, 1963 .... **$110.00-$220.00**

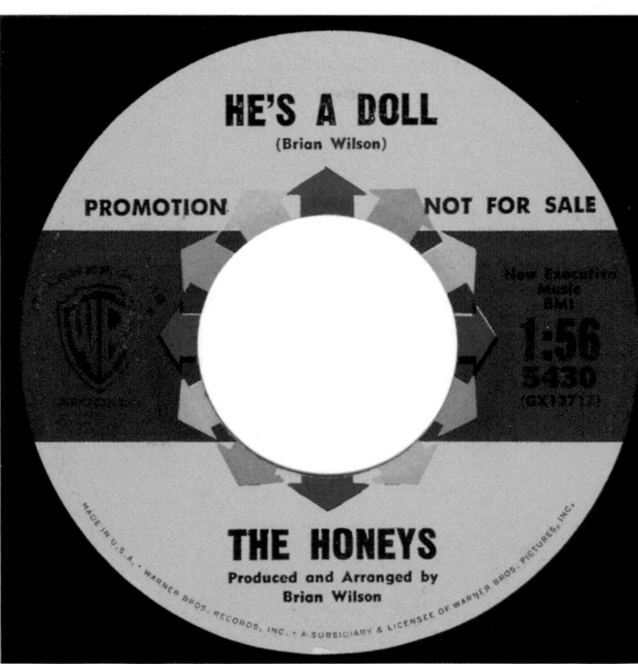

In the argot of the surf, "honeys" were the girlfriends of beach boys. This may explain why Brian Wilson renamed the Rozell Sisters "The Honeys," then wrote and produced their singles—and eventually married one of their members.
***$450**, VG+ condition*

Dot DLP-3516, Pipeline, 1963 .... **$25.00-$50.00**

Stereo LPs

Downey DLPS-1002, Pipeline, 1963 .... **$175.00-$350.00**
Dot 25516, Pipeline, 1963 .... **$40.00-$80.00**
25771, Two Sides of the Chantays, 1966 .... **$40.00-$80.00**

DICK DALE AND THE DEL-TONES:

45s

Deltone 5012, "Oh Whee Marie"/"Breaking Heart," 1959 .... **$30.00-$60.00**
5019, "Misirlou"/"Eight Till Midnight," 1962 .... **$12.50-$25.00**
5020, "Peppermint Man"/"Surf Beat," 1962 .... **$12.50-$25.00**
5028, "Run for Your Life"/"Lovin on My Brain," 1963 .... **$15.00-$30.00**
4939, "Misirlou"/"Eight Till Midnight," 1963 .... **$10.00-$20.00**
4940, "Surf Beat"/"Peppermint Man," 1963 .... **$10.00-$20.00**
Capitol 4963, "King of the Surf Guitar"/"Havah Nagilah," 1963 .... **$10.00-$20.00**
(with picture sleeve, add), 1963 .... **$40.00-$80.00**
5010, "Secret Surfin' Spot"/"Surfin and a-Swingin," 1963 .... **$10.00-$20.00**
Cougar 711, "Ramblin' Mari"/"You're Hurtin' Now," 1967 .... **$7.50-$15.00**
712, "Taco Wagon"/"Spanish Kiss," 1967 .... **$7.50-$15.00**
Columbia 38-07340, "Pipeline"/"Love Struck Baby," 1987 .... **$2.00-$4.00**
(with picture sleeve, add), 1987 .... **$3.00-$6.00**

Mono LPs

Deltone LPM-1001, Surfer's Choice, 1962 .... **$75.00-$150.00**
T 1886, Surfer's Choice, 1962 .... **$30.00-$60.00**
Capitol T 1930, King of the Surf Guitar, 1963 .... **$30.00-$60.00**
T 2293, Rock Out—Live at Ciro's, 1965 .... **$50.00-$100.00**

Stereo LPs

Capitol ST 1930, King of the Surf Guitar, 1963 .... **$50.00-$100.00**
ST 2002, Checkered Flag, 1963 .... **$40.00-$80.00**
ST 2053, Mr. Eliminator, 1964 .... **$40.00-$80.00**
ST 2111, Summer Surf (with bonus 45 by Jerry Cole, "Racing Waves"/"Movie' Surf," in front cover pocket) 1964 .... **$60.00-$120.00**
GNP Crescendo GNPS-2095, Greatest Hits, 1975 .... **$6.00-$12.00**
Rhino RNLP-70074, King of the Surf Guitar: The Best of Dick Dale and the Del-Tones, 1961-1964, 1986 .... **$6.00-$12.00**

DUANE EDDY:

45s

Ford 500, "Ramrod"/"Caravan" (credited to Duane Eddy and his Roc-a-Billies), 1957 .... **$1,000.00-$1,500.00**
Jamie 1101, "Moovin N' Groovin'"/"Up and Down"
(if pink label, first pressings), 1958 .... **$25.00-$50.00**
(if all yellow label, "Jamie" at top), 1958 .... **$12.50-$25.00**
1126, "Forty Miles of Bad Road"/"The Quiet Three" (mono), 1959 .... **$10.00-$20.00**
(if stereo 45), 1959 .... **$25.00-$50.00**
(with picture sleeve, add), 1959 .... **$25.00-$50.00**
RCA Victor 47-7999, "Deep in the Heart of Texas"/"Saints and Sinners," 1962 .... **$6.00-$12.00**
(with picture sleeve, add), 1962 .... **$12.50-$25.00**
47-8087, "(Dance with the) Guitar Man"/"Stretchin Out," 1962 .... **$7.50-$15.00**
(with picture sleeve, add), 1962 .... **$15.00-$30.00**
Colpix 779, "Trash"/"South Phoenix," 1965 .... **$7.50-$15.00**
788, "Don't Think Twice, It's All Right"/"House of the Rising Sun," 1965 .... **$7.50-$15.00**
(with picture sleeve, add), 1965 .... **$25.00-$50.00**

Mono LPs

Jamie JLP-3000, Have "Twangy" Guitar-Will Travel
(first cover, Eddy sitting with guitar case, title on cover in white), 1959 .... **$60.00-$120.00**
(second cover, Eddy sitting with guitar case, title on cover in green and red), 1959 .... **$50.00-$100.00**
(third cover, Eddy standing with guitar), 1959 .... **$25.00-$50.00**
JLPM-3014, $1,000,000.00 Worth of Twang, 1960 .... **$20.00-$40.00**
JLPM-3021, $1,000,000.00 Worth of Twang, Volume 2, 1962 .... **$20.00-$40.00**
RCA Victor LPM-2525, Twistin' 'N' Twangin, 1962 .... **$12.50-$25.00**
LPM-2648, Dance with the Guitar Man, 1962 .... **$12.50-$25.00**
Colpix CP-490, Duane A-Go-Go, 1965 .... **$15.00-$30.00**
Reprise R-6218, The Biggest Twang of Them All, 1966 .... **$15.00-$30.00**

Stereo LPs

Jamie JLPS-3000, Have "Twangy" Guitar—Will Travel
(first cover, Eddy sitting with guitar case, title on cover in white), 1959 .... **$200.00-$400.00**
(second cover, Eddy sitting with guitar case, title on cover in green and red), 1959 .... **$150.00-$300.00**
(third cover, Eddy standing with guitar, plays true stereo), 1959 .... **$50.00-$100.00**
(third cover, Eddy standing with guitar, plays fake rechanneled stereo), 196? .... **$25.00-$50.00**
JLPS-3011, Songs of Our Heritage (gatefold cover), 1960 .... **$50.00-$100.00**
(if red or blue vinyl), 1960 .... **$250.00-$500.00**
JLPS-3014, $1,000,000.00 Worth of Twang, 1960 .... **$35.00-$70.00**
JLPS-3021, $1,000,000.00 Worth of Twang, Volume 2, 1962 ... **$15.00-$30.00**
RCA Victor LSP-2525, Twistin' N' Twangin', 1962 .... **$20.00-$40.00**
LSP-2648, Dance with the Guitar Man, 1962 .... **$20.00-$40.00**
Colpix CPS-490, Duane A-Go-Go, 1965 .... **$20.00-$40.00**
CPS-494, Duane Eddy Does Bob Dylan, 1965 .... **$20.00-$40.00**

THE HONEYS:

45s

Warner Bros. 5430, "He's a Doll"/"The Love of a Boy and Girl," 1964 .... **$300.00-$600.00**
Capitol 4952, "Surfin' Down the Swanee River"/"Shoot the Curl," 1963 .... **$75.00-$150.00**
(with picture sleeve, add), 1963 .... **$400.00-$800.00**
5034, "Hide Go Seek"/"Pray for Surf," 1963 .... **$100.00-$200.00**
5093, "The One You Can't Have"/"From Jimmy With Tears," 1963 .... **$100.00-$200.00**
2454, "Goodnight My Love"/"Tonight You Belong to Me," 1969 .... **$40.00-$80.00**

JAN AND DEAN:

45s

Dore 522, "Baby Talk"/"Jeannette Get Your Hair Done," 1959 .... **$15.00-$30.00**
531, "There's a Girl"/"My Heart Sings," 1959 .... **$12.50-$25.00**
548, "Cindy"/"Whiter Tennis Sneakers," 1960 .... **$12.50-$25.00**
555, "We Go Together"/"Rosilane" (B-side also available as "Rosie Lane"), 1960 .... **$12.50-$25.00**
(with picture sleeve, add), 1960 .... **$60.00-$120.00**
576, "Gee"/"Such a Good Night to Be Together," 1960 .... **$12.50-$25.00**
(with picture sleeve, add), 1960 .... **$150.00-$300.00**
Liberty 55397, "A Sunday Kind of Love"/"Poor Little Puppet," 1961 .... **$12.50-$25.00**
55454, "Tennessee"/"Your Heart Has Changed Its Mind," 1962 .... **$12.50-$25.00**
55531, "Linda"/"When I Learn How to Cry," 1963 .... **$12.50-$25.00**
55580, "Surf City"/"She's My Summer Girl," 1963 .... **$7.50-$15.00**
(with picture sleeve, add), 1963 .... **$20.00-$40.00**
55613, "Honolulu Lulu"/"Someday," 1963 .... **$7.50-$15.00**
(with picture sleeve, add), 1963 .... **$20.00-$40.00**
55672, "Dead Man's Curve"/"The New Girl in School," 1964 ..... **$7.50-$15.00**
(with picture sleeve, add), 1964 .... **$20.00-$40.00**
55704, "The Little Old Lady (From Pasadena)"/"My Mighty G.T.O.," 1964 .... **$7.50-$15.00**
(with picture sleeve, add), 1964 .... **$20.00-$40.00**
55724, "Ride the Wild Surf"/"The Anaheim, Azusa, and Cucamonga Sewing Circle, Book Review and Timing Association," 1964 .... **$7.50-$15.00**
(with picture sleeve, add), 1964 .... **$20.00-$40.00**
Jan & Dean 10, "Hawaii"/"Tijuana," 1966 .... **$37.50-$75.00**
11, "Fan Tan"/"Love and Hate," 1966 .... **$60.00-$120.00**
Warner Bros. 7151, "Only a Boy"/"Love and Hate," 1967 .... **$20.00-$40.00**

Mono LPs

Dore LP-101, Jan and Dean (blue label), 1960 .... **$200.00-$400.00**
(with bonus photo, add), 1960 .... **$60.00-$120.00**
Liberty LRP-3248, Jan and Dean's Golden Hits, 1962 .... **$15.00-$30.00**
LRP-3294, Jan and Dean Take Linda Surfin', 1963 .... **$25.00-$50.00**
LRP-3314, Surf City and Other Swingin Cities, 1963 .... **$20.00-$40.00**
LRP-3377 , The Little Old Lady from Pasadena, 1964 .... **$15.00-$30.00**

Stereo LPs

Liberty LST-7294, Jan and Dean Take Linda Surfin', 1963 .... **$40.00-$80.00**
LST-7314, Surf City and Other Swingin' Cities, 1963 .... **$25.00-$50.00**
LST-7368, Ride the Wild Surf, 1964 .... **$20.00-$40.00**
LST-7444, Jan and Dean Meet Batman, 1966 .... **$35.00-$70.00**
Sunset SUS-5156, Jan and Dean, 1967 .... **$7.50-$15.00**
United Artists UAS-9961, Anthology (Legendary Masters Series, Vol. 3) (2 LPs), 1971 .... **$12.50-$25.00**

THE RIP CHORDS:

45s

42921, "Hey, Little Cobra"/"The Queen," 1963 .... **$10.00-$20.00**

(if "Hey Little Cobra" on both sides, yellow vinyl promo), 1963 ....$25.00-$50.00
43035, "Three Window Coupe"/"Hot Rod U.S.A.," 1964 ....$7.50-$15.00
(if "Three Window Coupe" on both sides, red vinyl promo), 1964 ....$25.00-$50.00

Mono LPs

Columbia CL 2151, Hey Little Cobra and Other Hot Rod Hits, 1964 ....$20.00-$40.00

Stereo LPs

CS 8951, Hey Little Cobra and Other Hot Rod Hits, 1964 ....$25.00-$50.00
9016, Three Window Coupe, 1964 ....$35.00-$70.00

RONNY AND THE DAYTONAS:

45s

Mala 481, "G.T.O."/"Hot Rod Baby," 1964 ....$12.50-$25.00
531, "Antique '32 Studebaker Dictator Coupe"/"Then the Rains Came," 1966 ....$10.00-$20.00
RCA Victor 47-8896, "All American Girl"/"Dianne, Dianne," 1966 ....$6.00-$12.00
(with picture sleeve, add), 1966 ....$12.50-$25.00

Mono LPs

Mala 4001, G.T.O., 1964 ....$60.00-$120.00
4002, Sandy, 1966 ....$40.00-$80.00

Stereo LPs

Mala 4002S, Sandy, 1966 ....$50.00-$100.00

THE SUNRAYS:

45s

Tower 148, "I Live for the Sun"/"Bye Baby Bye," 1965 ....$6.00-$12.00
191, "Andrea"/"You Don't Phase Me," 1966 ....$6.00-$12.00

Mono LPs

Tower T 5017, Andrea, 1966 ....$25.00-$50.00

Stereo LPs

Tower ST 5017, Andrea, 1966 ....$30.00-$60.00

THE SURFARIS:

45s

DFS 11/12, "Wipe Out"/"Surfer Joe," 1963 ....$2,250.00-$3,000.00
Princess 50, "Wipe Out"/"Surfer Joe"
(long versions of both songs), 1963 ....$200.00-$400.00
(short versions of both songs, "RE-1" stamped in dead wax), 1963 ....$75.00-$150.00
Dot 16479, "Wipe Out"/"Surfer Joe," 1963 ....$7.50-$15.00
16757, "Surfer Joe"/"Can't Sit Down," 1965 ....$15.00-$30.00
(if B-side credit is to the Challengers—who really performed the song), 1965 ....$25.00-$50.00
Decca 31538, "Point Panic"/"Waikiki Run," 1963 ....$7.50-$15.00
31561, "A Surfer's Christmas List"/"Santa's Speed Shop," 1963 ....$15.00-$30.00
32003, "Wipe Out"/"I'm a Hog for You," 1966 ....$5.00-$10.00
Dot 144, "Wipe Out"/"Surfer Joe"
(if black label, script "Dot" in multicolor letters), 1966 ....$5.00-$10.00
(if multicolored label, "DOT" in all capital letters in box at top), 1969 ....$3.00-$6.00
(if red vinyl promo, "Wipe Out" on both sides), 1966 ....$50.00-$100.00
(if red vinyl promo, "Surfer Joe" on both sides), 1966 ....$75.00-$150.00

Mono LPs

Dot DLP-3535, Wipe Out
(if back cover shows five Surfaris), 1963 ....$25.00-$50.00
(if back cover shows four Surfaris), 1963 ....$20.00-$40.00
(if back cover shows NO Surfaris), 1963 ....$15.00-$30.00
Decca DL 4470, The Surfaris Play Wipe Out, 1963 ....$12.50-$25.00
DL 4487, Hit City '64, 1964 ....$20.00-$40.00
DL 4614, Hit City '65, 1965 ....$20.00-$40.00

Stereo LPs

Dot DLP-25535, Wipe Out
(if back cover shows five Surfaris), 1963 ....$40.00-$80.00
(if back cover shows four Surfaris), 1963 ....$25.00-$50.00
(if back cover shows NO Surfaris), 1963 ....$20.00-$40.00
Decca DL 74487, Hit City '64, 1964 ....$25.00-$50.00
DL 74560, Fun City, U.S.A., 1964 ....$25.00-$50.00
DL 74663, It Ain't Me, Babe, 1965 ....$25.00-$50.00

THE TIGERS:

45s

Colpix 773, "GeeTO Tiger"/"The Prowl," 1965 ....$25.00-$50.00
(with picture sleeve of band on Pontiac GTO, add), 1965 ....$50.00-$100.00
SPEC-773, "GeeTO Tiger"/"The Big Sounds of the GeeTO Tiger," 1965 ....$40.00-$80.00
(with picture sleeve of tiger-skin rug on Pontiac GTO, add), 1965 ....$100.00-$200.00

THE VENTURES:

45s

Blue Horizon 100, "The Real McCoy"/"Cookies and Coke," 1960 ....$300.00-$600.00
101, "Walk Don't Run"/"Home," 1960 ....$12.50-$25.00
102, "Hold Me, Thrill Me, Kiss Me"/"No Next Time" (credited to "Scott Douglas and the Venture Quintet"), 1960 ....$100.00-$200.00
Dolton 25X, "Walk Don't Run"/"The McCoy," 1960 ....$10.00-$20.00
25, "Walk Don't Run"/"Home," 1960 ....$12.50-$25.00
94, "Fugitive"/"Scratchin'," 1964 ....$7.50-$15.00
96, "Walk Don't Run '64"/"The Cruel Sea," 1964 ....$7.50-$15.00
(with picture sleeve, add), 1964 ....$15.00-$30.00
Liberty 55967, "Strawberry Fields Forever"/"Endless Dream," 1967 ....$4.00-$8.00
55977, "Theme from "Endless Summer"/"Strawberry Fields Forever," 1967 ....$4.00-$8.00
56044, "Walk Don't Run-Land of 1000 Dances"/"Too Young to Know My Mind," 1968 ....$3.00-$6.00

Mono LPs

Dolton BLP 2003, Walk Don't Run
(if pale blue label, dolphins on top), 1960 ....$25.00-$50.00
(if dark label, logo on left), 1963 ....$10.00-$20.00
BLP 2006, Another Smash!!!
(if pale blue label, dolphins on top), 1961 ....$25.00-$50.00
(if dark label, logo on left), 1963 ....$10.00-$20.00
BLP 2037, The Ventures A-Go-Go, 1965 ....$12.50-$25.00
BLP 2050, Guitar Freakout, 1967 ....$10.00-$20.00
Liberty LRP-2052, Super Psychedelics, 1967 ....$10.00-$20.00
LRP-2055, Flights of Fancy, 1968 ....$15.00-$30.00

Stereo LPs

BST 8003, Walk Don't Run
(if pale blue label, dolphins on top), 1960 ....$30.00-$60.00
(if dark label, logo on left), 1963 ....$12.50-$25.00
BST 8006, Another Smash!!!
(if pale blue label, dolphins on top), 1961 ....$30.00-$60.00
(if dark label, logo on left), 1963 ....$12.50-$25.00
Liberty LST-8052, Super Psychedelics, 1967 ....$12.50-$25.00
LST-8053, Golden Greats by the Ventures, 1967 ....$10.00-$20.00
LST-8061, Hawaii Five-O, 1969 ....$7.50-$15.00

The Albany, N.Y.-based new wave band Blotto put out one of the funniest send-ups of surf music, when their song, "I Wanna Be A Lifeguard" was included in their debut EP, "Hello, My Name is Blotto, What's Yours?"

***$12**, NM condition*

CHAPTER 24

SWING MUSIC

History

Between 1935 and 1945, swing music was the most popular musical genre, a style that put couples on a dance floor to the Lindy Hop, the Charleston or any other number of popular dance steps. Swing music was different from straight jazz in that swing used melodic riffs, short snatches of melody that could be played between bandmembers in a rhythmic, call-and-response pattern. Instead of a small jazz trio or quartet, swing music was predominantly played by huge "big band" orchestras of ten to fifteen members, an uptempo symphony of brass, reeds, strings, and percussion.

With the growing popularity of radio in the 1930s, and a desire to have live entertainment available, many symphonic orchestras and 'big bands' received their own radio shows and plenty of airplay. Hotel ballrooms became instant broadcast studios, and the dance floor became a live studio audience. The big bands were essentially self-contained orchestras, with a featured vocalist or quartet, experienced sidemen, guest soloists, and a bandleader who did more than just swing a baton.

In 1935, Benny Goodman's orchestra was one of three groups appearing on the nationally broadcast radio show *Let's Dance*. Because of the show's timeslot (10:30 p.m. eastern to 4:30 a.m.), Goodman's orchestra would perform in the last third of the show, behind the orchestras of Ken Murray and Xavier Cugat. While East Coast listeners were already asleep by the time Goodman's band played, listeners on the West Coast got the chance to hear Goodman's uptempo performances. Working with Fletcher Henderson on song interpretations that would blow the doors off a hotel ballroom, Goodman took his band on tour, with an acclaimed performance on August 21, 1935, at Los Angeles'

The records by Glenn Miller and his Orchestra, arguably the most recognizable of swing artists, are easy to find today—this four-record 78-RPM "Smart Set" features many of Miller's biggest hits, including "Pennsylvania 6-5000" and "Chattanooga Choo Choo."
***$10**, VG condition*

Benny Goodman's "King Porter Stomp," one of the tracks that wowed the Palomar Ballroom crowd. The lineup in Goodman's Orchestra at the time included drummer Gene Krupa and saxophonist Bunny Berigan, both of whom would eventually lead their own swing bands.
***$20**, NM condition*

Palomar Ballroom, signaling the arrival of swing music. After that performance, and a Carnegie Hall concert that rocked the building down to its foundations, Benny Goodman became "the King of Swing."

By the late 1930s, swing music had accounted for 70% of all records sold in America, and big band members were idolized and scrutinized with the same fervor as one would follow a favorite baseball team. Sidemen like drummer Gene Krupa, guitarist Tony Mottola, trumpeters Roy Eldridge and Louis Armstrong, sax virtuoso Coleman Hawkins, and pianist Fats Waller became stars in their own right, many of them forming their own orchestras. Some sidemen would quit one band and join another—for example, when trumpeter Cootie Williams left Duke Ellington's orchestra to work with Benny Goodman's orchestra, fans of both bandleaders took great notice.

As the decade drew to a close, the top swing bands included the Glenn Miller Orchestra, the Tommy Dorsey Orchestra, the Jimmy Dorsey Orchestra, and the Artie Shaw Orchestra, as well as groups headed up by Duke Ellington and Benny Goodman. Interestingly, the uptempo swing sound permeated through other musical genres—Bob Wills and his Texas Playboys created "western swing," mixing swing music with a country and bluegrass twang. Spike Jones and his City Slickers recorded swing music with a ribald, humorous twist. In New York City, Sam Medoff and his Orchestra had a long-running radio broadcast in which they took old Yiddish folk melodies and gave them a swing beat.

By 1942, however, World War II draft boards called up musicians, vocalists, and bandleaders to serve their country on the front lines. Many of the musicians became part of special war-related services, playing swing and big band music for the soldiers and sailors overseas. Meanwhile, those who remained in America were locked in a bitter union sit-down strike against the record companies, in an

The vocal harmony quartet was just as important to a sing band as a horn section. Paula Kelly and The Modernaires were Glenn Miller's top vocal quartet, just as the Pied Pipers belonged to Tommy Dorsey's band.

***$5**, VG condition*

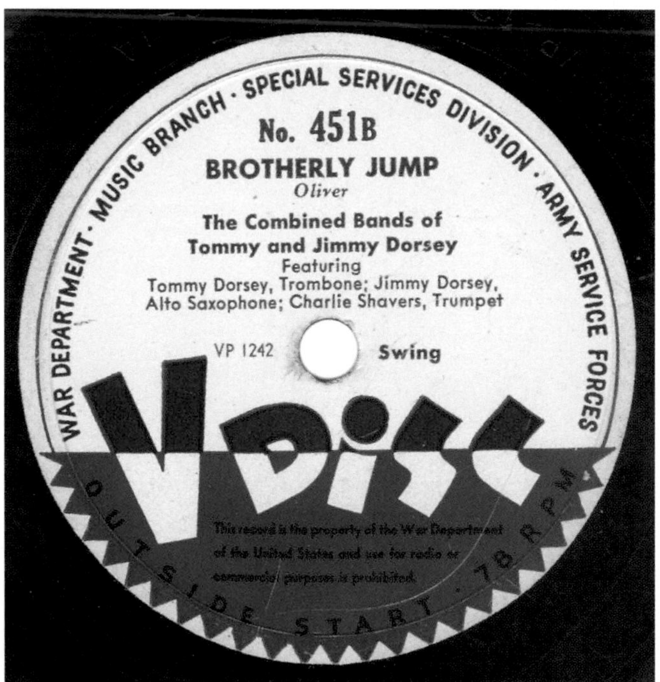

While Tommy and Jimmy Dorsey had two competing orchestras and seldom recorded together in the 1940s, they did record this V-Disc record for the soldiers and sailors overseas, and combined their orchestras for this once-in-a-lifetime recording session.

***$40**, NM condition*

Photo credit: From the collection of Henry Sapoznik.

Sam Medoff and His Yiddish Swing Orchestra mixed traditional Hebrew and Yiddish melodies with a swing beat—their versions of "Dayenu" and "The Bridegroom Special" were broadcast through New York City Yiddish radio stations in the 1940s. These acetates were later the subject of an NPR radio special.

***$40**, VG+ condition*

effort to extract more royalties from jukebox and radio airplay. The crippling strike lasted almost two years, during which time union musicians could not record for the major record companies.

They could, however, record for V-Disc, a record company created by the United States Army to provide recorded music for infantrymen and seabees. Freed from recording contracts that prevented musicians from rival labels from recording together, V-Disc brought artists and musicians together, recording 12-inch unbreakable vinylite 78s. With spoken-word introductions on each record, assuring the troops that the musical community supported them and wished them a safe return home, these V-Discs were as prized as a letter from home.

In the late 1990s, there was a revival of swing and jump blues music, as contemporary groups like the Cherry Poppin' Daddies, the Brian Setzer Orchestra, and the Royal Crown Revue took vintage melodies and riffs, and modernized them with electric guitars. Traditional swing music still tours the ballrooms and convention centers of America, as 'ghost bands' like the Glenn Miller Orchestra and the Tommy Dorsey Orchestra still entertain swing fans both young and old.

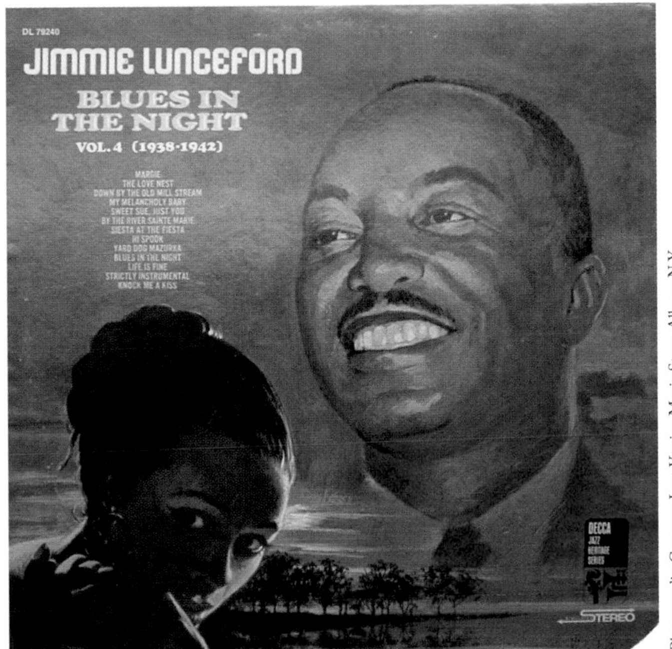

Photo credit: Courtesy Last Vestige Music Store, Albany, N.Y.

Unlike the other big band swing groups of Duke Ellington or Count Basie, Jimmie Lunceford's orchestra relied more on its ensemble work rather than on soloists. With the work of arranger Sy Oliver and singers Joe Thomas and Trummy Young, Lunceford's swing classics were a heavy influence on Glenn Miller's arrangements.

$10, *VG condition*

What To Look For

Swing 78s, especially those recorded between 1937 and 1942, are easily attainable and can be found in most yard sales and flea markets. The rare pieces are usually recordings by early swing pioneers like Bix Beiderbecke or Fletcher Henderson, or hard-to-find pressings by Duke Ellington or Count Basie.

That being said, if swing's your thing, you can quickly assemble a collection of the top big band and swing artists for a minimal cost. Clean copies of any of these records, however, are hard to come by, especially when one considers that these records were used for dancing—and were played over and over again, most often with steel-stylused phonographs. To be classified as a "near mint" swing 78, the records should be free of scratches, skips, scuffs or other telltale signs of a well-loved record.

Glenn Miller's 78s are easy to find, but the later 10-inch LP releases featuring his material have become collectible in their own right. Other 10-inch LPs from between 1949 to 1954 are very desirable, especially with clean covers and cleaner vinyl.

Web Pages

Any Swing Goes, a Web site for swing music and lifestyle: http://www.anyswinggoes.com

Artie Shaw's Web site: http://www.artieshaw.com

The Tommy Dorsey Orchestra's Web page: http://www.tommydorseyorchestra.com

The Glenn Miller Orchestra's home page: http://www.glennmillerorchestra.com

A place to hear Sam Medoff and the Yiddish Swing Orchestra: http://www.yiddishradioproject.com

Books

Knopper, Steve, *Musichound Swing! The Essential Album Guide*, Visible Ink Press, Farmington Hills, Mich., 1999.

ARTIST VG+ to NM

THE ANDREWS SISTERS:

78s

Decca 1562, "Bei Mir Bist Du Schön"/"Nice Work If You Can Get It," 1937 ....$5.00-$10.00

3598, "Boogie Woogie Bugle Boy"/"Bounce Me Brother," 1941 ...$3.00-$6.00

BIX BEIDERBECKE AND HIS GANG:

78s

Vocalion 3042, "At the Jazz Band Ball"/"The Jazz Me Blues," 1935 ....$20.00-$40.00

3149, "Sorry"/"Since My Best Gal Turned Me Down," 1936....$10.00-$20.00

Brunswick 8242, "Rhythm King"/"Somebody Stole My Gal," 1938 ....$25.00-$50.00

Mono LPs

Columbia Masterworks ML 4811, The Bix Beiderbecke Story, Volume 1, 1950 ....$35.00-$70.00

BUNNY BERIGAN:

10-inch LPs

RCA Victor LPT-10, Bunny Berigan 1937-38, 1951 ....$40.00-$80.00

12-inch LPs

RCA Victor LPT-1003, Bunny Berigan Plays Again, 1952 ....$25.00-$50.00

CAB CALLOWAY:

10-inch LPs

Brunswick 58101, Cab Calloway, 1954 ....$50.00-$100.00

12-inch LPs

RCA Victor LPM-2021, Hi De Hi De Ho (mono), 1958 ....$15.00-$30.00

(if on LSP-2021, stereo), 1958....................$20.00-$40.00

JIMMY DORSEY:

10-inch LPs

Columbia CL 6095, Dixie by Dorsey, 1950 ....$25.00-$50.00

Coral CRL 56004, Contrasting Music, Volume 1, 1950.............$25.00-$50.00

CRL 56033, Gershwin Music, 1950....................$25.00-$50.00

Decca DL 5091, Latin American Favorites, 1950....................$25.00-$50.00

12-inch LPs

Columbia CL 808, Dixie by Dorsey

(with red and black label with six eye logos), 1955 ....$15.00-$30.00

(with maroon label, gold print), 1955 ....$20.00-$40.00

TOMMY DORSEY:

78s

Victor 25236, "I'm Getting Sentimental Over You"/"I've Got a Note," 1935 ....$4.00-$8.00

10-inch LPs

RCA Victor LPT-3018, This is Tommy Dorsey, 1952....................$25.00-$50.00

Decca DL 5452, Your Invitation to Dance, 1952....................$25.00-$50.00

12-inch LPs

RCA Victor LPT-10, Getting Sentimental with Tommy Dorsey, 1951 ....$40.00-$80.00

TOMMY AND JIMMY DORSEY, COMBINED ORCHESTRAS:

78s

V-Disc 451 (Army), 'More Than You Know'/'Brotherly Jump', 1944 ....$20.00-$40.00

DUKE ELLINGTON:

78s

Victor 26788, "In a Mellotone"/"Rumpus In Richmond," 1940 ....$5.00-$10.00

10-inch LPs

Brunswick BL 58002, Ellingtonia, Volume 1, 1950 ....$50.00-$100.00

58012, Ellingtonia, Volume 2, 1950....................$50.00-$100.00

Columbia CL 2562, Here's the Duke, 1955....................$40.00-$80.00

CL 2593, Al Hibbler with the Duke, 1956....................$40.00-$80.00

12-inch LPs

Capitol T 521, Ellington '55 (turquoise label), 1955 ....$20.00-$40.00

(if black label with rainbow perimeter, logo at left), 1958 ....$10.00-$20.00

RCA Victor LPV-517, Jumpin' Punkins, 1965....................$10.00-$20.00

BENNY GOODMAN:

78s

Victor 25090, "King Porter"/"Sometimes I'm Happy," 1935 ....$10.00-$20.00

V-Disc 177 (Navy), "Sing Sing Sing" (Pt. 1)/(Pt. 2), 1945 ....$10.00-$20.00

10-inch LPs

Columbia CL 6033, Benny Goodman and Peggy Lee, 1949.......$40.00-$80.00

CL 6048, Dance Parade, 1949 ....$25.00-$50.00

RCA Victor WPT 12, Benny Goodman, 1951....................$25.00-$50.00

12-inch LPs

Columbia CL 817, The King of Swing, Volume 1, 1956..............$15.00-$30.00

CL 818, The King of Swing, Volume 2, 1956 ....$15.00-$30.00

CL 819, The King of Swing, Volume 3, 1956 ....$15.00-$30.00

CL 814, Carnegie Hall Jazz Concert, Volume 1 (red-black label, six eye logos), 1956....................$15.00-$30.00

(if red label, "Guaranteed High Fidelity" or "Mono" at bottom), 1963 ....$10.00-$20.00

GENE KRUPA:

78s

OKeh 5788, "Rhumboogie"/"Old, Old Castle in Scotland," 1940 ....$5.00-$10.00

Columbia 35454, "Tiger Rag"/"Sierra Sue," 1940....................$5.00-$10.00

10-inch LPs

Columbia CL 6017, Gene Krupa, 1949 ....$50.00-$100.00

CL 6066, Dance Parade, 1949 ....$50.00-$100.00

Clef MGC-514, Gene Krupa Trio, 1953 ....$40.00-$80.00

12-inch LPs

Verve MGV-8087, Drum Boogie, 1957....................$25.00-$50.00

MGV-8107, The Driving Gene Krupa, 1957....................$25.00-$50.00

JIMMIE LUNCEFORD:

10-inch LPs

Columbia GL 104, Lunceford Special, 1950 ....$40.00-$80.00

Decca DL 5393, For Dancers Only, 1952....................$30.00-$60.00

LPs

"X" LX-3002, Jimmie Lunceford and His Chickasaw Syncopators, 1954 ....$30.00-$60.00

Decca DL 8050, Jimmie Lunceford and His Orchestra, 1954.....$20.00-$40.00

DL 79240, Blues in the Night, Vol. 4, 1968....................$10.00-$20.00

SAM MEDOFF AND HIS ORCHESTRA:

12-inch Acetates

Empire Transcription, Yiddish Melodies in Swing, from radio broadcasts, 1940s....................$25.00-$50.00

GLENN MILLER AND HIS ORCHESTRA:

78s

Columbia 3058-D, "Solo Hop"/"In A Little Spanish Town," 1935 ....$10.00-$20.00

Bluebird 10286, "Little Brown Jug"/"Pavanne," 1939 ....$7.50-$15.00

10416, "In the Mood"/"I Want to Be Happy," 1939....................$7.50-$15.00

Victor 20-1564 through 20-1567, 4 78s in bound "Smart Set" folio, 1944 ....$10.00-$20.00

10-inch LPs

RCA Victor LPT-16, Glenn Miller Concert—Volume 1, 1951 ....$30.00-$60.00

LPT-30, Glenn Miller Concert—Volume 2, 1951 ....$30.00-$60.00

LPT-3067, Sunrise Serenade, 1954....................$30.00-$60.00

12-inch LPs

RCA Victor LPT-6700, Glenn Miller and His Orchestra Limited Edition (5 LPs, silver label, red print, leatherette spiral-bound binder), 1953 ....$75.00-$150.00

EPOT 6701, Glenn Miller and His Orchestra — Limited Edition, Volume Two (15 LPs, gold loose-leaf folder, numbered booklet), 1954 ....$100.00-$200.00

THE PIED PIPERS:

78s

Capitol CD 36, Johnny Mercer and the Pied Pipers (four 78s in folio), 194? ....$7.50-$15.00

ARTIE SHAW:

78s

Victor 26762, "Special Delivery Stomp"/ "Keepin' Myself For You," 1940 ....$4.00-$8.00

10-inch LPs

Decca DL 5286, Artie Shaw Dance Program, 195?....................$25.00-$50.00

RCA Victor LPT-3013, This Is Artie Shaw, 1952....................$25.00-$50.00

LPs

RCA Victor LPM-1241, Artie Shaw and His Gramercy Five, 1956 ....$20.00-$40.00

LPM-1244, Moonglow, 1956....................$20.00-$40.00

BOB WILLS AND HIS TEXAS PLAYBOYS:

78s

OKeh 6736, "Smoke on the Water"/"Hang Your Head in Shame," 1945 ....$12.50-$25.00

Section 3

Essential Collectible Artists

Chapter 25

The Beatles

History

John Lennon. Paul McCartney. George Harrison. Ringo Starr. These four men, along with their producer George Martin, revolutionized popular music forever. From their early days performing in the Liverpool Cavern Club, to their last public performance on the roof of their Apple Corps, Ltd. building, the Beatles were the heralds for a generation of music fans and collectors.

The group's history is a legendary and oft-told story, from their days as a skiffle band called the Quarry Men, then as the Silver Beatles; their nights at the Star Club in Hamburg, with a five-man lineup of John Lennon, George Harrison, Paul McCartney, Peter Best, and Stuart Sutcliffe; their days headlining the Cavern Club in Liverpool; Sutcliffe leaving and Best replaced with Ringo Starr; Decca Records passing over the Beatles in favor of Brian Poole and the Tremoloes; the foursome working with comedy album producer George Martin; the nationwide and eventual worldwide success; their seven years of evolution from moptop popsters to avant-garde album auteurs; and their eventual last concert together on the rooftop of their self-created record company building—and all the twists and turns in between.

In America, Beatlemania was at such a fevered pitch that in April 1964, the top five songs on the *Billboard* singles chart were Beatles songs. Of those five songs, two were official Capitol releases ("Can't Buy Me Love" and "I Wanna

The Beatles' picture sleeves are just as collectible as the records they hold. Capitol picture sleeves were printed on glossy stock with good color separations; counterfeits or reproductions exist on flat or thin paper.

***$120**, for NM sleeve*

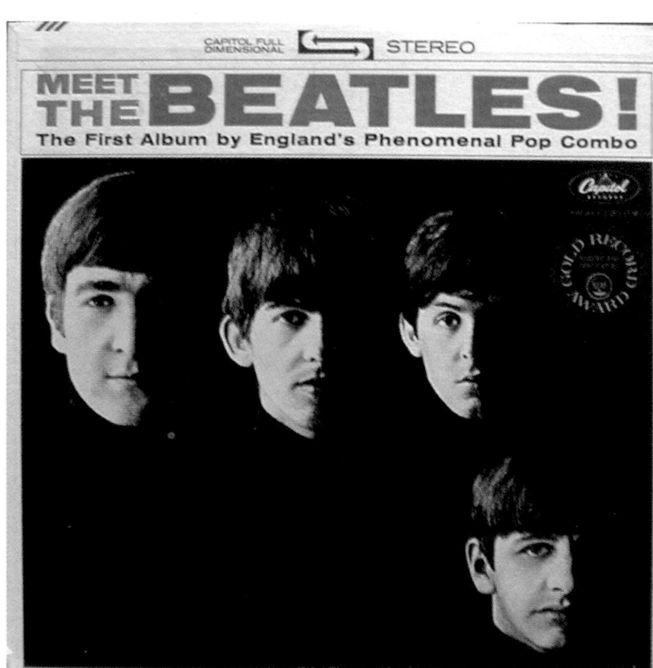

At first glance, this pressing of Meet the Beatles!, the group's first LP on the Capitol label, looks like a common reissue, as the "Gold Record Award" stamp on the jacket's right denotes that this title sold at least a million copies. However, look at the upper-left corner of the jacket and you will see three diagonal lines—denoting this record as a limited pressing from the Capitol Record Club, making it a very rare and collectible variation.

$NA

Three examples of early Beatles recordings on non-Capitol labels. "My Bonnie" features an early appearance by the Beatles, backing up Tony Sheridan as "The Beat Brothers." Stock copies featuring this Decca rainbow label can fetch over $10,000 in near-mint condition.

***$12,000**, VG+ condition*

As the Beatles dominated the music world, companies like Atco snapped up any Beatles tracks they could acquire—in this case, a cover of the old standard "Ain't She Sweet," recorded during the Beatles' days with Tony Sheridan, with Pete Best on drums—and released them as pop hits.

***$50**, NM condition*

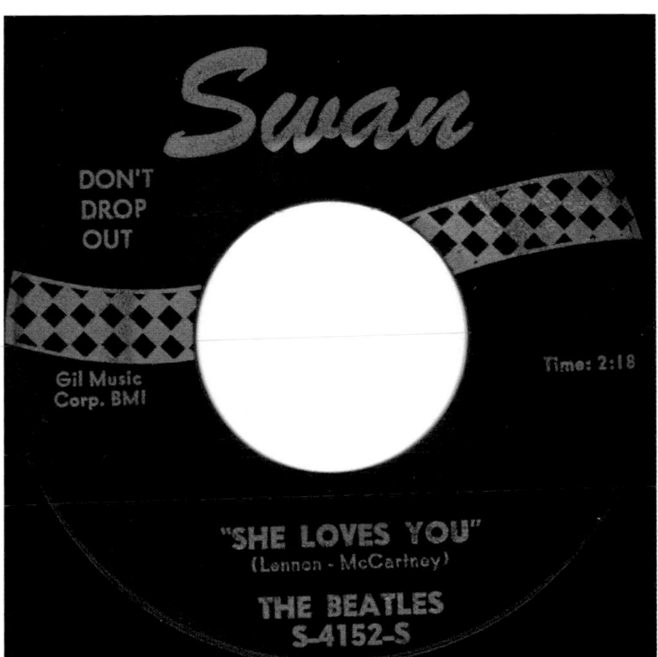

Swan Records, a dance label from Philadelphia, acquired the rights to this early Beatles track "She Loves You," which became the label's biggest-selling hit. Notice the words "Don't Drop Out" on the label, which were added by Swan owner Bernie Binnick as a subliminal message for kids to stay in school.

***$25**, VG+ condition*

Hold Your Hand"), while the other three were from Vee Jay and Swan Records, who both had previously been offered the license to certain early Beatles recordings. And as other labels like Atco and MGM were able to find Beatles recordings to release, it eventually gave the Beatles 14 songs in a single week on *Billboard*'s Hot 100 charts, a feat never duplicated. Demand for Beatles music was so great that "Roll Over Beethoven," a Capitol of Canada pressing, was able to cross the border and chart in America.

Even if the Beatles continued with the same Merseybeat rock that propelled them to stardom, their fans would have been satisfied. But one of the major strengths within the band was the ability to experiment within the studio, to challenge each other to write stronger songs, to raise the bar for every future album and single, and to make each recording better than the last. Within that framework, the talents and assistance of producer George Martin should not be forgotten. John Lennon and Paul McCartney would bounce ideas off Martin, who in turn would show the group what could and could not be done in a four-track studio. It was Martin, for example, who took two distinctly different recordings of "Strawberry Fields Forever" and, by using variable speed tape recorders, merged both versions into a seamless pop smash.

The Beatles were also pioneers in creating the "concept album," an LP where all or most of the tracks revolved around a certain theme. For the Beatles, that album was *Sgt. Pepper's Lonely Hearts Club Band*, with the Beatles dressed as orchestral military troubadours, their songs filled with the melodies and lyrics of their concert tours and of their trips to India and the Far East. Many have hailed *Sgt. Pepper* as the greatest Beatles album of all time; others have gone so far as to acclaim it as the greatest *album* of all time.

Although the Beatles officially disbanded in 1970, fans worldwide hoped for a reunion, a tour, possibly one more album. Those fans would have to be content with themed reissue LPs (*Rock and Roll Music*, *Love Songs*, *Reel Music*) and previously unreleased live concerts and demo tracks (*The Beatles at the Hollywood Bowl*, *Rarities*). All hopes of a live reunion show were dashed on December 8, 1980, when an assassin's bullet took John Lennon's life.

In the late 1990s, the three surviving Beatles (nicknamed by some media outlets as the "Threetles") recorded two new tracks for a televised documentary and concomitant album release, *The Beatles Anthology*. John Lennon was part of the sessions, as his voice was digitally enhanced from unreleased cassette tapes to create the songs "Free as a Bird" and "Real Love."

Interest in the Beatles has not wavered, even to this day. The release of *The Beatles 1*, a compilation of all their #1 hits, became a multiplatinum smash in the winter of 2000. Sadly, just one year later, on November 29, 2001, George Harrison passed away due to complications from brain cancer.

First pressings of the Beatles' classic album Sgt. Pepper's Lonely Hearts Club Band *have a track title misidentified as "A Little Help From My Friends." Subsequent pressings restored the word "With" to the beginning of the title.*

***$150**, VG condition*

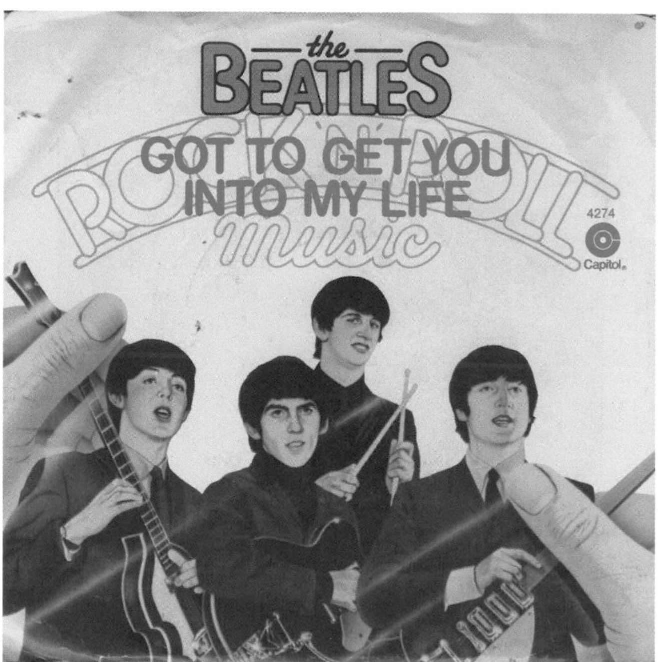

"Got To Get You Into My Life," originally a track from the Revolver *album, was released in 1976 as a single, and became a Top 10 hit.*

***$2.50** Good condition*

What To Look For

Without a doubt, the Beatles are the most highly collected music group of the rock era. Their early LPs can command thousands of dollars in near-mint condition. Because of this, bootlegs and counterfeits abound, and more than one collector has been fooled by a Beatles album with a price tag "too good to be true."

The two most highly sought American-pressed Beatles albums are 1963's *Introducing the Beatles* (Vee Jay 1062) and 1966's *Yesterday and Today* (Capitol 2553). The factors making these albums more collectible than other titles in the Beatles catalog are deep and varied, but will be explained in an abridged format below.

In 1963, the Beatles were dominating the UK pop scene, as their albums and 45s on Parlophone Records were rising up the charts. Parlophone's sister label in the USA, Capitol, was offered the opportunity to release Beatles records in America. Capitol initially refused, and Beatles songs appeared on other US labels—among them Swan, Tollie, Atco, and Decca.

The Chicago-based R&B label Vee Jay also released some Beatles material, and eventually released some 45s of "Please Please Me" and "From Me To You," two early Beatles hits. Even Vee Jay seemed to have the Beatles on their back burner—the early copies of "Please Please Me" misspell the group's name as the "Beattles."

One year later, Capitol released "I Want To Hold Your Hand," which shot to #1 and ushered in the American wave of Beatlemania. Suddenly every record company that ever owned a Beatles track flooded it onto the market, to the point where in April 1965, the five biggest selling 45s were Beatles records—"Can't Buy Me Love" and "I Want To Hold Your Hand" on Capitol, "She Loves You" on Swan, and "Love Me Do" and "Twist and Shout" on Tollie.

Along with all the new 45s came a new album, as Vee Jay had leased enough Beatles songs to issue a twelve-song LP. The album, *Introducing the Beatles*, was sold in both mono and stereo copies—then its running tracks were rearranged, with some songs added and others deleted—

Photo credit: From the collection of Bruce Spizer.

On this early pressing of "Please Please Me," their first American record company, Vee Jay, can't even get the group's name spelled correctly.

***$1,250**, VG+ condition*

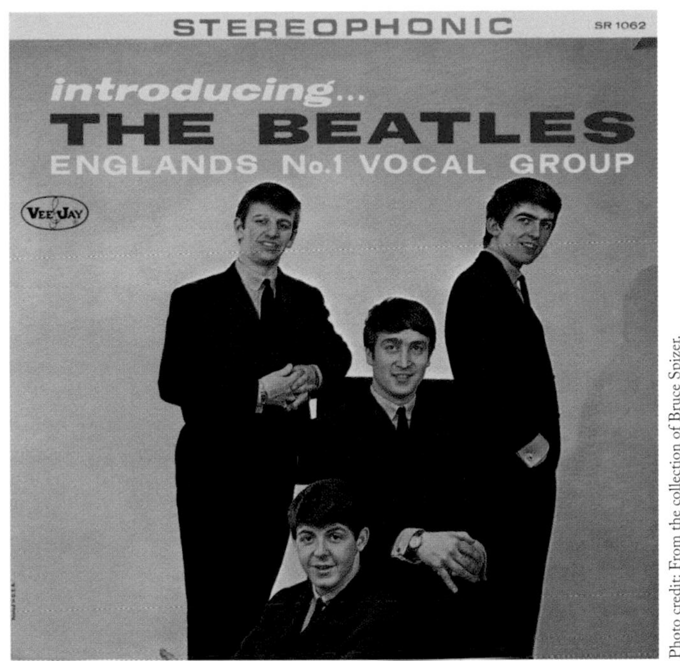

Photo credit: From the collection of Bruce Spizer.

A true stereophonic album cover, which includes good color separation, a shadow behind George Harrison, and the word "STEREOPHONIC" at the top of the jacket.

***$12,000**, NM condition*

then the disc was issued as part of a double-LP with Vee Jay's other pop hitmakers at the time, the Four Seasons.

The mono copies of *Introducing the Beatles* are rare enough, but legitimate stereo copies of this title are extremely hard to find. Notice that word "legitimate." Because stereo copies of this album can command up to $12,000 in near-mint condition, *Introducing the Beatles* is one of the most bootlegged and counterfeited albums of the rock era. When a stereo pressing of *Introducing the Beatles* can sell for a cool five figures, you don't want to discover that the pressing you thought was legitimate is actually a worthless reproduction.

To make sure your copy of *Introducing the Beatles* is a legitimate pressing, take a look at the front cover. Original covers will look shiny and glossy, as the initial pressing plants used coated paper stock. If either or both sides of the cover looks flat or glossless, it's a reproduction. A standing George Harrison must have a shadow in the background of the photograph. A sitting John Lennon wears a wristwatch; you might be able to make out what time the photograph was taken. The cover slicks should be bonded to brownish or tan cardboard, with a quarter-inch overlap of cardboard inside the jacket. All these can indicate a legitimate cover.

Reproduced covers will have poor photographic and text reproduction. The word "BEATLES" might have the "S" slightly cropped off the album opening, as the photo is slightly larger. George Harrison's shadow might be missing; John Lennon's watch might be unreadable. The album's front cover photograph might be enclosed in a rounded brownish frame; the Beatles themselves look deathly pink or jaundiced. All these are indications of a reproduced cover.

Look on the back cover. For stereo copies, if "Love Me Do" and "P.S. I Love You" are atop the columns of song titles, it's most likely a reproduction (only a dozen true stereo copies with this configuration are known to exist). Another telltale sign is the song "A Taste of Honey." All letters in that song should be crisp and straight; reproductions will look fuzzy and weathered; the "H" and "E" in "Honey" will look as if they are missing some corners or are notched, a sure sign of a reprinted copy.

Take the record out and examine the label. There should be no more than 1 inch from the edge of the final song to the label—any larger amount of runout groove indicates a reprinted copy. If the pressing has a rainbow perimeter, make sure all the colors are evenly spread throughout the rainbow—including green, which is missing from fake copies. The album title "INTRODUCING THE BEATLES" and the band name "THE BEATLES" should be above the spindle hole to indicate a legitimate copy; if those two lines are separated by a spindle hole, you could be purchasing a reprint. If your record has "Love Me Do," that Vee Jay logo better be an oval; if it's enclosed in brackets, you've got a fake copy in your hands. There are many other variations on this album; for more information on identifying the legitimacy or fraudulence of your copy of *Introducing the Beatles*, go to this Web site for more information: http://www.rarebeatles.com/photospg/introvj.htm.

Vee Jay's other Beatles albums have also been counterfeited. *Songs, Pictures and Stories of the Fabulous Beatles* has appeared as forged pressings with the title *Songs and Pictures of the Fabulous Beatles*. Another Vee Jay quickie album, *Jolly What! The Beatles and Frank Ifield On Stage*, was printed with two different covers—the first, a realistic

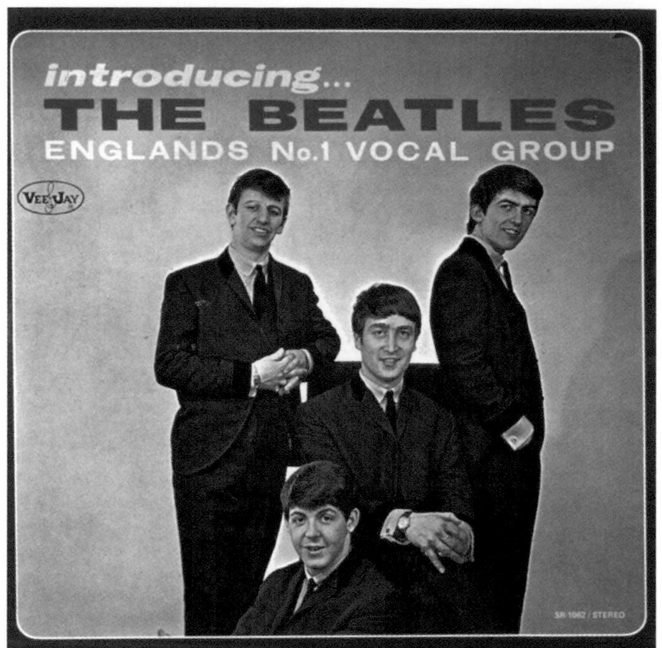

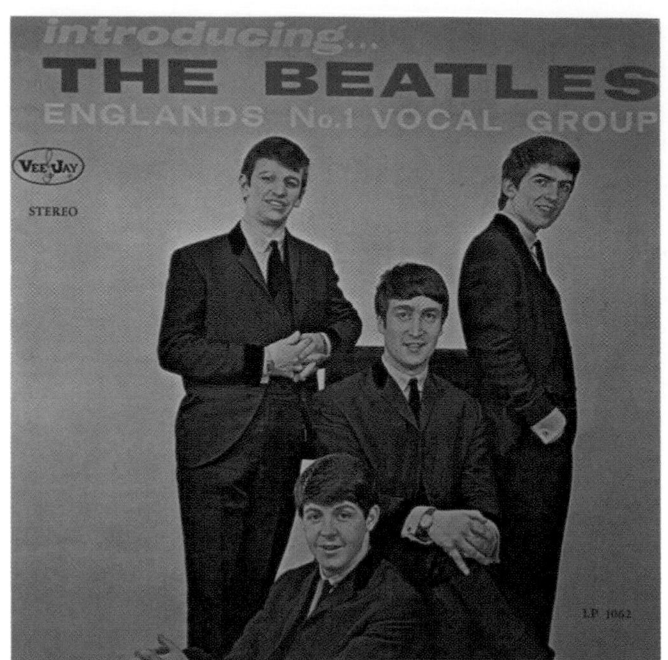

Photo credit: From the collection of Bruce Spizer

Two common and worthless stereo counterfeits of Introducing the Beatles. *Any copies with brown borders are fakes. If George Harrison, at the far right of the group, does not have a shadow behind him, the cover—and the album inside it—are fakes as well.*

(L and R) ***$20****, VG condition each*

drawing of the Beatles in their Pierre Cardin performance outfits; the second, with a drawing of an old man on the cover. Counterfeiters have recreated both covers with different color tones and paper stocks; the originals look crisp and well-focused, while the counterfeit covers look washed-out and airbrushed.

Since Vee Jay did not have its own pressing plant, they used independent facilities to manufacture their Beatles 45s and LPs. At one point during the pressing of "Please Please Me"/"From Me To You," when the pressing plants ran out of Vee Jay pre-printed labels, they simply made labels with the words "VEE JAY" or "VJ" in block printing—creating more than fifteen different label variations of that title.

Another highly collectible Beatles album is *Yesterday and Today* (Capitol 2553). During the Beatles' early hitmaking years, Capitol Records would trim two tracks from a British EMI/Parlophone album, and release the album with a new title (*Beatles '65* or *Something New*). By 1966, they were able to create an album featuring the Beatles' new hit single "Yesterday," along with tracks that had been culled from previous albums. Instead of the standard Beatles photographs that were used for Capitol album releases, the foursome posed for their new American album cover wearing butcher's smocks, their bodies covered with raw meat and baby doll parts. Capitol printed thousands of these covers before somebody realized the Beatles album cover looked like the Fab Four had just committed infanticide in a butcher shop.

The albums were recalled to the factories, and a new album jacket was printed, an innocuous photo of the Beatles sitting around a steamer trunk. Besides printing new album art, some of the Capitol factories recycled the old albums by applying the new "trunk" photo over the original "butcher" album art. Because of the major difference in cover art, *Yesterday and Today* is an extremely collectible album, if not the most collectible album cover in rock history. A "first

Legitimate mono and stereo pressings of Introducing the Beatles *have the group's name and album title both above the spindle hole, as can be seen in this genuine monaural pressing. Interestingly, the pressing plant actually ran out of Vee Jay album labels for a while, and pressed this record using 45-RPM Vee Jay labels!*

$100*, VG condition*

Photo credit: From the collection of Bruce Spizer.

An original "butcher" cover for the Beatles' Yesterday and Today *album. Were the Beatles posing for some unique "pop art" photographs, or were they sending a subtle message to Capitol Records that they weren't thrilled with their British releases getting "butchered" for the American market?*

***$8,000**, NM condition*

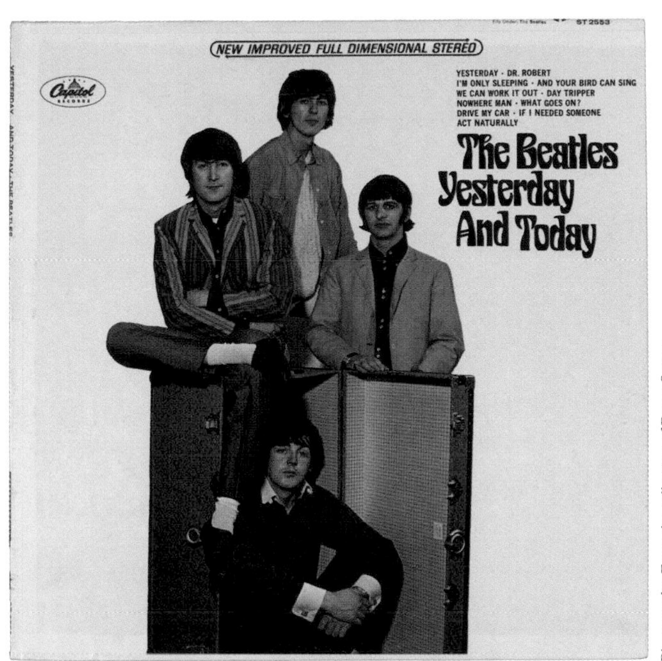

Photo credit: From the collection of Bruce Spizer.

If you see clues that your trunk-covered copy of Yesterday and Today *may have a butcher cover underneath, companies like Blue Jay Way Galleries of Downey, California can professionally steam off the trunk cover, revealing the butcher cover underneath. DO NOT TRY TO PEEL THE COVER OFF YOURSELF!! Many butcher covers have been ruined or torn by careless peels.*

***$1,000**, NM (value for the butcher cover underneath)*

state" cover features the Beatles in their butcher smocks. A "second state" cover will have the Beatles sitting around the steamer trunk, but with the "trunk" artwork covering up a "butcher" cover—if you see a black triangle on the right side of the "trunk" cover, that's Ringo Starr's black sweater in the "butcher" photo underneath. Without that triangle, it's a standard "trunk" cover.

Many of these "second state" covers have been steamed or peeled away to find the "butcher" artwork. A peeled cover is known as "third state." The value of a "third state" *Yesterday and Today* Beatles album is proportional to the success of the peel.

As for other fakes and counterfeits of Beatles 45s, picture sleeves and albums, there are the following:

"She Loves You"/"I'll Get You" on Swan, with machine-stamped numbers in the runout groove, without the pressing plant trademarks "Virtue Studio" or "Reco-Art" in the dead wax. Hand-etched numbers in the dead wax must contain the words "Don't Drop Out" on the Swan label, or else you have a reproduction.

Swan pressings of "Komm, Gib Mir Deine Hand" are fake "fantasy" pressings, as that title was on the Capitol *Something New* album. Other fantasy pressings include colored vinyl Tollie 45s of "Twist and Shout," or colored vinyl singles of "She Loves You" on Swan.

The Decca pressing of "My Bonnie," a very collectible record because the Beatles are backing up singer Tony Sheridan (as the "Beat Brothers"), has been counterfeited. Many counterfeits feature the Decca silver-print style of the 1950s, or a pink label with black print—by the time "My Bonnie" was recorded, Decca had already switched to a rainbow label that bisected the record's diameter.

While the Beatles' 45s and LPs were issued by several American companies during the group's early years, in Canada the Beatles appeared on Capitol releases from the start. Three albums were released up North—*Beatlemania! With the Beatles*, *Twist and Shout,* and *Long Tall Sally* (the final disc a renamed version of the American release *The Beatles' Second Album*, which would have been the group's third Canadian album). Several 45s were also issued in Canada on Capitol's 72000 series, including a coupling of "Roll Over Beethoven"/"Please Mister Postman," which charted in America as an import single.

By the mid-1980s, the surviving Beatles requested that all subsequent Beatles album and CD releases from around the world, including America, feature the original album artwork and track listings of the British Parlophone albums. This meant American titles like *Beatles '65*, *Something New,* and *Yesterday and Today* were deleted from the Capitol (U.S.) catalogs, to be replaced by the British titles *Beatles for Sale*, *With the Beatles,* and *Please Please Me*. Because of this, the value of near-mint copies of the original 1960s Capitol LPs has stayed high. The 1970s double-LP greatest hits packages are available on CD, but the other 1970s reissue compilations are not (including *Rock and Roll Music*, *The Beatles at the Hollywood Bowl*, *Rarities*, *Reel Music*, *Love Songs,* and *20 Greatest Hits*). While most of these 1970s LPs sound as if Capitol Records simply repurposed old Beatles hits in new packages, many of these compilations include different mixes or versions not heard on American releases until that time—for example, the 1980 album *Rarities* contained the Capitol of Canada 45 mix of "Love Me Do."

In 1968, beginning with the "Hey Jude"/"Revolution" 45 and *The Beatles* (the "White Album"), the Beatles switched their American label from Capitol to their own custom label, Apple (which Capitol distributed). One year later, however, every American Beatles release was reissued on Apple. On albums, these 1969 reissues can be identified by a Capitol logo on side two of the record label. The Beatles catalog was reissued again in 1971, these discs have the words "Mfd. by Apple" on the label. Another reissue, this time in 1975, will have the words "All Rights Reserved" on the label. Surprisingly, while the label on the record changed, albums that were originally released before 1968 still sported a prominent Capitol logo on their jackets!

In 1976, the Beatles' back catalog was reissued on Capitol. A two-LP collection of uptempo Beatles songs, *Rock and Roll Music*, was released, and both it and a single version of "Got To Get You Into My Life" hit the Top 10 on the charts. Capitol 45 reissues in 1976 were orange with a serifless "Capitol" printed on the bottom of the label. In 1978, Capitol went to an all-purple label with a geared perimeter, and the Beatles 45s appear in that format as well. Beatles reissues also appeared in Capitol's 1983 color scheme (black label with a rainbow on the perimeter), and their 1988 label pattern (light purple label, smooth label perimeter).

In 1994, the Beatles' greatest hits were reissued on 45, this time in colored vinyl. Most of these titles only sell for about $4 in near-mint condition, with the exception of "Birthday"/"Taxman" (Capitol S7-17488), which was "accidentally" pressed on black vinyl, and can sell for $50 in near-mint condition.

The Beatles' album titles and content have also changed in the post-Apple period. In 1978, three of the Beatles' two-LP sets were pressed, in a limited edition, on colored vinyl. They were *The Beatles: 1962-1966* (red vinyl), *The Beatles: 1967-1970* (blue vinyl), and *The Beatles* (on white vinyl). All feature the Capitol logo.

In 1987, while the Beatles' first albums were released on CD for the first time, their vinyl albums were re-released. Both the vinyl and CD versions of these albums followed the original EMI/Parlophone album art and track listings. These were released on the Capitol label. One year later, the American albums were re-released for the last time. These copies have UPC codes on the back covers. In 1995, the British album versions were re-released one more time on vinyl, with an Apple logo on the album and on the jacket.

This listing only contains a fraction of all known Beatles North American pressings. Many independent labels that possessed Beatles tracks, such as Vee Jay and Swan, used independent pressing plants to manufacture their records, and when certain printed labels ran out, the pressing plants sometimes improvised label artwork and background colors, thus the voluminous versions/variations listed below.

Because of its simple design, this Atco 45 picture sleeve for "Ain't She Sweet" has been counterfeited. Originals have blue lettering on the title and a straight cut on top; counterfeits may have green or red lettering, or a curved cut on top.

***$250**, VG+ condition*

The most notable variation between a Canadian and an American 45 release involves the song "Love Me Do." While the American version available on Tollie (and later Capitol) features session drummer Andy White on the track, while Ringo is relegated to playing a tambourine, the Capitol of Canada 45 features an earlier mix, in which Ringo is the drummer.

***$50**, Good condition*

One of fifteen different-colored vinyl Beatles 45s released by Capitol between 1994 and 1996. Capitol also released colored vinyl versions of Beatles solo records, including George Harrison's "My Sweet Lord," John Lennon's "(Just Like) Starting Over," and Paul McCartney's "Maybe I'm Amazed."

***$4**, NM condition*

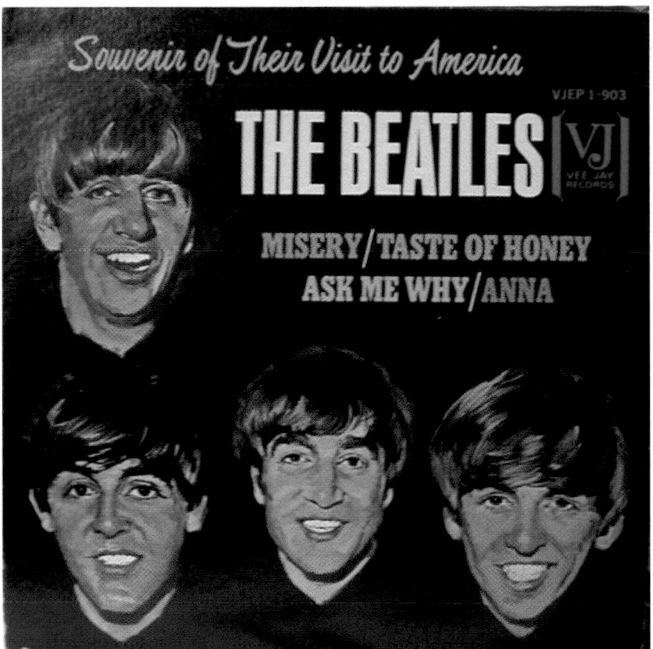

This cardboard sleeve was issued with Vee Jay's four-song EP of Beatles hits. The "Beatle heads" featured on this sleeve were also used for a Vee Jay 45 picture sleeve of "Do You Want to Know A Secret."

***$150**, NM condition*

Books

The Beatles Anthology, Chronicle Books LLC, San Francisco, CA, 2000.

Neely, Tim; Thompson, Dave, *Goldmine British Invasion Record Price Guide*, Krause Publications, Iola, WI, 1997.

Spizer, Bruce, *Songs, Pictures and Stories of the Fabulous Beatles Records on Vee Jay*, 498 Productions, New Orleans, LA, 1998.

Spizer, Bruce, *The Beatles' Story on Capitol Records* (two volumes), 498 Productions, New Orleans, LA, 2000.

Cox, Perry, *The Official Price Guide to the Beatles Records and Memorabilia*, House of Collectibles/Ballantine Publishing, New York, NY, 1999.

The Goldmine Beatles Digest, Krause Publications, Iola, WI, 2000.

Riley, Tim, *Tell Me Why: A Beatles Commentary*, Alfred A. Knopf, NY, 1988.

Spizer, Bruce, *The Beatles Are Coming!*, 498 Productions, New Orleans, LA, 2003.

Wiener, Allen J., *The Beatles: The Ultimate Recording Guide*, McFarland & Company, Inc., Jefferson, NC, 1994.

Web Pages

The Beatles' home page: http://www.beatles.com

Bruce Spizer's Beatles page: http://www.beatle.net

Mitch McGeary's Beatles online museum: http://www.rarebeatles.com

A Canadian Beatles Web site: http://www.thebeatles.ca

For identification of counterfeit Beatles LPs and 45s, go to these Web sites: http://members.aol.com/egweimi/btls2.htm; http://www.geocities.com/flangehead2/Counterfeits/_Counterfeits.html

Museums

The Beatles Story, Britannia Vaults, Albert Dock, Liverpool L3 4AA, England: http://www.beatlesstory.com.

Because of the adulation many Beatles fans had for the group in the 1960s, some companies produced special "Beatle labels" that could be applied to a 45 (and, despite all efforts to the contrary, won't come off without ripping the label underneath). This one, covering up a copy of "Please Please Me," was part of a collection that originally belonged to a John Lennon nut named Lisa.

Two 45s were released in conjunction with the Anthology albums. Both songs, "Free as a Bird" and "Real Love," feature performances by the three surviving Beatles, along with John Lennon's vocals from a previously unreleased cassette demo tape. ***$1.50**, VG condition*

THE BEATLES VG+ to NM

Vee Jay 45s

Vee Jay 498, "Please Please Me"/"Ask Me Why"
(if group listed as "The Beattles," number is "VJ 498"), 1963 .... **$1,125.00-$1,500.00**
(if group listed as "The Beattles," number is "#498"), 1963 .... **$1,200.00-$1,600.00**
(if group's name spelled correctly, number is "VJ 498," thick print), 1963 .... **$600.00-$900.00**
(if group's name spelled correctly, number is "#498"), 1963 .... **$1,200.00-$1,600.00**
(if group's name spelled correctly, number is "VJ 498," brackets label), 1963 .... **$1,500.00-$2,000.00**

522, "From Me to You"/"Thank You Girl"
(if black rainbow label, "Vee Jay" in oval), 1963 .... **$300.00-$600.00**
(if plain black label), 1963 .... **$400.00-$800.00**
(if black rainbow label, "VJ" in brackets), 1963 .... **$600.00-$900.00**

581, "Please Please Me"/"From Me to You"
(if plain black label, two horizontal lines), 1964 .... **$22.50-$45.00**
(if black rainbow label, oval logo), 1964 .... **$25.00-$50.00**
(if plain black label, "VEE JAY" stands alone), 1964 .... **$30.00-$60.00**
(if plain black label, oval logo), 1964 .... **$30.00-$60.00**
(if black rainbow label, brackets logo), 1964 .... **$30.00-$60.00**
(if plain black label, "VJ" stands alone), 1964 .... **$32.50-$65.00**
(if plain black label, brackets logo), 1964 .... **$37.50-$75.00**
(if yellow label), 1964 .... **$37.50-$75.00**
(if white label), 1964 .... **$80.00-$160.00**
(if purple label), 1964 .... **$400.00-$600.00**
(with picture sleeve, add), 1964 .... **$250.00-$500.00**
(with picture sleeve that says "The Record that Started Beatlemania," promo only, add), 1964 .... **$1,875.00-$2,500.00**

587, "Do You Want to Know a Secret"/"Thank You Girl"
(if black rainbow label, brackets logo), 1964 .... **$20.00-$40.00**
(if plain black label, two horizontal lines, "VJ" in brackets), 1964 .... **$22.50-$45.00**
(if black rainbow label, oval logo), 1964 .... **$25.00-$50.00**
(if plain black label, "VEE JAY" stands alone), 1964 .... **$25.00-$50.00**
(if plain black label, "Vee Jay" in oval), 1964 .... **$32.50-$65.00**
(if plain black label, "VJ" in brackets), 1964 .... **$32.50-$65.00**
(if plain black label, "VJ" stands alone), 1964 .... **$32.50-$65.00**
(if yellow label), 1964 .... **$300.00-$600.00**
(with picture sleeve, add), 1964 .... **$60.00-$120.00**

Capitol 45s

Capitol 72076, "Love Me Do"/"P.S. I Love You" (Canadian release, Ringo plays drums on A-side, no tambourine on record), 1963 .... **$37.50-$75.00**
72090, "Please Please Me"/"Ask Me Why" (Canadian release), 1963 .... **$25.00-$50.00**
72101, "From Me To You"/"Thank You Girl" (Canadian release), 1963 .... **$25.00-$50.00**
72125, "She Loves You"/"I'll Get You" (Canadian release), 1963 .... **$25.00-$50.00**
72133, "Roll Over Beethoven"/"Please Mister Postman" (Canadian release), 1963 .... **$25.00-$50.00**
72144, "All My Loving"/"This Boy" (Canadian release), 1964 ... **$25.00-$50.00**
72146, "Twist And Shout"/"There's A Place" (Canadian release), 1964 .... **$25.00-$50.00**
72159, "Do You Want To Know A Secret?"/"Thank You Girl" (Canadian release), 1964 .... **$25.00-$50.00**
72162, "Sie Liebt Dich"/"I'll Get You" (Canadian release), 1964 .... **$25.00-$50.00**

5112, "I Want to Hold Your Hand"/"I Saw Her Standing There"
(first pressings have "Walter Hofer" as publisher of B-side), 1964 .... **$20.00-$40.00**
(second pressings have "George Pincus and Sons" as publisher of B-side), 1964 .... **$17.50-$35.00**
(third pressing has "Gil Music" as publisher of B-side), 1964 .... **$15.00-$30.00**
(with picture sleeve, die-cut, crops George Harrison's head in photo, add), 1964 .... **$50.00-$100.00**
(with picture sleeve, straight cut, all of George Harrison's head intact, add), 1964 .... **$50.00-$100.00**
(if 20th anniversary reissue sleeve, "1984" in small print, Paul McCartney's cigarette is missing from hand), 1984 .... **$3.00-$6.00**
(if 30th anniversary reissue sleeve, "Reg. U.S. Pat. Off." has periods, plastic sleeve with "30th Anniversary" and bar code stickers, add), 1994 .... **$2.50-$5.00**

5150, "Can't Buy Me Love"/"You Can't Do That," 1964 .... **$15.00-$30.00**
(with extremely rare picture sleeve, add—be aware that numerous counterfeits exist), 1964 .... **$400.00-$800.00**

5222, "A Hard Day's Night"/"I Should Have Known Better"
(if "Unart" and "Maclen" are publishers), 1964 ....**$15.00-$30.00**
(if only "Maclen" credited as publishers), 1964 ....**$15.00-$30.00**
(with picture sleeve, add), 1964...**$50.00-$100.00**
5234, "I'll Cry Instead"/"I'm Happy Just to Dance with You," 1964
....**$20.00-$40.00**
(with picture sleeve, add), 1964...**$75.00-$150.00**
5235, "And I Love Her"/"If I Fell"
(if publisher listed as "Unart" and "Maclen"), 1964..................**$25.00-$50.00**
(if only "Maclen" credited as publishers), 1964 ....**$15.00-$30.00**
(with picture sleeve, add), 1964...**$60.00-$120.00**
5255, "Matchbox"/"Slow Down," 1964...**$15.00-$30.00**
(with picture sleeve, add), 1964...**$75.00-$150.00**
5237, "I Feel Fine"/"She's a Woman," 1964 ....**$15.00-$30.00**
(with picture sleeve, add), 1964...**$40.00-$80.00**
5371, "Eight Days a Week"/"I Don't Want to Spoil the Party," 1965
....**$15.00-$30.00**
(with die-cut picture sleeve, add), 1965 ....**$12.50-$25.00**
(with straight cut picture sleeve, add), 1965............................**$37.50-$75.00**
5407, "Ticket to Ride"/"Yes It Is," 1965 ....**$15.00-$30.00**
(with picture sleeve, add), 1965...**$50.00-$100.00**
5476, "Help!"/"I'm Down," 1965 ....**$15.00-$30.00**
(with picture sleeve, add), 1965...**$37.50-$75.00**
5498, "Yesterday"/"Act Naturally," 1965.....................................**$15.00-$30.00**
(with picture sleeve, add), 1965...**$50.00-$100.00**
5555, "We Can Work It Out"/"Day Tripper," 1965.........................**$15.00-$30.00**
(with picture sleeve, add), 1965...**$30.00-$60.00**
5587, "Nowhere Man"/"What Goes On"
(if "What Goes On" writers listed as "John Lennon-Paul McCartney"), 1966..**$12.50-$25.00**
(if "What Goes On" writers listed as "Lennon-McCartney-Starkey"), 1966
....**$25.00-$50.00**
(with picture sleeve, add), 1966...**$20.00-$40.00**
5651, "Paperback Writer"/"Rain," 1966 ....**$12.50-$25.00**
(with picture sleeve, add), 1966...**$37.50-$75.00**
5715, "Yellow Submarine"/"Eleanor Rigby," 1966 ....**$12.50-$25.00**
(with picture sleeve, add), 1966...**$50.00-$100.00**
5810, "Penny Lane"/"Strawberry Fields Forever"
(if "Penny Lane" listed at 3:00 in length), 1967 ....**$12.50-$25.00**
(if "Penny Lane" listed at 2:57 in length), 1967 ....**$15.00-$30.00**
(with picture sleeve, add), 1967...**$50.00-$100.00**
(if on Capitol P 5810, light green promo, trumpet solo at end of "Penny Lane"), 1967 ....**$150.00-$300.00**
(if on Capitol P 5810, light green promo, no trumpet solo at end of "Penny Lane"), 1967 ....**$300.00-$600.00**
5964, "All You Need Is Love"/"Baby, You're a Rich Man," 1967
....**$12.50-$25.00**
(with picture sleeve, add), 1967...**$20.00-$40.00**
2056, "Hello Goodbye"/"I Am the Walrus"
(if orange-yellow swirl, no "A Subsidiary of" in perimeter), 1967
....**$15.00-$30.00**
(with picture sleeve, add), 1967...**$50.00-$100.00**
(if light green label promo), 1967 ....**$125.00-$250.00**
(if orange-yellow swirl, "A Subsidiary of" printed in perimeter), 1968
....**$25.00-$50.00**
2138, "Lady Madonna"/"The Inner Light"
(if orange-yellow swirl, no "A Subsidiary of" in perimeter), 1968
....**$15.00-$30.00**
(if orange-yellow swirl, "A Subsidiary of" printed in perimeter), 1968
....**$25.00-$50.00**
(with picture sleeve, add), 1968...**$50.00-$100.00**
(with "Beatles Fan Club" glossy insert, included with sleeve, add)
....**$10.00-$20.00**
(if light green label promo), 1968 ....**$100.00-$200.00**
4274, "Got to Get You Into My Life"/"Helter Skelter"
(orange label, "Capitol" on bottom, George Martin's name on label), 1976
....**$5.00-$10.00**
(if George Martin's name is not on label), 1976 ....**$3.00-$6.00**
(with picture sleeve, add), 1976...**$2.50-$5.00**
4347, "Ob-La-Di, Ob-La-Da"/"Julia" (with orange label, "Capitol" at bottom), 1976 ....**$4.00-$8.00**
(with numbered picture sleeve, sleeves under the number 1000 can fetch premium prices), 1976 ....**$4.00-$8.00**
P-4506, "Girl" (mono/stereo promo pressing, black vinyl is legit, colored vinyl pressings are counterfeits), 1977 ....**$100.00-$200.00**
(with picture sleeve, advertising "You're Going to Lose That Girl" as B-side, stock copy never pressed), 1977 ....**$7.50-$15.00**
4612, "Sgt. Pepper's Lonely Hearts Club Band-With a Little Help from My Friends"/"A Day in the Life" (original has purple label, geared edge around label perimeter), 1978 ....**$4.00-$8.00**
(with picture sleeve, add), 1978...**$10.00-$20.00**
B-5100, "The Beatles' Movie Medley"/"Fab Four on Film," 1982
....**$25.00-$50.00**
(with picture sleeve, add), 1982...**$10.00-$20.00**
(if on PB-5100, promo), 1982 ....**$12.50-$25.00**
B-5107, "The Beatles' Movie Medley"/"I'm Happy Just to Dance with You," 1982 ....**$2.50-$5.00**
(with picture sleeve, add), 1982...**$2.50-$5.00**
B-5189, "Love Me Do"/"P.S. I Love You" (if orange-yellow swirl, black print, 20th anniversary pressing), 1982 ....**$2.50-$5.00**
(with picture sleeve, add), 1982...**$2.50-$5.00**
B-5624, "Twist and Shout"/"There's a Place," 1986 ....**$2.50-$5.00**

Apple 45s

Apple 2276, "Hey Jude"/"Revolution"
(if small Capitol logo on bottom of B-side of label), 1968...........**$7.50-$15.00**
(if "Mfd. by Apple" on label), 1968 ....**$5.00-$10.00**
2490, "Get Back"/"Don't Let Me Down"
(if small Capitol logo on bottom of B-side of label), 1969 ....**$5.00-$10.00**
(if "Mfd. by Apple" on label), 1969 ....**$5.00-$10.00**
2531, "The Ballad of John and Yoko"/"Old Brown Shoe"
(if small Capitol logo on bottom of B-side of label), 1969 ....**$5.00-$10.00**
(if "Mfd. by Apple" on label), 1969 ....**$5.00-$10.00**
(with picture sleeve, add), 1969...**$50.00-$100.00**
2654, "Something"/"Come Together"
(if small Capitol logo on bottom of B-side of label), 1969
....**$50.00-$100.00**
(if "Mfd. by Apple" on label), 1969 ....**$5.00-$10.00**
2764, "Let It Be"/"You Know My Name (Look Up My Number)"
(if small Capitol logo on bottom of B-side of label), 1970 ....**$6.00-$12.00**
(if "Mfd. by Apple" on label), 1970 ....**$5.00-$10.00**
(with picture sleeve, add), 1970...**$50.00-$100.00**
2832, "The Long and Winding Road"/"For You Blue"
(if small Capitol logo on bottom of B-side of label), 1970 ......**$10.00-$20.00**
(if "Mfd. by Apple" on label), 1970 ....**$5.00-$10.00**
(with picture sleeve, add), 1970...**$50.00-$100.00**
58348, "Baby It's You"/"I'll Follow the Sun"/"Devil in Her Heart"/"Boys," 1995 ....**$2.00-$4.00**
(with picture sleeve, add), 1995...**$2.00-$4.00**
58497, "Free as a Bird"/"Christmas Time (Is Here Again)" (small-holed 45), 1995 ....**$2.00-$4.00**
(with picture sleeve, add), 1995...**$2.00-$4.00**
58544, "Real Love"/"Baby's in Black (Live)" (small-holed 45), 1996
....**$1.50-$3.00**
(with picture sleeve, add), 1996...**$1.50-$3.00**

Other Label 45s

Decca 31382, "My Bonnie"/"The Saints" (credited to Tony Sheridan and the Beat Brothers, black label with rainbow, is legit—copies with 1950s label style, black label with star under Decca, is counterfeit), 1962
....**$11,250.00-$15,000.00**
(if on Decca 31382, pink label, star on label under "Decca," promotional copy), 1962...**$2,000.00-$3,000.00**
Atco 6302, "Sweet Georgia Brown"/"Take Out Some Insurance On Me Baby," 1964 ....**$100.00-$200.00**
6308, "Ain't She Sweet"/"Nobody's Child"
(if "Vocal by John Lennon" on left side of label), 1964 ....**$25.00-$50.00**
(if "Vocal by John Lennon" under "The Beatles"), 1964...........**$30.00-$60.00**
(with picture sleeve, add—be aware that black-green printed sleeves are reproductions), 1964 ....**$250.00-$500.00**
MGM 13213, The Beatles with Tony Sheridan, "My Bonnie (My Bonnie Lies Over the Ocean)"/"The Saints (When the Saints Go Marching In)" (no LP reference on label), 1964...**$20.00-$40.00**
(if reference to an LP number on label), 1964 ....**$25.00-$50.00**
(with picture sleeve, add), 1964...**$60.00-$120.00**
13227, "Why"/"Cry for a Shadow," 1964.....................................**$75.00-$150.00**
(with picture sleeve, add), 1964...**$200.00-$400.00**
Swan 4152, "She Loves You"/"I'll Get You"
(if black label, silver print, "Don't Drop Out" not on label, smaller numbers in trailoff area), 196? ....**$10.00-$20.00**
(if white label, red or maroon print, same as above), 196?..........**$25.00-$50.00**

(if semi-glossy white label, blue printing), 1963 .... **$300.00-$600.00**
(if semi-glossy white label, red print, "Don't Drop Out" not on label), 1963 .... **$300.00-$600.00**
(if flat white label, red print, "Don't Drop Out" not on label), 1963 .... **$325.00-$650.00**
(if semi-glossy white label, red print, "Don't Drop Out" on label), 1963 .... **$325.00-$650.00**
(if black label, silver print, "Don't Drop Out" on label), 1964 .... **$15.00-$30.00**
(if black label, silver print, "Don't Drop Out" not on label), 1964 .... **$20.00-$40.00**
(if black label, silver print, "Produced by George Martin" on both labels), 1964 .... **$25.00-$50.00**
(if black label, silver print, "Produced by George Martin" on only one label), 1964 .... **$25.00-$50.00**
(with picture sleeve, add), 1964 .... **$60.00-$120.00**
4182, "Sie Liebt Dich (She Loves You)"/"I'll Get You"
(if white label, A-side title split on two lines, wide red print), 1964 .... **$75.00-$150.00**
(if white label, A-side title on one line), 1964 .... **$75.00-$150.00**
(if white label, A-side title split on two lines, narrow print), 1964 .... **$75.00-$150.00**
(if white label, A-side title split on two lines, wide orange print), 1964 .... **$87.50-$175.00**

Tollie 9001, "Twist and Shout"/"There's a Place"
(if yellow label, black print, "TOLLIE" stands alone), 1964 .... **$25.00-$50.00**
(if yellow label, black print, black "tollie" in box), 1964 .... **$25.00-$50.00**
(if yellow label, green print, "tollie" in lower case), 1964 .... **$25.00-$50.00**
(if yellow label, black print, black "TOLLIE" in thin box), 1964 .... **$25.00-$50.00**
(if black label, silver print), 1964 .... **$30.00-$60.00**
(if yellow label, black print, purple "tollie" in box), 1964 .... **$30.00-$60.00**
(if yellow label, blue print), 1964 .... **$30.00-$60.00**
(if yellow label, black print, "TOLLIE" in brackets), 1964 .... **$37.50-$75.00**
(if yellow label, green print, "TOLLIE" in uppercase), 1964 ...... **$40.00-$80.00**
(if yellow label, purple print), 1964 .... **$40.00-$80.00**
9008, "Love Me Do"/"P.S. I Love You"
(if yellow label, blue-green print), 1964 .... **$25.00-$50.00**
(if yellow label, black print), 1964 .... **$25.00-$50.00**
(if black label, silver print), 1964 .... **$30.00-$60.00**

45 Reissues:

Oldies label, catalog 149-152, reissue of Vee Jay titles, 1964 .... **$7.50-$15.00**
Capitol "Starline" reissue of original Vee Jay titles, green swirl label, 1965 .... **$60.00-$120.00**
Any Capitol swirl label, "A subsidiary of" printed on perimeter in white), 1968 .... **$25.00-$50.00**
Any Capitol swirl label, "A subsidiary of" printed on perimeter in black), 1968 .... **$50.00-$100.00**
Any Capitol red-orange "target" label, Capitol round logo, 1969 .... **$10.00-$20.00**
Capitol red-orange "target" label, Capitol dome logo, 1969 .... **$30.00-$60.00**
Capitol "Starline" reissue, red-orange "target" label, 1971 .... **$15.00-$30.00**
Any Apple 45 reissue of Capitol title, same catalog number, star on A-side label, 1971 .... **$15.00-$30.00**
Any Apple 45 reissue of Capitol title, same catalog number, no star on A-side, 1971 .... **$5.00-$10.00**
Any Apple 45 reissue of Capitol title, same catalog number, "All Rights Reserved" on label, 1975 .... **$7.50-$15.00**
Any Apple 45 reissue of Apple title, "All Rights Reserved" on label, 1975 .... **$10.00-$20.00**
Capitol orange label, "Capitol" at bottom of label, 1976 .... **$3.00-$6.00**
Capitol purple label, geared edge around label, 1978 .... **$4.00-$8.00**
Capitol "Starline" reissue, blue labels, 1981 .... **$4.00-$8.00**
Collectables 45, catalog 1501-1515, reissue of original Decca audition tape singles, 1982 .... **$1.50-$3.00**
(with picture sleeve, add), 1982 .... **$1.50-$3.00**
Capitol black label, rainbow perimeter around label, 1983 .... **$3.00-$6.00**
Capitol purple label, smooth edge around label, 1988 .... **$2.50-$5.00**
Capitol reissue, S7-17488, 17688-17700, colored vinyl pressing, 1994 .... **$2.00-$4.00**
Capitol S7-17488, "Birthday"/"Taxman," black vinyl pressing (was supposed to be green), 1994 .... **$25.00-$50.00**
S7-18888, "Norwegian Wood"/"If I Needed Someone" (promo from Collector's Choice Music, 1000 copies made), 1994 .... **$75.00-$150.00**
Capitol reissue, S7-18889-18902, colored vinyl pressing, 1996 .... **$2.00-$4.00**

7-inch EPs

Vee Jay 1-903, Souvenir of their Visit to America (plays "Misery"/"A Taste of Honey"/"Ask Me Why"/"Anna"), value is for record and jacket
(if record has black rainbow label, oval logo), 1964 .... **$75.00-$150.00**
(if record has black rainbow label, brackets logo, all titles same size), 1964 .... **$75.00-$150.00**
(if record has black rainbow label, brackets logo, "Ask Me Why" in much larger print), 1964 .... **$92.50-$185.00**
(if record has plain black label, oval logo), 1964 .... **$92.50-$185.00**
(if record has plain black label, "VEE JAY" stands alone), 1964 .... **$105.00-$210.00**
(if record has plain black label, brackets logo), 1964 .... **$130.00-$260.00**
(if record has white-blue label, "Ask Me Why" in much larger print, promo sleeve plugs "Ask Me Why"), 1964 .... **$6,150.00-$8,300.00**
(if record has white-blue label, all titles same size, promo sleeve plugs "Ask Me Why"), 1964 .... **$6,200.00-$8,400.00**

Capitol SXA-2047, Meet the Beatles (stereo jukebox edition, plays "It Won't Be Long"/"This Boy"/"All My Loving"/"Don't Bother Me"/"All I've Got To Do"/"I Wanna Be Your Man," value is for record, jacket, title strips and miniature covers), 1964 .... **$500.00-$1,000.00**
SXA-2080, The Beatles' Second Album (stereo jukebox edition, contains "Thank You Girl"/"Devil in Her Heart"/"Money"/"Long Tall Sally"/"I Call Your Name"/"Please Mister Postman," value is for record, jacket, title strips and miniature covers), 1964 .... **$500.00-$1,000.00**
SXA-2108, Something New (stereo jukebox edition, plays "I'll Cry Instead"/"And I Love Her"/"Slow Down"/"If I Fell"/"Tell Me Why"/"Matchbox," value is for record, jacket, title strips and miniature covers), 1964 .... **$500.00-$1,000.00**

Capitol EAP 1-2121, Four by the Beatles (contains "Roll Over Beethoven"/"This Boy"/"All My Loving"/"Please Mr. Postman," value is for record and jacket), 1964 .... **$200.00-$400.00**
R-5365, 4-By The Beatles (contains "Honey Don't"/"I'm a Loser"/"Mr. Moonlight"/"Everybody's Trying to Be My Baby," value is for record and jacket), 1965 .... **$140.00-$280.00**

Mono LPs

Vee Jay LP 1062, Introducing the Beatles
(if song titles on back cover, "Please Please Me" and "Ask Me Why," plain Vee Jay logo on solid black label), 1964 .... **$125.00-$250.00**
(if song titles on back cover, "Please Please Me" and "Ask Me Why," brackets Vee Jay logo with rainbow perimeter), 1964 .... **$125.00-$250.00**
(if song titles on back cover, "Please Please Me" and "Ask Me Why," oval Vee Jay logo on solid black label), 1964 .... **$150.00-$300.00**
(if song titles on back cover, "Please Please Me" and "Ask Me Why," oval Vee Jay logo with rainbow perimeter), 1964 .... **$150.00-$300.00**
(if song titles on back cover, "Love Me Do" and "P.S. I Love You," oval Vee Jay logo with rainbow perimeter only!), 1964 .... **$400.00-$800.00**
(if blank back cover, with "Please Please Me" and "Ask Me Why," oval Vee Jay logo with rainbow perimeter only!), 1964 .... **$500.00-$1,000.00**
(if song titles cover, with "Please Please Me" and "Ask Me Why," brackets Vee Jay logo on solid black label), 1964 .... **$500.00-$1,000.00**
(if blank back cover, with "Love Me Do" and "P.S. I Love You," oval Vee Jay logo with rainbow perimeter only!), 1964 .... **$800.00-$1,200.00**
(if "Ad Back" cover, with "Love Me Do" and "P.S. I Love You," oval Vee Jay logo with rainbow perimeter only!), 1964 .... **$2,750.00-$4,000.00**
1085, Jolly What! The Beatles and Frank Ifield on Stage
(if man in Beatle wig on cover, printing on spine, dark blue/purple background), 1964 .... **$125.00-$250.00**
(if portrait of Beatles on cover, printing on spine), 1964 .... **$3,500.00-$5,000.00**
1092, Songs, Pictures and Stories of the Fabulous Beatles (gatefold cover, 2/3 width on front)
(if brackets Vee Jay logo with rainbow perimeter), 1964 ...... **$250.00-$500.00**
(if oval Vee Jay logo on solid black label), 1964 .... **$250.00-$500.00**
(if plain Vee Jay logo on solid black label), 1964 .... **$250.00-$500.00**
(if oval Vee Jay logo with rainbow perimeter), 1964 ...... **$1,600.00-$2,400.00**

Vee Jay DX-30, The Beatles vs. The Four Seasons (2 LPs), 1964 .... **$400.00-$800.00**
(with poster, add), 1964 .... **$150.00-$300.00**
Vee Jay 202, Hear the Beatles Tell All, 1964 .... **$150.00-$300.00**
PRO 202, Hear the Beatles Tell All, 1964 .... **$100.00-$200.00**
Atco 33-169, Ain't She Sweet, 1964 .... **$100.00-$200.00**
(if white label promo), 1964 .... **$500.00-$1,000.00**
Capitol T 6051, Beatlemania! with the Beatles (Canadian-only release), 1963 .... **$75.00-$150.00**
T 6054, Twist and Shout (Canadian-only release), 1964 .... **$75.00-$150.00**

T 6063, Long Tall Sally (Canadian-only release), 1964 .... **$75.00-$150.00**

Capitol (USA) T 2047, Meet the Beatles!

(if first pressings, black label with rainbow perimeter, "Beatles!" on cover in tannish brown print, no producer credit on back cover, no ASCAP or BMI credits on the label), 1964 .... **$200.00-$400.00**

(if second pressings, black label with rainbow perimeter, "Beatles!" on cover in tannish brown print, no producer credit on back cover, label has ASCAP and BMI credits), 1964 .... **$100.00-$200.00**

(if black label with rainbow perimeter, "Beatles!" on cover in green print, "Produced by George Martin" on back cover), 1965 .... **$50.00-$100.00**

(if black label with rainbow perimeter, "Beatles!" on cover in tannish brown print, "Produced by George Martin" on back cover, ASCAP and BMI credits on label), 1964 .... **$75.00-$150.00**

T 2080, The Beatles' Second Album, 1964 .... **$90.00-$180.00**

T 2108, Something New, 1964 .... **$75.00-$150.00**

TBO 2222, The Beatles' Story (2 LPs), 1964 .... **$100.00-$200.00**

T 2228, Beatles '65, 1964 .... **$60.00-$120.00**

T 2309, The Early Beatles, 1965 .... **$100.00-$200.00**

T 2358, Beatles VI

(if jacket says 'See label for correct playing order'), 1965 .... **$60.00-$120.00**

(if jacket has song titles in correct order on back cover), 1965 .... **$50.00-$100.00**

MAS 2386, Help!, 1965 .... **$75.00-$150.00**

T 2442, Rubber Soul, 1965 .... **$60.00-$120.00**

T 2553, Yesterday and Today

(if "first state" butcher cover), 1966 .... **$3,000.00-$4,000.00**

(if "second state" trunk cover over butcher cover), 1966 .... **$500.00-$1,000.00**

(if "third state" peeled trunk cover, value negotiable depending upon success of peel), 1966 .... **$800.00-$1,200.00**

(if trunk cover, no sign of butcher cover either peeled or pasted), 1966 .... **$75.00-$150.00**

T 2576, Revolver, 1966 .... **$100.00-$200.00**

MAS 2653, Sgt. Pepper's Lonely Hearts Club Band, 1967 .... **$150.00-$300.00**

MAL 2835, Magical Mystery Tour (with 24-page book bound into gatefold), 1967 .... **$150.00-$300.00**

CLJ-46436, With the Beatles

(if black label, print in rainbow, first Capitol version of British LP), 1987 .... **$10.00-$20.00**

(if purple label, small Capitol logo), 1988 .... **$12.50-$25.00**

(if on Capitol C1-46436, Apple logo on back cover), 1995 .... **$6.00-$12.00**

CLJ-46437, A Hard Day's Night

(if black label, print in rainbow, first Capitol version of British LP), 1987 .... **$10.00-$20.00**

(if purple label, small Capitol logo), 1988 .... **$12.50-$25.00**

(if on Capitol C1-4647, Apple logo on back cover), 1995 .... **$6.00-$12.00**

CLJ-46438, Beatles for Sale

(if black label, print in rainbow, first Capitol version of British LP), 1987 .... **$10.00-$20.00**

(if purple label, small Capitol logo), 1988 .... **$12.50-$25.00**

(if on Capitol C1-46438, Apple logo on back cover), 1995 .... **$6.00-$12.00**

C1-90445, Beatles VI (plays mono, lists stereo, 1988 reissue), 1988 .... **$12.50-$25.00**

MGM E-4215, The Beatles with Tony Sheridan, 1964 .... **$125.00-$250.00**

E-4215, The Beatles with Tony Sheridan and Their Guests, 1964 .... **$100.00-$200.00**

Metro M-563, This Is Where It Started, 1966 .... **$50.00-$100.00**

Phoenix PHX-352, Silver Beatles, Volume 1, 1982 .... **$6.00-$12.00**

PHX-353, Silver Beatles, Volume 2, 1982 .... **$6.00-$12.00**

United Artists UAL 3366, A Hard Day's Night

(if "I Cry Instead" listed), 1964 .... **$100.00-$200.00**

(if "I'll Cry Instead" listed), 1964 .... **$125.00-$250.00**

(if white label promo), 1964 .... **$1,500.00-$3,000.00**

(if on United Artists T-90828, Capitol Record Club edition), 1964 .... **$1,125.00-$1,500.00**

Stereo LPs

Vee Jay SR 1062, Introducing the Beatles

(if blank back cover, "Love Me Do" and "P.S. I Love You," oval Vee Jay logo with rainbow perimeter only!), 1964 .... **$1,250.00-$2,500.00**

(if blank back cover, "Love Me Do" and "P.S. I Love You" both in mono, oval Vee Jay logo with rainbow perimeter only!), 1964 .... **$8,000.00-$12,000.00**

(if song titles cover, "Please Please Me" and "Ask Me Why," brackets Vee Jay logo with rainbow perimeter), 1964 .... **$750.00-$1,500.00**

(if song titles cover, "Please Please Me" and "Ask Me Why," oval Vee Jay logo with rainbow perimeter), 1964 .... **$800.00-$1,600.00**

(if song titles cover, "Please Please Me" and "Ask Me Why," plain Vee Jay logo on solid black label), 1964 .... **$800.00-$1,600.00**

(if song titles cover; with "Love Me Do" and "P.S. I Love You"; oval Vee Jay logo with rainbow perimeter only; this album has been heavily counterfeited; please check the label of your copy before contacting the author. If the words "Introducing the Beatles" are above the center hole of the record, and the words "The Beatles" are below, it is automatically a counterfeit and virtually worthless), 1964 .... **$5,500.00-$8,000.00**

SR 1085, Jolly What! The Beatles and Frank Ifield on Stage

(if man in Beatle wig cover, "Stereo" on both cover and label), 1964 .... **$250.00-$500.00**

(if portrait of Beatles on cover, "Stereo" on both cover and label), 1964 .... **$8,000.00-$12,000.00**

VJS 1092, Songs, Pictures and Stories of the Fabulous Beatles (gatefold cover, 2/3 width on front, all copies have "Introducing the Beatles" records inside—NOTE: Any non-gatefold copy or any copy called "Songs and Pictures of the Fabulous Beatles" is a counterfeit)

(if brackets Vee Jay logo with rainbow perimeter), 1964 .... **$1,600.00-$2,400.00**

(if plain Vee Jay logo on solid black label), 1964 .... **$1,600.00-$2,400.00**

(if oval Vee Jay logo with rainbow perimeter), 1964 ...... **$1,600.00-$2,400.00**

DXS-30, The Beatles vs. the Four Seasons (2 LPs), 1964 .... **$2,250.00-$3,000.00**

(with poster, add), 1964 .... **$150.00-$300.00**

PRO 202, Hear the Beatles Tell All

(if white label promo, blue print), 1964 .... **$12,000.00-$18,000.00**

(if stereo reissue), 1979 .... **$5.00-$10.00**

(if shaped picture disc), 1987 .... **$10.00-$20.00**

Atco SD 33-169, Ain't She Sweet (if tan-purple label), 1964 .. **$200.00-$400.00**

(if yellow label), 1969 .... **$250.00-$500.00**

MGM SE-4215, The Beatles with Tony Sheridan, 1964 .... **$400.00-$800.00**

SE-4215, The Beatles with Tony Sheridan and Their Guests, 1964 .... **$300.00-$600.00**

MS-563, This Is Where It Started (stereo cover), 1966 .... **$75.00-$150.00**

Capitol ST 2047, Meet the Beatles!

(if first pressings, black label, rainbow perimeter, "Beatles!" on cover in tannish brown print, no publishing credits on label, no producer credit on back cover), 1964 .... **$200.00-$400.00**

(if second pressings, black label, rainbow perimeter, "Beatles!" on cover in tannish brown print, "ASCAP" and "BMI" credits listed, no producer credit on back cover), 1964 .... **$75.00-$150.00**

(if black label with rainbow perimeter; "Beatles!" on cover in tannish brown print; some labels have "ASCAP" and "BMI" credits listed, "Produced by George Martin" on back cover), 1964 .... **$60.00-$120.00**

(if black label with rainbow perimeter; "Beatles!" on cover in green print; "Produced by George Martin" on lower left of back cover; many of these have a label giving "BMI" credit to every song except "Don't Bother Me" and "Till There Was You"), 1965 .... **$37.50-$75.00**

ST 2080, The Beatles' Second Album (black label, rainbow perimeter), 1964 .... **$50.00-$100.00**

United Artists UAS 6366, A Hard Day's Night

(with "I Cry Instead" listed), 1964 .... **$100.00-$200.00**

(with "I'll Cry Instead" listed), 1964 .... **$125.00-$250.00**

(if pink-orange label), 1968 .... **$25.00-$50.00**

(if black-orange label), 1970 .... **$25.00-$50.00**

(if tan label), 1971 .... **$10.00-$20.00**

(if tan label, "All Rights Reserved" around perimeter of label), 1975 .... **$10.00-$20.00**

(if sunrise label), 1977 .... **$10.00-$20.00**

(if on United Artists ST-90828, Capitol Record Club edition), 1964 .... **$375.00-$750.00**

Capitol ST 2108, Something New (black label, rainbow perimeter), 1964 .... **$40.00-$80.00**

STBO-2222, The Beatles' Story (2 LPs) (black label, rainbow perimeter), 1964 .... **$75.00-$150.00**

ST 2228, Beatles '65 (black label, rainbow perimeter), 1964 ...... **$40.00-$80.00**

ST 2309, The Early Beatles (black label, rainbow perimeter), 1965 .... **$50.00-$100.00**

ST 2358, Beatles VI

(if songs titles listed in correct order on back cover), 1965 ...... **$37.50-$75.00**

(if "see label for correct playing order" on back cover), 1965 .... **$40.00-$80.00**

SMAS 2386, Help! (black label, rainbow perimeter), 1965 .... **$37.50-$75.00**

(if on SMAS-8-2386, Capitol Record Club edition, black label with rainbow perimeter, "8" on cover), 1965 .... **$300.00-$600.00**

(if on SMAS-8-2386, Capitol Record Club edition, black label with rainbow perimeter, no "8" on cover), 1965 .... **$200.00-$400.00**
ST 2442, Rubber Soul (black label, rainbow perimeter), 1965 .... **$30.00-$60.00**
ST 2553, Yesterday and Today
(if "first state" butcher cover), 1966............................... **$6,000.00-$8,000.00**
(if "second state" trunk cover over butcher cover), 1966....**$750.00-$1,000.00**
(if "third state," peeled butcher cover, value dependent upon success of peel), 1966..**$750.00-$1,500.00**
(if trunk cover, no butcher cover underneath, black label, rainbow perimeter), 1966..**$40.00-$80.00**
ST 2576, Revolver (black label, rainbow perimeter), 1966.......**$50.00-$100.00**
(if on Capitol ST-8-2576, Capitol Record Club edition, orange label, 1973 ....**$100.00-$200.00**
SMAS 2653, Sgt. Pepper's Lonely Hearts Club Band (black label, rainbow perimeter), 1967..**$50.00-$100.00**
(with cut-out inserts, add), 1967...**$1.50-$3.00**
(with red-white psychedelic inner sleeves, only in 1967 editions, add), 1967 ....**$7.50-$15.00**
SMAL 2835, Magical Mystery Tour, 1967............................**$50.00-$100.00**
(above Capitol titles have been reissued and remained in print for years; check the reissue listings later in this price guide for more information and identification on these reissues)

Apple SBC-100, The Beatles' Christmas Album (compilation of fan club Christmas messages, counterfeits exist), 1970 ....**$200.00-$400.00**
SWBO-101, The Beatles ("The White Album")
(if numbered copy, four individual posters and large poster; ringwear often appears on album, lower serial numbers have higher value), 1968 ....**$75.00-$200.00**
(if unnumbered copy, four individual posters and large poster), 197? ....**$30.00-$60.00**
(if "All Rights Reserved" on labels, title in black on cover, photos and poster on thinner paper stock), 1975 ....**$35.00-$70.00**
SW-153, Yellow Submarine
(with Capitol logo on bottom of side 2), 1969 ....**$25.00-$50.00**
(if "Mfd. by Apple" on label), 1971 ....**$10.00-$20.00**
(if "All Rights Reserved" on label), 1975....................................**$12.50-$25.00**
SO-383, Abbey Road
(if "Mfd. by Apple" on label, "Her Majesty" IS listed on the label), 1969 ....**$10.00-$20.00**
(if "Mfd. by Apple" on label, "Her Majesty" is NOT listed on the label), 1969..**$10.00-$20.00**
(with Capitol logo on bottom of side 2, "Her Majesty" IS listed on both jacket and label), 1969 ....**$20.00-$40.00**
(with Capitol logo on bottom of side 2, "Her Majesty" is NOT listed on either jacket or label), 1969...**$37.50-$75.00**
(if "All Rights Reserved" on label), 1975....................................**$12.50-$25.00**
SW-385, Hey Jude
(if "Mfd. by Apple" on label, label lists LP as "Hey Jude"), 1970 ....**$10.00-$20.00**
(if label lists LP as "The Beatles Again," catalog on label is SW-385), 1970 ....**$12.50-$25.00**
(if label lists LP as "The Beatles Again," catalog on label is SO-385), 1970 ....**$20.00-$40.00**
(with Capitol logo on bottom of side 2, label lists LP as "Hey Jude"), 1970 ....**$37.50-$75.00**
(with "All Rights Reserved" on label, label lists LP as "Hey Jude"), 1975 ....**$12.50-$25.00**
AR-34001, Let It Be (red Apple label, "Bell Sound" stamped in dead wax), 1970..**$12.50-$25.00**
SKBO-3403, The Beatles 1962-1966 (2 LPs), 1973 ....**$15.00-$30.00**
(if "All Rights Reserved" on labels), 1975 ....**$25.00-$50.00**
SKBO-3404, The Beatles 1967-1970 (2 LPs), 1973 ....**$15.00-$30.00**
(if "All Rights Reserved" on labels), 1975 ....**$25.00-$50.00**

Capitol SKBO-11357, Rock 'n' Roll Music (2 LPs), 1976 ....**$12.50-$25.00**
SMAS-11638, The Beatles at the Hollywood Bowl
(first pressings have embossed title and ticket on cover), 1977 ....**$10.00-$20.00**
(second pressings have flat cover), 1980.....................................**$7.50-$15.00**
(if UPC code on back cover), 1989..**$20.00-$40.00**
(if advance promo copy, plain white jacket, tan label), 1977 **$250.00-$500.00**
SKBL-11711, Love Songs (2 LPs)
(with booklet and embossed faux leather cover), 1977 ....**$10.00-$20.00**
(with booklet, cover not embossed), 1988..................................**$15.00-$30.00**
SHAL-12060, Rarities
(first pressing, says "There's a Place" debuts in stereo (false), says screaming at the end of "Helter Skelter" was a "classic Lennon statement," when Ringo actually said it), 1980 ....**$10.00-$20.00**
(if errors corrected, "Produced by George Martin" on back cover), 1980 ....**$7.50-$15.00**

Apple C1-97036, The Beatles 1962-1966 (2 LPs) (red vinyl), 1993 ....**$12.50-$25.00**
C1-97039, The Beatles 1967-1970 (2 LPs) (blue vinyl), 1993 ....**$12.50-$25.00**
C1-8-31796, Live at the BBC (2 LPs), 1994...............................**$25.00-$50.00**
C1-8-34445, Anthology 1 (3 LPs), 1995...................................**$20.00-$40.00**
C1-8-34448, Anthology 2 (3 LPs), 1996...................................**$20.00-$40.00**
C1-8-34451, Anthology 3 (3 LPs), 1996...................................**$15.00-$30.00**

Stereo LP reissues of previous single-LP Beatle titles
(if Capitol Record Club edition, catalog number begins with "ST-8," black label with rainbow perimeter, three diagonal lines on top of album jacket), 1964...**$250.00-$500.00**
(if Capitol black label, rainbow perimeter, "A Subsidiary of Capitol Industries, Inc." around perimeter of label), 1968...**$25.00-$50.00**
(if lime green Capitol label), 1969 ....**$20.00-$40.00**
(if Capitol Record Club edition, catalog number begins with "ST-8," lime green Capitol label), 1969 ....**$100.00-$200.00**
(if on Apple/Capitol logo, Capitol logo on bottom of side 2 label), 1968 ....**$20.00-$40.00**
(if on Apple/Capitol, "Mfd. by Apple" on label), 1971...............**$10.00-$20.00**
(if on Apple/Capitol, "All Rights Reserved" on label), 1975 ......**$12.50-$25.00**
(if orange Capitol label), 1976 ....**$6.00-$12.00**
(if purple Capitol label, large logo), 1978.......................................**$5.00-$10.00**
(if black Capitol label, print in rainbow perimeter), 1983 ....**$7.50-$15.00**
(if black label, print in rainbow perimeter, including American debuts of original British LPs), 1987..**$10.00-$20.00**
(if purple label, small Capitol logo, including final pressings of original American issues), 1988 ....**$12.50-$25.00**
(if Capitol label, Apple logo on back cover, 1995 reissues)...........**$6.00-$12.00**

Normally, a Sgt. Pepper's Lonely Hearts Club Band *album from the 1970s would not have a high collectible value. This record, however, features John Lennon's authentic signature, a personalization, a quick doodle, and an "80," symbolizing the year he signed the record. Although Beatles signatures are very valuable, one should always check with an autograph expert before investing or purchasing signed materials.*
***$710**, Good condition LP*
***$700** for John Lennon autograph*

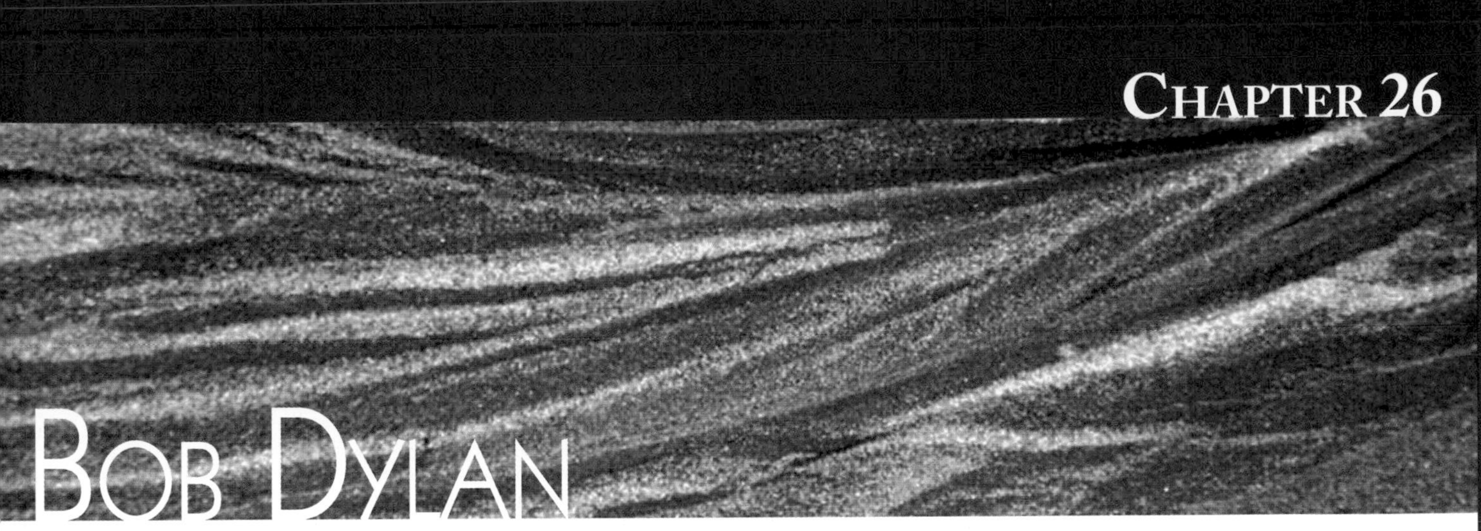

Chapter 26

Bob Dylan

History

Born in Hibbing, Minnesota in 1941, Robert Zimmerman learned how to play guitar and harmonica at an early age. By high school, he was already part of a rock band, the Golden Chords, and studied music at the University of Minnesota. While there, he performed at coffeehouses, taking his stage surname of "Bob Dylan" from another legendary poet, Dylan Thomas. By 1961, Dylan was a popular performer in Greenwich Village. While performing as an opening act for bluesman John Lee Hooker, Dylan was discovered and signed to a recording contract by Columbia Records' John Hammond.

While Dylan's first album featured mostly folk covers with only a couple of original tracks, Dylan's second album, *The Freewheelin' Bob Dylan*, embraced the protest movement of the early 1960s, and added direct messages about civil rights, war, and government intrusion. Tracks like "A Hard Rain's A-Gonna Fall," written during the height of the 1962 Cuban Missile Crisis, and the inquisitive "Blowin' In The Wind," spoke to a generation.

The version of *The Freewheelin' Bob Dylan* that most people recall contained the following "official" tracks— "Blowin' in the Wind," "Girl from the North Country," "Masters of War," "Down the Highway," "Bob Dylan's Blues," "A Hard Rain's A-Gonna Fall," "Don't Think Twice, It's All Right," "Bob Dylan's Dream," "Oxford Town," "Talking World War III Blues," "Corrina, Corrina," "Honey, Just Allow Me One More Chance" and "I Shall Be Free." But when the album was originally set for release, four more tracks were scheduled to be part of the project—"Let Me Die in My Footsteps," "Rocks and Gravel," "Talkin' John Birch Society Blues" and "Gamblin' Willie's Dead Man's Hand." The legend has it that Bob Dylan was scheduled to appear on the Ed Sullivan show, and wanted to perform "Talkin' John Birch Society Blues"—but the show's producers refused his request. Dylan reportedly stormed out of the building, and the next day Columbia re-mastered *The Freewheelin' Bob Dylan*, deleting that track—and three others—from the album. Some label and cover art still listed the four songs as available, so several variations—both in mono and stereo— on this album abound.

The impact of *Freewheelin'* was enormous. Dylan's music was now part of the catalog of other folk singers and groups (including Peter, Paul and Mary, who covered "Blowin' in the Wind," and the Four Seasons, who recorded his "Don't Think Twice, It's All Right"). Joan Baez would cover several of Dylan's songs, and the two were linked romantically for a time.

Bob Dylan's song "Subterranean Homesick Blues," with its stream-of-consciousness delivery, was Dylan's first Top 40 charted single. This promotional 45, like most of Columbia's promo singles of the 1960s, was pressed on red vinyl; the pressing plant didn't clean out all the black vinyl pellets before this initial pressing, giving this record a "mottled" appearance.

***$180**, VG+ condition*

This stereo label from one of the first pressings of The Freewheelin' Bob Dylan *shows such "deleted tracks" as "Rocks and Gravel" and "Let Me Die In My Footsteps," and is one of only two American stereo pressings to surface with those tracks. Interestingly, several monaural album jackets, with the "deleted" tracks listed on the front cover, have surfaced as Canadian issues. As can be seen in this closeup shot of the lower corner of the Canadian mono Freewheelin, the "deleted" titles of "Gamblin' Willie" and "Talkin' John Birch Society Blues" are clearly visible, although the albums themselves still play the "corrected" tracks.*
(at top left) ***$30,000,*** *NM condition*

$400, *NM condition Canadian cover*

But as the 1960s progressed, fans noticed a change in Dylan's music and his songwriting. Those expecting another protest album along the lines of *The Freewheelin' Bob Dylan* were instead presented with *Another Side of Bob Dylan*, in which Dylan focused on early blues music and sounds. After the fans got comfortable with that, Dylan recorded *Bringing it All Back Home*, with several of the tracks accompanied by rock music. Even songs that he gave to other artists were becoming electrified—the Byrds' performance of "Mr. Tambourine Man," for example. And *Highway 61 Revisited*, contained Dylan's strongest poetic imagery in lyrical tapestries like "Positively 4th Street" and "Like a Rolling Stone."

But to folk music fans, it was as if Dylan had slapped them in the face with an electric guitar. Many looked at Dylan's rock and roll excursions as a "betrayal," and when Dylan took the stage at the 1965 Newport Folk Festival with the Paul Butterfield Blues Band, his fans booed him lustily.

Undaunted, Dylan continued to record, working with a Canadian group, the Hawks (which he rechristened "The Band"), on several recordings and tours. In August 1966, however, Dylan suffered injury in a motorcycle accident, that kept him bedridden for nearly a year. During that time, he wrote and recorded several songs with The Band, eventually becoming the "Big Pink" sessions (so named for the pink house in Saugerties, New York, where Dylan resided). Originally the Big Pink sessions were circulated by Dylan's music publisher with the hopes that some of the songs would be covered by other artists; however, many of those tapes were pressed on bootleg albums and sold to fans as "Dylan's lost album." Those recordings finally surfaced as a legitimate release in 1975, as *The Basement Tapes*.

By the mid-1970s, Bob Dylan's music was more focused and direct, with his album *Blood on the Tracks* being hailed as a masterpiece. He also continued his efforts in social protest, documenting the case of boxer-turned prisoner Ruben "Hurricane" Carter in a hit song, "Hurricane." Dylan also went through his own period of self-examination and reflection, recording three gospel albums in the late 1970s and a reggae-influenced album, *Infidels*, in 1983.

In the 1990s, Dylan's recordings were few and far between, but the albums that did surface—1997's *Time Out of Mind* and 2001's *Love and Theft*—were hailed as Dylan's most significant and important recordings since *Blood on the Tracks*. Both albums received Grammy® awards for Best Contemporary Folk Album, with *Time Out of Mind* receiving the Grammy® for Album of the Year.

What To Look For

Bob Dylan spent most of his recording career with Columbia Records, with the exception of two albums and a few singles for Asylum Records in the early 1970s. Almost his entire catalog has remained in print since its initial release, meaning that one must undertake careful examination on an album cover or jacket to correctly identify the correct year of pressing, and to confirm if an album is an original or a reprint.

Columbia mono pressings in 1962 feature a red and black label, with six white "eye" logos, three at 9:00 on the record, three at 3:00 on the record. Dylan's first album *Bob Dylan* exists in this format.

Between 1962 and 1965, first mono pressings of *The Freewheelin' Bob Dylan*, *The Times They Are a-Changin'*, *Another Side of Bob Dylan,* and *Bringing It All Back Home* will have a red label, "COLUMBIA" in white lettering along the top perimeter of the label, and "GUARANTEED HIGH FIDELITY" in black at the bottom of the label. Between 1965 to 1968, the bottom perimeter of the label will say in white, either "360 SOUND MONO 360 SOUND," or simply "MONO." Columbia stopped making monaural albums for store purchases after 1968, although some pressings were made for radio stations.

As for Columbia's stereo output, pressings from 1962, including Dylan's first album *Bob Dylan*, contain a red-black label with six white "eye" logos, and the words "STEREO FIDELITY" in white along the bottom of the label.

Columbia's 1963 pressings, including *The Freewheelin' Bob Dylan*, feature the words "COLUMBIA" in white along the top of an all-red label, with "360 SOUND STEREO 360 SOUND" in black at the bottom of the label. Arrows were added to the bottom perimeter text at the end of 1963, this label style continued until 1965.

Between 1965 and 1970, the "360 SOUND STEREO 360 SOUND" was changed from black to white text. The label was redesigned in 1970 to an orange background, with the word "COLUMBIA" printed six times around the perimeter of the record label. This format lasted until 1990, when it was again changed to a red label with "COLUMBIA" in white along the top, and all other label print, including song titles, in black.

Several album cover variations exist, including a version of *Blood on the Tracks* without album liner notes (they were removed during the record's initial print run, then restored when the album won a Grammy® for Best Liner Notes). Many of the variations for Dylan 45s and LPs are listed below in the price section.

Bob Dylan, like many other popular artists, was plagued with bootleg releases of his concerts and commercially unreleased tracks. Although they are a historical part of Dylan's *catalog raisonne*, bootleg records are discussed in a separate chapter elsewhere in this book.

Be careful also of 45 RPM "fantasy" pressings, including a Columbia 45 featuring Dylan singing "Mr. Tambourine Man"—no such legitimate pressing existed, and the song's first 45 RPM release was when the Byrds recorded it.

Books

Dylan, Bob, *Bob Dylan: In His Own Words*, Omnibus Press, 1993.

Ellison, James, Ed., *Younger Than That Now: The Collected Interviews of Bob Dylan*, Thunder's Mouth Press, 2004.

Lee, C.P., *Bob Dylan: Like the Night*, Interlink Pub Group, 1998.

Web Pages

Bob Dylan's Web site: http://www.bobdylan.com

Over 600 different Dylan pages and links can be found at this site: http://www.worldgonewrong.com/

Photo credit: Courtesy Last Vestige Music Store, Albany, N.Y.

In the early 1970s, Dylan recorded two albums with Asylum Records; both with the Band. This album, Planet Waves, *was originally named "Ceremonies of the Horsemen," and although that title was never used, some covers were pressed with that title and are extremely rare items.*

***$7.50,** VG condition*

In 1985, the 5-LP set Biograph was issued, chronicling over 25 years of Dylan recordings, including hits and unreleased tracks.

***$20**, VG condition*

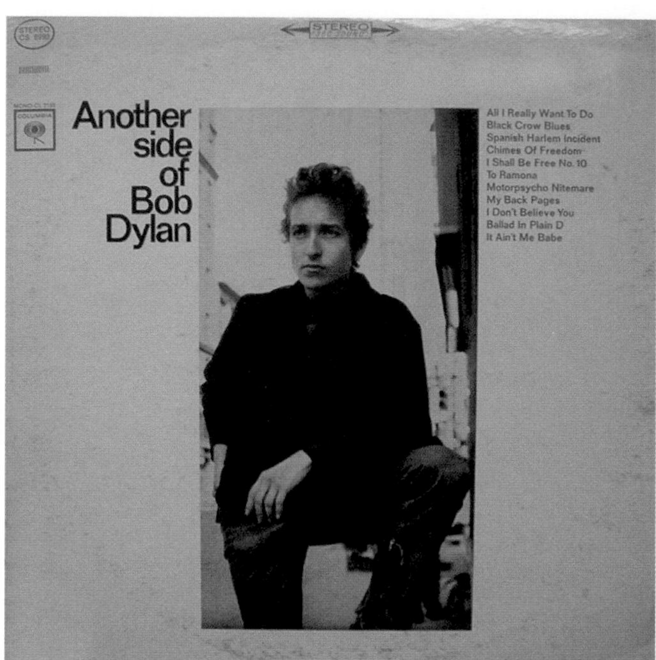

Part of the strength of Bob Dylan's catalog is that hundreds of artists have recorded his songs—"It Ain't Me, Babe," a track from this album, has been covered by such artists as the Turtles, Johnny Cash, Davy Jones, Glen Campbell, and Sebastian Cabot!

***$10**, Good condition*

In 2001, several of Dylan's albums were reissued on 180-gram virgin vinyl. This pressing of The Freewheelin' Bob Dylan *attempted to replicate as much of the original album as possible, but there are still some subtle differences in both pressings. The 2001 audiophile pressing on the right has a large sticker on the shrinkwrap and a UPC bar code on the back of the jacket—also, the "360 Sound" reference visible on the original 1963 release on the left has been deleted from the top of the audiophile album cover.*

*(L to R) **$50**, NM condition; **$20**, NM condition*

Bob Dylan VG+ to NM

45s

Columbia 42656, "Mixed-Up Confusion"/"Corrina, Corrina" (orange label), 1962 ....$1,000.00-$1,500.00
(if white label, promo pressing), 1962 ....$250.00-$500.00
42856, "Blowin' in the Wind"/"Don't Think Twice, It's All Right," 1963 ....$250.00-$500.00
(if white label promo), 1963 ....$150.00-$300.00
(with "Rebel with a Cause" promotional sleeve), 1963....................$400.00-$800.00
JZSP 75606/7, "Blowin' in the Wind"/"Don't Think Twice, It's All Right" (promo, "Special Album Excerpt"), 1963....................$150.00-$300.00
43242, "Subterranean Homesick Blues"/"She Belongs to Me," 1965 ....$10.00-$20.00
(if reissued on gray label, 1972 reissue), 1972 ....$15.00-$30.00
43346, "Like a Rolling Stone"/"Gates of Eden," 1965....................$10.00-$20.00
JZSP 110939/40, "Like a Rolling Stone (Part 1)"/"Like a Rolling Stone" (Part 2) (promo), 1965 ....$30.00-$60.00
43389, "Positively 4th Street"/"From a Buick 6," 1965 ....$10.00-$20.00
(if odd version, plays at 45, has small center hole, possibly for export), 1965 ....$15.00-$30.00
(if A-side contains alternate version of "Can You Please Crawl Out Your Window," must be heard to confirm), 1965....................$75.00-$150.00
(if reissued on gray label, 1972 reissue), 1972 ....$12.50-$25.00
(with picture sleeve, add), 1965....................$35.00-$70.00
43477, "Can You Please Crawl Out Your Window?"/"Highway 61 Revisited," 1965 ....$10.00-$20.00
43541, "One of Us Must Know (Sooner or Later)"/"Queen Jane Approximately," 1966....................$10.00-$20.00
JZSP 113096/147, "One Of Us Must Know (Sooner or Later)" (4:49)/(3:07) (promo only), 1966 ....$50.00-$100.00
43592, "Rainy Day Women #12 and 35"/"Pledging My Time," 1966 ....$7.50-$15.00
43683, "I Want You"/"Just Like Tom Thumb's Blues" (Live), 1966 ....$7.50-$15.00
(with picture sleeve, add), 1966....................$40.00-$80.00
43792, "Just Like a Woman"/"Obviously 5 Believers," 1966 ....$7.50-$15.00
44069, "Leopard-Skin Pill-Box Hat"/"Most Likely You'll Go Your Way and I'll Go Mine," 1967....................$10.00-$20.00
44826, "I Threw It All Away"/"Drifter's Escape," 1969 ....$4.00-$8.00
44926, "Lay Lady Lay"/"Peggy Day," 1969....................$4.00-$8.00
45004, "Tonight I'll Be Staying Here with You"/"Country Pie," 1969 ....$5.00-$10.00
45199, "Wigwam"/"Copper Kettle (The Pale Moonlight)" (different label styles, value is equal), 1970....................$3.00-$6.00
AE 25, "All the Tired Horses" (mono)/(stereo) (promo), 1970..$20.00-$40.00
AE7 1039, "If Not for You"/"Tomorrow Is a Long Time" (promo), 1971 ....$20.00-$40.00
45409, "Watching the River Flow"/"Spanish Is the Loving Tongue," 1971 ....$3.00-$6.00
45516, "George Jackson" (Acoustic version)/(Big Band version), 1971 ....$5.00-$10.00
45913, "Knockin' on Heaven's Door"/"Turkey Chase," 1973....................$2.50-$5.00
45982, "A Fool Such As I"/"Lily of the West," 1973 ....$3.00-$6.00
Asylum 11033, "On a Night Like This"/"You Angel You," 1974....................$3.00-$6.00
11035, "Something There Is About You"/"Going, Going, Gone," 1974 ....$3.00-$6.00
11043, "Most Likely You Go Your Way (And I'll Go Mine)"/"Stage Fright" (with The Band), 1974 ....$3.00-$6.00
45212, "All Along the Watchtower"/"It Ain't Me Babe," 1974....$6.00-$12.00
Columbia 10106, "Tangled Up in Blue"/"If You See Her Say Hello," 1975 ....$3.00-$6.00
10217, "Million Dollar Bash"/"Tears of Rage," 1975....................$5.00-$10.00
10245, "Hurricane" (Part 1)/"Hurricane" (Part 2), 1975....................$3.00-$6.00
(with picture sleeve, add), 1975....................$6.00-$12.00
10245, "Hurricane" (mono)/(stereo) (plays at 33-1/3 RPM, "Special Rush Reservice" on label), 1975 ....$7.50-$15.00
10245, "Hurricane" (mono)/(stereo) (plays at 33-1/3 RPM, no reference to "Special Rush Reservice" on label), 1975 ....$10.00-$20.00
(with special picture sleeve for mono/stereo pressing above, add), 1975 ....$7.50-$15.00
10298, "Mozambique"/"Oh, Sister," 1976....................$3.00-$6.00
10454, "Stuck Inside of Mobile with the Memphis Blues Again"/"Rita Mae," 1976....................$2.50-$5.00
(with picture sleeve, add), 1976....................$3.00-$6.00
10805, "Baby Stop Crying"/"New Pony," 1978....................$2.50-$5.00
10851, "Changing of the Guards"/"Senor (Tales of Yankee Power)," 1978 ....$2.00-$4.00
10851, "Changing of the Guards" (3:39)/(6:36) (promo), 1978.....$4.00-$8.00
11072, "Gotta Serve Somebody"/"Trouble in Mind," 1979....................$2.00-$4.00
11168, "Man Gave Names to All the Animals"/"When You Gonna Wake Up," 1979....................$2.00-$4.00
11235, "Slow Train"/"Do Right to Me Baby (Do Unto Others)," 1980 ....$2.00-$4.00
(with picture sleeve, add), 1980....................$2.50-$5.00
11318, "Solid Rock"/"Covenant Woman," 1980 ....$2.00-$4.00
11370, "Saved"/"Are You Ready" (hard to find stock copy), 1980 ....$12.50-$25.00
02510, "Heart of Mine"/"The Groom's Still Waiting at the Altar," 1981 ....$2.00-$4.00
(with picture sleeve, add), 1981....................$2.50-$5.00
04301, "Sweetheart Like You"/"Union Sundown," 1983....................$2.00-$4.00
(with picture sleeve, add), 1983....................$2.50-$5.00
04425, "Jokerman"/"Isis," 1984 ....$2.50-$5.00
04933, "Tight Connection to My Heart (Has Anybody Seen My Love)"/"We Better Talk This Over," 1985....................$2.00-$4.00
(with picture sleeve, add), 1985....................$2.00-$4.00
05697, "Emotionally Yours"/"When the Night Comes Falling from the Sky," 1985....................$2.00-$4.00
07970, "Silvio"/"Too Far from Home," 1988 ....$2.50-$5.00
73012, "Everything Is Broken"/"Dead Man, Dead Man," 1989.....$4.00-$8.00
CS7 32660, "Tweedle Dee & Tweedle Dum"/"Bye & Bye" (promotional record, red label, black cardboard sleeve), 2001 ....$5.00-$10.00

Red Vinyl Promo 45s

Columbia 43242, "Subterranean Homesick Blues" (same on both sides), 1965 ....$125.00-$250.00
(with picture sleeve, only issued with some promos), 1965 ....$1,000.00-$1,500.00
43346, "Like a Rolling Stone" (same on both sides), 1965.....$100.00-$200.00
43389, "Positively 4th Street" (same on both sides), 1965........$75.00-$150.00
43592, "Rainy Day Women #12 and 35" (same on both sides), 1966 ....$75.00-$150.00
43683, "I Want You" (same on both sides), 1966....................$75.00-$150.00

Mono LPs

Columbia CL 1779, Bob Dylan
(first pressings, black-red label, six white "eye" logos, three at 9:00, three at 3:00, stock copy), 1962....................$125.00-$250.00
(if six "eye" logos on label, "A New Star on Columbia" sticker on cover, promo stamp on label), 1962....................$250.00-$500.00
(if "Guaranteed High Fidelity" on label), 1963 ....$20.00-$40.00
(if "Mono" on label), 1966....................$15.00-$30.00
CL 1986, The Freewheelin' Bob Dylan ("Guaranteed High Fidelity" on label, corrected version record plays what label says), 1963 ....$20.00 $40.00
(if white label promo, label AND timing strip list, and record plays, "correct" tracks), 1963 ....$250.00-$500.00
(if white label promo, timing strip lists deleted tracks, label lists, and record plays, "correct" tracks), 1963 ....$400.00-$800.00
(if white label promo, label lists deleted tracks, timing strip lists, record plays, "correct" tracks), 1963 ....$1,000.00-$2,000.00
(if white label promo, label and timing strip lists the deleted tracks but plays the "correct" tracks), 1963 ....$2,000.00-$3,000.00
(if "Guaranteed High Fidelity" on label, plays "Let Me Die In My Footsteps," "Rocks and Gravel," "Talkin' John Birch Blues" and "Gamblin' Willie's Dead Man's Hand." Label does NOT list these. Matrix number in dead wax ends in "-1" followed by a letter), 1963........$8,000.00-$12,000.00
(if "Mono" on label, "correct" tracks on label), 1966....................$15.00-$30.00
CL 2105, The Times They Are a-Changin'
(if "Guaranteed High Fidelity" on label), 1964....................$20.00-$40.00
(if white label promo), 1964 ....$200.00-$400.00
(if "Mono" on label), 1965 ....$15.00-$30.00
CL 2193, Another Side of Bob Dylan
(if "Guaranteed High Fidelity" on label), 1964....................$20.00-$40.00
(if white label promo), 1964 ....$200.00-$400.00
(if "Mono" on label), 1965 ....$15.00-$30.00
CL 2328, Bringing It All Back Home
(if "Guaranteed High Fidelity" on label), 1965....................$25.00-$50.00
(if "Mono" on label), 1965 ....$15.00-$30.00
(if white label promo), 1965 ....$150.00-$300.00

CL 2389, Highway 61 Revisited, 1965 .... **$40.00-$80.00**
(if white label promo), 1965 .... **$200.00-$400.00**
C2L 41, Blonde on Blonde (2 LPs)
(if "female photos" inner gatefold with two women pictured), 1966
.... **$50.00-$100.00**
(if white label promo), 1966 .... **$500.00-$1,000.00**
(if no photos of women inside gatefold, late mono pressing), 1968
.... **$150.00-$300.00**
KCL 2663, Bob Dylan's Greatest Hits, 1967 .... **$25.00-$50.00**
(with poster, add), 1967 .... **$2.00-$4.00**
CL 2804, John Wesley Harding, 1968 .... **$75.00-$150.00**
Sundazed LP 5070, Bringing It All Back Home (audiophile mono reissue), 2001 .... **$7.50-$15.00**
LP 5071, Highway 61 Revisited (audiophile mono reissue), 2001
.... **$7.50-$15.00**
LP 5108, The Times They Are a-Changin' (audiophile mono reissue), 2001
.... **$7.50-$15.00**
LP 5115, The Freewheelin' Bob Dylan (audiophile mono reissue), 2001
.... **$7.50-$15.00**
LP 5121, Another Side of Bob Dylan (audiophile mono reissue), 2002
.... **$7.50-$15.00**
LP 5110, Blonde on Blonde (2 LPs) (audiophile mono reissue), 2002
.... **$12.50-$25.00**
LP 5156, Bob Dylan's Greatest Hits (audiophile mono reissue), 2003
.... **$7.50-$15.00**

Stereo LPs

Columbia CS 8579, Bob Dylan
(if red-black label, six white "eye" logos, three at 9:00, three at 3:00, stock copy), 1962 .... **$200.00-$400.00**
(if six "eye" logos on label, "A New Star on Columbia" sticker on cover and promo stamp on label), 1962 .... **$300.00-$600.00**
(if "360 Sound Stereo" in black on label), 1963 .... **$20.00-$40.00**
(if "360 Sound Stereo" in white on label), 1965 .... **$12.50-$25.00**
(if orange label), 1970 .... **$6.00-$12.00**
(if on Columbia JC 8579, some copies list the song "You're No Good" as "She's No Good," value is equal), 197? .... **$4.00-$8.00**
(if on Columbia KCS 8579, reissue), 197? .... **$5.00-$10.00**
(if on Columbia PC 8579, reissue), 198? .... **$4.00-$8.00**
(if on Columbia PC 8579, 180-gram audiophile vinyl reissue, sticker on sealed cover indicates this), 2001 .... **$6.00-$12.00**
CS 8786, The Freewheelin' Bob Dylan
(if "360 Sound Stereo" in black on label (no arrows); record plays, and label lists, "Let Me Die in My Footsteps," "Rocks and Gravel," "Talkin' John Birch Blues" and "Gamblin' Willie's Dead Man's Hand." No known stereo copies play these without listing them, but just in case, check the trail-off for the numbers "XSM-58719-1A" and "XSM-58720-1A." If the number after the dash is "2" or higher, it's the standard version), 1963
.... **$22,500.00-$30,000.00**
(if Canadian pressing, deleted tracks listed on the front cover—The label lists, and the record plays, the "correct" tracks, "Printed in Can." at bottom of label), 1963 .... **$200.00-$400.00**
(if "360 Sound Stereo" in black on label, no arrows), 1963
.... **$25.00-$50.00**
(if "360 Sound Stereo" in black on label, with arrows), 1964 ... **$20.00-$40.00**
(if "360 Sound Stereo" in white on label), 1965 .... **$12.50-$25.00**
(if orange label, "after hours" red vinyl pressing), 197? ...... **$500.00-$1,000.00**
(if orange label, black vinyl), 1970 .... **$6.00-$12.00**
(if on Columbia KCS 8786, 1970s reissue), 197? .... **$5.00-$10.00**
(if on Columbia PC 8786, 1980s reissue), 198? .... **$4.00-$8.00**
(if on Columbia PC 8786, 180-gram audiophile vinyl reissue, sticker on sealed cover indicates this), 2001 .... **$6.00-$12.00**
CS 8905, The Times They Are a-Changin'
(if "360 Sound Stereo" in black on label), 1964 .... **$20.00-$40.00**
(if "360 Sound Stereo" in white on label), 1965 .... **$12.50-$25.00**
(if orange label), 1970 .... **$6.00-$12.00**
(if on Columbia KCS 8905, 1970s reissue), 197? .... **$5.00-$10.00**
(if on Columbia PC 8905, 1980s reissue), 198? .... **$4.00-$8.00**
(if on Columbia PC 8905, 180-gram audiophile vinyl reissue, sticker on sealed cover indicates this), 2001 .... **$6.00-$12.00**
CS 8993, Another Side of Bob Dylan
(if "360 Sound Stereo" in black on label), 1964 .... **$20.00-$40.00**
(if "360 Sound Stereo" in white on label), 1965 .... **$12.50-$25.00**
(if orange label), 1970 .... **$6.00-$12.00**
(if on Columbia KCS 8993, 1970s reissue), 197? .... **$5.00-$10.00**
(if on Columbia PC 8993, 1980s reissue), 198? .... **$4.00-$8.00**
(if on Columbia PC 8993, 180-gram audiophile vinyl reissue, sticker on sealed cover indicates this), 2001 .... **$6.00-$12.00**
CS 9128, Bringing It All Back Home
(if "360 Sound Stereo" in white on label), 1965 .... **$12.50-$25.00**
(if "360 Sound Stereo" in black on label), 1965 .... **$20.00-$40.00**
(if orange label), 1970 .... **$6.00-$12.00**
(if on Columbia JC 9128 or KCS 9128, reissue), 197? .... **$5.00-$10.00**
(if on Columbia PC 9128, reissue), 198? .... **$4.00-$8.00**
(if on Columbia PC 9128, 180-gram audiophile vinyl reissue, sticker on sealed cover indicates this), 2001 .... **$6.00-$12.00**
CS 9189, Highway 61 Revisited
(with alternate take of "From a Buick 6," matrix number on Side 1 will end in "-1" plus a letter), 1965 .... **$125.00-$250.00**
(with regular take of "From a Buick 6," matrix number on Side 1 will end in "-2" or higher, plus a letter; "360 Sound Stereo" on label), 1965
.... **$15.00-$30.00**
(if orange label), 1970 .... **$6.00-$12.00**
(if on Columbia JC 9189 or KCS 9189, 1970s reissues), 197?
.... **$5.00-$10.00**
(if on Columbia PC 9189, reissue), 198? .... **$4.00-$8.00**
(if on Columbia PC 9189, 180-gram audiophile vinyl reissue, sticker on sealed cover indicates this), 2001 .... **$6.00-$12.00**
CL 2302/CS 9102, Bob Dylan In Concert (value is for cover slick, record was never pressed), 1965 .... **$3,000.00-$4,000.00**
C2S 841, Blonde on Blonde (2 LPs)
(if "female photos" inner gatefold with two women pictured), 1966
.... **$30.00-$60.00**
(if no photos of women inside gatefold, "360 Sound Stereo" on label), 1968
.... **$15.00-$30.00**
(if orange label), 1970 .... **$7.50-$15.00**
(if on Columbia CG 841, reissue), 198? .... **$6.00-$12.00**
CS 9463, Bob Dylan's Greatest Hits ("360 Sound Stereo" label), 1967
.... **$7.50-$15.00**
(if orange label), 1970 .... **$6.00-$12.00**
(if on Columbia JC 9463, reissue), 197? .... **$5.00-$10.00**
(if on Columbia JC 9463, 180-gram audiophile vinyl reissue, sticker on sealed cover indicates this), 2001 .... **$6.00-$12.00**
CS 9604, John Wesley Harding ("360 Sound Stereo" label), 1968
.... **$10.00-$20.00**
(if orange label), 1970 .... **$6.00-$12.00**
(if on Columbia JC 9604 or KCS 9604, 1970s reissue), 197? .... **$5.00-$10.00**
(if on Columbia PC 9604, 1980s reissue), 198? .... **$4.00-$8.00**
(if on Columbia PIC 9604, 180-gram audiophile vinyl reissue, sticker on sealed cover indicates this), 2001 .... **$6.00-$12.00**
CS 9825, Nashville Skyline ("360 Sound Stereo" label), 1969 ... **$15.00-$30.00**
(if on orange label), 1970 .... **$6.00-$12.00**
(if on Columbia JC 9825, 1970s reissue), 197? .... **$5.00-$10.00**
(if on Columbia PC 9825, 1980s reissue), 198? .... **$4.00-$8.00**
C2X 30050, Self Portrait (2 LPs) ("360 Sound Stereo" labels), 1970
.... **$75.00-$150.00**
(if on orange labels), 1970 .... **$10.00-$20.00**
(if on Columbia P2X 30050, 1970s reissue), 197? .... **$7.50-$15.00**
(if on Columbia CG 30050, 1980s reissue), 198? .... **$6.00-$12.00**
KC 30290, New Morning, 1970 .... **$7.50-$15.00**
(if on Columbia PC 30290, reissue), 197? .... **$4.00-$8.00**
(if on Columbia PC 30290, 180-gram audiophile vinyl reissue, sticker on sealed cover indicates this), 2001 .... **$6.00-$12.00**
KG 31120, Bob Dylan's Greatest Hits, Vol. II (2 LPs), 1971 .... **$7.50-$15.00**
(if on Columbia PG 31120, reissue), 197? .... **$6.00-$12.00**
(if on Columbia CG 31120, reissue), 198? .... **$5.00-$10.00**
KC 32460, Pat Garrett and Billy the Kid, 1973 .... **$7.50-$15.00**
(if on Columbia PC 32460, reissue), 197? .... **$4.00-$8.00**
Columbia PC 32747, Dylan, 1973 .... **$7.50-$15.00**
(if bar code on back cover), 1979 .... **$4.00-$8.00**
Asylum AB-201, Before the Flood (2 LPs), 1974 .... **$10.00-$20.00**
(if white label promo), 1974 .... **$25.00-$50.00**
7E-1003, Planet Waves, 1974 .... **$7.50-$15.00**
(with wraparound olive green second cover), 1974 .... **$10.00-$20.00**
(if white label promo), 1974 .... **$25.00-$50.00**
(if non-glued cover with original title of LP, "Ceremonies of the Horsemen," about 3 or 4 copies exist), 1974 .... **$2,250.00-$3,000.00**
Columbia PC 33235, Blood on the Tracks
(with liner notes), 1975 .... **$6.00-$12.00**
(with drawing on back cover, without liner notes), 1975 .... **$7.50-$15.00**
(with bar code on back cover), 1979 .... **$4.00-$8.00**

(if 180-gram audiophile vinyl reissue, sticker on sealed cover indicates this), 2001 .... $6.00-$12.00
(if white label promo), 1975 .... $15.00-$30.00
(if white label test pressing, alternate takes of five songs including "Idiot Wind" and "Tangled Up in Blue"), 1975 .... $3,750.00-$5,000.00
PC2 33682, The Basement Tapes (2 LPs), 1975 .... $10.00-$20.00
(if white label promo), 1975 .... $20.00-$40.00
(if on Columbia CG 33682, reissue), 198? .... $6.00-$12.00
PC 33893, Desire, 1976 .... $6.00-$12.00
(if white label promo), 1976 .... $15.00-$30.00
(if on Columbia JC 33893, reissue), 1977 .... $5.00-$10.00
(if on Columbia JC 33893, bar code on back cover), 1979 .... $4.00-$8.00
JC 35453, Street Legal, 1978 .... $6.00-$12.00
(if white label promo), 1978 .... $12.50-$25.00
(if on Columbia PC 35453, reissue), 198? .... $4.00-$8.00
PC2 36067, Bob Dylan at Budokan (2 LPs), 1979 .... $7.50-$15.00
(if white label promo), 1979 .... $15.00-$30.00
(if on Columbia CG 36067, reissue), 198? .... $6.00-$12.00
FC 36120, Slow Train Coming, 1979 .... $5.00-$10.00
(if white label promo), 1979 .... $12.50-$25.00
(if on Columbia PC 36120, reissue), 198? .... $4.00-$8.00
FC 36553, Saved, 1980 .... $5.00-$10.00
(if on Columbia PC 36553, reissue), 198? .... $4.00-$8.00
TC 37496, Shot of Love, 1981 .... $5.00-$10.00
(if on Columbia PC 37496, reissue), 198? .... $4.00-$8.00
PC 37637, Planet Waves (reissue of earlier Asylum pressing), 1981 .... $5.00-$10.00
CG 37661, Before the Flood (reissue of earlier Asylum pressing), 1983 .... $6.00-$12.00
QC 38819, Infidels, 1983 .... $5.00-$10.00
(if on Columbia PC 38819, reissue), 1986 .... $4.00-$8.00
FC 39944, Real Live, 1984 .... $5.00-$10.00
C5X 38830, Biograph (5 LPs), 1985 .... $15.00-$30.00
FC 40110, Empire Burlesque, 1985 .... $5.00-$10.00
OC 40439, Knocked Out Loaded, 1986 .... $5.00-$10.00
OC 40957, Down in the Groove, 1988 .... $5.00-$10.00
OC 45281, Oh Mercy, 1989 .... $6.00-$12.00
C 53200, Good As I Been to You, 1992 .... $10.00-$20.00
C2 67000, MTV Unplugged (2 LPs), 1995 .... $7.50-$15.00
C2 68556, Time Out of Mind (2 LPs), 1998 .... $7.50-$15.00
CK2-65759-1, The Bootleg Series Vol. 4: Bob Dylan Live 1966, The "Royal Albert Hall" Concert (2 LPs, 12 x 12 booklet, records individually packaged in cardboard jackets and sleeves), 1999 .... $50.00-$100.00
C2 85975 (2) Love and Theft, 2001 .... $7.50-$15.00

Quadraphonic LPs

Columbia KCQ 32825, Nashville Skyline, 1973 .... $15.00-$30.00
Asylum EQ-1003, Planet Waves, 1974 .... $25.00-$50.00
Columbia PCQ 33893, Desire, 1976 .... $15.00-$30.00

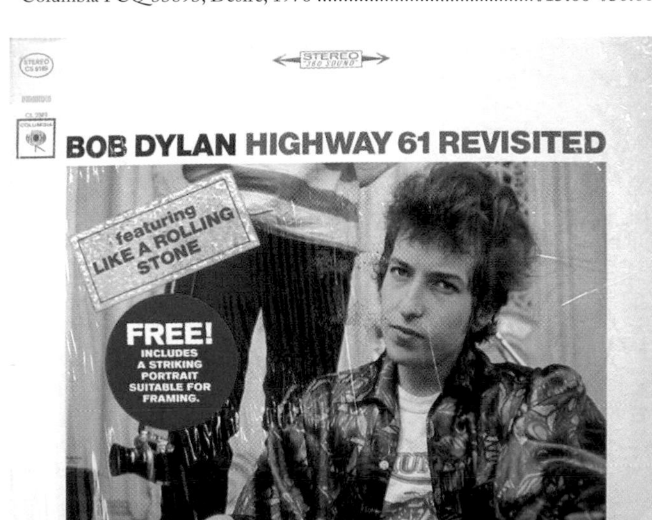

Columbia branded their stereo product as providing "360 Sound," and made sure all their albums featured it, both on the label and on the jacket. This pressing of Dylan's Highway 61 Revisited *is also collectible because it contains not only the accompany poster, but the stickers and its original shrinkwraps.*

***$30**, NM condition*

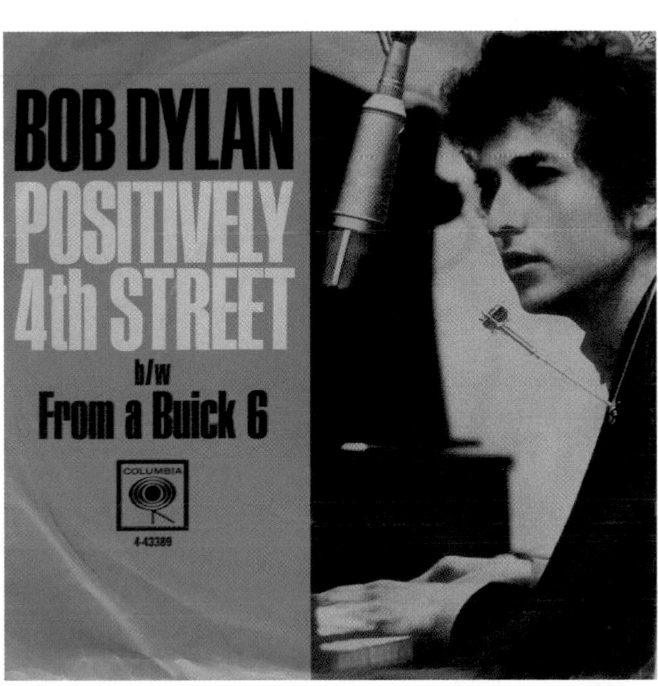

"Positively 4th Street" was one of Dylan's earliest 45s to be issued with a stock picture sleeve, as seen here.

***$35**, for VG condition sleeve*

A promotional 45 of "Tweedle Dee and Tweedle Dum," a single from Dylan's 2001 album Love and Theft, *was issued in this custom cardboard sleeve. The old "notes and microphone" logo design was last used by Columbia Records in the early 1950's, before they switched to the "eye" logotype.*

***$10**, NM condition*

Chapter 27

The Jimi Hendrix Experience

History

It seemed all too short. A superstar career that spanned less than half a decade, with a drug overdose taking the life of one of the greatest guitarists of all time. But if truth be told, Jimi Hendrix spent years working as a session guitarist, honing his skills by performing as a backup musician for everybody from the Isley Brothers to Little Richard, from Curtis Knight to Joey Dee and the Starliters.

But when the Jimi Hendrix Experience, a trio with bassist Noel Redding and drummer Mitch Mitchell, released their first singles and albums, they became instant superstars in England. And although Hendrix was originally from Seattle, Washington, his group was able to ride the wave of the British Invasion, becoming a popular and successful live act in America.

What set Jimi Hendrix apart from other guitarists of his era was his ability to use every part of his equipment—his guitar, his amplifier, and a wah-wah pedal—to create notes and effects never heard before. He could use controlled feedback from his amplifiers to generate new chords and complex orchestrations. He could make his guitar scream in pain, or moan in ecstasy.

Originally a struggling studio and club guitarist, Hendrix was discovered by Animals bass player Chas Chandler at Café Wha?, a New York City nightclub. Chandler

The Jimi Hendrix Experience's first album, Are You Experienced, *is difficult to find in a mono pressing. The top and side panels of the jacket have a black "MONO" box, which can be seen more clearly on this back cover photograph. Most monaural pressings in the late 1960's were designated for AM radio stations, as can be seen by the gold promotional sticker on the front cover.*

***$200**, mono, NM condition*

Photo credit: From the collection of Val Shively.

Jimi Hendrix's 45s were first released in the US on Reprise, and feature both an "r:" logo and the "W7" logo of Warner Bros.—Seven Arts, Reprise's parent company.

***$20**, VG+ condition*

Axis: Bold as Love, *the Jimi Hendrix Experience's second album, showed more studio experimentation, and contains such Hendrix classics as "If 6 Were 9" and "Little Wing."*

***$60**, VG+ condition*

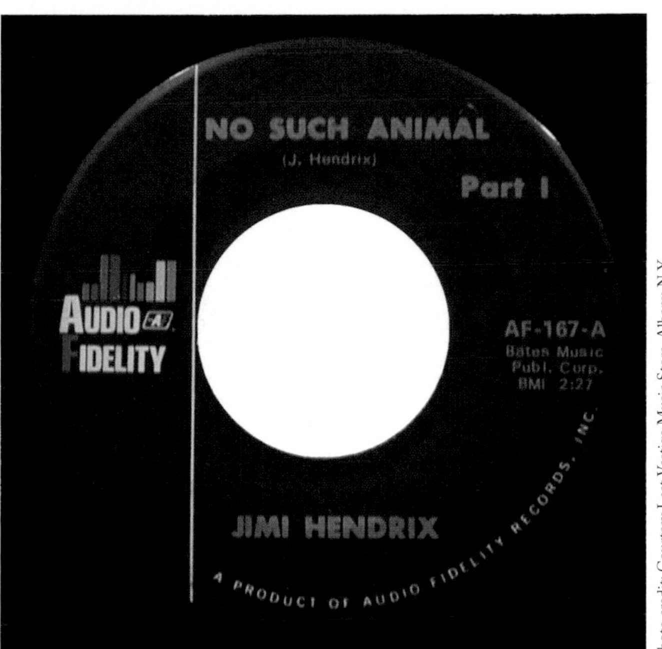

Photo credit: Courtesy Last Vestige Music Store, Albany, N.Y.

"No Such Animal" was one of many Hendrix recordings that were released without his consent or control.

***$7.50**, VG condition*

immediately brought Hendrix to England, where he teamed the guitarist with Noel Redding and Mitch Mitchell, and christened the trio as the Jimi Hendrix Experience.

The Experience's first singles, "Hey Joe" and "Purple Haze" rocketed to the top of the UK charts. By the time the Experience returned to America, they had a full-length album, *Are You Experienced?*, which reached the *Billboard* Top 10 in 1967.

In June 1967, at the Monterey International Pop Festival, the Jimi Hendrix Experience stole the show. During a performance of "Wild Thing," Hendrix played his guitar with his teeth, played it behind his back, then at he end of the performance, poured lighter fluid on the guitar and set it on fire. And although Hendrix's guitar cremations became a legendary memento of his live performances, he actually only burned two guitars in his career—once at the Monterey Pop Festival, and once at the London Astoria in 1967 (he later repaired the London Astoria guitar and re-torched it at the Miami Pop Festival in 1968).

The Experience would produce two more albums, *Axis: Bold as Love* and *Electric Ladyland*. Both albums showed Hendrix maturing as a musician and as a producer; the guitarist's legendary perfection in the studio required dozens of takes until the sound was just right. *Electric Ladyland* reached #1 on the *Billboard* album charts, and spawned Hendrix's first Top 40 hit in America, "All Along The Watchtower."

A common misperception is that unauthorized Hendrix albums were released only after the guitar legend died. In fact, Hendrix' legitimate releases were often competing with recordings he made years before. In his early years, Hendrix would record for anybody and everybody, and signed recording contracts as often as baseball players sign autographs. Thus, once he achieved stardom, his early recordings with Curtis Knight and with Little Richard were ripe for reissue.

By 1969, in fact, because of the rapacious contracts Hendrix signed, he found he was obligated to Capitol Records for an album, even though the Experience was bound to Reprise Records. By this time, he had already

*This pressing of "All Along the Watchtower" is part of a 45-RPM reissue boxed set released by the Experience Hendrix label. The record has a small hole; the yellow adapter is just part of the artwork. In box set would be **$60**, NM, total.*

broken up the Experience, and began work with other musicians. After a spectacular appearance at the Woodstock Festival, in which Hendrix woke the crowd with a feedback-influenced version of "The Star Spangled Banner," Hendrix recorded the album *Band of Gypsys* on New Year's Eve, 1969, at the Fillmore East.

On September 18, 1970, Jimi Hendrix, one of the greatest guitarists in music history, died of a drug overdose. His last studio album, *The Cry of Love*, was released posthumously.

But after Hendrix died, anybody who had as little as a Hendrix guitar riff on tape suddenly had Hendrix "previously unreleased" material on their hands, and could release it on LP for an avid legion of Hendrix devotees. A series of Hendrix legitimate releases were attempted by producer Alan Douglas. Douglas took some unfinished Hendrix recordings, fleshed them out with studio musicians, and released *Crash Landing* and *Midnight Lightning*, both with reasonable commercial success and mixed reviews.

In 1995, the rights to all of Jimi Hendrix' previous recordings reverted to Hendrix' father. Today, Experience Hendrix LLC is the umbrella company that maintains licensing, reissue, and repackaging of various classic and posthumous Hendrix songs.

What To Look For

Hendrix's classic albums came when record companies were finally phasing out separate-but-equal stereo and mono releases. A few mono pressings were made of Hendrix's first two albums (and a radio-only mono run for the third LP), making these discs extremely rare. Jimi Hendrix' work was best suited for albums. Although he had Top 40 hits in England, he only hit the U.S. Top 40 once in his entire career, with "All Along The Watchtower." Therefore, his other American singles are highly collectible, and their accompanying picture sleeves even more so.

The most valuable prices are for recordings made during Hendrix's lifetime. After he died in 1970, major and minor record companies continued to raid old tape vaults for unreleased works by the guitar virtuoso. These recordings sold well in their original release, some of them even cracking the Top 10 on the LP charts, but today do not have the same collectibility as Hendrix's early albums.

Photo credit: From the collection of Mark Pisani.

A vinyl release from Ryko Analogue that replicates a CD issue of a Hendrix live concert. The paper sash on the right side of the record is called an "obi," and is most often found on Japanese pressings.

***$15**, NM condition*

Books

Brown, Tony, *Jimi Hendrix: The Final Days*, Omnibus Press, 1997.

Hopkins, Jerry, *Hit and Run: The Jimi Hendrix Story*, Putnam Publishing, NY, 1983.

Murray, Charles S., *Crosstown Traffic: Jimi Hendrix and the Post-War Rock 'n' Roll Revolution*, Saint Martin's Press, NY, 1991.

Redding, Noel; Appleby, Carol, *Are You Experienced?: The Inside Story of Jimi Hendrix*, Fourth Estate, London, 1990.

Shapiro, Harry; Glebbeek, Caesar, *Jimi Hendrix: Electric Gypsy*, Mandarin, London, 1995.

Welch, Chris, *Hendrix: A Biography*, Omnibus Press, 1972.

Museums

Experience Music Project, 2901 Third Avenue Suite 400, 325 Fifth Ave N, Seattle, WA, 98121, (206) EMP-LIVE: http://www.emplive.com.

Web Pages

The official Jimi Hendrix home page: http://www.jimi-hendrix.com.

Jimi Hendrix was a sideman on many different records, see some of them at http://www.earlyhendrix.com.

The Jimi Hendrix Family Foundation, dedicated to developing resources and funds for charities: http://www.jimihendrix.org

Usenet newsgroups: alt.fan.jimi-hendrix, alt.music.jimi.hendrix

In the price guide, the first listings are for records that were released during Jimi Hendrix' lifetime, then post-death pressings.

THE JIMI HENDRIX EXPERIENCE:

45s

Reprise 0572, "Hey Joe"/"51st Anniversary," 1967 .... **$50.00-$100.00**
(with picture sleeve, add), 1967 .... **$500.00-$1,000.00**
0597, "Purple Haze"/"The Wind Cries Mary," 1967 .... **$12.50-$25.00**
0641, "Foxey Lady"/"Hey Joe," 1967 .... **$12.50-$25.00**
0665, "Up from the Skies"/"One Rainy Wish," 1968 .... **$15.00-$30.00**
0767, "All Along the Watchtower"/"Burning of the Midnight Lamp," 1968 .... **$15.00-$30.00**
0792, "Crosstown Traffic"/"Gypsy Eyes," 1968 .... **$15.00-$30.00**
0853, "If 6 Was 9"/"Stone Free," 1969 .... **$20.00-$40.00**
0905, "Stepping Stone"/"Izabella," 1970 .... **$50.00-$100.00**
1000, "Freedom"/"Angel," 1971 .... **$7.50-$15.00**
1044, "Dolly Dagger"/"Star Spangled Banner," 1971 .... **$7.50-$15.00**
1082, "Johnny B. Goode"/"Lover Man," 1972 .... **$7.50-$15.00**
1118, "The Wind Cries Mary"/"Little Wing," 1972 .... **$7.50-$15.00**
PRO 595, "Medley: The Little Drummer Boy-Silent Night"/"Auld Lang Syne," promo, 1974 .... **$75.00-$150.00**
(with picture sleeve saying "And a Happy New Year," add), 1974 .... **$40.00-$80.00**
EP 2239, "Gloria" (single-sided, included in "The Essential Jimi Hendrix, Volume 2," 1979 .... **$2.50-$5.00**
(with picture sleeve, add), 1979 .... **$2.50-$5.00**
29845, "Fire"/"Little Wing," 1982 .... **$3.00-$6.00**
Reprise "Back to Back Hits" 0728, "Purple Haze"/"Foxey Lady," 1968 .... **$7.50-$15.00**
0742, "All Along the Watchtower"/"Crosstown Traffic," 1971 .... **$3.00-$6.00**
Audio Fidelity 167, "No Such Animal" (Pt. 1)/(Pt. 2), 1970 .... **$7.50-$15.00**
(with picture sleeve, add) .... **$20.00-$40.00**
Experience Hendrix RTH-1007, The Jimi Hendrix Classic Singles Collection, 10 45s with custom picture sleeves in box with booklet, 1998 .... **$30.00-$60.00**
5651-7, "Little Drummer Boy-Auld Lang Syne"/"Three Little Bears," red vinyl, small hole, 1999 .... **$7.50-$15.00**
(if on green vinyl, small hole), 2001 .... **$2.50-$5.00**
(with picture sleeve for either pressing, add), 1999 .... **$2.50-$5.00**
MCA 55336, "Dolly Dagger"/"Night Bird Flying," promo, purple vinyl, 1997 .... **$5.00-$10.00**
(with picture sleeve, add), 1997 .... **$5.00-$10.00**
55434, "Can You Please Crawl Out Your Window?"/"Burning of the Midnight Lamp," promo, orange vinyl, 1998 .... **$2.50-$5.00**
(with picture sleeve, add), 1998 .... **$2.50-$5.00**
Trip 3002, "Hot Trigger"/"Suspicious," 1972 .... **$2.50-$5.00**

12-inch Singles

Capitol SPRO 11284, "The Star Spangled Banner" (same on both sides), blue vinyl record with eight die-cut stars in vinyl, 199? .... **$50.00-$100.00**

Mono LPs

Reprise R 6261, Are You Experienced?, 1967 .... **$100.00-$200.00**
R 6281, Axis: Bold As Love, 1968 .... **$1,250.00-$2,500.00**
2R 6307, Electric Ladyland, 2 LPs, promo, 1968 .... **$3,000.00-$4,000.00**
Capitol T-2856, Get That Feeling, 1967 .... **$40.00-$80.00**
T-2894, Flashing, 1968 .... **$50.00-$100.00**

Stereo LPs

Reprise RS 6261, Are You Experienced?
(if pink, gold and green label), 1967 .... **$25.00-$50.00**
(if two-tone orange label, with "W7" and "r:" logos), 1968 .... **$12.50-$25.00**
(if only "r:" logo on tan label), 1970 .... **$6.00-$12.00**
(if red-black or gold-blue label, reissue), 198? .... **$4.00-$8.00**
RS 6281, Axis: Bold As Love
(if pink, gold and green label), 1968 .... **$40.00-$80.00**
(if two-tone orange label, with "W7" and "r:" logos), 1968 .... **$12.50-$25.00**
(if SKAO-91441, Capitol Record Club pressing), 1968 .... **$20.00-$40.00**
(if only "r:" logo on tan label), 1970 .... **$6.00-$12.00**
(if red-black or gold-blue label, reissue), 198? .... **$4.00-$8.00**
2RS 6307, Electric Ladyland (2 LPs)
(if two-tone orange label, with "W7" and "r:" logos), 1968 .... **$50.00-$100.00**
(if STBO-91568, Capitol Record Club pressing), 1968 .... **$75.00-$150.00**
(if only "r:" logo on tan label), 1970 .... **$7.50-$15.00**
(if red-black or gold-blue label, reissue), 198? .... **$6.00-$12.00**
MS 2025, Smash Hits
(if two-tone orange label, with "W7" and "r:" logos), 1969 .... **$20.00-$40.00**
(with bonus poster, add), 1969 .... **$20.00-$40.00**
(if only "r:" logo on tan label), 1970 .... **$6.00-$12.00**
(if red-black or gold-blue label, reissue), 1989 .... **$4.00-$8.00**
(if on MSK-2776, reissue), 1977 .... **$5.00-$10.00**
MS 2029, Historic Performances as recorded at the Monterey International Pop Festival (Hendrix on side 1, Otis Redding on side 2), 1970 **$10.00-$20.00**
MS 2034, The Cry of Love
(with "W7" and "r:" logos on two-tone orange label, first pressing), 1971 .... **$250.00-$500.00**
(if on SMAS-93467, Capitol Record Club pressing), 1971 .... **$30.00-$60.00**
(solid background orange or tan label, second pressing), 1971 .. **$7.50-$15.00**
MS 2040, Rainbow Bridge, 1971 .... **$10.00-$20.00**
(if on SMAS-93972, Capitol Record Club edition), 1971 .... **$25.00-$50.00**
MS 2049, Hendrix in the West, 1972 .... **$10.00-$20.00**
MS 2103, War Heroes, 1972 .... **$10.00-$20.00**
2RS 6481, Soundtrack Recordings from the Film Jimi Hendrix, 2 LPs, 1973 .... **$12.50-$25.00**
MS 2204, Crash Landing, 1975 .... **$7.50-$15.00**
MS 2229, Midnight Lightning, 1975 .... **$7.50-$15.00**
2RS 2245, The Essential Jimi Hendrix, 2 LPs, 1978 .... **$10.00-$20.00**
HS 2293, The Essential Jimi Hendrix Volume Two, 1979 .... **$7.50-$15.00**
(with bonus single of "Gloria" with picture sleeve enclosed, add) .... **$7.50-$15.00**
HS 2299, Nine to the Universe, 1980 .... **$5.00-$10.00**
(if on Warner Bros. HS-2299, Reprise cover, possibly Columbia House pressing), 1980 .... **$6.00-$12.00**
22306, The Jimi Hendrix Concerts, 2 LPs, 1982 .... **$6.00-$12.00**
25119, Kiss the Sky, 1984 .... **$5.00-$10.00**
25358, Jimi Plays Monterey, 1986 .... **$5.00-$10.00**
Capitol ST 2856, Get That Feeling, 1967 .... **$20.00-$40.00**
ST 2894, Flashing, 1968 .... **$20.00-$40.00**
STAO-472, Band of Gypsys, 1970 .... **$10.00-$20.00**
SWBB-659, Get That Feeling/Flashing, 2 LPs, 1971 .... **$12.50-$25.00**
SN-16319, Band of Gypsys, budget reissue, 1985 .... **$5.00-$10.00**
01-96414, Band of Gypsys, numbered reissue, 1995 .... **$7.50-$15.00**
SJ-12416, Band of Gypsys 2, side 2 lists and plays three songs, 1986 .... **$5.00-$10.00**
SJ-12416, Band of Gypsys 2, side 2 lists three songs, plays four entirely different songs, look for four tracks on the vinyl, 1986 .... **$75.00-$150.00**
MLP-15022, Johnny B. Goode (EP), 1986 .... **$4.00-$8.00**
Experience Hendrix/Capitol ST-472, Band of Gypsys, "heavy vinyl" with booklet, 1997 .... **$12.50-$25.00**
Experience Hendrix/MCA 11599, First Rays of the New Rising Sun, 2 LPs, "heavy vinyl" with booklet, 1997 .... **$25.00-$50.00**
11600, Electric Ladyland, 2 LPs, "heavy vinyl" with booklet, 1997 .... **$20.00-$40.00**
11601, Axis: Bold As Love, "heavy vinyl" with booklet, 1997 .... **$25.00-$50.00**
11602, Are You Experienced?, 2 LPs, "heavy vinyl" with booklet, 1997 .... **$25.00-$50.00**
11684, South Saturn Delta, "heavy vinyl" with booklet, 1997 .... **$12.50-$25.00**
11671, Experience Hendrix: The Best of Jimi Hendrix, "heavy vinyl," numbered edition, 1998 .... **$12.50-$25.00**
11742, BBC Sessions, 3 LPs, 1998 .... **$15.00-$30.00**
Accord SN-7101, Kaleidoscope, 1981 .... **$5.00-$10.00**
SN-7112, Before London, 1981 .... **$5.00-$10.00**
SN-7139, Cosmic Feeling, 1981 .... **$5.00-$10.00**
Maple 6004, Jimi Hendrix and Lonnie Youngblood: Two Great Experiences Together, 1971 .... **$25.00-$50.00**
Nutmeg 1001 High, Live 'N' Dirty (red or black vinyl, value is equal), 1978 .... **$12.50-$25.00**
1002, Cosmic Turnaround, 1981 .... **$6.00-$12.00**
Pickwick SPC-3528, Jimi, 197? .... **$5.00-$10.00**
Ryko Analogue RALP-0038, Live at Winterland, 2 LPs, 1988 .... **$7.50-$15.00**
RALP-0078, Radio One, clear vinyl, 2 LPs, 1988 .... **$7.50-$15.00**
Track 612003, Axis: Bold as Love, mono reissue of UK edition, 2000 .... **$12.50-$25.00**
Trip 3509, Superpak (2 LPs), 197? .... **$7.50-$15.00**
TLP-9500, Rare Hendrix, 1972 .... **$7.50-$15.00**
9501, Roots of Hendrix, 1972 .... **$6.00-$12.00**
9512, Moods, 1973 .... **$6.00-$12.00**
9523, The Genius of Jimi Hendrix, 1973 .... **$6.00-$12.00**
United Artists UA-LA-505-E, The Very Best of Jimi Hendrix, 1975 .... **$6.00-$12.00**

CHAPTER 28

ELVIS PRESLEY

History

Singer, performer, cultural icon. In simple terms, these words describe Elvis Presley. The emotional attachment millions of his fans have to his music surpasses simple adoration. To his fans, Elvis was the greatest pop singer of his generation, rivaling Frank Sinatra, Bing Crosby, and Enrico Caruso as the greatest male vocalist of the 20th century.

Elvis' first Sun recordings, a fusion of country twang with rhythm and blues, became early rockabilly classics. His early output for RCA included such rock classics as "Heartbreak Hotel," "Don't Be Cruel," "Hound Dog," and "Jailhouse Rock." His gyrating stage performances in the 1950s drove female fans into ecstasy; his late 1960s television specials proved that despite suggestions to the contrary, the King had not left the building. And upon his death in 1977, Presley's soul may have ascended into heaven—but his legend ascended into icon status.

Among Presley's most coveted and collectible recordings are the ten sides he recorded for Sam Phillips' Sun Records. These Memphis-based recordings were Elvis' first commercial tracks, but within these songs were the beginnings of a musical legend. He could sing deep haunting ballads like "Blue Moon," he could belt out the blues like "I Got A Woman" and "Milkcow Blues Boogie," and rock the room with "That's All Right" and "Blue Moon of Kentucky." Those Sun sessions, where Presley performed with bassist Bill Black and guitarist Scotty Moore, became hits—first in Memphis, then throughout the South.

Eventually Presley acquired a new manager, Col. Tom Parker, who had previously worked with country legend

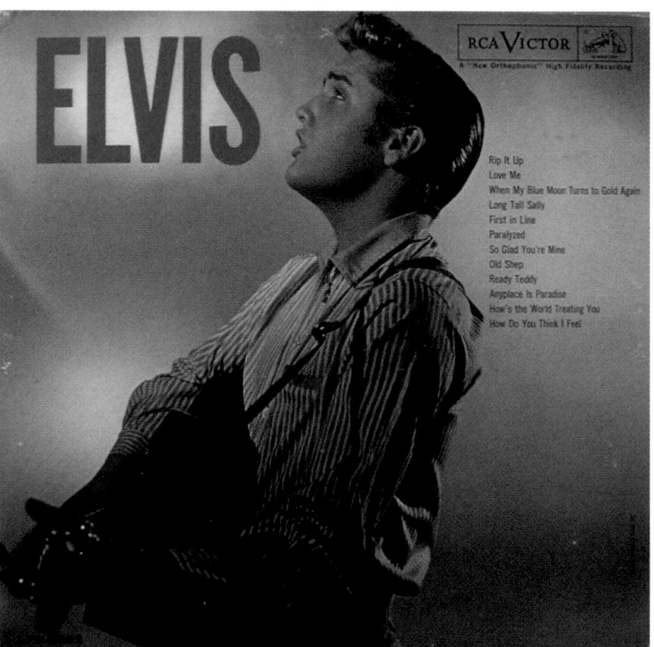

*One of Elvis Presley's early albums. Some copies of this album feature an alternate take of his song "Old Shep," with the words "he grew old AND his eyes were growing dim..." Those copies can be worth **$800** in near-mint condition.*

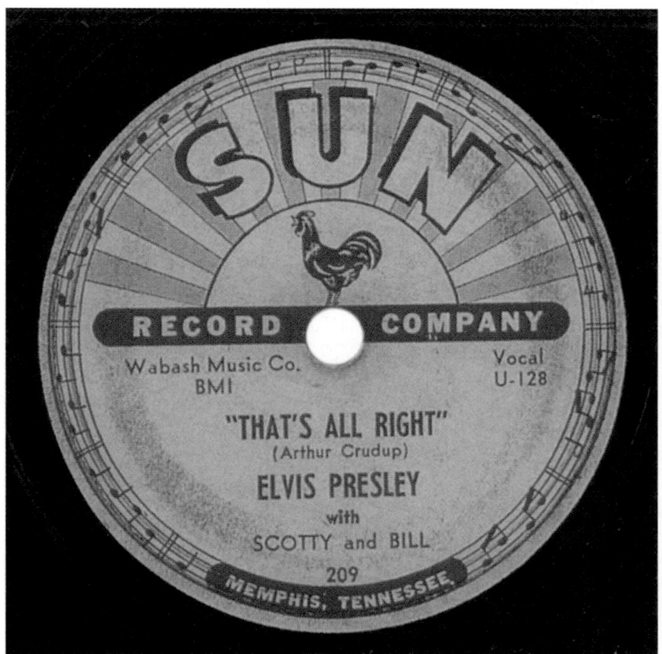

Photo credit: From the Tom Kelly Archives, St. Louis, Mo.

Elvis Presley's first Sun single, "That's All Right"/"Blue Moon of Kentucky." While Presley's original Sun 45s can sell for thousands of dollars, his five Sun 78s can command high prices as well.

***$1,500**, VG condition*

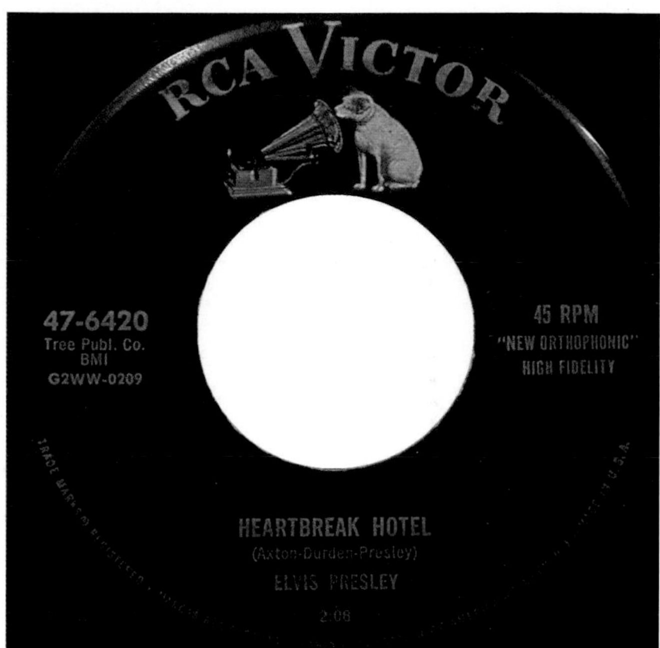

"Heartbreak Hotel," Elvis Presley's first national hit on RCA Victor. Presley's earliest RCA hits have very thin serifless lettering on the record title, with the song's running time at the 6:00 position.

***$40**, NM condition*

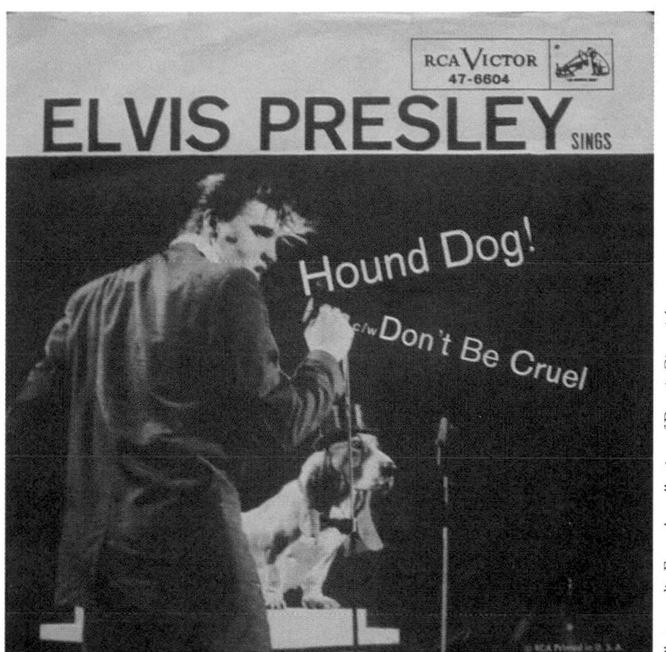

Photo credit: From the collection of Dennis Gingerich

Two versions of this picture sleeve exist, with either "Don't Be Cruel" or "Hound Dog" receiving top billing. The photo of Elvis singing to a top-hatted basset hound came from his appearance on the Steve Allen show.

***$120**, NM picture sleeve*

Eddy Arnold. He also acquired a new recording label—Sam Phillips sold Presley's contract, as well as the Sun recordings, to RCA Victor for the unheard-of sum of $35,000.00. No record company ever paid that much for an artist—but in retrospect, RCA Victor received a bargain.

The original Sun recordings were reissued with RCA catalog numbers and labels. They were quickly followed by Presley's first RCA recording, "Heartbreak Hotel." The song stormed up the charts, hitting #1 on both the pop and country listings. There was no turning back. By 1956, Elvis Presley was the #1 recording artist in the country.

Not since the days when Frank Sinatra's bobbysoxed followers swooned *en masse* before the Brooklyn Paramount had there ever been such a show of adulation for any singer. Presley's impact in 1956 was nearly unstoppable—as a rock and roll singer, he influenced a new generation of musicians, vocalists, and songwriters. As an entertainer, his swiveling hips and deep vocals drove female fans into hysteria. In fact, when performing on the *Ed Sullivan* variety show, Sullivan ordered the cameras to show the performing Presley only from the chest up, so as not to offend the viewing public with the singer's pelvic gyrations.

For the next twenty years, Elvis Presley released a stream of albums and 45s, appeared in over 30 motion pictures, and performed on television with Frank Sinatra (during a musical number, Sinatra sang "Love Me Tender," while Presley sang "Witchcraft"). With the Jordanaires as his backup singers, Presley now branched into different musical styles—tender ballads like "Love Me Tender" and "Are You Lonesome Tonight," uptempo rockers like "Hard Headed Woman" and "Jailhouse Rock," and puppy love songs like "(Let Me Be Your) Teddy Bear" and "Return to Sender."

Nothing could dim Presley's popularity—not a stint in the Army, not the declining quality of his movies—even though other musicians' careers were curtailed during the British Invasion, he was able to have hits like "Crying in the Chapel," he was one of the few Americans to still have hits during this period. His return to prominence came during a

This copy of "Love Me Tender" has a silver horizontal line that bisects the label. Until 1957, RCA Victor 45s exist both with and without the horizontal line—in Presley's case, that includes his 45s up to and including RCA Victor 47-7150, "Don't"/"I Beg of You." Other than for completists who want each label variation, there is no different in price between lined and line-less pressings.

***$15**, VG condition*

1968 television variety special, in which a leather-clad Elvis still showed he could rock and roll with the best of them.

In 1973, Presley gave another stellar broadcast performance—this time from Hawaii, to an audience of over one billion television viewers. The subsequent soundtrack album from that concert, *Hello From Hawaii Via Satellite*, was a worldwide million-seller, both in stereo and the new quadraphonic (four speakers) album format.

When Presley passed away on August 16, 1977, his millions of loyal fans grieved. Then they went to the stores and bought nearly every Elvis Presley 45 and LP they could. RCA's pressing plants worked round the clock to satisfy the demand for Presley's back catalog. They also released new Presley singles, either as "in concert" performances ("My Way"), remixed versions ("Guitar Man"), or even novelty recordings ("The Elvis Medley").

Today, Elvis Presley's music is still as popular as ever, as new compilations and reissues continue to appear on store shelves. His opulent Memphis estate Graceland is now a museum and tourist attraction, attracting legions of Elvis followers every year.

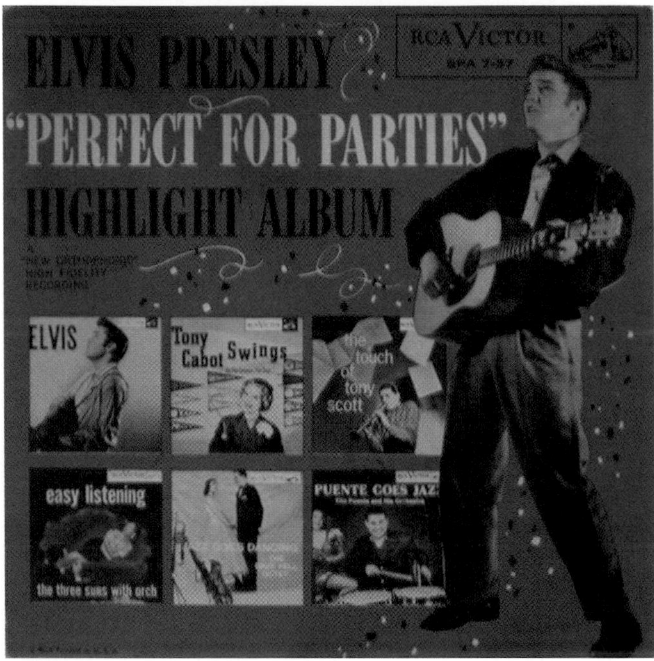

Although this six-song promotional EP contains only one Elvis Presley song, "Love Me," it does feature Presley introducing songs from several other RCA Victor artists, including Tito Puente, The Three Suns, and Tony Scott.

***$50**, VG+ condition*

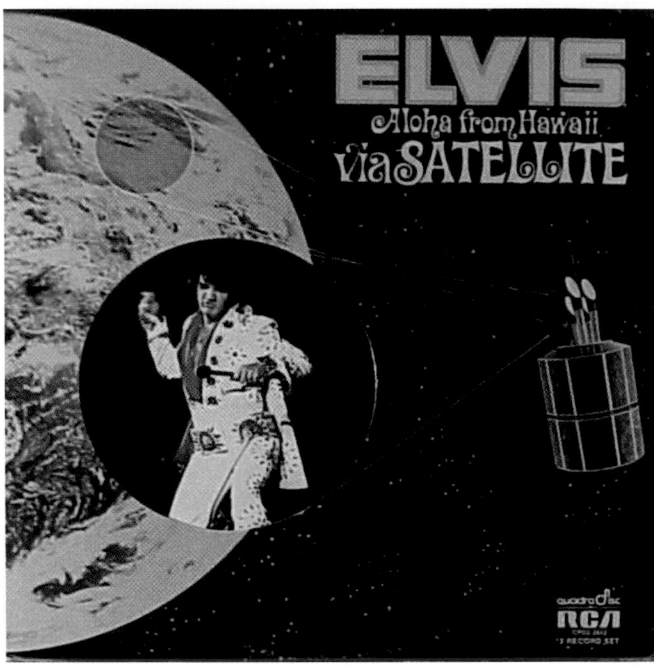

Aloha from Hawaii Via Satellite sold over one million copies in RCA Victor's "QuadraDisc" four-speaker format.

***$25**, VG+ condition*

What To Look For

The toughest task for an Elvis collection is to find his five Sun 45s (they are also available on 78s). Reproductions abound on these titles, and some of the reproductions actually use original out-of-stock Sun labels.

Any Sun Elvis recording pressed on colored or swirled vinyl is a reproduction; the originals were pressed only in black. There were never any "picture sleeves" for Elvis Sun recordings, either. And Sun never made any four-song EPs of Elvis' songs, so any that you find are phonies.

Of Presley's five Sun releases, legitimate copies of his first four releases have "push marks"—three circles pressed into the label itself. Not all the originals have push marks, but because the collectible value of a Sun 45 is extremely high, and since so many counterfeit and reproduced Sun 45s exist because of this, collectors look for the "push marks" to confirm a true Memphis pressing.

Presley's fifth Sun release, "Mystery Train"/"I Forgot to Remember to Forget" (Sun 223) does not contain push marks on the label. If the record has a triangle in the dead wax, the record was pressed by Monarch Record Pressing in Los Angeles. Even before his signing with RCA Victor, Elvis was already an established country music star from these Sun recordings, with "I Forgot To Remember To Forget" hitting #1 on the *Billboard* country charts.

During Presley's RCA tenure, the record company pressed millions of copies of his 45s and LPs. Within this, it is important to know not only the variations in label design throughout Elvis' recording career, but also when RCA changed their label patterns so that a collector can determine an original from a repressing.

Even though the front of an Elvis Presley album may contain the traditional RCA logos and trademarks of the 1950s, oftentimes the company would continue to press an old-style jacket with old-style logos, while inserting a new recording inside. The following is a short list of label variations for RCA 45s and LPs, as well as the first and last Presley records in each format.

Photo credit: From the collection of Rodney Branham.

If you look carefully on this Sun 45 label, you can see the circular "push mark" indentations, especially near the letters "TUC" in "Kentucky," and just to the right of the "Peer BMI" at 9:00.

***$6,000**, NM condition*

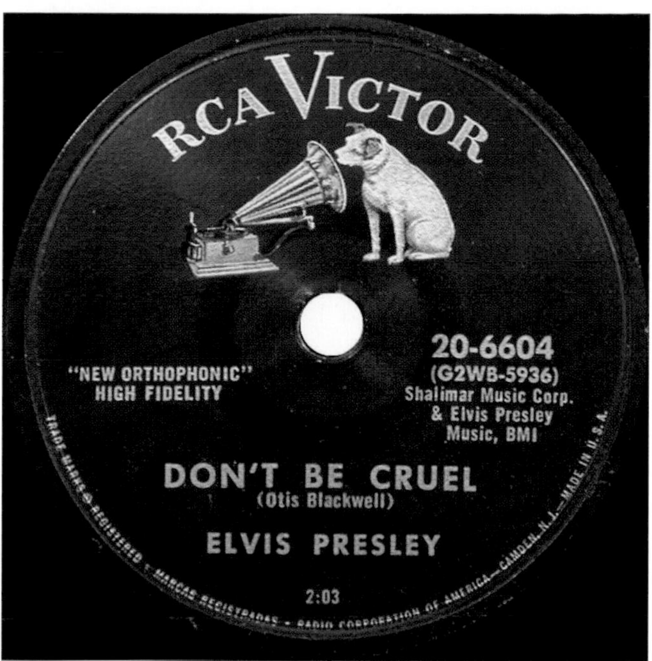

Until 1959, Elvis Presley's music was available on 10-inch 78s, with titles like "Hard Headed Woman" and "I Got Stung" among RCA's final 78s pressed in America. Two final Presley 78-RPM titles were sold in Canada, "A Fool Such As I," and "A Big Hunk O' Love."

***$75**, VG+ condition*

Elvis Presley RCA 45s

1955-1965—"RCA VICTOR" in white or grey capital serif letters, along the 12:00 perimeter (top of label). Beneath the letters, in full color, is the RCA dog and gramophone trademark ("Nipper"). Black background. Copies exist with a grey-white horizontal line through the spindle hole; copies also exist without the line. Unless specifically listed below, the value for the copies with a horizontal line bisecting the center hole is equivalent to line-less pressings. Elvis' first RCA-recorded 45 in this format: "Heartbreak Hotel"/"I Was The One" (RCA Victor 47-6420). Presley's five Sun 45s were also reissued on this label prior to the release of "Heartbreak Hotel." The last Elvis 45 on this format: "Do the Clam"/"You'll Be Gone" (RCA 47-8500).

1965-1968—"RCA VICTOR" in thin tall white letters, at 3:00; full-color Nipper at 9:00. Black background. The first Elvis 45 on this format was actually part of the RCA "Gold Standard" reissue series: "Crying in the Chapel"/"I Believe In The Man In The Sky" (RCA Victor 447-0643). The first Elvis 45 in the standard numbering series in this format: "(Such An) Easy Question"/"It Feels So Right") (RCA Victor 47-8585). Last Elvis 45 on this format: "A Little Less Conversation"/"Almost In Love" (RCA Victor 47-9610).

1968-1976—"RCA" in futuristic print at 9:00, orange label. First Elvis 45 on this format: "If I Can Dream"/"Edge of Reality" (RCA 47-9670). Now here's where it gets tricky.

1974-1975—"RCA" in futuristic print at 9:00, tan or grey label. At this time, RCA had three major record pressing plants—Indianapolis, Indiana; Hollywood, California, and Rockaway, New York. Although Rockaway had ceased pressing records by 1974, Indianapolis and Hollywood were still cranking out Elvis vinyl. However, Hollywood still used orange labels for their 45s, the last Elvis record that plant pressed with an orange label was "Bringing It Back"/"Pieces Of My Life" (RCA PB-10401).

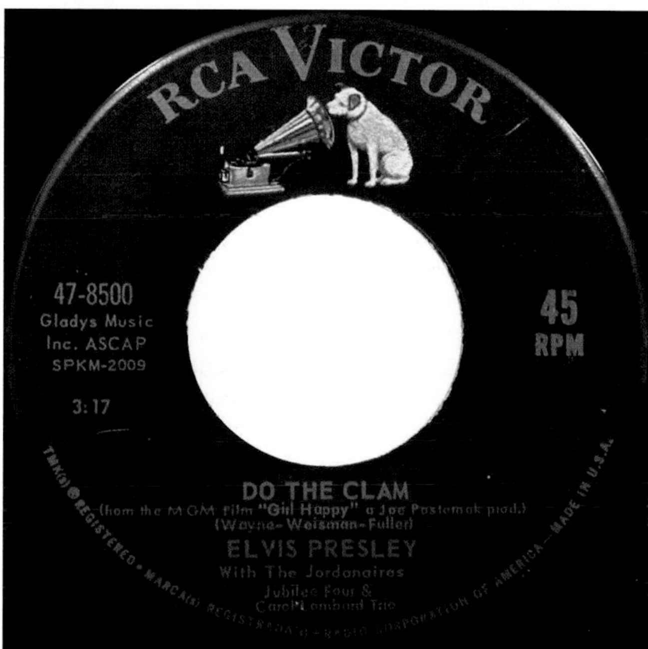

After this 45, the RCA "His Master's Voice" trademark moved from the 12:00 position to 9:00.

***$6**, VG condition*

In 1968, RCA jettisoned Nipper and the gramophone in favor of a stylized futuristic logo.

***$6**, NM condition*

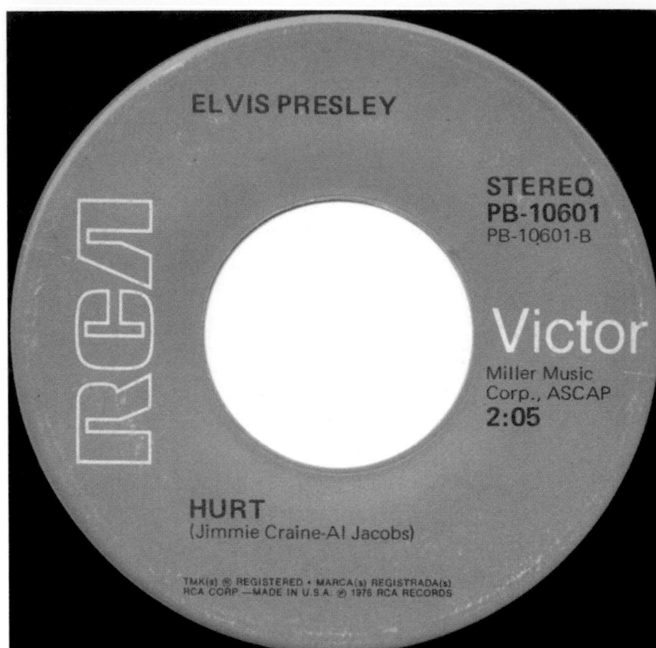

The last Elvis Presley 45 with a tan background was "Hurt"/"For The Heart" (RCA PB-10601). Eventually Elvis would be reunited with his "hound dog," and subsequent RCA pressings would restore "His Master's Voice" to the paper label.

***$4**, NM condition*

Beginning in 1974, the Indianapolis plant pressed RCA 45s first with a grey label. Among Elvis 45s, the only single in this color was "Promised Land"/"It's Midnight" (PB-10074). By the time the next Elvis 45, "My Boy"/"Thinking About You" (RCA PB-10191) was pressed, the Indianapolis factor used a tan label. So until RCAs pressing plants were consolidated into one Indianapolis factory, some Presley records exist with both tan backgrounds and orange backgrounds.

1976-1988—Futuristic "RCA" at 12:00, Nipper returns at 1:00, black label. Elvis' last living recordings are on this label format. The first Elvis 45 on this format was a second pressing of "Hurt"/"For The Heart" (RCA PB-10601). The last living Elvis 45 on this format was "Way Down"/"Pledging My Love" (RCA PB-10998). Presley died as that record was rising up the pop charts.

2000-present—Presley's name at the top, no sign of Nipper, RCA logo almost non-existent, replaced by a BMG label at 3:00. This was used for all current Presley pressings, including his two "remixed" hits, "A Little Less Conversation," and "Rubberneckin." The record labels also have bar codes.

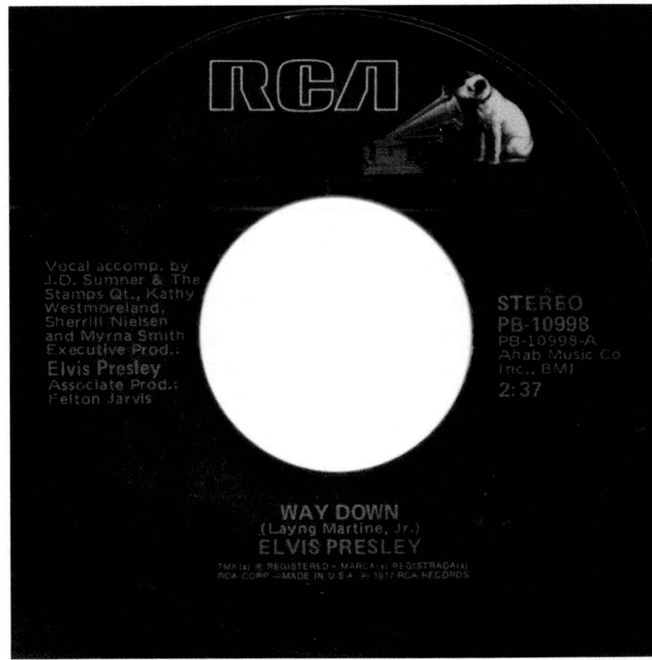

RCA 45s from the late 1970s often have a frosty dust layer on the paper label, this frost can be removed by gently wiping with a soft cloth.

***$4**, VG condition*

Elvis Presley RCA 78s

In addition to his five Sun releases, several of Elvis Presley's biggest hits were released on 78 RPM records. The catalog numbers on these pressings will begin with "20-," and feature a black label with "RCA Victor" in silver around the top perimeter, with a full-color "His Master's Voice" trademark above the spindle hole. The words "New Orthophonic High Fidelity" often appear on the label; copies that do not have those words are pressings from RCA's Rockaway, New York, plant. Although the 78 RPM format died out in 1958, RCA continued to press several popular Presley titles in that format, with the last American release being 20-7410, "One Night"/"I Got Stung." After that, two more Elvis Presley 78 titles were manufactured by RCA's Canadian pressing plant, with full color labels and possibly available for export to America. The last 78 pressing made in Canada was 20-7600, "A Big Hunk O' Love"/"My Wish Came True."

The last Presley 78-RPM title manufactured in North America was this pressing of "A Big Hunk O' Love." While previous Canadian Presley 78s had a monochromatic label with a grey Nipper trademark above the spindle hole, this pressing has a full-color "His Master's Voice" logo, possibly indicating the 78 was available for American export.

***$150**, VG+ condition*

Elvis Presley RCA Albums

Mono LPs from 1956 to 1963 will say "Long Play" on the label, which was replaced by "Mono" in 1963, then "Monaural" in 1964. After 1964, albums that were recorded only in mono were pressed in electronically rechanneled stereo, and will have an (e) at the end of the catalog number.

As for stereo pressings, from 1956 to 1964, "RCA VICTOR" appears in grey capital serif letters, along the 12:00 perimeter. The "His Master's Voice" trademark, Nipper and the gramophone, sits underneath the letters, above the spindle hole. First Elvis album on this format: *Elvis Presley* (RCA LPM-1254). Last Elvis album on this format: *Roustabout* (RCA LSP-2999).

From 1964 to 1968, "RCA VICTOR" appears in white serif letters, along the 12:00 perimeter. The letters are fatter and take up more of the perimeter than do previous grey-letter pressings. Nipper sits underneath the letters, above the spindle hole. First Elvis album in this format: *Girl Happy* (RCA LSP-3338). The last Elvis album with this label design: *Speedway* (RCA LSP-3989).

1968-1975—"RCA" in futuristic print at 9:00, orange label. No sign of Nipper. First Elvis album on this format: *The Elvis TV Special ('68 Special)* (RCA LPM-4088). Last Elvis album on this format: *Today* (RCA APL-1039).

1975-1976— "RCA" in futuristic print at 9:00, tan label. Still no sign of Nipper. These were pressed in Indianapolis,

Several of Elvis Presley's earlier titles, including some Christmas-related or movie-related albums, were re-released on RCA's budget label Camden, or were licensed to the Pickwick reissue label. Unlike their RCA Victor counterparts, these budget label pressings do not command a high collectible value.

***$10**, NM condition*

after RCA's record pressing facilities in Hollywood and Rockaway were shut down. *The Elvis Sun Sessions* (RCA APM-1675) and *From Elvis Presley Boulevard, Memphis, Tennessee* (RCA APL-1506) have these tan labels.

1976-1988—"RCA" at 1:00, Nipper returns at 2:00, black label. Elvis' last living recordings are on this label format. First Elvis album on this format: *Welcome To My World* (RCA APL-2274). Last living Elvis album on this format: *Moody Blue* (RCA AFL-2428).

Any RCA 45 with the words "Gold Standard Series," no matter what the format, is a reissue. These records will contain a "447" before the serial number. Although some of these "447" numbers became hits on their own, such as "Crying in the Chapel," Presley is one of a very few artists whose company-produced reproductions have collectible value.

In 1984, to honor Presley's 50th birthday, RCA released two box sets of six 45s apiece, each one pressed on golden vinyl. In 1986, Collectibles Records released a boxed set of Presley's greatest hits on black vinyl. Six years later, they re-released the set on gold vinyl. And, in 1997, they released a second set, this time on marbled grey vinyl.

Many of the rarest Presley recordings are pressings that have some slight variation from the standard pressing. The name of the song might be misspelled, a songwriting or backup singer's credit might be added or deleted, the record might have been mastered at an incorrect speed, or the RCA "His Master's Voice" trademark might have disappeared from some copies. If an album or single may have an alternate track, and you don't have a phonograph available to confirm this, look at the stamper numbers in the dead wax. Certain stamper numbers may provide the clue to an alternate pressing, and those records, for which the stamper number will provide a clue to its contents, are listed below in the selected discography.

Almost all of Elvis Presley's RCA releases came with a picture sleeve. After Presley's death, RCA reissued most of Presley's releases as "Gold Standard Singles," and printed new picture sleeves for them. Picture sleeves printed for singles with serial numbers RCA 47-9610 and lower (between the years 1956 and 1968) should have the old-style serifed "RCA VICTOR" logo, along with Nipper and the gramophone. Reprinted sleeves will have the futuristic "RCA" logo, and no sign of Nipper. They may also say "COLLECTOR'S EDITION" or "GOLD STANDARD SERIES" on the sleeve.

Elvis' albums, especially the soundtracks to his movies, may contain promotional postcards or posters. For an album to qualify as near-mint, these postcards and posters must be part of the package, with no tack holes or pen marks.

Books

Jorgensen, Ernst, *Elvis Presley, A Life In Music: The Complete Recording Sessions*, St. Martin's Press, New York, NY, 1998.

Hawkins, Martin; Escott, Colin, *Elvis: The Illustrated Discography*, Omnibus Press, London, 1981.

Kingsbury, Paul; Axelrod, Alan, Eds. *Country: The Music and the Musicians*, Abbeville Press, New York, NY, 1988.

Worth, Fred L.; Tamerous, Steven, *Elvis: His Life From A-Z*, Contemporary Books, Chicago, IL, 1988.

Helling, André, *Elvis Presley's 78's Around the World*, self-published, Wilhelmshaven, Germany, fa.helling@t-online.de

Museums

Graceland, Elvis' home and current museum/shrine to the King, 3734 Elvis Presley Boulevard, Memphis, Tennessee, 38186-0508. (800) 238-2000. *http://www.elvis.com/graceland*

The Elvis-A-Rama Museum, 3401 Industrial Road, Las Vegas, NV, 89109. (702) 309-7200. *http://www.elvisarama.com*

Elvis Is Alive Museum, SE 170 Exit, Wright City, MO, 63390. (636) 745-3154.

Web Pages

Elvis Presley's official page: *http://www.elvis.com*
Usenet newsgroups: *alt.fan.elvis-presley, alt.elvis.king*

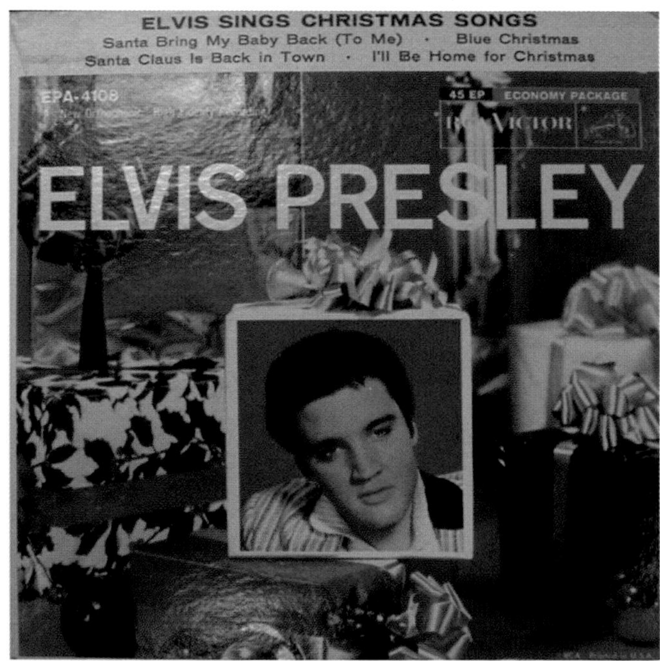

A hard-to-find Christmas EP featuring several of Presley's seasonal songs.
$125, *VG+ condition*

45s

Sun 209, "That's All Right"/"Blue Moon of Kentucky"
(first pressings, label credits "Elvis Presley, Scotty and Bill"), 1954 .... **$4,000.00-$6,000.00**
(second pressings, label credits "Elvis Presley with Scotty and Bill"), 1954 .... **$4,000.00-$6,000.00**
210, "Good Rockin' Tonight"/"I Don't Care if the Sun Don't Shine," 1954 .... **$2,500.00-$3,500.00**
215, "Milkcow Blues Boogie"/"You're a Heartbreaker," 1955 .... **$3,500.00-$5,000.00**
217, "Baby Let's Play House"/"I'm Left, You're Right, She's Gone," 1955 .... **$2,000.00-$3,000.00**
223, "I Forgot To Remember To Forget"/"Mystery Train," 1955 .... **$1,250.00-$2,500.00**
RCA Victor 47-6357, "I Forgot to Remember to Forget"/"Mystery Train," 1955 .... **$30.00-$60.00**
47-6380, "That's All Right"/"Blue Moon of Kentucky," 1955 ... **$30.00-$60.00**
47-6381, "Good Rockin' Tonight"/"I Don't Care If the Sun Don't Shine," 1955 .... **$30.00-$60.00**
47-6382, "Milkcow Blues Boogie"/"You're a Heartbreaker," 1955 .... **$30.00-$60.00**
47-6383, "Baby Let's Play House"/"I'm Left, You're Right, She's Gone," 1955 .... **$30.00-$60.00**
47-6420, "Heartbreak Hotel"/"I Was the One," 1956 .... **$20.00-$40.00**
47-6540, "I Want You, I Need You, I Love You"/"My Baby Left Me," 1956 .... **$20.00-$40.00**
47-6604, "Don't Be Cruel"/"Hound Dog," 1956 .... **$15.00-$30.00**
(with picture sleeve, "Don't Be Cruel" receives top billing), 1956 .... **$100.00-$200.00**
(with picture sleeve, "Hound Dog" receives top billing), 1956 .... **$60.00-$120.00**
47-6643, "Love Me Tender"/"Anyway You Want Me (That's How I Will Be)," 1956 .... **$15.00-$30.00**
(if no reference to movie "Love Me Tender" on label), 1956 ... **$20.00-$40.00**
(with black and white picture sleeve, add), 1956 .... **$90.00-$180.00**
(with black and green picture sleeve, add), 1956 .... **$37.50-$75.00**
(with black and dark pink picture sleeve, add), 1956 .... **$20.00-$40.00**
(with black and light pink picture sleeve, add), 1956 .... **$15.00-$30.00**
47-6800, "Too Much"/"Playing for Keeps," 1957 .... **$15.00-$30.00**
(with picture sleeve, add), 1957 .... **$45.00-$90.00**
47-6870, "All Shook Up"/"That's When Your Heartaches Begin," 1957 .... **$15.00-$30.00**
(with picture sleeve, add), 1957 .... **$45.00-$90.00**
47-7000, "Let Me Be Your TEDDY BEAR"/"Loving You," 1957 .... **$20.00-$40.00**
(if label has parentheses around "Let Me Be Your"), 1957 ...... **$15.00-$30.00**
(with picture sleeve, add), 1957 .... **$60.00-$120.00**
47-7305, "Jailhouse Rock"/"Treat Me Nice," 1957 .... **$15.00-$30.00**
(with picture sleeve, add), 1957 .... **$50.00-$100.00**
47-7150, "Don't"/"I Beg of You," 1958 .... **$12.50-$25.00**
(with picture sleeve, add), 1958 .... **$45.00-$90.00**
47-7240, "Wear My Ring Around Your Neck"/ "Don'tcha Think It's Time," 1958 .... **$12.50-$25.00**
(with picture sleeve, add), 1958 .... **$45.00-$90.00**
47-7280, "Hard Headed Woman"/"Don't Ask Me Why," 1958 .... **$12.50-$25.00**
(with picture sleeve, add), 1958 .... **$12.50-$25.00**
47-7410, "One Night"/"I Got Stung," 1958 .... **$12.50-$25.00**
(with picture sleeve, add), 1958 .... **$35.00-$70.00**
47-7506, "(Now and Then There's) A Fool Such As I"/"I Need Your Love Tonight," 1959 .... **$12.50-$25.00**
(with picture sleeve that promotes "Elvis Sails" EP, add), 1959 .... **$500.00-$1,000.00**
(with picture sleeve that lists EPs and Gold Standard singles, add), 1959 .... **$30.00-$60.00**
47-7600, "A Big Hunk O' Love"/"My Wish Came True," 1959 .... **$12.50-$25.00**
(with picture sleeve, add), 1959 .... **$35.00-$70.00**
47-7740, "Stuck on You"/"Fame and Fortune," 1960 .... **$10.00-$20.00**
(with picture sleeve, add), 1960 .... **$30.00-$60.00**
47-7777, "It's Now or Never"/"A Mess of Blues"
(if "It's Now or Never" is missing the piano part, stamper numbers L2WW-0100-3S or L2WW-0100-4S), 1960 .... **$500.00-$1,000.00**
(if "It's Now or Never" has the overdubbed piano), 1960 .... **$10.00-$20.00**
(with picture sleeve, add), 1960 .... **$30.00-$60.00**
(if on RCA 61-7777, stereo single, 45 RPM, large hole), 1960 .... **$200.00-$400.00**
47-7850, "Surrender"/"Lonely Man," 1961 .... **$10.00-$20.00**
(with picture sleeve, add), 1961 .... **$30.00-$60.00**
(if on RCA Victor 61-7850, "Living Stereo" single, 45 RPM, large hole), 1961 .... **$400.00-$800.00**
(if on RCA Victor 61-7850, "Compact Stereo 33," in "Living Stereo"), 1961 **$1,500.00-$2,000.00**
47-7968, "Can't Help Falling In Love"/"Rock-a-Hula Baby," 1961 .... **$10.00-$20.00**
(with picture sleeve, add), 1961 .... **$20.00-$40.00**
47-8360, "Viva Las Vegas"/"What'd I Say," 1964 .... **$6.00-$12.00**
(with "Coming Soon" on picture sleeve, add), 1964 .... **$12.50-$25.00**
(with "Ask For" on picture sleeve, add), 1964 .... **$25.00-$50.00**
47-9425, "Guitar Man"/"High Heel Sneakers," 1968 .... **$5.00-$10.00**
(with picture sleeve ["Coming Soon" and "Ask For" variations have equal value], add), 1968 .... **$12.50-$25.00**
47-9600, "You'll Never Walk Alone"/"We Call On Him," 1968 .... **$6.00-$12.00**
(with rare picture sleeve, add), 1968 .... **$50.00-$100.00**
47-9670, "If I Can Dream"/"Edge of Reality," 1968 .... **$4.00-$8.00**
(with picture sleeve [some sleeves mention his NBC special, some don't, value is equal], add), 1968 .... **$10.00-$20.00**
47-9764, "Suspicious Minds"/"You'll Think of Me," 1969 .... **$4.00-$8.00**
(with picture sleeve, add), 1969 .... **$10.00-$20.00**
74-0651, "He Touched Me"/"The Bosom of Abraham"
(if stamper number is AWKS-1277, "He Touched Me" incorrectly mastered at 35 RPM), 1972 .... **$75.00-$150.00**
(if stamper number is APKS-1277, both songs play correctly), 1972 .... **$4.00-$8.00**
(with picture sleeve, add), 1972 .... **$60.00-$120.00**
74-0769, "Burning Love"/"It's A Matter Of Time"
(if on orange label), 1972 .... **$3.00-$6.00**
(with picture sleeve, add), 1972 .... **$7.50-$15.00**
(if on grey label, very rare reissue), 1974 .... **$75.00-$150.00**
APBO-0280, "If You Talk In Your Sleep"/"Help Me"
(if A-side title is all on one line), 1974 .... **$6.00-$12.00**
(if title is split to two lines), 1974 .... **$3.00-$6.00**
(with picture sleeve, add), 1974 .... **$7.50-$15.00**
PB-10278, Elvis Presley, "T-R-O-U-B-L-E"/"Mr. Songman"
(if on orange label), 1975 .... **$2.50-$5.00**
(if on tan label), 1975 .... **$5.00-$10.00**
(if on grey label), 1975 .... **$50.00-$100.00**
(with picture sleeve, add), 1975 .... **$5.00-$10.00**
PB-10401, "Bringing It Back"/"Pieces Of My Life"
(if on orange label), 1975 .... **$100.00-$200.00**
(if on tan label), 1975 .... **$2.50-$5.00**
(with picture sleeve, add), 1975 .... **$5.00-$10.00**
PB-10601, "Hurt"/"For the Heart," black label with Nipper, 1976 .... **$50.00-$100.00**
PB-10857, "Moody Blue"/"She Thinks I Still Care," 1976 .... **$2.50-$5.00**
(with picture sleeve, add), 1976 .... **$2.50-$5.00**
PB-10998, "Way Down"/"Pledging My Love," 1977 .... **$2.50-$5.00**
(with picture sleeve, add), 1977 .... **$2.50-$5.00**
60575, "A Little Less Conversation" (remix)/(original version), remixed by JXL, 2002 .... **$4.00-$8.00**
61937, "Rubberneckin" (remix)/(original), 2003 .... **$3.00-$6.00**

45 Reissues

RCA Victor "Gold Standard Series," reissues:
(if catalog number begins with "447-," black label, Nipper at 12:00), 1959 .... **$7.50-$15.00**
(if catalog number begins with "447-," black label, Nipper at 3:00), 1965 .... **$5.00-$10.00**
(if promotional pressing for radio only), 1964 .... **$50.00-$100.00**
(with picture sleeve for promo pressings, add), 1964 .... **$100.00-$200.00**
(if catalog number begins with "447-," orange label, no Nipper), 1969 .... **$12.50-$25.00**
RCA "Gold Standard Series" reissues:
(if on black label, modern RCA logo, Nipper at 12:00 on label), 1977 .... **$2.00-$4.00**

Collectables, any title with catalog number 4500-4522, black vinyl, 1986 ....**$1.50-$3.00**
Collectables, any title with catalog number 4500-4522, gold vinyl, 1992 ....**$2.00-$4.00**
Collectables, any title with catalog number 80001-80028, grey marbled vinyl, 1997 ....**$2.00-$4.00**
COL-0103, Elvis #1 Hit Singles Collection, 23 singles in box set, red vinyl —contains five Sun-labeled 45s on red vinyl, 2001 ....**$50.00-$100.00**
COL-0134, Elvis Hit Singles Collection Volume 2, 23 singles in box set, red vinyl, 2002 ....**$50.00-$100.00**
RCA DMEI-18038, "King of the Whole Wide World"/"King Creole," red vinyl, 3,000 pressed, 1997 ....**$7.50-$15.00**
(if above on gold vinyl, about 7,000 pressed), 1997 ....**$4.00-$8.00**
(if on green, blue, white and clear vinyl, test pressings, value is equal), 1997 ....**$200.00-$400.00**

7-inch 33-1/3, "Compact Singles"

RCA Victor 37-7850, "Surrender"/"Lonely Man," 1961 ....**$300.00-$600.00**
(with picture sleeve, add), 1961 ....**$500.00-$1,000.00**
37-7880, "I Feel So Bad"/"Wild in the Country," 1961 ....**$500.00-$1,000.00**
(with picture sleeve, add), 1961 ....**$600.00-$1,200.00**
37-7968, "Can't Help Falling In Love"/"Rock-a-Hula Baby," 1961 ....**$1,500.00-$2,000.00**
(with picture sleeve, add), 1961 ....**$3,000.00-$4,000.00**
DTF0-02006, Aloha from Hawaii Via Satellite, 1973 ....**$40.00-$80.00**
(with picture sleeve, add), 1973 ....**$50.00-$100.00**

78s

Sun 209, "That's All Right"/"Blue Moon of Kentucky," 1954 ....**$1,500.00-$3,000.00**
210, "Good Rockin' Tonight"/"I Don't Care if The Sun Don't Shine," 1954 ....**$900.00-$1,800.00**
215, "Milkcow Blues Boogie"/"You're A Heartbreaker," 1955 ....**$1,250.00-$2,500.00**
217, "Baby Let's Play House"/"I'm Left, You're Right, She's Gone," 1955 ....**$750.00-$1,500.00**
223, "I Forgot To Remember To Forget"/"Mystery Train," 1955 ....**$500.00-$1,000.00**
RCA Victor 20-6357, "I Forgot To Remember To Forget"/"Mystery Train," 1955 ....**$75.00-$150.00**
20-6380, "That's All Right"/"Blue Moon of Kentucky," 1955 ....**$75.00-$150.00**
20-6381, "Good Rockin' Tonight"/"I Don't Care if The Sun Don't Shine," 1955 ....**$75.00-$150.00**
20-6382, "Milkcow Blues Boogie"/"You're A Heartbreaker," 1955 ....**$75.00-$150.00**
20-6383, "Baby Let's Play House"/"I'm Left, You're Right, She's Gone," 1955 ....**$75.00-$150.00**
20-6420, "Heartbreak Hotel"/"I Was The One," 1956 ....**$50.00-$100.00**
20-6540, "I Want You, I Need You, I Love You"/"My Baby Left Me," 1956 ....**$50.00-$100.00**
20-6604, "Don't Be Cruel"/"Hound Dog," 1956 ....**$50.00-$100.00**
20-6636, "Blue Suede Shoes"/"Tutti-Frutti," 1956 ....**$50.00-$100.00**
20-6637, "I Got a Woman"/"I'm Counting On You," 1956 ....**$50.00-$100.00**
20-6638, "I'll Never Let You Go"/"I'm Gonna Sit Right Down and Cry," 1956 ....**$50.00-$100.00**
20-6639, "Tryin' to Get To You"/"I Love You Because," 1956 ....**$50.00-$100.00**
20-6640, "Blue Moon"/"Just Because," 1956 ....**$50.00-$100.00**
20-6641, "Money Honey"/"One Sided Love Affair," 1956 ....**$50.00-$100.00**
20-6642, "Shake, Rattle and Roll"/"Lawdy Miss Clawdy," 1956 ....**$50.00-$100.00**
20-6643, "Love Me Tender"/"Anyway You Want Me," 1956 ....**$50.00-$100.00**
20-6800, "Too Much"/"Playing for Keeps," 1957 ....**$50.00-$100.00**
20-6870, "All Shook Up"/"That's When Your Heartaches Begin," 1957 ....**$50.00-$100.00**
20-7000, "Teddy Bear"/"Loving You," 1957 ....**$50.00-$100.00**
20-7035, "Jailhouse Rock"/"Treat Me Nice," 1957 ....**$50.00-$100.00**
20-7150, "Don't"/"I Beg of You," 1958 ....**$50.00-$100.00**
20-7240, "Wear My Ring Around Your Neck"/"Doncha' Think It's Time," 1958 ....**$60.00-$120.00**
20-7280, "Hard Headed Woman"/"Don't Ask Me Why," 1958 ....**$60.00-$120.00**
20-7410, "One Night"/"I Got Stung" (RCA Victor 20-7410) (last Elvis Presley 78 pressed in America), 1958 ....**$250.00-$500.00**
20-7506, "A Fool Such As I"/"I Need Your Love Tonight," Canadian pressing, 1959 ....**$100.00-$200.00**
20-7600, "A Big Hunk o' Love"/"My Wish Came True," Canadian pressing (last Elvis Presley 78 issued in Canada), 1959 ....**$100.00-$200.00**

Mono LPs

LPM-1254, Elvis Presley
(if first version, "Long Play" on label, "Elvis" in pale pink, "Presley" in pale green on cover, pale green logo box in upper right front cover), 1956 ....**$250.00-$500.00**
(if second version, "Long Play" on label, "Elvis" in pale pink, "Presley" in neon green on cover, neon green logo box in upper right front cover), 1956 ....**$200.00-$400.00**
(if third version, "Long Play" on label, "Elvis" in pale pink, "Presley" in neon green on cover, black logo box in upper right front cover), 1956 ....**$125.00-$250.00**
(if fourth version, "Long Play" on label, "Elvis" in neon reddish-pink, "Presley" in neon green on cover, black logo box in upper right front cover), 1958 ....**$100.00-$200.00**
(if "Mono" on label, cover photo is slightly left of center, otherwise same color scheme as fourth version above), 1963 ....**$60.00-$120.00**
(if "Monaural" on label), 1964 ....**$30.00-$60.00**
LPM-1382, Elvis
(if matrix number is 15S, 17S or 19S, containing alternate take of "Old Shep" with lyrics "he grew old AND his eyes were growing dim"), 1956 ....**$400.00-$800.00**
(if songs are listed as "Band 1" through "Band 6" on label), 1956 ....**$200.00-$400.00**
(if back cover has ads for other albums), 1956 ....**$150.00-$300.00**
(if back cover has no ads for other albums, "Long Play" on label), 1956 ....**$150.00-$300.00**
(if "Mono" on label), 1963 ....**$40.00-$80.00**
LPM-1515, Loving You
(if "Long Play" on label), 1957 ....**$150.00-$300.00**
(if "Mono" on label), 1963 ....**$50.00-$100.00**
(if "Monaural" on label), 1964 ....**$25.00-$50.00**
LPM-1707, Elvis' Golden Records
(if title on cover in light blue letters, no song titles listed on front cover), 1958 ....**$125.00-$250.00**
(if title on cover in light blue letters, no song titles listed on front cover, "RE" on back cover), 1958 ....**$75.00-$150.00**
(if "MONO" on cover, title in white letters, song titles added to front cover), 1963 ....**$30.00-$60.00**
(if "Monaural" on label, "RE2" on back cover), 1964 ....**$20.00-$40.00**
LPM-1884, King Creole
(if "Long Play" on label), 1958 ....**$100.00-$200.00**
(if "Mono" on label), 1963 ....**$40.00-$80.00**
(if "Monaural" on label), 1964 ....**$30.00-$60.00**
LPM-2075, Elvis' Golden Records Volume 2—50,000,000 Elvis Fans Can't Be Wrong
(if "Long Play" on label, "Magic Millions" on upper right front cover with RCA Victor logo), 1960 ....**$100.00-$200.00**
(if "Mono" on label, "RE" on lower right front cover), 1963 ....**$40.00-$80.00**
(if "Monaural" on label, label says "50,000,000 Elvis Presley Fans Can't Be Wrong"), 1964 ....**$25.00-$50.00**
(if "Monaural" on label, label only says "Elvis' Gold Records—Vol. 2"), 1964 ....**$25.00-$50.00**
LPM-2756, Fun in Acapulco
(if "Mono" on label), 1963 ....**$40.00-$80.00**
(if "Monaural" on label), 1964 ....**$25.00-$50.00**
LPM-2999, Roustabout
(if "Mono" on label), 1964 ....**$50.00-$100.00**
(if "Monaural" on label), 1965 ....**$30.00-$60.00**
LPM-3989, Speedway (last mono LP), 1968 ....**$1,000.00-$2,000.00**
(with bonus photo, add), 1968 ....**$25.00-$50.00**

Stereo LPs

LSP-1254(e), Elvis Presley
(if "Stereo Electronically Reprocessed," silver "RCA Victor" on label), 1962 ....**$100.00-$200.00**
(if "Stereo Electronically Reprocessed," white "RCA Victor" on label), 1965 ....**$20.00-$40.00**
(if orange label, non-flexible vinyl), 1968 ....**$15.00-$30.00**

(if tan label), 1975 ....$7.50-$15.00
(if black label with Nipper at 1:00), 1976....................................$6.00-$12.00
(if on AFL1-1254(e), some copies have stickers over original catalog numbers), 1977 ....$6.00-$12.00

LSP-1382(e), Elvis
(if "Stereo Electronically Reprocessed" and silver "RCA Victor" on label), 1962...$100.00-$200.00
(if "Stereo Electronically Reprocessed" and white "RCA Victor" on label), 1964...$25.00-$50.00
(if orange label, non-flexible vinyl), 1968................................$15.00-$30.00
(if orange label, flexible vinyl), 1971 ....$10.00-$20.00
(if tan label), 1975...$7.50-$15.00
(if black label with Nipper at 1:00), 1976 ....$6.00-$12.00
(if on RCA Victor AFL1-1382(e), some copies have stickers over original catalog numbers), 1977..$6.00-$12.00

LSP-1515(e), Loving You
(if "Stereo Electronically Reprocessed" and silver "RCA Victor" on label), 1962...$75.00-$150.00
(if "Stereo Electronically Reprocessed" and white "RCA Victor" on label), 1964...$25.00-$50.00
(if orange label, non-flexible vinyl), 1968................................$20.00-$40.00
(if orange label, flexible vinyl), 1971 ....$10.00-$20.00
(if tan label), 1975...$10.00-$20.00
(if black label with Nipper at 1:00), 1976 ....$6.00-$12.00
(if on RCA Victor AFL1-1515(e), some copies have stickers over original catalog numbers), 1977..$6.00-$12.00

LSP-1884(e), King Creole
(if "Stereo Electronically Reprocessed" and silver "RCA Victor" on label), 1962...$75.00-$150.00
(if "Stereo Electronically Reprocessed" and white "RCA Victor" on label), 1964...$30.00-$60.00
(if on orange label, non-flexible vinyl), 1968...........................$20.00-$40.00
(if on orange label, flexible vinyl), 1971 ....$10.00-$20.00
(if on tan label), 1975...$10.00-$20.00
(if on black label with Nipper at 1:00), 1976 ....$6.00-$12.00
(if on RCA Victor AFL1-1884, some copies have stickers over original catalog numbers), 1977..$6.00-$12.00

LSP-1707(e), Elvis' Golden Records
(if "Stereo Electronically Reprocessed" and silver "RCA Victor" on label), 1962...$100.00-$200.00
(if "Stereo Electronically Reprocessed" and white "RCA Victor" on label), 1964...$25.00-$50.00
(if orange label, non-flexible vinyl), 1968................................$15.00-$30.00
(if orange label, flexible vinyl), 1971 ....$10.00-$20.00
(if tan label), 1975...$10.00-$20.00
(if black label with Nipper at 1:00), 1976 ....$6.00-$12.00
(if on RCA Victor AFL1-1707(e), some copies have stickers over original catalog numbers), 1977..$6.00-$12.00
(if on RCA Victor AQL1-1707(e), reissue with new prefix), 1979 ....$5.00-$10.00
(if on RCA 07863-67642 1, with six extra tracks, sold through Tower Records stores), 1997...$15.00-$30.00

LSP-2075(e), Elvis' Golden Records Volume 2—50,000,000 Elvis Fans Can't Be Wrong
(if "Stereo Electronically Reprocessed," label says "50,000,000 Elvis Presley Fans Can't Be Wrong"), 1962...$75.00-$150.00
(if "Stereo Electronically Reproduced" and white "RCA Victor" on label), 1964...$25.00-$50.00
(if orange label, non-flexible vinyl), 1968................................$15.00-$30.00
(if orange label, flexible vinyl), 1971 ....$10.00-$20.00
(if tan label), 1975...$12.50-$25.00
(if black label with Nipper at 1:00), 1976 ....$6.00-$12.00
(if on RCA Victor AFL1-2075(e), some copies have stickers over original catalog numbers), 1977..$6.00-$12.00
(if on RCA 07863-67631-1, with ten extra tracks, sold through Tower Records stores), 1997...$15.00-$30.00

LSP-2756, Fun in Acapulco
(if "stereo" and silver "RCA Victor" on black label), 1963 ....$50.00-$100.00
(if "stereo" and white "RCA Victor" on black label), 1964 ....$30.00-$60.00
(if orange label, non-flexible vinyl), 1968................................$20.00-$40.00
(if tan label), 1975...$12.50-$25.00
(if black label with Nipper at 1:00), 1976 ....$6.00-$12.00
(if on RCA Victor AFL1-2756, some copies have stickers over original catalog numbers), 1977..$6.00-$12.00

LSP-2999, Roustabout
(if "stereo" and silver "RCA Victor" on black label), 1963....$300.00-$600.00
(if "stereo" and white "RCA Victor" on black label), 1964 ....$30.00-$60.00
(if orange label, non-flexible vinyl), 1968................................$20.00-$40.00
(if orange label, flexible vinyl), 1971 ....$10.00-$20.00
(if tan label), 1975...$10.00-$20.00
(if black label with Nipper at 1:00), 1976 ....$6.00-$12.00
(if on RCA Victor AFL1-2999, some copies have stickers over original catalog numbers), 1977..$6.00-$12.00

LSP-3989, Speedway
(if "stereo" on black label), 1968 ....$30.00-$60.00
(if orange label, non-flexible vinyl), 1968................................$20.00-$40.00
(if orange label, flexible vinyl), 1971 ....$10.00-$20.00
(if tan label), 1975...$10.00-$20.00
(if black label with Nipper at 1:00), 1976 ....$6.00-$12.00
(if on RCA Victor AFL1-3989, some copies have stickers over original catalog numbers), 1977..$6.00-$12.00

LSP-4460, Elvis Country (I'm 10,000 Years Old)
(if on orange label, non-flexible vinyl), 1971...........................$20.00-$40.00
(if on orange label, flexible vinyl), 1971 ....$12.50-$25.00
(with bonus photo, add), 1971 ....$7.50-$15.00
(if on tan label), 1975...$12.50-$25.00
(if on black label, dog near top), 1976.......................................$7.50-$15.00
(if on green vinyl, black label, dog near top), 197? ....$1,000.00-$2,000.00
(if on RCA Victor AFL1-4460, some copies have stickers over original catalog numbers), 1977..$6.00-$10.00
(if on RCA Victor A&L1-3956, budget reissue), 1981 ....$4.00-$8.00

AFL1-2428, Moody Blue
(if on blue vinyl), 1977..$5.00-$10.00
(if on black vinyl, short printed), 1977................................$100.00-$200.00
(if on any other color vinyl, promo copies only), 1977...$1,000.00-$2,000.00
(if on RCA AQL1-2428, reissue with new prefix), 1979.........$12.50-$25.00

RCA Special Products DML5-0263, The Elvis Story, 5 LPs, available only through Candelite Music TV mail-in, 1977 ....$30.00-$60.00

RCA CPL8-3699, Elvis Aron Presley, 8 LPs, 1980 ....$50.00-$100.00
(if box says "Reviewer Series" on cover), 1980.......................$125.00-$250.00
(if on RCA DJL1-3781, promo-only selections on one disc from album

Reader's Digest RD-10/A, Elvis Presley, His Greatest Hits), 8 LPs, 1979 ....$50.00-$100.00
(if on Reader's Digest 010/A, 7 LPs, yellow box), 1983..........$30.00-$60.00
(if on Reader's Digest 010/A, 7 LPs, white box), 1990............$20.00-$40.00

Premore PL-589, Early Elvis (1954-1956 Live at the Louisiana Hayride), 1989 ....$15.00-$30.00

Photo credit: From the collection of Dennis Gingerich.

Almost every Presley 45 on RCA had a concomitant picture sleeve; these sleeves not only advertised Presley's upcoming albums and films, but they also were suitable for tacking on bedroom walls or pasting into scrapbooks.
***$90**, for NM condition sleeve*

Chapter 29

The Rolling Stones

History

Without a doubt, the Rolling Stones have earned their nickname, "The Greatest Rock and Roll Band in the World." From their early years at the Ealing Club, performing with Alexis Korner's Blues Incorporated, to their years of cutting-edge live shows and envelope-opening lyrics, the Rolling Stones have done it all. They have lived the rock and roll lifestyle—sometimes to excess, sometimes to distress. But other than the Beatles and Elvis Presley, the Rolling Stones are arguably the most collectible rock band worldwide.

The nucleus of the Rolling Stones has always been lead singer Mick Jagger and guitarist Keith Richards. The songs they co-wrote have become rock anthems—"I Can't Get No Satisfaction," "Paint It, Black," "Honky Tonk Women," "19th Nervous Breakdown," "Brown Sugar," and "Start Me Up."

It was a love of early American blues music—Leadbelly, Muddy Waters, Willie Dixon, and Chuck Berry—that provided an early bond between schoolmates Jagger and Richards in 1961. As the story goes, while Jagger and Richards were waiting at a Dartford railway station, Richards noticed some blues records in Jagger's hands. Before long, both Jagger and Richards were singing and performing with mutual friend Dick Taylor in a band called "Little Boy Blue and the Blue Boys." They eventually added pianist Ian Stewart and guitarist Brian Jones to form an early combo.

Taking their name from the Muddy Waters classic "Rollin' Stone," the newly christened Rolling Stones made their live debut at England's Marquee Club. By 1963, the band

The Stones' fragile picture sleeves, especially those pressed by London Records, are very collectible. This one, from the song "She's A Rainbow," is hard to find in good condition.

***$50**, for NM sleeve*

Photo credit: From the collection of Tom Grosh

The B-side of "Not Fade Away" was this instrumental called "Stoned." This song was yanked off the B-side, and another track was inserted in its place, making this pressing one of the rarest American 45s to a Rolling Stones collector.

***$9,000**, NM condition*

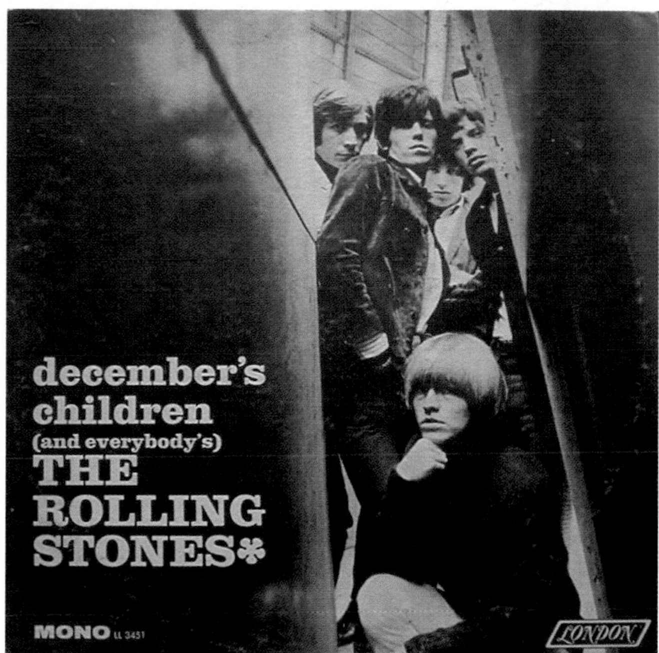

The World's Greatest Rock and Roll Band, on the cover of one of their monaural pressings.

***$12.50**, Good condition*

Only a few copies of this picture sleeve for "Street Fighting Man" exist; as the image of police beating up a protestor at the 1968 Democratic National Convention was deemed too sensitive for record stores.

***$10,000**, NM condition*

Photo credit: From the collection of Tom Grosh.

added drummer Charlie Watts and bass player Bill Wyman (allegedly added because Wyman owned his own amplifier), and made a steady living performing at the Ealing Jazz Club and the Station Hotel Crawdaddy. A promoter named Andrew Loog Oldham signed the band to a management deal, and immediately began promoting the group as a musical alternative to the Beatles. He even created a successful newspaper campaign, taking out ads with the tagline "Would you let your daughter marry a Rolling Stone?"

The campaign paid off, and the Stones signed a recording contract with the British label Decca (apparently by the person who passed on signing the Beatles to that label). The group's covers of "Not Fade Away" and "Come On" immediately brought them a new legion of fans—and some detractors, who couldn't understand why this band wasn't as sweet and polite as the Beatles.

Eventually the Stones' success translated into American hits—and some American controversy. Their first release on London Records, Decca's American subsidiary label, was the UK hit "I Wanna Be Your Man." The song's B-side, an instrumental called "Stoned," was quickly yanked from the shelves because of the "drug reference" of the song's title. Eventually "I Wanna Be Your Man" returned to the stores, as the B-side of the group's first hit, a remake of the Buddy Holly song "Not Fade Away." Their first Top 40 hit in America, "Tell Me (You're Coming Back)," was a Jagger-Richards original, and showed the band could write their own material, as well as perform killer versions of blues classics.

Other hits followed—"It's All Over Now," "Play With Fire," and "Time Is On My Side." In fact, by 1965, the Rolling Stones were chart-toppers in England, and their songs' airplay in America proved that there was more to British music than moptops, cheeky humor and "Yeah, Yeah, Yeah."

While their fans enjoyed the Stones' music, the band was constantly harangued by reporters who were eager for a story on how "bad" the "bad boys of rock" really were. Everything from drug arrests to urinating on the wall of a gas station were fodder for journalists and reporters, but these news stories did not diminish the Stones' popularity—rather, they actually *enhanced* the group's reputation.

And in 1965, the group recorded some of the most popular songs of their career—beginning with "I Can't Get No Satisfaction," and following with "Get Off of My Cloud," "As Tears Go By," "19th Nervous Breakdown," "Paint It, Black," "Mother's Little Helper," "Have You Seen Your Mother, Baby, Standing in the Shadow?," and "Ruby Tuesday." The group introduced new instruments into their repertoire, including Brian Jones' sitar on "Paint It, Black." Their record sleeves also show a fiercer experimentation than in their previous efforts—while their early covers show the band standing at attention or relaxing on a grassy knoll, "Have You Seen Your Mother, Baby, Standing in the Shadow?" shows the band dressed as women. Another picture sleeve, this one for "Street Fighting Man," shows the violent aftermath of the police and protestors at the 1968 Democratic Convention.

By the late 1960s, the Rolling Stones continue to raise the bar, both musically and artistically. Songs like "Let's Spend the Night Together" and "Jumpin' Jack Flash" kept the Stones' music at the top of the charts, while their live performances and concert tours were greeted by frenzied fans worldwide.

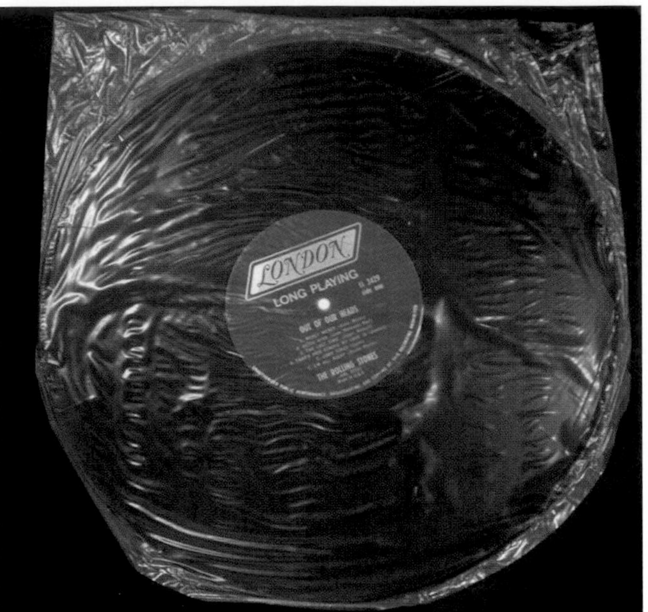

As opposed to other record companies, who packaged their albums with paper inner sleeves, London preferred to seal their albums with a thin plastic sheet before inserting them in a jacket, as can be seen on this copy of the Rolling Stones' Out of Our Heads *album.*

***$150**, VG+ condition*

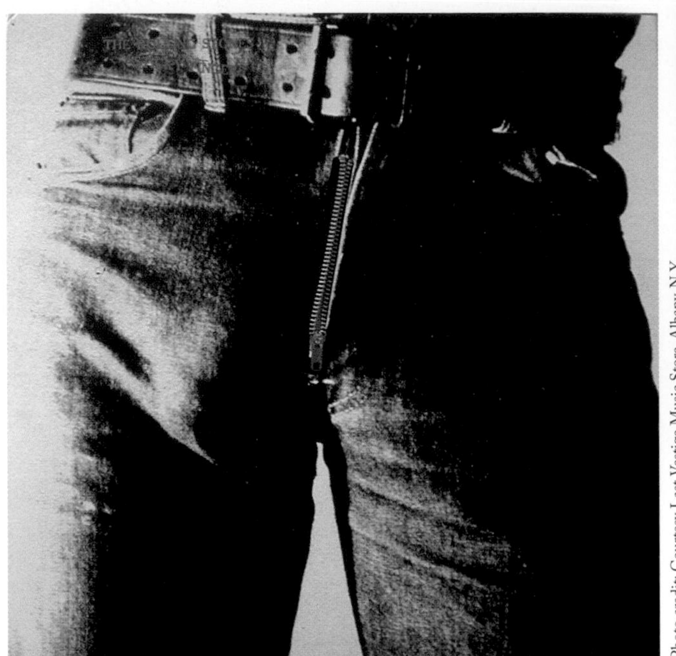

Photo credit: Courtesy Last Vestige Music Store, Albany, N.Y.

Finding copies of the Rolling Stones' Sticky Fingers *album with a working zipper is not difficult – but make sure that the back cover of the album doesn't have any scrape marks. As these records were packed in shipping boxes and sent to record stores, the metal zippers often scuffed the other copies in the box.*

***$8**, VG+ condition*

1969 should have been as successful a year for the Rolling Stones as any other. But the year will be remembered for two tragedies that nearly shook the band to its foundation. On June 8, 1969, Brian Jones left the Rolling Stones to form his own group, and was replaced by former Bluesbreaker Mick Taylor. Less than a month after Jones left the band, however, the founding Stones member was found dead in his swimming pool, the victim of an accidental drowning. The band continued on, performing a concert in Hyde Park in Jones' memory.

The second tragedy happened in late December, 1969. The Rolling Stones were part of a free concert at California's Altamont Speedway. During the concert, a fan was beaten to death by Hell's Angels, who were hired as concert security.

In 1970, the Rolling Stones switched labels, from Decca/London to their own custom Rolling Stones Records (initially distributed by Atlantic Records). Their first single on their new label, "Brown Sugar," was a Top 5 hit, and the album *Sticky Fingers* (featuring an Andy Warhol-designed front cover of a pair of jeans—with a fully functional zipper) shot to #1 on the album charts.

By 1972, *Exile on Main Street* was released, hailed by critics as one of the greatest Stones albums ever released. By this time, the band's tours outgrew concert halls and arenas, as their multimedia productions now required stadium tours. The next Stones personnel change occurred in 1974, when Mick Taylor left for a solo career. Ronnie Wood, formerly of Faces, joined the Stones as their new guitarist.

Even in the 1970s, the Stones never lost their love for blues and soul—or their reputation for controversy. Billboards promoting their album *Black and Blue*, featuring a rope-bound, bruised woman saying she loved the album, were quickly removed after protests from anti-abuse groups. Their 1978 album *Some Girls* featured images of Marilyn Monroe and Lucille Ball—until lawsuits forced changes to the artwork. One of the tracks from *Some Girls*, "Miss You," not only became another #1 hit for the Rolling Stones, but also became a #1 hit in discos and clubs, forcing the release of a 12-inch "disco" version of the track.

Even in the 1980s, the Rolling Stones were still pushing the envelope as far as possible. Some of the lyrics to their 1981 song "Start Me Up," including "You make a dead man come," received a few edits on some conservative radio stations. While their 1985 single "Undercover of the Night" featured lyrics of militias and terrorism, their album *Undercover* featured a naked woman on the cover, her body parts covered by peelable stickers.

By 1985, Mick Jagger recorded his first solo album, *She's The Boss*, and collaborated with David Bowie for a remake of "Dancing In The Streets." The track, recorded for the world famine relief concert Live Aid, was a runaway smash. Keith Richards and Ronnie Wood also appeared at Live Aid, performing with Bob Dylan in the closing ceremonies.

Sadly, 1985 was also the year Ian Stewart, the Stones' piano player and road manager, died at the age of 47 of a massive heart attack. Stewart was an original member of the Stones, but eventually faded into the background, working behind the scenes and playing piano whenever the band needed him.

In 1986, the band changed distribution for their vanity label, from Atlantic to CBS. With their first song, "Harlem Shuffle," the Stones showed they still had a love for classic

Photo credit: Courtesy Last Vestige Music Store, Albany, N.Y.

The images of Lucille Ball, Joan Crawford, and Marilyn Monroe were later removed in subsequent pressings, with covers featuring the words "Under Construction" or simply showing a solid color shape where a face should be.

$15, *NM condition*

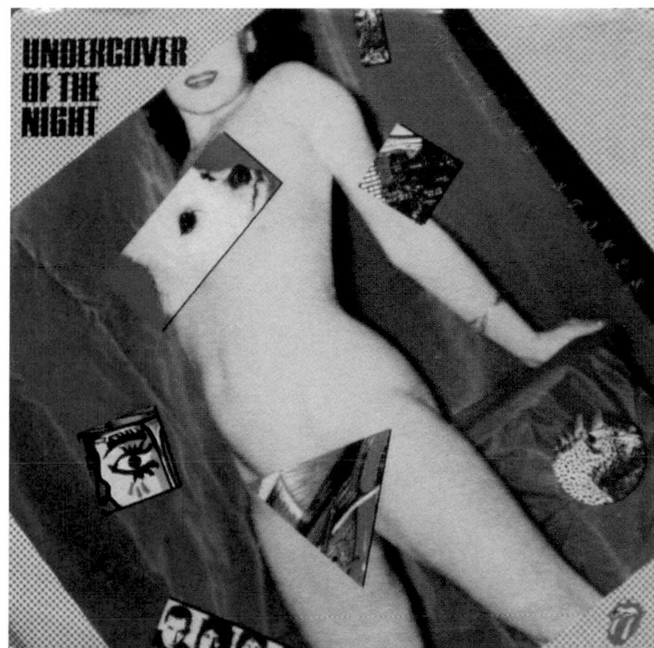

The Stones' 1983 hit "Undercover of the Night" was released with this picture sleeve; while first pressings of the Undercover album jacket have peel-off decals that cover the cover subject's modesty, no such revealing decals exist on this picture sleeve

$2, *VG+ condition*

soul and blues ("Harlem Shuffle" was a mid-chart hit for Bob and Earl in the early 1960s).

But there was a growing friction in the band, most notably between Mick Jagger and Keith Richards. Both men recorded solo albums, and fans checked every lyric and liner note to find some clue to what each band member thought about the other. Eventually Jagger and Richards put their disagreements behind them and, with the Stones, recorded the album *Steel Wheels*, and the Top 40 hit "Mixed Emotions."

In 1993, after 30 years with the Rolling Stones, Bill Wyman retired from the band. The group still continues to record and tour, with Darryl Jones working as a "side musician" in place of Wyman. Like its name implies, the Rolling Stones continue to roll on.

What To Look For

Rolling Stones picture sleeves—especially those from the London years—are currently commanding high prices. Although most sleeves simply feature stock photos of the band itself, some sleeves contained controversial covers ("Street Fighting Man" and "Beast of Burden," for example) and were quickly deleted. Beware of counterfeits—most 1960s Rolling Stones picture sleeves have been counterfeited.

Conversely, the Stones' stock recordings from 1971 forward have not equally increased in value. Rare pieces from this period include stereo and mono radio pressings of *Sticky Fingers*, the aforementioned "Beast of Burden" picture sleeve, any stock copies of the single "Too Tough" with "Miss You" on the B-side, and a Mobile Fidelity multi-album audiophile boxed set. In 1986, ABKCO Records, who currently owns the Rolling Stones' London Records catalog, reissued those albums as part of an audiophile series. Although they did return some of the lost art and liner notes to public view—including the rare "toilet graffiti" from *Beggars Banquet*—these reissues have minimal collectible value when compared to the originals.

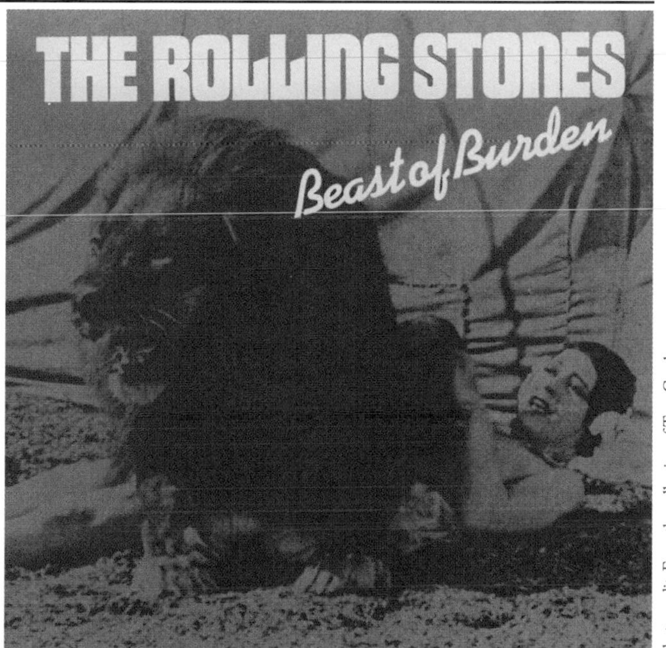

Photo credit: From the collection of Tom Grosh.

A controversial Rolling Stones picture sleeve from 1978, for the song Beast of Burden, *is extremely difficult to find.*

$2,000, *NM condition*

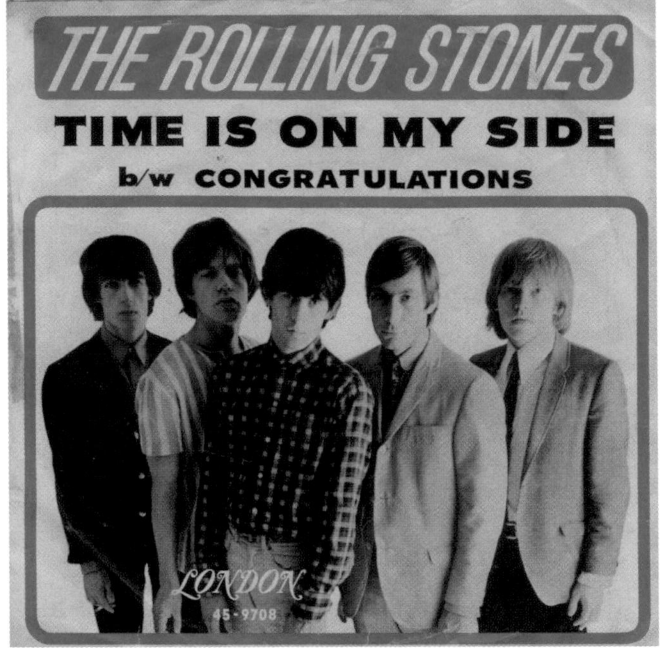

This picture sleeve for the Rolling Stones' "Time Is On My Side" is not difficult to find; but, like most picture sleeves of the 1950s and 1960s, they may suffer from split seams (when the record's sharp edge pierces through the sleeve folds) or the repairs from split seams. As can be seen from the yellowing tape residue on the seam edges, time was NOT on the side of this picture sleeve. ***$25****, Fair condition*

Books

Booth, Stanley, *Dance With The Devil: The Rolling Stones And Their Times*, Random House, NY, 1984.

Dowley, Tim, *The Rolling Stones*, Hippocrene Books, Inc., New York, NY, 1983.

Greenfield, Robert, *S.T.P.: A Journey Through America with the Rolling Stones*, Saturday Review Press/E.P. Dutton & Co., Inc., NY, 1974.

Norman, Philip, *Symphony for the Devil: The Rolling Stones Story*, Linden Press/Simon and Schuster, New York, NY, 1984.

Wyman, Bill, with Ray Coleman, *Stone Alone: The Story of a Rock and Roll Band*, Da Capo Press, New York, NY, 1997.

Web Pages

The Rolling Stones' official home page: http://www.therollingstones.com

The Rolling Stones Internet Index: http://members.aol.com/hummer1954/links.html

A page listing the Top 100 Rolling Stones Internet sites: http://hometown.aol.com/lorand/index.html.

Usenet newsgroups: alt.rock-n-roll.stones

Rolling Stones — VG+ to NM

45s

London 9641, "I Wanna Be Your Man"/"Stoned"
(if on white-purple-blue label), 1964 .... **$6,000.00-$9,000.00**
(if promo, similar label, except in white, black and gray), 1964 .... **$500.00-$1,000.00**
(if promo, white label, black print, script "London" at top), 1964 .... **$750.00-$1,500.00**

9657, "Not Fade Away"/"I Wanna Be Your Man"
(if on white-purple-blue label), 1964 .... **$20.00-$40.00**
(if promo, similar label, except in white, black and gray), 1964 .... **$400.00-$900.00**
(if on blue swirl label), 1964 .... **$4.00-$8.00**
(with picture sleeve, add), 1964 .... **$300.00-$450.00**

9682, "Tell Me (You're Coming Back)"/"I Just Want to Make Love to You"
(if white-purple-blue label), 1964 .... **$20.00-$40.00**
(if blue swirl label), 1964 .... **$5.00-$10.00**
(with picture sleeve, add), 1964 .... **$125.00-$175.00**

9687, "It's All Over Now"/"Good Times, Bad Times"
(if on white-purple-blue label), 1964 .... **$20.00-$40.00**
(if on blue swirl label), 1964 .... **$5.00-$10.00**
(with picture sleeve, add), 1964 .... **$85.00-$125.00**

9708, "Time Is On My Side"/"Congratulations"
(if on white-purple-blue label), 1964 .... **$15.00-$30.00**
(if on blue swirl label), 1964 .... **$5.00-$10.00**
(with picture sleeve, add), 1964 .... **$50.00-$100.00**

9725, "Heart of Stone"/"What a Shame"
(if on white-purple-blue label), 1964 .... **$15.00-$30.00**
(if on blue swirl label), 1964 .... **$5.00-$10.00**
(with picture sleeve, add), 1964 .... **$400.00-$800.00**

9741, "The Last Time"/"Play with Fire"
(if on white-purple-blue label), 1965 .... **$12.50-$25.00**
(if on blue swirl label, "LONDON" in black letters), 1965 .... **$5.00-$10.00**
(if on blue swirl label, "LONDON" in black letters), 1965 .... **$7.50-$15.00**
(with picture sleeve, add), 1965 .... **$75.00-$150.00**

9766, "(I Can't Get No) Satisfaction"/"The Under Assistant West Coast Promotion Man," 1965 .... **$10.00-$20.00**
(with picture sleeve, add), 1965 .... **$250.00-$500.00**
(if on orange swirl label, catalog number 5N-9766, reissue), 1975 .... **$30.00-$60.00**

9792, "Get Off of My Cloud"/"I'm Free," 1965 .... **$10.00-$20.00**
(with picture sleeve, add), 1965 .... **$30.00-$60.00**

9808, "As Tears Go By"/"Gotta Get Away," 1965 .... **$7.50-$15.00**
(with picture sleeve, add), 1965 .... **$30.00-$60.00**

9823, "19th Nervous Breakdown"/"Sad Day," 1966 .... **$7.50-$15.00**
(with picture sleeve, add), 1966 .... **$30.00-$60.00**

901, "Paint It, Black"/"Stupid Girl," 1966 .... **$7.50-$15.00**
(with picture sleeve, add), 1966 .... **$30.00-$60.00**

902, "Mothers Little Helper"/"Lady Jane," 1966 .... **$7.50-$15.00**
(with picture sleeve, add), 1966 .... **$30.00-$60.00**

903, "Have You Seen Your Mother, Baby, Standing in the Shadow?"/"Who's Driving My Plane," 1966 .... **$7.50-$15.00**
(with picture sleeve, add), 1966 .... **$30.00-$60.00**

904, "Ruby Tuesday"/"Let's Spend the Night Together," 1967 .... **$7.50-$15.00**
(with picture sleeve, add), 1967 .... **$30.00-$60.00**

905, "Dandelion"/"We Love You," 1967 .... **$10.00-$20.00**
(if on orange swirl label, full-length version of "We Love You"), 1967 .... **$50.00-$75.00**
(if on orange swirl label, 3:10 edition of "We Love You"), 1967 .... **$100.00-$150.00**
(with picture sleeve, add), 1967 .... **$300.00-$600.00**

906, "She's a Rainbow"/"2000 Light Years from Home," 1967 .... **$10.00-$20.00**
(if on orange swirl label, promo), 1967 .... **$50.00-$75.00**
(with picture sleeve, add), 1967 .... **$25.00-$50.00**

907, "In Another Land"/"The Lantern," 1967 .... **$12.50-$25.00**
(if on orange swirl label, promo), 1967 .... **$50.00-$75.00**
(with picture sleeve, add), 1967 .... **$40.00-$80.00**

908, "Jumpin' Jack Flash"/"Child of the Moon," 1968 .... **$7.50-$15.00**
(if on orange swirl label, promo), 1968 .... **$50.00-$75.00**
(with picture sleeve, add), 1968 .... **$20.00-$40.00**

909, "Street Fighting Man"/"No Expectations," 1968 .... **$10.00-$20.00**
(if on orange swirl label, promo), 1968 .... **$50.00-$75.00**
(with extremely rare picture sleeve, add), 1968 .... **$8,000.00-$10,000.00**

910, "Honky Tonk Women"/"You Can't Always Get What You Want," 1969 ......$7.50-$15.00
(with picture sleeve, add), 1969......$15.00-$30.00
Rolling Stones 19100, "Brown Sugar"/"Bitch," 1971......$2.50-$5.00
19101, "Wild Horses"/"Sway," 1971......$2.50-$5.00
(if mono-stereo full-length promo), 1971......$20.00-$30.00
(if long-short promo version), 1971......$30.00-$50.00
19103, "Tumbling Dice"/"Sweet Black Angel," 1972......$2.50-$5.00
(with tongue die-cut sleeve, add), 1972......$4.00-$8.00
19104, "Happy"/"All Down the Line," 1972......$2.50-$5.00
19105, "Silver Train"/"Angie" ("Silver Train" is Side One), 1973..$6.00-$12.00
(if above, "Angie" is listed as Side One, or no distinction to sides), 1973 ......$2.50-$5.00
19109, "Doo Doo Doo Doo Doo (Heartbreaker)"/"Dancing with Mr. D," 1973......$2.50-$5.00
19301, "It's Only Rock 'N' Roll (But I Like It)"/"Through the Lonely Nights," 1974......$2.50-$5.00
19302, "Ain't Too Proud to Beg"/"Dance Little Sister," 1974......$2.50-$5.00
19304, "Fool to Cry"/"Hot Stuff," 1976......$2.00-$4.00
(if promo, "Fool to Cry" same length on both sides), 1976......$20.00-$30.00
(if promo, "Fool to Cry" long-short versions), 1976......$25.00-$35.00
(if promo, "Fool to Cry" and "Hot Stuff" are both on disc), 1976 ......$100.00-$200.00
(if promo, "Hot Stuff" same length on both sides), 1976......$20.00-$30.00
(if promo, "Hot Stuff" long-short versions), 1976......$25.00-$35.00
19307, "Miss You"/"Far Away Eyes," 1978......$2.00-$4.00
(if promo, "Miss You" on both sides), 1978......$20.00-$30.00
(if promo, "Far Away Eyes" on both sides), 1978......$100.00-$250.00
(with picture sleeve, add), 1978......$2.00-$4.00
19309, "Beast of Burden"/"When the Whip Comes Down," 1978 ......$2.00-$4.00
(with extremely rare picture sleeve, add), 1978......$1,500.00-$2,000.00
19310, "Shattered"/"Everything Is Turning to Gold," 1978......$2.00-$4.00
(if promo), 1978......$10.00-$20.00
(with picture sleeve, add), 1978......$3.00-$6.00
20001, "Emotional Rescue"/"Down in the Hole," 1980......$2.00-$4.00
(with picture sleeve, add), 1980......$2.00-$4.00
21001, "She's So Cold"/"Send It to Me," 1980......$2.00-$4.00
(with picture sleeve, add), 1980......$3.00-$6.00
21003, "Start Me Up"/"No Use in Crying," 1981......$2.00-$4.00
(with picture sleeve, add), 1981......$2.00-$4.00
21004, "Waiting on a Friend"/"Little T & A," 1981......$2.00-$4.00
(with picture sleeve, add), 1981......$2.00-$4.00
21300, "Hang Fire"/"Neighbours," 1982......$2.00-$4.00
(with die-cut tongue sleeve, add), 1982......$4.00-$8.00
21301, "Going to A-Go-Go"/"Beast of Burden," 1982......$2.00-$4.00
(with picture sleeve, add), 1982......$2.00-$4.00
99978, "Time is On My Side"/"Twenty Flight Rock," 1982......$2.50-$5.00
(with picture sleeve, add), 1982......$2.50-$5.00
99813, "Undercover of the Night"/"All the Way Down," 1983......$1.50-$3.00
(with picture sleeve, add), 1983......$1.50-$3.00
99788, "She Was Hot"/"Think I'm Going Mad," 1984......$1.50-$3.00
(with picture sleeve, add), 1984......$1.50-$3.00
99724, "Too Tough"/"Miss You," 1984......$20.00-$40.00
38-05802, "Harlem Shuffle"/"Had It with You," 1986......$1.50-$3.00
(with picture sleeve, add), 1986......$1.50-$3.00
(with picture sleeve that says "Demonstration-Not For Sale," no B-side listed), 1986......$10.00-$20.00
38-05906, "One Hit (To the Body)"/"Fight," 1986......$1.50-$3.00
(with picture sleeve, add), 1986......$1.50-$3.00
(with picture sleeve that says "Demonstration-Not For Sale," no B-side listed), 1986......$10.00-$20.00
38-69008, "Mixed Emotions"/"Fancy Man Blues," 1989......$1.50-$3.00
38-73057, "Rock and a Hard Place"/"Cook Cook Blues," 1989....$1.50-$3.00
38-73093, "Almost Hear You Sigh"/"Break the Spell," 1989......$1.50-$3.00
38-73742, "Highwire"/"2000 Light Years from Home," 1991......$2.50-$5.00
38-73789, "Sexdrive"/"Undercover of the Night," 1991......$4.00-$8.00
Virgin NR-38446, "Love Is Strong"/"The Storm"/"Love Is Strong (Teddy Riley Remix)," 1994......$2.50-$5.00
(with picture sleeve, add), 1994......$2.50-$5.00
NR-38459, "Out of Tears" (2 versions)/"I'm Gonna Drive," 1994.$2.50-$5.00
(with picture sleeve, add), 1994......$2.50-$5.00
NR-38626, "Saint of Me"/"Anyway You Look At It," 1998......$1.00-$2.00
(with picture sleeve, add), 1998......$1.00-$2.00

Promotional 45s

London 9682-9823, 901-910, orange swirl label, 1964-69......$50.00-$75.00
Rolling Stones 19101-19307, mono-stereo versions of A-side or "edited"/"full-length" versions, 1971-78......$20.00-$30.00
20001-21301, same song on both sides, 1979-82......$10.00-$20.00

12-inch Singles

Rolling Stones PR 70, "Hot Stuff"/"Crazy Mama," black-blue splash vinyl, counterfeits have black spots in the blue vinyl areas), 1976......$40.00-$80.00
DSKO 119, "Miss You" (8:36) (same on both sides), 1978......$25.00-$50.00
DSKO 174, "Miss You" (8:34)/"Hot Stuff" (5:21), 1979......$20.00-$40.00
DK 4609, "Miss You"/"Far Away Eyes," with die-cut "The Rolling Stones Miss You" sleeve, 1978......$6.00-$12.00
(if above, with "Atlantic-Atco Disco" sleeve), 1978......$5.00-$10.00
PR 367, "Emotional Rescue" (2 versions), 1980......$20.00-$40.00
DMD 253, "If I Was a Dancer" (Dance Pt. II)/"Dance" (instrumental), 1981 ......$15.00-$30.00
PR 397, "Start Me Up" (same on both sides), 1981......$15.00-$30.00
PR 574, "She Was Hot"/"Think I'm Going Mad," 1983......$20.00-$40.00
DMD 685, "Undercover of the Night" (6:22) (album version 4:31) (yellow label promo), 1983......$7.50-$15.00
PR 692, "Too Much Blood" (3 versions), 1983......$10.00-$20.00
CAS 2275, "Harlem Shuffle" (same on both sides), 1986......$7.50-$15.00
44-05365, "Harlem Shuffle" (NY Mix)/(London Mix), 1986......$5.00-$10.00
CAS 2340, "One Hit (To the Body)" (2 versions), 1986......$10.00-$20.00
44-05388, "One Hit (To The Body)" (2 versions)/"Fight," 1986....$4.00-$8.00
44-73133, "Rock and a Hard Place" (3 versions and "Bonus Beats"), 1989 ......$7.50-$15.00
CAS 1765, "Mixed Emotions" (2 versions), 1989......$20.00-$40.00
CAS 4051, "Sexdrive" (3 versions), 1991......$30.00-$60.00
Virgin Y-38446, "Love is Strong" (6 versions), 1994......$4.00-$8.00
Y-38468, "You Got Me Rocking" (4 versions)/"Jump On Top of Me," 1995 ......$4.00-$8.00
SPRO-12746, "Anybody Seen My Baby?" (3 versions), 1997....$20.00-$40.00
SPRO-12788, "Saint of Me" (7 versions, 2 discs), 1988......$35.00-$70.00
Y-38626, "Saint of Me" (3 versions)/"Anyway You Look At It," 1998 ......$4.00-$8.00

Mono LPs

London LL 3375, England's Newest Hit Makers -The Rolling Stones
(maroon label, "Full Frequency Range Recording" inside horizontal lines that go through the center hole, lower left-hand corner of cover advertises a bonus photo), 1964......$150.00-$300.00
(maroon label, "London" unboxed at top), 1965......$30.00-$60.00
(maroon or red label, "London" boxed at top), 1966......$20.00-$40.00
LL 3402, 12 x 5
(maroon label, "London ffrr" in a box at top), 1964......$100.00-$200.00
(maroon label, "London" unboxed at top), 1964......$30.00-$60.00
(maroon label, "London" unboxed at top, blue vinyl pressing?), 1964 ......$7,500.00-$10,000.00
(maroon or red label, "London" boxed at top), 1965......$20.00-$40.00
LL 3420, The Rolling Stones, Now!
(maroon label, "London ffrr" in a box at top, add 20% for complete liner notes (or sticker) on back of cover, both columns of type about equal in length), 1965......$100.00-$200.00
(maroon label, "London" unboxed at top, no lines on label; add 20% for complete liner notes (or sticker) on back of cover, both columns of type about equal in length), 1965......$30.00-$60.00
(maroon label, "London" unboxed, "ffrr" ear above "London," "Full Frequency Range Recording" inside horizontal lines that go through the center hole), 1965......$200.00-$400.00
(maroon label, "London" unboxed, horizontal lines that go through the center hole, NO "ffrr" ear at top, NO "Full Frequency Range Recording" between horizontal lines), 1965......$200.00-$400.00
(red or maroon label, "London" boxed at top, edited liner notes—second column an inch shorter than first column), 1966......$20.00-$40.00
LL 3429, Out of Our Heads
(maroon label, "London ffrr" in a box at top), 1965......$100.00-$200.00
(maroon label, "London" unboxed at top), 1965......$20.00-$4.00
(red or maroon label, "London" boxed at top), 1966......$12.50-$25.00
LL 3451, December's Children (and Everybody's)
(maroon label, "London" unboxed at top), 1965......$20.00-$40.00
(maroon label, "London" boxed at top), 1966......$12.50-$25.00
LL 3476, Aftermath, 1966......$20.00-$40.00

NP 1, Big Hits (High Tide and Green Grass)
(with two lines of type on the front cover, all in small letters), 1966 ......**$4,000.00-$8,000.00**
(with five lines of type on the front cover, all in capital letters), 1966 ......**$20.00-$40.00**
NP 2, Their Satanic Majesties Request, 1967 ......**$125.00-$250.00**
LL 3493, Got Live If You Want It! 1966......**$20.00-$40.00**
LL 3499, Between the Buttons, 1967 ......**$20.00-$40.00**
LL 3509, Flowers, 1967......**$25.00-$50.00**
Any of the above titles, if "Digitally Remastered from Original Master Recording" on cover, red label, 1986......**$4.00-$8.00**
Rolling Stones COC 59100, Sticky Fingers (white label promo), 1971 ......**$250.00-$500.00**

Stereo LPs

London PS 375, England's Newest Hit Makers-The Rolling Stones
(if dark blue label, lower left-hand corner of cover advertises a bonus photo), 1964......**$150.00-$300.00**
(if dark blue label, "London" unboxed at top), 1965......**$12.50-$25.00**
PS 402, 12 x 5
(if dark blue label, "London" unboxed at top), 1964 ......**$12.50-$25.00**
(if dark blue label, "London" boxed at top), 1965......**$5.00-$10.00**
PS 420, The Rolling Stones, Now!
(dark blue label with "London" unboxed at top; add 205 for complete liner notes (or sticker) on back cover, both columns of type about equal in length), 1965 ......**$12.50-$25.00**
(dark blue label with "London" boxed at top; add 205 for censored liner notes (or sticker) on back cover, second column an inch shorter, "offensive" notes quietly restored in the 1970s), 1966 ......**$5.00-$10.00**
PS 429, Out of Our Heads
(if dark blue label, "London ffrr" in box at top, "Made in England by the Decca Record Co. Ltd." at top edge), 1965 ......**$50.00-$100.00**
(if dark blue label, "London" unboxed at top), 1965......**$12.50-$25.00**
(if dark blue label, "London" boxed at top), 1966......**$5.00-$10.00**
PS 451, December's Children (and Everybody's)
(if dark blue label, "London" unboxed at top), 1965......**$12.50-$25.00**
(if dark blue label, "London" boxed at top), 1966......**$5.00-$10.00**
PS 476, Aftermath, 1966 ......**$5.00-$10.00**
NPS 1, Big Hits (High Tide and Green Grass), 1966......**$5.00-$10.00**
PS 493, Got Live If You Want It!, 1966 ......**$5.00-$10.00**
PS 499, Between the Buttons, 1967......**$5.00-$10.00**
PS 509, Flowers, 1967 ......**$5.00-$10.00**
PS 539, Beggars Banquet
(if original "toilet graffiti" cover slick, not on a cover), 1968 ......**$5,000.00-$10,000.00**
(if all songs credited to "Jagger-Richard"), 1968......**$12.50-$25.00**
(if Rev. Wilkins, credited as composer of "Prodigal Son"), 1968 ......**$5.00-$10.00**
2PS 606/7, Hot Rocks 1964-1971 (2 LPs)
(if alternate mixes of "Brown Sugar" and "Wild Horses," "11-5-71" or "11-18-71" in the trail-off vinyl of side 4), 1971......**$500.00-$1,000.00**
(with regular mixes of all tracks), 1971......**$10.00-$20.00**
2PS 626/7, More Hot Rocks (Big Hits and Fazed Cookies) (2 LPs) 1972 ......**$10.00-$20.00**
NPS 2, Their Satanic Majesties Request
(with 3-D cover), 1967......**$20.00-$40.00**
(without 3-D cover), 197? ......**$4.00-$8.00**
NPS 3, Through the Past, Darkly (Big Hits Vol. 2)
(if hexagonal cover), 1969......**$5.00-$10.00**
(if square cover), 197? ......**$10.00-$20.00**
(if prototype picture disc, uses cover art from "Big Hits (High Tide and Green Grass)" either on one or both sides), 1969 ......**$4,500.00-$6,000.00**
NPS-4, Let It Bleed
(with poster), 1969 ......**$7.50-$15.00**
(without poster), 1969 ......**$5.00-$10.00**
(if after-hours pressing, multicolored vinyl, value is speculative), 1970 ......**$7,500.00-$10,000.00**
NPS-5, Get Yer Ya-Yas Out!, 1970......**$5.00-$10.00**
Rolling Stones COG 59100, Sticky Fingers
(with working zipper), 1971......**$6.00-$12.00**
(white label stereo promo), 1971......**$150.00-$300.00**
(if on Atlantic COG 39105, working zipper, reissue), 1977 ......**$5.00-$10.00**
(if on Atlantic COG 39105, photo of zipper), 1977 ......**$4.00-$8.00**
COG 59101, Goats Head Soup (with photo; deduct 25% if photo is absent), 1973......**$7.50-$15.00**
(if on Atlantic 39106, reissue), 1977......**$4.00-$8.00**
COG 2-2900, Exile on Main Street (2 LPs)
(if original covers, gatefold has to be opened to remove the records, add 33% to value if postcards still in package), 1972......**$7.50-$15.00**
(if reissue, two pockets, one for each record), 1973......**$6.00-$12.00**
COG 79101, It's Only Rock'n' Roll, 1974 ......**$5.00-$10.00**
COG 79102, Made in the Shade, 1975 ......**$5.00-$10.00**
(if on Atlantic COG 39107, reissue), 1977......**$4.00-$8.00**
COG 79104, Black and Blue, 1976 ......**$5.00-$10.00**
COG 2-9001, Love You Live (2 LPs), 1977......**$6.00-$12.00**
COG 39108, Some Girls
(first cover, shows all women's faces visible; nine different color schemes for front cover, value is equal), 1978......**$7.50-$15.00**
(if "cover under reconstruction"), 1978 ......**$5.00-$10.00**
COG 16015, Emotional Rescue
(with poster wrapped around the record jacket), 1980......**$7.50-$15.00**
(without poster), 1980 ......**$5.00-$10.00**
COG 16028, Sucking in the Seventies, 1981 ......**$5.00-$10.00**
COC 16052, Tattoo You, 1981 ......**$5.00-$10.00**
COG 39113, Still Life (American Concert 1981), 1982......**$5.00-$10.00**
90120, Undercover (with stickers), 1983......**$6.00-$12.00**
(without stickers), 1983 ......**$4.00-$8.00**
90176, Rewind (1971-1984), 1984 ......**$12.50-$25.00**
OC 40250, Dirty Work (add 50% if cover still has red shrink-wrap) 1986 ......**$4.00-$8.00**
OC 45333, Steel Wheels, 1989 ......**$5.00-$10.00**
C 47456, Flashpoint, 1991......**$10.00-$20.00**
Virgin V 2750, Voodoo Lounge (2 LPs), 1994......**$10.00-$20.00**
V 2801, Stripped (2 LPs), 1995 ......**$7.50-$15.00**
8 44712 1, Bridges to Babylon (2 LPs), 1997......**$7.50-$15.00**
8 46740 1, No Security (2 LPs), 1998......**$7.50-$15.00**
47863, Sticky Fingers (with working zipper), 1999......**$12.50-$25.00**
47864, Exile on Main St. (2 LPs, all original inserts), 1999......**$25.00-$50.00**
47867, Some Girls (with "cover under reconstruction" sleeve), 1999 ......**$12.50-$25.00**
Any title from 1970s reissued on CBS, single disc, 1986 ......**$4.00-$8.00**
Any 2-LP set from 1970s reissued on CBS, 1986 ......**$5.00-$10.00**

Section 4

Notable Collectible Labels

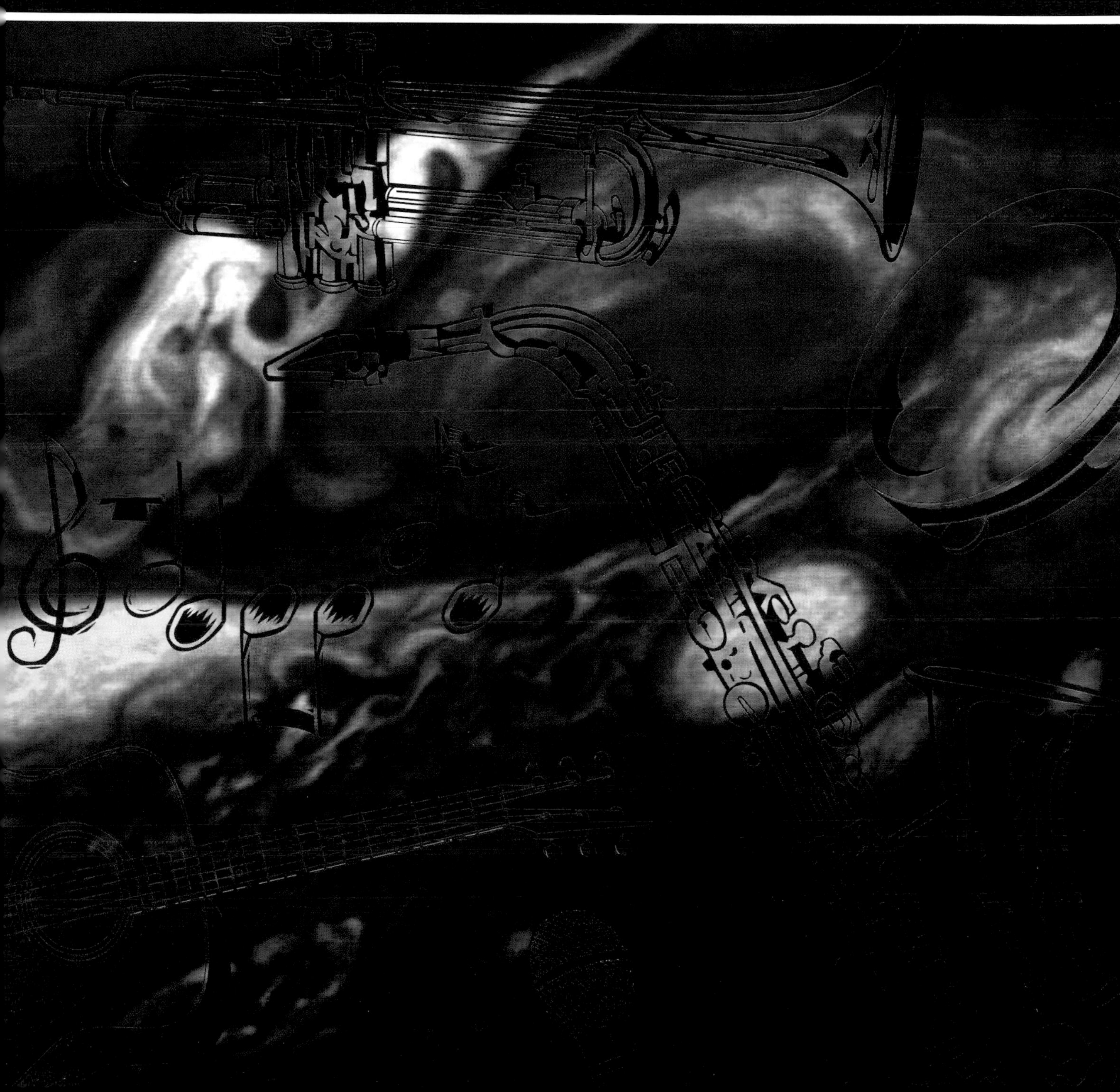

Chapter 30

Apple Records

History

Apple Corps Ltd. was born in early 1968, as an attempt by the Beatles to create their own corporate empire. Ostensibly, Apple was a record company, a clothing boutique, a book publishing company and an electronics firm. While the non-musical projects folded after only a few months, Apple Records survived for almost eight years. It was still around when the Beatles broke up in 1970, and was the home of all four Beatles' solo projects until 1975.

Apple was also the home for other groups, some of whom received songwriting and/or instrumental assistance by the Beatles, eventually achieving Top 10 hits of their own. The biggest of these "non-Beatles" groups on Apple was the band Badfinger. The British group, led by lead singer/songwriter Peter Ham, was originally signed to the Apple label as the Iveys, and charted with the song "Maybe Tomorrow," before being renamed. Badfinger was also one of the early proponents of "power pop," which combined intricate melodies and ear-catching hooks, laced with jangly guitar solos. The lyrics to power pop songs were intricate and emotional, mixing love ballads with passionate energy, throwing a wry rhyme or a terse verse into an unrestrained refrain. Badfinger originally benefited from their early association with the Beatles, but songs like "Day After Day" and "Baby Blue" showed they could produce hits on their own.

Another Apple success story is Welsh singer Mary Hopkin. In 1968, she took the old Russian folk song "Dear For Me" and, with new lyrics written by Paul McCartney, had a Top 5 hit with "Those Were The Days." Hopkin also hit the Top 40 with songs like "Goodbye" and "Temma Harbour." Other artists who recorded singles or albums for Apple include Ronnie Spector, who recorded a George

Apple Records' 45-RPM logo featured a green Granny Smith apple for the A-side. The B-side showed a sliced apple.

***$10**, VG+ condition*

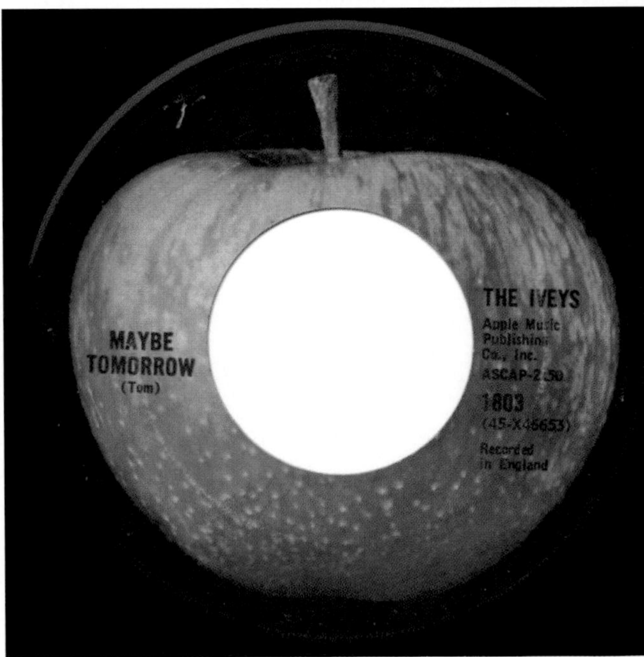

Badfinger's first charted hit, "Maybe Tomorrow," came when the group was originally known as the Iveys.

***$20**, NM condition*

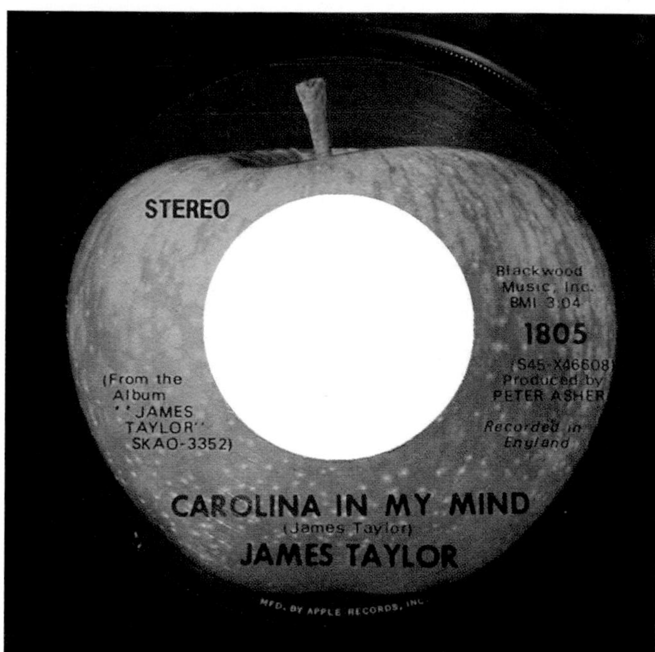

*James Taylor's first single, "Carolina in My Mind," on Apple. If the B-side is "Taking It In," the record can be worth as much as **$300** in near-mint condition.*

Harrison composition called "Try Some, Buy Some;" Billy Preston, whose Apple singles included a version of Harrison's "My Sweet Lord;" Jackie Lomax, a blue-eyed soul singer from Liverpool who once played the same small clubs and bars as the Beatles did in their formative years; and James Taylor, who had a minor chart hit with an early version of "Carolina In My Mind."

Between 1968 and 1970, Apple 45s contained a tiny

George Harrison's 3-LP boxed set, All Things Must Pass, was the first solo Beatles album to sell over a million copies. This album spiked in value when Harrison passed away in 2002; it has since returned to a more reasonable $40 near-mint price.

***$30**, VG+ condition*

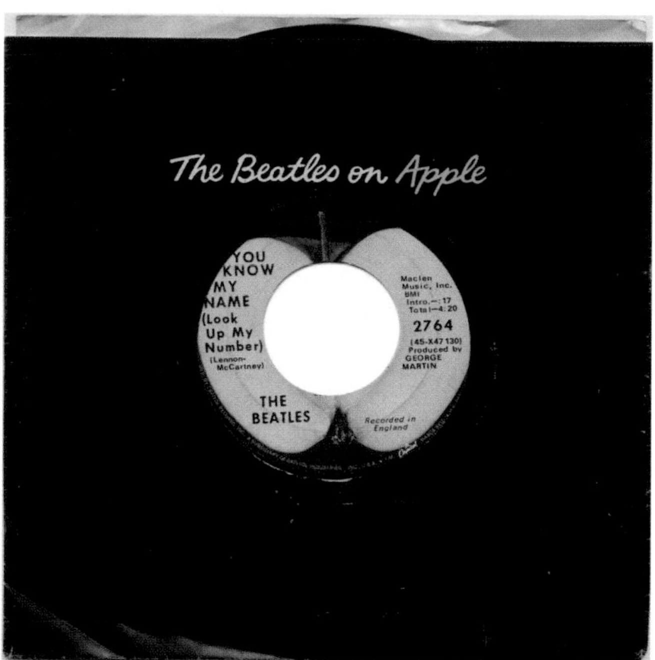

While most Apple artists received a generic Apple company sleeve, the Beatles were provided their own company sleeve. If you look at the perimeter of the label for this Beatles 45, the B-side of "Let It Be," you can see a tiny Capitol logo, denoting this record as an original first pressing and not a reissue.

***$8**, VG+ condition*

Capitol logo on the label's B-side. This is a key point in identifying the age of an Apple 45. In 1971, the Beatles' entire singles catalog, going back to "Love Me Do" and "Please Please Me," was re-released on Apple, and the Capitol logo disappeared from the B-side label. If these 1971 re-releases have a star on the A-side, they are worth $7.50 in VG condition, $30 in near-mint. Without the star,

The Beatles' "Free as a Bird," which resurrected the Fab Four's Apple label. Note that the 45 contains a small center hole; this allowed the record to be exported to England, where small holed-45s are the norm.

***$3**, VG+ condition*

their value drops to one-third of those pressings with a star. In 1975, the Beatles' entire Apple-Capitol singles catalog once again re-released; these recordings have the words "All Rights Reserved" on the label, and are worth $3.75 to $15, depending on condition.

After the Beatles broke up, the four solo members remained signed with Apple, and released some of the most memorable albums with that imprint. The rarity of these albums and 45s depends mostly on the popularity of the initial release. For example, George Harrison's triple-disc opus, *All Things Must Pass*, was a million-selling album. However, to qualify as a near-mint pressing, the album must still contain its poster and lyric-sheet album sleeves, and the box cover must still be intact, with no splits, rips or surface wear.

After 1976, Apple Records remained silent for almost 20 years. In 1996, however, the label was resurrected as the imprint for the Beatles' *Live at the BBC* album and three double-disc *Anthology* releases, as well as for the 45s "Baby, It's You," "Free As A Bird," and "Real Love."

What To Look For

The Beatles' material will always be collectible, no matter what label they appear on. Apple's single releases were first pressed with a black star on the "A" side—these first pressings command higher prices than non-starred material. In 1975, Apple re-released their entire Beatles and solo artist catalog. These reissues are identified by the words "All Rights Reserved" on the label.

Beatles picture sleeves are always collectible, and picture sleeves from their Apple labelmates are also desirable. Since Apple was distributed by Capitol, and Capitol releases had a grooved, gear-like ridge along the label, many of these picture sleeves will have a circular groove or wear pattern in their center. This wear pattern automatically brings the sleeve down one grade—a near-mint sleeve containing this wear pattern is downgraded to VG+.

Until 1976, all four Beatles released their solo works on Apple. When a Beatle moved on to another record company, the receiving label often re-released the original Apple solo albums with a new record company imprint. For example, Paul McCartney's *McCartney* album exists with an Apple label—as well as on Columbia and Capitol labels, his post-Apple destinations.

Apple's promotional 45s have a mono version of the artist's hit on the A-side, while a stereo pressing will exist on the B-side. They are very collectible, as are Apple's promotional sleeves.

Photo credit: Courtesy Last Vestige Music Store, Albany, N.Y.

Look at the center of this picture sleeve for John Lennon's "Instant Karma." You can see the geared edge that perforated the sleeve around Lennon's face. Finding copies without this geared edge is difficult.

***$5**, Fair condition*

Ringo Starr's most successful post-Beatles pop chart run came with a series of albums and singles produced by Richard Perry.

***$10**, VG+ condition*

Books

Spizer, Bruce, *The Beatles on Apple Records*, 498 Productions, New Orleans, La., 2003.

Wiener, Allen I., *The Beatles: The Ultimate Recording Guide* (3rd Revised Ed.), Bob Adams, Inc., Holbrook, MA, 1994.

Web Pages

Mitch McGeary's Beatles Web site, which contains label scans of many Apple artists: http://www.rarebeatles.com.

A listing of all the Apple albums, at this Web site: http://meltingpot.fortunecity.com/kirkland/266/apple/applp.htm

ARTIST VG+ to NM

BADFINGER:

45s

Apple 1815, "Come and Get It"/"Rock of All Ages," 1969 ....**$3.00-$6.00**
(if Capitol logo on B-side of label), 1969..**$4.00-$8.00**
1822, "No Matter What"/"Carry On Till Tomorrow," 1970..........**$3.00-$6.00**
(with star on A-side of label), 1970 ....**$10.00-$20.00**
1841, "Day After Day"/"Money," 1971 ....**$3.00-$6.00**
(with star on A-side of label), 1971 ....**$10.00-$20.00**
(if white label promo), 1971 ....**$60.00-$120.00**

LPs

Apple ST-3364, Magic Christian Music, 1970..........................**$10.00-$20.00**
(if Capitol logo on bottom of side 2 label), 1970 ....**$15.00-$30.00**

THE BEATLES:

45s

Apple 2276, "Hey Jude"/"Revolution"
(if small Capitol logo on bottom of B-side of label), 1968...........**$7.50-$15.00**
(if "Mfd. by Apple" on label), 1968 ....**$5.00-$10.00**
(if "All Rights Reserved" on label), 1975 ....**$10.00-$20.00**
2490, "Get Back"/"Don't Let Me Down"
(if small Capitol logo on bottom of B-side of label), 1969 ....**$5.00-$10.00**
(if "Mfd. by Apple" on label) , 1969...**$5.00-$10.00**
(if "All Rights Reserved" on label), 1975.................................**$10.00-$20.00**
2764, "Let It Be"/"You Know My Name (Look Up My Number)"
(if small Capitol logo on bottom of B-side of label), 1970 ....**$6.00-$12.00**
(if "Mfd. by Apple" on label), 1970 ....**$5.00-$10.00**
(if "All Rights Reserved" on label), 1975.................................**$10.00-$20.00**
(with picture sleeve, add), 1970...**$50.00-$100.00**
2832, "The Long and Winding Road"/"For You Blue"
(if small Capitol logo on bottom of B-side of label), 1970 ......**$10.00-$20.00**
(if "Mfd. by Apple" on label), 1970 ....**$5.00-$10.00**
(if "All Rights Reserved" on label), 1975.................................**$10.00-$20.00**
(with picture sleeve, add), 1970...**$50.00-$100.00**
58348, "Baby It's You"/"I'll Follow the Sun"/"Devil in Her Heart"/"Boys," 1995 ....**$2.00-$4.00**
(with picture sleeve, add), 1995..**$2.00-$4.00**
58497, "Free as a Bird"/"Christmas Time (Is Here Again)" (small-holed 45), 1995 ....**$2.00-$4.00**
(with picture sleeve, add), 1995..**$2.00-$4.00**
58544, "Real Love"/"Baby's in Black (Live)" (small-holed 45), 1996 ....**$1.50-$3.00**
(with picture sleeve, add), 1996..**$1.50-$3.00**

LPs

Apple SBC-100, The Beatles' Christmas Album (compilation of fan club Christmas messages, counterfeits exist), 1970 ....**$200.00-$400.00**
SWBO-101, The Beatles ("The White Album")
(if numbered copy, four individual posters and large poster; ringwear often appears on album, lower serial numbers have higher value), 1968 ....**$75.00-$200.00**
(if unnumbered copy, four individual posters and large poster), 197? ....**$30.00-$60.00**
(if "All Rights Reserved" on labels, title in black on cover, photos and poster on thinner paper stock), 1975 ....**$35.00-$70.00**
SW-153, Yellow Submarine
(with Capitol logo on bottom of side 2), 1969 ....**$25.00-$50.00**
(if "Mfd. by Apple" on label), 1971 ....**$10.00-$20.00**
(if "All Rights Reserved" on label), 1975.................................**$12.50-$25.00**
SW-385, Hey Jude
(if "Mfd. by Apple" on label, label lists LP as "Hey Jude"), 1970 ....**$10.00-$20.00**
(if label lists LP as "The Beatles Again," catalog on label is SW-385), 1970 ....**$12.50-$25.00**
(if label lists LP as "The Beatles Again," catalog on label is SO-385), 1970 ....**$20.00-$40.00**
(with Capitol logo on bottom of side 2, label lists LP as "Hey Jude"), 1970 ....**$37.50-$75.00**
(with "All Rights Reserved" on label, label lists LP as "Hey Jude"), 1975 ....**$12.50-$25.00**
AR-34001, Let It Be (red Apple label, "Bell Sound" stamped in dead wax), 1970 ....**$12.50-$25.00**
C1-8-34445, Anthology 1 (3 LPs), 1995 ....**$20.00-$40.00**
C1-8-34448, Anthology 2 (3 LPs), 1996 ....**$20.00-$40.00**
C1-8-34451, Anthology 3 (3 LPs), 1996 ....**$15.00-$30.00**

GEORGE HARRISON:

45s

Apple 1828, "What Is Life"/"Apple Scruffs," 1971 ....**$4.00-$8.00**
(with star on A-side of label), 1971 ....**$7.50-$15.00**
(with picture sleeve, add), 1971 ....**$20.00-$40.00**
1836, "Bangla-Desh"/"Deep Blue," 1971 ....**$4.00-$8.00**
(with star on A-side of label), 1971 ....**$12.50-$25.00**
(with picture sleeve, add), 1971...**$10.00-$20.00**
1862, "Give Me Love (Give Me Peace on Earth)"/"Miss O'Dell"
(if B-side time is 2:20, correct), 1973...**$4.00-$8.00**
(if B-side time is 2:30, incorrect), 1973 ....**$4.00-$8.00**
(if white label promo, "Give Me Love" on both sides, mono/stereo versions), 1973..**$25.00-$50.00**
1877, "Dark Horse"/"I Don't Care Anymore"
(if light blue-white custom label), 1974...**$4.00-$8.00**
(if white label, stock copy), 1974...**$5.00-$10.00**
(with picture sleeve, add), 1974..**$40.00-$80.00**
(if on Apple P-1877, white label promo, "Dark Horse" on both sides, full length mono/stereo versions), 1974 ....**$20.00-$40.00**
(if on Apple P-1877, white label promo, "Dark Horse" on both sides, edited mono/stereo versions), 1974 ....**$30.00-$60.00**

LPs

Apple ST-3350, Wonderwall Music
(if "Mfd. by Apple" on label), 1968 ....**$12.50-$25.00**
(with Capitol logo on bottom of side 2 label), 1968 ....**$75.00-$150.00**
(with bonus photo, add), 1968 ....**$2.50-$5.00**
STCH-639, All Things Must Pass (3 LPs) (custom inner sleeves and poster), 1970 ....**$20.00-$40.00**

MARY HOPKIN:

45s

Apple 1801, "Those Were the Days"/"Turn, Turn, Turn," 1968 ....**$5.00-$10.00**
1806, "Goodbye"/"Sparrow," 1969 ....**$4.00-$8.00**
(with picture sleeve, add), 1969...**$6.00-$12.00**
1816, "Temma Harbour"/"Lantano Dagli Occhi," 1970...............**$4.00-$8.00**
(with picture sleeve, add), 1970...**$6.00-$12.00**
1823, "Que Sera, Sera (Whatever Will Be, Will Be)"/"Fields of St. Etienne," 1970..**$4.00-$8.00**
1825, "Think About Your Children"/"Heritage," 1970..................**$4.00-$8.00**
(if A-side has star on label), 1970 ....**$6.00-$12.00**
(with picture sleeve, add), 1970...**$6.00-$12.00**
1843, "Water, Paper and Clay"/"Streets of London," 1972 ....**$4.00-$8.00**
(if A-side has star on label), 1972 ....**$6.00-$12.00**
1855, "Knock Knock Who's There"/"International," 1972 ....**$4.00-$8.00**

LPs

Apple ST-3351, Post Card, 1969 ....**$12.50-$25.00**
(if on Apple ST-5-3351, Capitol Record Club Edition), 1969 ....**$15.00-$30.00**
SMAS-3381, Earth Song/Ocean Song, 1970..........................**$12.50-$25.00**
SW-3395, Those Were the Days, 1972 ....**$20.00-$40.00**

THE IVEYS:

45s

Apple 1803, "Maybe Tomorrow"/"And Her Daddy's a Millionaire," 1969 .... **$10.00-$20.00**

(with star on A-side of label), 1969 .... **$15.00-$30.00**

LPs

Apple ST-3355, Maybe Tomorrow (album not released in America, price is for an American LP slick, which does exist), 1969 .... **$1,000.00-$2,000.00**

JOHN LENNON/PLASTIC ONO BAND:

45s

Apple 1809, "Give Peace a Chance"/"Remember Love," 1969 .... **$2.50-$5.00**

(with picture sleeve, add), 1969 .... **$7.50-$15.00**

1813, "Cold Turkey"/"Don't Worry Kyoko (Mummy's Only Looking for a Hand in the Snow)"

(if copy skips on A-side on the third chorus because of a pressing defect) , 1969 .... **$2.50-$5.00**

(if label has wider, bolder print, pressings don't skip), 1969 .... **$5.00-$10.00**

(with picture sleeve, add), 1969 .... **$20.00-$40.00**

1818, "Instant Karma! (We All Shine On)"/Yoko Ono Lennon, "Who Has Seen the Wind?," 1970 .... **$2.00-$4.00**

(if white label promo, "Instant Karma!" on one side, B-side blank), 1970 .... **$100.00-$200.00**

(with picture sleeve, add), 1970 .... **$7.50-$15.00**

1840, "Imagine"/"It's So Hard"

(if tan label), 1971 .... **$4.00-$8.00**

(if green label, "All Rights Reserved"), 1975 .... **$6.00-$12.00**

1842, "Happy Xmas (War Is Over)"/"Listen, the Snow Is Falling"

(if green vinyl, Apple label), 1971 .... **$5.00-$10.00**

(if green vinyl, faces label), 1971 .... **$7.50-$15.00**

(with picture sleeve, add), 1971 .... **$10.00-$20.00**

(if on Apple S45X-47663/4, white label promo on styrene pressing) .... **$400.00-$800.00**

LPs

Apple T-5001, Two Virgins — Unfinished Music No. 1

(without brown bag), 1968 .... **$25.00-$50.00**

(with die-cut bag), 1968 .... **$75.00-$150.00**

(with brown bag), 1968 .... **$75.00-$150.00**

(with flat label, reissue), 1985 .... **$7.50-$15.00**

SMAX-3361, Wedding Album (contains photo strip, postcard, poster of wedding photos, poster of lithographs, "Bagism" bag, booklet, photo of slice of wedding cake. Missing inserts reduce the value), 1969 .... **$75.00-$150.00**

SVBB-3392, Some Time in New York City (2 LPs), 1972 .... **$15.00-$30.00**

(if white label promo), 1972 .... **$500.00-$1,000.00**

JACKIE LOMAX:

45s

Apple 1802, "Sour Milk Sea"/"The Eagle Laughs at You"

(B-side author may be either Jackie Lomax or George Harrison, value is equal), 1968 .... **$10.00-$20.00**

1807, "New Day"/"Thumbin' a Ride," 1969 .... **$30.00-$60.00**

(if A-side has star on label), 1969 .... **$37.50-$75.00**

1819, "How the Web Was Woven"/"I Fall Inside Your Eyes," 1970 .... **$4.00-$8.00**

(with picture sleeve, add), 1970 .... **$5.00-$10.00**

LPs

Apple ST-3354, Is This What You Want?, 1969 .... **$12.50-$25.00**

PAUL McCARTNEY (AND WINGS):

45s

Apple 1829, "Another Day"/"Oh Woman, Oh Why," 1971 .... **$4.00-$8.00**

(if A-side has star on label), 1971 .... **$6.00-$12.00**

1847, "Give Ireland Back to the Irish"/"Give Ireland Back to the Irish" (Version), 1972 .... **$5.00-$10.00**

(with picture sleeve with large center hole, add), 1972 .... **$15.00-$30.00**

1851, "Mary Had a Little Lamb"/"Little Woman Love," 1972 .... **$5.00-$10.00**

(if white label promo, artist is "Paul McCartney," not "Wings"), 1972 .... **$150.00-$300.00**

(with picture sleeve, mentions "Little Woman Love," add), 1972 .... **$20.00-$40.00**

(with picture sleeve, no mention of "Little Woman Love," add), 1972 .... **$12.50-$25.00**

1861, "My Love"/"The Mess," 1973 .... **$4.00-$8.00**

(if white label promo), 1973 .... **$100.00-$200.00**

1863, "Live and Let Die"/"I Lie Around," 1973 .... **$4.00-$8.00**

1869, "Helen Wheels"/"Country Dreamer," 1973 .... **$4.00-$8.00**

(if white label promo, both songs listed), 1974 .... **$1,000.00-$2,000.00**

(if on Apple PRO-6786, "Helen Wheels" on both sides, mono/stereo), 1973 .... **$25.00-$50.00**

(if on Apple PRO-6787, "Country Dreamer" on both sides, mono/stereo), 1973 .... **$200.00-$400.00**

LPs

Apple STAO-3363, McCartney

(if only "McCartney" on label; back cover does NOT say "An Abkco managed company"), 1970 .... **$10.00-$20.00**

(if "McCartney" and "Paul McCartney" on separate lines on label; New York address on back cover), 1970 .... **$12.50-$25.00**

(if only "McCartney" on label; back cover says "An Abkco managed company"), 1970 .... **$12.50-$25.00**

(if "McCartney" and "Paul McCartney" on separate lines on label; California address on back cover), 1970 .... **$15.00-$30.00**

(if Apple label, small Capitol logo on B-side), 1970 .... **$40.00-$80.00**

(if on Apple SMAS-3363, new prefix), 197? .... **$10.00-$20.00**

(if on Apple SMAS-3363, "All Rights Reserved" on label), 1975 .... **$50.00-$100.00**

YOKO ONO:

45s

Apple GM/OYB-1, "Greenfield Morning"/"Open Your Box" (six copies pressed for Yoko Ono's personal use and distribution), 1971 .... **$400.00-$800.00**

1859, "Death of Samantha"/"Yang Yang," 1973 .... **$3.50-$7.00**

1867, "Woman Power"/"Men, Men, Men," 1973 .... **$3.50-$7.00**

LPs

Apple SW-3373, Yoko Ono Plastic Ono Band, 1970 .... **$10.00-$20.00**

SVBB-3380, Fly (2 LPs), 1971 .... **$12.50-$25.00**

SVBB-3399, Approximately Infinite Universe (2 LPs), 1973 .... **$12.50-$25.00**

SW-3412, Feeling the Space, 1973 .... **$10.00-$20.00**

BILLY PRESTON:

45s

Apple 1808, "That's the Way God Planned It"/"What About You," 1969 .... **$4.00-$8.00**

(if "Mono" on both sides of record, reference to the LP), 1972 .... **$4.00-$8.00**

(with picture sleeve, add), 1969 .... **$5.00-$10.00**

(if on Apple P-1808/PRO-6555, "That's The Way God Planned It," mono/stereo versions), 1969 .... **$30.00-$60.00**

LPs

Apple ST-3359, That's the Way God Planned It

(if cover has close-up of Billy Preston), 1969 .... **$25.00-$50.00**

(if cover has multiple images of Billy Preston), 1972 .... **$10.00-$20.00**

RINGO STARR:

45s

Apple 2969, "Beaucoups of Blues"/"Coochy-Coochy"

(if "Mfd. by Apple" on label, no star on label), 1970 .... **$4.00-$8.00**

(if small Capitol logo on bottom of B-side label, star on A-side of label), 1970 .... **$12.50-$25.00**

(if "Mfd. by Apple" on label, star on A-side of label), 1970 .... **$20.00-$40.00**

(with picture sleeve with correct catalog number Apple 2969, add), 1970 .... **$25.00-$50.00**

(if picture sleeve has incorrect catalog number Apple 1826, add), 1970 .... **$20.00-$40.00**

LPs

Apple SW-3365, Sentimental Journey, 1970 .... **$10.00-$20.00**

SMAS-3368, Beaucoups of Blues, 1970 .... **$10.00-$20.00**

SW-3417, Goodnight Vienna, 1974 .... **$6.00-$12.00**

SW-3422, Blast from Your Past, 1975 .... **$7.50-$15.00**

JAMES TAYLOR:

45s

Apple 1805, "Carolina in My Mind"/"Taking It In," 1969 .... **$150.00-$300.00**

(if promo, A-side erroneously listed as "Carolina ON My Mind"), 1970 .... **$15.00-$30.00**

1805, "Carolina in My Mind"/"Something's Wrong," 1970 .... **$4.00-$8.00**

(with star on A-side of label), 1970 .... **$5.00-$10.00**

LPs

Apple SKAO-3352, James Taylor

(if title in black print), 1969 .... **$12.50-$25.00**

(if title in orange print), 1970 .... **$10.00-$20.00**

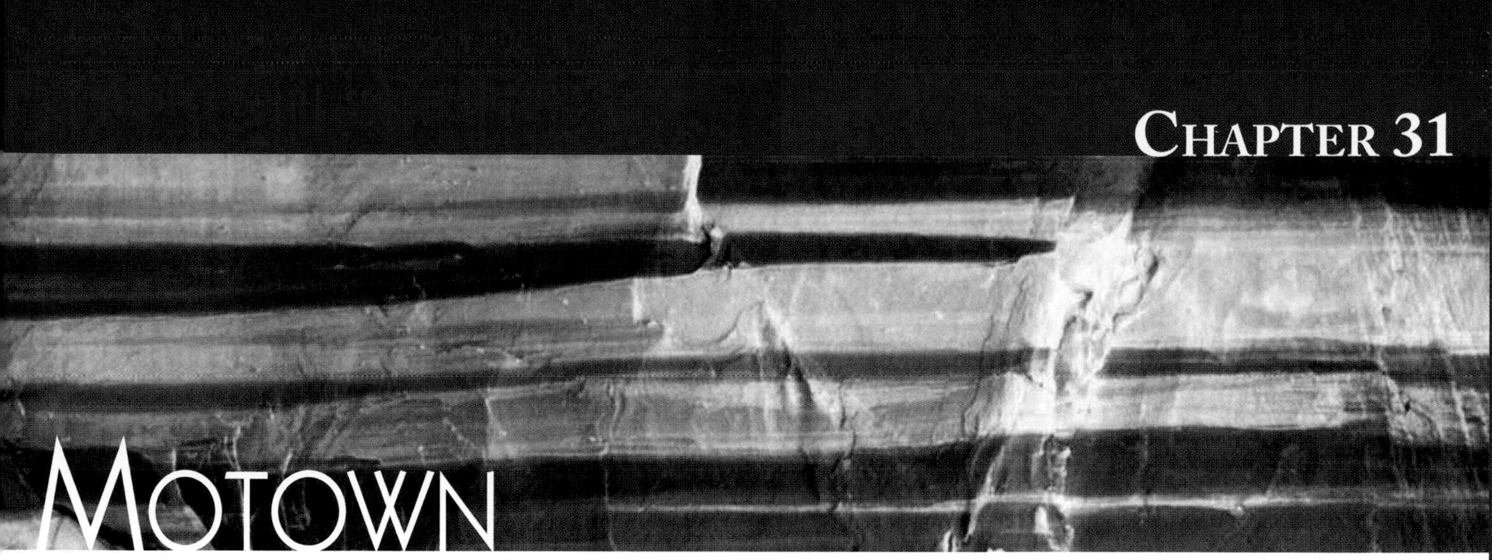

Chapter 31

Motown

History

From its inception, Motown was a success in both business and in music. Its fusion of black soul and white pop was as dominant during the 1960s as the music of the Beatles or the Rolling Stones. The singing groups that formed Motown's musical core—the Supremes, the Temptations, the Four Tops, Smokey Robinson and the Miracles, Stevie Wonder, Marvin Gaye, the Jackson Five—were part of a sound that, for lack of any other descriptive term, came to be known as the "Motown Sound."

Motown Records, as well as its sister labels Tamla and Gordy, were created by Berry Gordy, Jr., in 1958. After several songs Gordy wrote for Jackie Wilson, including "Reet Petite" and "Lonely Teardrops," became big hits, Gordy left his job at the Detroit Lincoln-Mercury assembly line to form his own recording studio and record company, Tamla Records. Tamla's earliest recordings were eventually licensed to other national labels, including Marv Johnson's "Come To Me" on United Artists, and the Miracles' "Bad Girl" on Chess. But by 1960, Gordy stopped licensing tracks to other labels, instead concentrating on making Tamla a national label.

Tamla's first successful group was the Miracles. Led by tenor William "Smokey" Robinson, the Miracles evolved from a successful doo-wop group to a pop-soul band that regularly dominated the pop charts. Songs like "Shop Around," "Mickey's Monkey," "You Really Got A Hold On Me," and "What's So Good About Good-By" established the Miracles as Gordy's first superstars, and helped pave the way for Gordy's other acts. Eventually Berry Gordy moved his record company into a house at 2648 West Grand Boulevard, which became as important an address

A picture sleeve for one of Motown's biggest hitmakers, the Supremes. Motown often used the "titles on top, picture on the bottom" artwork template for its sleeves in the 1960s.

***$20**, for VG+ sleeve*

Photo credit: From the collection of Scott Primeau, Primeau Music Corp.

The Miracles' first hit, "Got a Job," was licensed to George Goldner's End label, and is shown here on an extremely rare 78-RPM pressing.

***$150**, NM condition*

Marvin Gaye's second album, Stubborn Kind of Fellow, *features background vocals from Martha and the Vandellas on the title track. It also features several of his early hits, including "Hitch Hike" and "Pride and Joy," as well as "Wherever I Lay My Hat (That's My Home)," which British soul singer Paul Young would record as a UK #1 hit.*

***$450**, VG+ condition*

It was not uncommon for Motown's top acts to collaborate on hits—Marvin Gaye recorded with many of Motown's leading female singers. This superstar collaboration features Motown's top two singing groups at the time, the Temptations and Diana Ross & the Supremes.

***$7**, NM condition*

in popular music as the Cavern Club, Graceland, or the Fillmore East.

Other groups in Tamla's early years included the Marvelettes, a four-member girl group from Detroit's Inkster High School who brought the company its first chart-topper, "Please Mr. Postman," as well as Marvin Gaye, a charismatic solo singer whose voice drove women crazy in hits like "Pride and Joy" and "Can I Get A Witness."

Eventually two other labels appeared from the company—Gordy Records, named after the founder; and Motown Records, from the nickname for Detroit. Gordy Records made its initial splash with the Contours' raucous "Do You Love Me," while Motown's first big star, Mary Wells, cooed a series of up-tempo ballads like "Bye By Baby," "You Beat Me To The Punch," and "Two Lovers."

In 1963, a blind piano/harmonica player named Stevie Wonder joined the Motown lineup. His recording of "Fingertips" became the first concert recording to top the pop charts, beginning a 40-year-long association with Berry Gordy's record company. Wonder would eventually grow from a child prodigy to a musical *wunderkind*, embracing soul, pop, funk and rock into albums filled with new grooves and beats. Some of Stevie Wonder's biggest hits in the 1960s included "Uptight—Everything's Alright," "For Once In My Life," "A Place In The Sun," and "Signed, Sealed, Delivered, I'm Yours."

But Motown's biggest artists made their claim to fame in 1964. That's when the Supremes, after recording a dozen singles that failed to chart, finally broke through with their #1 hit "Baby Love." The Supremes would have five straight #1 songs in a row, and twelve #1 songs overall. What began as three girls from Detroit's Brewster housing projects developed into a trio of international singing superstars, playing Las Vegas and the *Ed Sullivan* show on a regular basis.

1964 was also the year when the Temptations established themselves as hit makers extraordinaire. The group was formed in 1960, as the merger of two vocal groups, the Primes and the Elgins. With the dueling lead vocal skills of David Ruffin and Eddie Kendricks, the Temptations had major hits with songs like "The Way You Do the Things You Do," "Beauty Is Only Skin Deep," and their #1 smash, "My Girl."

One could argue that Motown was a solitary recording act with multiple lead singers. Whether the vocalists were the Supremes or the Vandellas, the Temptations or the Miracles, the Motown house band provided top-of-the-line musicianship for all of them. Led by keyboardist Earl Van Dyke, the house band consisted of bassist James Jamerson, guitarists Robert White and Joe Messina, and drummer Benny Benjamin. It's their orchestrations that can be heard on nearly every Motown record during the 1960s. Their ability to tailor their musical style for each artist—whether it was the party-dance sound of Martha Reeves and the Vandellas, the icy roughness of Marvin Gaye, or the emotional cries of the Four Tops—provided their artists with a flexibility previously unheard of in studio bands.

Motown could also take pride in its songwriting teams. The Brian Holland-Lamont Dozier-Eddie Holland triumvirate composed chart-topping smashes for Diana Ross and the Supremes, while Norman Whitfield and

Barrett Strong gave the Temptations some of their greatest hits. Another songwriting duo, Nickolas Ashford and Valerie Simpson, wrote their first big hits for the duo of Marvin Gaye and Tammi Terrell.

Not only was one expected to be a top-notch singer in the Motown stable, one also had to be able to perform on stage. Everything, from the Supremes' hand-signals during "Stop! In the Name of Love," to the Temptations' dance steps during "My Girl," were choreographed by Motown's Cholly Atkins. Artists were groomed on everything from stage appearance to diction, as Gordy wanted his stars to appeal both to black and white audiences.

By the late 1960s, Motown was a dominant force on the pop and soul charts. Songs like Marvin Gaye's "I Heard It Through The Grapevine," Smokey Robinson and the Miracles' "The Tears of a Clown," the Temptations' "Just My Imagination (Running Away With Me)," and Diana Ross and the Supremes' "Love Child" were part of every radio station's play lists.

The 1970s were a time of sweeping change in the Motown studios. Albums full of three-minute pop songs, a formula that had sustained Motown's album division for over a decade, changed as Marvin Gaye's social awareness album *What's Goin' On* and Stevie Wonder's innovative double-LP *Songs in the Key of Life* both topped the album charts. Motown itself moved in a different direction, as Berry Gordy moved his musical hit factory to Los Angeles in 1972, in an effort to help Motown enter the motion picture industry, and to establish Diana Ross as an actress.

While Diana Ross did have major hits in the 1970s, including "Ain't No Mountain High Enough," "Love Hangover" and "Theme From 'Mahogany' (Do You Know Where You're Going To)," the group she left, the Supremes, continued to have major hits, including "Up The Ladder To The Roof," "Nathan Jones," and "Stoned Love."

In fact, during the 1970s, many of Motown's greatest acts splintered apart, yet still were able to garner Top 10 hits. Such successes included former Temptations Eddie Kendricks ("Keep On Truckin'") and David Ruffin ("Walk Away From Love"); both Smokey Robinson ("Cruisin'") and the Miracles ("Love Machine"); and the Jackson 5's Jermaine Jackson ("Let's Get Serious") and Michael Jackson ("Ben," "Rockin' Robin").

In the 1980s, Motown's most successful stars were Stevie Wonder, Lionel Richie, and Rick James. Wonder continued to dominate the pop, soul and adult contemporary charts with songs like, "I Just Called To Say I Love You," "That Girl" and "Part-Time Lover." Lionel Richie, the former lead singer of the Commodores, strung together a series of number one ballads like "Truly," "You Are," "My Love," and "All Night Long (All Night)."

Today, Motown is a subsidiary of Universal Music Group, and Berry Gordy has long since sold his stock in the company. The label still continues on, however, as artists like Boyz II Men, Erykah Badu, and Brian McKnight continue the tradition that began with Berry Gordy and the house-turned studio on 2648 West Grand Boulevard.

The Temptations' "Ain't Too Proud to Beg" on Gordy, featuring Eddie Kendrick on lead vocal. After working with several Motown songwriters, including Smokey Robinson, this was the Temptations' first hit with songwriters Norman Whitfield and Barrett Strong.

***$5**, VG condition*

When Motown purchased Detroit's tiny Ric-Tic label, Edwin Starr was one of the label's performers. His biggest hit for Gordy, "War," was covered by such diverse artists as the Jam and Bruce Springsteen.

***$4**, VG condition*

The late Rick James' "Street Songs" featured his hits "Super Freak" and "Give It To Me Baby," as well as a duet with Motown soul singer Teena Marie on "Fire and Desire."

***$6**, VG+ condition*

As Motown Records entered the 21st century, their 45s abandoned the full-color "Map of Detroit" artwork, in favor of a simple stylized "M" logo. The label artwork also noted that Motown is one of many record companies under the aegis of Universal Music.

***$4**, NM condition*

What To Look For

The most collectible Motown/Tamla/Gordy recordings are the earliest ones. The pre-1964 recordings by artists such as Marv Johnson, Mary Wells, the Miracles, Eddie Holland, the Elgins, and "Little" Stevie Wonder are difficult to find. Early albums by these groups are also collectible; be aware that Motown has reissued their back catalog many times, and will often place a "originally recorded" statement, along with its date of original release, on the back of the album jacket.

The earliest Tamla and Motown record labels have vertical lines. From 1962 to 1964, Tamla used a tan label with two circles at the top; one circle was a globe, the other was the name "TAMLA." From 1964 until the label was shut down in the mid-1980s, the word "TAMLA" appeared in a box at the top of the 45 label.

Motown went from their vertical lines label to a map of Detroit in 1962, with the word "MOTOWN," in red-gold-green letters, superimposed over the map. The bottom of the label was a dark blue, with the recording information stamped in white or silver.

Gordy Records, the home of the Temptations and Rick James, originally had the name "Gordy" in script at the 12:00 of the label, with the words "It's what's in the grooves that count" surrounding the "Gordy." By 1965, that was replaced with a magenta label and a yellow triangle running from the label's 9:00 edge to the 3:00 edge. The word "GORDY" appeared inside the triangle, with a large "G" as part of the artwork.

The 1960s Motown classics were recorded to be heard on AM car radios. Because of this, many of Motown's greatest songs sound better in mono than in stereo. Some of the stereo recordings were rechanneled, putting the drums in one speaker and the rest of the instruments in the other. On Marvin Gaye's "I Heard It Through The

The Miracles' picture sleeves can run anywhere from $150-$200 in near-mint condition. This sleeve for their 1961 hit "Everybody's Gotta Pay Some Dues" is the group's most collectible picture sleeve.

***$50**, VG+ condition*

Grapevine," Gaye's voice is in both speakers, but the drums are in the left channel and the strings are in the right.

Some records are surprisingly expensive on the collectible market. One of the reasons is that many Motown records that did not become hits upon their first release eventually became hits overseas, in the "Northern Soul" British dance clubs. This makes the few copies that were pressed extremely rare today. Other times, a song was pulled from production at the last minute, many times for reasons known only to Berry Gordy. The few copies that were pressed became instant collectibles.

Besides Motown, Tamla, and Gordy, there were several other labels and imprints from the company. Jr. Walker and the All-Stars, Gladys Knight and the Pips, the Fantastic Four, and Shorty Long all recorded for Motown's "Soul" label. An R&B rock band called the Sunliners were signed in 1970 to Motown's Rare Earth rock label. The group changed their name to match the label, and had a string of Top 10 hits. Motown even had a country music label, Melodyland, and topped the country charts with T.G. Sheppard's hit "Devil in the Bottle."

In 1981, Motown reissued many of their classic albums from the 1960s as part of a budget line. These pressings will have an "M5" or "M6" in their catalog number, and only fetch a fraction of the value of the original pressings.

By the late 1960s, Motown used their paper sleeves to promote upcoming album releases. This sleeve was manufactured in September 1968; among the albums Motown promoted that month was a Martin Luther King tribute album, "In Loving Memory," as seen in the lower right-hand corner of the sleeve.

***$4**, VG condition*

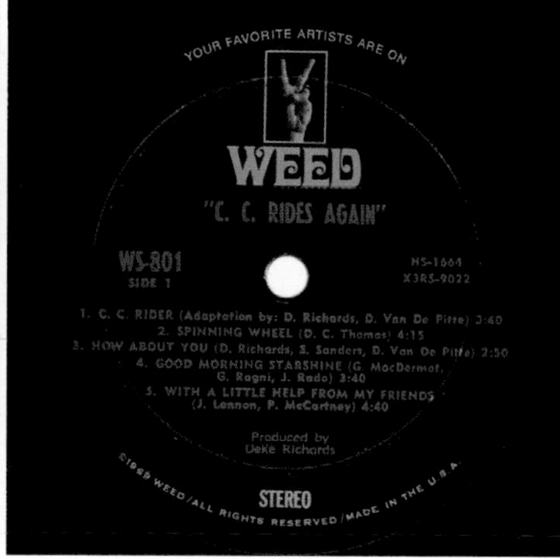

Not every Motown subsidiary label was a success. In 1984, Motown developed the Morocco label as an imprint for rock bands like Duke Jupiter. "The Crown," Gary Byrd and the G.B. Experience's 10-minute pro-education and pan-African history rap record, was the only release on a Stevie Wonder vanity label, Wondirection. And although only one record was ever released on Motown's Weed label, an album of pop standards by Chris Clark, notice the unintentionally funny advertising slogan above the Weed peace sign.

*(L to R) **$6**, NM condition; **$25**, NM condition; **$10**, NM condition*

Museums

The Motown Historical Museum, 2648 West Grand Boulevard, Detroit, MI 48208-1237. Phone: (313) 875-2264. E-mail: MotownMus@aol.com

Web Pages

Motown's home page, celebrating the company's 40th anniversary: http://www.motown.com

A page devoted to Mary Wilson of the Supremes: http://www.marywilson.com

The Unofficial Stevie Wonder Internet Archive: http://www.insoul.com/stevie

The Motown Alumni Association, a 10,000-member organization dedicated to maintaining a brotherhood among former musicians, singers and employees of Motown: http://members.aol.com/maainc

Books

Smith, Suzanne E., *Dancing In The Street: Motown and the Cultural Politics of Detroit*, Harvard University Press, Cambridge, Mass., 1999. ISBN: 0-674-00063-3.

Walker, Don, *The Motown Story*, Charles Scribner's Sons, New York, N.Y., 1985.

ARTIST VG+ to NM

THE ANDANTES:

45s

VIP 25006, "If You Were Mine"/"(Like A) Nightmare," 1964 ..... **$3,000.00-$4,000.00**

JERRY BUTLER:

45s

Motown 1403, "The Devil in Mrs. Jones"/"Don't Wanna Be Reminded," 1976 ..... **$2.50-$5.00**

(with picture sleeve, add), 1976 ..... **$5.00-$10.00**

1414, "I Wanna Do It To You"/"Don't Wanna Be Reminded," 1977 ..... **$2.50-$5.00**

12-inch Singles:

Motown M00004D1, "Chalk It Up"/Smokey Robinson, "Vitamin U," 1977 ..... **$10.00-$20.00**

LPs

Motown M6-850, Love's on the Menu, 1976 ..... **$6.00-$12.00**

M6-878, Suite for the Single Girl, 1977 ..... **$5.00-$10.00**

M6-892, It All Comes Out In My Songs, 1977 ..... **$5.00-$10.00**

THE COMMODORES:

45s

Mowest 5009, "I'm Looking for Love"/"At the Zoo (The Human Zoo)," 1972 ..... **$4.00-$8.00**

Motown 1307, "Machine Gun"/"There's A Song in My Heart," 1974 ..... **$2.50-$5.00**

1381, "Sweet Love"/"Better Never Than Forever," 1976 ..... **$2.00-$4.00**

1443, "Three Times a Lady"/"Look What You've Done To Me," 1978 ..... **$2.00-$4.00**

12-inch Singles

Motown M00007D1, "Brick House" (2 versions), promo, 1977 ..... **$7.50-$15.00**

PR-56, "Still"/"Sail On," promo, 1979 ..... **$10.00-$20.00**

PR-166, "Nightshift" (3 versions), promo, 1985 ..... **$6.00-$12.00**

4533MG, "Nightshift" (3 versions), 1985 ..... **$4.00-$8.00**

LPs

Motown M6-798, Machine Gun, 1974 ..... **$7.50-$15.00**

M6-867, Hot on the Tracks, 1976 ..... **$5.00-$10.00**

6044 ML2, Anthology (2 LPs), 1983 ..... **$6.00-$12.00**

THE FOUR SEASONS:

45s

Mowest 5026, "Walk On, Don't Look Back"/"Sun Country," 1972 ..... **$5.00-$10.00**

LPs

Mowest MW 108L, Chameleon, 1972 ..... **$6.00-$12.00**

THE FOUR TOPS:

45s

Motown 1062, "Baby I Need Your Loving"/"Call On Me," 1964 ..... **$7.50-$15.00**

1073, "Ask the Lonely"/"Where Did You Go," 1965 ..... **$7.50-$15.00**

(with picture sleeve, add), 1965 ..... **$40.00-$80.00**

1076, "I Can't Help Myself"/"Sad Souvenirs," 1965 ..... **$7.50-$15.00**

1098, "Reach Out I'll Be There"/"Until You Love Someone," 1966 ..... **$7.50-$15.00**

(with picture sleeve, add), 1966 ..... **$40.00-$80.00**

1113, "You Keep Running Away"/"If You Don't Want My Love," 1967 ..... **$6.00-$12.00**

Mono LPs

Motown 622, Four Tops, 1964 ..... **$15.00-$30.00**

647, 4 Tops on Top, 1966 ..... **$12.50-$25.00**

689, Yesterday's Dreams, 1968 ..... **$15.00-$30.00**

Stereo LPs

Motown MS-622, Four Tops, 1964 ..... **$20.00-$40.00**

(if on M5-122V1, reissue), 1981 ..... **$4.00-$8.00**

MS-647, 4 Tops on Top, 1966 ..... **$15.00-$30.00**

MS-660, Four Tops Reach Out, 1967 ..... **$12.50-$25.00**

MARVIN GAYE:

45s

Tamla 54041, "Let Your Conscience Be Your Guide"/"Never Let You Go," 1961 ..... **$200.00-$400.00**

54068, "Stubborn Kind of Fellow"/"It Hurts Me Too," 1962 ..... **$15.00-$30.00**

54176, "I Heard It Through The Grapevine"/"You're What's Happening (In The World Today)," 1968 ..... **$5.00-$10.00**

Mono LPs

Tamla T 221, The Soulful Moods of Marvin Gaye, 1961 ..... **$500.00-$1,000.00**

T 239, That Stubborn Kinda Fellow, 1963 ..... **$300.00-$600.00**

(if on Motown M5-218V1, reissue), 1981 ..... **$5.00-$10.00**

T 285, In the Groove, 1968 ..... **$25.00-$50.00**

Stereo LPs

Tamla TS 258, How Sweet It Is To Be Loved By You, 1965 ..... **$25.00-$50.00**

TS 285, In the Groove, 1968 ..... **$12.50-$25.00**

MARVIN GAYE AND TAMMI TERRELL:

45s

Tamla 54149, "Ain't No Mountain High Enough"/"Give a Little Love," 1967 ..... **$4.00-$8.00**

54156, "Your Precious Love"/"Hold Me Oh My Darling," 1967 ... **$4.00-$8.00**

Mono LPs

Tamla T 277, United, 1967 ..... **$15.00-$30.00**

284, You're All I Need, 1968 ..... **$25.00-$50.00**

Stereo LPs

Tamla TS 277, United, 1967 ..... **$12.50-$25.00**

(if on Motown M5-200V1, reissue), 1981 ..... **$5.00-$10.00**

TS 284, You're All I Need, 1968 ..... **$10.00-$20.00**

(if on Motown M5-142V1, reissue), 1981 ..... **$5.00-$10.00**

MICHAEL JACKSON:

45s

Motown 1107, "Rockin' Robin"/"Love is Here and Now You're Gone," 1972 ..... **$2.50-$5.00**

1202, "I Wanna Be Where You Are"/"We Got A Good Thing Going," 1972 ..... **$2.50-$5.00**

(with picture sleeve, add), 1972 ..... **$5.00-$10.00**

LPs

Motown M 755, Ben

(if Michael Jackson is on top half of cover, rats on the bottom half), 1972 ..... **$30.00-$60.00**

(if only Michael Jackson on front cover), 1972 ..... **$7.50-$15.00**

(if on Motown M5-153V1, reissue), 1981 .... **$5.00-$10.00**
6099 ML, Michael Jackson, Michael Jackson and the Jackson 5—14 Greatest Hits (picture disc with white glove), 1984 .... **$5.00-$10.00**

THE JACKSON FIVE:

45s

Motown 1157, "I Want You Back"/"Who's Lovin' You," 1969 .... **$4.00-$8.00**
1183, "ABC"/"The Young Folks," 1970 .... **$4.00-$8.00**
1177, "Mama's Pearl"/"Darling Dear," 1971 .... **$3.00-$6.00**
(with picture sleeve, add), 1971 .... **$7.50-$15.00**
1286, "Dancing Machine"/"It's Too Late to Change the Time," 1974 .... **$3.00-$6.00**

LPs

Motown MS 700, Diana Ross Presents the Jackson 5, 1969 .... **$12.50-$25.00**
(if on Motown M5-129V1, reissue), 1981 .... **$4.00-$8.00**
709, ABC, 1970 .... **$12.50-$25.00**
718, Third Album, 1970 .... **$7.50-$15.00**

RICK JAMES:

45s

Gordy 7197, "Give It To Me Baby"/"Don't Give Up on Love," 1981 .... **$2.00-$4.00**
7205, "Super Freak" (Pt. 1)/(Pt. 2), 1981 .... **$2.00-$4.00**

LPs

Gordy G7-984, Bustin' Out of L. Seven, 1979 .... **$5.00-$10.00**
G8-1002, Street Songs, 1981 .... **$4.00-$8.00**

GLADYS KNIGHT AND THE PIPS:

45s

Soul 35033, "Take Me in Your Arms and Love Me"/"Do You Love Me Just a Little More?," 1967 .... **$4.00-$8.00**
35039, "I Heard It Through the Grapevine"/"It's Time to Go Now," 1967 .... **$5.00-$10.00**
35078, "If I Were Your Woman"/"The Tracks of My Tears," 1970 .... **$3.50-$7.00**

Mono LPs

Soul S 706, Everybody Needs Love, 1967 .... **$10.00-$20.00**
S 707, Feelin' Bluesy (white label promo only, cover has "Monaural Record DJ Copy" sticker), 1968 .... **$20.00-$40.00**

Stereo LPs

Soul SS 706, Everybody Needs Love, 1967 .... **$12.50-$25.00**
SS 707, Feelin' Bluesy, 1968 .... **$12.50-$25.00**
S 737L, Neither One of Us, 1973 .... **$7.50-$15.00**

MARTHA AND THE VANDELLAS:

45s

Gordy 7014, "Come and Get These Memories"/"Jealous Love," 1963 .... **$15.00-$30.00**
7022, "Heat Wave"/"A Love Like Yours," 1963 .... **$10.00-$20.00**
7033, "Dancing in the Street"/"There He Is (At My Door)," 1964 .... **$7.50-$15.00**
(with picture sleeve, add), 1964 .... **$60.00-$120.00**
7058, "Jimmy Mack"/"Third Finger, Left Hand," 1967 .... **$5.00-$10.00**

Mono LPs

Gordy G-902, Come and Get These Memories, 1963 .... **$200.00-$400.00**
G-907, Heat Wave, 1963 .... **$75.00-$150.00**
G-920, Watchout!, 1966 .... **$12.50-$25.00**
G-926, Ridin High (mono is promo only), 1968 .... **$20.00-$40.00**

Stereo LPs

GS-902, Come and Get These Memories, 1963 .... **$400.00-$800.00**
GS-907, Heat Wave
(if "Stereo" banner pre-printed on cover), 1963 .... **$75.00-$150.00**
(if mono cover, "Stereo" sticker), 1963 .... **$200.00-$400.00**
GS-920, Watchout!, 1966 .... **$15.00-$30.00**
GS-926, Ridin' High, 1968 .... **$10.00-$20.00**

THE MARVELETTES:

45s

Tamla 54046, "Please Mr. Postman"/"So Long Baby," 1961 .... **$12.50-$25.00**
(with picture sleeve, add), 1961 .... **$60.00-$120.00**
54054, "Twistin' Postman"/"I Want a Guy," 1962 .... **$10.00-$20.00**
(with picture sleeve, add), 1962 .... **$50.00-$100.00**
54065, "Beechwood 4-5789"/"Someday, Someway," 1962 .... **$10.00-$20.00**
54105, "Two Many Fish in the Sea"/"A Need for Love" (A-side incorrect title), 1964 .... **$20.00-$40.00**
54105, "Too Many Fish in the Sea"/"A Need for Love," 1964 .... **$5.00-$10.00**

Mono LPs

Tamla T-228, Please Mr. Postman (white label), 1961 .... **$300.00-$600.00**
(if on yellow label with globes logo), 1963 .... **$150.00-$300.00**
(if on Motown 5266 ML, budget reissue), 1982 .... **$5.00-$10.00**
T-229, Smash Hits of '62 (Title as listed on front cover, large black "M" with song titles in circles), 1962 .... **$900.00-$1,200.00**
(if T-229, "The Marveletts Sing," group name misspelled, all-black cover with circles), 1962 .... **$250.00-$500.00**
(if T-229, "The Marveletts Sing," group name misspelled, yellow label with side-by-side globes logo), 1963 .... **$125.00-$250.00**

Stereo LPs

Tamla TS-253, Greatest Hits (yellow cover), 1966 .... **$20.00-$40.00**
(if green cover), 1967 .... **$10.00-$20.00**
TS-286, Sophisticated Soul, 1968 .... **$10.00-$20.00**

THE MIRACLES (also SMOKEY ROBINSON AND THE MIRACLES):

45s

Motown TLX-2207, "Bad Girl"/"I Love Your Baby," 1959 .... **$1,875.00-$2,500.00**
Tamla 54034, "Shop Around"/"Who's Lovin' You" (Original take, withdrawn shortly after release. In trail-off wax is " H55518A"), 1960 .... **$90.00-$180.00**
(if trail-off wax is "L-1," horizontal lines label, hit version of "Shop Around"), 1960 .... **$15.00-$30.00**
(if trail-off wax is "L-1," globe label, hit version of "Shop Around"), 1960 .... **$6.00-$12.00**
54118, "The Tracks of My Tears"/"A Fork in the Road," 1965 ..... **$7.50-$15.00**
54178, "Baby, Baby Don't Cry"/"Your Mother's Only Daughter," 1968 .... **$4.00-$8.00**
54199, "The Tears of a Clown"/"Promise Me," 1970 .... **$3.00-$6.00**
54262, "Love Machine" (Part 1)/"Love Machine" (Part 2), 1975 ... **$2.50-$5.00**

Mono LPs

Tamla T 220, Hi We're the Miracles, 1961 .... **$300.00-$600.00**
(if on Motown M5-160V1, budget reissue), 1981 .... **$4.00-$8.00**
T 223, Cookin' with the Miracles, 1962 .... **$400.00-$800.00**
T 238, The Fabulous Miracles, 1963 .... **$150.00-$300.00**
T 238, You've Really Got a Hold on Me, 1963 .... **$100.00-$200.00**

Stereo LPs

Tamla TS 245, Doin' Mickey's Monkey, 1963 .... **$150.00-$300.00**
TS 267, Going to a Go-Go, 1966 .... **$20.00-$40.00**
TS 276, Make It Happen, 1967 .... **$15.00-$30.00**
TS 276, The Tears of a Clown, 1970 .... **$7.50-$15.00**
T6-339, City of Angels, 1975 .... **$6.00-$12.00**

RARE EARTH:

45s

Rare Earth 5010, "Generation (Light of the Sky)"/"Magic Key," 1969 .... **$6.00-$12.00**
5017, "(I Know) I'm Losing You"/"When Joanie Smiles," 1970 .... **$3.00-$6.00**
5031, "I Just Want to Celebrate"/"The Seed," 1971 .... **$3.00-$6.00**
(with picture sleeve, add), 1971 .... **$5.00-$10.00**

LPs

Rare Earth RS-507, Get Ready
(first pressing with rounded top), 1969 .... **$15.00-$30.00**
(second pressing, square cover), 1970 .... **$6.00-$12.00**
RS-520, One World, 1971 .... **$6.00-$12.00**

DIANA ROSS:

45s

Motown 1165, "Reach Out and Touch (Somebody's Hand)"/"Dark Side of the World," 1970 .... **$2.50-$5.00**
(with picture sleeve, add), 1970 .... **$6.00-$12.00**
1169, "Ain't No Mountain High Enough"/"Can't It Wait Until Tomorrow," 1970 .... **$2.50-$5.00**
(with picture sleeve, add), 1970 .... **$6.00-$12.00**

LPs

Motown MS 711, Diana Ross, 1970 .... **$7.50-$15.00**
MS-719, Diana!, 1971 .... **$7.50-$15.00**
M-758D, Lady Sings the Blues (with booklet, 2 LPs), 1972 .... **$7.50-$15.00**
M6-861S1, Diana Ross (different album from Motown MS 711), 1976 .... **$6.00-$12.00**

THE SUPREMES (also DIANA ROSS AND THE SUPREMES):

45s

Tamla 54038, "I Want a Guy"/"Never Again"
(if horizontal lines on label), 1961 .... **$62.50-$125.00**
(if globes on label), 1961 .... **$30.00-$60.00**
Motown 1008, "I Want a Guy"/"Never Again," 1961 .... **$150.00-$300.00**
1027, "Your Heart Belongs to Me"/"(He's) Seventeen," 1962 .... **$12.50-$25.00**

(with picture sleeve, add), 1962 .... **$200.00-$400.00**
1044, "A Breath Taking, First Sight Soul Shaking, One Night Love Making, Next Day Heart Breaking Guy"/"Rock and Roll Banjo Band," 1963 .... **$50.00-$100.00**
(if A-side is shortened to "A Breath Taking Guy"), 1963 .... **$12.50-$25.00**
1094, "Love Is Like an Itching in My Heart"/"He's All I Got," 1966 .... **$7.50-$15.00**
1135, "Love Child"/"Will This Be the Day," 1968 .... **$4.00-$8.00**
1156, "Someday We'll Be Together"/"He's My Sunny Boy," 1969 .... **$4.00-$8.00**
1162, "Up the Ladder to the Roof"/"Bill, When Are You Coming Home," 1970 .... **$3.00-$6.00**
1172, "Stoned Love"/"Shine on Me," 1970 .... **$3.00-$6.00**

Mono LPs

Motown M 606, Meet the Supremes
(if girls are sitting on stools), 1963 .... **$450.00-$900.00**
(if girls are in close-up photos), 1963 .... **$15.00-$30.00**
M 621, Where Did Our Love Go, 1964 .... **$15.00-$30.00**
M 623, A Bit of Liverpool, 1964 .... **$20.00-$40.00**
M 627, More Hits by the Supremes, 1965 .... **$12.50-$25.00**

Stereo LPs

Motown MS 606, Meet the Supremes (close-up photos of faces), 1964 .... **$20.00-$40.00**
MS 621, Where Did Our Love Go, 1964 .... **$20.00-$40.00**
MS 627, More Hits by the Supremes, 1965 .... **$15.00-$30.00**
MS 649, The Supremes A' Go-Go, 1966 .... **$15.00-$30.00**

THE SUPREMES AND THE FOUR TOPS:

45s

Motown 1173, "River Deep-Mountain High"/"Together We Can Make Such Sweet Music," 1970 .... **$3.00-$6.00**

LPs

Motown MS 717, The Magnificent Seven, 1970 .... **$7.50-$15.00**
MS 736, The Return of the Magnificent Seven, 1971 .... **$7.50-$15.00**

DIANA ROSS AND THE SUPREMES AND THE TEMPTATIONS:

45s

Motown 1137, "I'm Gonna Make You Love Me"/"A Place in the Sun," 1968 .... **$3.50-$7.00**
(with picture sleeve, add), 1968 .... **$10.00-$20.00**

Mono LPs

Motown M 679, Diana Ross and the Supremes Join the Temptations, 1968 .... **$15.00-$30.00**

Stereo LPs

Motown MS 679, Diana Ross and the Supremes Join the Temptations, 1968 .... **$10.00-$20.00**
MS 682, TCB, 1968 .... **$10.00-$20.00**

THE TEMPTATIONS:

45s

Gordy 7001, "Dream Come True"/"Isn't She Pretty," 1962 .... **$20.00-$40.00**
7028, "The Way You Do the Things You Do"/"Just Let Me Know," 1964 .... **$7.50-$15.00**
7038, "My Girl"/"Nobody But My Baby," 1965 .... **$7.50-$15.00**
(with picture sleeve, add), 1965 .... **$60.00-$120.00**
7049, "Get Ready"/"Fading Away," 1966 .... **$7.50-$15.00**
7057, "(I Know) I'm Losing You"/"I Couldn't Cry If I Wanted To," 1966 .... **$7.50-$15.00**

Mono LPs

Gordy G 911, Meet the Temptations, 1964 .... **$15.00-$30.00**
G 912, The Temptations Sing Smokey, 1965 .... **$15.00-$30.00**
G 914, Temptin' Temptations, 1965 .... **$12.50-$25.00**

Stereo LPs

Gordy GS 911, Meet the Temptations
(if "Gordy" in script on label), 1964 .... **$20.00-$40.00**
(if "Gordy" in block letters inside large "G" on label), 1967 .... **$10.00-$20.00**
GS 914, Temptin' Temptations
(if "Gordy" in script on label), 1965 .... **$15.00-$30.00**
(if "Gordy" in block letters inside large "G" on label), 1967 .... **$10.00-$20.00**
GS 922, With a Lot o' Soul
(if "Gordy" in script on label), 1967 .... **$12.50-$25.00**
(if "Gordy" in block letters inside large "G" on label), 1967 .... **$10.00-$20.00**
Gordy GS 927, The Temptations Wish It Would Rain, 1968 .... **$10.00-$20.00**
GS 949, Puzzle People, 1969 .... **$10.00-$20.00**
G7-97551 The Temptations Do the Temptations, 1976 .... **$7.50-$15.00**

THE VELVELETTES:

45s

V.I.P. 25007, "Needle in a Haystack"/"Should I Tell Them," 1964 .... **$12.50-$25.00**
25013, "He Was Really Sayin' Somethin'"/"Throw a Farewell Kiss," 1965 .... **$12.50-$25.00**
25021, "A Bird in the Hand (Is Worth Two in the Bush)"/(B side unknown), 1965 .... **$400.00-$800.00**
25030, "A Bird in the Hand (Is Worth Two in the Bush)"/"Since You've Been Loving Me," 1965 .... **$10.00-$20.00**

MARY WELLS:

45s

Motown 1003, "Bye Bye Baby"/"Please Forgive Me," 1960 .... **$25.00-$50.00**
1024, "The One Who Really Loves You"/"I'm Gonna Stay," 1962 .... **$10.00-$20.00**
(with picture sleeve, add), 1962 .... **$40.00-$80.00**
1032, "You Beat Me to the Punch"/"Old Love (Let's Try It Again)," 1962 .... **$10.00-$20.00**
(with picture sleeve, add), 1962 .... **$60.00-$120.00**
1056, "My Guy"/"Oh Little Boy (What Did You Do to Me)," 1964 .... **$10.00-$20.00**

Mono LPs

Motown M 605, The One Who Really Loves You
(with map, label address above the center hole), 1962 .... **$80.00-$160.00**
(with map, label address around lower part of label), 1964 .... **$20.00-$40.00**

Stereo LPs

Motown MS 616, Greatest Hits, 1964 .... **$20.00-$40.00**
MS 653, Vintage Stock, 1967 .... **$25.00-$50.00**

STEVIE WONDER:

45s

Tamla 54061, "I Call It Pretty Music But The Old People Call It the Blues" (Pt. 1)/(Pt. 2), 1962 .... **$15.00-$30.00**
(with picture sleeve, add), 1962 .... **$40.00-$80.00**
54080, "Fingertips" (Pt. 2)/(Pt. 1), 1963 .... **$10.00-$20.00**
(with picture sleeve, add), 1963 .... **$25.00-$50.00**
54124, "Uptight (Everything's Alright)"/"Purple Rain Drops," 1965 .... **$7.50-$15.00**
54136, "Blowin' in the Wind"/"Ain't That Asking for Trouble," 1966 .... **$6.00-$12.00**
(with picture sleeve, add), 1966 .... **$12.50-$25.00**
54174, "For Once in My Life"/"Angie Girl," 1968 .... **$4.00-$8.00**

Mono LPs

Tamla T 232, Tribute to Uncle Ray, 1962 .... **$75.00-$150.00**
T 240, Recorded Live/Little Stevie Wonder/The 12 Year Old Genius, 1963 .... **$60.00-$120.00**
T 255, Stevie at the Beach, 1964 .... **$40.00-$80.00**
T 268, Up-Tight Everything's Alright, 1966 .... **$12.50-$25.00**

Stereo LPs

TS 268, Up-Tight Everything's Alright, 1966 .... **$15.00-$30.00**
TS 279, I Was Made to Love Her, 1967 .... **$12.50-$25.00**
T13-340C2, Songs in the Key of Life (2 LPs and bonus 7-inch EP), 1976 .... **$10.00-$20.00**
T8-37381, Hotter Than July, 1980 .... **$6.00-$12.00**
6134 TL, In Square Circle, 1985 .... **$5.00-$10.00**

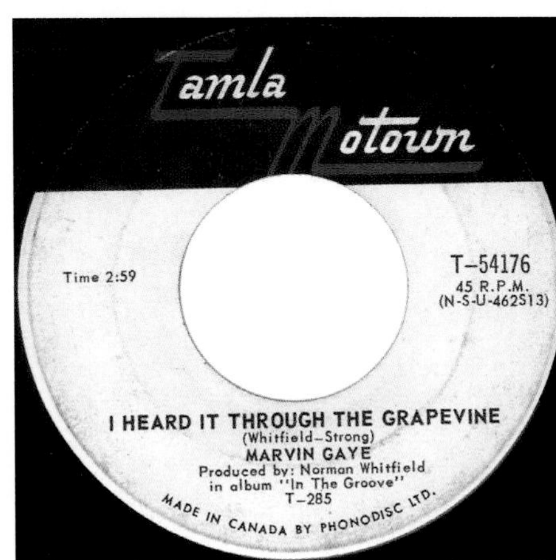

Outside the United States, there was no distinction between Motown, Tamla, Gordy, or any of the company's other subsidiary labels. Songs in Canada, for example, were released on the "Tamla Motown" label pictured here. Different countries had different label artwork, but most pressings outside of America used the "Tamla Motown" logo above.

***$8**, NM condition*

CHAPTER 32

SUN RECORDS

History

To say that the only thing Sun Records ever brought to rock and roll was Elvis Presley, is equivalent to erroneously stating the New York Yankees are only known for Babe Ruth. During the 1950s, Sun Records and its creator, Sam Phillips, recorded seminal blues records, nurtured a new musical format called "rockabilly," and started the careers of rock and roll legends.

Sam Phillips was born in 1923, the youngest of eight children born to an Alabama tenant farmer. After working in radio stations throughout Alabama and Tennessee, Phillips set up his own recording studio at 706 Union Avenue, Memphis, Tennessee, in 1950. His early recordings were sessions for local blues artists, such as B.B. King and Howlin' Wolf, which Phillips would then lease to national record labels like Chess, Modern, and RPM.

During one of these sessions, Phillips produced "Rocket 88" by Ike Turner and his Kings of Rhythm. Chess Records licensed the track and credited it to "Jackie Brenston and his Delta Cats" (Brenston was a member of Turner's band, and sang lead on the track). The song, cited by many experts as the first true "rock and roll record," hit #1 on the R&B charts and gave Phillips his first national exposure.

Unfortunately, many of the blues artists that recorded for Sun eventually went north and recorded with Chess and the other Chicago labels, effectively eliminating the Memphis Recording Service middleman. Phillips eventually fought back by creating his own record label, Sun. Sun's first releases were by blues singers and disc jockeys around the Memphis area, including saxophonist Johnny London, disc

Photo credit: From the Tom Kelly Archives, St. Louis, Mo.

Sun Records' first big hit was the song "Bear Cat," an answer record to Big Mama Thornton's "Hound Dog." Rufus Thomas would record one more side for Sun before moving on to other labels, including a long stay with Stax Records.

***$120**, NM condition*

Photo credit: From the collection of Rodney Branham.

There are two label variations on Elvis Presley's first 45, "That's All Right." First pressings list the artist and his backup musicians as "Elvis Presley, Scotty and Bill." Subsequent pressings credit the performers as "Elvis Presley With Scotty and Bill."

***$6,000**, NM condition*

Photo credit: From the Tom Kelly Archives, St. Louis, Mo.

The Prisonaires' 1953 hit "Just Walking in the Rain" was later covered by pop singer Johnnie Ray, who took it to the top of the charts. Of the five inmates that made up the Prisonaires, Johnny Bragg was the only one to stay in the music business after his release from prison, recording some songs for the Decca and Elbejay labels.

***$100**, NM condition*

Jerry Lee Lewis pounded out several Top 10 hits for Sun Records. His version of Otis Blackwell's "Breathless" was later covered by the alternative band X for a motion picture of the same name, starring Richard Gere.

***$20**, VG condition*

jockey Rufus Thomas, and songwriter Little Junior Parker.

During this time, Phillips had an open-door policy at Sun—he would record anybody and everybody, all the while looking for someone who could be Sun's next big superstar. Somebody who could sing the blues like he had lived it all his life, someone who could master country and western bop, somebody who could bring Sun Records the same national prominence it once had in the "Rocket 88" days.

In 1954, Elvis Presley walked into the Memphis Recording Service, hoping to make an acetate recording for his mother. Even though Phillips nurtured Presley's early talent and provided him with his top studio musicians Scotty Moore and Bill Black, Phillips continued to record other artists, experimenting with a new sound called "rockabilly"—a mixture of blues, bluegrass, and western bop, with a "slapback" echo and roadhouse energy. While Elvis Presley recorded his seminal Sun singles and performed with Scotty Moore and Bill Black on tour, other Sun recording artists, like Charlie Feathers, Billy Lee Riley, and Sonny Burgess, spread the gospel of rockabilly through every roadhouse and dance hall in the South.

Signing Elvis Presley was proof that Sam Phillips was not afraid to record new and different sounds, whether it involved Presley, some up-and-coming blues or hillbilly sounds—or even taking a chance on a vocal group who couldn't tour. In 1953, Phillips recorded a vocal harmony group from the Tennessee State Prison, calling them the "Prisonaires." The lineup featured Johnny Bragg (six counts of rape), Ed Thurman (99 years for murder), William Stewart (99 years for murder), John Drue (three years for larceny), and Marcel Sanders (involuntary manslaughter), whose harmonies were overheard by a radio newscaster who thought they should make a record. With armed guards transporting the quintet to the Sun studios, the Prisonaires cut "Just Walking in the Rain," which became a major hit for the label.

Carl Perkins' "Blue Suede Shoes" is one of the easiest Sun 45s or 78s to find. The record was a Top 10 smash on the pop and country charts, and so many copies were pressed that some error pressings got out—including this one, where the spindle hole, which should be directly under the Sun rooster logo, is slightly out of true.

***$30**, VG+ condition*

Phillips eventually sold Presley's contract to RCA Victor for $35,000.00, which he invested into his Sun studio and into the new Holiday Inn motel organization. For an independent record label, losing their biggest singer might have meant a death knell for the label. But there was something new under the Sun, a stable of artists that would bring the label Top 10 hits of its own.

Carl Perkins, who played in local clubs and bars around Memphis, brought Sun Records their first national Top 5 rock and roll hit, "Blue Suede Shoes." Sun also had a string of hits from a flamboyant piano-pounder from Louisiana, Jerry Lee Lewis. Another Sun performer, Johnny Cash, brought a darker side to rockabilly, with songs like "Cry! Cry! Cry!," "Ballad of a Teenage Queen," and "I Walk The Line." A group from Texas called the Teen Kings had some minor hits on Sun, but it was the first musical exposure for the Teen Kings' singer and lead guitarist, Roy Orbison.

The glory era of Sun ended in the early 1960s. Although the label's hits at that time were few and far between (Cash and Perkins signed with Columbia, Orbison joined the Monument label, and Lewis' career never survived the negative publicity of his incestuous marriage), the label found success across the Atlantic, as the Beatles added two of Carl Perkins' hits, "Honey Don't" and "Matchbox," to their growing musical repertoire.

In 1969, Sam Phillips sold Sun Records to Shelby Singleton, and the company became a reissue label, selling re-released classic 1950s hits. The legendary Sun Studio in Memphis is now a museum, and equipment from the Elvis Presley recording sessions is now on permanent display at the Rock and Roll Hall of Fame in Cleveland, Ohio.

What To Look For

Where to start? Sun has a little bit of everything for collectors—early blues legends, the evolution of rockabilly, the Million Dollar Quartet (the solo recordings of Presley, Cash, Perkins, and Lewis).

Sun 45s with a catalog number lower than 222 will have "push marks" on the label, three circular indentations around the spindle hole, caused when the record label was pressed onto the vinyl. Counterfeits will not have push marks. Because Sun was an independent record label and had their records pressed at other factories, there are variations in how the labels were attached to the vinyl. And although "push marks" make the record a legitimate copy, the absence of "push marks" does not necessarily mean the record is not an original. If you're unsure about the legitimacy of your Sun 45, don't be afraid to consult an expert, especially one versed in Elvis Presley recordings.

All five of Elvis Presley's Sun 45s have been replicated in one form or another. Many will say "Reproduction" in the dead wax. Others will be pressed in colored vinyl; legitimate Presley 78s were pressed only on black vinyl. Presley never had a picture sleeve or a four-song EP during his Sun career; any that exist are counterfeits.

There is a Sun 45, catalog number 1129, with the songs "That's All Right" and "Blue Moon of Kentucky," with no artist listed. This record also appears under Sun catalog number 1136 in 1978, as part of a four-song EP with "Misty" and "D.O.A." These are **not** rare Elvis recordings, the tracks are actually by singer Jimmy Ellis. Ellis (who also recorded under the name Orion) was capable of sounding almost like the King—enough to fool some people into thinking Presley was recording under a pseudonym. In the late 1970s, Ellis sang some duets with Jerry Lee Lewis, which some people mistook as Presley-Lewis duets from the 1950s. How confusing did it get? In 1978, Ellis recorded a song on the Boblo label, called "I'm Not Trying To Be Like Elvis."

Elvis records may be tough to find, but regional hits by the Prisonaires and blues harmonica player Hot Shot Love are even tougher to uncover. Rockabilly legend Charlie Feathers also recorded for Sun, and his sides are among the most difficult titles to find for Feathers and rockabilly collectors.

During Sun's hitmaking days, the label released only 12 albums, concentrating instead on their singles hits. The Sun albums included tracks from Johnny Cash, Carl Perkins, Roy Orbison, and Jerry Lee Lewis, as well as one "Best of Sun"

"Push marks," three circular indentations in the label, shown in red in this enhanced photograph, were made by the pressing plant Sun Records used. Four of Elvis Presley's 45s contain these "push marks," the last one ("Mystery Train") does not.

***$40**, NM condition*

album. After 1969, when Phillips sold the label to Shelby Singleton, much of the Sun catalog was reissued, especially on the Sun International label. There is a distinct redesign of the Sun label artwork, and the following was added to the label's bottom perimeter: "Sun International Corp.—A Division of the Shelby Singleton Corp.—Nashville, U.S.A." Many of the albums in the Sun International 1000 series are available both in gold vinyl and in black vinyl.

There is a design change for Sun International 45s, and can help you in determining whether the 45 you purchase is an original or a repressing. Although both 45 labels have the music scale perimeter and the letters "SUN" against a sunbeam background, Sun International pressings have two-tone "bull's-eyes" on the lower half of the label, and the numbering system begins with "S1."

Sun's first singles were released on the 78 RPM format. Although Sun 174, a track called "Blues In My Condition" by Little Walter Horton and Jack Kelly, does exist on a promotional-only 45, the first commercially released Sun 45 was Johnny London's "Drivin' Slow" (Sun 175). Sun continued to press 78s and 45s concurrently until 1958, when 78s were eventually phased out of the Sun catalog.

Of the thirteen albums Sun Records released between 1956 and 1965, seven of them were by Johnny Cash, including this collection of his earliest Sun recordings. Although this album has an "SLP" in front of the catalog number, indicating a stereo release, all the tracks on this LP are actually in mono.

***$25**, VG+ condition*

Books

Kennedy, Rick; McNutt, Randy, *Little Labels—Big Sound*, Indiana University Press, Bloomington, IN, 1999.

Morrison, Craig, *Go Cat Go: Rockabilly Music and Its Makers*, University of Illinois Press, Chicago, IL, 1998.

Museums

Sun Studio, 706 Union Avenue, Memphis, TN 38103, 1-800-441-6249: http://www.sunstudio.com

Web Pages

Mike Callahan's Both Sides Now: Sun Label Discography: http://www.bsnpubs.com/suna.html

The official Sun Records home page: http://www.sunrecords.com.

Take a tour of the original Sun Studios: http://www.sunstudio.com.

The Gentrys recorded several sides for Sun, including this Neil Young song, after the success of their MGM-labeled hit "Keep On Dancing." One of the Gentrys, Jimmy Hart, later achieved fame as a professional wrestling manager and promoter.

***$5**, NM condition*

DUSTY BROOKS AND HIS TONES WITH JUANITA BROWN:

45s

Sun 182, "Heaven or Fire"/"Tears and Wine," 1953 .... **$2,250.00-$3,000.00**

JOHNNY CASH:

45s

Sun 221, "Hey Porter"/"Cry, Cry, Cry," 1955 .... **$20.00-$40.00**
232, "Folsom Prison Blues"/"So Doggone Lonesome," 1956 .... **$15.00-$30.00**
241, "I Walk the Line"/"Get Rhythm," 1956 .... **$20.00-$40.00**
258, "Train of Love"/"There You Go," 1956 .... **$15.00-$30.00**
266, "Next in Line"/"Don't Make Me Go," 1957 .... **$15.00-$30.00**
279, "Home of the Blues"/"Give My Love to Rose," 1957 .... **$15.00-$30.00**
283, "Ballad of a Teenage Queen"/"Big River," 1958 .... **$12.50-$25.00**
295, "Guess Things Happen That Way"/"Come In Stranger," 1958 .... **$12.50-$25.00**
(with picture sleeve, add), 1958 .... **$20.00-$40.00**
302, "The Ways of a Woman in Love"/"You're the Nearest Thing to Heaven," 1958 .... **$12.50-$25.00**
309, "It's Just About Time"/"Just Thought You'd Like to Know," 1958 .... **$12.50-$25.00**
316, "Luther Played the Boogie"/"Thanks a Lot," 1959 .... **$10.00-$20.00**
321, "Katy Too"/"I Forgot to Remember to Forget," 1959 .... **$10.00-$20.00**
331, "Goodbye Little Darlin"/"You Tell Me," 1959 .... **$10.00-$20.00**
334, "Straight A's in Love"/"I Love You Because," 1960 .... **$10.00-$20.00**
343, "The Story of a Broken Heart"/"Down the Street to 301," 1960 .... **$10.00-$20.00**

78s

Sun 241, " I Walk The Line"/"Get Rhythm," 1956 .... **$12.50-$25.00**
258, "Train of Love"/"There You Go," 1956 .... **$15.00-$30.00**

7-inch EPs (4 songs on EP, value is for record and cover)

Sun EPA-111, Johnny Cash Sings Hank Williams, 1956 .... **$50.00-$100.00**
EPA-112, Country Boy, 1956 .... **$40.00-$80.00**
EPA-113, I Walk the Line, 1958 .... **$40.00-$80.00**
EPA-114, His Top Hits, 1958 .... **$40.00-$80.00**
SEP-116, Home of the Blues, 1959 .... **$40.00-$80.00**
SEP-117, Johnny Cash, 1959 .... **$40.00-$80.00**

Mono LPs

Sun SLP-1220, Johnny Cash with His Hot and Blue Guitar, 1956 .... **$50.00-$100.00**
SLP-1235, The Songs That Made Him Famous, 1958 .... **$50.00-$100.00**
SLP-1240, Johnny Cash's Greatest!, 1959 .... **$25.00-$50.00**
SLP-1245, Johnny Cash Sings Hank Williams, 1960 .... **$25.00-$50.00**
SLP-1255, Now Here's Johnny Cash, 1961 .... **$25.00-$50.00**
SLP-1270, All Aboard the Blue Train, 1963 .... **$25.00-$50.00**
SLP-1275, The Original Sun Sound of Johnny Cash, 1965 .... **$25.00-$50.00**

Stereo LPs

Sun SLP-1220, Johnny Cash with His Hot and Blue Guitar (front cover says "STEREO," rechanneled reissue), 196? .... **$10.00-$20.00**
SLP-1235, The Songs That Made Him Famous (front cover says "STEREO," rechanneled reissue), 196? .... **$10.00-$20.00**
SLP-1245, Johnny Cash Sings Hank Williams (front cover says "STEREO," rechanneled reissue), 196? .... **$10.00-$20.00**
SLP-1255, Now Here's Johnny Cash (front cover says "STEREO," rechanneled reissue), 196? .... **$10.00-$20.00**
Sun LP-100, Original Golden Hits, Volume I, 1969 .... **$6.00-$12.00**
LP-101, Original Golden Hits, Volume II, 1969 .... **$6.00-$12.00**
LP-104, Story Songs of the Trains and Rivers, 1969 .... **$6.00-$12.00**
LP 105, Get Rhythm, 1969 .... **$6.00 $12.00**
LP-106, Showtime, 1969 .... **$6.00-$12.00**
LP-115, The Singing Story Teller, 1970 .... **$6.00-$12.00**
LP-118, Johnny Cash—The Legend (2 LPs), 1970 .... **$10.00-$20.00**
LP-122, The Rough Cut King of Country Music, 1971 .... **$6.00-$12.00**
LP-126, Johnny Cash: The Man, The World, His Music (2 LPs), 1971 .... **$10.00-$20.00**
LP-127, Original Golden Hits, Volume III, 1972 .... **$6.00-$12.00**
LP-139, I Walk the Line, 1979 .... **$5.00-$10.00**
LP-140, Folsom Prison Blues, 1979 .... **$5.00-$10.00**
LP-141, The Blue Train, 1979 .... **$5.00-$10.00**
LP-142, Johnny Cash Sings the Greatest Hits, 1979 .... **$5.00-$10.00**
1002, Superbilly (1955-58), 198? .... **$5.00-$10.00**
1006, The Original Johnny Cash, 1980 .... **$5.00-$10.00**

JAMES COTTON:

45s

Sun 199, "My Baby"/"Straighten Up, Baby," 1954 .... **$750.00-$1,500.00**
206, "Cotton Crop Blues"/"Hold Me in Your Arms," 1954 **$900.00-$1,800.00**

78s

Sun 199, "My Baby"/"Straighten Up, Baby," 1954 .... **$300.00-$600.00**
206, "Cotton Crop Blues"/"Hold Me in Your Arms," 1954 ... **$350.00-$700.00**

JIMMY DEBERRY:

45s

Sun 185, "Take a Little Chance"/"Time Has Made a Change," 1953 .... **$1,500.00-$3,000.00**

EMERSON, BILLY:

45s

Sun 195, "No Teasin' Around"/"If Lovin' Is Believin'," 1954 .... **$200.00-$400.00**
203, "I'm Not Going Home"/"The Woodchuck," 1954 .... **$400.00-$600.00**
214, "Move, Baby, Move"/"When It Rains, It Pours," 1955 .... **$25.00-$50.00**
219, "Red Hot"/"No Greater Love," 1955 .... **$50.00-$100.00**
233, "Something for Nothing"/"Little Fine Healthy Thing," 1956 .... **$25.00-$50.00**

CHARLIE FEATHERS:

45s

Sun 231, "Defrost Your Heart"/"Wedding Gown of White," 1956 .... **$400.00-$600.00**
503, "I've Been Deceived"/"Peeping Eyes," 1956 .... **$400.00-$600.00**

THE FIVE TINOS:

45s

Sun 222, "Sitting By My Window"/"Don't Do That," 1955 .. **$600.00-$1,200.00**

78s

Sun 222, "Sitting By My Window"/"Don't Do That," 1955 ..... **$300.00-$600.00**

HARDROCK GUNTER:

45s

Sun 201, "Fallen Angel"/"Gonna Dance All Night," 1954 .... **$1,000.00-$2,000.00**

THE JONES BROTHERS:

45s

Sun 213, "Every Night"/"Look to Jesus," 1954 .... **$400.00-$800.00**

JERRY LEE LEWIS:

45s

Sun 259, "Crazy Arms"/"End of the Road"
(if credited to "Jerry Lee Lewis and his Pumping Piano"), 1957 .... **$25.00-$50.00**
(if credited to "Jerry Lee Lewis," 1957 .... **$50.00-$100.00**
267, "Whole Lot of Shakin' Going On"/"It'll Be Me," 1957 ..... **$20.00-$40.00**
281, "Great Balls of Fire"/"You Win Again," 1957 .... **$20.00-$40.00**
(with picture sleeve, add), 1957 .... **$40.00-$80.00**
288, "Breathless"/"Down the Line," 1958 .... **$20.00-$40.00**
296, "High School Confidential"/"Fools Like Me," 1958 .... **$15.00-$30.00**
(with picture sleeve, add), 1958 .... **$40.00-$80.00**
301, "Lewis Boogie"/George and Louis, "The Return of Jerry Lee," 1958 .... **$15.00-$30.00**
303, "I'll Make It All Up to You"/"Break-Up," 1958 .... **$12.50-$30.00**
312, "I'll Sail My Ship Alone"/"It Hurt Me So," 1958 .... **$12.50-$25.00**
317, "Lovin' Up a Storm"/"Big Blon' Baby," 1959 .... **$12.50-$25.00**
324, "Let's Talk About Us"/"Ballad of Billy Joe," 1959 .... **$12.50-$25.00**
330, "Little Queenie"/"I Could Never Be Ashamed of You," 1959 .... **$12.50-$25.00**
337, "Old Black Joe"/"Baby Baby, Bye Bye," 1960 .... **$10.00-$20.00**
344, "Hang Up My Rock and Roll Shoes"/"John Henry," 1960 **$10.00-$20.00**
352, "Love Made a Fool of Me"/"When I Get Paid," 1960 .... **$10.00-$20.00**
356, "What'd I Say"/"Livin' Lovin' Wreck," 1961 .... **$10.00-$20.00**
364, "Cold, Cold Heart"/"It Won't Happen with Me," 1961 ..... **$10.00-$20.00**
367, "Save the Last Dance for Me"/"As Long As I Live," 1961 . **$10.00-$20.00**
371, "Money"/"Bonnie B," 1961 .... **$10.00-$20.00**
374, "I've Been Twistin'"/"Ramblin' Rose," 1962 .... **$10.00-$20.00**
379, "Sweet Little Sixteen"/"How's My Ex Treating You," 1962 **$10.00-$20.00**
382, "Good Golly Miss Molly"/"I Can't Trust Me," 1962 .... **$10.00-$20.00**
384, "Teenage Letter"/"Seasons of My Heart," 1963 .... **$10.00-$20.00**

78s

Sun 259, "Crazy Arms"/"End of the Road," 1957 .... **$150.00-$300.00**
267, "Whole Lot of Shakin' Goin' On"/"It'll Be Me," 1957 ... **$100.00-$200.00**
281, "Great Balls of Fire"/"You Win Again," 1957 .... **$100.00-$200.00**

288, "Breathless"/"Down the Line," 1958 .... **$100.00-$200.00**

LPs

Sun LP-102, Original Golden Hits — Volume 1, 1969 .... **$7.50-$15.00**

LP-103, Original Golden Hits — Volume 2, 1969 .... **$7.50-$15.00**

LP-107, Rockin' Rhythm and Blues, 1969 .... **$7.50-$15.00**

LP-108, The Golden Cream of the Country, 1969 .... **$7.50-$15.00**

(if white label promo mono pressing, "MONO" at 9:00 on the label), 1969 .... **$20.00-$40.00**

LP-114, A Taste of Country, 1970 .... **$7.50-$15.00**

1018, Trio+ (featuring Lewis, Carl Perkins, Charlie Rich, and Jimmy "Orion" Ellis), 1979 .... **$6.00-$12.00**

145, Roots, 1982 .... **$6.00-$12.00**

LITTLE MILTON:

45s

Sun 194, "Beggin' My Baby"/"Somebody Told Me," 1954 .... **$150.00-$300.00**

200, "If You Love Me"/"Alone and Blue," 1954 .... **$300.00-$600.00**

220, "Looking for My Baby"/"Lonesome for My Baby," 1955 .... **$400.00-$800.00**

HOT SHOT LOVE:

45s

Sun 196, "Wolf Call Boogie"/"Harmonica Jam," 1954 .... **$2,000.00-$4,000.00**

78s

Sun 196, "Wolf Call Boogie"/"Harmonica Jam," 1954 .... **$250.00-$500.00**

CARL MANN:

45s

Phillips International 3539, "Mona Lisa"/"Foolish One," 1959 .... **$12.50-$25.00**

3546, "Pretend"/"Rockin' Love," 1959 .... **$12.50-$25.00**

LPs

Phillips International PLP-1960, Like Mann, 1960 .... **$300.00-$600.00**

ROY ORBISON:

45s

Sun 242, "Ooby Dooby"/"Go! Go! Go!," 1956 .... **$50.00-$100.00**

251, "Rockhouse"/"You're My Baby," 1956 .... **$30.00-$60.00**

353, "Devil Doll"/"Sweet and Easy to Love," 1960 .... **$125.00-$250.00**

78s

Sun 242, "Ooby Dooby"/"Go! Go! Go!," 1956 .... **$100.00-$200.00**

LPs

Sun LP-1260, Roy Orbison at the Rock House, 1961 .... **$300.00-$600.00**

LITTLE JUNIOR'S BLUE FLAMES (JUNIOR PARKER):

45s

Sun 187, "Feelin' Good"/"Fussin' and Fightin' Blues," 1953 ...... **$200.00-$400.00**

78s

Sun 187, "Feelin' Good"/"Fussin' and Fightin' Blues," 1953 .... **$50.00-$100.00**

CARL PERKINS:

45s

Sun 224, "Gone, Gone, Gone"/"Let the Jukebox Keep On Playing," 1955 .... **$50.00-$100.00**

234, "Blue Suede Shoes"/"Honey Don't!," 1956 .... **$30.00-$60.00**

243, "Boppin' the Blues"/"All Mama's Children," 1956 .... **$20.00-$40.00**

249, "Dixie Fried"/"I'm Sorry, I'm Not Sorry," 1956 .... **$15.00-$30.00**

78s

234, "Blue Suede Shoes"/"Honey Don't!," 1956 .... **$20.00-$40.00**

243, "Boppin' the Blues"/"All Mama's Children," 1956 .... **$20.00-$40.00**

LPs

Sun SLP-1225, The Dance Album of Carl Perkins, 1957 ..... **$600.00-$1,200.00**

ELVIS PRESLEY:

45s

Sun 209, "That's All Right"/"Blue Moon of Kentucky"

(first pressings, label credits "Elvis Presley, Scotty and Bill"), 1954 .... **$4,000.00-$6,000.00**

(second pressings, label credits "Elvis Presley with Scotty and Bill"), 1954 .... **$4,000.00-$6,000.00**

210, "Good Rockin' Tonight"/"I Don't Care if the Sun Don't Shine," 1954 .... **$2,500.00-$3,500.00**

215, "Milkcow Blues Boogie"/"You're a Heartbreaker," 1955 .... **$3,500.00-$5,000.00**

THE PRISONAIRES:

45s

Sun 186, "Just Walking in the Rain"/"Baby Please," 1953 .... **$250.00-$500.00**

(if on red vinyl), 1953 .... **$3,750.00-$5,000.00**

189, "Softly and Tenderly"/"My God Is Real," 1953 .... **$350.00-$700.00**

191, "A Prisoner's Prayer"/"I Know," 1953 .... **$250.00-$500.00**

207, "There Is Love in You"/"What'll You Do Next," 1954 .... **$8,500.00-$12,000.00**

78s

Sun 186, "Just Walking in the Rain"/"Baby Please," 1953 .... **$50.00-$100.00**

189, "Softly and Tenderly"/"My God Is Real," 1953 .... **$200.00-$400.00**

191, "A Prisoner's Prayer"/"I Know," 1953 .... **$150.00-$300.00**

207, "There Is Love in You"/"What'll You Do Next," 1954 .... **$1,000.00-$2,000.00**

SLIM RHODES:

45s

Sun 216, "Don't Believe"/"Uncertain Blues," 1955 .... **$50.00-$100.00**

225, "Are You Ashamed of Me"/"The House of Sin," 1955 ... **$150.00-$300.00**

238, "Bad Girl"/"Gonna Romp and Stomp," 1956 .... **$50.00-$100.00**

256, "Do What I Do"/"Take and Give," 1956 .... **$25.00-$50.00**

CHARLIE RICH:

45s

Philips International 3532, "Whirlwind"/"Philadelphia Baby," 1959 .... **$12.50-$25.00**

3542, "Rebound"/"Big Man," 1959 .... **$12.50-$25.00**

3552, "Lonely Weekends"/"Everything I Do Is Wrong," 1960 .. **$12.50-$25.00**

LPs

Phillips International PLP-1970, Lonely Weekends, 1960 ...... **$300.00-$600.00**

Sun LP 110, Lonely Weekend, 1970 .... **$6.00-$12.00**

RUFUS THOMAS:

45s

Sun 181, "Bear Cat (The Answer to Hound Dog)"/"Walking in the Rain," 1953 .... **$175.00-$350.00**

(if A-side is just titled "Bear Cat," no subtitle), 1953 .... **$100.00-$200.00**

188, "Tiger Man (King of the Jungle)"/"Save Your Money," 1953 .... **$250.00-$500.00**

78s

Sun 181, Bear Cat (The Answer to Hound Dog)"/"Walking in the Rain," 1953 .... **$60.00-$120.00**

(if A-side is just titled "Bear Cat," no subtitle), 1953 .... **$40.00-$80.00**

188, "Tiger Man (King of the Jungle)"/"Save Your Money," 1953 .... **$100.00-$200.00**

Photo credit: From the Tom Kelly Archives, St. Louis, Mo.

Country music legend and disc jockey Hardrock Gunter had plenty of success with songs like "Birmingham Bounce" and "Sixty Minute Man" before signing with Sun; his biggest hit for the label would be this song, "Fallen Angel." Notice the big red "Hillbilly" stamp on the label, apparently this song was not designated for the rhythm and blues crowd.

***$2,000**, NM condition*

Proper Care and Maintenance of Your Record Collection

Records need attention. They need to be cleaned. They need to be properly stored. When you want to play them, they must be played on proper equipment. Some common sense tips can also ensure that your near-mint records stay in near-mint condition.

Albums and 45s must be stored vertically, never laid flat. Laying albums flat on a pile can cause ringwear on the album cover, and can create problems if you want to play a certain LP on the bottom of the pile. For small collections, most standard bookshelves will suffice. Make sure there is a 13" spacing between each shelf, so that you can easily extract albums.

For larger collections, think about building your own bookshelf or purchasing a rack system. Stay away from metal shelving units; besides their lack of supporting walls, which could cause the first or last album on the shelf to get scraped or notched against the shelving unit screws, poorly assembled metal shelving units can become top-heavy and will eventually fall down or collapse. Many record collecting magazines have advertisers who offer stackable shelving units (such as ICE for CDs, and the Rackit series for LPs and tapes); make sure that whatever cabinets you choose will allow you easy access to your records.

You can also build your own customized shelving units. Your local home improvement store will have modular closet shelves that can easily hold your albums and 45s. Depending on your collection, you may outgrow that unit fast and have to buy a second (or third) one. Be aware that closet shelves from a home improvement store are made from pressed wood, and a shelf with two feet of albums on it may start to sag.

Overexposure to sunlight and humidity, over time, can damage your record collection. Make sure that wherever you store your records, they are located away from direct sunlight or radiators. If you want to store your collection in a basement, make sure you invest in a dehumidifier and pour out its excess water every day.

If you want to keep your picture sleeves and rare company sleeves in mint condition, it's a good idea to store the records and sleeves separately. 45 sleeves are more prone to ringwear, seam splits and tearing; some 1970s Capitol 45s can also produce gear-like ridges around the center of your picture sleeve. The best way to store your 45s is in plain white paper sleeves. Place your picture sleeves in separate plastic or mylar cover sleeves and store them elsewhere. You can also use Disc-o-Files, which consists of a heavy paper sleeve with a coded section in the upper-right corner of the sleeve. The owner can write information about the record—its condition, value, age, stamper number, etc., there.

Vinyl albums and 45s become magnetized after several plays—dust and airborne particles can magically attach to the grooves, as a needle rotating along a record's grooves actually increases the static charge on the vinyl. After playing a record, you should use a zerostat gun, a plastic appliance that sprays harmless neutral ions on your record and removes the record's static charge. Or spray a non-alcohol-based static spray into a dry cloth and wipe the record with the cloth.

White paper sleeves are also acceptable for albums, but if you can find a dealer that still sells rice-paper sleeves, buy as many as you can. Rice-paper sleeves envelop your album in a thin, pillowy material that both protects the vinyl from everyday use, and keeps it scratch-free inside. Placing your records in polyethylene protective sleeves is also a good idea, and you can purchase them at companies like Bags Unlimited for a very reasonable price.

If you choose to use standard poly-lined sleeves, don't use them for your most expensive or rarest albums—standard poly-lined sleeves have a tendency to break down in heat and stick to albums, as opposed to mylar sleeves, which do not break down over time.

There has been considerable discussion about whether to leave shrink-wrap on an album cover or to remove it. If you haven't opened the disc up, you can leave the shrink-wrap alone. If you've already opened the disc, unless the shrink-wrap has some identifying sticker on it, you should remove it before it gets too tattered and dusty. There are 12-inch clear mylar sleeves available if you want to protect your album art, and some companies sell shrink-wrap machines so you can hermetically re-seal your discs.

Some people actually believe that if shrink-wrap remains on a record, it will be protected from water damage. This is wrong. In reality, records that sustain water damage (floods, rain storms, leaky pipes dripping on collections) can be more damaged if the shrink-wrap is left on. Often the water will seep through a hole in the shrink-wrap. Once the water gets inside the shrink-wrap to the jacket, the shrink-wrap actually keeps the moisture inside the record, causing it to stain and mold quickly.

If your records and album jackets have been damaged from floods or rain, there are ways to make them playable and storable again. Take the water-damaged records out of the sleeves, wash them with a mixture of distilled lukewarm water and very mild detergent. Dab off the excess water with a soft sponge and store the records in a dish rack until dry. Place your album covers between dry white paper towels (insert paper towels in the jackets themselves through the album opening if necessary). Stack them for 24 hours in a dry warm room, then replace the paper towels with clean ones. The sleeves may show signs of water damage, but they can be re-used in a few days.

Everybody has an opinion on what to use to clean your vinyl—rubbing alcohol, distilled water, hydrogen peroxide, de-ionized water, etc. A serious collector should invest in a cleaning machine with a built-in vacuum, like a Nitty Gritty or a VPI machine. Cleaning fluids like Discwasher D4 and Vinyl-Zyme Gold will clean your grooves when used in conjunction with a carbon fiber brush. After cleaning out the grooves, rinse your records thoroughly with distilled water—not spring water or mineral water or tap water, all of which have impurities that can settle in the grooves. Use a clean cloth diaper or chamois to wipe any excess water off, then place your disc in a rack to dry. If you use a home brew, test it out on some old 45s to make sure you have mixed the right formula.

Never use any "home brew" originally concocted for 45s and LPs on 78s—an alcohol-based cleaner will eat shellac like candy. You can, however, use a non-alcoholic, non-ammonia window cleaner to clean 78s. Spray the window cleaner onto a clean white cloth or woolen towel. Wiping carefully, gently and firmly, following the path of the grooves, you should be able to remove dirt and grime from 78s. Depending on the age of the 78, you may even find yourself removing minuscule iron filings from the grooves, the residue of steel needles from generations past.

If you've invested all this money in your record collection, you should also think about adding an insurance policy. Talk with an insurance agent to make sure you receive the right insurance policy for your needs, and remember that the agent who sells insurance is not the same person who will settle the damage claim. Insurance is only for the physical property, not for the equivalent of the music.

In conjunction with your insurance policy, you should maintain an itemized list of your collection. If you have a computer, you should invest in inventory software—nobody can remember every single album or 45 they own at the snap of a finger. There are music-specific databases, which have specific fields (artist, title, label, condition). Or you can invest in a standard spreadsheet database program like Quattro Pro, Excel, or dBASE, and tailor the information to your specific needs (variations in label design, RCA master number, beats per minute, etc.). Be sure that the company you purchase your data software from provides upgrades—I know one person who's forced to still use his Apple IIe because the software he stored his 10,000 classical albums on is incompatible with modern computers.

Once you've inputted all the information into your database, you should print out an inventory list at least once every two months and store it in a binder with your record collection. Not only will this tell you at a glance what records you have and their condition, you can take this binder to any record show and avoid spending $25 for a $15 record you forgot you owned.

Naturally you want to listen to your music whenever it suits your fancy. This means we come to the most important part of your record collection outside of the vinyl itself—your record player. No matter how cool it looks to play your priceless 50s records on a 1950s-era turntable, don't play them on those players unless they have been upgraded and updated with new needles. There are many phonograph repair and upgrade services on the Internet that specialize in modifying your RCA 45-Y-3, Silvertone, or GE Wildcat, so that it can play today's music without sacrificing its original looks and charm.

And although multi-record drop-changing turntables are great examples of 1970s kitsch, don't use them without serious upgrades to their needles and tonearm tracking. Even then, although the myth of record grooves scraping against each other on dropchanger phonographs is apocryphal at best (since the album edge and label are raised, stacked grooves seldom touch), the labels do rub together, causing scrapes and label wear.

If you want to play large-holed 45s in your collection and can't find the 45 adaptor that came with your turntable, it never hurts to pick up some single-use 45 adaptors. Plastic three-armed adaptors are cheap enough, and 10-20 inserts for a dollar is a fair price. Zinc Pfanstiehl "Push-Up" adaptors are more expensive—about 6 inserts for a dollar, and if you place it in a record, it should not be removed (zinc Pfanstiehl's won't do damage to your discs, unlike Webster Chicago steel adaptors that were made in the 1950s, which can cause damage to 45s if they're removed improperly).

By following these simple guidelines for record care, your discs should last a lifetime; your investment will not depreciate over time; and your friends and family will be amazed at the fantastic record collection you've maintained over the years.

Here are some links to several record collecting supply companies, where you can acquire items like replacement needles, phonograph upgrades and cleaning solutions:

Bags Unlimited, for all your record storage needs: http://www.bagsunlimited.com

Nauck's Vintage Records, home of the Disc-O-File: http://www.78RPM.com

KAB Sound Equipment, where one can purchase specialty turntables: http://www.kabusa.com

Jerry Raskin's Needle Doctor: http://www.needledoctor.com

un-DU sticker removal compound: http://www.un-du.com

Technics turntables: http://www.technicsusa.com

Victrola Repair Service, specializing in restoration of vintage phonographs: http://www.together.net/~victrola/

Wyatt's Musical Repair, fixing Victrolas and other phonographs: http://www.wyattsmusical.com/

For Your Listening Pleasure, a company that fixes and upgrades 1960s and 1970s phonographs and electronics: http://www.everythingradio.com/

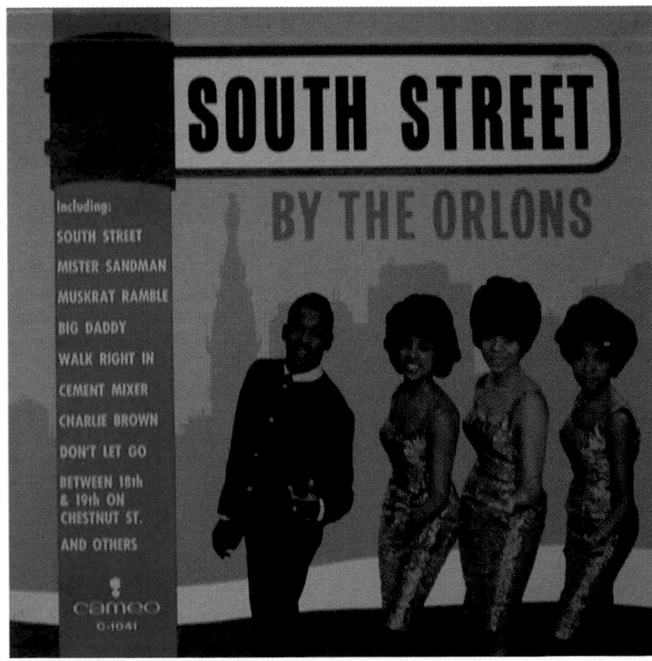

The Orlons were one of many soul groups, including the Tymes and the Dreamlovers, who recorded at Phhiladelphia's Cameo-Parway Studios in the 1960s. Their hit "South Street" was actually inspired by all the shops and clubs on Philadelphia's South Street.

***$30**, VG+ condition*

The Million Dollar Pages

Gathered from across various record collecting genres are twelve of the most expensive and highly collectible 78s, 45s, and LPs ever pressed. Many of these pressings are extremely rare—in some cases, only one or two copies of a certain record still exist. Should you happen to win the lottery, or come into a huge inheritance, these titles would be a crown jewel in your collection. These twelve titles can easily command thousands of dollars for a single copy—in some cases, only a single copy of a certain title exists. Some of these records contain the first recorded output or first national exposure of an artist or group. Some titles capture an artist's last performances, or their first on a new musical format. Many of these titles have been counterfeited or reprinted. The records shown here are not the only pressings that command such prices, but are twelve "Holy Grails" for record collectors of various genres.

Robert Johnson, "Cross Road Blues"/"Rambling on My Mind," Vocalion 03519, 78 RPM.

NM price: **$10,000**

Photo Credit: John Tefteller

Why: Robert Johnson's 78s are almost impossible to find in good condition; this title is maddeningly rare. This record also plays into the mythology of Robert Johnson meeting the devil at the crossroads, who bestows upon Johnson the power to play a guitar.

King Oliver and His Creole Jazz Band, "Zulus Ball"/"Workingman's Blues," Gennett 5275, 78 RPM.

Near-mint price: **$32,000**

Photo Credit: Mark Berresford/Russell Shor

Why: The rarest jazz 78 in existence, only one copy has survived to this day. A young Louis Armstrong plays cornet on this disc. A King Oliver pressing on Gennett 5276, "That Sweet Something Dear," still remains undiscovered to this day.

Nirvana, "Love Buzz"/"Big Cheese", Sub Pop 23, 45 RPM with picture sleeve.

NM price: **$1,500**

Counterfeited: Both the sleeve and the 45 have been heavily reproduced.

Why: The first record from Seattle's grunge-rock pioneers; also the first pressing from the Sub Pop Singles Club. Each picture sleeve was hand-numbered in thin red felt-tip pen; lower-numbered pressings can be worth twice the price listed above. The #1 pressing, by the way, is currently owned by Courtney Love.

Elvis Presley, "That's All Right"/"Blue Moon of Kentucky," Sun 209, 45 RPM.

NM price: **$6,000**

Counterfeits exist: Legitimate copies are on black vinyl, have three circular "push marks" in the label.

Why: Elvis Presley's first commercially released 45, one of five records produced for the small Sun label. First pressings list artist credits as "Elvis Presley, Scotty and Bill," second pressings say "Elvis Presley with Scotty and Bill."

The Five Sharps, "Stormy Weather"/ "Sleepy Cowboy," Jubilee 5104, 78 RPM.

NM price: **$25,000**
Photo Credit: Kurt Nauck

Counterfeited: Yes, on 45 (all-blue label, non-black vinyl).

Reproduced: Yes, on 45 (Bim Bam Boom records, red vinyl)

Why: The most collectible Doo-wop record, only a handful of 78s exist on this title; stories of a legit pressing on 45 RPM are apocryphal. A copy with a "tight crack" sold at auction in 2003 for $19,000.

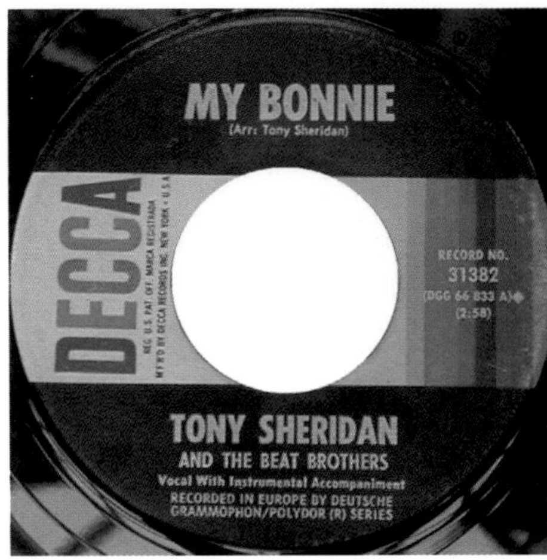

Tony Sheridan and the Beat Brothers, "My Bonnie"/"The Saints (When the Saints Go Marching In)," Decca 31382, 45 RPM.

NM price: **$15,000**

Counterfeited: Yes, all black label with silver print, star under "Decca" are counterfeits; pink label pressings are legit promo copies.

Reproduced: Yes, on MGM in 1964.

Why: The "Beat Brothers" were the Beatles, backing up popular European singer Tony Sheridan on this record. It was initially released by Decca in America a year before the Beatles' "official" American pressings.

Art Kassel and His Orchestra, "Queen for a Day"/"At the End of a Perfect Day," Vogue R784, 78-RPM picture disc.

NM price: **$5,000**
Photo Credit: Kurt Nauck

Why: Vogue Picture Records had varying print runs; only a few copies of this record exist. The A-side was later used as the opening theme for the TV reality show of the same name.

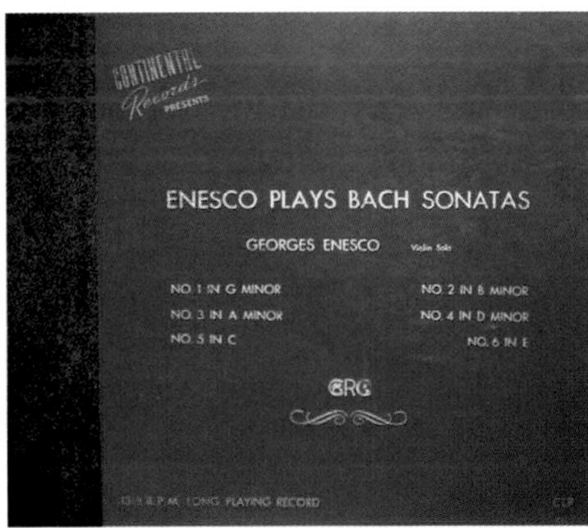

George Enesco, Bach: Six Sonatas and Partitas for Unaccompanied Violin, *Continental CLP 104, 3 LPs in box.*

NM price: **$10,000**

Reproduced: Yes, both on LP and CD.

Why: The great violinist, composer and teacher, whose pupils included Yehudi Menuhin, made one of his final recordings in 1949. His hands wrecked with arthritis and old age, Enesco painfully but passionately played through all six Bach sonatas in one single recording session. Fewer than 100 copies exist today.

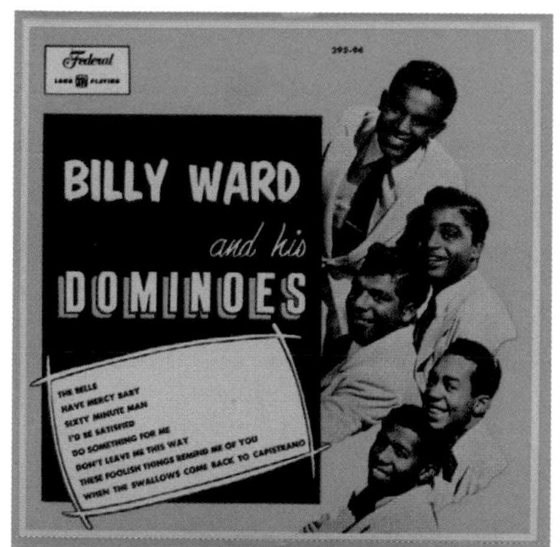

Billy Ward and His Dominoes, *Federal 295-94, 10-inch LP.*
NM price: **$13,000**

Reproduced: Yes, on 12-inch LP.

Why: 10-inch LPs were manufactured between 1948 and 1955, and are much rarer than their 12-inch LP counterparts, and Federal only made albums for its biggest-selling artists. This record contains most of the Dominoes' early hits, including "Sixty Minute Man" and "The Bells." Clyde McPhatter, who would later form the Drifters, is also heard on this record.

Bob Dylan, The Freewheelin' Bob Dylan, *Columbia CS 8786, stereo LP.*
NM price: **$30,000**

Why: The first few stereo pressings of this album feature four songs, "Let Me Die in My Footsteps," "Rocks and Gravel," "Talkin' John Birch Blues," and "Gamblin' Willie's Dead Man's Hand," that were taken off the record days later. Only two true stereo copies of this album exist. Label must list these titles and play them—in stereo—to command such a high price.

The Rolling Stones, "I Wanna Be Your Man"/"Stoned," London 9641, white-purple-blue label format, 45 RPM.
NM price: **$9,000**
Photo Credit: Tom Grosh

Why: The Stones' first American 45, the "Stoned" instrumental was quickly withdrawn due to the supposition that the song title might imply drug use. One of the rarest Rolling Stones 45s of them all.

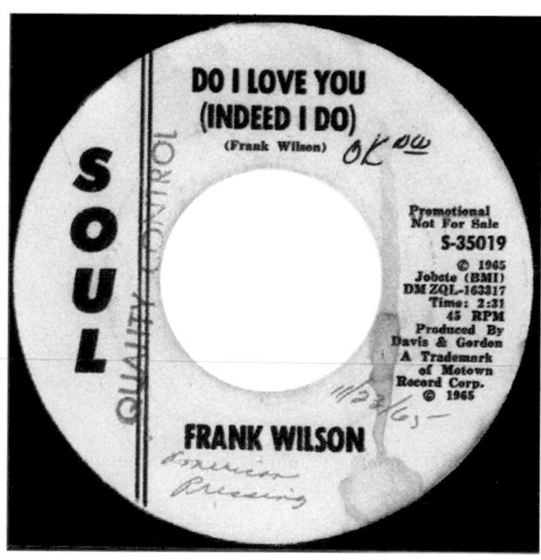

Frank Wilson, "Do I Love You (Indeed I Do)"/"Sweeter as the Days Go By," Soul 35019, 45 RPM.
NM price: **$20,000**
Photo Credit: Kev Roberts/ David S. Carne

Reproduced: Yes, including bootlegs on In Records (credited to Eddie Foster).

Why: One of the rarest Northern Soul titles of all time, originally resigned to the Motown archives, a copy was "borrowed" and later turned up at a northern England dance club, where the crowd danced to it every night. As many as 7 copies may exist of this record, but only two have surfaced to this day.

How to Un-Warp a Record

A warped record is one where the disc does not lay flat on the turntable, but has one of its edges curled or bent, causing the tonearm to ride up and down as the record spins. Warps are often caused by heat, as the shellac or PVC expands when stored near a radiator or furnace, or even over prolonged exposure to sunshine. There are also compression warps, which occur when a record is stored flat or on a table edge, with other records stacked on top, and the vinyl actually bows or bends as the years go by. Warping is an equal-opportunity problem; it affects shellac 78s, vinyl LPs and styrene 45s with similar malevolence. And, of course, the more severe the warp, the lower the collectible value.

There are ways to un-warp a record, but it is not a project that should be undertaken with your rarest disc. Some solutions are listed below, but understand the following before you begin: (a) not every technique will work for every type of record; (b) un-warping a record is a very tricky process and requires a lot of skill, patience and perseverance; (c) you need to practice these techniques with records to which you have NO emotional attachment. And many of these un-warping methods have varying degrees of success and failure; even if you do get the record flat, you may still hear a hiss in the grooves, or the record may still mistrack. Neither myself nor Krause Publications is responsible for any damage caused by an attempt to un-warp a record—in other words, if your Robert Johnson Vocalion 78 gets damaged, don't come crying to me. Make sure to take all safety precautions, for example, safety glasses and hand protection.

1. The "Oven Baking" method (has been known to work on shellac 78s and thick vinyl LPs)

Many people swear that they can unwarp a record by using an oven. For this recipe, you need two 14-inch square sheets of tempered glass and an oven. Begin by preheating your oven to 150 degrees. Clean your record and rinse with distilled water, to make sure there is no dust, dirt, or other residue in the grooves. Place the record between the two sheets of tempered glass, then place in your oven. Wait 12 minutes. Carefully take your glass-and-record sandwich out of the oven and place on a cooling rack for 30 minutes. Then gently remove the glass and inspect the record. It should have returned to its original flatness. Oven temperatures and cooking times may vary; you may have to add an extra two or three minutes in the oven to achieve the desired results. (For more information, visit this Web site: *http://home.comcast.net/~analyst18/unwarp.htm*)

2. The "Solar Baking" method (works best on shellac 78s).

This method was discovered at the Roadhouse Web site, a gathering place for eBay record buyers and sellers (*http://www.angelfire.com/fl5/roadhouse/warped.html*). The formula requires two 14-inch pieces of 3/8" thick glass, two large pieces of approx. 3/16" "place mat/craft" vinyl/foam, one quality album sleeve, five pieces of cork and common household glue. Trace the outline of a 12" vinyl LP on the craft foam (make two of them, one for top and one for bottom). Cut out the center on each craft foam sheet, so that only the vinyl grooves are covered by the mats. Use common household glue to attach five (5) pieces of cork on the bottom piece of glass to avoid any clanking when setting it down, plus it makes it easy to pick back up. Clean the LP and place it inside a protective sleeve, such as a Discwasher VIP sleeve. Then place the record and sleeve between the craft foam mats, and place all that between the two sheets of glass. Take outside on a sunny day and let sit for 10 to 15 minutes (sun times may vary whether you live in Houston or in Seattle). Bring the glass-and-record sandwich inside and let it cool for a day. Then inspect.

3. The "Hot Towel" method (may work better on 45s).

For this you need a thick towel and heavy books. Place a thin towel on top of the dryer for a full cycle (on top, not inside). Once the dryer cycle is finished, take the towel off the dryer, and place it on your table. Lay a record flat on one end of the towel, cover the other side of the record with the rest of the towel. Place heavy books on top. Inspect after 30 minutes.

4. The "Heat and Bath" method

I came across this one by using an Internet search engine: (*http://www.google.com/search?q=cache:jg_ggFZ2dhMC:chronictronic.org/spin/warped.htm+warped+record+fix&hl=en*)

Once again, you place your records between two plates of tempered glass and bake in the oven. While your record is baking, go to your bathroom and fill your tub with cold water, at least four inches deep. After your record has baked for twelve minutes or so, take the glass-and-vinyl sandwich out of the oven, carry it to your bathroom and submerge the entire mixture into the cold tub water. After a few seconds, you should be able to remove a flat record from your tub. Make sure you have used tempered glass when cooking and submerging; some types of glass will fracture after going from extreme heat to extreme cold.

Some of the other un-warping formulae involve hand-held hair dryers, microwaves, wrapping in a towel and flattening it with a steam iron - but no matter what method you use to flatten a record, be aware that the following can happen:

- Un-warping a record can cause other heat warps or ripples, and the groove itself could flatten out, causing the needle to mistrack.

- If the record is not carefully cleaned beforehand, you can actually melt dirt and debris into the grooves.

Finally, be aware that these un-warping techniques will only work on *slightly* warped records. If your record is severely warped, to the point where your tonearm looks as if it's riding a roller coaster as it tracks in the grooves, your best bet is to either toss the record and get a new one if you can; or really take a heat source to it and create some decorative art.

Board of Advisors

The following is a list of experts who have helped with the completion of *Warman's American Records*, and have expertise in various subgenres of record and music collecting. Many of these experts have provided rare images from their own personal archives; others have helped by offering information, details, and data. Their assistance in the completion of this book, along with others who have helped along the way, is greatly appreciated.

Pete Battistini
6576 Lake Forest Drive
Avon, IN 46123-7405
e-mail: at40@aol.com
Specialty: American Top 40 radio show

Rodney Branham
Rerun Records
P.O. Box 148
Chelsea, MI 48118
e-mail: rerun45@aol.com

Michael Cumella
P.O. Box 67
Planetarium Station
New York, NY 10024
e-mail: me@michaelcumella.com
http://www.michaelcumella.com
Specialty: flexidiscs and vinyl oddities

David Diehl
1814 East Washington Avenue, #94NA
Harlingen, TX 78550-5707
Specialty: Stag records

Leslie Gerber
Parnassus Records
51 Goat Hill Road
Saugerties, NY 12477-3008
(845) 246-3332
Specialty: Classical music

Tim Gracyk
9180 Joy Lane
Granite Bay, CA 95746-9682
e-mail: tgracyk@garlic.com
Specialty: Cylinder recordings, Edison Diamond Discs, acoustic 78s

Thomas R. Grosh
P.O. Box 7061
Lancaster, PA 17604-7061
e-mail: vears@lancnews.infi.net
http://www.veryenglish.com
Specialty: British Invasion, Rolling Stones

Barry Hansen
"Doctor Demento"
The Demento Society
P.O. Box 884
Culver City, CA 90232
http://www.drdemento.com
Specialties: Comedy/Novelty music, Blues, Jazz, 60s Rock

Piers A. Hemmingsen
40 Edgecombe Avenue
Toronto, ON M5N 2X3
e-mail: babs@istar.ca
http://www.capitol6000.com
Specialty: Canadian Beatles releases, Canadian Capitol series

Ken Jarrell
4314 16th Street, #5
Lubbock, TX 79416-5834
e-mail: vinylville@door.net
http://members.tripod.com/~Vinylville

Norm Katuna
P.O. Box 80154
San Diego, CA 92138
e-mail: normk@operamail.com

Allen Koenigsberg
The Antique Record and Phonograph Collector
502 E. 17th Street
Brooklyn, NY 11226
http://www.phonobooks.com
Specialty: pre-1950 recordings

Rocky Kruegel
6814 West Highland Road 128N
Mequon, WI 53092
(262) 236-4391

Craig Moore
Younger Than Yesterday
2615 N. University Street
Peoria, IL 61604
(309) 682-1116
Specialty: Garage

Peter Muldavin
173 W. 78th Sreet
New York, NY 10024
e-mail: kiddie78s@aol.com
http://www.kiddierekordking.com
Specialty: Children's records

Kurt Nauck
Nauck's Vintage Records
22004 Sherrod Lane
Spring, TX 77389
http://www.78RPM.com
Specialty: Pre-World War II 78s

Tim Neely
c/o Krause Publications
700 East State Street
Iola, WI 54990-0001
e-mail: neelyt@krause.com

Bob Perry
Blue Note Records
16401 NE 15th Avenue
North Miami Beach, FL 33162
e-mail: bluenote@netrox.net

Martin Popoff
P.O. Box 65208, 358 Danforth Ave.
Toronto, ON, Canada M4K 2Z2
http://www.martinpopoff.com
Specialty: Heavy Metal, Southern Rock

Kev Roberts
Hartford House
Common road
Thorpe Salvin
Notts, UNITED KINGDOM
http://www.goldsoul.co.uk
Specialty: Northern Soul

Catherine Saunders-Watson
P.O. Box 622
Center Harbor, NH 03226
Specialty: Punk, British Invasion, Jazz

Robert Schoenfeld
Nighthawk Records
P.O. Box 1432
Maryland Heights, MO 63043
http://www.nghthwk.com/rkr/
Specialty: Ska, Reggae

Val Shively
Box B
Havertown, PA 19083
Specialties: Doo-wop, 1950s music

Bruce Spizer
925 Common Street
New Orleans, LA 70112
e-mail: bruce@beatle.net
Specialty: Beatles

Bob Szuszzewicz
Boo's Blasts From The Past
3875 Alberta Place
Philadelphia, PA 19154
Specialty: Oldies, Motown

John Tefteller
P.O. Box 1727
Grants Pass, OR 97528-0200
http://www.tefteller.com
Specialty: Blues, Rockabilly, 78s

Loren Van Sinclair
Box 2383
Orillia, ON, Canada L3V 6V7
Specialty: Canadian pressings

David Whatmough
284 Main Street West
Hamilton, ON, Canada L8P 1J8
Specialty: Canadian 45s

INDEX

The pages in boldfaced type are pages from the listing sections. The non-bolded page numbers are entries for text references and images.

A

B

C

T

U

V

W

X

Y

Z